ORACLE®

Oracle Press™

Oracle Database 10*g* XML & SQL: Design, Build & Manage XML Applications in Java, C, C++ & PL/SQL

ORACLE®

Oracle Press™

Oracle Database 10*g* XML & SQL: Design, Build & Manage XML Applications in Java, C, C++ & PL/SQL

Mark V. Scardina
Ben Chang
Jinyu Wang

McGraw-Hill/Osborne

New York Chicago San Francisco
Lisbon London Madrid Mexico City Milan
New Delhi San Juan Seoul Singapore Sydney Toronto

The McGraw-Hill Companies

McGraw-Hill/Osborne
2100 Powell Street, 10th Floor
Emeryville, California 94608
U.S.A.

To arrange bulk purchase discounts for sales promotions, premiums, or fund-raisers, please contact **McGraw-Hill**/Osborne at the above address. For information on translations or book distributors outside the U.S.A., please see the International Contact Information page immediately following the index of this book.

Oracle Database 10*g* XML & SQL: Design, Build & Manage XML Applications in Java, C, C++ & PL/SQL

1234567890 CUS CUS 01987654

ISBN 0-07-222952-7

Publisher
Brandon A. Nordin

Vice President & Associate Publisher
Scott Rogers

Acquisitions Editor
Lisa McClain

Project Editors
LeeAnn Pickrell, Lisa Wolters-Broder, Emily Wolman

Acquisitions Coordinator
Athena Honore

Technical Editors
Olivier Le Diouris, Anjana Manian

Copy Editor
William McManus

Proofreader
John Gildersleeve

Indexer
Irv Hershman

Composition
Apollo Publishing Services, Jim Kussow

Illustrators
Kathleen Edwards, Michael Mueller, Melinda Lytle

Series Design
Jani Beckwith

Cover Series Design
Damore Johann Design, Inc.

This book was composed with Corel VENTURA™ Publisher.

To my family for their understanding, tolerance, and support through the late nights and lost weekends. To my coworkers for accepting without complaint my interruptions for technical help and advice.

—Mark Scardina

To my family for their support.

—Ben Chang

I would like to thank first and foremost my husband, Yong, for his support when I worked on this book. I'd also like to thank my colleagues on the Oracle XML development team who gave me invaluable help.

—Jinyu Wang

About the Authors

Mark V. Scardina is Oracle's XML Evangelist for Server products and is the Group Product Manager for the CORE and XML Development Group tasked with providing the XML infrastructure components used throughout the Oracle product stack, including the Oracle XML Developer's Kit. Mark chairs the Oracle XML Standards committee and is an editor on the W3C XSL Working Group. He is a frequent speaker at industry trade shows and conferences, a writer for industry journals and is co-author of *Oracle9i XML Handbook* and *Oracle XML Handbook*. Prior to joining Oracle, he worked at Socket Communications and ACE Technologies. He holds a B.S. in Information Systems Management from USF.

Mark lives in San Francisco with his wife and twin boys. His hobbies include DanceSport, high-end audio/video, and working on his house.

Ben Chang is a 15-year veteran at Oracle Corp., where he heads the CORE and XML Development Group as Director. In addition to working on Oracle6 to Oracle Database 10*g* releases, he served the longest tenure as Development Release Manager for Oracle 8.0, spanning five releases. He also served three years as chair of Oracle's C Coding Standards Committee, and he was a W3C DOM Working Group editor. He is co-author of *Oracle9i XML Handbook* and *Oracle XML Handbook*. Before coming to Oracle, he worked at IBM Corp., Pacific Bell, Bellcore, and GE Corporate R&D. He holds an M.S. in Electrical Engineering (Computer Systems) from Stanford University and a B.S. in Electrical Engineering and Computer Science from the University of California at Berkeley.

Jinyu Wang is a Senior Product Manager for Oracle XML Product management, in charge of the Oracle XML Developer's Kit, which provides the XML infrastructure components used across Oracle product stacks. As an Oracle Certified Professional with an extensive database background, she leads a variety of projects that successfully apply XML technologies to enterprise business applications. While completing her master's degree in computer science at the University of Southern California and electrical engineering at Northern Jiaotong University, she worked on artificial intelligence and computer vision, focusing on motion analysis.

Contents

PART II

Oracle XML Management for DBAs

PART IV

Oracle XML for C Developers

PART VI

Oracle XML for PL/SQL Developers

Introduction

ML is now six years old, having been published as a W3C recommendation in February 1998. It was around that time that Oracle began to take a serious look at this new promising technology. In fact the Architectural Review Board decided that XML was going to be of company-wide importance and handed down a development charter to the CORE Development group as follows:

> *Deliver the best platform for developers to productively build and cost-effectively deploy reliable and scaleable Internet applications exploiting XML.*

This charter has proven to be prescient as not only has XML become a dominant Internet technology, but also has spawned an entire family of standards that are becoming the foundation of electronic publishing, business, and application development. The impact of XML has been felt to no greater measure than within Oracle and has kept the now CORE and XML Development group busy these many years. The authors are members of this group and have had the opportunity to not only participate in the XML standards process and produce the implementations but also work with over a hundred development groups across Oracle and countless customers in putting this family of technologies to work in a myriad of ways. Thus we hope to bring to you not only the means to put Oracle's XML technology to work, but also new ways and new ideas for using XML in your applications.

Over the years, the XML dialog has changed. It used to be asked, when talking with new users or businesses contemplating XML, *What is all this fuss about? Why would I want to exchange data in a bloated form having lost its binding? What is the one killer XML application?*

These were tough questions, primarily because XML is not an end but a means. Its strength and its weakness are in its ability to be infinitely flexible and extensible. Fortunately, as companion standards such as XSL, XML Schema, Namespaces, XPath, and so on, were developed and rolled out businesses and their developers stopped asking *Why XML?* and started asking *How XML?* which leads us to why we wrote this book.

You may be surprised to learn that Oracle does not have a research and development division. All development is done in the context of a product. This can make developing new technologies difficult as these standards efforts evolve, have bugs, and have taken years to stabilize. This can be seen in the years it took to publish XML Schema and that XML Query is in its fifth year and still not out the door. Nevertheless, Oracle has been an early adopter in all of these technologies, putting them to work within all Oracle products.

This situation gave birth to the Oracle XML Developer's Kit in 1999 as a vehicle to expose implementations of these technologies to both the internal and external development community. This was desirable, as it would allow us to bring these implementations to production quicker using the beta facilities of the Oracle Technology Network (OTN), getting feedback from a broad spectrum of developers looking for XML functionality. Productizing Oracle's XML infrastructure for external use meant that we had to develop a license. At that time the only Oracle licenses available were either a product license that limited usage to one's own deployment or a development one that forbid deployment. Neither of these made sense for a software development kit that we weren't charging for and wanted people to develop against seriously. We were able to successfully navigate Oracle's legal system to create a deployment and redistribution license for the XDK that exists to this day.

The license wasn't enough as we were looking for serious enterprise-level development and deployments. We needed support as well. Therefore we again successfully negotiated to have the XDK be included as part of the Oracle server support contracts for the database, application server, and tools at the same service level at no additional charge. Additionally, we were able to offer standalone support agreements for non-Oracle customers. Finally, for those who could not afford or did not need formal support, we opened a support forum on OTN, which has rapidly grown to six forums that we directly support. Over the last five years we have released both beta and production XDKs at roughly three month intervals. Beta versions have a time-based development-only license but the production releases have the full redistribution license.

Finally we come to this book. While this is the third book for two of us, it represents a totally different effort from the previous *Oracle XML Handbook* and *Oracle9*i *XML Handbook*. Those previous editions provided a survey of Oracle and XML and in-depth discussions about the XDK. This edition is totally rewritten with almost all new content. While the previous editions came with CDs, this one does not for two very important reasons. First, all the code in the book will be downloadable from the Oracle Press web site. As distinct from a CD, this allows us to update it should any bugs appear. In the previous editions we provided Oracle software on the CD; however, it forced us to include only Oracle software, so we made most of the code available on OTN. This had the unanticipated effect of lessening the book's value in some reader's minds. This edition does not suffer under those limitations, so you will find more original and innovative content and all of the code available for download.

The book is divided into six parts and is organized to be accessible by managers, DBAs, and developers alike. Part I includes Chapters 1 through 7 and focuses on the family of XML standards that are important to Oracle and that should be considered when designing XML-enabled solutions. These not only discuss the common standards of DOM, SAX, XSLT, and XML Schema, but venture into new standards, some of which are not complete, such as XML Query, XML Pipeline, StAX, and JAXB. These chapters are not intended to be comprehensive in their coverage, as whole books have been written on many of them. They do intend to give you a good feel for the functionality offered and to compare and contrast similar standards thus providing guidance in their optimum usage.

Part II includes Chapters 8 through 12 and focuses on XML and the Oracle database. Beginning in Oracle9*i* Release 2, native XML support was introduced along with significant XML functionality integrated into other database features such as Oracle Text and Advanced Queuing. These chapters provide an in-depth look at this functionality and its evolution into Oracle Database 10*g*. After getting started in Chapter 8, the chapters are arranged along task lines such as storing XML, retrieving and generating XML, searching and querying XML, and managing the Oracle XML DB. These chapters are designed to be accessible to both developers and DBAs.

Parts III through VI consists of Chapters 13 through 28 and focus on how to use Oracle's XML technology for real application development. These chapters are split into Oracle's major development languages of Java, C, C++, and PL/SQL. Each language begins with a getting started chapter covering environment, IDE setup, runtime setup, and so on. The subsequent chapters in these parts discuss real-use case application scenarios. In many instances, these were drawn from actual customer projects. While they include extensive source code, each example is explained in detail and the code is available for download from Oracle Press.

This book was written during the development of Oracle Database 10*g* and as such could not have been completed without the help of many within Oracle. The authors wish to especially thank the following:

K Karun	Tomas Saulys	Tim Yu
Bill Han	Anjana Manian	Meghna Mehta
Kongyi Zhou	Stanley Guan	Ian Macky
Dimitry Lenkov	Anguel Novoselsky	Mark Drake
Stephen Buxton	Asha Tarachandani	Ravi Murthy
Nipun Agarwal	Jim Warner	Olivier LeDiouris
Bhushan.Khaladkar	Dan Chiba	

PART I

Oracle and the XML Standards

CHAPTER 1

Introducing XML

Extensible Markup Language (XML) is a meta-markup language, meaning that the language, as specified by the World Wide Web Consortium's (W3C) XML 1.0 specification, enables users to define their own markup languages to describe and encapsulate data into XML files. These files can then be transformed into HTML (as well as into any other markup language) and displayed within browsers such as Netscape Navigator and Microsoft Internet Explorer, exchanged across the Internet between applications and businesses, or stored in and retrieved from databases. The power of XML comes from its simplicity, its being part of an open standard, and the incorporation of user-defined markup tags that lend semantics to the embedded data.

XML's origins come from the *Standard Generalized Markup Language (SGML)*—ratified by the International Standards Organization (ISO) in 1986—on which *Hypertext Markup Language (HTML),* created in 1990, is based. While SGML is still a widely used standard in the document world, and HTML is still widely used as the basis of millions of web pages on the World Wide Web, XML is rapidly gaining widespread acceptance because of its advantages in data exchange, storage, and description over the existing markup languages. Since the publication of its v1.0 specifications by the W3C in February 1998, XML has been widely seen as the language and data interchange of choice for e-commerce.

What Is an XML Document?

While this book is not meant to be a full XML tutorial, as with any standard, numerous concepts and technical terms need to be explained. Because XML was developed to convey data, a relevant example is a data record of a book listing from a standard database. A complex SQL query could return data in the following format:

```
History of Interviews, Juan, Smith, 99999-99999, Oracle Press, 2003.
```

If XML is used as the output form, however, this record now has additional context for each piece of data, as evidenced in the following:

```
<book>
 <title>History of Interviews</title>
  <author>
   <firstname>Juan</firstname>
   <lastname>Smith</lastname>
  </author>
  <ISBN>99999-99999</ISBN>
  <publisher>Oracle Press</publisher>
  <publishyear>2003</publishyear>
  <price type="US">10.00</price>
</book>
```

Certain items of note in this example are explored in detail later. Notice that the file has symmetry, and each piece of data has its context enclosing it in the form **<context> ... </context>**. The angle brackets and text inside are called *tags,* and each set of tags and its enclosed data is called an *element.* This relationship can be thought of as similar to a column in a database table in which the text of the tag is the column heading and the text between the tags is the data from a row in that column. In the preceding example, **title** could be the name of the column and **History of Interviews** could be the data in a row.

Notice, too, that several tags contain tags instead of data. This is a significant feature of XML, which permits nesting of data to define relationships better. Returning to the database metaphor, the **<author>** tag could be modeled as a table whose columns were **<firstname>** and **<lastname>**. In XML terminology, these column tags are referred to as *children* of the *parent* **<author>** tag.

Now look at the **<price>** tag and you see that it includes text of the form *name="value"*. These name-value pairs are called *attributes,* and one or more of these can be included in the start tag of any element. Attributes, however, are not legal in end tags (for example, **</tag name="foo">**). Notice that attribute values *must* be framed by quotes (single or double, as long as the closing and opening quotes are the same) as specified by SGML. HTML is much more permissive in this area.

One final terminology note: the entire XML example is enclosed by **<book> ... </book>**. These tags are defined as the *root* of the document, and only one may exist in any particular document. XML documents that follow these rules of having only one root and properly closing all open tags are considered *well formed.*

XML's basic concepts and terminology are straightforward and are formalized in an open Internet standard. As the W3C XML 1.0 specification states, "XML documents are made up of storage units called *entities,* which contain either parsed data or unparsed data. Parsed data [or PCDATA] is made up of *characters,* some of which form *character data,* and some of which form *markup.* Markup encodes a description of the document's storage layout and logical structure." XML documents have both physical and logical structure. The physical structure of the XML document simply refers to the XML file and the other files that it may import, whereas the *logical structure* of an XML document refers to the prolog and the body of the document.

The XML of the book example represents the body of an XML document, but it is missing important information that helps identify its nature. This information is in the prolog, discussed in the following section.

The Prolog

The *prolog* consists of the XML declaration (that is, the version number), a possible language encoding hint, other attributes (name-value pairs), and an optional grammar or data model specified by either an *XML Schema Definition (XSD)* or a *Document Type Definition (DTD)* referred to by a URL. The prolog may also contain the actual XSD or DTD. An example with a reference to an external DTD would look like the following:

```
<?xml version="1.0" encoding="UTF-8" standalone="no" ?>
<!DOCTYPE book SYSTEM "book.dtd">
```

Note that a line containing **<? ... ?>** is an example of an XML *processing instruction (PI).* In this example, **xml** is the name of the XML PI. In addition, the character set encoding supported in the example is a compressed version of Unicode called *UTF-8.* While XML processors usually detect the encoding from the first 3 bytes in the file, this declaration can be used as a hint to indicate the expected encoding. Finally, the **standalone** attribute refers to whether the processor needs to include or import other external files.

The second line of this prolog refers to a **DOCTYPE**. This is where the declaration of the grammar or data model for this XML document is done. Why is this important? Remember, an

XML file has both physical and logical representations. In some applications, it may be sufficient to process the XML without knowing whether information is missing, but most of the time, an application wants to validate the XML document it receives to confirm everything is there. To do this, the application must know which elements are required, which ones can have children, which ones can have attributes, and so forth. In XML terms, the grammar or data model in this example is referred to as DTD. This DTD can reside within the XML file itself or simply be referred to so that the processor can locate it, as in this example.

The preceding example might look as follows with an XML Schema declaration:

```
<?xml version="1.0"?>
<xsd:schema xmlns:xsd=http://www.w3.org/2001/XMLSchema
   xmlns:bk="http://www.mypublishsite.com/books">
```

To begin with, note that the XML Schema declaration has a prefix **xsd:**, which is associated with the XML Schema namespace through the declaration **xmlns:xsd="http://www.w3.org/2001/XMLSchema"**. This prefix is used on the names of the data types defined in the referenced XSD to differentiate them from others using the same name. The **xsd:schema** declaration denotes the beginning of this XML Schema incorporated in this XML document, along with one other declaration, **xmlns:bk="http://www.mypublishsite.com/books"**, which defines the namespace of the prefix **bk:** so as to identify these types as defined by the author of this data model.

Note also that the schema declaration is within the **<book>** tag instead of in the prolog. This is a distinct difference between XSDs and DTDs. Thus, the XML schema declaration is an attribute of the root element of the document and is part of the body, which we discuss next.

The Body

The root element, which contains the remainder of the XML document, follows the prolog and is called the *body* of the XML document. This part is composed of elements, processing instructions, content, attributes, comments, entity references, and so forth. As previously mentioned, elements must have start tags and corresponding end tags nested in the correct order; otherwise, the XML document is not well-formed, and XML parsers may signal errors because of this. Elements can also have attributes, or name-value pairs, such as **<author firstname="Juan" lastname="Smith">**. Built-in attributes defined by the XML 1.0 specification also exist, such as **xml:space="preserve"** to indicate that the whitespace between the elements be considered as data and thus preserved.

Entity references, defined only in DTDs, are similar to macros in that entities are defined once, and references to them, such as **&nameofentity**, can be used in place of their entire definitions. For example, in a DTD, **<!ENTITY Copyright "Copyright 2000 by Smith, Jones, and Doe – All rights reserved">** could be declared, and then **&Copyright** could be used as a shortcut throughout the XML document. An XML parser must recognize entities defined in DTDs, even though the validity check may be turned off and an additional XML Schema is specified. Again, built-in entities also exist as defined by the XML 1.0 specifications, such as those for the ampersand, **&** apostrophe, **'** less than, **<** and so forth. Comments are recognized when they are enclosed in the **<!-- -->** construct.

Within the body of the XML document instance, certain element and attribute names may have prefixes, which are XML namespaces identified by *Uniform Resource Identifier (URI)* references that qualify the names of these elements and attributes and locate resources that could be on different machines or XML documents. For example, if the declaration **xmlns:bk="http://www.mypublishsite.com/books"** is made in a parent element, the prefix **bk:title** stands for **http://www.mypublishsite.com/books:title**. You can use identical names for either elements or attributes if they are qualified with URIs to differentiate the names. For example, **bk:hello** is called a qualified name; the namespace prefix **bk** is mapped to the URI, **http://www.mypublishsite.com/books**, and the local part is **hello**. Note that URI references can contain characters not allowed in element names; that is why **bk** serves as a substitute for the URI. It is important to mention that the **bk** prefix belongs to the document in which it is declared. Another document declaring the prefix **book** instead of **bk** but referencing the same URI would be considered equivalent when parsed by an XML parser.

Finally, the body may contain *character data (CDATA)* sections to mark off blocks of text that would otherwise be regarded as markup, comments, entity references, processing instructions, and so forth. The *CDATA* syntax is

```
<![CDATA[ characters including <, >, /, ?, & not legal anywhere else]]>
```

These sections are simply skipped by XML parsers as if they were opaque. Later in the book, you will see how you use them to embed SQL statements in XML documents.

Thus, the body of the XML document contains the root element with its schema declarations, child and sibling nodes, elements, attributes, text nodes that represent the textual content of an element or attribute, and *CDATA* sections.

Well-Formed XML Documents

As mentioned previously, an XML document is well formed if only one root exists and all start tags have corresponding end tags, with the correct nesting. For example, the following is not well formed:

```
<bookcatalog>
 <book>
  <title>History of Interviews</ti>
   <author>
    <firstname>Juan</firstname>
    <lastname>Smith</author></lastname>
    <ISBN>99999-99999</ISBN>
    <publisher>Oracle Press</publisher>
    <publishyear>2003</publishyear>
    <price type="US">10.00</price>
 </book>
</bookcatalog>
<bookcatalog2>
...
</bookcatalog2>
```

The following are the reasons why it is not well formed:

- Two roots exists, **bookcatalog** and **bookcatalog2**.
- The **<title>** tag does not have a correct corresponding end tag, as in **</title>**.

- The end tag **</author>** is not nested correctly, because the **</lastname>** end tag is after it instead of before it.

XML parsers will reject this document without further processing.

Valid XML Documents

A valid XML document is one that conforms to either a specified DTD or XML Schema, meaning that the elements, attributes, structural relationships, and sequences in the XML document are the same as the ones specified in the DTD or XML Schema. For example, the following XML is valid with respect to the DTD, which follows it:

```
<bookcatalog>
 <book>
  <title>History of Interviews</title>
  <author>
   <firstname>Juan</firstname>
   <lastname>Smith</lastname>
  </author>
  <ISBN>99999-99999</ISBN>
  <publisher>Oracle Press</publisher>
  <publishyear>2003</publishyear>
  <price type="US">10.00</price>
 </book>
</bookcatalog>
```

The following is the DTD to which the XML document conforms:

```
<!-- DTD bookcatalog may have a number of book entries -->
<!DOCTYPE bookcatalog [
 <!ELEMENT bookcatalog (book)*>
 <!-- Each book element has a title, 1 or more authors, etc. -->
 <!ELEMENT book (title, author+, ISBN, publisher, publishyear, price)>
 <!ELEMENT title (#PCDATA)>
 <!ELEMENT author (firstname, lastname)>
 <!ELEMENT firstname (#PCDATA)>
 <!ELEMENT lastname (#PCDATA)>
 <!ELEMENT ISBN (#PCDATA)>
 <!ELEMENT publisher (#PCDATA)>
 <!ELEMENT publishyear (#PCDATA)>
 <!ELEMENT price (#PCDATA)>
 <!ATTLIST price type (US|CAN|UK|EURO) #REQUIRED>
]>
```

The **DOCTYPE** declaration of the DTD specifies the root element—in this case, the **<bookcatalog>** element. An element simply consists of a start tag, for example, **<title>**; all of the text in between, **History of Interviews**; and the corresponding end tag, for example, **</title>**. Only one root element, however, may exist within an XML document. The root element marks the beginning of the document and is considered the parent of all the other elements, which are nested within its start tag and end tag. For XML documents to be considered *valid* with respect to this DTD, the root element **bookcatalog** must be the first element to start off the body of the XML document.

Following this are the *element declarations,* which stipulate the child elements that must be nested within the root element **bookcatalog**, the content model for the root element. Note that all the child elements of **bookcatalog** are explicitly called out in its element declaration, and that **author** has **a +** as a suffix. This is an example of the *Extended Backus-Naur Format (EBNF)* that can be used to describe the content model. The allowed suffixes are

? For 0 or 1 occurrence
* For 0 or more occurrences
+ For 1 or more occurrences
No suffix means 1 and only 1.

Note also the use of **#PCDATA** to declare that the element text must not be marked-up text, and that **price**'s required attribute values are explicitly declared. The difference between **CDATA** and **PCDATA** is that **CDATA** sections are simply skipped by the parser and aren't checked for well-formedness; hence, they can be viewed as "non-parsed character data."

Thus a validating XML parser, by parsing the XML document according to the rules specified in this DTD, tries to determine whether the document conforms to the DTD (is valid), meaning that all the required elements, attributes, structural relationships, and sequences are as declared.

XML Namespaces

Earlier in the chapter, we introduced XML namespaces. This W3C XML standard introduces the following terms with regard to XML namespaces:

- *Local name* Represents the name of the element or attribute without the prefix. In the previous example, **book**, **title**, **author**, **ISBN**, and so forth are considered local names. These are used whenever there is no concern over duplicate tag or attribute names. *Local name* is also used to refer to the name part of a qualified name.
- *Qualified name* Represents the fully prefixed name. For example, as a continuation of the previous examples, **bk:title**, **bk:book**, and so forth are considered qualified names. Qualified names are being used more often because XML Schemas are defining standard types, such as address, customer, purchase order, and so on, and there is a need to differentiate semantics.
- *Namespace prefix* Represents the namespace prefix declared using the special prefix, **xmlns**. The previous example defined one namespace prefix: **bk**. Prefixes are scoped and thus must be unique within the children of the parent element that declared the namespace, but prefixes may be overridden by a new declaration on a descendent element or attribute.
- *Expanded name* Represents the result of applying the namespace defined by the namespace prefix to the qualified name. For example, **bk:booklist** could be expanded to **http://www.mypublishsite.com/books:booklist**. The expanded name is never seen in the XML document itself, but is conceptually important.

Two kinds of namespace attributes exist: *prefixed* and *default*. A prefixed namespace attribute is of the form **nsprefix:attr**, where **nsprefix** is the namespace prefix defined previously. Once a prefix has been declared, it can be used to specify a namespace for any elements or attributes in the scope of the element where it was declared. You would, therefore, need to declare global prefixes—that is, prefixes you want to use everywhere in your document—as attributes of the root element.

The default namespace attribute is **xmlns**. **xmlns** has the effect of specifying a default namespace for the entire scope of an element (including the element itself). This default does not apply to the attributes in the subtree, however. For example, consider the following example:

```
<booklist xmlns="http://www.osborne.com/books>
 <book isbn="1234-5678-1234">
  <title>Oracle XML Handbook</title>
  <author>Oracle XML Team</author>
 </book>
 <book isbn="24345-564478-1344234">
  <title>The C programming language</title>
  <author>Kernighan and Ritchie</title>
 </book>
</booklist>
```

This root element declaration has the effect of specifying that all the elements under **booklist** (**book**, **title**, **author**) are in the **http://www.osborne.com/books** namespace. The attribute **isbn**, however, is not. Default namespaces can be specified at any level of the document and have the effect of overriding previous declarations. Setting **xmlns=""** has the effect of removing the default namespace declaration for a particular document subtree.

Namespaces complicate the determination of attribute uniqueness. For example, consider the following example:

```
<booklist xmlns:dollars="USA" xmlns:pounds="Britain">
 <book dollars:price="7.99" pounds:price="3.99">
  <title>The Code of the Woosters</title>
  <author>P.G. Wodehouse </author>
 </book>
</booklist>
```

The two **price** attributes should be considered different, even though they have the same local name, because their expanded names are different. The following document would not be considered well-formed, however:

```
<booklist xmlns:dollars="USA" xmlns:currency="USA">
 <book dollars:price="7.99" currency:price="3.99">
  <title>The Code of the Woosters</title>
  <author>P.G. Wodehouse </author>
 </book>
</booklist>
```

Here, even though **dollars:price** and **currency:price** have different qualified names, they have the same expanded name, which means they are, in fact, the same attribute declared twice on the book element. For a similar reason, only one default namespace is allowed per document.

XML and the Database

Databases and XML offer complementary functionality for storing data. Whereas databases store data for efficient retrieval, XML offers an easy information exchange that enables interoperability between applications due to its ability to encapsulate the data with the metadata. Oracle8*i*, Oracle9*i*, and, to an even larger extent, Oracle Database 10*g* enable you to store XML natively and build XML-enabled applications. Storing XML collections in databases enables you to benefit from not only the full power of a SQL engine but also database administration, business intelligence, and recovery tools and procedures, such as Oracle Enterprise Manager, Discoverer, and RMAN. You can use them to enforce rules about data and security, and to block operations that compromise data integrity by embedding rules and logic in a database. Also, converting database tables into XML documents enables you to take advantage of XML's features while preserving SQL data types, indexes, and enterprise-level scalability. You can present XML documents as HTML pages with XSLT stylesheets, search them using XML-based query languages, or use them as a data-exchange format.

Oracle's object-relational features have been extended to support hierarchical storage thus enabling you to capture the complex structure of XML data. You can operate and manage XML data on a desired level of granularity which lends itself readily to efficiently construct dynamic XML documents from the stored fragments. You can also store XML documents in a new XMLType data type that supports storing XML as a single document in a virtually unbounded text data type called *Character Large Object (CLOB),* as data without tags distributed in object-relational tables or as both. You can use Oracle Text to perform searches on XML documents stored in CLOBs.

NOTE
A CLOB is one of the Oracle internal Large Objects (LOBs) whose value is composed of character data and can store up to 4GB of data. Meanwhile, a VARCHAR2 column in a table has a limit of 4000 bytes, and a VARCHAR2 in a PL/SQL variable has a limit of 32767 bytes (32K).

CLOBs can be indexed to search the XML as plain text or as document sections for more precise searches. For example, you can find **Oracle** WITHIN **<title>**, ignoring it elsewhere in the document. Oracle Text also provides full-text indexing of documents and the capability to do SQL queries over documents, along with XPATH-like searching. Finally, Oracle's Advanced Queuing (AQ) now supports XML-based message queuing in the database, supporting both synchronous and asynchronous communications of XML messages defined in the standard *Simple Object Access Protocol (SOAP)* format for both the server and client.

Database Schema and XML Documents

XML documents consist of text that conforms to a hierarchy or tree structure specified by a DTD or XML Schema. As distinct from other strictly relational databases, you can easily store this hierarchical data in an optimal internal form using Oracle's object-relational tables, which serve as the foundation for the native XMLType storage. All the existing and future internal applications can work with the information in the most efficient way possible. When you retrieve information, for sharing with partners or other applications, you can present the appropriate view of data and document content specific to the task at hand as integrated XML. These XMLType views enable you to present data in any number of "logical" combinations, hiding any details of their underlying physical storage. You can effectively transform the structure of one or more underlying tables into a more useful or more appropriate structure for the demands of a specific application. When you link views of information with other views of related information, they quite naturally form "trees" or "graphs" of related data. When you represent database information as XML, the previous related views provide the foundation for many different tree-structured XML documents.

Here, we offer a simple example of how a database table would be expressed as an XML DTD:

```
<!DOCTYPE table [
 <!ELEMENT table (rows)*>
 <!ELEMENT rows (column1, column2, ...)>
 <!ELEMENT column1 (#PCDATA)>
 <!ELEMENT column2 (#PCDATA)>
...]>
```

Note, however, that the actual data types in these columns remain unspecified. We can instead use an XML Schema of the following form:

```
<xs:element name="table">
 <xs:sequence>
  <xs:element name="rows">
  <xs:sequence >
  <xs:element name="column1" type="xs:integer" xdb:SQLType="NUMBER"/>
  <xs:element name="column2" type="xs:string" xdb:SQLType="CLOB"/>
 . . .
```

This does provide us with the column data types through the **type** attribute which can further constrain the data as we will discuss later in the database chapters. However, a database provides even more capability to express rules than does a DTD or an XML Schema. The database schema defines type information and constraints—not only simple constraints, such as permissible value ranges, but also constraints between columns and tables. A database schema enables you to define relationships or dependencies. For example, your e-commerce business might receive orders as XML documents. By using a database, you can link customer and order information, and define a rule about not processing orders for closed accounts. In spite of the limitations in DTDs or XML Schemas, mapping a database schema to a DTD or an XML Schema presents the database as a virtual XML document to the tools that need XML documents as input.

Mapping XML Documents to a Database Schema

When mapping XML documents associated with an XML DTD or an XSD to a database schema for the purpose of storing XML in Oracle, three basic strategies exist:

- Map the complete XML document as a single, intact object, such as an XMLType CLOB.

- Store the data in relational or object-relational tables and create XMLType views over the data to present it as an XML document.
- Map XML documents to an Oracle Native XMLType.

You can choose one of the previous approaches, depending on the structure of the XML document and the operations performed by the application. Each of these three approaches is described in turn next. You can also store the XML DTD or Schema in the database to validate the XML documents.

XML Documents Stored As XMLType CLOBs

Storing an intact XML document in an XMLType CLOB is a good strategy if the XML document contains static content that will only be retrieved as a whole or updated by replacing the entire document. Examples include written text such as articles, advertisements, books, legal briefs, and contracts. Applications that use a repository of this nature are known as *document-centric* and operate on the stored XML outside the database. Storing this kind of document intact within OracleX gives you the advantages of an industry-proven database and its reliability over file system storage. Upon insertion, XML documents are checked and only committed if well formed. Oracle Text can provide both content and path indexes to search, but data retrievals need to be done by processing the whole document. The *Oracle XML Developer's Kit (XDK)* provides the functionality to use standards-based interfaces to access, modify, transform, and validate these documents.

XMLType CLOBs can also be used in conjunction with XMLType views and the Native XMLType described in the following sections. In these cases, the XML is a well-formed fragment that is treated as a whole.

XML Documents Stored As XMLType Views

When an application is using XML merely as an encapsulation of its data, it is considered to be *data-centric*. Typically, the XML document contains elements and attributes that have complex structures, but in reality this structure is simply metadata to convey the actual data of interest. Examples of this kind of document include sales orders, invoices, and airline flight schedules. In this case, there is value to maintaining the storage as SQL data because the actual data types need to be exposed to the application. Oracle Database 10g, with its XMLType object-relational extensions, has the capability to capture the structure of the data in the database present it in an XMLType view while still you can easily update, query, rearrange, and reformat as needed using SQL. The important distinction to remember is that this view cannot convey document order, comments, processing instructions, or the whitespace between elements and attributes that are preserved in the CLOB type.

Using XMLType views is especially useful when you are XML-enabling existing applications or database schemas. This view can serve to abstract the underlying database schema, thereby eliminating the need to modify it to support XML. In fact, since you can have multiple views of differing XML structure over the same database schema, you can directly support a different XML schema for each view without the need to apply XSL to transform the documents to a structure compatible with your database schema.

Applications built against XMLType views have the flexibility of using SQL and SQL-XML interfaces to process within the database and using the XDK to process either in JServer, middle tier, or client.

XML Documents Stored As Native XMLTypes

Finally, you can store an XML document as a *Native XMLType,* where the underlying storage is dictated and created by its XML schema. This type has the advantages of the other two types together because it stores the XML as SQL data and preserves byte-for-byte fidelity. Creating this native type is as simple as registering its XML schema, which not only creates the underlying database schema but also creates a database resource that can be used for access and updates with the Internet-standard protocols HTTP, FTP, and WebDAV.

Applications that need both a document and data view can make full use of this type, because an extensive array of SQL, PL/SQL, Java, C, and C++ interfaces is available. Inserts, updates, and deletes are simplified due to Native XMLType's support for query rewrites, thereby eliminating the triggers needed by the XMLType views. The Native XMLType can, however, be used in conjunction with these views to expose differing or subset XML documents. To further support large documents, a "virtual" or "lazy" DOM is provided through the XDK to access only those elements that are needed at any one time.

While the native XMLType exposes broad functionality, you need to remember that the underlying storage is intimately tied to the XML schema that created it. Therefore, it will most likely not be the best choice for applications that need to support multiple schemas or a nontrivial evolving schema.

Summary

Oracle provides you with differing strategies to map XML documents into a database schema. Since XML is an enabling technology and not an application, there is no one strategy that will work optimally for all scenarios. XML is an abstraction born from the need to exchange content or data in an interoperable manner. XML's cost is the increased overhead to process its structure and tags, thus your correct selection of XML storage model will have a significant performance impact on your application. In later chapters, we will walk you through the process of using each of these strategies with appropriate example applications.

CHAPTER 2

Accessing XML with DOM, SAX, JAXB, and StAX

The importance of XML and its related technologies being open standards is that components, libraries, and applications built to these standards have the potential for a high level of interoperability and reuse. To parse and access XML documents, you can call upon a number of components and utilities. You can use the W3C-specified *Document Object Model (DOM)* APIs to query and manipulate a parsed document or create a new document from scratch. You can use the *Simple API for XML (SAX)* event-based APIs for the same purpose without building a full-blown DOM tree in memory. You can use the Sun Microsystems Java Extension standard *Java Architecture for XML Binding (JAXB)* APIs to generate Java code from an XML Schema, which enables you to create and access a conformant XML document. Finally, the Sun Microsystems Java Extension standard *Streaming API for XML (StAX)*APIs enable you to perform stream parsing on an XML document in a manner that is similar to, yet simpler than, using SAX. The following sections discuss parsing and various accessor APIs and provide examples of how to use them.

Parsing and Binding an XML Document

Application programs invoke the parse function to read an XML document and provide access to its content and structure by DOM or SAX APIs. Usually, initialization and termination functions must also be invoked in association with the parse function. Note that various flags, such as to discard white space and to turn on validation, can be set with some initialization functions before the parse function is invoked by the application program. For example, whereas some XML parsers are only nonvalidating, meaning they cannot check to see whether the XML document conforms to the DTD or XML Schema, other parsers, such as those from Oracle, have optional validation, meaning users can specify validation or nonvalidation before invoking the parse function. In addition, the parse routine must be able to accept different language encodings as specified in the XML document.

The *Oracle XML Parser for Java* makes it easy for Java programmers to extend their existing Java applications seamlessly to support XML. It processes XML documents and provides access to the information contained in them through a variety of user-friendly APIs. The parser fully supports both the tree-based DOM and event-based SAX standards. It also has a built-in XSLT processor that makes transforming XML documents from one format to another extremely simple. The parser can be used in any environment that supports JDK 1.2.*x* or higher, and it can also be run inside the Oracle9*i* and Oracle Database 10*g* OJVM. The parser is completely internationalized and supports every character set supported by Java, in addition to numerous others. This support means that the parser provides error messages in nearly every language supported by Oracle9*i* and Oracle Database 10*g*, making it an invaluable tool if you're writing XML applications for non–English- speaking users.

The *Oracle XML Parser for C* with its integrated XSLT processor is provided in two forms: as a stand-alone, command-line executable, and as a library for linking with applications. Most users write their own applications and use the XML library. The executable is provided as a quick way to familiarize new users with XML by parsing and validating their own test documents, and it is also used to apply stylesheets to the XML document.

The C library contains APIs for initializing, parsing a file or buffer, resetting and shutting down the parser, plus full DOM, SAX, and XSLT implementations. Typically, you would use the following sequence: initialize(), parse(), terminate(). If multiple documents are to be parsed, the sequence would be initialize(), parse(), parse(), ..., terminate(). All data presented by a parse remains valid until termination or cleanup. If you need only the results on each parse without retaining older data, the sequence would be initialize(), parse(), clean(), parse(), clean(),..., terminate(). To apply stylesheets to the XML documents, an additional call to **xslprocess** before terminate() or clean() would be necessary. See the C header, **xml.h**, in the XDK distribution for details on available functions.

The *Oracle XML Parser for C++* calls the C parser with a wrapper to make it accessible from C++, with both interfaces provided in the same XML library, **oraxml10.lib** or **libxml10.a**. Everything about the C APIs holds true for the C++ APIs, except that the C++ APIs are able to provide APIs in an object-oriented manner corresponding to the class and method names in the DOM specification. See the C++ header, **xml.hpp**, for details on available functions.

Finally, functionality exists by way of class generators in both Java and C++ to automate the mapping between XML documents and code, so that generated code can create, access, update, and validate XML documents against XML Schema. Among the advantages are speed (the generated code is easily generated from input schema), ease of use (application programmers can easily call these generated routines rather than code their own), and data conversion (XML document data can be converted to that language's data types). Using this type of functionality makes marshalling and unmarshalling XML content back and forth into the language representation very easy and facilitates the programming of XML applications.

Accessing XML Using the DOM

DOM is based on an object structure that closely resembles the structure of the documents it models. For instance, consider the following XML document:

```
<booklist>
 <book isbn="0-07-213495-X">
  <title>Oracle9i XML Handbook</title>
  <author>Chang, Scardina and Kiritzov</author>
  <publisher>Osborne</publisher>
  <price>49.99</price>
 </book>
</booklist>
```

In DOM, documents have a logical structure that is similar to a tree, also known as a *structure model*. In the example document, you can see the root element **booklist** serves as the root of the DOM tree, as you would expect. The root element contains one child, **book**, which has four children: **title**, **author**, **publisher**, and **price**; and one attribute, **ISBN**. The leaf nodes of the tree are simple text string values. The nodes in the DOM tree can be reached by using *tree-walking* methods (this does not include attributes). One important property of DOM structure models is *structural isomorphism*: if any two DOM implementations are used to create a representation of the same document, they create the same structure model. This means implementations are free to choose any data structure (not necessarily a tree) to implement DOM. When the XML parser parses the XML document, such a representation can be formed in memory.

W3C has created a set of DOM APIs for accessing and navigating this structure. Again, the components of this structure are the root element of the document; elements; attributes; text nodes that represent the textual content of an element or attribute; CDATA sections to mark off blocks of text that would otherwise be regarded as markup; comments; entity references; processing instructions; and so forth. XML parsers that provide all the DOM APIs are considered to be compliant with the W3C DOM recommendation.

The following Java code sample demonstrates a simple use of the parser and DOM APIs. This sample demonstrates how to set parser options, parse the XML file given to the application, and print the element nodes and attribute values in the document.

```
import java.io.*;
import java.net.*;
import org.w3c.dom.*;
import org.w3c.dom.Node;
import oracle.xml.parser.v2.*;

public class DOMSample {
 static public void main(String[] argv){
  try {
   if (argv.length != 1){
    // Must pass in the name of the XML file.
    System.err.println("Usage: java DOMSample filename");
    System.exit(1);
   }

   // Get an instance of the parser
   DOMParser parser = new DOMParser();

   // Generate a URL from the filename.
   URL url = createURL(argv[0]);

   // Set various parser options: validation on,
   // warnings shown, error stream set to stderr.
   parser.setErrorStream(System.err);
   parser.showWarnings(true);

   // Parse the document.
   parser.parse(url);

   // Obtain the document.
   Document doc = parser.getDocument();

   // Print document elements
   System.out.print("The elements are: ");
   printElements(doc);

   // Print document element attributes
   System.out.println("The attributes of each element are: ");
   printElementAttributes(doc);
   }
   catch (Exception e){
    System.out.println(e.toString());
   }
  }

  static void printElements(Document doc) {
```

```
    NodeList nl = doc.getElementsByTagName("*");
    Node n;

    for (int i=0; i<nl.getLength(); i++){
     n = nl.item(i);
     System.out.print(n.getNodeName() + " ");
    }
    System.out.println();
   }

  static void printElementAttributes(Document doc){
    NodeList nl = doc.getElementsByTagName("*");
    Element e;
    Node n;
    NamedNodeMap nnm;

    String attrname;
    String attrval;
    int i, len;

    len = nl.getLength();

    for (int j=0; j < len; j++){
     e = (Element)nl.item(j);
     System.out.println(e.getTagName() + ":");
     nnm = e.getAttributes();

     if (nnm != null){
      for (i=0; i<nnm.getLength(); i++){
       n = nnm.item(i);
       attrname = n.getNodeName();
       attrval = n.getNodeValue();
       System.out.print(" " + attrname + " = " + attrval);
      }
     }
     System.out.println();
    }
   }
}
```

Introducing the DOM APIs

The power of the DOM lies in its capability to provide access to an in-memory structure representation of the entire XML document. Using the DOM, applications can perform tasks such as searching for specific data in an XML document, adding or deleting elements and attributes in the XML document, and transforming the DOM to an entirely different document. Along with the org.w3c.dom interfaces provided by W3C, the Oracle Java XML parser comes with a set of classes that implement the DOM APIs and extend them to provide other useful features, such as printing a document fragment or retrieving namespace information.

The following code demonstrates some of the DOM functionality in an XML parser:

```
// This example demonstrates a simple use of the DOMParser
// An XML file is parsed and some information is printed out.

import java.io.*;
import java.net.*;
import oracle.xml.parser.v2.DOMParser;
import org.w3c.dom.*;
import org.w3c.dom.Node;
// Extensions to DOM Interfaces for Namespace support.
import oracle.xml.parser.v2.XMLElement;
import oracle.xml.parser.v2.XMLAttr;

public class DOMExample {
 public static void main(String[] argv){
  try {
   // Generate a new input stream from given file
   FileInputStream xmldoc = new FileInputStream(argv[0]);

   // Parse the document using DOMParser
   DOMParser parser = new DOMParser();
   parser.parse(xmldoc);

   // Obtain the document.
   Document doc = parser.getDocument();

   // Print some information regarding attributes of elements
   // in the document
   printElementAttributes(doc);
  }
  catch (Exception e){
   System.out.println(e.toString());
  }
 }
 static void printElementAttributes(Document doc){
  NodeList nl = doc.getElementsByTagName("*");
  Element e;
  XMLAttr nsAttr;
  String attrname, attrval, attrqname; NamedNodeMap nnm;

  for (int j=0; j < nl.getLength(); j++) {
   e = (Element) nl.item(j);
   System.out.println(e.getTagName() + ":");
   nnm = e.getAttributes();

   if (nnm != null) {
    for (int i=0; i < nnm.getLength(); i++) {
     nsAttr = (XMLAttr) nnm.item(i);

     // Use the methods getQualifiedName(), getLocalName(),
     // getNamespace(), and getExpandedName() in NSName
```

```
      // interface to get Namespace information.

      attrname = nsAttr.getExpandedName(
      attrqname = nsAttr.getQualifiedName();
      attrval = nsAttr.getNodeValue();

      System.out.println(" " + attrqname + "(" + attrname +
       ")" + " = " +attrval);
     }
    }
   System.out.println();
  }
 }
}.
```

The DOM APIs, unlike the SAX APIs, can be used only after the XML document is completely parsed. The downside of this is that large XML documents can occupy a lot of memory, which could ultimately affect the performance of your application. In pure functionality terms, however, the DOM APIs are definitely more powerful. The first thing you need to do before you begin using any of the DOM APIs is to parse your document using a new instance of **DOMParser**:

```
// Parse the document using DOMParser
DOMParser parser = new DOMParser();
parser.parse(xmldoc);
```

Then, you need to request the parser to return a handle to the root of the Document Object Model, which it has constructed in memory:

```
// Obtain the document.
Document doc = parser.getDocument();
```

Using the preceding handle, you can access every part of the XML document you just parsed. The **DOMExample** class assumes you want to access the elements in the document and their attributes. To do this, you first need to obtain a list of all the elements in the document. A DOM method called **getElementsByTagName** enables you to retrieve, recursively, all elements that match a given tag name under a certain level. It also supports a special tag named "*", which matches any tag. Given this information, you need to invoke this method at the top level of the document via the handle to the root you obtained earlier in this section:

```
NodeList nl = doc.getElementsByTagName("*");
```

The preceding call generates a list of all the elements in the document. Each of these elements contains the information regarding its attributes. To access this information, you need to traverse this list:

```
len = nl.getLength();
for (int j=0; j < len; j++) {
 e = (Element) nl.item(j);
   ...
}
```

To obtain the attributes of each element in the loop, you can use a DOM method called **getAttributes**. This method generates a special kind of DOM list called **NamedNodeMap**. Once you obtain this list, traversing it to obtain information about the attributes themselves is straightforward.

DOM Level 2

As DOM evolved into Level 2, it became a modular specification, meaning that some of the new APIs can be stand-alone modules. Though the specifications are "Level 2," they are actually 1.0 versions, which can be confusing, especially when the same DOM Core names are reused. In addition to DOM Level 2 Core, there are Events, Style, HTML, Traversal and Range, and Views modules. References to these specifications can be found in the appendix of this book.

The introduction of XML namespaces was the primary force behind the development of the DOM Core Level 2 specification, because all the element and attribute functions now had to accept or retrieve namespaces. The following snippet uses the Oracle XML Parser's DOM 2.0 XML Namespace support to retrieve additional information regarding the attributes of each element:

```
for (int i=0; i < nnm.getLength(); i++){
 nsAttr = (XMLAttr) nnm.item(i);

 // Use the methods getQualifiedName() and getExpandedName()
 // in NSName interface to get Namespace information.

 attrname = nsAttr.getExpandedName();
 attrqname = nsAttr.getQualifiedName();
 attrval = nsAttr.getNodeValue();

 System.out.println(" " + attrqname + "(" + attrname +
                  ")" + " = " + attrval);
}
```

This kind of code is useful if the XML document you have to parse has elements with many attributes that belong to different namespaces. For example, suppose the **booklist** XML document from the preceding section looked like this:

```
<booklist xmlns:osborne="http://www.osborne.com"
          xmlns:bookguild="http://www.bookguild.com"
          xmlns:dollars="http://www.currency.org/dollars">
 <book osborne:isbn="0-07-213495-X" title="Oracle9i XML Handbook"
       author="Chang, Scardina, and Kiritzov" bookguild:publisher="Osborne"
       dollars:price="49.99"/>
 <book osborne:isbn="1230-23498-2349879" title="Emperor's New Mind"
       author="Roger Penrose" bookguild:publisher="Oxford Publishing
              Company"
       dollars:price="15.99"/>
</booklist>
```

The generated output with namespaces would look like this:

```
xmlns:osborne(http://www.w3.org/2000/xmlnls/:osborne)=http://www.osborne.com
xmlns:bookguild(http://www.w3.org/2000/xmlns/:bookguild)=http://www.bookguild.com
xmlns:dollars(http://www.w3.org/2000/xmlns/:dollars=http://www.currency.org/dollars
book:
 osborne:isbn(http://www.osborne.com:isbn) = 0-07-213495-X
 title(title) = Oracle9i XML Handbook
 author(author) = Chang, Scardina, and Kiritzov
```

The DOM Level 2 Traversal and Range functionality includes methods that create *Iterators* and *TreeWalkers* to traverse a node and its children in document order. Objects using a TreeWalker to navigate a document tree or subtree use the view of the document defined by their **whatToShow** flags and filters. An example of such stub code would be the following:

```
// This filter accepts everything
NodeFilter n1 = new nf1();
// Node iterator doesn't allow expansion of entity references
NodeIterator ni =
doc.createNodeIterator(elems[0],NodeFilter.SHOW_ALL,n1,false);
// Move forward
XMLNode nn =(XMLNode) ni.nextNode();
while (nn != null){
 System.out.println(nn.getNodeName() + " " + nn.getNodeValue());
 nn = (XMLNode)ni.nextNode();
}
// Move backward
nn = (XMLNode)ni.previousNode();
while (nn != null){
 System.out.println(nn.getNodeName() + " " + nn.getNodeValue());
 nn = (XMLNode)ni.previousNode();
}

// Node iterator allows expansion of entity references
ni = doc.createNodeIterator(elems[0],NodeFilter.SHOW_ALL,n1,true);
// Move forward
nn =(XMLNode) ni.nextNode();
while (nn != null){
 System.out.println(nn.getNodeName() + " " + nn.getNodeValue());
 nn = (XMLNode)ni.nextNode();
}
// Move backward
nn = (XMLNode)ni.previousNode();
while (nn != null){
 System.out.println(nn.getNodeName() + " " + nn.getNodeValue());
 nn = (XMLNode)ni.previousNode();
}

// This filter doesn't accept expansion of entity references
NodeFilter n2 = new nf2();

// Node iterator allows expansion of entity references
```

```
ni = doc.createNodeIterator(elems[0],NodeFilter.SHOW_ALL,n2,true);
// Move forward
nn =(XMLNode) ni.nextNode();
while (nn != null){
 System.out.println(nn.getNodeName() + " " + nn.getNodeValue());
 nn = (XMLNode)ni.nextNode();
}
// Move backward
nn = (XMLNode)ni.previousNode();
while (nn != null){
 System.out.println(nn.getNodeName() + " " + nn.getNodeValue());
 nn = (XMLNode)ni.previousNode();
}

// After detaching, all node iterator methods throw an exception
ni.detach();
try {
 nn = (XMLNode)ni.nextNode();
}
catch(DOMException e) {
 System.out.println(e.getMessage());
}
try {
 nn = (XMLNode)ni.previousNode();
}
catch(DOMException e){
 System.out.println(e.getMessage());
}
// TreeWalker allows expansion of entity references
TreeWalker tw =
    doc.createTreeWalker(elems[0],NodeFilter.SHOW_ALL,n1,true);
nn = (XMLNode)tw.getRoot();
// Traverse in document order
while (nn != null) {
 System.out.println(nn.getNodeName() + " " + nn.getNodeValue());
 nn = (XMLNode)tw.nextNode();
}

tw = doc.createTreeWalker(elems[0],NodeFilter.SHOW_ALL,n1,true);
nn = (XMLNode) tw.getRoot();
// Traverse the depth left
while (nn != null){
 System.out.println(nn.getNodeName() + " " + nn.getNodeValue());
 nn = (XMLNode)tw.firstChild();
}
tw = doc.createTreeWalker(elems[0],NodeFilter.SHOW_ALL,n2,true);
nn = (XMLNode)tw.getRoot();
// Traverse in document order
while (nn != null){
```

```
 System.out.println(nn.getNodeName() + " " + nn.getNodeValue());
 nn = (XMLNode)tw.nextNode();
}
tw = doc.createTreeWalker(elems[0],NodeFilter.SHOW_ALL,n2,true);
nn = (XMLNode) tw.getRoot();
// Traverse the depth right
while (nn != null) {
 System.out.println(nn.getNodeName() + " " + nn.getNodeValue());
 nn = (XMLNode)tw.lastChild();
}
...
class nf1 implements NodeFilter {
 public short acceptNode(Node node) {
  return FILTER_ACCEPT;
 }
}
class nf2 implements NodeFilter {
 public short acceptNode(Node node) {
  short type = node.getNodeType();

  if ((type == Node.ELEMENT_NODE) || (type == Node.ATTRIBUTE_NODE))
   return FILTER_ACCEPT;
  if ((type == Node.ENTITY_REFERENCE_NODE))
   return FILTER_REJECT;
  return FILTER_SKIP;
 }
}
```

DOM Level 3

As in Level 2, the DOM Level 3 W3C Working Draft consists of DOM Level 3 modules of Core, Load and Save, Validation, Events, and XPath, which provide further functionality identified by DOM users as useful and necessary for their applications. References to these can be found in the Appendix.

A DOM application can use the **hasFeature()** method of the **DOMImplementation** object to determine whether the module is supported. A **DOMImplementation** object can be retrieved from a **Document** using the **getImplementation()** method. Examples of these feature strings for their respective modules are **XML**, **HTML**, **Events**, and **Validation**.

The basis of the DOM, as previously stated, is a tree consisting of **Node** objects. Different kinds of **Nodes** are used to represent an XML document: **Document**, **Element**, **Attr**, **Text**, **DocumentFragment**, **DocumentType**, **ProcessingInstruction**, **Comment**, **CDATASection**, **EntityReference**, and **Notation**. The DOM also defines some other types that represent a list of nodes—**NodeList** and **NamedNodeMap**—and introduces a **DOMString** type, which is a string of *UTF-16* encoded characters. Finally, DOM introduces an exception type, **DOMException**, which is raised by the various DOM interfaces if an erroneous operation is performed or if some other error occurred during execution.

Table 2-1 and Table 2-2 list the DOM types and the corresponding types supported by the Oracle XML parsers for Java, PL/SQL, C and C++.

DOM Type	Java	PL/SQL
Node	XMLNode	DOMNode
Document	XMLDocument	DOMDocument
Element	XMLElement	DOMElement
Attr	XMLAttr	DOMAttr
Text	XMLText	DOMText
DocumentFragment	XMLDocumentFragment	DOMDocumentFragment
ProcessingInstruction	XMLPI	DOMPI
DocumentType	DTD	XMLDTD
EntityReference	XMLEntityReference	DOMEntityReference
Comment	XMLComment	DOMComment
CDATASection	XMLCDATA	DOMCDataSection
NodeList	XMLNodeList	DOMNodeList
NamedNodeMap	N/A (private class)	DOMNamedNodeMap
Notation	XMLNotation	DOMNotation
DOMString	java.lang.String	VARCHAR2
DOMException	XMLDOMException	EXCEPTION

TABLE 2-1. *DOM Types with Corresponding Java and PL/SQL Oracle Types*

DOM Type	C	C++
Node	xmlnode	NodeRef
Document	xmldocnode	DocumentRef
Element	xmlelemnode	ElementRef
Attr	xmlattrnode	AttrRef
Text	xmltextnode	TextRef
DocumentFragment	xmlfragnode	DocumentFragmentRef
ProcessingInstruction	xmlpinode	ProcessingInstructionRef
DocumentType	xmldtdnode	DocumentTypeRef

TABLE 2-2. *DOM Types with Corresponding C and C++ Oracle Types*

DOM Type	C	C++
EntityReference	xmlentrefnode	EntityReferenceRef
Comment	xmlcommentnode	CommentRef
CDATASection	xmlcdatanode	CDATASectionRef
NodeList	xmlnodelist	NodeListRef
NamedNodeMap	xmlnamedmap	NamedNodeMapRef
Notation	xmlnotenode	NotationRef
DOMString	oratext *	DOMString
DOMException	N/A	N/A

TABLE 2-2. *DOM Types with Corresponding C and C++ Oracle Types* (continued)

Oracle DOM APIs in C

Because the DOM is an object-oriented specification and the C language is *not* object oriented, some changes had to be made. In particular, the C function namespace is flat, so the names of DOM methods that are the same in several different classes have been changed to make them unique, as detailed in Table 2-3.

The documentation that is included with the C XDK details each of these functions and can also be seen in the parser header file, **xml.h**.

DOM Name	C Name
Attr::getName, ...	XmlDomGetAttrName, ...
CharacterData::getData, ...	XmlDomGetCharData, ...
DocumentType::getName, ...	XmlDomGetDocTypeName, ...
Entity::getPublicId, ...	XmlDomGetEntityPublicID, ...
NamedNodeMap::item	XmlDomGetChildNode
NamedNodeMap::getLength	XmlDomGetNodeMapLength
NodeList::item	XmlDomGetChildNode
NodeList::getLength	XmlDomGetNodeMapLength
Notation::getPublicId, ...	XmlDomGetNotationPubID, ...

TABLE 2-3. *Oracle DOM APIs in C*

Accessing XML with SAX

Simple API for XML (SAX) is a standard interface for event-based XML parsing. This means that notification of certain events and data encountered during the parsing of the XML document can be reported by callback functions to the application program. On notification of these events, the application program then must deal with them. For example, the application program can have data structures using *callback event handlers*. Finally, the types of information and notifications passed back by these callback functions are in the vein of such things as the start and end of elements and information related to an element's content, such as CDATA, processing instructions, and subelements.

SAX, initially developed by David Megginson, has become a W3C XML standard. One advantage of using SAX parsing over using the DOM is that an in-memory representation of the parse structure doesn't have to be built, thus saving memory and resulting in better performance for certain types of operations, such as searching. On the other hand, modifying, updating, and performing other structural operations may be made more efficient by using a DOM parser.

SAX Level 1 and Level 2

The SAX API consists of a set of interfaces and classes. Some of these interfaces are implemented by a SAX parser (such as the Oracle XML Parser for Java). Others need to be implemented/extended by your application. In addition, with SAX Level 2, the interfaces and methods now have namespace support, along with other functionality such as filters. Consequently, because of the namespace support, some of the interfaces were deprecated and replaced with new ones.

SAX interfaces and classes are classified into five groups:

- Interfaces implemented by the parser
- Interfaces implemented by the application
- Standard SAX classes
- Optional Java-specific helper classes in the **org.xml.sax.helpers** package
- Java demonstration classes in the **nul** package

However, as an application writer, you only need to focus on at most two of the interfaces, as described in Table 2-4.

SAX 1.0 Interface	SAX 2.0 Interface	Description
DocumentHandler	ContentHandler	Receives notifications from parser
ErrorHandler	ErrorHandler	Optional interface for special error handling
DTDHandler	DTDHandler	Optional interface needed to work with notations and unparsed (binary) entities
EntityResolver	EntityResolver	Optional interface needed to do redirection of URIs in documents

TABLE 2-4. *Interfaces Implemented by Applications*

SAX 1.0 Interface	SAX 2.0 Interface	Description
ParserFactory	XMLReaderFactory	Class to support loading SAX parsers dynamically
AttributeListImpl	AtrributeImpl	Convenience class to make a persistent copy of an AttributeList
LocatorImpl	LocatorImpl	Convenience class to make a persistent snapshot of a Locator's values at a specific point in the parse
N/A	NamespaceSupport	Convenience class to add namespace support
N/A	XMLFilerImpl	Base class to be subclassed when applications need to modify the event stream
HandlerBase	DefaultHandler	Base class with default implementations of all four SAX2 handler classes

TABLE 2-5. *Oracle SAX Helper Classes*

In addition to the application interfaces, most SAX parsers, including the Oracle XML Parser for Java, implement helper classes that provide static methods that are useful in integrating SAX parsers. These helper classes are described in Table 2-5.

The following code sample demonstrates a simple use of the parser and SAX API. The XML file given to the application is parsed and prints some information about the contents of this file. Sample code of various useful interfaces is also provided.

```
import org.xml.sax.*;
import java.io.*;
import java.net.*;
import oracle.xml.parser.v2.*;

public class SAXSample extends DefaultHandler {
 // Store the locator
 Locator locator;

 static public void main(String[] argv) {
  try {
   if (argv.length != 1) {
   // Must pass in the name of the XML file.
    System.err.println("Usage: SAXSample filename");
    System.exit(1);
   }
   // Create a new handler for the parser
   SAXSample sample = new SAXSample();

   // Get an instance of the parser
```

```
    Parser parser = new SAXParser();

    // Set Handlers in the parser
    parser.setDocumentHandler(sample);
    parser.setEntityResolver(sample);
    parser.setDTDHandler(sample);
    parser.setErrorHandler(sample);

    // Convert file to URL and parse
    try {
     parser.parse(fileToURL(new File(argv[0])).toString());
    }
   }
  }
//////////////////////////////////////////////////////////////////////
// Sample implementation of ContentHandler interface.
//////////////////////////////////////////////////////////////////////

 public void setDocumentLocator (Locator locator) {
  System.out.println("SetDocumentLocator:");
  this.locator = locator;
 }

 public void startDocument(){
  System.out.println("StartDocument");
 }

 public void endDocument() throws SAXException {
  System.out.println("EndDocument");
 }
 public void startElement(String namespaceURI, String localName,
                          String qName,  AttributeList atts)
                          throws SAXException  {
  System.out.println("StartElement:"+name);
  for (int i=0;i<atts.getLength();i++) {
   String aname = atts.getName(i);
   String type = atts.getType(i);
   String value = atts.getValue(i);
   System.out.println("    "+aname+"("+type+")"+"="+value);
  }
 }
 public void endElement(String namespaceURI, String localName, String qName)
  throws SAXException {
   System.out.println("EndElement:"+name);
  }

  public void characters(char[] cbuf, int start, int len) {
   System.out.print("Characters:");
   System.out.println(new String(cbuf,start,len));
  }
```

```
  public void ignorableWhitespace(char[] cbuf, int start, int len) {
   System.out.println("IgnorableWhiteSpace");
  }
  public void processingInstruction(String target, String data)
   throws SAXException {
    System.out.println("ProcessingInstruction:"+target+" "+data);
  }

//////////////////////////////////////////////////////////////////////
// Sample implementation of the EntityResolver interface.
//////////////////////////////////////////////////////////////////////

  public InputSource resolveEntity (String publicId, String systemId)
   throws SAXException {
   System.out.println("ResolveEntity:"+publicId+" "+systemId);
   System.out.println("Locator:"+locator.getPublicId()+" "+
                      locator.getSystemId()+
                      " "+locator.getLineNumber()+" "
                      +locator.getColumnNumber());
   return null;
  }

//////////////////////////////////////////////////////////////////////
// Sample implementation of the DTDHandler interface.
//////////////////////////////////////////////////////////////////////

  public void notationDecl (String name, String publicId,
                            String systemId) {
   System.out.println("NotationDecl:"+name+" "+publicId+" "+systemId);
  }

  public void unparsedEntityDecl (String name, String publicId,
                                  String systemId, String notationName) {
   System.out.println("UnparsedEntityDecl:"+name + " "+publicId+" "+
                     systemId+" "+notationName);
  }
...
```

Using SAX APIs

Quite often, applications that require only SAX (Level 1 and Level 2) support do not want to be burdened with a parser that always builds a full-blown DOM tree in memory. The Oracle XML SAX parser's high-performance, event-based, run-time engine addresses this requirement. Using the SAX parser, applications can leverage the full power of the SAX model to parse extremely large documents without incurring prohibitive memory costs.

The following code demonstrates how the SAX APIs can be used to extract useful information from an XML document:

```
// This example demonstrates a simple use of the SAXParser.
// An XML file is parsed and some information is printed out.
```

```
import org.xml.sax.*;
import java.io.*;
import java.net.*;
import oracle.xml.parser.v2.*;

public class SAXHandler extends DefaultHandler {
 public static void main(String[] argv) {
  try {
   // Get an instance of the parser
   Parser parser = new SAXParser();

   // Create a SAX event handler and register it with the parser
   SAXHandler handler = new SAXHandler();
   parser.setContentHandler(handler);

   // Convert file to InputSource and parse
   InputSource xmldoc = new InputSource(new FileInputStream(argv[0]));
   parser.parse(xmldoc);
  }
  catch (Exception e) {
   System.out.println(e.toString());
  }
 }
   // Sample implementation of DocumentHandler interface.
  public void startElement(String name, Attributes atts)
   throws SAXException {
   System.out.println("StartElement:"+name);
   for (int i=0;i<atts.getLength();i++) {
    String aname = atts.getName(i);
    String type = atts.getType(i);
    String value = atts.getValue(i);
    System.out.println("    "+aname+"("+type+")"+"="+value);
   }
  }

  public void characters(char[] cbuf, int start, int len) {
   System.out.print("Characters:");
   System.out.println(new String(cbuf,start,len));
  }
}
```

To use the Oracle XML parser's SAX support, you need to use the **SAXParser** class to parse your XML document. The first thing to do, therefore, is to get an instance of this class:

```
Parser parser = new SAXParser();
```

You then need to register your SAX event handler with the parser, so that it knows what methods to invoke when a particular event occurs. Because not all events may be of interest to you, make sure the handler you register extends the **org.xml.sax.DefaultHandler** class. This class provides some default behavior for handling events (typically these do nothing). You can then override the methods for those events of interest to you. In the preceding example, the assumption is that the only events of interest are a subset of those specified by the **org.xml.sax.ContentHandler** interface, namely, **startElement** and **characters**. Arguably, these are the most important SAX events generated because XML documents typically consist of markup and text. This handler can be registered with **SAXParser** with a simple API call:

```
parser.setContentHandler(handler);
```

The **startElement** event is triggered every time a new element is encountered within the XML document by **SAXParser**. When this event occurs, you can print the element name and its attributes:

```
public void startElement(String namespaceURI, String localName, String
                           qName,Attribute
 throws SAXException {
        ...
 }
```

The **characters** event is triggered every time unmarked-up text is encountered by **SAXParser**. This text is often the "value" of an element and can be retrieved by listening for this event:

```
public void characters(char[] cbuf, int start, int len) {
        ...
}
```

Once the handler has been registered, all that remains is to parse an XML document using **SAXParser**:

```
parser.parse(xmldoc);
```

The input XML document could contain a list of book data, such as the following:

```
<booklist>
 <book isbn="0-07-213495-X">
  <title>Oracle9i XML Handbook</title>
  <author>Chang, Scardina and Kiritzov</author>
  <publisher>Osborne</publisher>
  <price>49.99</price>
 </book>
 <book isbn="1230-23498-2349879">
  <title>Emperor's New Mind</title>
  <author>Roger Penrose</author>
  <publisher>Oxford Publishing Company</publisher>
  <price>15.99</price>
 </book>
</booklist>
```

The following output would be generated:

```
StartElement:booklist
StartElement:book
   isbn(CDATA)= 0-07-213495-X
StartElement:title
Characters: Oracle9i XML Handbook
StartElement:author
Characters: Chang, Scardina and Kiritzov
StartElement:publisher
Characters: Osborne
StartElement:price
Characters:49.99
StartElement:book
   isbn(CDATA)=1230-23498-2349879
StartElement:title
Characters:Emperor's New Mind
StartElement:author
Characters:Roger Penrose
StartElement:publisher
Characters:Oxford Publishing Company
StartElement:price
Characters:15.99
```

Implementation of SAX Level 2 comes mainly in the form of support of XML namespaces, and querying or setting features or properties in the parser. With namespace support, element and attribute names may now return an optional namespace URI followed by a *local name*, e.g., **<foo:bar xmlns:foo="http://www.oracle.com/"/>**, where **http://www.oracle.com/** is the namespace URI and **bar** is the local name. In addition, the qualified name (or **qName**), **foo:bar**, may also be returned. Without namespace support, element and attribute names simply return a local name. The SAX Level 2 interfaces affected by namespace support are **XMLReader**, **Attributes**, and **ContentHandler**. An example of SAX 2 namespace support, followed by code for the **startElement** and **endElement** callback methods in the **ContentHandler** interface, might look like this:

```
// This example demonstrates how to use SAX Level 2 Namespace
// support, followed by how to use the callback
// methods startElement and endElement.

import java.io.*;
import java.net.URL;
import java.net.MalformedURLException;
import org.xml.sax.*;
import org.xml.sax.helpers.*;
import oracle.xml.parser.v2.SAXParser;

public class SAX2Namespace {
 static public void main(String[] args) {
```

```
  String fileName;
  //Get the file name
  fileName = args[0];
  try {
   // Create handlers for the parser
   // For all the other interfaces use the default provided by
   // Handler base
   DefaultHandler defHandler = new XMLDefaultHandler();
   SAXParser parser = new SAXParser();
   parser.setContentHandler(defHandler);
   parser.setErrorHandler(defHandler);
   parser.setEntityResolver(defHandler);
   parser.setDTDHandler(defHandler);
   try {
    parser.parse(createURL(fileName));
   }
  }
 }
 static URL createURL(String fileName) {
  URL url = null;
  try {
   url = new URL(fileName);
  } catch (MalformedURLException ex) {
  try {
   File f = new File(fileName);
   url = f.toURL();
  }
  catch (MalformedURLException e) {
   System.out.println("Cannot create url for: " + fileName);
   System.exit(0);
  }
      }
    return url;
 }
}
class XMLDefaultHandler extends DefaultHandler {
 public void XMLDefaultHandler() {
 }
 public void startElement(String uri, String localName,
                          String qName, Attributes atts)
  throws SAXException {
   System.out.println("ELEMENT Qualified Name:" + qName);
   System.out.println("ELEMENT Local Name    :" + localName);
   System.out.println("ELEMENT Namespace     :" + uri);

   for (int i=0; i<atts.getLength(); i++) {
    qName = atts.getQName(i);
    localName = atts.getLocalName(i);
    uri = atts.getURI(i);
```

```
        System.out.println(" ATTRIBUTE Qualified Name    :" + qName);
        System.out.println(" ATTRIBUTE Local Name        :" + localName);
        System.out.println(" ATTRIBUTE Namespace         :" + uri);

        // You can get the type and value of the attributes either
        // by index or by the Qualified Name.

        String type = atts.getType(qName);
        String value = atts.getValue(qName);

        System.out.println(" ATTRIBUTE Type              :" + type);
        System.out.println(" ATTRIBUTE Value             :" + value);
        System.out.println();
       }
     }

    public void endElement(String uri, String localName,
                           String qName) throws SAXException {
     System.out.println("ELEMENT Qualified Name:" + qName);
     System.out.println("ELEMENT Local Name    :" + localName);
     System.out.println("ELEMENT Namespace     :" + uri);
    }
}
```

For SAX Level 2, the additional parameters being passed in are the **namespace URI**, the **local name**, and the **qName**. Other SAX Level 2 enhancements include the querying and setting of features and properties in the parser. For example, getter/setter methods such as **getFeature**, **setFeature**, **getProperty**, **setProperty**, are available supporting namespaces as demonstrated in the following listing:

```
void process(String filename) throws SAXException, IOException{
 URL url = createURL(filename);

 // Validating, Namespace = true, NamespacePrefix = true
 parser.setFeature("http://xml.org/sax/features/validation", true);
 parser.setFeature("http://xml.org/sax/features/namespaces", true);
 parser.setFeature("http://xml.org/sax/features/namespace-prefix", true);

 try {
  parser.parse(url.toString());
 }
 catch (XMLParseException e) {
  System.out.println();
  System.out.println(e);
 }

 // Non-validating, NamespacePrefix = false
 parser.setFeature("http://xml.org/sax/features/validation", true);
```

```
 parser.setFeature("http://xml.org/sax/features/namespace-prefix", true);

 try {
  parser.parse(url.toString());
 }

 catch (XMLParseException e) {
  System.out.println();
  System.out.println(e);
 }
}
```

For this code example, note that you can control namespace support in SAX Level 2 processing. In default processing, **namespace-prefix** is false, meaning that **qNames** are optionally reported and namespace declarations (**xmlns** attributes) are not reported. In our example, however, the code stub sets **validation**, **namespaces**, and **namespace-prefix** to be true, which when given

```
<foo:bar xmlns:foo="http://www.oracle.com/" foo1="bar1" foo:stock="wayout.com"/>,
```

an element will have the namespace URI of **http://www.oracle.com/**, a local name of **bar**, and a **qName** of **foo:bar**; one attribute will have no namespace URI, no local name, and a **qName** of **xmlns:foo**; another attribute will have no namespace URI, a local name, and a **qName** of **foo1**; and the last attribute will have the namespace URI **http://www.oracle.com/** and a local name of **stock**.

Oracle SAX APIs in C

To use the Oracle SAX APIs, a set of callback functions is passed to **xmlinit()**. The parser then invokes these functions as the matching parts of a document are encountered. Compare this to the DOM, in which the document is parsed and a node tree is constructed in memory, which can then be queried and modified through the DOM API. SAX functions are invoked as the document is parsed. Each SAX function returns a **(sword)** error code. If the code is nonzero, an error is indicated and parsing stops immediately.

The SAX callback structure (**xmlsaxcb**) is defined as follows:

```
struct xmlsaxcb {
 sword (*startDocument)(void *ctx);
 sword (*endDocument)(void *ctx);
 sword (*startElement)(void *ctx, const oratext *name,
                       const struct xmlnodes *attrs);
 sword (*endElement)(void *ctx, const oratext *name);
 sword (*characters)(void *ctx, const oratext *ch, size_t len);
 sword (*ignorableWhitespace)(void *ctx, const oratext *ch,
                              size_t len);
 sword (*processingInstruction)(void *ctx, const oratext *target,
                                const oratext *data);
 sword (*notationDecl)(void *ctx, const oratext *name,
```

```
                         const oratext *publicId,
                         const oratext *systemId);
 sword (*unparsedEntityDecl)(void *ctx, const oratext *name,
                              const oratext *publidId,
                              const oratext *systemId,
                              const oratext *notationName);
 sword (*nsStartElement)(void *ctx, const oratext *qname,
                          const oratext *local,
                          const oratext *nsp,
                          const struct xmlnodes *attrs);
}
```

Any or all callback functions may be specified; none are required. An optional context pointer may be provided, and it will be passed to each callback function. Its use is entirely up to the user. The callback functions are described in detail in Table 2-6.

Callback Function	Description
startDocument	Invoked immediately before the parse begins.
endDocument	Invoked immediately after a successful parse ends.
startElement	Invoked when an element start-tag is found. If the namespace version of this callback is also supplied, it is called instead.
endElement	Invoked when an element end-tag is found.
characters	Invoked for each CDATA or #PCDATA.
ignorableWhitespace	Invoked for each run of ignorable white space, unless all white space is being retained (in which case characters is invoked).
processingInstruction	Invoked for each processing instruction.
notationDecl	Invoked for each NOTATION declaration in the DTD.
unparsedEntityDecl	Invoked for each unparsed entity (those with NDATA defined).
nsStartElement	Invoked when a namespace qualified start-tag is found returning the namespace, local part, etc.

TABLE 2-6. *SAX Callback Functions*

The following program fragments show how to declare, register, and use the SAX callbacks:

```
/* declare SAX callback functions */
sword startdocument(void *ctx);
sword enddocument(void *ctx);
sword startelement(void *ctx, const oratext *name,
                   const xmlnodes *attrs);
sword endelement(void *ctx, const oratext *name);
sword characters(void *ctx, const oratext *ch, size_t len);
sword whitespace(void *ctx, const oratext *ch, size_t len);
sword pi(void *ctx, const oratext *target,
         const oratext *data);
sword notation(void *ctx, const oratext *name,
               const oratext *publicId,
               const oratext *systemId);
sword entity(void *ctx, const oratext *name,
             const oratext *publidId,
             const oratext *systemId,
             const oratext *notationName);
/* declare SAX callback context */
typedef struct saxcontext {
  uword    depth;  /* nested element level, for indenting */
} sax_context;

/* declare SAX callback structure */
xmlsaxcb sax_callback = {
 startdocument, enddocument, startelement, endelement,
 characters, whitespace, pi, notation, entity
};
/* declare SAX context and initialize */
sax_context saxctx = { 0 };  /* depth = 0 */
/* initialize parser specifying SAX callbacks */
xmlinit(&ecode, NULL, NULL, NULL, NULL,
        &sax_callback, (void *) &saxctx, NULL, NULL);

/* ----- SAX CALLBACKS ----- */
sword startdocument(void *context) {
 puts("StartDocument");
 return 0;  /* success */
}

sword enddocument(void *context) {
 puts("EndDocument");
 return 0;  /* success */
}

sword startelement(void *context, const oratext *name,
                   const xmlnodes *attrs) {
```

```
 sax_context *saxctx = (sax_context *) context;
 indent(saxctx->depth);
 printf("<%s", name);
 if (attrs) {
  for (i = 0; i < numAttributes(attrs); i++) {
   attr = getAttributeIndex(attrs, i);
   printf(" %s=\"%s\"", getAttrName(attr), getAttrValue(attr));
  }
 }
 puts(">");
 saxctx->depth++;
 return 0;  /* success */
}

sword endelement(void *context, const oratext *name) {
 sax_context *saxctx = (sax_context *) context;

 indent(--saxctx->depth);
 printf("</%s>\n", name);
 return 0;  /* success */
}

sword characters(void *context, const oratext *ch, size_t len) {
 sax_context *saxctx = (sax_context *) context;

 indent(saxctx->depth);
 putchar('"');
 print_string((oratext *) ch, (sword) len);
 puts("\"");
 return 0;  /* success */
}

sword whitespace(void *context, const oratext *ch, size_t len)
{
 sax_context *saxctx = (sax_context *) context;

 indent(saxctx->depth);
 putchar('\'');
 print_string((oratext *) ch, (sword) len);
 puts("'");
 return 0;  /* success */
}

sword pi(void *context, const oratext *target,
         const oratext *data) {
 sax_context *saxctx = (sax_context *) context;

 indent(saxctx->depth);
 fputs("PI", stdout);
```

```
 if (target)
  printf(" target=\"%s\"", target);
 if (data)
  printf (" data=\"%s\"", data);
 putchar('\n');
 return 0;  /* success */
}

sword notation(void *context, const oratext *name,
               const oratext *publicId,
               const oratext *systemId) {
 sax_context *saxctx = (sax_context *) context;

 indent(saxctx->depth);
 printf("NOTATION '%s'", name);
 if (publicId)
  printf (" PUB:%s", publicId);
 if (systemId)
  printf(" SYS:%s", systemId);
 putchar('\n');
 return 0;  /* success */
}

sword entity(void *context, const oratext *name,
             const oratext *publidId,
             const oratext *systemId,
             const oratext *notationName) {
 sax_context *saxctx = (sax_context *) context;

 indent(saxctx->depth);
 printf("ENTITY '%s'", name);
 if (publidId)
  printf(" PUB:%s", publidId);
 if (systemId)
  printf(" SYS:%s", systemId);
 if (notationName)
  printf(" NAME:%s", notationName);
 putchar('\n');
 return 0;  /* success */
}
```

The following is a sample XML document that includes an inline DTD:

```
<?xml version="1.0"?>
<!DOCTYPE PLAY [
 <!ELEMENT top    (second*)>
 <!ELEMENT second (third*)>
 <!ELEMENT third  (#PCDATA)*>
 <!NOTATION note1 SYSTEM "foo.exe">
```

```
 <!NOTATION note2 PUBLIC "bar" "bar.ent">
 <!ENTITY ent SYSTEM "http://www.w3.org/" NDATA n>
]>
<?dummy this is a sample processing instruction?>
<top>
 <second>
  <third>third level</third>
 </second>
</top>
```

This is the resulting output from the preceding sample program:

```
StartDocument
NOTATION 'note1' SYS:foo.exe
NOTATION 'note2' PUB:bar SYS:bar.ent
ENTITY 'ent' SYS:http://www.w3.org/ NAME:n
PI target=dummy data=this is a sample processing instruction
<top>
    '\n  '
    <second>
        '\n    '
        <third>
            "third level"
        </third>
        '\n  '
    </second>
    '\n'
</top>
EndDocument
```

Accessing XML with Java Binding

The JAXB APIs create Java source files from an XML Schema to assist in programmatically creating valid document instances from dynamic data. This is useful when you want an application to send an XML message to another application according to an agreed-upon XML Schema, or you want a web form to construct an XML document. You can construct, optionally validate, and print XML documents that comply with the input XML Schema in your Java applications using the generated classes. The JAXB APIs work in conjunction with the Oracle XML Parser for Java, which parses the XML Schema and passes the parsed XML Schema to the JAXB compiler.

The JAXB APIs then query the XML Schema for all the elements. A Java class is generated for each of these elements. These classes have methods to set the attributes and add child nodes by the corresponding content model. The Java class corresponding to the root element also has methods to validate and print the constructed XML document. The following subsections use an example to show how the JAXB APIs can be used to process an XML Schema and generate classes for the XML Schema's elements. The example then shows how to use the methods of the element classes to programmatically construct a valid XML document.

The Input XML Schema

The following XML Schema for book data, **bookcatalog.xsd**, is used as the input to the JAXB Compiler. Here, the schema specifies that the XML document root is BOOKCATALOG. BOOKCATALOG consists of one or more BOOKs. Each BOOK contains a required ISBN attribute as a unique identifier, as well as several optional attributes and child elements, such as TITLE for the book title, AUTHORNAME for the author's name, PUBLISHER for the publisher, and so on. Optional attributes and children are followed by a **?** in the element definition.

```
<xsd:element name="PRICE" type="xsd:decimal"/>
   </xsd:sequence>
 </xsd:complexType>
</xsd:schema>
```

Generating XML Classes

The following code sample processes an XML Schema and generates the corresponding classes for elements in the DTD. The sample uses an external DTD file along with the name of the root element. The JAXB APIs can also parse an XML document and use the DTD defined in the document. Running the JAXB compiler on the preceding XML Schema creates Java classes for each element (BOOKCATALOG, BOOK, TITLE, and so on). A Java application can then use the methods defined on these classes to create a valid XML document containing book data. The Oracle XDK 10*g* includes a JAXB compiler that can generate these classes with the following command line:

```
java -classpath %CLASSPATH% oracle.xml.jaxb.orajaxb -schema bookcatalog.xsd
 -targetPkg generated
```

Binding to an XML Instance

The following Java code shows how generated methods might be used. Here, two BOOK records are created: book1 and book2. The required attributes are enforced by adding them as parameters to the constructor. In this case, ISBN is a required attribute for the BOOK element. Elements for each column are also created (title1, authorname1, and so on). If an element has an enumerated attribute, a static constant is defined in the class for each value in the enumeration. To build an XML document tree, the various data elements are grouped by assigning them to each row element as tree nodes. Each BOOK element is then added as a node to the document root element BOOKCATALOG. In this example, classes generated are in uppercase.

```
import javax.xml.bind.JAXBContext;
import javax.xml.bind.Marshaller;
import java.util.List;

public class CreateBooksDemo {
  public static void main (String args[]) {
    try {
      // Instantiate the object factory
      CreateBooks.ObjectFactory objFactory = new CreateBooks.ObjectFactory();
```

```
        // New Book Catalog
        CreateBooks.BOOKCATALOG bookCatalogue = objFactory.createBOOKCATALOG();

        // New book book1
        CreateBooks.BOOK book1 = objFactory.createBOOK();
        book1.setISBN("7654");
        book1.setTITLE("The Adventures of Don Quixote");
        book1.setAUTHORNAME("Miguel Cervantes");
        book1.setPUBLISHER("Oracle Press");
        book1.setPUBLISHYEAR("2000");
        book1.setPRICE(new java.math.BigDecimal("1.0"));

        // Create new book book2
        CreateBooks.BOOK book2 = objFactory.createBOOK();
        book2.setISBN("7788");
        book2.setTITLE("The Iliad");
        book2.setAUTHORNAME("Homer");
        book2.setPUBLISHER("Oracle Press");
        book2.setPUBLISHYEAR("1000");
        book2.setPRICE(new java.math.BigDecimal("2.0"));

        // Getting the list
        List bookList = bookCatalogue.getBOOK();

        // Setting a book item
        bookList.add(book1);
        bookList.add(book2);

        // Get the JAXB Context
        JAXBContext  jc = JAXBContext.newInstance("CreateBooks");

        // Print to System.out
        Marshaller m = jc.createMarshaller();
        m.setProperty(Marshaller.JAXB_FORMATTED_OUTPUT, new Boolean(true));
        m.marshal(bookCatalogue, System.out);
        System.out.println();
        System.out.println();
        }
        catch (Exception e) {
        e.printStackTrace();
        }
    }
}
```

XML Document Created by Java Application

The input for the preceding Java application can be received from various sources, such as a web form, SAX parser, or JDBC result set. The preceding Java application creates an XML document that can then be transformed or stored in the database. The XML document created is similar to the following:

```
<?xml version="1.0" encoding="UTF-8"?>
<BOOKCATALOG xmlns:xsi="http://www.w3.org/2001/XMLSchema-instance"
xsi:noNamespaceSchemaLocation="bookcatalog.xsd">
  <BOOK>
      <TITLE>The Adventures of Don Quixote</TITLE>
      <AUTHORNAME>Miguel Cervantes</AUTHORNAME>
      <ISBN>7654</ISBN>
      <PUBLISHER>Oracle Press</PUBLISHER>
      <PUBLISHYEAR>2000</PUBLISHYEAR>
      <PRICE>50.00</PRICE>
  </BOOK>
  <BOOK>
      <TITLE>The Iliad</TITLE>
      <AUTHORNAME>Homer</AUTHORNAME>
      <ISBN>5354</ISBN>
      <PUBLISHER>Oracle Press</PUBLISHER>
      <PUBLISHYEAR>1000</PUBLISHYEAR>
      <PRICE>5.00</PRICE>
  </BOOK>
</BOOKCATALOG>
```

Accessing XML with StAX

Pull parsing or *StAX (Streaming API for XML)* is a new Java standards effort to address some of the limitations of SAX parsing yet still maintain a streaming model. Defined under JSR-173 in the Java Community Process, XML Pull Parsing was designed with simplicity and performance in mind.

As in SAX parsing, StAX delivers events; however, these events are less granular and can be returned as objects. These events, listed next, are derived from XMLEvent:

```
StartDocument, EndDocument
StartElement, EndElement
Characters, CDATA, Comment
Processing Instruction
Entity Reference
```

A StAX parser has factories to create readers, writers, and events. They consist of the following:

```
javax.xml.stream.XMLInputFactory
javax.xml.stream.XMLOutputFactory
javax.xml.stream.XMLEventFactory
```

Each of these factory instances is obtained through the **newInstance()** static method. Specific implementations can be plugged into these interfaces as is done in the Oracle version.

As distinct from SAX, you don't need to register handlers for every type of event that the parser will stream to you. Instead, once a reader in instantiated, you simply call the **next()**

method on the reader to get the events. The following example shows this being done on the booklist.xml file:

```
XMLStreamReader reader =
XMLInputFactory.newInstance().createXMLStreamReader
 (new FileInputStream("booklist.xml"));

while(reader.hasNext()) {
 int eventType = reader.next();
 if (eventType == XMLEvent.START_ELEMENT &&
  reader.getLocalName().equals("\title")) {
  reader.next();
  System.out.println(reader.getText());
 }
}
```

Note that the element to be searched for could be "pulled" while the rest is ignored. This is the *cursor style* of pull parsing and it provides fine-grained access to the document content.

There is a second style to StAX parsing that is more natural to Java programmers because it returns the events as objects with get and set type methods. The following is an example of this *iterator style* performing the same task:

```
XMLEventReader eventReader =
   XMLInputFactory.newInstance().createXMLEventReader
   (new FileInputStream("booklist.xml"));
while(reader.hasNext()) {
  XMLEvent event = reader.next();
  if (event instanceof StartElement &&
   ((StartElement)event).getLocalName().equals("book\title"))
  {
    System.out.println( ((Characters)reader.next()).getData());
  }
}
```

Note that the **getLocalName()** method had to be called on the event to pull the title, and the **getData()** method to extract the data to print it.

As you can see in these examples, it is the application, not the parser, that controls the process. This type of parsing is excellent for filtering XML, especially when dealing in small fragments.

The StAX writer can be used for limited transformation when a single pass is all that is necessary creating a subset or derivative XML document. However, the inability to traverse the document bidirectionally makes it a poor replacement for a DOM parser.

Pull parsing generally can be used wherever SAX parsing can be used—and in most cases with fewer lines of code. Pull parsing really has application in situations in which namespaces need to be supported. As in the DOM, there is the concept of scope to namespaces, where children inherit their parent's namespace even when it is not explicitly declared. StAX supports retrieving this namespace information from elements, whereas SAX does not. Finally, the ability of StAX to support multiple data or input sources easily provides a uniform programming model that can produce more reliable XML processing in distributed environments. This reliability is due once again to the pull model, where a single parser can poll multiple data sources or inputs and merge their contents into a single context without the need for multiple threads. This is why StAX is the parsing method of choice for web service specifications such as *JAX-RPC (Java API for XML-based RPC).*

Best Practices

This chapter has demonstrated various ways to parse and programmatically access the content of XML documents. Each method has different strengths and weaknesses, as discussed in its respective section. However, as the following sections discuss, there are some particular features and solutions to common problems.

DTD Caching

When parsing a collection or batch of XML documents with the same DTD, performance is improved significantly if you cache the DTD, which eliminates its being parsed over and over again. While DTD caching is not enabled automatically, the Oracle XML Parser for Java provides the validating/nonvalidating DTD caching through the **setDoctype()** function. After you set the DTD using this function, the parser will cache this DTD for further XML parsing. This is illustrated in the following code fragment:

```
// Parse the first document and set the DTD for caching
parser.setValidationMode(DOMParser.DTD_VALIDATION);
parser.setAttribute(DOMParser.USE_DTD_ONLY_FOR_VALIDATION,Boolean.TRUE);
parser.parse("{XML_Document_URL}");
DTD dtd =parser.getDoctype();
parser.setDoctype(dtd);

// loop of XML parsing
for(...) {
  // XML Parsing with DTD Cached
}
```

Note that you also should set the following if the cached DTD object is used only for validation:

```
parser.setAttribute(DOMParser.USE_DTD_ONLY_FOR_VALIDATION,Boolean.TRUE);
```

Otherwise, the XML parser copies the DTD object and adds it to the resultant DOM tree. While the preceding example is for an internal DTD, the same method is used for external DTDs.

Skipping the <!DOCTYPE> Tag

A common problem when parsing an XML document that has an external DTD declaration is retrieving that DTD. In many cases, it may not be necessary, and frequently firewalls, permissions, etc., prevent retrieving it. Fortunately, this can be ignored in the Java parser in either of two ways. If you have write access to the document, you can add standalone="yes" as an attribute to the DOCTYPE element. Alternatively, within the application, you can add

```
xmlparser.setAttribute(XMLParser.STANDALONE, Boolean.TRUE)
```

which has the same effect.

Cutting and Pasting Across Documents

Using the DOM parser is the appropriate way to modify an XML document in most cases. However, when the modification needs to be across different documents, as you would do when cutting and pasting, the approach is not obvious. Fortunately, this has been made easy with the DOM 3.0 **adoptNode()** method. As distinct from **importNode()**, which simply copies the node from one document to another, **adoptNode()** actually removes it from one document and inserts it into the other document, as illustrated in the following code fragment:

```
XMLDocument doc1 = new XMLDocument();
XMLElement element1 = (XMLElement)doc1.createElement("foo");
doc1.appendChild(element1);
XMLDocument doc2 = new XMLDocument();
XMLElement element2 = (XMLElement) doc2.createElement("bar");
doc2.appendChild(element2);
...
// Using adoptNode()
element2 = (XMLElement)doc1.adoptNode(element2);
element1.appendChild(element2);
```

We will illustrate further parsing examples in the third part of the book when we illustrate actual applications that you can build.

CHAPTER 3

Transforming XML with XSLT and XPath

To continue the theme from the last chapter, one open XML standard that has caught tremendous traction in the industry is the W3C *Extensible Stylesheet Transformation (XSLT)* specification. Many companies have built XSLT engines and applications according to this specification, which is traditionally embodied in an XSLT processor, to be generally invoked following the parsing and validating of the XML document.

Because XSLT is a function-based language, programmers who are used to procedure-based and object-oriented programming languages may have difficulty picking it up. An XSLT stylesheet will include one or more templates formatted in XML that are applied to the entire input XML document. XSLT is a feature-rich language, and version 2.0 will extend it considerably in the area of supporting XML Schema and data types. Whole books have been written on the language, so we are not going to cover that here. Instead, we will focus on integrating the Oracle XSLT processors into your applications.

Using an XSLT processor, you can transform an XML document into another XML document, an HTML document, or a variety of other text formats. The processor can be invoked either programmatically (using the given APIs) or from the command line, and takes, as input, the XML document (to be transformed) and the XSLT stylesheet that operates on it. It performs the transformation specified by the XSLT stylesheet and generates either a result DOM tree or a text output stream. The diagram shown in Figure 3-1 represents the architecture of the XSLT processor.

As mentioned, the XSLT processor operates on two inputs: the XML document to transform and the XSLT stylesheet to use. It calls out to an XPath engine whenever it needs to match patterns. The XPath engine often needs to traverse the XML DOM tree to retrieve nodes; it passes these nodes back to the XSLT processor. Whenever the XSLT processor needs to generate a result node, it generates a special XSLT event. This event is handled by an XSLT event handler, serving as a midtier caching agent, which waits for subsequent events that affect the same result node. A simple example of this is when the result node to be built is an **XMLElement**. Multiple XSLT events, such as one to create the element simply followed by several that depict its attributes, may be generated by the XSLT processor. Once the XSLT event handler gets complete information about a node, it generates an appropriate SAX event, which can then be processed by a registered SAX handler.

Currently, two output mechanisms are supported by the XSLT Processor for Java: a DOM tree and a text output stream. Either of these mechanisms can be invoked through appropriate API

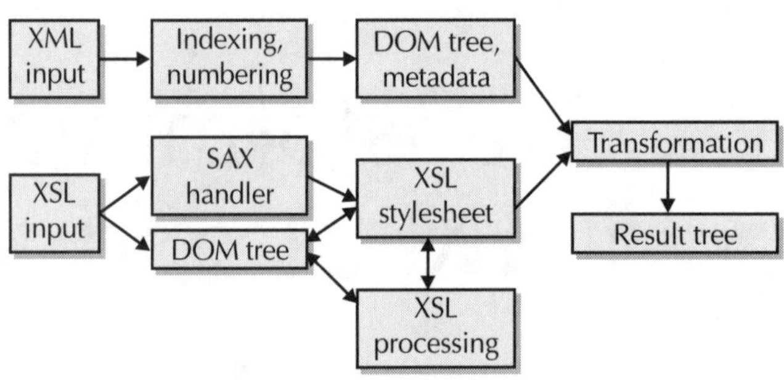

FIGURE 3-1. *The Java XSLT processor architecture*

calls made using the **XSLProcessor** class. If the API to build a result DOM tree is invoked, a DOM tree builder is registered as the SAX event handler for XSLT. Similarly, if the API to output to a text stream is invoked, an **OutputWriter** is registered as the SAX event handler. The advantage of this architecture is that a DOM tree is not built as the result tree unless you require it. If your XSLT application simply needs a text output (such as HTML), you can use the less memory-intensive **OutputWriter** mechanism to do the processing. Remember, if your XSLT stylesheet contains **xsl:output** instructions, you must use the **OutputWriter** mechanism for these instructions to be interpreted correctly.

Programmatic Invocation of the XSLT Processor

The XSLT processor exposes two Java classes that you need to use to perform an XSL transformation: **XSLProcessor** and **XSLStylesheet**. An **XSLStylesheet** object holds all information about an XSLT stylesheet, such as its templates, keys, variables, and attribute sets. This object, once constructed, can be used multiple times to apply the same transformation to a variety of XML documents. It can also be "tweaked" periodically by setting suitable stylesheet parameter values from the outside.

The following code demonstrates how the XSLT APIs could be used:

```
import java.util.*;
import java.io.*;
import java.net.*;
import org.w3c.dom.*;
import oracle.xml.parser.v2.*;

/**
 * This is a simple example of how to use the XSL processing
 * capabilities of the Oracle XML Parser V2.0. An input XML document
 * is transformed using a given input stylesheet
 */
public class XSLExample {
  public static void main (String args[]) throws Exception {
    DOMParser parser;
    XMLDocument xmldoc, xsldoc, out;
    FileInputStream xmlstream, xslstream;
    try {
      // Create an instance of the DOMParser
      parser = new DOMParser();
      parser.setPreserveWhitespace(true);

      // parse input XML file
      xmlstream = new FileInputStream(args[0]);
      parser.parse(xmlstream);
      xmldoc = parser.getDocument();

      // parse input XSL file
      xslstream = new FileInputStream(args[1]);
      parser.parse(xslstream);
      xsldoc = parser.getDocument();
```

```
        // instantiate a stylesheet
        XSLStylesheet xsl = processor.newXSLStylesheet(xsldoc);
        // Apply stylesheet
        XSLProcessor processor = new XSLProcessor();
        XMLDocumentFragment result =
        processor.processXSL(xsl, xmldoc);

        // print the transformed document
        result.print(System.out);
        } catch (Exception e) {
          e.printStackTrace();
        }
    }
}
```

The preceding example is fairly straightforward. It accepts as input, the XML input file, and the XSL stylesheet to apply. The first thing you need to do is to parse these using the **DOMParser** and to retrieve the roots of their respective DOM trees:

```
// Create an instance of the DOMParser
  parser = new DOMParser();
  parser.setPreserveWhitespace(true);

// parse input XML file
xmlstream = new FileInputStream(args[0]);
parser.parse(xmlstream);
xmldoc = parser.getDocument();

// parse input XSL file
xslstream = new FileInputStream(args[1]);
parser.parse(xslstream);
xsldoc = parser.getDocument();
```

The important thing to note is that the new parser is explicitly configured to preserve whitespace (by default, it is not unless a DTD is present). This is crucial, as it allows XSLT whitespace rules to determine how white space should be dealt with.

The next step is to construct a stylesheet object:

```
// instantiate a stylesheet
    XSLStylesheet xsl = processor.newXSLStylesheet(xsldoc);
```

This example, being extremely simple, assumes that the input stylesheet does not reference anything external, such as included stylesheets, external entities, and so forth. Only in such a case can you get away with passing a null as the second argument to the **XSLStylesheet** constructor. Otherwise, you need to create a URL to serve as a reference point for resolving external references within the stylesheets.

The next step is to create a new **XSLProcessor** and use it to apply the stylesheet on the input XML document:

```
// Apply stylesheet
XSLProcessor processor = new XSLProcessor();
DocumentFragment result = processor.processXSL(xsl, xml);
```

The transformed output is now available to you as a document fragment, which can be further manipulated using the regular DOM APIs. For the sake of simplicity, this example prints the results:

```
// print the transformed document
result.print(System.out);
```

A simple yet powerful stylesheet is the identity stylesheet:

```
<?xml version="1.0"?>
<!-- Identity transformation -->
<xsl:stylesheet version="1.0" xmlns:xsl="http://www.w3.org/1999/XSL/Transform">
  <xsl:template match="*|@*|comment()|processing-instruction()|text()">
      <xsl:copy>
          <xsl:apply-templates select="*|@*|comment()|processing-
          instruction()|text()"/>
      </xsl:copy>
  </xsl:template>
</xsl:stylesheet>
```

If you apply this stylesheet to any XML document, you get the same document back. You can test the preceding example by passing it a reference to a file containing the identity stylesheet and (say) the **booklist** example from Chapter 2. The output generated would be as expected:

```
<booklist>
  <book isbn="0-07-213495-X">
    <title>Oracle9i XML Handbook</title>
    <author>Chang, Scardina and Kiritzov</author>
    <publisher>Osborne</publisher>
    <price>49.99</price>
  </book>
  <book isbn="1230-23498-2349879">
    <title>Emperor's New Mind</title>
    <author>Roger Penrose</author>
    <publisher>Oxford Publishing Company</publisher>
    <price>15.99</price>
  </book>
</booklist>
```

Navigating XML with XPath

The *XML Path* (*XPath*) language provides a way to address parts of an XML document and some basic functionality for the manipulation of strings, numbers, and Booleans. XPath is also a W3C standard, currently at version 1.0 but soon to be 2.0. However, as distinct from other standards, it is designed to be used by host languages. XSLT, XPointer, and the new XQuery standards use it. Because the use of XPath with XSLT is well documented in XSLT books, we do not provide an extensive discussion here. However, to help with the examples, we provide a brief summary.

XPath models an XML document as a tree of nodes. These nodes are of the following types: root nodes, element nodes, text nodes, attribute nodes, namespace nodes, processing instruction nodes, and comment nodes. As you can see, these are the same nodes used by DOM.

XPath defines a declarative syntax to navigate these nodes to point to a document subtree or item. Referring to our sample XML document in the previous section, paths are expressed in a similar fashion to how files and URLs are expressed: the XPath **/** refers to the entire document, where **/booklist/book/title** refers to the **<title>** element that is a child of the **book** element. Attributes can also be selected using the @ symbol prepended to their name. For example, **/booklist/book[@id]** refers to the **id** attribute on the **book** element.

XPath also defines a way to compute a string-value for each type of node. For some node types, the string-value is part of the node; for other types of node, the string-value is computed from the string-value of descendant nodes. For nodes that have a name (for example, element nodes), XPath models these as an expanded name—that is, a name-value pair, consisting of a local name and a namespace value.

XPath Expressions

XPath expressions are the heart of XPath's functionality and are used extensively in XSLT. When an XPath expression is evaluated, the result is an object of one of the types: *node-set* (an unordered collection of nodes without duplicates), *Boolean* (true or false), *number* (a floating-point number), or *string* (a sequence of UCS characters). Expression evaluation occurs with respect to a context, and according to a set of rules and the order in which to apply them. Since XPath is dependent on the host language, XSLT and XPointer each specify how this context is determined relative to their use in their respective languages.

The example paths in the previous sections are actually expressions when used in an XSLT stylesheet. Taking a look at our identity stylesheet, we see the following expression:

```
Match="*|@*|comment()|processing-instruction()|text()"
```

This is evaluated as matching a set of all XML items where the | signifies "or." Therefore, it matches elements as the first *, attributes as @*, comments as **comment()**, processing instructions as **processing-instruction**, and text as **text()**.

Expressions can be constructed not only with path syntax but also by using a rich array of functions that support operations on node sets, numbers, strings, and Booleans. Table 3-1 provides examples that could be used in a stylesheet that accepts our **booklist.xml** file as input.

These expressions are used as predicates within the XSLT language to activate a template or perform an operation on selected XML content. They also serve as parameters to XSLT functions, which are distinct from XPath functions.

Example	Description
`//book`	Selects all of the <book> elements in the document
`//book[@id="121"]`	Selects the <book> element whose id is 121
`Book[position()=1]`	Selects the first <book> in the document
`//title | //author`	Selects all <title> and <author> elements
`number sum(//book/price)`	Returns the sum of all <price> elements whose parent is <book>
`string concat (//book/title, //book/author)`	Returns a concatenated list of titles and authors
`Count (/booklist)`	Returns a count of all books, which is 2
`ancestor::book`	Selects the ancestor node of <book>, which is <booklist>

TABLE 3-1. *Example XPath Expressions*

Introducing XSLT Stylesheets

XSLT is used to describe rules for transforming a source tree into a result tree. The transformation is achieved by associating patterns with templates contained within a stylesheet. An XSLT processor matches patterns against elements in the source tree and instantiates associated templates to create various parts of the result tree. While constructing the result tree, the processor might filter and reorder elements from the source tree and add arbitrary structure, as specified by the XSLT transformation. The result tree is separate from the source tree—that is, no nodes are shared between the two—and its structure can be completely different from the structure of the source tree.

XSLT stylesheets are well-formed XML documents that contain elements and attributes in the XSLT namespace (**http://www.w3.org/1999/XSL/Transform**). These elements and attributes are used to provide instructions to an XSLT processor regarding the transformation it needs to effect. A stylesheet may also contain elements and attributes that are not in the XSLT namespace. XSLT processors typically interpret these as markup to be directly added to the result tree. An exception is the case of extension-elements, which serve as XSLT processor instructions and are in a separate namespace defined using a special mechanism.

XSLT instructions are contained within templates. The result tree is constructed by finding the template rule for the root node and instantiating its template. When a template is instantiated, each instruction within it is executed and replaced by the result tree fragment it creates. These instructions may select and process descendant source elements, which may entail instantiating other templates. It is important to note that elements are only processed when they have been selected by the execution of an instruction. XSLT uses the XPath language to select elements from the source tree and to do conditional processing.

An XSLT processor instantiates templates based on pattern-matching rules. In the process of finding an applicable template rule, more than one template rule may have a pattern that matches a given element. The processor then uses special conflict-resolution logic (which uses template priorities) to ensure the best template rule is applied.

XSL Templates

Templates can be compared to procedures in a structural programming language. Templates contain programming logic expressed in terms of XSLT instructions that process the source tree and change the result tree. In some cases, even a single template can be used to transform your source tree into a result tree. In fact, XSLT has a special mechanism called *Literal Result Element as Stylesheet,* which enables you to embed all your XSLT processing logic in the body of the result document you want to create.

Templates can either be explicitly named or contain a match expression. When the XSLT processor encounters an **xsl:apply-templates** instruction, it attempts to match the nodes that were selected with the most appropriate template (using the match expression). Sometimes, more than one template might match. XSLT specifies a complex set of rules to help resolve this conflict by assigning priorities to various kinds of match expressions (patterns). Additionally, a template may itself specify an explicit priority, which the XSLT processor considers while determining which template to instantiate.

The XSLT Process Model

XSLT comes with a full-fledged set of instructions that enable you to use it almost like a programming language of its own. Conditional statements, variables, parameters, and loops exist, just as you would expect in any programming language. Obviously, XSLT is geared more to do transformations than to write general-purpose programs, but its rich instruction set makes it a powerful tool, indeed.

The various instructions you can use in XSLT, their syntax, and a brief explanation of what they do are described in the next few sections.

<xsl:apply-imports/>

This instruction, when encountered while processing a node within a template, directs the processor also to apply template rules imported into the stylesheet on that node. It has no attributes or content.

<xsl:apply-templates>

The following instruction directs the processor to instantiate a template that matches the XPath expression given by the value of the **select** attribute. In the absence of a **select** attribute, the instruction processes all the children of the current node, including text nodes. The optional **mode** attribute can be used to specify the mode of the template to be used if a conflict occurred. This instruction can also be made to pass parameters to the template being instantiated (using **xsl:with-param**) and change the order of processing the selected nodes (as given by **xsl:sort**):

```
<xsl:apply-templates select = node-set-expression mode = qname>
  <!-- Content: (xsl:sort | xsl:with-param)* -->
</xsl:apply-templates>
```

Introducing XSLT 2.0

When the XSLT 1.0 standard was released, there was no XML Schema standard. Consequently, stylesheets were extremely limited in the types of transformations and XML operations that they could perform. As of this writing, the XSLT 2.0 standard is in its final stages and will bring significant enhancements along with expanded functionality and support for XML Schema. Because the Oracle Java XSLT processor will support this standard, the following sections provide a brief overview of it.

NOTE
There is also a companion XPath 2.0 standard that incorporates an extensive set of functions and operators on XML Schema data types. This standard will not be discussed because there is not as yet an Oracle implementation.

Grouping

In XSLT 1.0, stylesheet writers had great difficulty in creating templates that grouped items. In fact, the most popular method was one developed by Steve Muench of Oracle that involves using **<xsl:key>** to create keys for grouping. In 2.0, **<xsl:for-each-group>** has been introduced to perform this function. An example of its usage to subset and sort the **booklist.xml** example by author is as follows:

```
<xsl:for-each-group select="book" group-by="author">
 <xsl:sort select="current-grouping-key()" />
  <author>
   <xsl:value-of select="current-grouping-key()" />
    <xsl:for-each select="current-group()">
     <book>
       <xsl:value-of select="title" />
     </book>
    </xsl:for-each>
  </author>
</xsl:for-each-group>
```

This produces the following XML output:

```
<book isbn="0-07-213495-X">
    <title>Oracle9i XML Handbook</title>
    <author>Chang, Scardina and Kiritzov</author>
  </book>
  <book isbn="1230-23498-2349879">
    <title>Emperor's New Mind</title>
    <author>Roger Penrose</author>
  </book>
```

Function Definitions

In XSLT 2.0, functions can be defined via the **xsl:function** declaration, callable from any XPath expression in the stylesheet. The name of the function must be a QName, along with any parameters defined via **xsl:param** elements. In this manner, stylesheet creators can define their own functions in much the same way that functions are created in other programming or scripting languages. The following example defines a function that takes an integer and returns its lexical name in uppercase:

```
<xsl:function name="str:numtostr" as="xs:string">
 <xsl:param name="value" as="xs:integer"/>
  <xsl:number value="$value" format="N"/>
</xsl:function>
```

This can be used in a template:

```
<xsl:template match="/">
 <output>
  <xsl:value-of select="str:numtostr(9)"/>
 </output>
</xsl:template>
```

This template returns the following:

```
<output>NINE</output>
```

Multiple Result Documents

In XSLT 2.0, stylesheet writers can invoke **<xsl:result-document>** to create a result tree that can then be validated. The root node of this tree is the document node. The utility of this is that different output formats can be specified for the result tree and validation can occur on these different formats. Turning once again to **booklist.xml**, the following template will split it into separate files, **book1.html** and **book2.html**:

```
<xsl:template match="/">
 <xsl:for-each-group select="/booklist/book">
  <xsl:result-document href="book{position()}.html"
         format="book-format" validation="strip">
    <html xmlns="http://www.w3.org/1999/xhtml">
    <head><title><xsl:value-of select="./title"/></title></head>
    <body>
     <xsl:copy-of select="current-group()"/>
    </body>
   </html>
  </xsl:result-document>
 </xsl:for-each-group>
</xsl:template>
```

The output of **book1.html** will be

```
<html xmlns="http://www.w3.org/1999/xhtml">
 <head><title>Oracle9i XML Handbook</title></head>
  <body>
   <title>Oracle9i XML Handbook</title>
   <author>Chang, Scardina and Kiritzov</author>
   <publisher>Osborne</publisher>
   <price>49.99</price>
  </body>
 </html>
```

Temporary Trees

In XSLT 2.0, temporary trees are available for processing. In this manner, intermediate results of transformations can be accessed and then discarded. These trees can be constructed by evaluating an **xsl:variable**, **xsl:param**, or **xsl:with-param** element that has nonempty content (referred to as the variable-binding element), the value of which becomes the document node of the temporary tree.

The advantage is that now, instead of employing one large template, complex XSLT transformations can be broken down and modularized. Since values can be passed in, lookup tables for various mappings can be employed. The following is example syntax showing how to pass the tree between templates that may apply successive styles:

```
<xsl:import href="modern.xsl">
<xsl:import href="sophisticated.xsl">
<xsl:variable name="style">
 <xsl:apply-templates select="/" mode="modern" />
</xsl:variable>
<xsl:template match="/" />
 <xsl:apply-templates select="$style" mode="sophisticated"/>
</xsl:template>
```

The Oracle XSLT Extensions

For Oracle XSLT extensions, you need to understand that once you define an XSLT extension in a certain programming language, the XSL file can be used only with XSL processors that can invoke such an extension. For example, if you define an XSLT extension function in Java, this function can be invoked only by an XSL processor that can invoke Java calls. Currently, no extensions exist for Oracle XSL processors in C/C++.

In addition, you should use XSLT extensions only if the built-in XSL functions can't help you solve the problem. For example, instead of creating an arc tangent function, you can use the built-in cosine and sine functions to achieve this functionality.

Finally, if you are thinking of using a specific XSL processor, you need to have the namespace of the extension class start with the proper URL. For example, when using the Oracle XSLT extensions, the namespace to prefix is **http://www.oracle.com/XSL/Transform/java**.

Useful Built-in Java Oracle XSLT Extensions

Defined for use by the Java Oracle XSLT processor, two such extensions are **<ora:output>** element and **<ora:node-set>**, where **xmlns:ora="http://www.oracle.com/XSL/Transform/java"**. When **<ora:output>** is used as a top-level element, it is similar to the **<xsl:output>** extension function, except that **<ora:output>** has an additional attribute **name** that is used as an identifier. When **<ora:output>** is used in an XSL template, again, it is similar to the **<xsl:output>** extension function, except that it has two additional attributes, **use** and **href**, which specify the name of the top-level **<ora:output>** to be used and give the output URL for the subtree of the XSLT result, respectively.

<xsl:output> is very useful when you need to create multiple outputs from one XSLT transformation, such as the product specifications. Using **<xsl:output>**, you can create the index pages with links to the set of subpages for the topic details.

The second built-in extension function, **<ora:node-set>**, converts a result tree fragment into a node-set, which makes it a very useful convenience function. This function is useful if you need to refer the existing text or intermediate text result in XSL for further XSL transformation.

The XSLT Virtual Machine

New in Oracle Database 10*g* is an *XSLT Virtual Machine (XSLTVM)* available for C and C++. It is the software implementation of a CPU designed to run compiled XSLT code. To do this, XSL stylesheets need to be compiled into the code the XSLTVM understands. Therefore, an XSL compiler is also included that is compliant with the XSLT 1.0 standard. This compilation can occur at runtime or can be stored for runtime retrieval. Thus, transformations are performed more quickly with higher throughput, as the stylesheet not only doesn't need to be parsed, but the templates are applied with an index lookup instead of an XML operation.

Using the XSLTVM involves a bit different processing model and APIs. The following is a code listing of this process:

```
/* Create or re-use an XML meta context object. /
  xctx = XmlCreate(&err,...);
/* Create or re-use an XSLT Compiler object. /
  comp = XmlXvmCreateComp(xctx);
/* Compile an XSL stylesheet and store/cash the result bytecode. /
  code = XmlXvmCompileFile(comp, xslFile, baseuri, flags, &err);
/* Create or reuse an XSLTVM object. The explicit stack size setting is needed
when XSLTVM terminates with "... Stack Overflow" message or when smaller
memory footprints are required (see XmlXvmCreate). /
  vm = XmlXvmCreate(xctx, "StringStack", 32, "NodeStack", 24);
/* Set a stylesheet bytecode to the XSLTVM object. */
  len = XmlXvmGetBytecodeLength(code, &err);
  err = XmlXvmSetBytecodeBuffer(vm, code, len);
/* Transform an instance XML document. */
  err = XmlXvmTransformFile(vm, xmlFile, baseuri);
/* Clean up. */
  XmlXvmDestroy(vm);
```

```
XmlXvmDestroyComp(comp);
XmlDestroy(xctx);
```

We discuss the XSLTVM in more detail in Chapter 21, in which we use it in an application.

XSLT and the Database

Many application developers are putting their business data to work over the Web as the Internet drives an explosive demand for flexible information exchange. Developers require standards-based solutions to this problem. SQL, XML, and XSLT are the standards that can get the job done in practice.

SQL is the standard you are already familiar with for accessing appropriate views of database-stored business information in your production systems. XML provides an industry-standard, platform-neutral format for representing the results of SQL queries as datagrams for exchange. XSLT defines the industry-standard way to transform XML datagrams into target XML, HTML, or text format as needed.

Beginning in Oracle9*i*, XSLT transformations can be invoked from SQL with the **xsltransform()** function. It is also available as **xmltype.transform()**. This function invokes the C XSLT 1.0 processor from the XDK that is linked into the kernel of the Oracle database. The function takes as parameters an XMLType and the stylesheet, as shown in the following example:

```
SELECT XMLTransform(booklist.xmlcol,
  (select stylesheet from stylesheet_tab where id = 1)).getStringVal()
 AS result FROM book_tab booklist;
```

This function can also take an explicit stylesheet or a DBURI to the stored location. The following is the same query using a DBURI:

```
SELECT XMLTransform(booklist.xmlcol,
    dburiType('/SCOTT/STYLESHEET_TAB/ROW[ID = 1]
      /STYLESHEET/text()').getXML()).getStringVal()
    AS result FROM book_tab booklist;
```

We will discuss the SQL XML functions in greater detail in the chapters that deal with the Oracle XML database.

Best Practices

The following sections describe some best practices to follow when employing XSL and XSLT functionality. Simply put, these sections go over some common problems that you may encounter and explain how to solve them.

Tuning Tips for XSLT

Here are two tips for tuning XSLT. First, avoid unconstrained axes such as **//foo** because they cause the entire tree to be traversed. Second, if element whitespace is not needed by the transformed output, then **<xsl:strip-space elements="*"/>** can be set in the stylesheet, dramatically reducing the size of the DOM tree built and thus improving the transformation performance. Note that when using **<xsl:strip-space elements="*"/>**, a prebuilt DOM for the input XML document cannot be passed as a parameter to the XSLT processor. Instead, you need to pass in an URL or a text stream.

The document() Function in XSLT

This function is useful when the XSLT transformation needs data from multiple XML documents. In addition, when the XSLT output includes a large section of XML data, use the **<xsl:copy>** extension function to copy the XML document content returned from the **document()** function. Finally, when using the **document()** function in the XSL file, make sure that the **setBaseURL()** is correctly set; if it is not set, the XSL file will not be found by the XSLT processor.

Improving the Overall Performance of XSLT for Multiple Transformations

In Oracle Database 10*g*, the Oracle XML Developer's Kit provides an XSLT that is useful when you need to reuse XSL stylesheets for a large number of XSL transformations. It precompiles the XSL in binary format with optimizations for use in the XSL TVM. This greatly speeds up the overall XSL transformation, up to 200 percent, especially if you have large XSL stylesheets.

Using Java, you can also reuse the **XSLStylesheet** objects by prebuilding them and reusing them in the **XSLProcessor.process()** procedures. The Java XSLT processor also allows multiple processors in different threads to share the same XSL stylesheet, because it is *threadsafe.*

CHAPTER 4

Validating XML with DTDs and XML Schemas

Although XML enables users to define their own markup languages to describe and encapsulate data into XML files, all XML documents must conform to basic "grammar" rules so that application developers can develop software with the assurance that all XML documents conform to certain basic rules of syntax. Document type definitions (DTDs) and XML schemas (XSDs) help you to ensure that your XML documents adhere to specified structures, constraints, and in the case of XSDs, datatypes so that they can be used by applications. This chapter discusses both of these methods while comparing and contrasting how and when they should be used. It will then discuss how these relate to database data and specifically the XML support in Oracle Database 10*g*.

Introducing the DTD

DTDs are inherited from SGML and are not in XML syntax. They specify the structure of an XML document including the hierarchical relationship between specified elements and their included attributes. A DTD can be associated with an XML document either by its being included in that document or by internally referencing an external file. If the DTD is contained in an external file, it is referenced through a *uniform resource locator (URL)* of the form **http://www.foobar.com/book.dtd**.

For example, the following **booklist.xml** file can have a DTD associated as an embedded decalarion within the XML file itself:

```
<?xml version = "1.0"?>
<!-- DTD bookcatalog may have a number of book entries -->
<!DOCTYPE bookcatalog [
  <!ELEMENT bookcatalog (book)*>
  <!-- Each book element has a title, 1 or more authors, etc. -->
  <!ELEMENT book (title, author+, ISBN, publisher, publishyear, price)>
  <!ELEMENT title (#PCDATA)>
  <!ELEMENT author (firstname, lastname)>
  <!ELEMENT firstname (#PCDATA)>
  <!ELEMENT lastname (#PCDATA)>
  <!ELEMENT ISBN (#PCDATA)>
  <!ELEMENT publisher (#PCDATA)>
  <!ELEMENT publishyear (#PCDATA)>
  <!ELEMENT price (#PCDATA)>
  <!ATTLIST price type (US|CAN|UK|EURO) #REQUIRED>
]>
<bookcatalog>
 <book>
  <title>History of Interviews</title>
  <author>
   <first name>Juan</first name>
   <last name>Smith</last name>
  </author>
  <ISBN>99999-99999</ISBN>
  <publisher>Oracle Press</publisher>
  <publishyear>2000</publishyear>
  <price type="US">1.00</price>
 </book>
</bookcatalog>
```

Following the **DOCTYPE** declaration of the DTD is the root element declaration **<!ELEMENT>** of **bookcatalog**. An element simply consists of a start tag, other elements or text and an end tag. For example, the **<bookcatalog>** element contains all of the elements, attributes, and text within the document. Such an element is called the *root* element. Only one root element may exist within an XML document. The root element marks the beginning of the document and is considered the parent of all the other elements, which are nested within its start tag and end tag. For XML documents to be considered "valid" with respect to this DTD, the root element **<bookcatalog>** must be the first element to start off the body of the XML document.

Following this is the *element declaration,* which stipulates the child elements that must be nested within the root element **<bookcatalog>**, the content model for the root element. Note that all the child elements of **<bookcatalog>** are explicitly called out in its element declaration, and **author** has a **+** as a suffix. This is an example of the *Extended Backus-Naur Format (EBNF)* that can be used for describing the content model. The allowed suffixes are

- **?** For 0 or 1 occurrence
- * For 0 or more occurrences
- \+ For 1 or more occurrences

Note also the use of **#PCDATA** to declare that the element text must be non-marked-up text, and the price's required attribute values are explicitly declared. The difference between **CDATA** and **PCDATA** is that **CDATA** sections are simply skipped by the parser and aren't checked for well-formedness; hence, they can be viewed as *non-parsed character data.*

A DTD in an external file can also be used. In this case only a reference is embedded in the XML document as this other version of the **booklist.xml** file.

```
<?xml version="1.0" encoding="UTF-8" standalone="no" ?>
<!DOCTYPE bookcatalog SYSTEM "booklist.dtd">
<bookcatalog>
 <book>
  <title>History of Interviews</title>
   <author>
    <first name>Juan</first name>
    <last name>Smith</last name>
   </author>
   <ISBN>99999-99999</ISBN>
   <publisher>Oracle Press</publisher>
   <publishyear>2000</publishyear>
   <price type="US">1.00</price>
 </book>
</bookcatalog>
```

Note that within the <!DOCTYPE> processing instruction, in place of the actual DTD content, is **SYSTEM "booklist.dtd"**, which refers to the external DTD. This DTD is then of the following form:

```
<!ELEMENT bookcatalog (book)*>
<!-- Each book element has a title, 1 or more authors, etc. -->
<!ELEMENT book (title, author+, ISBN, publisher, publishyear, price)>
```

```
<!ELEMENT title (#PCDATA)>
<!ELEMENT author (firstname, lastname)>
<!ELEMENT firstname (#PCDATA)>
<!ELEMENT lastname (#PCDATA)>
<!ELEMENT ISBN (#PCDATA)>
<!ELEMENT publisher (#PCDATA)>
<!ELEMENT publishyear (#PCDATA)>
<!ELEMENT price (#PCDATA)>
<!ATTLIST price type (US|CAN|UK|EURO) #REQUIRED>
```

When it comes to validating XML documents, functionally these two methods are the same.

Validating XML Against DTDs

A validating XML parser, by parsing the XML document according to the rules specified in the DTD, tries to determine whether the document conforms to the DTD (valid), meaning that the structural relationships and sequences are the same. Depending on the implementation of the parser, if an error is encountered during validation, processing may stop, as in "panic mode" exception processing, or continue with internal corrections. Warnings or errors may be reported either as processing occurs or at the very end of the processing. Finally, most processors have a mode whereby validation can be turned off; however, with DTDs, certain constructs defined in DTDs not discussed here, such as entity definitions, must still be processed.

Introducing the XML Schema Language

In February 1999, a W3C Note detailing the XML Schema Working Group's XML Schema requirements was published. This document, titled "XML Schema Requirements," includes an overview, purpose, usage scenarios, design principles, and the structural, datatype, and conformance requirements for the XML Schema language.

The "Overview" section states that the XML Schema Working Group, by charter, is assigned to look into a more informative constraint on the XML document than is provided by DTDs, namely one that would also, among other things:

- Support both primitive and complex datatypes
- Support restrictions or extensions on datatypes
- Be written in XML

For example, consider the following snippet of a DTD:

```
<!ELEMENT book (title, author, publisher, price)>
<!ELEMENT title (#PCDATA)>
<!ELEMENT author (#PCDATA)>
<!ELEMENT publisher (#PCDATA)>
<!ELEMENT price (#PCDATA)*>
```

This could appear in XML Schema format as the following XSD file:

```
<?xml version="1.0"?>
<xsd:schema xmlns:xsd="http://www.w3.org/2001/XMLSchema"
  xmlns:bk=http://www.mypublishsite.com/book>
 <xsd:annotation>
 <xsd:documentation xml:lang="en">
  Possible XML Schema equivalent of a DTD shown in Listing 1.
 </xsd:documentation>
 </xsd:annotation>
 <xsd:element name="title" type="xsd:string" minOccurs="1"
     maxOccurs="1"/>
 <xsd:element name="author" type="xsd:string" minOccurs="1"
     maxOccurs="unbounded"/>
 <xsd:element name="publisher" type="xsd:string" minOccurs="1"
     maxOccurs="unbounded"/>
 <xsd:element name="price" type="xsd:string" minOccurs="0"
     maxOccurs="*"/>
 <xsd:element name="Book"/>
 <xsd:complexType>
   <xsd:sequence>
     <xsd:element ref="bk:title"/>
     <xsd:element ref="bk:author"/>
     <xsd:element ref="bk:publisher"/>
     <xsd:element ref="bk:price"/>
    </xsd:sequence>
  </xsd:complexType>
 </xsd:element>
</xsd:schema>
```

The "Purpose" section of the "XML Schema Requirements" Note succinctly states the purpose of a schema:

> The purpose of a schema is to define and describe a class of XML documents by using these constructs to constrain and document the meaning, usage and relationships of their constituent parts: datatypes, elements and their content, attributes and their values, entities and their contents and notations. Schema constructs may also provide for the specification of implicit information such as default values. Schemas document their own meaning, usage, and function. Thus, the XML schema language can be used to define, describe and catalogue XML vocabularies for classes of XML documents.

The "Usage Scenarios" section of the Note lists the types of XML applications and activities that should benefit from an XML schema:

- Publishing and syndication
- Electronic commerce transaction processing
- Supervisory control and data acquisition

- Traditional document authoring/editing governed by schema constraints
- Use schema to help query formulation and optimization
- Open and uniform transfer of data between applications, including databases
- Metadata Interchange

The "Design Principles" section set forth specific goals for the XML Schema language to be met in order to meet the design requirements. These included that it must be a simple, self-describing language in XML that was widely usable by applications across the Internet and was coordinated with core XML specifications such as XML Information Set, Links, Namespaces, Pointers, Style and Syntax.

The final section, "Requirements," lists the structural requirements of what the XML Schema language must define, the datatype requirements of the language, and the conformance requirements. The XML Schema Working Group took these requirements and produced a number of working drafts, which culminated in the May 2001 "W3C Recommendation for XML Schema." This document consists of three parts: "XML Schema Part 0: Primer"; "XML Schema Part 1: Structures"; and "XML Schema Part 2: Datatypes."

Simple and Complex Datatypes

XML Schema Part 1 and 2 goes over the basic concepts of what datatypes can be declared in an XML schema and the properties associated with such datatypes. Simple built-in datatypes exist, along with complex datatypes defined by the XML schema designer. An example of a complex type definition for an address in a purchase order follows:

```
<xsd:complexType name="USAddress">
 <xsd:sequence>
  <xsd:element name="name" type="xsd:string"/>
  <xsd:element name="street" type="xsd:string"/>
  <xsd:element name="city" type="xsd:string"/>
  <xsd:element name="state" type="xsd:string"/>
  <xsd:element name="zip" type="xsd:decimal"/>
 </xsd:sequence>
 <xsd:attribute name="country" type="xsd:NMTOKEN" fixed="US"/>
</xsd:complexType>
```

Important things to note are that XML Schema namespace prefixes appear even on the built-in datatypes, such as **string**, and that a complex data type is surrounded by an inner sequence tag. In addition, constraints such as **minOccurs** and **maxOccurs**, whose default values equal 1, could have been put on the **name** element for number of occurrences, as in the following:

```
<xsd:element name="name" type="xsd:string" minOccurs="1" maxOccurs="2"/>
```

XML Schema Part 2 lists all the possible simple built-in datatypes for XML Schema, as outlined in Table 4-1.

These simple datatypes can also be used as a base type for ones that you can create. You can create these user-defined types by specifying constraints in three ways. First you can define a type by **restriction** by specifying additional aspects such as a pattern, value range, etc. Secondly,

Simple Built-in Data Type	Example (Comments)
string	*this is a string*
normalizedString	*this is a string* (newlines, tabs, carriage returns, etc., are translated into spaces)
token	*this is another string* (newlines, tabs, carriage returns, etc., are translated into spaces; adjacent spaces are collapsed into 1 space; trailing and leading spaces are removed)
byte	–1, 126
unsignedByte	0, 126
base64Binary	GpM7
hexBinary	0fff
integer	–126789, 0, 126789 (integer values only)
positiveInteger	1, 2, 126789 (positive integer values only)
negativeInteger	–126789, –2, –1 (negative integer values only)
nonNegativeInteger	0, 1, 126789
nonPositiveInteger	–126789, –1, 0
int	–1, 0, 2, 126789675
unsignedInt	0, 1, 1267896754
long	–1, –2, 0, 12678967543233
unsignedLong	0, 1, 3, 12678967543233
short	–1, –2, –5, 0, 1, 12678
unsignedShort	0, 1, 5, 12678
decimal	–1.2, 0, 1.2, 10000.00
Float	–0, 0, 12, INF, NaN 1.0E-2 (32-bit floating point)
Double	–0, 0, 13, INF, NaN 1.0E-20 (64-bit floating point)
Boolean	true, false, 1, 0
Time	21:21:21.000–01:00 (UTC)
dateTime	2001–01–01T121:21:21.000–01:00 (date + time zone + UTC)
duration	P1Y2M3DT10H30M12.0S (year, month, day, hour, minute, second)
date	1999–05–31

TABLE 4-1. *XML Schema Built-in Datatypes*

Simple Built-in Data Type	Example (Comments)
gMonth	–01–
gYear	2001
gYearMonth	2001–01
gDay	–31
gMonthDay	–05–31
Name	anyname (XML 1.0 Name)
QName	xsd:anyname (XML Namespace Qualified Name)
NCName	anyname (XML Namespace Qualified Name without the prefix and colon)
anyURI	http://www.oracle.com
language	en-US
ID	(a unique token, XML 1.0 ID attribute)
IDREF	(a token that matches an ID, XML 1.0 IDREF attribute)
IDREFS	(list of IDREF, XML 1.0 IDREFS attribute)
ENTITY	(XML 1.0 ENTITY attribute)
ENTITIES	(XML 1.0 ENTITIES attribute)
NOTATION	(XML 1.0 NOTATION attribute)
NMTOKEN	US, Canada (XML 1.0 NMTOKEN attribute)
NMTOKENS	US UK Canada (XML 1.0 NMTOKENS attribute)

TABLE 4-1. *XML Schema Built-in Datatypes* (continued)

you can define a **list** type made up of a set of simple datatypes. Finally, you can define a **union** type which can be satisfied from a set of types. There are, however, no extension constraints. Some additional examples are the **string**, **normalizedString**, **token**, **base64Binary**, **hexBinary**, **Name**, **QName**, **NCName**, **anyURI**, **language**, **ID**, **IDREFS**, **ENTITY**, **ENTITIES**, **NOTATION**, **NMTOKEN**, and **NMTOKENS** datatypes all can take the following facets: **length**, **minLength**, **maxLength**, **pattern** (this can be a regular expression such as a date format like MM/DD/YYYY), **enumeration**, and **whiteSpace**. The number-oriented datatypes, such as **byte**, **unsignedByte**, **integer**, **positiveInteger**, **negativeInteger**, **nonNegativeInteger**, **nonPositiveInteger**, **int**, **unsignedInt**, **long**, **unsignedLong**, **short**, **unsignedShort**, and **decimal**, all can take the following facets: **maxInclusive**, **maxExclusive**, **minInclusive**, **minExclusive**, **totalDigits**, and **fractionDigits**.

The following examples illustrate the syntax of restrictions on simple types:

```
<!-- Range -->
 <xsd:simpleType>
  <xsd:restriction base="xsd:integer">
      <xsd:minInclusive value="0"/>
      <xsd:maxInclusive value="100"/>
  </xsd:restriction>
 </xsd:simpleType>

<!-- Enumeration -->
 <xsd:simpleType>
  <xsd:restriction base="xsd:string">
   <xsd:enumeration value="Audi"/>
   <xsd:enumeration value="Golf"/>
   <xsd:enumeration value="BMW"/>
  </xsd:restriction>
 </xsd:simpleType>

<!-- Patterns -->
 <xsd:simpleType>
  <xsd:restriction base="xsd:string">
   <xsd:pattern value="[a-zA-Z0-9]{8}"/>
  </xsd:restriction>
 </xsd:simpleType>

<!-- Whitespace: preserve, collapse, replace -->
<xsd:simpleType>
 <xsd:restriction base="xsd:string">
  <xsd:whiteSpace value="preserve"/>
 </xsd:restriction>
</xsd:simpleType>

<!-- String length -->
 <xsd:simpleType>
 <xsd:restriction base="xsd:string">
   <xsd:minLength value="5"/>
   <xsd:maxLength value="8"/>
  </xsd:restriction>
</xsd:simpleType>
```

Complex types also can be constrained, but they have the flexibility of accepting both restriction and extension constraints. The following examples illustrate the syntax for complex types along with their constraints:

```
<!-- Element Extensions -->
<xsd:complexType name="fpersont">
 <xsd:complexContent>
   <xsd:extension base="personinfo">
     <xsd:sequence>
       <xsd:element name="address" type="xsd:string"/>
```

```
        <xsd:element name="city" type="xsd:string"/>
        <xsd:element name="country" type="xsd:string"/>
      </xsd:sequence>
    </xsd:extension>
  </xsd:complexContent>
</xsd:complexType>

<!-- Attribute only -->>
<xsd:element name="product">
  <xsd:complexType>
    <xsd:attribute name="prodid" type="xsd:positiveInteger"/>
  </xsd:complexType>
</xsd:element>

<!--Simple Content - Extension/Restriction -->
<xsd:element name="shoesize">
  <xsd:complexType>
    <xsd:simpleContent>
      <xsd:extension base="xsd:integer">
        <xsd:attribute name="country" type="xsd:string" />
      </xsd:extension>
    </xsd:simpleContent>
  </xsd:complexType>
</xsd:element>

<!-- Mixed Content -->
<xsd:element name="letter">
  <xsd:complexType mixed="true">
    <xsd:sequence>
      <xsd:element name="name" type="xsd:string"/>
      <xsd:element name="orderid" type="xsd:positiveInteger"/>
      <xsd:element name="shipdate" type="xsd:date"/>
    </xsd:sequence>
  </xsd:complexType>
</xsd:element>
```

XML Schema extends the DTD functionality of IDs and IDREFs by introducing user-defined KEYs and KEYREFs. The following examples illustrate their syntax:

```
<element name="purchaseReport">
  <complexType>
    <sequence>
     <element name="regions" type="r:RegionsType">
      <keyref name="dummy2" refer="r:pNumKey">
       <selector xpath="r:zip/r:part"/>
       <field xpath="@number"/>
      </keyref>
     </element>
     <element name="parts" type="r:PartsType"/>
    </sequence>
```

```
    <attribute name="period" type="duration"/>
    <attribute name="periodEnding" type="date"/>
  </complexType>

  <unique name="dummy1">
    <selector xpath="r:regions/r:zip"/>
    <field xpath="@code"/>
  </unique>

  <key name="r:pNumKey">
    <selector xpath="r:parts/r:part"/>
    <field xpath="@number"/>
  </key>
</element>
```

Note that there is an XPath selector to specify the path to the named key as well as the attribute value to be used for the key's value.

NOTE
The Oracle XML Database does not currently support KEY/KEYREFs directly; however, this functionality can be implemented using SQL constraints.

Additionally, union types such as **<xsd:union memberTypes="mystates allstate"/>**, complexTypes from simple types, mixed attributes for complexTypes to indicate data between child elements, anyType such as **type="xsd:anyType"** to indicate that the element could be of any datatype, are also allowed. Annotations such as **<xsd:annotation>** are also allowed, because they are simply mechanisms to embed documentation in the schema, such as in this example:

```
<xsd:annotation>
 <xsd:documentation xml:lang="en">
  hi there
  </xsd:documentation>
</xsd:annotation>
```

Finally, user-defined mechanisms such as an attribute group can be created to have a number of attributes associated with an element. This includes **<xsd:attributeGroup name="BookDelivery">** with a reference like **<xsd:attributeGroup ref="BookDelivery">** within the definition of the **complexType**. We recommend that you review the XML Schema Part 0:Primer for a full discussion of the specification. See the Appendix for the locations of all the XML Schema specifications.

Validating XML with XML Schemas (XSDs)

A validating XML parser, by parsing the XML document according to the rules specified in the XML schema, tries to determine whether the document conforms to the XML schema (valid), meaning that the structural relationships and sequences are the same and that conformance to the datatype rules specified in the XML schema are observed. Depending on the implementation of the parser, as with parsers that validate XML documents against DTDs, if an error is encountered during validation, processing may stop (as in "panic mode" exception processing) or continue with internal corrections. Warnings or errors may be reported either as processing occurs or at the very end of the processing. For a validating XML Schema parser, one final requirement is that if a DTD is also included by the XML document and entity definitions are encountered in the DTD, these must be taken into account by the XML schema, along with any other constructs possibly defined in the DTD. However, since the XML Schema specification does not exactly define what occurs if both a DTD and an XML schema exist for an XML document, such a situation is left to the validating parser to determine what exactly to do, which creates an implementation-dependent scenario.

Oracle produces, as part of the XDK, three XML Schema processors, Java, C, and C++, that can perform both DTD and XSD validations. In addition, the Oracle XML DB can perform validation on XML documents as they are inserted or updated. This is built in to the support for XMLType but can also be directly invoked from PL/SQL. Specific code illustrating schema validation will be presented later in the chapter, but it is useful to understand the underlying process model.

Schema validation can be triggered in two ways: external to the input document or as a result of the input document. This means that an XML schema can be passed in when the XML parser is invoked or, if the input document includes an XML Schema declaration providing a URL to the location, the XML schema can be fetched during the process. The following is the syntax of this type of declaration with and without namespaces:

```
<root xmlns:xsi=http://www.w3.org/2001/XMLSchema-instance
      xsi:schemaLocation="[target_namespace] [schemafile_location]">

 <root xmlns:xsi="http://www.w3.org/2001/XMLSchema-instance"
       xsi:noNamespaceSchemaLocation="[schemafile_location]">
```

The schema processor needs not only to build an object of the input document through parsing but also to parse the schema document into an object for the validation process to begin. This is where the different processors depart. For Java, the input and schema documents are parsed using SAX with a DOM built as needed from these SAX events. If validation is only required, then it is completely SAX based. For C and C++ processors, DOM parsing and processing is used throughout the validation process.

The Oracle XML DB, even though it uses the C XDK components, performs this processing quite differently. If it has a registered copy of the XML schema, it has already compiled and stored it as a database object, so no schema parsing is required. Upon inserting a document, the C SAX parser is invoked and the validation occurs against the compiled schema.

In all cases, if the XML schema has one or more **<xsd:import>** or **<xsd:include>** elements, as illustrated next, they will be retrieved and expanded into one aggregated schema before any validation occurs.

```
<xsd:import namespace=http://www.w3schools.com/schema
   schemaLocation="http://www.w3schools.com/schema/customer.xsd"/>
<xsd:include schemaLocation="http://www.w3schools.com/schema/customer.xsd"/>
```

XML Document Models and the Database

XML documents consist of text that conforms to a hierarchy or tree structure specified by a DTD or XML schema. In most cases you can easily store this hierarchical data in an optimal internal form using object-relational tables. All the existing and future internal applications can work with the information in the most efficient way possible. When you retrieve information, for sharing with partners or other applications, you can present the appropriate view of data and document content specific to the task at hand as integrated XML. Oracle Database's 10*g* XMLType views enable you to present data in any number of "logical" combinations, hiding any details of their underlying physical storage. You can effectively transform the structure of one or more underlying tables into a more useful or more appropriate structure for the demands of a specific application. When you link views of information with other views of related information, they quite naturally form "trees" or "graphs" of related data. When you represent database information as XML, the previous related views provide the foundation for many different tree-structured XML documents.

Mapping DTDs to Database Schemas

Here, we offer a simple example of mapping a database table to an XML DTD of the following form:

```
<!ELEMENT table (rows)*>
<!ELEMENT rows (column1, column2, ...)>
<!ELEMENT column1 (#PCDATA)>
<!ELEMENT column2 (#PCDATA)>
...
```

However, a database provides even more capability than a DTD for expressing rules. Using DTDs, you cannot define type information other than numbers, strings, and IDs. The database schema defines type information and constraints, such as permissible value ranges. A database schema enables you to define relationships or dependencies. For example, your e-commerce business might receive orders as XML documents. By using a database, you can link customer and order information, and define a rule about not processing orders for closed accounts. In spite of the limitations in DTDs, mapping a database schema to a DTD presents the database as a virtual XML document to the tools that need XML documents as input.

A database consists of a schema associated with each database user. Each schema associated with a user is a collection of schema objects accessible to the user. While mapping a database scheme to a DTD, each user is mapped as a child element of the top-level element identified by the SID of the database instance. An element representing a user schema and its child elements uses a unique namespace to avoid conflicts with schema objects defined in other user schemas.

You can perform the following steps to generate a simple DTD from a relational schema:

1. For each table, create an element.
2. For each column in a table, create a PCDATA-only child element.
3. For each object or nested table column, create an ELEMENT-content only child element with attributes or nested columns as child elements.

For example, the following DTD corresponds to a simple database schema:

```
<!ELEMENT dbschema (sys, scott, ...)>
<!ATTLIST dbschema
        xmlns CDATA #FIXED "http://www.oracle.com/xml/dbschema"
        sid   CDATA #REQUIRED>
<!ELEMENT scott (BookList, ...)>
<!ATTLIST scott
        xmlns CDATA #FIXED "http://www.oracle.com/xml/dbschema/scott">
<!ELEMENT BookList (Book)*>
<!ATTLIST Book row_num CDATA #IMPLIED>
<!ELEMENT Book (Title, ISBN, Author, Publisher, (Review)*)>
...
```

Unfortunately, a number of drawbacks exist to mapping a database schema to a DTD. For example, there is no way to predict datatypes or column lengths definitively from the DTD. The solution to this problem is to use datatypes in XML documents using XML schemas.

Mapping XML Documents to a Database Schema

The format for DTDs is an existing worldwide standard and will likely exist and be improved upon for years. However, because of the inherent limitations of DTDs and the increasingly data-oriented role that XML is being asked to assume because of developments in e-business and e-commerce, the W3C standards body is promoting XML Schema, rather than attempting to push the current DTD standards any further. Using an XML schema, you can map the simple database table into an XML schema of the following form:

```
<schema targetNamespace="some NSURI">
<xsd:complexType  name="table">
 <xsd:sequence>
  <xsd:element name="rows" minOccurs="0" maxOccurs="unbounded"/>
 </xsd:sequence>
 </xsd:complexType>
  <xsd:complexType name="rows" >
   <xsd:sequence>
    <xsd:element name="column1" type="xs:string"/>
    <xsd:element name="column2" type="xs:date"/>
     ...
    </xsd:sequence>
   </xsd:complexType>
  </xsd:schema>
```

Note that you can specify additional datatypes using the **<xsd:element>** attribute of the form ***type="xsd:datatype"*** where ***datatype*** is either an XML Schema simple datatype or a named type defined in the XML schema.

Supported Database Mappings

To transfer data between an XML document and a database, you must map a document structure defined by a DTD or an XML schema to a database schema and vice versa.

When mapping XML documents associated with a DTD or an XML schema to a database schema for the purpose of storing XML in Oracle XML DB, four basic strategies exist:

- Map the complete XML document as a single, intact object, such as CLOBs
- Map XML elements to object-relational tables and columns in the database schema
- Map fragments of XML documents as CLOBs and the rest of the document as object-relational tables
- Map XML documents to an Oracle XMLType

You can choose one of the previous approaches, depending on the structure of the XML document and operations performed by the application. You can also store the XML DTD or schema in the database to validate the XML documents.

XML Documents in CLOBs

Storing an intact XML document in a *Character Large Object (CLOB)* or *Binary Large Object (BLOB)* is a good strategy if the XML document contains static content that will only be updated by replacing the entire document. Examples include written text such as articles, advertisements, books, and legal contracts. Documents of this nature are known as document-centric and are delivered from the database as a whole. Storing this kind of document intact within the database gives you the advantages of an industry-proven database and its reliability over file system storage. If you choose to store an XML document outside the database, you can still use the database features to index, query, and efficiently retrieve the document through the use of BFILES, URLs, and text-based indexing.

XML Documents as Object-Relational Data

If the XML document has a well-defined structure and contains data that is updatable or used in other ways, the document is data-centric. Typically, the XML document contains elements or attributes that have complex structures. Examples of this kind of document include sales orders, invoices, and airline flight schedules. Oracle Database 10*g*, with its object-relational extensions, has the capability to capture the structure of the data in the database using object types, object references, and collections. Two options exist for storing and preserving the structure of the XML data in an object-relational form:

- Store the attributes of the elements in a relational table and define object views to capture the structure of the XML elements
- Store the structured XML elements in an object table

Once stored in the object-relational form, the data can be easily updated, queried, rearranged, and reformatted as needed using SQL. The XML SQL Utility then provides the means to store an XML document by mapping it to the underlying object-relational storage and, conversely, provides the capability to retrieve the object-relational data as an XML document. If an XML document is structured, but the structure of the XML document is incompatible with the structure of the underlying database schema, you must transform the data into the correct format before writing it to the database. You can achieve this using XSL stylesheets or other programming approaches; but, depending on your needs, you might want to store the data-centric XML document as an intact single object. Or, you can define object views corresponding to the various XML document structures and define INSTEAD OF triggers to perform the appropriate transformation and to update the base data.

XML Documents as Fragment Documents and Object-Relational Data

You can use Oracle Database 10g's views to view and operate a combination of structured and unstructured XML data as a whole. Views enable you to construct an object on-the-fly by combining XML data stored in a variety of ways. So, you can store structured data (such as employee data, customer data, and so on) in one location within object-relational tables and store related unstructured data (such as descriptions and comments) within a CLOB. When you need to retrieve the data as a whole, you simply construct the structure from the various pieces of data using type constructors in the view's SELECT statement. The XML SQL Utility then enables you to retrieve the constructed data from the view as a single XML document.

XML Documents as XMLTypes

Finally, you can store an XML document in an Oracle XML DB's XMLType. XMLType supports searches and queries using XPATH-like syntax. It can be created as a database table, view, columns, and as the parameter and return type of SQL, PL/SQL, and Java functions. For example, the SYS_XMLGEN and SYS_XMLAGG Oracle SQL functions, which generate an XML document and aggregate a number of XML documents, respectively, can take as a parameter an XMLType object and return an XMLType object. These functions can be embedded in SQL queries as in a simple SELECT statement and return XML:

```
SELECT SYS_XMLGEN(book) FROM bookcatalog WHERE title LIKE '%ELLISON%';
```

and

```
SELECT SYS_XMLAGG(SYS_XMLGEN(book)).getClobVal() book_list FROM bookcatalog
GROUP BY title;
```

The first would return the XML of a book entry and the second would return a list of all the titles of the book entries.

Similarly, the DBMS_XMLGEN PL/SQL package converts the result set from SQL queries to an XML stored in an XMLType, as in

```
SELECT SYS_XMLAGG(SYS_XMLGEN(book)).getClobVal() book_list FROM bookcatalog
GROUP BY title
```

resulting in a listing of all the book titles in XML.

Table creation using XMLType columns and database manipulation language (DML) operations to insert, update, and delete values is allowed with this new data type, along with datatype member functions such as **existsNode()** and **extract()** that take arguments with XPATH-like syntax to return fragments of XML in the XMLType, such as

```
SELECT book.extract('//title/text()').getStringVal() FROM bookcatalog;
```

and

```
SELECT * FROM bookcatalog where book.existsNode('//book/title') != 0;
```

Best Practices

The following are some best practices to follow when employing DTDs and XML schemas.

Designing Your Schema

Defining a schema from scratch can be a daunting task. The following are a set of guidelines that will make your job easier, reduce errors, and ease maintenance.

1. Name the XML Schema document file to reflect the root element.
2. Ensure the root element is defined as the first top-level element and based on the **rootType**.
3. Ensure XML Schemas are versioned using the optional **version** attribute in the **<schema/ >** element.
4. Use **xsd:token** instead of **xsd:string** because the lexical space of a token is the set of strings that do not contain the line feed (#xA) nor tab (#x9) characters, that have no leading or trailing spaces (#x20) and that have no internal sequences of two or more spaces. The base type of token is **normalizedString**.
5. XML element and attribute names should be entirely upper case and use the underscore to separate word boundaries. This makes the database objects easier to create and use when registering the XML schema to Oracle XML DB.

Elements vs. Attributes

A classic question that every XML schema and DTD designer faces at some point is this: Shall I design my DTD or XML schema modeling the data as elements or attributes? It is also a very crucial question as its answer can be the difference between a successful future-proof design and one that fails. To illustrate this, consider the following two fragments describing an instance of an address. The first is attribute-based:

```
<Address Street="123 Main St." City="San Francisco" State="CA" Zip="94127"/>
```

Notice how it reads very nicely and appears to be a compact representation because there are no end tags. Now consider the following element-based instance:

```
<Address>
 <Street>123 Main St.</Street>
 <City>San Francisco</City>
 <State>CA<State>
 <Zip>94127</Zipcode>
</Address>
```

While this version does not read left to right as conveniently, its DOM representation is not significantly larger than the first one because both elements and attributes are nodes. More importantly, if at a later time you want to add structure to any one of the elements, you can with the second one but not the first, because attributes cannot have structure or be more than a simple type. An example would be where you want to support extended ZIP codes:

```
<Zip>
 <Code>94127</Code>
 <Ext>8522</Ext>
</Zip>
```

Designing Element and Attribute Names

XML has the characteristic of being human-readable with no effective limit to the number of characters used in element and attribute names. The temptation is therefore to create very explicit names, the result being an instance document that is many times larger than the data it is conveying, as shown in this XML fragment:

```
<ArrivalInfo>
 <TripCityTimeInfo>
  <CodeDescription>
   <Code>CVG</Code>
    <Description>CVG - Cincinnati,OH, United States - Northern Kentucky
       Intl</Description>
    <AdditionalData>Northern Kentucky Intl</AdditionalData>
   </CodeDescription>
   <Date>
    <Month>5</Month>
    <Day>21</Day>
    <Year>2002</Year>
   </Date>
   <Time Format="Military">0759</Time>
   <FlightSearchByTimeType Type="Arriving"/>
 </TripCityTimeInfo>
</ArrivalInfo>
```

This actual XML fragment contains 471 bytes yet only 114 bytes of data. This does add significantly to the processing costs in both resources and time. Remember, ultimately XML is a machine-processed document; therefore, it is important for names to be reasonable.

Loading External DTDs from a JAR File

A very convenient way to handle multiple DTDs is to put them in a JAR file, so that when the XML parser needs one of the DTDs, it can access it from the JAR. The Oracle XML parser supports a base URL (setBaseURL()), but that just points to a place where all the DTDs are exposed. The solution involves the following steps:

1. Load the DTD as an **InputStream** using

   ```
   InputStream is = YourClass.class.getResourceAsStream("/foo/bar/your.dtd");
   ```

   This opens **./foo/bar/your.dtd** in the relative location on the CLASSPATH so that it can be found in your JAR.

2. Parse the DTD with the following code:

```
DOMParser d = new DOMParser();
d.parseDTD(is, "rootelementname");
d.setDoctype(d.getDoctype());
```

3. Parse your document with the following code:

```
d.parse("yourdoc");
```

CHAPTER 5

XML Operations with XQuery

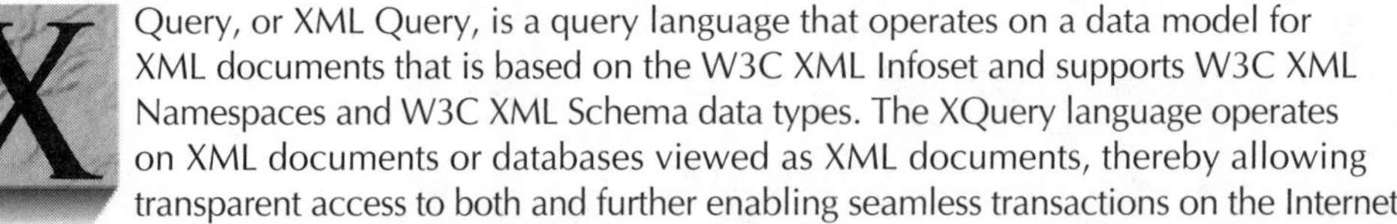

XQuery, or XML Query, is a query language that operates on a data model for XML documents that is based on the W3C XML Infoset and supports W3C XML Namespaces and W3C XML Schema data types. The XQuery language operates on XML documents or databases viewed as XML documents, thereby allowing transparent access to both and further enabling seamless transactions on the Internet.

From the requirements set out by the user community, the XQuery functionality should be able to perform queries on XML that are in the form of human-readable documents, data-oriented documents, mixed document-oriented and data-oriented, administrative data, streaming data, DOM objects, native repositories and web servers, and catalogs.

This chapter will introduce the basics of XQuery, introduce the Oracle XQuery engine and describe how it interacts with the Oracle database, and present XQuery best practices.

Introducing XQuery

XQuery is described at length in the following W3C Last Call Working Draft specifications per www.w3.org/TR/xquery/ (referenced in a prior chapter):

- **XQuery 1.0: An XML Query Language** Describes how the language is an extension of XPath 2.0 and describes in-depth the grammar and how it is processed. It describes the different expressions that are allowed (such as primary, path, sequence, arithmetic, comparison, logical, and so on), how the expressions can be nested, and the possible data types for the various expressions, operators, and functions. The module section describes the main module and the prolog that can be type-checked on a stand-alone basis.
- **XQuery 1.0 and XPath 2.0 Data Model** Describes the data model of the XML document on which the XQuery operators function. The *data model* is simply a representation of the XML document, e.g., elements, attributes, namespaces, processing instructions, and so on, that is provided as input to an XML processor, along with how that information is qualified in terms of data types and allowed values. This specification also describes the different accessor functions to this information. Users do not need to concern themselves with this specification because it is aimed at implementers of XQuery processors.
- **XQuery 1.0 and XPath 2.0 Formal Semantics** Describes the formal semantics of the language with a formal notation governed by grammar productions. It complements the first specification in this list and the XML Path Language (XPath) 2.0 specification by strictly defining the meaning of the language's objects, such as expressions, values, and data types, with formal notations. With this specification's formal semantics, reference implementations can easily be prototyped and problems with this language can thereby be eliminated. Like the preceding specification in this list, this specification is not intended for users.
- **XQuery 1.0 and XPath 2.0 Functions and Operators** Introduces new functions and operators to the XPath 2.0 language and includes error, trace, constructor, strings, qualified names, context, and casting functions. It also introduces functions and operators on the XML Schema simple data types such as numeric types and values, Booleans, durations, dates, time, any URI, base64Binary, hexBinary, and NOTATION as well as on nodes, and on sequences.

- **XML Syntax for XQuery 1.0 (XQueryX)** Maps the grammar productions outlined in the "XQuery 1.0 and XPath 2.0 Formal Semantics" specification into XML. Thus, XML parsers and XSLT stylesheets can process, query, generate, modify, and reuse the XQuery operations. It makes the productions more easy for humans to read and the queries themselves more easy to deal with.

Basics

XPath is used quite extensively in the XQuery specification, along with regular expressions, which explains the joint data model. As mentioned in previous chapters, XPath is simply a way to select of create portions of an XML document, and XQuery makes extensive use of this syntax in its queries and expressions. The joint data model upon which XQuery operators operate defines the input and output of XQuery operators. This data model relies on the concept of a *sequence*, which is an ordered collection, (e.g., in document order) of zero or more items, which are defined to be a node (e.g., element, attribute, text, document, comment, PI or namespace node), or an atomic value that is typed via XML Schema data types (one special value is an error value). The language itself is simply composed of keywords and such operators defined via these expressions or constructors. For example, variables, which are prefixed by $ signs, can be used in various expressions, such as loops or assignments, or in function calls or constructors.

Expressions

A number of expressions exist within the XQuery language, so we will concentrate on just the three that we think will be the most heavily used:

- FLWOR expression
- Path expression
- Predicate expression

For these expressions, the following variation of the **book.xml** file will be used:

```
<book xmlns:bk="http://www.mcgraw-hill.com" bk:ISBN="99999-99999">
 <title>Oracle Database 10g XML and SQL</title>
 <author>
  <name bk:type="person">
   <first>Mark</first>
   <last>Scardina</last>
  </name>
  <name bk:type="person">
   <first>Ben</first>
   <last>Chang</last>
  </name>
  <name bk:type="person">
   <first>Jinyu</first>
   <last>Wang</last>
  </name>
 </author>
```

```
 <publisher>Oracle Press</publisher>
 <publishyear>2003</publishyear>
 <price type="US">10.00</price>
</book>
```

FLWOR Expression

The FLWOR expression consists of the FOR, LET, WHERE, ORDER BY, and RETURN keywords. For example, the following code loops over all book instances, finds the respective authors, and returns result nodes containing the book's title and the authors for each book:

```
<Result>
{
FOR $book in fn:doc("book.xml")/book
LET $author:=collection('author')/$book/author
WHERE count($author)>0
ORDER BY $author/name/last
RETURN
   <title> {$book/title} </title>
  <author>
   {fn:string-join(($author/name/first/text(), $author/name/last/text(),)," ")}
  </author>
)
</result>
```

The following is the result of this XQuery:

```
<result>
 <title>Oracle Database 10g XML and SQL</title>
 <author> Ben Chang, Mark Scardina, Jinyu Wang</author>
</result>
```

Examining the operation of this XQuery entails the following steps:

1. The iteration is set to the **<book>** element by FOR and assigned to the **$book** variable.
2. The variable **$author** is assigned via LET to **/<book>/<author>** for all input books.
3. The predicate WHERE ensures that only books with authors are selected.
4. ORDER BY causes the results to return sorted based on the author's last name.
5. RETURN defines the actual format of the result.

Note that in this case an XML document is constructed as the result in a similar fashion to the result from an XSLT template, and we will be discussing XQuery versus XSLT in the "Best Practices" section.

Path Expression

The path expression is based on the abbreviated syntax of XPath 1.0 and is extended in 2.0 with dereference operators and range predicates—i.e., expressions enclosed in square brackets that are often used to filter a sequence of values. These expressions are evaluated by performing node tests on one or more steps delineated by **/** or **//** by performing a node test. There are two types of node tests. The *Kind Test* checks for whether the type of XML item is either an *ElementTest, AttributeTest, PITest, CommentTest, TextTest* or *AnyKindTest*. The *Name Test* adds the further qualification of matching the QName as well. For example, the following are several node tests:

```
Element(child::book) - matches all child elements of book
Element(child::/book/author/name, person) - matches all names of child element,
author, of type person
Attribute() - matches any single attribute node regardless of name
Attribute(/book/@bk:ISBN) - matches all book elements containing ISBN attributes
   in the XML namespace associated with the br prefix.
```

Predicate Expression

The predicate expression can be used to identify certain nodes (e.g., the expression starting with **title** used in **book[title="Oracle Database 10*g* XML and SQL"]**), to help determine values (e.g., the expression **price** in **book[price > 10]** or **book[price –10]**), or to determine the ordinal position (such as **book[5]**).

Query Prolog

The query prolog, along with the query body, comprises an XQuery query. It contains constructs such as namespace declarations, function and variable definitions, and module imports such as XML Schema imports. The query body thus references the constructs defined or declared in the query prolog, and utilizes the aforementioned expressions to determine the result of an XQuery query. Some of the other constructs mentioned in the XQuery specification that are contained in the query prolog are version declaration, validation declaration, default namespace declaration, xmlspace declaration, and default collation.

With a namespace declaration in the query prolog, a prefix can be used in qualified names to differentiate names of elements, attributes, etc. For example,

```
declare namespace bk = "http://www.oracle.com/book"
```

can be used to uniquely define an element **<mybook>** as in the qualified name **<bk:mybook>**. A default namespace declaration could also be made to apply to all unqualified elements, attributes, etc., such as:

```
declare default namespace element namespace bk = "http://www.oracle.com/book"
```

without which these unqualified elements, attributes, etc., would be considered to be in no namespace.

In addition to namespace declarations, the query prolog can also contain function definitions that can be called within the query body. The **function definition** consists of the function name, with an optional prefix, preceded by the **define** function keyword and followed by a parameter list and the expressions that make up the function body. For example, in

```
declare default namespace element namespace bk = http://www.oracle.com/book
define function bk:getbookname($node) {
  let $name := $node/bookname
  return $name
}
```

the function name is **bk:getbookname**, which contains the namespace prefix to prevent it from colliding with other **getbookname** functions. It takes a node as a parameter, and in its body it creates a return variable, **$name**, that is used to return the **<bookname>** nodes that are children of the passed-in node.

Finally, the **import** keyword can be used in the query prolog to include other bodies of definitions, such as XML schemas, which can then be referenced in the query body. For example,

```
import schema namespace mybook=http://www.mcgrawhill.com/book
   at "http://xmlns.mcgraw-hill.com/mybook.xsd"
declare default namespace element namespace bk = http://www.oracle.com/book
define function bk:getbookname($node) {
  let $name := $node/bookname
  return $name
}
```

Introducing XQueryX

XQueryX is simply an XML representation of an XQuery query. The XQueryX specification maps the grammar productions outlined in the XQuery 1.0 and XPath 2.0 Formal Semantics specification into XML. Thus, using XML parsers you can process, query, generate, modify, and reuse the XQuery expressions. It enables XML processes such as XSLT stylesheets to generate productions. At the time of this writing, this specification is undergoing significant rewriting and thus may not exit the W3C process as it currently stands. We mention it here for informational purposes because the Oracle XQuery prototype discussed in the following section supports the original syntax.

To give you a specific example of how the XQuery XML looks, the following FLWOR expression is transformed from

```
FOR $b IN document("book.xml")//book
WHERE $b/publisher = "Oracle Press" AND $b/year = "2003"
RETURN
    $b/title
```

to the following XML representation:

```
<q:query xmlns:q="http://www.w3.org/2001/06/xqueryx">
  <q:flwr>
    <q:forAssignment variable="$b">
      <q:step axis="SLASHSLASH">
        <q:function name="document">
          <q:constant datatype="CHARSTRING">book.xml</q:constant>
        </q:function>
        <q:identifier>book</q:identifier>
      </q:step>
    </q:forAssignment>
    <q:where>
      <q:function name="AND">
        <q:function name="EQUALS">
          <q:step axis="CHILD">
            <q:variable>$b</q:variable>
```

```
            <q:identifier>publisher</q:identifier>
          </q:step>
          <q:constant datatype="CHARSTRING">Oracle Press</q:constant>
        </q:function>
        <q:function name="EQUALS">
          <q:step axis="CHILD">
            <q:variable>$b</q:variable>
            <q:identifier>year</q:identifier>
          </q:step>
          <q:constant datatype="CHARSTRING">2003</q:constant>
        </q:function>
      </q:function>
    </q:where>
    <q:return>
      <q:step axis="CHILD">
        <q:variable>$b</q:variable>
        <q:identifier>title</q:identifier>
      </q:step>
    </q:return>
  </q:flwr>
</q:query>
```

The Oracle XQuery Engine

The Oracle XQuery engine is a prototype implementation of the evolving XQuery language, with Oracle extensions. Written in Java, the engine can be invoked via its OJXQI Java API, or via its XQLPlus command-line utility. This engine can be used either within the Oracle database or outside, as in a web application server or client. The only other requirements are Oracle XDK 9*i* or above, an associated JDBC driver, and JDK 1.3. This prototype is based on the November 15, 2002 draft of the specification.

Setting Up the Environment

On Windows platforms, **xq.zip** needs to be downloaded and unzipped. The directory contains the JAR file, **xquery.jar**, an example XQuery file and XML file, and a Javadoc directory. The next step is to include in your CLASSPATH the location of this JAR and the JARs in the Oracle XDK, along with your desired JDK or JRE.

Similarly, on UNIX platforms, the **xq.tar.gz** file needs to be downloaded, unzipped, and extracted; and the CLASSPATH needs to be set properly. These distributions contain the same files and can also be used on any Oracle-supported platform with the appropriate port of the JDK or JRE.

Testing Your Installation

On both Windows and UNIX platforms, in order to test the installation, after you make sure the CLASSPATH has been set correctly, run XQLPlus via the following command:

```
java oracle.xquery.XQLPlus exmpl1.xql
```

This will process the following XQuery contained in **exmpl1.xql**:

```
<bib>
  {
    FOR $b IN document("bib.xml")/bib/book
    WHERE $b/publisher = "Addison-Wesley" AND $b/@year > 1991
    RETURN
      <book year="{ $b/@year }">
        { $b/title }
      </book>
  }
</bib>
```

The preceding query parses **bib.xml**, iterating over all the **<book>** elements that it has assigned to the **$b** variable. For each **<publisher>** element, it attempts to match the string value as well as a numeric comparison against the **year** attribute. For each entry that satisfies both conditions, it creates an XML output of the title and year published. The matched portion of **bib.xml** and the result is as follows:

```
<bib>
 <book year="1994">
  <title>TCP/IP Illustrated</title>
  <author><last>Stevens</last><first>W.</first></author>
  <publisher>Addison-Wesley</publisher>
  <price> 65.95</price>
 </book>
 <book year="1992">
  <title>Advanced Programming in the Unix environment</title>
  <author><last>Stevens</last><first>W.</first></author>
  <publisher>Addison-Wesley</publisher>
  <price>65.95</price>
 </book>
...
</bib>
Result
--------------------------------------------------------
<bib>
 <book year="1994">
  <title>TCP/IP Illustrated</title>
 </book>
 <book year="1992">
  <title>Advanced Programming in the Unix environment</title>
 </book>
</bib>
```

Note that the file being queried, **bib.xml**, is in the query itself and is not passed on the command line.

Querying XML Documents

Using the Oracle XQuery engine, it is quite simple to query XML documents either interactively via the command line or programmatically.

Running in Interactive Mode

XQLPlus can be run in interactive mode in the same way as SQLPlus. In fact, where appropriate, it uses the same commands. To run XQLPlus in interactive mode, invoke the following command:

```
java oracle.xquery.XQLPlus
```

Then, an XQuery can be entered from the XQL prompt, terminated by **/**, or a script invoked via **@exmpl**. Typing **help** returns the following:

```
XQuery Command Line Tool
Enter XQuery statements followed by /;
To execute queries in a file from the XQL prompt, enter @ followed by
the <fileName>
To execute queries in a file from the shell prompt, enter
java XQLPlus <fileName>
Set command helps set environment variables:
set sqlconn default=<jdbc-connect-string>
set sqlconn <name> =<jdbc-connect-string>
set echo   (ON | OFF)
set timing (ON | OFF)
set var <variable name> <value>
set print_plan  (ON | OFF)
```

Querying XML from the Command Line

In addition to interactive mode XQLPlus can be invoked with arguments:

```
java oracle.xquery.XQueryContext -xqfile /private/exmp11.xql
```

These can be the XQuery file containing the query, an optional base URL to be used when accessing filenames inside document functions in the XQuery, and optional debug features. For example:

```
java oracle.xquery.XQueryContext -xqfile /private/exmp11.xql
   -baseurl /private -debug
```

Querying XML with XQueryX

The XQueryX XML file can also be run from the XQLPlus engine via

```
java oracle.xquery.XQLPlus @foo.xml
```

or at the command-line prompt after invoking XQLPlus.

XQuery and the Oracle Database

The Oracle XQuery engine enables you to connect to the Oracle database and execute XQuery queries over the data stored in the database, the result sets of which are returned via an XQueryResultSetObject object. This capability is made possible through Oracle extensions that allow the execution of XQuery expressions over traditional database tables viewed as XML. Hence, the power of XQuery has been significantly enhanced with the Oracle implementation.

XQuery API for Java

OJXQI is the Java API for XQuery proposed by Oracle, and includes various extensions that Oracle supports for connecting to the database and binding variables, among other things. OJXQI provides an **XqueryResultSet** class that can be used to obtain the results of executing the XQuery.

To use OJXQI, you first need to construct a context. To do so, use the default constructor or pass in the connection information, prepare an XQuery or XQueryX statement by calling prepareXQuery() or prepareXQueryX(), respectively, bind any values to the return object of these calls, PreparedXQuery, execute the PreparedXQuery object, and then iterate over the XQueryResultSetObject. The following code fragment illustrates this:

```
XQueryContext ctx = new XQueryContext();
   try    {
  // create a string from the file
     Reader strm = new FileReader("exmpl1.xql");
  // prepare the query
     PreparedXQuery xq = ctx.prepareXQuery(strm);
  // get a resultset
     XQueryResultSet rset = xq.executeQuery();
       while (rset.next()) {
  // get result nodes
       XMLNode node = rset.getNode();
       System.out.println(" NODE "+ node.getNodeName());
       node.print(System.out);
     }
   }
   catch (Exception e) {
    // do something..
   }
```

A number of Oracle enhancements were made to support embedding SQL inside XQuery queries, to support bind variables so that the XQuery query is not re-executed, and to support XMLType.

Querying XML in the Database

Invoking the methods defined in OJXQI in a Java program enables you to query the database using XQuery expressions and operators. For example, the following XQuery will return the results of all the names and titles from an author table:

```
FOR $i IN sqlquery("select * from booklist.author"/ROW)
RETURN
```

```
$i/NAME,
$i/TITLE
```

The code to convert that to a Java program would look something like this:

```
// get the connection
DriverManager.registerDriver(new oracle.jdbc.driver.OracleDriver());
Connection conn = DriverManager.getConnection("jdbc:oracle:@", "scott", "tiger");
// create the context using that connection
XqueryContext ctx = new XQueryContext(conn);
// create a string from the file
Reader strm = new StringReader("For $i IN sqlquery(\"select * from
booklist.author\"), "+  " RETURN $i/NAME, $i/TITLE");
// prepare the query
PreparedXQuery xq = ctx.prepareXQuery(strm);
// get a result set
XqueryResultSet rset = xq.executeQuery();
while (rset.next()) {
  XMLNode node = rset.getNode();
  System.out.println(" NODE "+ node.getNodeName());
  Node.print(System.out);
}
```

Best Practices

Obviously, since XQuery has not been finalized, there is little user experience with it. However, we feel there is value in comparing its functionality with two alternative technologies—XSLT 2.0 and SQL/XML. Oracle Database 10*g* has implementations of both of these technologies.

XQuery Versus XSLT 2.0

XSLT is a mature language that has Oracle implementations in Java, C, and C++ as well as SQL access. XSLT 2.0, as discussed in Chapter 3, is incorporating more functionality, including support for data types and XPath 2.0. XQuery, which also uses XPath 2.0, is also still brewing even as this is being written, and as seen from the examples supports similar functionality. Therefore, the following are legitimate questions: *Do we need both XSLT and XQuery?* and *Are there advantages of one over the other?*

Since XSLT is a function-based language in which each template needs to be evaluated against the entire document, its processing model is considered recursive. This can produce less-than-optimum performance when processing large documents, not only because XSLT processors require an in-memory representation of the entire document, such as DOM, to traverse, but also because the frequent XPath traversals reduce throughput of the processing.

XQuery, on the other hand, while still using XPath, is neither function-based nor recursive. Therefore, its processing model can be optimized by compiling the queries, potentially producing more efficient processing. However, XQuery, without XQueryX, is not an XML syntax, thus limiting its integration into an XML processing stack.

Finally, between the work being done to compile XSLT stylesheets and the fact that few XQuery implementations exist due to the standard's draft status, the verdict is still out as to whether both will find a niche or one will prevail.

XQuery Versus SQL/XML

In the case of XQuery versus SQL/XML, they are two emerging standards that can be considered to be competing for the same function space. We will be discussing SQL/XML in detail in later chapters because its functionality is included in Oracle Database 10*g*. Of particular note is that SQL/XML depends on SQL for its datatype support and not XML Schema. Thus, as its name implies, SQL/XML integrates XML processing with SQL and therefore would be the technology of choice for SQL environments or when you need to mix table-based, structured data with XML or document data.

On the other hand, XQuery is designed for an XML environment where a database is not a required component. While it will access collections of documents, it does not depend on any particular repository model. It is also designed to work with XML Schema data types. Therefore, taking into account the XSLT issues, XQuery will generally be the choice where your XML processing doesn't have access to or will not benefit from a SQL engine and requires XML Schema support.

CHAPTER 6

XML Messaging and RPC with SOAP

he Oracle E-Business Suite of applications offers companies a new and better way to conduct business. The E-Business Suite combines customer relationship management (CRM), supply chain management, and internal operations as a fully integrated solution. The Oracle E-Business XML Services component, which is available in release 11.5.6 of Oracle Applications, provides a framework and system infrastructure for deployment, management, and run-time execution of XML Services, the foundation for developing a new generation of Web-enabled e-business applications. Central to this notion of XML Services is the concept of XML messaging based on SOAP, which underlies the communication of these applications via their key integration points (for example, XML Services, how XML Services are invoked, what events trigger them, and how event subscribers are able to handle them).

Introducing SOAP

The Simple Object Access Protocol (SOAP) is a lightweight, XML-based protocol for exchanging information in a decentralized, distributed environment. SOAP consists of three parts:

- The SOAP Envelope, which defines an overall framework for expressing what is in the message, who should process the message, and whether the processing is optional or mandatory.
- A set of encoding rules for expressing instances of application-defined data types. These rules define a serialization mechanism that converts the application data types to XML and vice versa.
- A SOAP remote procedure call (RPC) convention for representing remote procedure calls and responses.

The major design goal for SOAP is simplicity and extensibility. SOAP has a looser coupling between the client and the server than some similar distributed computing protocols, such as Common Object Request Broker Architecture/Internet Inter-ORB Protocol (CORBA/IIOP). All this makes the protocol even more compelling. SOAP is transport protocol independent and thus can be used with any transport protocol. At the same time, when used with HTTP for remote service invocation over the Internet, SOAP emerged as a de facto standard for delivering programmatic content over the Web. SOAP 1.2 became a W3C recommendation in June 2003; however, the Oracle XFK 10*g* implementation is based on SOAP 1.1, which is a W3C note.

Since SOAP is XML based, it is platform and operating system independent. It supports communication between a client and server that use different programming languages. SOAP requests are easy to generate, and a client can easily process the responses. By using SOAP, one application can become a programmatic client of another application's services, with the two applications exchanging rich, structured information. SOAP provides a robust programming model that creates the possibility to aggregate powerful, distributed web services (such as XML services) to turn the Internet into an application development platform of the future.

Literal, Encoded SOAP Messages

The SOAP specification describes a standard, XML-based way to encode requests and responses, including:

- Requests to invoke a method/function as a service, including in parameters
- Responses from a service method/function, including return value and out parameters
- Errors from a service

An illustration of a SOAP message format appears in Figure 6-1.

Basically, the message itself is the key for a SOAP message; the payload is encoded in XML and has no knowledge of processing, while the header may contain processing details.

Consider the following example: a GetLastTradePrice SOAP request is sent to a StockQuote service. The request takes a string parameter, the company ticker symbol, and returns a float in the SOAP response. The XML document represents the SOAP message. The SOAP Envelope element is the top element of the XML document. XML namespaces are used to disambiguate SOAP identifiers from application-specific identifiers. The example uses HTTP as the transport protocol. The rules governing XML payload format in SOAP are entirely independent of the fact that the payload is carried in HTTP (because SOAP is transport independent). The SOAP request message embedded in the HTTP request looks like this:

```
POST /StockQuote HTTP/1.1
Host: www.stockquoteserver.com
Content-Type: text/xml; charset="utf-8"
Content-Length: nnnn
SOAPAction: "Some-URI"

<SOAP-ENV:Envelope  xmlns:SOAP-   ENV="http://schemas.xmlsoap.org/soap/envelope/"
SOAP-ENV:encodingStyle="http://schemas.xmlsoap.org/soap/encoding/">
 <SOAP-ENV:Body>
  <m:GetLastTradePrice xmlns:m="Some-URI">
   <symbol>ORCL</symbol>
  </m:GetLastTradePrice>
 </SOAP-ENV:Body>
</SOAP-ENV:Envelope>
```

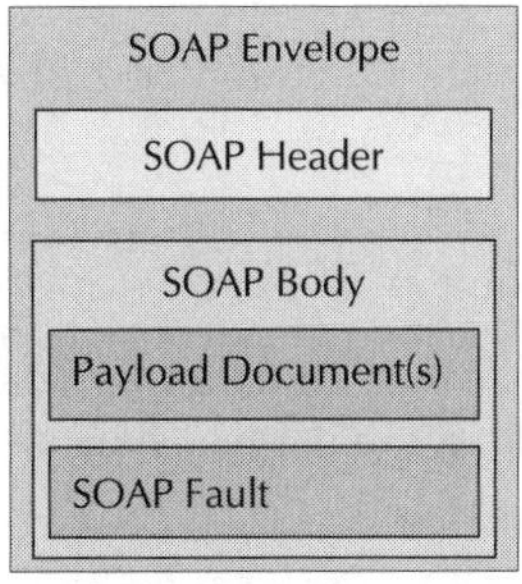

FIGURE 6-1. *SOAP message format*

What follows is the response HTTP message containing the XML message in SOAP format as the payload:

```
HTTP/1.1 200 OK
Content-Type: text/xml; charset="utf-8"
Content-Length: nnnn

<SOAP-ENV:Envelope xmlns:SOAP-ENV=http://schemas.xmlsoap.org/soap/envelope/
SOAP-ENV:encodingStyle="http://schemas.xmlsoap.org/soap/encoding/"/>
 <SOAP-ENV:Body>
  <m:GetLastTradePriceResponse xmlns:m="Some-URI">
   <Price>34.5</Price>
  </m:GetLastTradePriceResponse>
 </SOAP-ENV:Body>
</SOAP-ENV:Envelope>
```

One-Way and Two-Way SOAP Messaging and RPCs

The preceding example is an example of two-way SOAP messaging in that both the request and response are encapsulated in SOAP messages. A one-way SOAP message is one that simply sends out a request or a message, without needing an acknowledging SOAP message in return. In addition, SOAP allows the encapsulation and exchange of RPCs and responses.

Using SOAP for RPCs is not limited to HTTP requests and responses. In order to invoke a method, the following is needed:

- A method name
- An optional method signature
- The parameters to the method
- The URI of the target object
- Optional header data

The method calls and responses are embedded in the SOAP Body using the following representation:

- The method invocation is a data structure whose name and type is the same as the method name.
- The data structure contains fields that act as accessors for each parameter of the method, each of whose name, type, and order are the same as in the method signature.
- The method response is also a data structure, similar to the data structure that models the data invocation, except that the name is typically *name_Response* and the first accessor is the return value.
- A method fault is encoded in the SOAP Fault section.

If additional information relevant to the encoding of a method request exists, it must be expressed within the SOAP Header section. For example, an alternative book ID may be embedded in the SOAP Header when passing along a SOAP message concerning the sale of a book, since this book ID would not be part of the method signature and can be extracted from the header by code on the receiving side.

Using SOAP and the Oracle XDK

XML Services included in Oracle XDK 10*g* uses the Oracle SOAP implementation that is part of Oracle AS 10*g* version 9.0.4 as its SOAP run-time engine, which is part of the Oracle XDK. The Oracle SOAP implementation is based on the Apache SOAP implementation and is SOAP 1.1. Therefore, the XML Services are SOAP services and can be invoked by any SOAP-compatible client, the description of which follows.

SOAP Client

The SOAP client must perform the following steps:

1. Gather all parameters that are needed to invoke a service.
2. Create a SOAP service request message. This is an XML message, built according to the SOAP protocol, that contains all of the values of all input parameters encoded in XML. This process is called *serialization* of the parameters.
3. Submit the request to a SOAP server using some transport protocol that is supported by the SOAP server.
4. Receive a SOAP response message.
5. Determine the success or failure of the request by handling the SOAP Fault element.
6. Convert the returned parameter from XML to a native data type. This process is called *deserialization.*
7. Use the result as needed.

To enable you to avoid dealing with XML and SOAP at a very low level, a number of SOAP clients are available that will do most of this work for you. To facilitate easy application development and to insulate the application developers from all details of using SOAP, XML Services includes a SOAP client API. This API provides an easy way to invoke SOAP services from the XML Services framework. The XML Services SOAP client API supports a synchronous invocation model for requests and responses.

SOAP Server

Any SOAP server follows the following general steps while executing a SOAP service request:

1. The server receives the service request.
2. After parsing the XML request, the server must decide whether to execute the message or reject it.
3. If the message is to be executed, the server finds out if the service that is requested exists.
4. The server converts all input parameters from XML into data types that the service understands.
5. The server invokes the service.
6. The server converts the return parameter to XML and generates a SOAP response message.
7. The server sends the response message back to the caller.

SOAP Handlers

A SOAP handler is simply a mechanism that is used to intercept the SOAP message to do either pre- or post-processing as indicated by the SOAP request or response. These can be used on the client or server side, or both, and can add additional features to XML services, such as security, error handling, and so forth. For the Java language binding, all SOAP handlers live in the package namespace **user.soap.handlers** hierarchy.

An example of such a handler would be the following in a SOAP XML configuration file:

```
<osc:handlers>
 <osc:handler name="book" class="opress.soap.handlers.book.BookLogger">
  <osc:option name="BookLogDirectory"
    value="/private1/opress/app/product/tv02/soap/webapps/soap/WEB-INF"/>
  <osc:option name="filter" value="(!(host=localhost))"/>
 </osc:handler>
</osc:handlers>
<osc:requestHandlers names="book"/>
<osc:responseHandlers names="book"/>
<osc:errorHandlers names="book"/>
```

Using SOAP and the Oracle Database

Using the Oracle Database with SOAP as the underlying messaging protocol to queue and operate on messages from applications working on top of the database allows all the traditional features, such as performance, scalability, security, high reliability, and recoverability, to be associated with such messages. In addition, an Oracle Advanced Queuing (AQ) servlet allows clients to interpret and communicate with the back-end database to extract information and to retrieve, update, enqueue, and dequeue these messages, which are stored in message queue tables in the database.

Finally, allowing AQ messages in SOAP format and the XML-based Internet Data Access Presentation (iDAP) formats allows transformation, extraction, and other standards-based operations associated with XML to occur.

Oracle Streams AQ Support

Oracle's AQ acts as the hub for either native XML or XML defined using iDAP, meaning that such messages can be sent over HTTP or SMTP protocols. In either case, clients such as browsers and servers such as Oracle can communicate through enqueue, dequeue, publish, and register functionality encapsulated by Oracle-specific tags such as **AQXMLSend**, **AQXMLReceive**, **AQXMLPublish**, **AQXMLRegister**, **AQXMLReceiveResponse**, **AQXMLPublishResponse**, **AQXMLNotification**, and along with other required elements. For example, a client can construct the following iDAP XML message and send it over HTTP to be processed by Oracle:

```
<?xml version="1.0"?>
 <Envelope xmlns=http://www.oracle.com/schemas/IDAP/envelope>
  <Body>
   <AQXMLSend xmlns=http://www.oracle.com/schemas/AQ/access>
```

```
    <!-- mandatory -->
    <producer_options>
     <!--mandatory -->
     <destination>BOOKLIST.BOOK_QUEUE</destination>
    </producer_options>
    <!-- mandatory
    <message_set>
     <message>
      <message_number>1</message_number>
       <!-- mandatory -->
       <message_header>
        <correlation>BOOK</correlation>
        <sender_id>
         <agent_name>Juan</agent_name>
        </sender_id>
       </message_header>
       <message_payload>
        <Book>
         <Title>Introducing XML</Title>
         <Author_Lastname>Smith</Author_Lastname>
         <ISBN>11-0342000123</ISBN>
        </Book>
       </message_payload>
       </message>
      </message_set>
     </AQXMLSend>
    </Body>
  </Envelope>
```

In this manner, messages can be intelligently managed, so that data about them can be extracted at a later point to help in configuring the architecture and viewing the messages through SQL.

AQ Servlet

Oracle Advanced Queuing (AQ) is a database facility that provides an integrated message queuing capability, enabling and managing asynchronous communication between applications using Oracle messaging formats. The AQ servlet is simply a servlet that operates in the middle tier that acts on AQ messages in both SOAP format and the IDAP format, a format that uses XML for the data representation and HTTP and e-mail protocols as the transport mechanism. The servlet then can interpret the incoming message from the client and communicate back to it, and can connect to the Oracle database from the middle tier to perform operations on the message queues.

Enqueuing and Dequeuing Messages

To begin with, Oracle message queues can be created with messages that contain XML messages—these are encapsulated by the XMLType data type. To do this, a queue table is created using the **dbms_aqadm.create_queue_table** call, with the **queue_payload_type** as **SYS.XMLType**; the table can be populated via the **dbms_aqadm.create_queue** call. For example, a book order queue table and a queue with different priorities could be created in PL/SQL via the following code.

```
BEGIN
…
EXECUTE dbms_aqadm.create_queue_table (
 queue_table                 => 'book_order_table',
 sort_list                   => 'book_order, 'ship_book_order',
 comment                     => 'book order message queue table',
 multiple_consumers          => TRUE,
 queue_payload_type          => 'SYS.XMLType',
 compatible                  => '8.1',
 primary_instance            => 2,
 secondary_instance          => 1);
…
END;
BEGIN
…
EXECUTE dbms_aqadm.create_queue (
    queue_name               => 'book_order_queue',
    queue_table              => 'book_order_table');
…
END;
```

To enqueue a message using SOAP, the following could be an XML representation of the message:

```
<?xml version="1.0"?>
 <Envelope xmlns=http://schemas.xmlsoap.org/soap/envelope/>
  <Body>
   <AQXmlSend xmlns=http://ns.oracle.com/AQ/schemas/access>
    <producer_options>
     <destination>book.book_order_queue</destination>
    </producer_options>
    <message_set>
     <message_count>1</message_count>
     <message>
       <message_number>1</message_number>
       <message_header>
        <correlation>order1</correlation>
        <priority>1</priority>
        <sender_id>
         <agent_name>JuanL</agent_name>
        </sender_id>
       </message_header>
       <message_payload>
         <BOOKORDER_TYPE>
           <BOOKORDER>5</BOOKORDER>
           <BOOKORDER_SHIP>5</BOOKORDER_SHIP>
           <BOOKCUSTOMER>
              <BOOKCUSTOMER_ID>99999999</BOOKCUSTOMER_ID>
              <BOOKCUSTOMER_LASTNAME>Loaiza</BOOKCUSTOMER_LASTNAME>
              <BOOKCUSTOMER_STREET>1 Oracle Parkway</BOOKCUSTOMER_STREET>
              <BOOKCUSTOMER_CITY>Redwood Shores</BOOKCUSTOMER_CITY>
              <BOOKCUSTOMER_STATE>California</BOOKCUSTOMER_STATE>
```

```
              <BOOKCUSTOMER_ZIP>94065</BOOKCUSTOMER_ZIP>
              <BOOKCUSTOMER_COUNTRY>USA</BOOKCUSTOMER_COUNTRY>
             </BOOKCUSTOMER>
             <BOOKTITLE>Oracle and XML</BOOKTITLE>
             <BOOKID>3333333333333</BOOKID>
             <BOOKPRICE>49.99</BOOKPRICE>
            </BOOKORDER_TYPE>
          </message_payload>
         </message>
        </message_set>
        <AQXmlCommit/>
       </AQXMlSend>
     </Body>
   </Envelope>
```

To dequeue a message using SOAP, the following could be an XML representation of the message:

```
<?xml version="1.0"?>
<Envelope xmlns=http://schemas.xmlsoap.org/soap/envelope/>
 <Body>
  <AQXmlReceive xmlns=http://ns.oracle.com/AQ/schemas/access>
    <consumer_options>
     <destination>book.book_order_queue</destination>
     <consumer_name>JuanL</consumer_name>
     <wait_time>0</wait_time>
     <selector>
      <correlation>order1</correlation>
     </selector>
    </consumer_options>
    <AQXmlCommit/>
  </AQXmlReceive>
 </Body>
</Envelope>
```

Using SOAP from PL/SQL

PL/SQL Java stored procedures that encapsulate SOAP services are invoked in exactly the same manner as any other Java stored procedure. The SOAP JAVA jar file created during the translation/deployment of a PL/SQL package is also needed on the client side to compile application programs that invoke the SOAP service. As in the example given above, the basics are to declare a set of variables to represent the request and the response, and to declare the XMLType that would represent the message itself. Since this is more RPC-style, PL/SQL functions would be created to build a SOAP message body and envelope, build a SOAP request to invoke a web service, invoke the web service, process any SOAP faults or exceptions, and possibly extract information from the returned SOAP message.

Best Practices

Web services are simply XML services that are shared by and used as components of web-based applications. Depending on different technologies, scenarios, and computer configurations, these services can reside on dissimilar computers and can be accessed and transported using different standard protocols. Though these protocols are different, these services are made interoperable because XML is the language used as the message format, the services themselves can be encapsulated via XML, and the services can be accessed on the Internet from the different applications. The following sections will go over some alternative mechanisms for transporting messages.

SOAP vs. JAX-RPC

Java API for XML-based RPC (JAX-RPC) is a Sun Microsystems Java Specification Request (JSR) that specifies the client API for invoking a web service. The **java.xml.rpc** interfaces consist of the main client interface, the factory class for creating the main client interfaces, the client proxy for invoking the operations of a web service, the call interface used to dynamically invoke a web service, and an exception class that is thrown if a web service error occurs. This specification is more interface-driven, i.e., methods, parameters, return values, and synchronous, meaning that the client waits for the response; in short, more RPC-style.

SOAP vs. JMS

Java Message Service (JMS)—or message Enterprise Java Beans (EJBs)—is more message-style than SOAP, in that it's more message-based and asynchronous and involves sending or receiving an XML document. Inherently, with the use of EJBs, the traditional facilities of persistence, security, transactions, and concurrency are available with these messages. Essentially, two types of operations exist with JMS: operations that send data and operations that receive data. JMS can send messages to the JMS destination, which then forwards it on the client, and JMS can also receive messages from the JMS destination that received a message from the client.

These operations contrast with SOAP in that there needs to be a Java-compatible JMS client receiving these messages, whereas the SOAP message is platform independent and can support a broadcast protocol that doesn't depend on getting responses.

CHAPTER 7

Putting It All Together with XML Pipeline, JSPs, and XSQL

ML processing has evolved quite a bit over the last few years. Previously, XML application developers needed to come up with quite a bit of code to parse an XML file, apply a stylesheet to it, and transmit the results. With the acceptance of XML in modern business applications, the demands on the processing infrastructure to access and exchange business data in the form of XML also grew; and associated with that growth came even higher application development and maintenance cost.

To reduce this cost, Oracle XML Developer's Kit 10*g* (XDK) extends and supports XML standards and introduces new processing technologies and features that simplify XML creation, access, transformation, and validation. With these new mechanisms, XML application developers can more easily process XML within their business-to-business (B2B), business-to-customer (B2C), and Enterprise Application Integration (EAI) applications. This chapter explains how the XML Pipeline Processor, JSPs, and the XSQL Servlet enable Oracle XML application developers to achieve this goal of greatly reducing the complexity of today's XML processing.

Introducing the XML Pipeline Processor

The XML Pipeline Processor establishes a reusable component framework that supports declarative pipelining of XML resources so that different processes, such as XML parsing, XML schema validation, and XSL transformations, can be performed for an application within this framework. Compliant with the W3C XML Pipeline Definition Language Version 1.0 Note (**http://www.w3.org/TR/2002/NOTE-xml-pipeline-20020228/**), Oracle's implementation of this processing framework allows developers to avoid dealing with all of these different process interfaces individually, in a sense "pipelining" the processing of XML in one module.

To begin with, an XML document detailing this pipeline must be created according to the rules specified in the W3C Note. For the XML Pipeline Processor to act upon it, the use of the available XML processing components and the inputs and outputs for these processes must be established in this document. For Oracle's XML Pipeline Processor, these available components include the DOM and SAX XML parsers for parsing the XML documents, the XML Schema Processor for the XML schema validations, the XSL Processor for transforming XML documents, SAXSerializer for printing XML, and the XML Compressor to compress XML into binary format.

Put simply, the XML Pipeline Processor executes the chain of XML processing according to the descriptions in the pipeline document and returns a particular result. The following is an example of an XML Pipeline document that performs an XSLT transformation of **book.xml** using **book.xsl** and producing **booklist.html**:

```
<pipeline xmlns=http://www.w3.org/2002/02/xml-pipeline
                   xml:base="http://example.org/">
 <param name="target" select="booklist.html"/>

 <processdef name="domparser.p"
        definition="oracle.xml.pipeline.processes.DOMParserProcess"/>
 <processdef name="xslstylesheet.p"
        definition="oracle.xml.pipeline.processes.XSLStylesheetProcess"/>
 <processdef name="xslprocess.p"
        definition="oracle.xml.pipeline.processes.XSLProcess"/>
```

```
 <process id="p2" type="xslstylesheet.p" ignore-errors="false">
     <input name="xsl" label="book.xsl"/>
     <outparam name="stylesheet" label="xslstyle"/>
 </process>

 <process id="p3" type="xslprocess.p" ignore-errors="false">
     <param name="stylesheet" label="xslstyle"/>
     <input name="document" label="xmldoc"/>
     <output name="result" label="booklist.html"/>
 </process>

 <process id="p1" type="domparser.p" ignore-errors="true">
   <input name="xmlsource" label="book.xml "/>
   <output name="dom" label="xmldoc"/>
   <param name="preserveWhitespace" select="true"></param>
   <error name="dom">
    <html xmlns="http://www/w3/org/1999/xhtml">
     <head>
       <title>DOMParser Failure!</title>
     </head>
     <body>
       <h1>Error parsing document</h1>
     </body>
    </html>
   </error>
 </process>
</pipeline>
```

Note that any error is returned as an HTML document, which is consistent with the output format.

Multistage XML Processing

Multistage XML processing is quite straightforward, allowing processing of XML components in parallel and at different stages. Thus, the output from processing an XML document can immediately act as one input or multiple inputs to other stages of processing XML. All of this multistage XML processing is encapsulated within an XML Pipeline document.

Parsing, then Validation, then Serialization or Transformation

When users need to process and access XML data, the first step is to parse the XML document by using an XML parser. XML parsers are the components that read in XML documents and provide the programmatic access to the content and structure of XML. Depending on whether the structure of the document is governed by a DTD or an XML schema, the validating parser performs the checking operations necessary during the parsing. In Oracle's Java XML Schema Processor, a lax validation mode also exists, in addition to the strict validation mode, whereby synchronous retrieval of the metadata information and the validation processing status from the XML Schema Processor during the SAX XML parsing can occur.

The management of handlers for SAX events streaming from XML SQL Utility (XSU) output after SQL queries return rowset data is greatly simplified with a new Java interface, **oracle.xml.parser .v2.SAXSerializer**, which provides output options to specify if the pretty printing format is needed, what the XML declaration and encoding information is, which if any are the elements whose content needs to be set as CDATA sections, and what the DTD **system-id** and **public-id** are. To use this new feature, you simply use it as another type of SAX content handler. For example, you can register it to the XSU's SAX output interface as follows:

```
OracleXMLQuery.getXMLSAX(sample);
```

This generates unbounded XML documents from result sets returned from queries, with warnings or errors reported either as processing occurs or at the very end of the processing.

Alternatively, XSL Transformation (XSLT) stylesheets can then be applied to either the streaming XML data or the input XML documents to transform and apply formatting semantics on the text output.

SAX vs. DOM

SAX parsing is event-based XML parsing, meaning that when certain events occur or are encountered when processing the XML document—for example, when the root node of the document is encountered—the event handlers or functions, **startDocument** for this example, are then invoked through function callbacks. Compared to DOM parsing, SAX is much faster and less memory-intensive in that an in-memory tree representation is not constructed. For multistage XML processing, this lightweight XML parsing is ideal when you need to filter and search from large XML documents, but the drawbacks are that the XML content cannot be changed in place and dynamic access to the content is not as efficient as with DOM. In the case of the current Pipeline Processor implementation, the SAX Parser can be connected to the XML Compressor and the SAXSerializer but not to the XSLT Processor, because that requires a DOM.

Processing XML with JSPs and XML Beans

Many XML developers today use Oracle JDeveloper as an integrated development environment (IDE) to speed their development cycle and take advantage of the component approach in building applications based on numerous prebuilt components. The JavaBeans component model is fully supported in Oracle JDeveloper. In JDeveloper, you can build JavaBeans that can later be reused in other projects, or install and use JavaBeans that are built by Oracle or third-party vendors.

You can install the beans in JDeveloper on the JDeveloper Tools palette and later customize and include them in your application. Once the beans are installed, you can use drag-and-drop to add beans from the Tools palette to your application. When you add a bean to your application design surface, JDeveloper automatically generates the code needed to instantiate and customize the bean. This usually includes creating an instance of the bean, setting the bean properties to customize the bean, and adding action listeners to the bean to enable the application to handle the events generated by the bean. Because this technology is so powerful and easy to use, it is natural to encapsulate key XML functionality into JavaBeans.

The Oracle XML JavaBeans are a set of XML components for Java applications or applets that make adding XML support to an application easy. These Java components can be integrated into Oracle JDeveloper to enable developers to create and deploy XML-based database applications quickly. The following beans are provided:

- DOMBuilder bean
- XSLTransformer bean

- DBAccess bean
- XMLDBAccess bean
- XMLDiff bean
- XMLCompress bean
- XSDValidator bean

If you install these beans into your JDeveloper environment, as described in Chapter 13, you benefit by the automatic code generation that JDeveloper performs when you include the beans in your application. If you do not use JDeveloper and work in a command-line JDK environment, you can also use the beans to visualize and transform XML. In this case, you simply use the beans as you would any other classes. The examples in this chapter were developed using JDeveloper.

DOMBuilder Bean

The DOMBuilder bean encapsulates the Java XML Parser with a bean interface and extends its functionality to permit asynchronous parsing. By registering a listener, Java applications can parse large or successive documents by having the control return immediately to the caller. The following sample code shows a program that takes a list of XML files as parameters and parses all of these files concurrently:

```
package sample;
import java.awt.event.*;
import oracle.xml.async.*;
import oracle.xml.parser.v2.*;
import org.w3c.dom.*;
import java.net.*;
import java.io.*;

public class MParse extends Object
  implements DOMBuilderListener, DOMBuilderErrorListener{
  int numArgs,i;
  String Args[];
  DOMBuilder tParser;

  public MParse(String[] args) {
     Args=args;
  }
  public void parse() {
     for (i=0;i<Args.length;i++) {
        // new instance of the asynchronous parser
        tParser=new DOMBuilder(i);
        // add this Listener object to be notified when parsing is complete
        tParser.addDOMBuilderListener(this);
        // or when an error occurs
        tParser.addDOMBuilderErrorListener(this);
        System.out.println("Start parsing "+Args[i]);
        try {
```

```
            tParser.parse(new URL("file:"+(String)Args[i]));
         } catch (Exception e) {
            System.out.println(e.toString());
         }
      }
      System.out.println("Multiple files parsed in background threads");
   }
   public static void main(String[] args) {
     MParse mParse = new MParse(args);
     mParse.parse();
   }
   // Implementing DOMBuilderListener Interface
   // Method called by DOMBuilder when document parsing starts
   public void domBuilderStarted(DOMBuilderEvent p0) {

   }
   // Method called by DOMBuilder when document parsing returns an error.
   public void domBuilderError(DOMBuilderEvent p0) {

   }
   // Method called by DOMBuilder when document parsing is completed.
   public void domBuilderOver(DOMBuilderEvent p0) {
      DOMBuilder parser;
      XMLDocument xmlDoc;
      int id;
      // Get a reference to the parser instance that finished parsing.
      parser=(DOMBuilder)p0.getSource();
      // Get the parser id to identify the file being parsed
      id=parser.getId();
      System.out.println("Parse completed for file "+Args[id]);
      // get the dom tree
      xmlDoc=parser.getDocument();
      // You can add custom code here to work with the parsed document.
   }

 // Implementing DOMBuilderErrorListener Interface

   // This method is called when parsing error occurs.
   public void domBuilderErrorCalled(DOMBuilderErrorEvent p0) {
      int id=((DOMBuilder)p0.getSource()).getId();
      System.out.println("Parse error for "+Args[id]+": "+
      p0.getException().getMessage());
   }
 }
```

If you run this program using the following command, you get the output displayed in Figure 7-1.

```
java Sample.mParse booklist1.xml booklist2.xml booklist3.xml
```

```
Start parsing booklist1.xml
Start parsing booklist2. xml
Start parsing booklist3.xml
Multiple files parsed in background threads
Parse completed for file booklist2.xml
Parse completed for file booklist1.xml
Parse completed for file booklist3.xml
```

FIGURE 7-1. *Example output in JDeveloper that uses the DOMBuilder bean*

If you have to parse a large number of files, the DOMBuilder bean can deliver significant time savings. Depending on the system and the number of concurrent threads (instances of DOMBuilder), we have achieved up to 40 percent faster times compared to parsing the files one after another.

The asynchronous parsing in a background thread implemented in DOMBuilder can also be used in interactive visual applications. If the application parses a large file using the normal parser, the user interface will freeze until the document is parsed completely. This can easily be avoided if the DOMBuilder bean is used instead. After calling the parse method of DOMBuilder, the application receives the control back immediately. The application can then display a window with the message "Parsing, please wait." The window can also show a Cancel button, so that the user can abort the operation if they decide to do so. If no user action is taken, the program resumes when **domBuilderOver()** is called by the DOMBuilder bean upon completion of the parsing task in the background.

XSLTransformer Bean

The XSLTransformer bean encapsulates the Java XML Parser's XSLT processing engine with a bean interface and extends its functionality to permit asynchronous transformation. By registering a listener, Java applications can transform large or successive documents by having the control returned immediately to the caller. Because the XSL transformations are time-consuming, you may consider using this asynchronous interface for XSL transformations. The XSLTransformer bean can benefit applications that transform large numbers of files by transforming multiple files concurrently. It also can be used for visual applications to achieve responsive user interfaces. The considerations here are the same as with the DOMBuilder bean. From a programming standpoint, the preceding sample demonstrates the general approach that can also be applied to the XSLTransformer bean. The main point is that by implementing the XSLTransformerListener interface, the calling application is notified when the transformation is over. Therefore, the calling application can do something else between requesting the transformation and getting the result.

DBAccess Bean

The DBAccess bean maintains CLOB tables that are used to store XML documents. This functionality is quite useful when you are storing a wide range of XML documents and you are most interested in storing and retrieving them quickly without performing any XML processing within the database. This type of storage is also important when you wish to preserve any entities within the XML document instead of having them expanded, as would occur with an XMLType CLOB.

The database access is through JDBC to the CLOB tables that may store the XML and XSL files, or even files resulting from applying the XSL stylesheet to the XML file. The DBAccess bean provides the following functionality:

- Creates and deletes CLOB tables.
- Lists a CLOB table's contents.
- Adds, replaces, or deletes XML documents in the CLOB table.

The following code fragments demonstrate this functionality. These fragments assume the appropriate strings are passed in on the command line or through prompts.

```
// Create a new XML CLOB Table
  void createXMLCLOBTable(String tableName) {
     log.println("\nDemo for createXMLTables():");
     try {
        db.createXMLCLOBTable(con, tableName);
     } catch (Exception ex) {
        log.println("Error creating XML CLOB table: " + ex.getMessage());
     }
     log.println("Table +'" + tableName + "' successfully created.");
     return;
  }
// Replace XML Data in CLOB Table
  void replaceXMLCLOBData( String tablename, String xmlname,
                           String filename) {
     log.println("\nDemo for replaceXMLCLOBData() (similar to insert):");
     String xmldata = loadFile(filename);
     try {
        db.replaceXMLCLOBData(con, tablename, xmlname, xmldata);
     } catch (Exception ex) {
        log.println("Error inserting into XML CLOB table: " +
                    ex.getMessage());
      }
      log.println("XML Data from +'" + filename + "' successfully
                  replaced in table '" + tablename + "'.");
      return;
  }
// Retrieve XML Data from CLOB Table
  void getXMLCLOBData(String tablename, String xmlname) {
      log.println("\nDemo for getXMLCLOBData():");
      String xmlText=null;
      try {
         xmlText=db.getXMLCLOBData(con, tablename, xmlname);
      } catch (Exception ex) {
         log.println("Error getting XML data: " + ex.getMessage());
         return;
      }
      log.println("XML CLOB data fetched: ");
```

```
        log.println(xmlText);
        return;
    }
// List all XML CLOB Tables
  void listXMLCLOBTables() {
        // list all recognized XML CLOB tables
        log.println("\nDemo for listXMLCLOBTables():");
        String tableNames[];
        int i;
        try {
           tableNames=db.getXMLCLOBTableNames(con,"");
           for (i=0;i<tableNames.length;i++) {
              log.println("tablenamename="+tableNames[i]);
           }
        } catch (Exception ex) {
           log.println("Error listing XML CLOB tables: "
                       + ex.getMessage());
        }
  }
```

The complete DBAccess bean demo code is available as DBAccessDemo.java in the source download.

XMLDBAccess Bean

The XMLDBAccess bean is a simple extension of the DBAccess bean to support XMLType CLOBs that were introduced in Oracle9*i*. This bean has different packaging because it additionally depends upon the **xdb.jar** file that provides Java access to the XMLType. While the functionality includes all the equivalent methods to the DBAccess bean, it adds one useful function based upon the fact that the document is parsed on insert as XML. The **getXMLXPathTextData()** method retrieves the value of an XPath expression from the XML document stored in the table. The following code fragment illustrates this:

```
  void getXMLTypeData(String tablename, String xmlname) {
        log.println("\nDemo for getXMLTypeData():");
        String xmlText=null;
        try {
           xmlText=db.getXMLTypeData(con, tablename, xmlname);
        } catch (Exception ex) {
          log.println("Error getting XMLType data: " + ex.getMessage());
          return;
        }
        log.println("XMLType data fetched: ");
        log.println(xmlText);
        return;
  }
```

On the surface it would appear that you should always use the XMLDBAccess bean over the DBAccess bean because of this increased functionality. Note, however, that since the XML documents are parsed, any referenced DTDs will need to be fetched and entities replaced. Thus, the document stored will not be identical to its inserted state when it is retrieved.

XMLDiff Bean

At some time, you may be faced with the task of determining whether two XML documents are the same. In practice this is usually not a simple character-for-character comparison, because for many XML documents, white space and linefeeds are insignificant. Instead, what is important is to determine how the structure and text content differ. The XMLDiff bean was created for just this purpose. It does a DOM tree comparison of file A to file B while producing an XSL stylesheet to convert A into B. There is additional visual functionality available that uses JPanel to visually display the differences detected.

This bean has many uses and, since it uses the standards-based XSLT language to indicate the differences, it is an excellent component for pipeline applications. One particular application would be to keep track of document revisions. As each XML document is submitted, it can be compared to its previous version, and the resulting XSLT stylesheet can be stored. Another application would be to use it to detect whether material differences have occurred between XML files, such as XML schemas. You will be building such an application using the XMLDiff bean in Chapter 17.

XMLCompress Bean

One of the disadvantages of XML is the fact that whenever it is received in serialized form, it needs to be parsed in order for any operations to be performed. There is the additional disadvantage of the growth in size caused by the tag encapsulation of the data. We have seen real production schemas where the instance XML documents were 10 to 100 times the size of the data they contained! The XMLCompress bean provides an efficient solution to these situations. It encapsulates the XMLCompress serialization method that creates a binary format from the DOM that tokenizes the XML tags, resulting in a more compact XML stream. Additionally, Oracle XML processors such as XSL and XSD can read from the compressed stream directly to re-create the DOM without reparsing the document.

To maximize the flexibility of the bean, both **DOMCompress()** and **SAXCompress()** are provided, which support a full range of input sources, including files, strings, and streams. Additionally, the DOM method supports the XMLType, CLOB, and BLOB Oracle SQL datatypes. It should be noted that there is only a complementary **DOMExpand()** method, as applications that don't need the DOM can work exclusively with SAX input and output events, therefore making a **SAXExpand()** function unnecessary.

XSDValidator Bean

Rounding out the set of XML beans is the XSDValidator bean. While, like the other beans, it encapsulates the XSDValidator class in the XML parser, it has one significant feature that makes it the choice for visual or editor applications. The XSDValidator bean includes a **getStackList()** method that returns the list of DOM tree paths that lead to the invalid node if a validation error is returned. To use this function, you need to use the **java.util.vector** and **java.util.stack** classes, which are populated with the path list as follows:

```
static void printError(XSDValidator xsdval) {
// Initialize list of paths
  Vector vectPath = xsdval.getStackList();
```

```
// Register error handler
  DocErrorHandler errHndl =
       DocErrorHandler)xsdval.getError().getErrorHandler();
// Initialize list of errors
  Vector errlist =  errHndl.getErrorList();
    if (vectPath.isEmpty()) {
    System.out.println("Schema validation successful! No errors.");
    }
    if (!(vectPath.isEmpty())) {
// Initialize Stack for nodes
      Stack tempStack ;
      XMLNode xnode;
      Enumeration enum1 = vectPath.elements();
      Enumeration enum2 = errlist.elements();
// Print paths and corresponding nodes that had errors
    while (enum1.hasMoreElements() && enum2.hasMoreElements()) {
      System.out.println(enum2.nextElement());
      tempStack = (Stack)enum1.nextElement();
        while (!(tempStack.empty())) {
          xnode = (XMLNode)((tempStack).pop());
          System.out.print(xnode.getNodeName());
            if (!(tempStack.empty()))
               System.out.print("->");
        }
        System.out.println();
      }
    }
  }
```

Using XML Beans in JSPs

You can use the Oracle XML beans in your JSP pages just like you would any other bean because they all conform to the Sun JavaBeans specification and include the requisite **BeanInfo** class that extends **java.beans.SimpleBeanInfo**. By using the **<jsp:usebean>** tags, you can embed your Java program code easily into an HTML page as follows:

```
<%@ page language="java"
contentType="text/xml; charset=UTF-8" %>
<jsp:useBean class="XMLDiff" id="xml_diff"
scope="request" >
<%
<jsp:setProperty name="booklist" property="file" value="booklist.xml"/>
// Your Java Code
%>
```

Note that you can set properties for the execution of the class using one or more **<jsp:setproperty>** tags.

Introducing the XSQL Page Publishing Framework

Building upon the functionality of the XML SQL Utility and the XML parser is the XSQL Servlet. Written in Java, this servlet provides a high-level declarative interface to developers and webmasters to render data across the Internet dynamically and in custom formats. Able to run with the servlet engines of most web servers, the XSQL Servlet delivers the capability to transform a single data source automatically in terms of the client browser and the format best suited to its capabilities and those of the platform.

The XSQL Pages

The heart of the XSQL Servlet is the XSQL page. This page is simply an XML file that contains specific elements to direct the action of the servlet. The following **booklist.xsql** file is a simple XSQL page:

```
<?xml version="1.0"?>
<?xml-stylesheet type="text/xsl" href="booklist.xsl"?>
<xsql:query connection="demo" xmlns:xsql="urn:oracle-xsql">
  select * from Booklist
</xsql:query>
```

Figure 7-2 shows the process flow when an Internet browser requests this page and the web server hands over the request to the XSQL Servlet after it registers the **xsql** extension with the server. The servlet then hands the page to the XML parser to retrieve its instructions. In this case, it is asked to open a JDBC connection with the alias of **demo** and submit the query Select * from Booklist. It does this by passing this data to the XML SQL Utility, which performs the query as described previously and returns the result as an XML DOM object. Finally, the servlet passes the stylesheet reference along with the DOM object to the XML parser's XSLT processor to apply the transformation to HTML for display in the client's browser.

The essential elements of the file are the **<xsql:query>** element, which includes the database connection information within its **connection** attribute, and the SQL query within its body. The connection value is an alias contained within the **<connectiondefs>** section of the **XMLConfig.xml** file:

```
<connectiondefs>
   <connection name="demo">
      <username>scott</username>
      <password>tiger</password>
      <dburl>jdbc:oracle:thin:@localhost:1521:ORCL</dburl>
      <driver>oracle.jdbc.driver.OracleDriver</driver>
   </connection>

   <connection name="xmlbook">
      <username>xmlbook</username>
      <password>xmlbook</password>
      <dburl>jdbc:oracle:thin:@localhost:1521:ORCL</dburl>
      <driver>oracle.jdbc.driver.OracleDriver</driver>
   </connection>
```

```
   <connection name="lite">
      <username>system</username>
      <password>manager</password>
      <dburl>jdbc:Polite:POlite</dburl>
      <driver>oracle.lite.poljdbc.POLJDBCDriver</driver>
   </connection>
</connectiondefs>
```

This section from the default **XMLConfig.xml** file shows the declaration of the database connection string and the JDBC driver that will be used by the XML SQL Utility. Because you can have this file reside on the server in a directory that is not accessible to the client, this information remains secure.

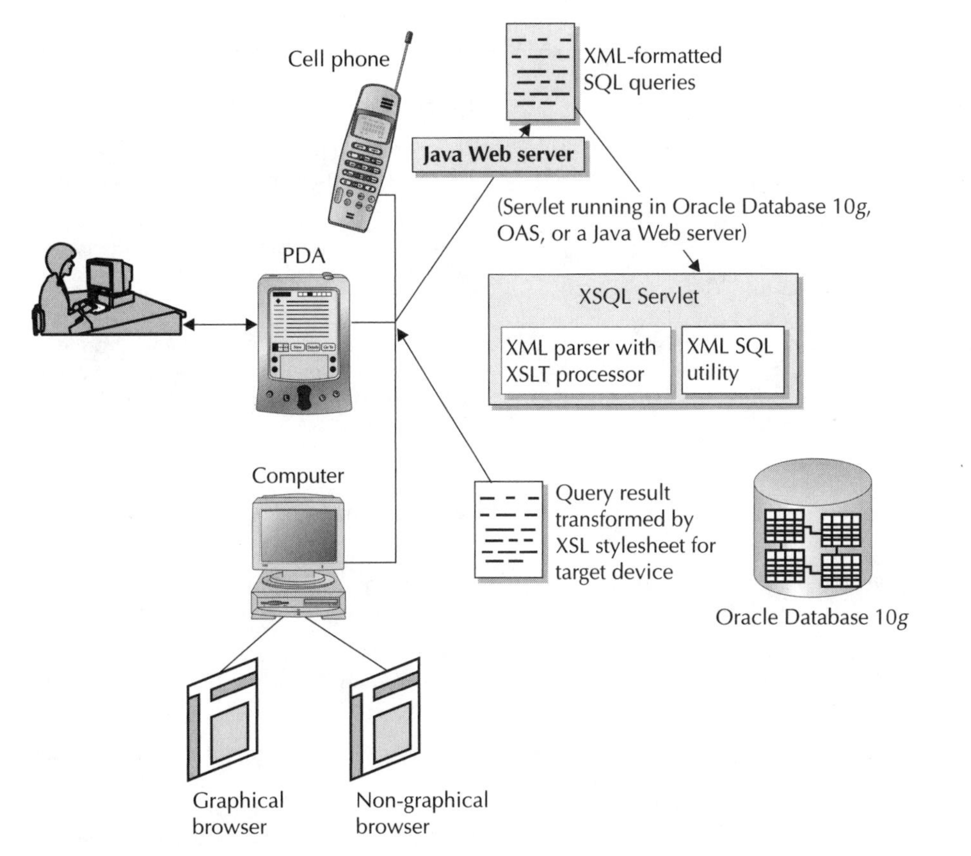

FIGURE 7-2. *XSQL page process*

Installing the XSQL Servlet

The XSQL Servlet is designed to be quite flexible in its installation and setup. It may be used in any Java 1.2 or greater JVM and with any JDBC-enabled database. Specific testing has been done with JDK 1.2.2, 1.3.1, and 1.4.2 on Windows and several Unix platforms, including Solaris, Linux, and HP-UX. Even though it has previously supported 1.1.8, the 10*g* libraries no longer support this JDK version, nor does Sun.

Submitting Queries to the XSQL Servlet

The XSQL Servlet is designed to create dynamic web pages from database queries. The XSQL pages can be linked to any web site and can contain one or more queries whose results will replace the respective **<xsql:query>** section in the page. These results can be further customized through the use of attributes within the **<xsql:query>** tag. Table 7-1 shows the various options that are available.

Attribute	Default	Description
rowset-element	<ROWSET>	Element name for the query results. Set equal to the empty string to suppress printing a document element.
row-element	<ROW>	Element name for each row in the query results. Set equal to the empty string to suppress printing a row element.
max-rows	Fetch all rows	Maximum number of rows to fetch from the query. Useful for fetching the top *N* rows or, in combination with skip-rows, the next *N* rows from a query result.
skip-rows	Skip no rows	Number of rows to skip over before returning the query results.
id-attribute	Id	Attribute name for the id attribute for each row in the query result.
id-attribute-column	Row count value	Column name to supply the value of the id attribute for each row in the query result.
null-indicator	Omit elements with a NULL value	If set to **y** or **yes**, causes a null-indicator attribute to be used on the element for any column whose value is NULL.
tag-case	Use the case of the column name or alias from the query	If set to **upper**, the element names for columns in the query result appear in uppercase letters. If set to **lower**, the element names for columns in the query result appear in lowercase letters.

TABLE 7-1. *Attribute Options for the <xsl:query> Element*

Parameters can also be passed into the query from the HTTP request line. By prefixing an @ to the parameter name, the XSQL Servlet will search the HTTP request parameters and then the **<xsql:query>** attributes to find a match. Once a match is found, a straight lexical substitution is performed. The following is an example of an XSQL page using this function when the HTTP request line is **http://localhost/xsql/demo/booksearch.xsql?year=2001**:

```
<?xml version="1.0"?>
<xsql:query xmlns:xsql="urn:oracle-xsql" connection="demo"
    SELECT TITLE, AUTHOR, DESCRIPTION FROM BOOKLIST
      WHERE YEAR = {@year}
</xsql:query>
```

Queries that return no rows can also be handled by adding an optional **<xsql:no-rows-query>** element within the **<xsql:query>** tags. This allows the user to see a formatted page instead of the raw error. The following is an example that initially tries to retrieve the listings corresponding to the author's name; failing that, it attempts to do a fuzzy match on the submitted name:

```
<?xml version="1.0"?>
<xsql:query xmlns:xsql="urn:oracle-xsql" connection="demo"
    SELECT TITLE, AUTHOR, DESCRIPTION FROM BOOKLIST
      WHERE AUTHOR = UPPER ('{@author}')

  <xsql:no-rows-query>
    SELECT TITLE, AUTHOR, DESCRIPTION FROM BOOKLIST
      WHERE AUTHOR LIKE UPPER ('%{@author}%')
      ORDER BY AUTHOR
  </xsql:no-rows-query>

</xsql:query>
```

Transforming the XSQL Output with Stylesheets

The real power of the XSQL Servlet lies in its capability to dynamically transform query results by applying XSL stylesheets. The stylesheet declaration is included in the XSQL file and is applied once the XML output from the query is received. It most commonly transforms query results into HTML, as can be seen in the following example; however, the stylesheet can perform any text-based transformation. The following XSQL page and its associated stylesheet will return the results to the requesting browser as an HTML table:

```
<?xml version="1.0"?>
<xsql-stylesheet type="text/xsl" href="totable.xsl"?>
<xsql:query xmlns:xsql="urn:oracle-xsql" connection="demo"
    SELECT Title, Author, Description FROM Booklist
      WHERE Author = UPPER ('{@author}')
  <xsql:no-rows-query>
    SELECT Title, Author, Description FROM Booklist
      WHERE Author LIKE UPPER ('%{@author}%')
      ORDER BY Author
  </xsql:no-rows-query>
</xsql:query>
```

This is the **Totable.xsl** stylesheet:

```
<html xmlns:xsl="http://www.w3.org/1999/XSL/Transform">
  <head>
    <title>Book Listing</title>
  </head>
  <body>
    <table border="1" cellspacing="0">
        <tr>
          <th><b>Author</b></th>
          <th><b>Title</b></th>
          <th><b>Description</b></th>
        </tr>
      <xsl:for-each select="ROWSET/ROW">
        <tr>
          <td><xsl:value-of select="TITLE"/></td>
          <td><xsl:value-of select="AUTHOR"/></td>
          <td><xsl:value-of select="DESCRIPTION"/></td>
        </tr>
      </xsl:for-each>
    </table>
  </body>
</html>
```

Figure 7-3 shows the query result and subsequent transformation.

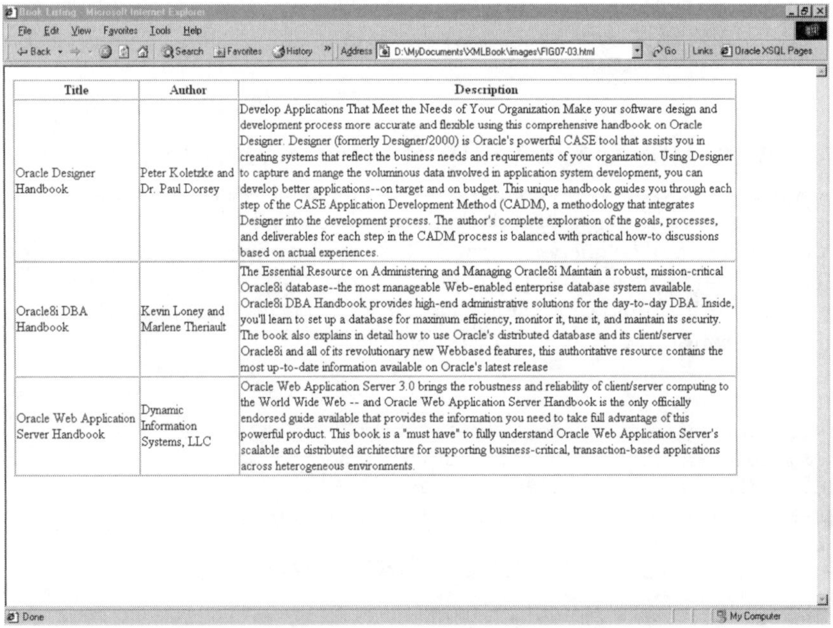

Book Listing - Microsoft Internet Explorer

Title	Author	Description
Oracle Designer Handbook	Peter Koletzke and Dr. Paul Dorsey	Develop Applications That Meet the Needs of Your Organization Make your software design and development process more accurate and flexible using this comprehensive handbook on Oracle Designer. Designer (formerly Designer/2000) is Oracle's powerful CASE tool that assists you in creating systems that reflect the business needs and requirements of your organization. Using Designer to capture and mange the voluminous data involved in application system development, you can develop better applications--on target and on budget. This unique handbook guides you through each step of the CASE Application Development Method (CADM), a methodology that integrates Designer into the development process. The author's complete exploration of the goals, processes, and deliverables for each step in the CADM process is balanced with practical how-to discussions based on actual experiences.
Oracle8i DBA Handbook	Kevin Loney and Marlene Theriault	The Essential Resource on Administering and Managing Oracle8i Maintain a robust, mission-critical Oracle8i database--the most manageable Web-enabled enterprise database system available. Oracle8i DBA Handbook provides high-end administrative solutions for the day-to-day DBA. Inside, you'll learn to set up a database for maximum efficiency, monitor it, tune it, and maintain its security. The book also explains in detail how to use Oracle's distributed database and its client/server Oracle8i and all of its revolutionary new Webbased features, this authoritative resource contains the most up-to-date information available on Oracle's latest release
Oracle Web Application Server Handbook	Dynamic Information Systems, LLC	Oracle Web Application Server 3.0 brings the robustness and reliability of client/server computing to the World Wide Web -- and Oracle Web Application Server Handbook is the only officially endorsed guide available that provides the information you need to take full advantage of this powerful product. This book is a "must have" to fully understand Oracle Web Application Server's scalable and distributed architecture for supporting business-critical, transaction-based applications across heterogeneous environments.

FIGURE 7-3. *Formatted output from the SearchAuthor.xsql page*

Multiple stylesheet declarations are also supported. In such instances, the XSQL Servlet chooses the transformation method by matching the **user-agent** string in the HTTP header to an optional **media** attribute in the **<xml-stylesheet>** element. The match is case-insensitive, and the first match in file order is the one applied. The following example shows how multiple browsers are supported.

```
<?xml version="1.0"?>
<?xml-stylesheet type="text/xsl" media="lynx" href="booklist-lynx.xsl"?>
<?xml-stylesheet type="text/xsl" media="msie" href="booklist-ie.xsl"?>
<?xml-stylesheet type="text/xsl" href="booklist.xsl"?>

<xsql:query connection="demo" xmlns:xsql="urn:oracle-xsql">
  select * from BOOKLIST
</xsql:query>
```

Note that the last stylesheet declaration has no **media** attribute. It will be applied to any HTTP requests that do not match the others and thus acts as the default stylesheet. Table 7-2 shows the allowable attributes that can be added to the **<xml-stylesheet>** element and their functions.

The final way to apply a stylesheet is to pass its URL as an HTTP parameter as follows:

```
http://localhost/yourdatapage.xsql?param1=value&xml-stylesheet=yourstyle.xsl
```

This techniqvue is especially useful for prototyping and development. By replacing the stylesheet URL with **none**, you ensure that the raw XML document is sent without any stylesheet processing.

Attribute	Required	Description
type	Yes	Must be set to the value **text/xsl**; otherwise, the **<?xml-stylesheet?>** instruction is ignored by the XSQL Page Processor.
href	Yes	Indicates the relative or absolute URL of the stylesheet to be used.
media	No	If set, this attribute's value is used to perform a case-insensitive match on the **User-Agent** string of the requesting browser, so the appropriate stylesheet is used, depending on the requesting software/device.
client	No	If set to **yes**, will download the raw XML to the client and include the **<?xml-stylesheet?>** processing instruction for processing in the browser. If not specified, the default is to perform the transform in the server.

TABLE 7-2. *Attribute Options for the <?xml-stylesheet?> Element*

Inserting XML Documents with the XSQL Servlet

By leveraging the full capability of the XML SQL Utility, you can set up an XSQL page to insert XML documents into a database. An XML document can be submitted to the **OracleXMLSave** class of the XML SQL Utility by employing the Action Element, **<xsql:insert-request>**. As discussed previously, the schema must already exist in the database to save a document. While at first this may be considered a limitation, the XSQL Servlet's capability to apply a stylesheet to the XML document on submission provides the necessary functionality to filter or transform documents as needed.

Returning to the book listing example presented earlier in the chapter, an XSQL page can be set up to accept book listings not only in the prescribed format of the database but also from virtually any text-based format. For example, consider the case in which a local bookseller would like to list his books on the pages, but his book listings use a different set of tags from the database schema. By creating an XSLT stylesheet and applying it on receipt of his listings, his selections could be accommodated. The following XSQL page could accept the book feed from "Joe's Books" via HTTP and transform it into the Booklist database schema by applying the **joesbooks.xsl** stylesheet and then submitting the resulting XML to the **OracleXMLSave** class for insertion:

```
<?xml version="1.0">
<xsql:insert-request xmlns:xsql="urn:oracle-xsql"
          connection = "demo" table = "BOOKLIST"
          transform = "joesbooks.xsl"/>
```

However, one more item must be set up to make this example function properly. The database generates the BookID column; therefore, this column's entry must be created for each new insertion. This can be done by setting up a trigger on the Booklist table that generates this ID whenever an insertion is made. The following SQL script will create a new BookID when each new listing is added, assuming you have already created a sequence named **bookid_seq**:

```
CREATE TRIGGER booklist_autoid
BEFORE INSERT ON BOOKLIST FOR EACH ROW
BEGIN
   SELECT bookid_seq.nextval
   INTO :new.BookID
   FROM dual;
END;
```

Other Action Elements that are supported by the XSQL Servlet and their functions are listed in Table 7-3.

Updating Data with the XSQL Servlet

Many applications require that data or documents be updated instead of wholly replaced. In a similar manner to the way the BookID was automatically generated, you can use a form of trigger to provide this functionality.

Oracle makes available an INSTEAD OF trigger that allows a stored procedure in PL/SQL or Java to be called whenever an INSERT of any kind is attempted. These triggers utilize Oracle's Object Views to be associated with the INSERT.

Action Element	Description
<xsql:set-stylesheet-param>	Sets the value of a top-level XSLT stylesheet parameter.
<xsql:set-page-param>	Sets a page-level (local) parameter that can be referred to in subsequent SQL statements in the page.
<xsql:set-session-param>	Sets an HTTP session-level parameter.
<xsql:set-cookie>	Sets an HTTP cookie.
<xsql:query>	Executes an arbitrary SQL statement and includes its result set in canonical XML format.
<xsql:ref-cursor-function>	Includes the canonical XML representation of the result set of a cursor returned by a PL/SQL stored function.
<xsql:include-param>	Includes a parameter and its value as an element in your XSQL page.
<xsql:include-request-params>	Includes all request parameters as XML elements in your XSQL page.
<xsql:include-xml>	Includes arbitrary XML resources at any point in your page by relative or absolute URL.
<xsql:include-owa>	Includes the results of executing a stored procedure that uses the Oracle Web Agent (OWA) packages inside the database to generate XML.
<xsql:if-param>	Includes nested actions and/or literal XML content if some condition based on a parameter value is true.
<xsql:include-xsql>	Includes the results of one XSQL page at any point inside another.
<xsql:insert-request>	Inserts the XML document (or HTML form) posted in the request into a database table or view.
<xsql:update-request>	Updates an existing row in the database based on the posted XML document supplied in the request.
<xsql:delete-request>	Deletes an existing row in the database based on the posted XML document supplied in the request.
<xsql:insert-param>	Inserts the XML document contained in the value of a single parameter.
<xsql:dml>	Executes a SQL DML statement or PL/SQL anonymous block.
<xsql:action>	Invokes a user-defined action handler, implemented in Java, for executing custom logic and including custom XML information into your XSQL page.

TABLE 7-3. *Action Elements and Their Functions for XSQL Pages*

For example, if you wanted to have the Booklist table be updatable, you could initially search for the unique combination of title and author and, if one is found, perform an UPDATE instead of doing an INSERT. To set this up, you must create an Object View corresponding to the Booklist table. This can be done using the following SQL:

```
CREATE VIEW Booklistview AS
SELECT * FROM Booklist;
```

Next, the trigger needs to be created and associated with this view. In this example, PL/SQL is being used, but the job could also be done with a Java stored procedure.

```
CREATE OR REPLACE TRIGGER insteadOfIns_booklistview
INSTEAD OF INSERT ON booklistview FOR EACH ROW
DECLARE
  notThere BOOLEAN := TRUE;
  tmp      VARCHAR2(1);
  CURSOR chk IS SELECT 'x' FROM BOOKLIST
         WHERE TITLE = :new.title AND AUTHOR  = :new.author;
BEGIN
  OPEN chk;
  FETCH chk INTO tmp;
  notThere := chk%NOTFOUND;
  CLOSE chk;

  IF notThere THEN
    UPDATE INTO Booklist(TITLE, AUTHOR, PUBLISHER, YEAR,
                         ISBN, DESCRIPTION)
         VALUES (:new.title, :new.author, :new.Publisher,
                 :new.Year, :new.ISBN, :new.Description);
  END IF;
END;
```

Finally, the XSQL file needs to be changed as follows to update the Booklistview instead of the Booklist table:

```
<?xml version="1.0">
<xsql:insert-request xmlns:xsql="urn:oracle-xsql"
             connection = "demo"
             table = "Booklistview"
             transform = "joesbooks.xsl"/>
```

As a final note, since the uniqueness is being checked in terms of the combination of the title and author, a unique index can be created to speed up the check and improve performance. The following SQL statement will create the index:

```
CREATE UNIQUE INDEX booklist_index ON booklist(Title, Author);
```

While the previous example explained how to perform an update using the trigger functionality of an object view, you can also use the XML SQL Utility update capability from the XSQL Servlet using the following very simple **.xsql** file:

```
<?xml version="1.0"?>
<xsql:dml connection="demo" xmlns:xsql="urn:oracle-xsql">
  update Booklist set status='S' where BookID = '1';
</xsql:dml>
```

This example illustrates the simplicity and power of the XSQL's XML-based interface.

Using JSPs and XSQL Pages

While you can extend XSQL pages with custom action handlers to call Java classes, you can also use JSP pages to include XSQL pages using **<jsp:include>** or forward to them using **<jsp:forward>**. For example, this allows you to bind variables into a SQL query that would be run by an XSQL page. Consider the query used earlier with a simple **booksearch.xsql** page:

```
<?xml version="1.0"?>
<xsql:query xmlns:xsql="urn:oracle-xsql" connection="demo"
    bind-param={@param}
SELECT TITLE, AUTHOR, DESCRIPTION FROM (@table)
</xsql:query>
```

This XSQL page can be called from the following JSP fragment to pass in the bound parameters:

```
<jsp:forward page="booksearch.xsql">
  <jsp:param name="table" value="BOOKLIST WHERE YEAR = ?"/>
  <jsp:param name="YEAR" value="2001"/>
  <jsp:param name="param" value="YEAR"/>
</jsp:forward>
```

When you want to include the results of an XSQL page within a JSP, you can use **<jsp:include>** in the following manner:

```
<jsp:include page="booksearch.xsql">.
```

Best Practices

In this chapter you have seen several techniques that can be used to put together XML-enabled applications. The common theme is that whether you use the Pipeline Processor, JSPs, or the XSQL Servlet, the code is almost entirely declarative. This is distinctly different from normal compiled and linked applications in that the code can be changed, customized, or updated at any time. This approach has the advantage of allowing you to develop generic, high-quality, reusable components that can be easily put together in the same way that integrated circuits simplified and improved electronic circuit design over discrete transistors.

Creating a More Secure Connection

In most applications, you will use the XSQL Servlet to connect to a database. The **XSQLConfig.xml** file must be kept secure on the server. This file should never be in any directory tree that is mapped to a virtual path of your web server. You should set up an account that owns your servlet engine for your application and make sure that only this account has read permissions on the file.

It is also important that you control the parameters passed by the URL into the XSQL Servlet. By default, it will accept a stylesheet using the **xml-sytlesheet** parameter unless you add the attribute **allow-client-style="no"** to the document element of your page.

Finally, you saw how to use lexical substitution of variables into SQL queries. This is a common feature of many Oracle products. It is also potentially a dangerous one. Therefore, you can guard against abuses by limiting the scope of database access permitted to users of your application. You can also bind variables (as shown in the "Using JSPs and XSQL Pages" section) or, even better, perform the entire database transaction in a custom action handler call.

When You Need Simple JSP XML Functionality

Besides all of this powerful XML functionality provided by the XDK, Oracle does supply an XML JSP tag library with its OC4J J2EE container. This library is called **xml.jar** and can be found in the **/j2ee/jsp/lib/tlds** directory. It provides the following custom JSP tags to perform simple XML processing:

- **xml:transform** Takes a stylesheet and applies it to the XML in the tag's body
- **xml:styleSheet** Declares and locates the stylesheet to be used for **xml:transform**
- **xml:parsexml** Parses the XML in the body of the tag into a DOM for node access
- **xml:cacheXMLObject** Allows for XML objects such as DOMs to be cached in the Web Object cache

In Oracle XML Database 10*g* or earlier, these tags do not use the XDK libraries, but instead use the XML ones included in JDK 1.4.

PART II

Oracle XML Management for DBAs

CHAPTER 8

Getting Started with the Oracle XML Database

he *Oracle XML Database (XML DB)* refers to the collection of XML technologies built into the Oracle Database 10*g* database, providing high-performance and native storage, retrieval, and processing of XML. This native XML functionality is seamlessly integrated with the Oracle relational database server to bridge the gap between the relational table-row and XML hierarchical storage. Therefore, you have the advantage of leveraging the power of both.

As companies are seeking XML technologies to automate and enhance their core business processes over the Internet, the Oracle XML Database, along with the programming interfaces in the *Oracle XML Developer's Kit (XDK),* provides a platform to efficiently build and deploy XML solutions.

This chapter discusses what the Oracle XML database is, what the related XML features are, and how to set up the environment to make sure that these features are ready for use. It will then work though some examples to help you get familiar with the basic XML DB functionality. Finally, it will provide information to help you make decisions regarding when and how to use the XML database features. Specifically, it will

- Show how to set up the XML database environment
- Discuss various uses of the native XMLType data type
- Explore the various XML storage and processing options
- Investigate the effective design of XML database solutions

A Brief History of XML Support in Oracle Database

The support of XML in the Oracle database began with Oracle8*i*, in which users could load the Java packages from the Oracle XDK into Oracle JServer as well as create the XML PL/SQL packages built on the Java stored procedures. The XML PL/SQL packages include the DBMS_XMLSAVE and the DBMS_XMLQUERY packages, which are packaged as the *XML SQL Utility (XSU),* and the XMLPARSER, XMLDOM, and XSLPROCESSOR packages. The two XSU PL/SQL packages allow users to insert XML documents into the database tables and retrieve SQL data in XML format through a canonical mapping. The XMLPARSER package is used for parsing XML, the XMLDOM package is used for XML DOM operations, and the XSLPROCESSOR package is used for XSLT transformations.

Since all of these packages are built on Java stored procedures, you need to initialize the *Oracle Java Virtual Machine (Oracle JVM)* and load the Java packages before using the functionality. This leads additional database management complexity and high maintenance cost.

In Oracle9*i* Release 1, a new native XML data type—XMLType—was introduced to store and query XML data in the database. XMLType provides member functions to access, extract and query XML data using XPath expressions, such as XMLType.**extract()**, XMLType.**extractValue()** and XMLType.**existsNode()**. Additionally, the C-based DBMS_XMLGEN PL/SQL package and a set of SQL functions, including the SYS_XMLGEN() and SYS_XMLAGG(), are provided to create XMLTypes. The new **DBUri-refs** allow URL-based content references in database. With these built-in XML functions and operators, processing XML is simplified, because you do not need to initialize and maintain the Java classes in the Oracle database. However, these XML functions do not scale well, because XMLTypes are stored as CLOBs and requires the building of DOM in memory before processing XML content. In addition, in this release, the text-search functionality in `Oracle Text` provides the XPATH support within the CONTEXT index.

Oracle9*i* Release 2 introduces additional XML Schema–based data storage for XMLType, which allows users to register XML schemas that conform to the W3C XML Schema recommendation. After an XML schema is registered, sets of object types and object tables are created to store XML instances conforming to the schema. The XML instance documents are "shredded" and stored in the objects. This "preparsed" storage of XML helps avoid the run-time DOM parsing needed by the CLOB-based XMLTypes in Oracle9*i* R1. Additionally, the Oracle XML DB is capable of rewriting the XML queries with XPath expressions into the relational SQL queries for fast data access. In this release, a new text-search index—CTXXPATH index—is integrated in XMLType to speed up the performance of XPath searching when using XMLType.existNode() function.

Along with the new storage model, Oracle9*i* Release 2 provides a document-centric *XML DB Repository* for high-performance document management in the Oracle database. The XML DB Repository provides the protocol interfaces in addition to the SQL interfaces, such as FTP, HTTP, and WebDAV, to help users easily access and manipulate the XML documents stored in the Oracle database.

Furthermore, the SQL and PL/SQL support for XML processing is enhanced in this release by including the new XMLType member functions, the new SQL/XML functions, and the C-based PL/SQL packages for processing XML data. A set of PL/SQL packages and XDBUriType are also provided for the resource management of the XML DB Repository. As previously discussed, the built-in C functions and PL/SQL packages have less management and processing overhead than the Java-based PL/SQL packages.

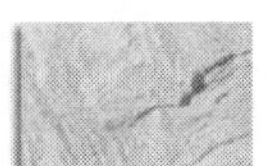

NOTE
*Because C-based PL/SQL packages provide compatible APIs with better performance, the Java-based XML PL/SQL packages, including XMLPARSER, XMLDOM, and XSLPROCESSOR, are deprecated and are not included in the Oracle Database 10*g *release.*

In Oracle Database 10*g*, native XML support is further enhanced by supporting a certain level of XML Schema evolution. This allows you to update the registered XML schemas for XMLTypes without performing an import/export on your data. Additionally, the existing XML applications can now have a single code line for multi-tier XML application deployment as Oracle XDK in Oracle Database 10*g* provides unified DOM interfaces to access XMLTypes. This support speeds up the XML processing by eliminating the need to reparse the XML documents in mid-tier and directly utilize the DOM objects stored in the database with "lazy" DOM manifestation. This feature is initially available in C and C++ for OCI and OCCI applications respectively.

The Oracle Database 10*g* database now contains extensive native XML functionality within the database server. The technical details of this technology will be discussed in later chapters. Table 8-1 provides a summary of the evolution of Oracle XML features.

NOTE
In OracleX, most of the functionality in DBMS_XMLQUERY and DBMS_XMLSAVE is covered by the C-based PL/SQL packages—the DBMS_XMLGEN and DBMS_XMLSTORE, respectively. For better performance, you should always use the C-based packages if they cover the functionality you need. However, you generally cannot mix the two within a single XML process.

Database Version	Major XML Features
Oracle8*i*	Java-based XML SQL Utility (XSU): DBMS_XMLQUERY, DBMS_XMLSAVE Java-based XML PL/SQL packages: XMLPARSER, XSLPROCESSOR, XMLDOM Text search for XML: Searching within XML elements/attributes using the AUTO_SECTION_GROUP/XML_SECTION_GROUP in the CONTEXT index
Oracle9*i* Release 1	XMLType with CLOB storage: XMLType.**extract()**, XMLType.**extractValue()**, XMLType.**existsNode()** SQL functions for XML generation and aggregation: SYS_XMLGEN(), SYS_XMLAGG() C-based PL/SQL package for XML generation: DBMS_XMLGEN Native DBURI-refs: **UriType**, **DBUriType**, **HttpUriType**, **UriFactoryType** Text search for XML: XPATH searching using the PATH_SECTION_GROUP in the CONTEXT index Text search integration within XMLType: CTXXPATH index integrated within XMLType.**existsNode()**
Oracle9*i* Release 2	XML Schema–based XMLType and CLOB-based XMLType New XMLType member functions such as XMLType.**transform()** XML DB Repository and protocol data access interfaces: HTTP, WebDAV over HTTP, FTP, SQL/XML support Oracle SQL extensions for XML Processing: UPDATEXML(), XMLSEQUENCE() C-based XML PL/SQL packages: DBMS_XMLDOM for XML DOM operations DBMS_XSLPROCESSOR for XSLT transformations and XPath-based data extraction DBMS_XMLPARSER for XML parsing DBMS_XMLTRANSFORM for XSLT transformations DBMS_XMLSCHEMA for XML Schema operations such as XML Schema registration and validation DBMS_XDB for XML DB Repository configuration DBMS_XDBZ for XML DB hierarchical indexing DBMS_XDB_VERSION for XML document versioning in XML DB Repository Additional native DBUri-refs: **XDBUriType**
Oracle Database 10*g* Release 1	XML Schema evolution New C-based XML PL/SQL package for inserting XML data: DBMS_XMLSTORE Unified DOM interfaces to XMLType for OCI/OCCI applications

TABLE 8-1. *XML Features in Oracle Database*

Along with the XML functionality centralized in the Oracle database, you can also take advantage of the XML interfaces in the Oracle XDK and connect to databases through JDBC or OCI to build mid-tier XML database applications. This will be discussed in the following chapters.

Setting Up the Oracle XML Database

To make sure that you can run the examples in the upcoming chapters, you need to have access to Standard or Enterprise Edition of the Oracle Database 10*g* database and follow the setup procedures explained in this section.

NOTE
*Most of the Oracle XML DB functionality discussed in this section also works in Oracle 9.2.0.2 and later releases. However, the directory structures for SQL files may be different from Oracle Database 10*g.

Installing Oracle XML Database

If you installed the Oracle Database 10*g* database using *Database Configuration Assistant (DBCA),* you do not need to perform extra steps to set up Oracle XML DB because it is set up by default. Otherwise, after the database installation, you need to perform the following steps to enable the Oracle XML DB functionality:

1. Create an Oracle XML DB tablespace (as XDB) for Oracle XML DB Repository.
2. Enable protocol access.

You need to connect as the SYS user and run the SQL scripts in the **$ORACLE_HOME/rdbms/admin** (or **%ORACLE_HOME%\rdbms\admin** for Windows) directory. These steps assume your Oracle Database 10*g installation is in* **D:\oracle**, which is the Oracle home directory.

NOTE
The term XDB, which will be introduced, was the original name used by Oracle development for XML DB. Therefore, it can be confusing as it is used internally for labeling users, schemas, tablespaces, etc. For clarification, XML DB will continue to be used to refer to functionality and the Repository, and XDB to describe XML DB metadata, users, and where it is used by default.

1. Log in to a SQL*Plus session and connect as the SYS user with SYSDBA privilege:

   ```
   OSPrompt> SQLPLUS "SYS/<sys_password> as sysdba"
   ```

2. Create a new XDB tablespace as follows:

   ```
   CREATE TABLESPACE XDB LOGGING
    DATAFILE 'D:\oracle\oradata\ORCLX\xdb.dbf'
    SIZE 25M REUSE AUTOEXTEND ON NEXT 1280K MAXSIZE 100M
    EXTENT MANAGEMENT LOCAL;
   ```

3. Then, run the **catqm.sql** script to create the XDB database registry, PL/SQL packages, and so forth:

   ```
   SQL> @catqm.sql <XDBUSER_password> <XDB_TS_NAME> <TEMP_TS_NAME>
   ```

   For example, the following command creates the *XDB* user using the *XDB* tablespace and sets the temporary tablespace to be *TEMP* (the password for the XDB user is *XDBPW*):

   ```
   SQL> @catqm XDBPW XDB TEMP
   ```

4. After all the tablespaces and built-in PL/SQL packages are created, you can reconnect to SQL*Plus as a SYS user with the SYSDBA privilege and run the catxdbj.sql script to load XML DB Java libraries:

```
SQL> @catxdbj
```

5. If you like to install the XDK packages, such as the DBMS_XMLQUERY and DBMS_XMLSAVE PL/SQL packages, you need to run initxml.sql as follows:

```
SQL> @initxml.sql
```

6. Finally, you need to shut down and restart the database.

Now, you have set up the database schema for Oracle XML DB, created the supporting PL/SQL packages, and set up the associated component registries in the Oracle database. Next, you need to set up the XML DB HTTP and FTP listeners to allow users to connect to XML DB Repository through the WebDAV/HTTP and FTP protocols.

First, you need to make sure the Oracle Net Services are started. To check the status, you can use the **lsnrctl status** command in a command-line window.

As shown in Figure 8-1, the XML DB service, *orclXXDB,* (<Oracle SID>XDB naming convention), and the XML DB HTTP and FTP listeners have started. By default, the HTTP listener listens on port 8080 and the FTP listener uses port 2100.

If the status is not as shown in Figure 8-1, you need to perform the following steps, assuming you have the default port 1521 registered for the database listener:

```
Command Prompt
D:\>lsnrctl status

LSNRCTL for 32-bit Windows: Version 10.1.0.2.0 - Production on 09-FEB-2004 12:16:05

Copyright (c) 1991, 2003, Oracle.  All rights reserved.

Connecting to (DESCRIPTION=(ADDRESS=(PROTOCOL=IPC)(KEY=EXTPROC)))
STATUS of the LISTENER
------------------------
Alias                     LISTENER
Version                   TNSLSNR for 32-bit Windows: Version 10.1.0.2.0 - Production
Start Date                09-FEB-2004 11:56:05
Uptime                    0 days 0 hr. 20 min. 1 sec
Trace Level               off
Security                  OFF
SNMP                      OFF
Listener Parameter File   d:\oracle\network\admin\listener.ora
Listener Log File         d:\oracle\network\log\listener.log
Listening Endpoints Summary...
  (DESCRIPTION=(ADDRESS=(PROTOCOL=ipc)(PIPENAME=\\.\pipe\EXTPROCipc)))
  (DESCRIPTION=(ADDRESS=(PROTOCOL=tcp)(HOST=my-laptop)(PORT=1521)))
  (DESCRIPTION=(ADDRESS=(PROTOCOL=tcp)(HOST=my-laptop)(PORT=8080))(Presentation=HTTP)(S
ession=RAW))
  (DESCRIPTION=(ADDRESS=(PROTOCOL=tcp)(HOST=my-laptop)(PORT=2100))(Presentation=FTP)(Se
ssion=RAW))
Services Summary...
Service "ORCLXDB" has 1 instance(s).
  Instance "orcl", status READY, has 1 handler(s) for this service...
Service "PLSExtProc" has 1 instance(s).
  Instance "PLSExtProc", status UNKNOWN, has 1 handler(s) for this service...
Service "orcl" has 1 instance(s).
  Instance "orcl", status READY, has 1 handler(s) for this service...
The command completed successfully

D:\>
```

FIGURE 8-1. *Oracle Net Services status*

Initializing the Oracle JVM

If the Oracle JVM is not initialized, you must initialize it before loading the Java package for the XSU PL/SQL packages. To initialize the JVM:

1. Run the initjvm.sql and initdbj.sql scripts in the **$ORACLE_HOME/javavm/install** (**%ORACLE_HOME%\javavm\install** for Windows) directory.
2. When you upgrade the XDK PL/SQL packages, you need to uninstall the XDK with the rmxml.sql utility and reload the new XDK PL/SQL packages into Oracle JServer with the **initxml.sql** utility in the **$ORACLE_HOME/rdbms/admin** directory. However, you *do not* need to reinitialize the Oracle JVM during this reloading process.
3. By default, the XDK PL/SQL packages are loaded into the SYS or SYSTEM user. However, for easier maintenance when reloading Java packages is needed, it is suggested to load them into a specific user schema. For example, you can create a user named XDK and load the Java classes to this user's schema. This keeps them separated from the other Java classes, thus eliminating potential compatibility problems during upgrades. You should also notice that, by default, the public synonyms are created for the package names, and the execution privileges are granted to PUBLIC.

To set up the TCP dispatcher, you need to add the **dispatchers** parameter to a server parameter file (SPFILEORCLX.ORA) first:

```
dispatchers="(PROTOCOL=TCP) (SERVICE=<SID>XDB)"
```

For example, assuming your instance is ORCLX, you need to run the following command as the SYS user:

```
SQL> ALTER SYSTEM SET dispatchers='(PROTOCOL=TCP)(SERVICE=ORCLXXDB)'
SCOPE=SPFILE;
SQL> SHOW PARAMETERS dispatchers;
```

Then, you need to stop and restart the listener by running the following in the command-line window:

```
OSPrompt> lsnrctl stop
OSPrompt> lsnrctl start
```

Finally, you need to shut down and restart the database from SQL*Plus:

```
SQL> shutdown immediate;
SQL> startup
```

To make sure the listeners work properly and the XML DB service is registered, you can check the listener status by running the following command:

```
OSPrompt> lsnrctl status
```

You should now be able to see the XML DB service and the HTTP and FTP listeners up and running.

NOTE
After Oracle9i, instead of updating the init<SID>.ora file to change the initialization parameters of the Oracle database, normally you need to update the Stored Parameter File (SPFILE), which is used by default. To do this, you can run the ALTER SYSTEM command in the SYS user:

```
ALTER SYSTEM set parameter = value SCOPE = MEMORY
| SPFILE | BOTH;
```

The SCOPE clause allows you to set the scope parameters: MEMORY affects the current running database but will not be in place after a database is restarted, SPFILE does not change the current database setting of the parameter but will modify the SPFILE *so that this parameter will take effect when the database is restarted, and BOTH changes system parameters in the current database instance and updates the SPFILE.*

If the database listener does not use the default 1521 port (i.e., 1581), the XML DB service and FTP and HTTP listeners cannot be dynamically registered to the listener. Therefore, you need extra setup steps. For example, if you have the following Oracle Net Service defined in **$ORACLE_HOME/network/admin/tnsname.ora** (or **`%ORACLE_HOME%\network\admin\tnsname.ora`** on Windows):

```
ORCLX =
  (DESCRIPTION =
    (ADDRESS_LIST =
      (ADDRESS = (PROTOCOL = TCP)(HOST = mylaptop)(PORT = 1581))
    )
    (CONNECT_DATA =
      (SERVER = DEDICATED)
      (SERVICE_NAME = ORCLX)
    )
  )
```

and you have the listener defined in the following section of the **listener.ora**:

```
LISTENER =
  (DESCRIPTION_LIST =
    (DESCRIPTION =
      (ADDRESS_LIST =
        (ADDRESS = (PROTOCOL = IPC)(KEY = EXTPROC0))
```

```
      )
      (ADDRESS_LIST =
        (ADDRESS = (PROTOCOL = TCP)(HOST = mylaptop)(PORT = 1581))
      )
    )
  )
```

then you need to configure the LOCAL_LISTENER parameter in the initialization parameter file referring to the TNSNAME entry specified in the **tnsnames.ora** that points to the correct listener. You can run the following command in SQL*Plus to update the SPFILE file:

```
SQL> ALTER SYSTEM SET dispatchers='(PROTOCOL=TCP)(LISTENER=ORCLX)' SCOPE=SPFILE;
SQL> SHOW PARAMETERS local_listener;
```

Finally, you also need to shut down and restart the database as follows:

```
SQL> shutdown immediate;
SQL> startup
```

Oracle XML DB allows you to change the default configurations of the HTTP and FTP ports. However, that process is not discussed here, because the preceding setups are enough for you to get started to run the XML DB samples. Such management and setup details are discussed in Chapter 12, which presents some tips and techniques for using the XML DB features.

Installing the Sample Database Schemas

The Oracle sample database schemas are used in the examples for the book. However, the installation of the sample schema is an option when creating a database with DBCA in Oracle Database 10*g*. If the sample schemas are not installed during database creation, you need to start SQL*Plus to run the following command in the **$ORACLE_HOME** or **%ORACLE_HOME%** directory:

```
SQL> @demo\schema\mksample <SYS_PASSWORD> <SYSTEM_PASSWORK> HR OE PM QS SH BI
EXAMPLE TEMP D:\temp\log
```

The **mksample.sql** script requires you to supply the SYS and SYSTEM password followed by the password for the six sample schema users, HR, OE, PM, QS, SH, and BI. To help remember the password for each user, you can specify the password same as the user names. For example, the password for user HR is HR. Then, you need to specify the default tablespace (i.e., EXAMPLE), the temporary tablespace (i.e., TEMP), and the directory where you want the log file to be generated for the sample schema installation.

Upon installation, the sample schemas are created. The six sample schemas build up a general database schema for company management, which consists of different divisions represented by different users:

- **HR** The Human Resource division contains information about the company's employees and the organizational structure.
- **OE** The Ordering Entry division tracks the product inventory and fulfills purchase orders of products through different channels.

- **PM** The Product Media division maintains the product-related information.
- **QS** The Quality Shipping division manages the shipping of the products to customers.
- **SH** The Sale History division tracks business statistics.
- **BI** The Business Intelligence division provides decision support information.

The XML generation and Object-Relational (O-R) XMLType storage examples will use the HR schema, and the XML-based content management samples will be built on the PM schema.

Creating a User to Run the XMLType Samples

You need to create a temporary user account to run the examples of XMLType in this chapter. For example, you can run the following SQL commands in SYS user to create a user named **demo**:

```
CREATE USER demo IDENTIFIED BY demo
 DEFAULT TABLESPACE USERS
 QUOTA 50M ON USERS
 TEMPORARY TABLESPACE TEMP;
```

This user needs to have the following privileges:

- CREATE SESSION
- CREATE TABLE
- CREATE PROCEDURE
- CREATE TYPE
- CTXAPP ROLE

You can grant the privileges as follows:

```
GRANT CREATE SESSION TO demo;
GRANT CREATE TABLE TO demo;
GRANT CREATE PROCEDURE to demo;
GRANT CREATE TYPE TO demo;
GRANT CTXAPP TO demo;
```

The first three privileges are granted for basic DDL operations. The third one has to be granted to create object types during the XML Schema registration. The CTXAPP role is used to create and synchronize Oracle Text indexes.

Setting Up a WebDAV Folder

WebDAV support in Oracle XML DB allows you to create WebDAV folders in the Windows environment. It makes accessing the Oracle XML DB Repository just like accessing any other folder on your disk drive. The following instructions work through the procedure to set up a WebDAV Folder in a Windows XP system:

1. From the START menu, open *My Network Places.*
2. Click *Add A Network Place,* which allows you to pick up the kind of network place to add.
3. Click *Next,* choose *Choose Another Network Connect,* and then type **http://<host-name>:8080/** as the address. You can also use **127.0.0.1** or **localhost** for your hostname.
4. Click *Next.* A window pops up asking for login information. You can type any valid database username and password here to log in to XML DB. Note that different users may have different views of data because of the security protection in the XML DB Repository.
5. Click OK. In the next wizard window, type in the name **XML DB Repository** and click *Next.*
6. Deselect the *Open Folder By Default* option and then click Finish to complete the wizard.
7. Back in the window My Network Places window, you will now see that the folder XML DB Repository has been created, as shown in Figure 8-2.
8. Double-click the XML DB Repository folder icon. You will be asked to log in. You can use the same database username and password to log in. The web folder opens, as shown in Figure 8-3.

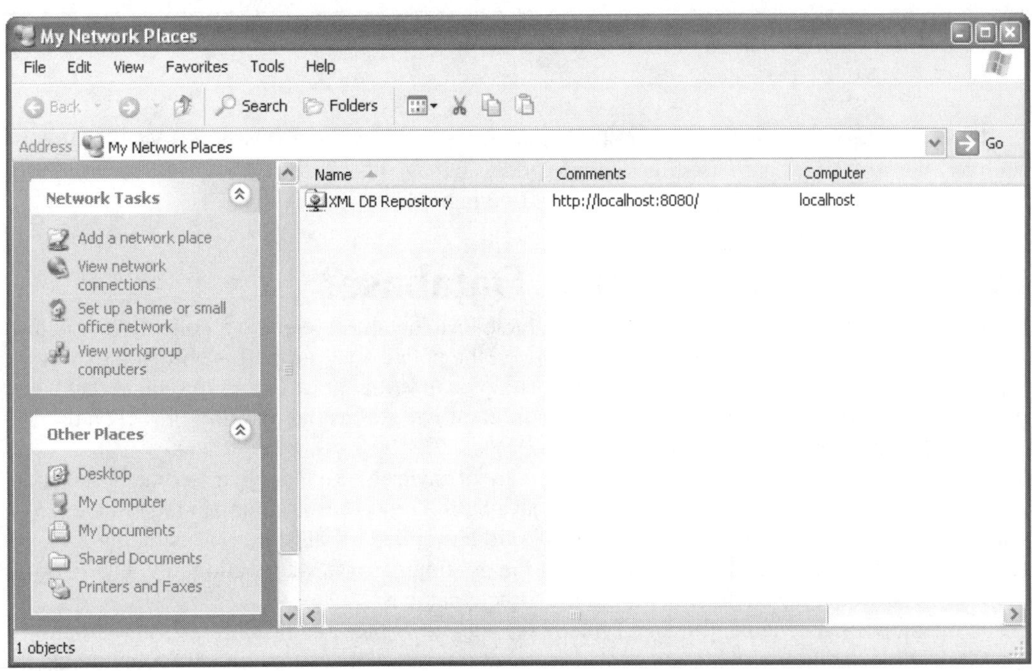

FIGURE 8-2. *WebDAV folder created*

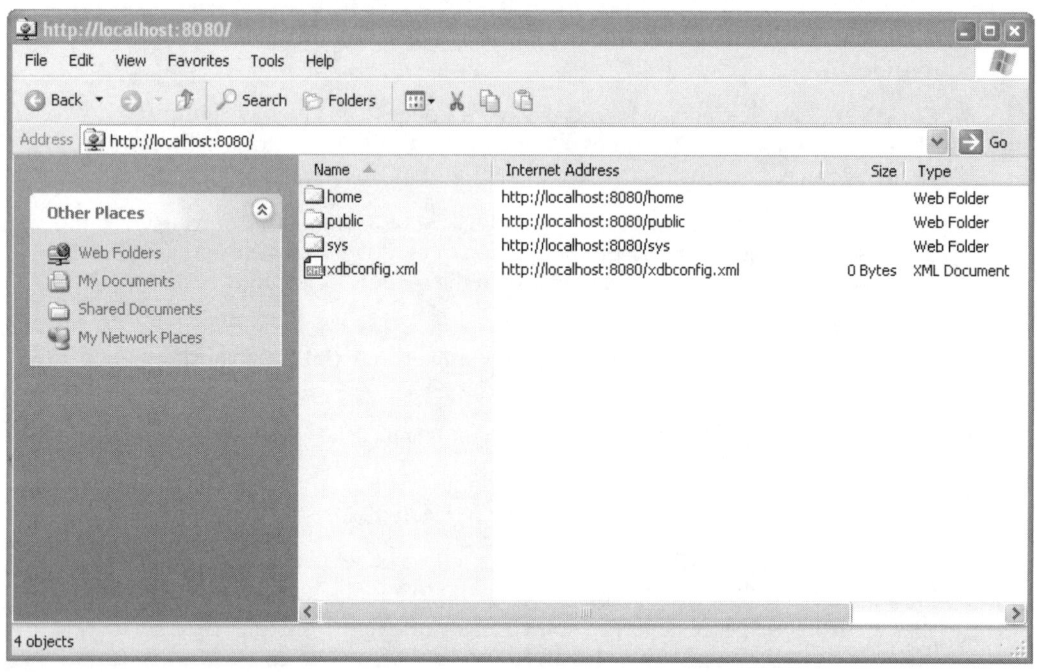

FIGURE 8-3. *Example Oracle XML DB Repository*

Now that you have created the WebDAV folder, any application that supports WebDAV, such as Microsoft Word, can use this folder to access or save files in the XML DB Repository. The setup of the folder is complete and will be used later.

What Is the Oracle XML Database?

As stated at the beginning of the chapter, the Oracle XML database refers to a collection of native XML technologies in the database server. However, the native XML support is only one part of the XML infrastructure in the Oracle database. The overall XML infrastructure in Oracle database provides both high-performance native XML support and an extensible platform on which users can build and deploy their own solutions.

The native XML DB functionality is available without having to run through a separate installation process. The extension platform is based on the Java Stored Procedures running in the Oracle JVM and the C-based external procedures. You can build customized XML solutions using the XML functionality in the Oracle XDK to compliment the existing native XML functionality. Figure 8-4 illustrates the overall XML infrastructure in the Oracle database.

In the native XML engine, the XMLType tables and views provide the storage of XML data. The XML DB Repository provides an XML document repository that is optimized for handling

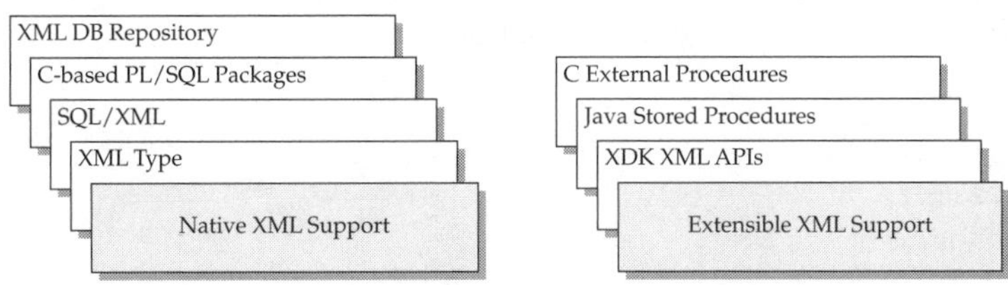

FIGURE 8-4. *Oracle database XML support*

XML documents, and the PL/SQL and SQL/XML functions allow XML operations on SQL data and XML content. The Java and C XML programming APIs in the Oracle XDK can be used to add functionality by building external procedures, such as creating a Java Stored Procedure for SAX stream-based XML processing, which is not available as part of the native XML support.

Exploring the native XML features is the focus in this section. The examples for building Java or C extensions using XDK will be included in later chapters to demonstrate the value of the entire Oracle XML infrastructure.

In the coming section, the following features will be demonstrated:

- The native XMLType data type used to store and manage XML documents
- XMLType functions and SQL/XML functions operating on XMLType data in SQL
- XML DB Repository and its protocols interfaces including the FTP, HTTP, and WebDAV interfaces on XMLTypes
- Oracle Text search on XMLTypes
- Oracle Advanced Queuing extensions for XMLTypes

XMLType

XMLType is the native data type for storing XML data in the Oracle database. It is similar to the DATE data type in that you can use it to define table columns or use it as parameters, return values, or variables in the PL/SQL procedures.

XMLType provides a set of built-in member functions that operate on XML content, enabling you to create an XMLType instance from various resources, extract XML content, validate XML against XML Schemas, apply XSL transformations, and so on.

NOTE
The content stored in XMLType must be well-formed XML, or you will get an ORA-31011: XML parsing failed error. All the entity references in the XML document will be resolved to ensure it is well formed during the data insertion into XMLTypes.

The following example creates a product table called **product** with an XMLType column called **description** for storing the product descriptions:

```
CREATE TABLE product(
 id VARCHAR(10),
 name VARCHAR2(100),
 description XMLType);
```

You insert sample data into this table using the following SQL:

```
INSERT INTO product(id, name, description)
  VALUES('xdk', 'XML Developer''s Kit',
    XMLTYPE('<DESCRIPTION><KEYWORD>xdk</KEYWORD> is a set of
    standards-based utilities that help to build XML applications.
    It contains XDK Java, C/C++ components.</DESCRIPTION>'));
```

In this example, the **XMLType()** construction function is used to create an XMLType instance from a string input.

As previously discussed, you can process XML by creating the PL/SQL procedures taking XMLType as parameters, variables, or return types. To demonstrate this, you create a PL/SQL procedure, in which the descriptions of each product are passed in as an XMLType parameter called **p_desc**. Using the **UPDATEXML()** SQL function, you update this product description by substituting all of the **<KEYWORD>** elements whose content equals **p_id** that are passed in by the **p_name** parameter:

```
CREATE OR REPLACE FUNCTION MYTRANSFORM (p_desc IN XMLTYPE,
  p_id IN VARCHAR2, p_name IN VARCHAR2) RETURN XMLTYPE AS
  v_result XMLType;
BEGIN
 SELECT UPDATEXML(p_desc,
        '//KEYWORD[text()='''||p_id||''']/text()',p_name) INTO v_result
 FROM dual;
 RETURN v_result;
END MYTRANSFORM;
```

After you have created the PL/SQL procedure, you can run the following SQL command:

```
SQL> set long 10000
SQL> SELECT MYTRANSFORM(description, id, name) FROM product;
```

You will see the following output:

```
MYTRANSFORM(DESCRIPTION,ID,NAME)
----------------------------------------------------------------------
<DESCRIPTION> <KEYWORD>XML Developer&apos;s Kit</KEYWORD> is a set of
standards-based utilities that help to build XML applications. It
contains XDK Java, C/C++ components.</DESCRIPTION>
```

When storing XML in XMLTypes, there are several storage options. Basically, you can create XMLTypes as:

- **XML Schema–based XMLTypes** Stored under an object-relational structure specified by a registered XML schema unless you specify the storage options when creating the objects.
- **Non XML Schema–based XMLTypes** Stored in CLOBs.

The XML Schema defines how to "shred" the content of an XML document and store it as a set of SQL objects. For example, you can register an XML Schema as follows:

```
BEGIN
 DBMS_XMLSCHEMA.registerSchema(
  SCHEMAURL=>'http://xmlns.oracle.com/xml/content.xsd',
  SCHEMADOC=>'<?xml version="1.0" encoding="UTF-8"?>
<xs:schema
 xmlns:xs="http://www.w3.org/2001/XMLSchema" elementFormDefault="qualified">
  <xs:element name="DESCRIPTION">
   <xs:complexType mixed="true">
    <xs:choice minOccurs="0" maxOccurs="unbounded">
     <xs:element name="KEYWORD" type= "xs:string" maxOccurs="unbounded"/>
    </xs:choice>
   </xs:complexType>
  </xs:element>
 </xs:schema>',
  LOCAL=>TRUE,
  GENTYPES=>TRUE,
  GENTABLES=>FALSE);
 END;
```

In the Oracle XML database, each XML schema is registered under a unique URL so that XMLTypes can identify the XML schemas when referring to them. The preceding example uses the **http://xmlns.oracle.com/xml/content.xsd** URL.

During the XML Schema registration, Oracle XML DB generates SQL objects to store XMLTypes that are complaint with the XML schema and, optionally, generates a default table. This example does not generate the default tables for the XMLTypes, but we will discuss this later in the "Oracle XML DB Repository" section. You can look at the objects generated using the following SQL commands:

```
SQL> COLUMN object_name format a30
SQL> COLUMN object_type format a30
SQL> SELECT object_name, object_type FROM user_objects;
```

The objects created by the XML Schema registration are listed as follows:

```
OBJECT_NAME                    OBJECT_TYPE
------------------------------ ------------------------------
DESCRIPTION163_T               TYPE
KEYWORD164_COLL                TYPE
```

```
PRODUCT                           TABLE
SYS_LOB0000042735C00004$$         LOB
```

You will see the SQL object types created for each complex type in the XML schema, such as the **DESCRIPTION163_T** and **KEYWORD164_COLL**. You can use the **desc** command to show the details of the object types:

```
SQL> desc DESCRIPTION163_T
 DESCRIPTION163_T is NOT FINAL
 Name                                      Null?    Type
 ----------------------------------------- -------- ------------------------
 SYS_XDBPD$                                         XDB.XDB$RAW_LIST_T
 KEYWORD                                            KEYWORD164_COLL
SQL> desc KEYWORD164_COLL
 KEYWORD164_COLL VARRAY(2147483647) OF VARCHAR2(4000)
```

A VARRAY of VARCHAR2(4000) is created for elements such as **<KEYWORD>** where its occurrence is unbounded. By default, its size is 2147483647 bytes! Not only is the default size of VARRAY too large for storing XML documents, the extra SYS_XDBPD$ column created to preserve the DOM fidelity of XML content may not be needed by your application. To customize these storage modes, you can annotate the XML schemas. How can you annotate the XML schema? What is the **SYS_LOB0000042735C00004$$** column? We will answer these kinds of XMLType storage–related questions in Chapter 9.

By default, XMLTypes are stored in CLOBs unless you associate a registered XML schema URL with the XMLType columns or XMLType object tables. For example, in the previous **product** table, the **description** column is an XMLType in CLOB storage. Instead, you can define the column **description** as an XML Schema–based XMLType using the registered **http://xmlns.oracle.com/xml/content.xsd** schema as follows:

```
CREATE TABLE product(
 id VARCHAR(10),
 name VARCHAR2(100),
 description XMLType)
XMLType COLUMN description
XMLSCHEMA "http://xmlns.oracle.com/xml/content.xsd"
ELEMENT "DESCRIPTION";
```

The **description** column uses the structured storage of XMLType. The following example shows that when inserting the same XML data into XML Schema–based XMLType columns, you need to use the XMLType.**createSchemaBasedXML()** function:

```
INSERT INTO product(id, name, description)
 VALUES('xdk', 'XML Developer''s Kit', XMLTYPE('<DESCRIPTION>
 <KEYWORD>xdk</KEYWORD> is a set of standards-based utilities that
 helps to build<KEYWORD>XML</KEYWORD> applications. It contains XDK
 Java, C/C++ Components.</DESCRIPTION>').CreateSchemaBasedXML(
 'http://xmlns.oracle.com/xml/content.xsd'));
```

NOTE
*If you do not specify the registered XML schema URL for XMLTypes using the XMLType.**createSchemaBasedXML()**, you will get the error - ORA-19007: Schema and element do not match.*

After XML is stored in XMLTypes, you can use the XMLType member functions to operate on the XML content. We will discuss this with more examples in Chapter 10. In this section, we just look at a simple example, which extracts XML nodes using the XMLType.**extract()** function. The following query extracts all **<KEYWORD>** elements in the product description.

```
SQL> SELECT p.description.extract('//KEYWORD') FROM product p;
P.DESCRIPTION.EXTRACT('//KEYWORD')
----------------------------------------------------------------------
<KEYWORD>xdk</KEYWORD>
<KEYWORD>XML</KEYWORD>
```

XMLType Views

XMLType can be used to define views, called *XMLType Views*. For example, you can create an XMLType view based on the **employees** table in the HR user schema:

```
CREATE OR REPLACE VIEW employee_vw AS
 SELECT XMLELEMENT("Employee",
        XMLATTRIBUTES(employee_id AS "empno"),
        XMLFOREST(first_name, last_name, job_id))AS result
 FROM hr.employees;
```

You may not be familiar with the SQL/XML functions used in the example. Do not worry. We will discuss these in the next section. Simply query the view, and you will see the XML content that is returned:

```
SQL> SELECT * FROM employee_vw WHERE ROWNUM<2;
RESULT
-----------------------------------------------------------------------------
<Employee empno="100">
  <FIRST_NAME>Steven</FIRST_NAME>
  <LAST_NAME>King</LAST_NAME>
  <JOB_ID>AD_PRES</JOB_ID>
</Employee>
```

From this example, you can see that the XMLType view provides an option to wrap up existing object-relational data in XML, which then can be used for both Web publishing and data exchange. Additionally, XMLType views can serve as an XML interface for XML-centric processing, such as XPath-based content navigation and updates. You can build XMLType views based on XML schemas. The major difference between these XML Schema–based XMLType views and XMLType views that are not based on XML schemas is that the XML Schema validation can occur, which brings rich data-type constraints and XPath query optimization.

SQL/XML Processing

SQL is the standard for efficiently managing relational data. The XML extensions of SQL in Oracle XML Database allow SQL operations previously limited to relational data to operate on XML data as well. Table 8-2 outlines the overall functionality of SQL/XML and Oracle extension support in Oracle Database 10*g*.

By using Oracle SQL extensions and the SQL/XML functions for XML processing, you can easily leverage the relational data model and XML data model in one SQL query. This gives you

Type	Function	Description
Oracle SQL extensions	EXISTSNODE()	Takes an XPath expression and returns true (1) if the XML document contains the node specified by XPath.
	EXTRACT()	Takes an XPath expression and returns the node or node set that matches the XPath.
	EXTRACTVALUE()	Takes an XPath expression and returns the text of the XML nodes that match the XPath.
	UPDATEXML()	Takes an XPath expression and updates the XML nodes that match the XPath.
	XMLCOLATTVAL()	Generates an XML fragment converting each passed column name to an attribute name-value pair within a **<column>** element.
	SYS_XMLGEN()	Generates XML from SQL queries passed as parameters.
	XMLSEQUENCE()	Returns a sequence of XMLType using VARRAY of the top-level elements.
SQL/XML functions	XMLELEMENT()	Creates an XML element in XMLType by taking an element name, an optional collection of attributes for the element, and the element content.
	XMLATTRIBUTES()	Used within XMLELEMENT() to specify attributes of that element.
	XMLFOREST()	Converts each of its argument parameters to XML, and then returns an XML fragment that is the concatenation of these converted arguments.
	XMLCONCAT()	Takes as input a series of XMLType instances, concatenates the series of elements for each row, and returns the complete series.
	XMLAGG()	Aggregates XML fragments to build up an XML document.

TABLE 8-2. *Basic Functions for SQL XML Processing*

the maximum flexibility to solve business problems. In the previous example, the SQL/XML functions are used to create XMLType views. We will use additional SQL operators and functions in later chapters, and discuss the technical details of how to use these SQL functions in Chapter 10.

Oracle XML DB Repository

Oracle XML DB Repository is a queryable, hierarchically organized repository, which is ideal for managing document- or content-centric documents in various formats including XML. With this repository, you can

- Store and view XML content stored in XML DB as a directory hierarchy of folders.
- Use the hierarchical metaphors, such as XPath and URLs, to access XML documents and represent the relationships between documents.

XML documents stored in the repository can be accessed through the protocol interfaces such as HTTP, WebDAV, and FTP. In addition, you can access the repository from SQL and PL/SQL scripts using the two public views, RESOURCE_VIEW and PATH_VIEW. We will discuss the Oracle XML DB Repository in detail in Chapter 10 and the memory- and performance-tuning techniques for the repository in Chapter 12.

Oracle Text

XML data stored as XMLTypes in either CLOBs or XML Schema–based structured storage can be indexed by Oracle Text. For example, to create an Oracle Text index and query the **product** table, you can use the following code:

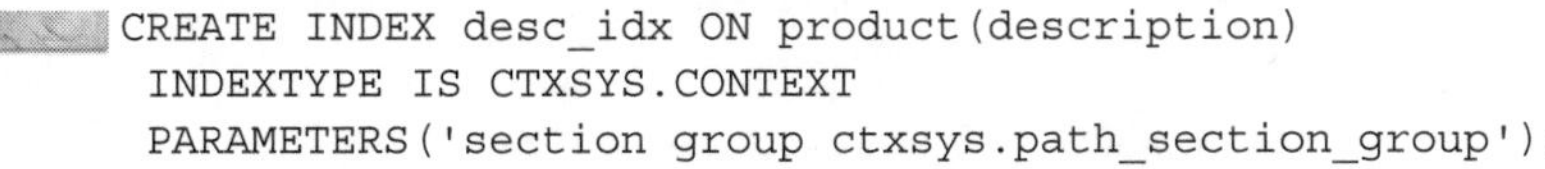

```
CREATE INDEX desc_idx ON product(description)
 INDEXTYPE IS CTXSYS.CONTEXT
 PARAMETERS('section group ctxsys.path_section_group');
```

NOTE
You must have the CTXAPP role granted to create the Oracle Text indexes.

Thereafter, you can use the CONTAINS() function in SQL queries to search the XML content as follows:

```
SELECT name
FROM product
WHERE CONTAINS(description,'about(xml utilities)')>0;
```

The **about()** is provided in Oracle Text to allow semantic search. There are additional XML search capabilities. For example, you can do the following:

- Use the ora.contains() function in XMLType.**existsNode()** for text searches within XPath-based searches.
- Use the HASPATH() and INPATH() operators to optimize XML data searches within the content specified by the XPath expressions.

Additionally, Oracle Text searching capabilities are integrated into XMLType by introducing the new CTXXPATH index. This is detailed in Chapter 11, where we will also discuss how you can create various SQL indexes on XMLTypes, such as B*Tree indexes, bitmap indexes, and functional indexes to speed up queries on the XML documents.

Oracle Advanced Queuing

Oracle Advanced Queuing supports XMLType as a message type. In other words, users can enqueue and dequeue XML messages from and into XMLTypes. In later chapters, you will see examples using the XMLType message queues and how to use XMLType functions for message processing.

XML Database and Standards

At this point, we have introduced the broad extent of Oracle XML support. Equally important is that its XML infrastructure is built on a family of open standards. These standards and the corresponding XML functionality are summarized in Table 8-3.

Standard	Current Status	Oracle XML Functionality
XML 1.0	Extensible Markup Language 1.0 W3C Recommendation Oct. 2000 www.w3.org/TR/REC-xml	XMLType DBMS_XMLPARSER (DOM Parser) XDK XML PARSERS (DOM and SAX Parser) in C, C++ and Java
XML Namespaces	XML Namespaces www.w3.org/TR/REC-xml-names	
XML Schema 1.0	XML Schema 1.0 W3C Recommendation May 2001 www.w3.org/TR/xmlschema-0	XML Schema–based XMLType with XML DB XML Schema annotations; used as the basis for mapping XML to SQL data types DBMS_XMLSCHEMA XDK XML SCHEMA PROCESSORS in C, C++ and Java
DOM 1.0 & 2.0	Document Object Model Level 2 W3C Recommendation Jan. 2003 www.w3.org/TR/DOM-Level-2-HTML	DBMS_XMLDOM XDK DOM Parser in C, C++ and Java
XSLT 1.0	XSLT Transformation 1.0 W3C Recommendation Nov. 1999 www.w3.org/TR/xslt	XMLType.**transform()** DBMS_XSLPROCESSOR C/C++ XDK XSL Processor in C, C++ and Java

TABLE 8-3. *XML DB Standards and Functionality*

Standard	Current Status	Oracle XML Functionality
XPath 1.0	XML Path Language 1.0 W3C Recommendation Nov. 1999 www.w3.org/TR/xpath	Used for hierarchical queries against XML documents: XMLType.extract() XMLTypes.extractValue() XMLType.**existsNode()** The **selectNodes(),valueOf()** and **selectSingleNode()** functions in: DBMS_XSLPROCESSOR XDK XML Parser in Java XDK XSL Processor in C
XQuery 1.0	XML Query Language 1.0 W3C Working Draft, Nov. 2002 www.w3.org/TR/xquery/	Standard XML query interfaces independent from the storage model
SQL/XML	XML-Related Specifications ISO-ANSI Working Draft www.sqlx.org	SQL/XML functions Oracle SQL extension functions for XML operations
WebDAV	Web-based Distributed Authoring and Versioning IETF RFC 2518 in 1999 http://asg.web.cmu.edu/rfc/rfc2518.html	WebDAV for Oracle XML DB Repository
HTTP 1.1	Hypertext Transfer Protocol www.w3.org/Protocols/rfc2616/rfc2616.html	WebDAV for Oracle XML DB Repository DBURI Servlet XML DB Servlet
FTP	File Transfer Protocol www.ietf.org/rfc/rfc959.txt	FTP for Oracle XML DB Repository

TABLE 8-3. *XML DB Standards and Functionality* (continued)

We will cover these features in detail in later chapters. If you are not familiar with these standards, check out the associated URLs in the Appendix.

Designing the XML Database

When you start to design XML applications using Oracle XML DB, you need to make several decisions, including how to store XML data in a database, what is the strategy to retrieve or generate XML, and how to create proper indexes for searching the content in the XML documents. In this section, we will discuss some helpful approaches to these decisions.

How to Store XML Data

As you have learned, there are different ways to store XML documents inside an Oracle XML database, and each of them offers different trade-offs in both performance and functionality. From experience, we find that the design flow depicted in Figure 8-5 is helpful in simplifying the selections.

By walking through this flowchart, you can explore the design strategy for using different storage types. First, you can start by asking whether you need to store XML documents in relational tables or as XMLType objects. This greatly affects the application development process, the technologies you use, and the performance of your application.

XMLType or Relational Tables?

This initial decision can generally be based on the format of the XML data and the DOM fidelity requirement on XML content. For format, the XML documents generally can be categorized as the data-centric or the document-centric document.

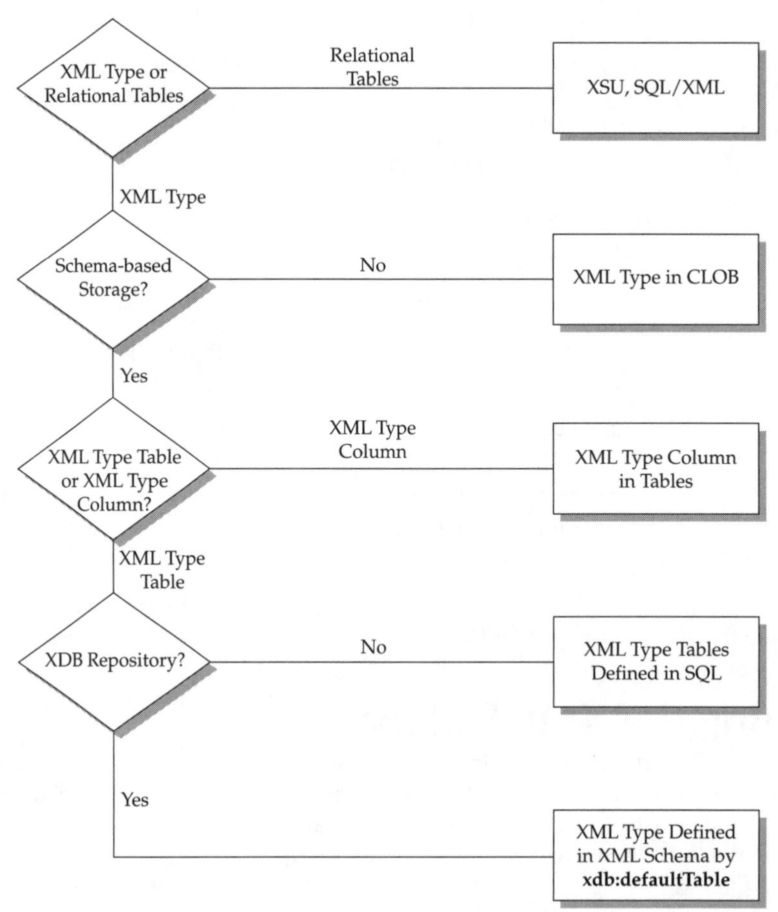

FIGURE 8-5. *Decision flowchart for storing XML in Oracle XML DB*

Data-centric XML documents are characterized by the regular structure for the data, in which the smallest data unit is either an XML element with simple content or an XML attribute. In such XML document, there is little or no mixing content (i.e., tags within an XML element's string content). Additionally, the DOM Fidelity for the document is not required to preserve. The following XML document is an example data-centric XML document:

```
<?xml version="1.0"?>
<purchaseOrder orderDate="1999-10-20">
 <shipTo country="US">…</shipTo>
  <billTo country="US">…</billTo>
   <items>
    <item partNum="872-AA">
     <productName>Lawnmower</productName>
      <quantity>1</quantity>
       <USPrice>148.95</USPrice>
       <comment>Confirm this is electric</comment>
     </item> …
   </items>
</purchaseOrder>
```

All the data in the above purchase order document are represented either as XML elements or as the attributes for XML elements.

Most of the data-centric XML documents are created based on the relational data for exchanging and sharing data between applications. You can think of XML as the boxes used for moving things around. When relocating them to another place, you need to put items in boxes in order to protect them and organize them for easy delivery. However, when the items reach the destination, there is no need to keep them in the box.

Likewise, for data-centric XML documents, there is no need to keep data in XML once it reaches the database. For a data-centric XML document, if XML elements and attributes are properly stored in relational table columns, it has the optimized storage for further processing, which avoids the overhead of keeping and managing the XML structure in the database. Whenever you need the data in XML for data exchange and Web publishing, you can build up XMLType views to wrap up data in XML.

On the other hand, there are document-centric XML documents, which are characterized by less regular or irregular data structure with lots of mixing content. For example, the following **faq.xml** is a document-centric XML document, in which the **<ANSWER>** element contains the mixing content of both text and **<KEY>** and **<CODE>** elements.

```
<FAQ>
 <TITLE>What is wrong if I got "ClassNotFoundException"? </TITLE>
 <ANSWER> If you get this kind of error, you need to check if the
<KEY>CLASSPATH</KEY> is correctly set. Basically you need to add the
 following <KEY>jar files</KEY> in your Java CLASSPATH environment
variable:
  <CODE> xmlparserv2.jar: XML Parser V2 for Java
         xschema.jar: XML Schema Processor for Java
         xsu12.jar(xsu12.jar): XML SQL Utility for Java
         …
  </CODE>
```

```
 </ANSWER>
 <CATEGORY>xdk</CATEGORY>
 <LANGUAGE>java</LANGUAGE>
</FAQ>
```

Dealing with the document-centric XML documents, you can store them in the native XMLTypes that well preserves the original XML data structure. If there are many queries on the XML content, the XML Schema–based XMLType is suggested as it well maintains the XML structure in the database and provides high-performance data retrieval and updates using the XML metadata.

However, sometimes no clear line exists between these two categories. A document may be highly structured without mixed content, but still cannot be shredded into tables if it has some XML-specific information—such as comments, processing instructions, and document order—that needs to be preserved. The following document shows a variation of the previous purchase order that now contains processing instructions (PIs) in the XML content. To keep the information, such as namespace prefixes, processing instructions, and even the order of the elements, in the XML document, you can choose to use the native XMLType to preserve the DOM byte for byte.

```
<?xml version="1.0"?>
<?dml name="Welcome"?>
<purchaseOrder orderDate="1999-10-20">
 <shipTo country="US">…</shipTo>
 <?dml name="Welcome"?>
 <billTo country="US">…</billTo>
  <items>
   <item partNum="872-AA">
    <productName>Lawnmower</productName>
    <quantity>1</quantity>
    <USPrice>148.95</USPrice>
    <comment>Confirm this is electric</comment>
   </item> …
  </items>
</purchaseOrder>
```

In general, when selecting between relational and native XML storage, you need to ask yourself whether your application really needs the full XML document preserved. Otherwise, you should leverage the database's ability to generate XML from relational tables using XMLType views to void the overhead for preserving the XML markups, the whitespaces for XML indentations, and so on.

Note that if you store XML in relational tables but construct XML interfaces with XMLType views that are deeply nested, the data queries and operations with many table joins may degrade the performance. In this case, you should choose the native XMLType data type because it well preserves the hierarchical structure of the XML documents and thus optimizes the related XML queries or operations.

Finally, the native XML Schema–based XMLType storage binds the underlying database schema tightly to the XML schemas. Currently, there are limitations on how much the schema can evolve before an export and import of the data set would be needed.

XML Schema–Based Types or CLOB XMLTypes?

If you decide to use XMLType, you need to decide whether you want to store XML in CLOBs or use the XML Schema–based XMLTypes by shredding the XML content and storing it in a set of SQL objects.

If you store XML in CLOBs, you keep the document in the original format byte for byte and can use the XMLType functions and the SQL commands to update and query the XML data. This type of storage is optimum for DTD-based documents and XML Schema–based documents where the schemas are changing or varied. Since the storage is not based upon the XML structure, documents of any size and hierarchical depth can be accommodated equally. However, since the XML data is not stored in a preparsed structure, it takes time to parse the documents before accessing the XML content. If your application requires intensive data retrievals or updates on XML element or attributes, or you want to extract the data out of XML documents for different use, you should not use the CLOB storage.

In the XML Schema–based XMLTypes, the XML documents are shredded and stored as a set of SQL objects. The XML content is validated and stored in a preparsed format. This storage is optimized in database for the fine-grained data queries and retrievals. Because this kind of XMLType is stored using offsets based on its XML Schema, called *XML Objects (XOBs),* and not materialized into the DOM tree until needed, it saves system resources. In addition, you have the option to preserve the byte-for-byte DOM fidelity, such as the order of XML elements and attributes, the whitespace between elements and attributes, XML comments, XML PIs, namespace declarations, and so on. However, XML Schema–based XMLTypes have high cost for schema evolutions.

NOTE
Because extra information is needed to preserve the DOM fidelity, you should avoid using it unless necessary.

After discussing all the storage models for XML documents in the Oracle Database 10*g* database, Table 8-4 compares the three types of XML storage and show the pros (+) and cons (-) based on the different application design considerations.

In summary, using the relational tables to create XMLType views or simply deliver XML encapsulated output using SQL/XML functions or the DBMS_XMLGEN package, you have the normalized data storage with high-performance SQL queries. However, the DOM fidelity of the XML documents is lost.

The CLOB storage best preserves the original XML document and has the flexibility to handle XML Schema evolution. However, the run-time DOM building and DOM tree transversal slows down the SQL queries.

The XML Schema–based XMLTypes store XML in Object-Relational tables preserving the XML document with high-performance SQL queries resulting from query rewrite support. However, it has limited support of XML schema evolution and limited data replications support. You should analyze your application requirements and pick the best storage that meets your needs.

XMLType Object Tables or XMLType Columns?

Creating XMLType as a table column or as an object table is determined by whether you want to store relational data along with the XML documents. If there is relational data associated with the XML documents, such as the document create time and the current owner of the XML document, you can create a set of columns in relational tables to store such information and use XMLType columns to store XML documents.

Category	Relational Storage with XMLType Views	CLOB XMLType	Schema-Based XMLType
Modeling	(+) Relational modeling with data normalization (+) Relational storage that handles the schema evolution well (+) No XML overhead after data is stored in database (+) Easy reuse of the data	(–) No data normalization (+)Flexible storage when XML Schemas evolve or document size varies (–) Document view of the XML data prevents reuse as SQL data	(–) No data normalization (–) Limited XML Schema evolution support (+) Data reused by building up multiple views on XML data
Loading	(–) Low throughput for data uploading	(+) Fast XML uploading	(–) Low throughput for data uploading
Query	(+) High performance for SQL queries (–) Requires table joins for XML queries	(–) Low performance for XPath queries with run-time DOM building and DOM tree transversal.	(+) XPath queries are rewritten to SQL queries for high-performance data retrieval
XML fidelity	(+) No DOM fidelity	(+) Maintains the original XML byte for byte	(+) DOM fidelity as an option when setting the **xdb:maintainDOM= "true"**
Data replication	Full support	Full support	Limited support

TABLE 8-4. *Comparison of XML Storage*

On the other hand, there are options on how to create XMLType object tables. You can create an XMLType object table using the "CREATE TABLE ... OF XMLType" command or create the XMLType object table when registering XML schemas to the Oracle XML DB. However, the latter option allows you to use the Oracle XML DB Repository to manage the XML documents. By looking at what the Oracle XML DB Repository offers and what you need or how you can take advantage of the functionality, you can decide how to create the XMLType object tables.

Use Oracle XML DB Repository?

To use the Oracle XML DB Repository, you need to create XMLType tables by specifying the **xdb:defaultTable** attribute for the root element of the XML document in the XML schema. After you do so, Oracle XML DB will create XMLType Object tables when registering the XML schemas. Using XML DB Repository, you have the high-performance hierarchical document navigation and easy-to-use protocol interfaces for document management.

How to Retrieve and Generate XML

After you decide how to store XML documents, you need to figure out how to build the indexes and views for querying XML data, generating new XML based on the existing XML/non-XML data, and securing the XML data by controlling user access. We will discuss the details of these XML features in Chapter 11 and explore several solutions in the application development chapters.

How to Search XML Data

In Oracle Database 10*g*, there are two ways to search XML data using the XPath-based queries: Oracle Text searches using the CONTAINS() function and the XPath search using the XMLType.**existsNode()** function. In Oracle Database 10*g*, you can produce efficient searches by creating the CTXXPATH index for the XMLType.**existsNode()** queries. We will discuss this in Chapter 11.

How to Design XML Database for Web Applications

XML is widely used in content management and Web publishing systems. One of the reasons is that data in XML format can be easily transformed using XSLT to various presentation formats, such as HTML, WML (Wireless Markup Language), SVG, or any other Web publishing format that clients request. These kinds of applications normally have the structure shown in Figure 8-6.

In this type of application, an XML document can be stored in XML Schema–based XMLTypes so that you can extract the data for different content-publishing purposes and uses the Oracle XML DB Repository for easy document management. To reuse the XML data, XMLType views can be created, which provide "pretransformed" XML documents. Finally, indexes are usually created for frequently executed queries to speed XML retrieval from the database.

How to Design XML Database for Messaging Application

XML is widely used for application integration where applications run on different platforms or are from different vendors that need to exchange the application data. Figure 8-7 illustrates the architecture of an example XML-based messaging system. In this kind of application, you should think about using precompiled XSLT or XMLType views to transform the XML data into appropriate formats for the application receiving the XML messages.

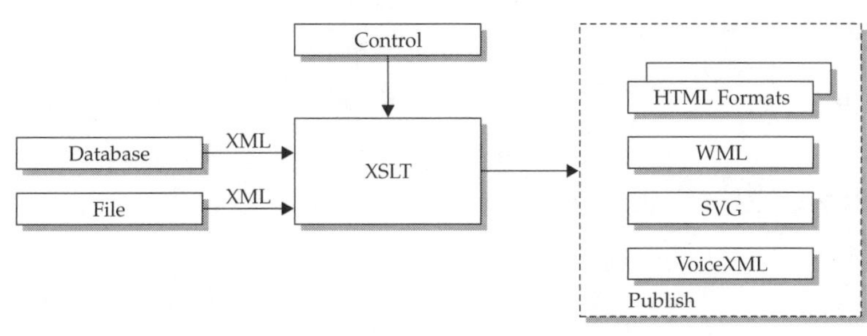

FIGURE 8-6. *XML-based web application architecture*

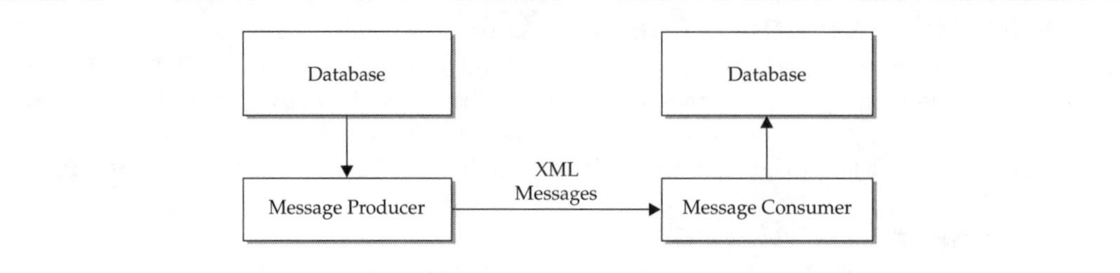

FIGURE 8-7. *XML messaging application*

Summary

The Oracle XML DB provides high-performance XML functionality seamlessly integrated with SQL. The standards-based XML loading, update, query, and transform interfaces greatly simplify your working with XML. Additionally, the Oracle Database 10*g* database provides an extensible platform from which the Oracle XDK can be used to build your customized solutions. Oracle Database 10*g* is a platform for building and deploying successful XML applications; however, you still need to follow some simple design steps to make best use of it. Now we are ready to show you the technical details of the Oracle XML DB functionality.

CHAPTER 9

Storing XML Data

In Oracle Database 10*g*, you have a number of choices for storing XML data. You can shred the XML documents and store the data in one or more relational tables, put them intact in CLOB XMLTypes, or register an XML schema and store them in an XML Schema–based XMLType with object-relational storage. If there is no requirement for updating the XML content, you can also store the XML documents externally by creating *External Tables*.

This chapter gives an overview of the XML storage options available in Oracle Database 10*g* and shows you various examples of how to use the technologies. You will also learn how to use the Oracle utilities including the SQL*Loader and XML SQL Utility (XSU) to load XML documents into either XMLType tables or relational tables in Oracle Database 10*g*. We start with the simplest storage format: the CLOB XMLTypes.

Storing XML Documents in CLOB XMLTypes

Using the CLOB XMLType, XML documents are stored as CLOBs with a set of XML interfaces provided by the XMLType. Though you can optionally carry out any XML processing during the data ingestion, such as validating the input XML against an XML schema or a DTD, the CLOB XMLType storage does not require any XML processing except well-formedness checking and entity resolution.

Updating and Querying CLOB XMLTypes

The CLOB XMLType storage best preserves the original format of XML documents and gives the maximum flexibility for XML schema evolution. However, storing XML documents in CLOB XMLTypes results in expensive processing overhead when querying the XML content, such as using the **XMLType.Extract()** or **XMLType.ExistsNode()** functions, because these operations require building an XML DOM tree in memory at run time and performing functional XPath evaluations. In addition, any update operation can be performed only at the document level. This means that you need to update the entire XML document for even a small change to one XML element. Therefore, normally you should avoid using XMLType functions to perform fine-grained XML updates or XPath-based queries on CLOB XMLTypes.

Instead, for XPath-based queries on CLOB XMLTypes, Oracle Text provides a full text search supporting a limited set of XPaths. This functionality allows you to perform XPath queries on CLOB XMLTypes utilizing the CONTEXT index created by Oracle Text, and it has proven very useful and scalable for enterprise applications, which we will discuss in Chapter 11.

Dealing with Character Encoding for CLOB XMLTypes

When storing XML documents in the Oracle database, you should know that a character set conversion is automatically performed during data insertions, which converts all the text data, including XML documents, to the database character set, except when stored as BLOB, NCHAR, or NCLOB data types.

Because of this implicit character set conversion, the actual XML data encoding and the encoding declaration in the **<?XML?>** prolog may not be the same. In the current Oracle Database 10*g* release,

XMLType APIs ignore the encoding declaration in the **<?XML?>** prolog and assume that XML data in CLOB XMLTypes is stored in the database character set. Therefore, when loading XML data from the client side, you need to make sure this conversion is properly performed.

To ensure proper conversion from the client character set to the database character set, you are required to set up the NLS_LANG environment variable to reflect the client character set encoding if the XML document is originally stored in a client character set that is different from the database character set. Otherwise, if the variable is set to be the same as the database character set, the original text will be stored as-is in the database without character validation and conversion.

In other words, if the NLS_LANG environment variable is not set or is set incorrectly and the XML document does not have the same encoding as the database, garbage data will be stored in the database.

NOTE
If the XML document contains characters that are invalid in the database character set, you will get an Invalid Character error during the data insertions to CLOB XMLTypes. The current solution for this is to use the NCLOB or BLOB for data storage in the database and build mid-tier XML applications or PL/SQL external procedures using the XDK APIs to process the XML data.

Because the character set conversion may result in conflict between the actual encoding and the encoding declaration in the **<?XML?>** prolog, when reading the XML data out of CLOB XMLTypes, you must do the reverse character set conversion or update the encoding declaration in the **<?XML?>** prolog to make them consistent. This is important because although an XML parser can use the first 4 bytes of the **<?XML?>** prolog to detect the encoding of XML documents, it can determine only whether the character encoding is an ASCII-based encoding or EBCDIC encoding. If it is an ASCII-based encoding, an XML parser can detect only whether it is UTF-8 or UTF-16. Otherwise, it depends on the encoding attributes in **<?XML?>.** Therefore, if you have XML documents not in UTF-8 or UTF-16 encoding, you *must* include a correct XML encoding declaration indicating which character encoding is in use, as follows:

```
<?xml version="1.0" encoding='Shift-JIS'?>
```

Storing XML Documents in XML Schema–based XMLTypes

To speed up the XPath queries and fine-grained updates on XMLTypes, you can create XML Schema–based XMLTypes. One way of doing this is to associate registered XML schemas with the XMLType columns or XMLType tables using XMLSCHEMA. You can also create XMLType tables by specifying the DEFAULT TABLE annotation in the registered XML schemas.

All these approaches create XML Schema–based XMLTypes, where sets of object-relational tables/objects are bound to the XML entities defined in the XML schema. The only difference between creating a default table during XML schema registration and using the XMLSCHEMA keyword is that the former approach allows XML documents conforming to the registered XML schema to be managed by Oracle XML DB repository. With the support of the XML DB repository, you can not only retrieve or update XML in SQL, but also manage XML documents stored in the XML DB repository using protocol interfaces such as FTP and HTTP/WebDAV.

XML Schema Registration

XML schema registration defines the XML-to-SQL mapping and a hierarchical object-relational structure for storing XML documents in the Oracle database. We will explore this using the DEMO user and the WebDAV folder created in Chapter 8.

First, you need to copy the XML schema for customer records, **contact_simple.xsd**, into the **/public** WebDAV folder. The following is the content of this schema:

```
<xsd:schema xmlns:xsd="http://www.w3.org/2001/XMLSchema">
 <xsd:element name="Customer" type="CustomerType"/>
  <xsd:complexType name="CustomerType">
   <xsd:sequence>
    <xsd:element name="NAME" type="xsd:string"/>
    <xsd:element name="EMAIL" type="xsd:string"/>
    <xsd:element name="ADDRESS" type="xsd:string"/>
    <xsd:element name="PHONE" type="phoneType"/>
    <xsd:element name="DESCRIPTION" type="contentType"/>
   </xsd:sequence>
  </xsd:complexType>
  <xsd:complexType name="ContentType" mixed="true">
   <xsd:sequence>
    <xsd:any minOccurs="0" maxOccurs="unbounded" processContents="skip"/>
   </xsd:sequence>
  </xsd:complexType>
  <xsd:simpleType name="phoneType">
   <xsd:restriction base="xsd:string">
    <xsd:pattern value="\(\d{3}\)\d{3}-\d{4}"/>
   </xsd:restriction>
  </xsd:simpleType>
</xsd:schema>
```

To register this XML schema to the XML DB, you can call the following PL/SQL procedure:

```
ALTER SESSION SET EVENTS='31098 trace name context forever';
BEGIN
 DBMS_XMLSCHEMA.registerURI(
     'http://localhost:8080/public/contact_simple.xsd',
     '/public/contact_simple.xsd',
      LOCAL=>TRUE, GENTYPES=>TRUE, GENBEAN=>FALSE, GENTABLES=>TRUE);
END;
```

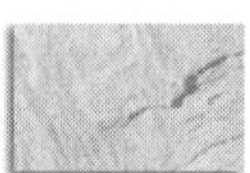

NOTE
To use the ALTER SESSION command, you need to log in as SYS and grant the ALTER SESSION *privilege to the DEMO user using "*GRANT ALTER SESSION TO DEMO*". Otherwise, you will get an ORA-01031: Insufficient Privileges error.*

In the **DBMS_XMLSCHEMA.registerURI()** function, the first parameter is the schema URI, **http://localhost:8080/public/contact_simple.xsd**, which uniquely identifies the registered XML schema in the XML DB. The second parameter is an XML DB URI (XDBUri), **/public/contact_simple.xsd**, pointing to the **contact_simple.xsd** file in the /**public** folder of the XML DB repository. The following parameters control whether the XML schema is registered as a local (LOCAL=>TRUE) or global (LOCAL=>FALSE) schema, whether object types (GENTYPES=>TRUE) and default tables (GENTABLES=>TRUE) will be created. The GENBEAN parameter is optional and does not perform any function at this time. If the XML schema is registered as a global XML schema in the XML DB, it can be shared across different database users. Otherwise, XML schema sharing is not allowed.

You can set GENTABLES=>FALSE if you do not want Oracle XML DB to create default tables during the XML schema registration. In this case, you can create XMLType tables using the XMLSCHEMA keyword, as in:

```
CREATE TABLE customer_xmltype_tbl OF XMLTYPE
 XMLSCHEMA "http://localhost:8080/public/contact_simple.xsd"
 ELEMENT "Customer";
```

Additionally, you can use the following syntax to define XMLType columns using XML Schema–based storage:

```
CREATE TABLE customer_col_tbl(
 id NUMBER,
 record XMLType)
XMLTYPE COLUMN record STORE AS OBJECT RELATIONAL
XMLSCHEMA "http://localhost:8080/public/contact_simple.xsd"
ELEMENT "Customer";
```

Since the same storage techniques apply to both XMLType tables and XMLType columns, we will discuss only the details of how to use XML Schema-based XMLType tables in later sections.

During XML schema registration, you can use the following command to create a trace file in the USER_DUMP_DIR showing the DDLs used to create the object tables and datatypes:

```
ALTER SESSION SET EVENTS='31098' TRACE NAME CONTEXT FOREVER;
```

To locate the trace file, you need to check the current session ID by querying the V$SESSION and V$PROCESS views. Before selecting from the V$SESSION and V$PROCESS views in the DEMO user, you need to log in as SYS and grant to the DEMO user the SELECT privilege on V_$SESSION and V_$PROCESS views, as follows:

```
GRANT SELECT ON V_$SESSION TO DEMO;
GRANT SELECT ON V_$PROCESS TO DEMO;
```

NOTE
Since V$SESSION and V$PROCESS are just synonyms for the views, you cannot grant any privileges on them.

By issuing the following SQL command, you can find the ID of the session corresponding to the trace file:

```
SELECT a.spid
FROM V$PROCESS a, V$SESSION b
WHERE a.addr=b.paddr
AND b.audsid=userenv('sessionid');
```

This returns the following:

```
SPID
------------
2796
```

The trace file has a name structured as **orclX_ora_<Session_Id>.trc,** and you can get the USER_DUMP_DIR by issuing the following command in a SYS user account:

```
SQL> SHOW PARAMETERS user_dump_dest
NAME              TYPE         VALUE
-----------------------------------------------------------
user_dump_dest    string       D:\ORACLE\ADMIN\ORCLX\UDUMP
```

Thus, the trace file is **orclX_ora_2796.trc,** in the USER_DUMP_DIR verified by running the following:

```
SQL> host ls d:\oracle\admin\orclX\udump\orclX_ora_2796.trc
orclX_ora_2796.trc
```

Because this file lists the set of DDLs used to create the object table and data types, it is a good reference when debugging XML schema registrations.

Now, let's examine the created storage structure in more detail by issuing the following command in SQL*Plus:

```
SQL> SELECT object_name, object_type
  2  FROM USER_OBJECTS
  3  WHERE object_name LIKE '%Customer%';
OBJECT_NAME                 OBJECT_TYPE
-------------------------- --------------------
Customer260_TAB             TABLE
Customer260_TAB$xd          TRIGGER
CustomerType259_T           TYPE
```

The result shows that three objects were created during the XML schema registration. If you further examine the types and the table's definitions, you will see that the objects created are not limited to these. First, you can describe the **Customer260_TAB** table as follows:

```
SQL> DESC "Customer260_TAB";
```

This results in the following:

```
Name                                      Null?    Type
----------------------------------------- -------- ----------------------------
TABLE of SYS.XMLTYPE(XMLSchema "http://localhost:8080/public/contact_
simple.xsd" Element "
Customer") STORAGE Object-relational TYPE "CustomerType259_T"
```

NOTE
*If an XML element uses mixed case or lowercase, the default table and object names by default will be case sensitive. Therefore, you need to use double quotes when referring these names, as in **"Customer260_TAB"**.*

The preceding description shows that:

- **Customer260_TAB** is an XMLType table.
- The XMLType objects in the table are associated with the registered XML schema, **http://localhost:8080/public/contact_simple.xsd**.
- The root element of the XML document is **<Customer>.**
- The object type used to store the XMLTypes is **CustomerType259_T**.

Looking at the description of **CustomerType259_T**, you can see that this type contains

```
SQL> DESC "CustomerType259_T"
 "CustomerType259_T" is NOT FINAL
   Name                                      Null?    Type
 ----------------------------------------- -------- ----------------------------
 SYS_XDBPD$                                           XDB.XDB$RAW_LIST_T
 NAME                                                 VARCHAR2(4000 CHAR)
 EMAIL                                                VARCHAR2(4000 CHAR)
 ADDRESS                                              VARCHAR2(4000 CHAR)
 PHONE                                                VARCHAR2(4000 CHAR)
 DESCRIPTION                                          contentType257_T
```

All the XML elements in XMLTypes are mapped to the corresponding database data types. In this example, the NAME, EMAIL, ADDRESS, and PHONE elements as simple types in the XML schema are stored as VARCHAR2. Since there is no limit on the string length in the XML schema, Oracle XML DB sets 4000 characters as the default length for these columns. On the other hand, new object types are created for the complex types defined in the XML schema. In this example, **contentType257_T** is created to store the customer descriptions, which is further shown as follows:

```
SQL> DESC "contentType257_T";
 "contentType257_T" is NOT FINAL
 Name                                      Null?    Type
 ----------------------------------------- -------- ----------------------------
 SYS_XDBPD$                                         XDB.XDB$RAW_LIST_T
 SYS_XDBANY258$                                     VARCHAR2(4000 CHAR)
```

Note that Oracle XML DB defines the SYS_XDBANY258$ column as a VARCHAR2 (4000) to store the **<xsd:any/>** element defined in the **<DESCRIPTION>** element. The SYS_XDBPD$ column is a *position descriptor* column created by the XML DB to preserve the DOM fidelity of XML documents. Information, such as comments, processing instructions, namespace prefixes, and the order of sibling XML elements, is stored in this SYS_XDBPD$ column. Therefore, this column is used to preserve the integrity of the original XML document for the DOM transversals.

To examine further details of the **Customer260_TAB** table, you can query the USER_TAB_COLS view:

```
SQL> SELECT column_name,data_type,
       CASE WHEN hidden_column='YES' THEN 'hidden'
            WHEN virtual_column='YES' THEN 'virtual'
            ELSE null END as attr
     FROM USER_TAB_COLS
     WHERE table_name='Customer260_TAB'
     ORDER by virtual_column desc, column_name;

COLUMN_NAME          DATA_TYPE                 ATTR
-------------------- ------------------------- -------
SYS_NC_ROWINFO$      XMLTYPE                   virtual
XMLDATA              CustomerType259_T         hidden
ACLOID               RAW                       hidden
OWNERID              RAW                       hidden
SYS_NC00007$         RAW                       hidden
SYS_NC00014$         RAW                       hidden
SYS_NC_OID$          RAW                       hidden
SYS_NC00009$         VARCHAR2                  hidden
SYS_NC00010$         VARCHAR2                  hidden
SYS_NC00011$         VARCHAR2                  hidden
SYS_NC00012$         VARCHAR2                  hidden
SYS_NC00016$         VARCHAR2                  hidden
SYS_NC00008$         XDB$RAW_LIST_T            hidden
SYS_NC00015$         XDB$RAW_LIST_T            hidden
XMLEXTRA             XMLTYPEEXTRA              hidden
SYS_NC00004$         XMLTYPEPI                 hidden
SYS_NC00005$         XMLTYPEPI                 hidden
SYS_NC00013$         contentType257_T          hidden
```

Note that the CASE expression selects a result from one or more alternatives. It uses an optional SELECTOR, to specify an expression whose value determines which alternative to return. A normal CASE expression has the following form:

```
CASE selector
   WHEN expression1 THEN result1
   WHEN expression2 THEN result2
   ...
   WHEN expressionN THEN resultN
  [ELSE resultN+1]
END;
```

From the query, you can see that the **Customer260_TAB** table contains one virtual column called SYS_NC_ROWINFO$ and several hidden columns, including XMLDATA, ACLOID, OWNERID, XMLEXTRA and a set of **$SYS_NC<number>$** columns.

The virtual column, SYS_NC_ROWINFO$, is an XMLType object that identifies the rows of the XMLType table. For example, in the triggers of XMLType tables, you can use **:new.SYS_NC_ROWINFO$** to refer to the current row of data.

The XMLDATA column refers to the SQL objects used for storing the XMLTypes. It is useful when you want to query or create indexes on XMLTypes by directly working on the SQL objects. In the preceding example, XMLDATA is an alias for the **CustomerType259_T** object. Therefore, you can add a unique constraint on the EMAIL element by referring to it as XMLDATA.EMAIL, as follows:

```
ALTER TABLE Customer260_TAB ADD UNIQUE(XMLDATA.EMAIL);
```

The XMLDATA.EMAIL refers to the object storing the content of the EMAIL elements in the customer records. With the UNIQUE constraint added, if you try to insert the same customer record multiple times, you get the following error:

```
ORA-00001: unique constraint (DEMO.SYS_C003626) violated
```

Some of the hidden columns in **Customer260_TAB** are for Oracle XML DB repository use. For example, in Oracle XML DB repository, the *Access Control List (ACL)* defines the permissions for each resource. The ACLOID specifies the ACL permissions for the XMLType table and the OWNERID specifies the ID of the table owner. The other hidden columns are used to create the hierarchical relationships between XML elements.

Except for XMLDATA and SYS_NC_ROWINFO$, you should never access or manipulate these XMLType table columns directly.

XML Schema Annotations

To control the mapping between XMLType storage and XML schemas, you need to use Oracle XML DB annotations. In Oracle Database 10*g*, these XML Schema annotations are a set of attributes added to an XML schema declaring the SQL object names, data types, and various storage options. All of these annotations are in the Oracle XML DB namespace, **http://xmlns.oracle.com/xdb**, normally using the **xdb** prefix. Basically, you can use these annotations to specify the following:

- **DefaultTable** The name and storage attributes of the default XMLType table storing the XML documents.
- **SQLNames** The SQL names for the XML elements defined in the XML schema.
- **SQLTypes** The names of the SQL data types used to store simple or complex data types defined in the XML schema. For an unbounded XML element mapping to a collection SQL type, **xdb:SQLCollType** is used to specify the type name.
- **MaintainDOM** The attribute that tells Oracle XML DB whether to preserve DOM fidelity of the element on output.
- **Storage Options** The XML DB annotations, such as **xdb:storeVarrayAsTable**, **xdb:mapUnboundedStringToLob, xdb:maintainOrder**, and **xdb:SQLInline**, specify the options for optimizing storage.

Let's examine the following annotated XML schema for the customer records, **customer_simple_ann.xsd**, explore some useful design techniques, and then register it to the XML DB.

```
<xsd:schema xmlns:xsd="http://www.w3.org/2001/XMLSchema"
 xmlns:xdb="http://xmlns.oracle.com/xdb" xdb:storeVarrayAsTable="true">
 <xsd:element name="Customer" type="CustomerType"
      xdb:defaultTable="CUSTOMER"/>
 <xsd:complexType name="CustomerType" xdb:maintainDOM="false">
  <xsd:sequence>
   <xsd:element name="NAME" type="xsd:string"
      xdb:SQLName="NAME" xdb:SQLType="VARCHAR2"/>
   <xsd:element name="EMAIL" type="xsd:string"
      xdb:SQLName="EMAIL" xdb:SQLType="VARCHAR2"/>
   <xsd:element name="ADDRESS" type="xsd:string" maxOccurs="unbounded"
      xdb:SQLName="ADDRESS" xdb:SQLCollType="ADDRESS_TYPE"
       xdb:SQLType="VARCHAR2" xbd:maintainOrder="false"/>
   <xsd:element name="PHONE" type="phoneType" xdb:SQLName="PHONE"/>
   <xsd:element name="DESCRIPTION" type="contentType"/>
  </xsd:sequence>
 </xsd:complexType>
 <xsd:complexType name="contentType" mixed="true"
       xdb:SQLType="CLOB" xdb:maintainDOM="true">
  <xsd:sequence>
   <xsd:any minOccurs="0" maxOccurs="unbounded" processContents="skip"/>
  </xsd:sequence>
 </xsd:complexType>
 <xsd:simpleType name="phoneType">
  <xsd:restriction base="xsd:string">
   <xsd:pattern value="\(\d{3}\)\d{3}-\d{4}"/>
  </xsd:restriction>
 </xsd:simpleType>
</xsd:schema>
```

Looking at the preceding example, the first thing to do when annotating the XML schema is to include the Oracle XML DB namespace declaration, **xmlns:xdb="http://xmlns.oracle.com/xdb"**, in the **<schema>** element. This namespace prefix is then used to qualify all the Oracle XML DB annotations.

Next, **xdb:storeVarrayAsTable="true"** is a global XML DB annotation, which tells the XML DB to store all the VARRAY elements in nested object tables. This annotation helps to speed up the queries on XML elements that are defined with **maxOccurs > 1**. For example, in **customer_simple_ann.xsd**, this annotation affects the storage of the **<ADDRESS>** elements.

In addition, you can specify an XML DB annotation **xdb:mapUnboundedStringToLob="true"** in the **<schema>** element to map unbounded strings to CLOB and unbounded binary data to BLOB with out-of-line table storage. By default, it is set to be **false** so that all unbounded strings defined in the XML schema map to VARCHAR2(4000) and unbounded binary data maps to RAW(2000) with inline table storage. Since inline table storage does not efficiently store large XML documents, you should set **xdb:mapUnboundedStringToLob="true"**.

For all the global complex and simple types, you can define the following XML DB annotations to specify the corresponding SQL names and data types:

- **xdb:SQLType** Specifies the SQL type mapped to the XML schema type definition. You can use this annotation to avoid having the XML DB generate names for the SQL data types.
- **xdb:maintainDOM** Specifies whether the complex type should maintain DOM fidelity. Normally, you should set this to **false**. Otherwise, the XML DB by default will add the SYS_XDBPD$ attribute (position descriptor) to each created object type to preserve information such as comments, processing instructions, and the sibling element orders in XML, and thus increases the storage overhead. For example, to avoid maintaining the DOM fidelity in the customer records, **xdb:maintainDOM="false"** is set on **CustomerType**.

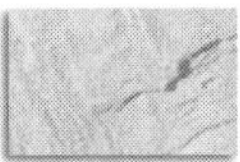

NOTE
***xdb:SQLName** is not allowed on the complexType or simpleType definitions. Otherwise, you will get the following error:* ORA-30937: No schema definition for 'SQLName' (namespace 'http://xmlns.oracle.com/xdb') in parent 'complexType'

For the root element of the XML document, you should specify the **xdb:defaultTable** attribute and optionally use **xdb:tableProps** to set the table attributes:

- **xdb:defaultTable** Specifies the name of the table into which XML instances of this schema should be stored. It establishes a link between the XML DB repository and this default table so that any insertion, update, or deletion of the XML documents conforming to this XML schema in the XML DB repository will have the corresponding changes in the default table, and vice versa. In the example, a **customer** table will be created as the default table.
- **xdb:tableProps** Specifies the default table properties in SQL syntax that is appended to the CREATE TABLE clause.

For all XML elements, you should specify the element names and the element type if the type they are based on is not among the global types defined in the XML schema that have already been annotated. The following lists the XML DB annotations for the XML elements:

- **xdb:SQLName** Specifies the name of the SQL object that maps to the XML element.
- **xdb:SQLType** Specifies the name of the SQL type corresponding to the XML element.
- **xdb:SQLInline** Specifies whether Oracle XML DB should generate a new object table and define XMLType REFs to store the XML elements. The default setting is **true**, which specifies not to define REFs. The **true** setting of this annotation affects all the top-level elements declared in the XML schema and the XML element with **maxOccurs > 1**. You need to set this to **false** for out-of-line storage. This will give better performance by avoiding table locks.
- **xdb:SQLCollType** Specifies the name of the SQL collection type corresponding to the XML element that has **maxOccurs > 1**. For example, in the **<ADDRESS>** element, the xdb:SQLCollType="ADDRESS_TYPE" is added. By default, the collection will use a VARRAY. Because **xdb:storeVarrayAsTable="true"** is set, the storage of the VARRAY

is a Ordered Collections in Table (OCTs) instead of LOBs (default). This is useful when you want to create constrains on the element.

Instead of covering all the possible annotations, we listed the most frequently used XML DB annotations. In summary, you should keep the following points in mind when annotating XML schemas.

First, you should specify the name of the default table using **xdb:defaultTable** and a SQL name for each XML element and data type in the XML schema using **xdb:SQLName**, **xdb:SQLCollType**, or **xdb:SQLType**. You should notice that, in the example:

- **xdb:SQLName** defines the SQL names for the XML elements
- **xdb:SQLCollType** defines the SQL names only for the XML elements with **maxOccurs>1**.
- **xdb:SQLType** defines the SQL names for all the complexTypes or the simpleTypes that do not use the default mapping provided by Oracle XML DB.

Specifying the SQL names using XML schema annotations is useful because the system-generated names are not easy to remember. You should also consider specifying all SQL names capitalized to eliminate case-sensitive names in the database, which require using double quotes when referring to the SQL objects. For example, without capitalization, you have to use **"**Customer260_TAB" versus CUSTOMER260_TAB to refer to the default table storing the customer records.

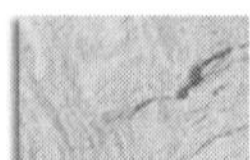

NOTE
*For XML elements and types, if no **xdb:SQLName**, **xdb:SQLType**, or **xdb:SQLCollType** is specified, Oracle XML DB will use the name of the element or data type to create the SQL name. Because XML is case sensitive, the SQL name will be case sensitive, requiring you to use quotes around it for all references. These annotations are also useful if the XML element or type name is long, or has a name conflict in the XML schema.*

Next, you should define the storage minimizing any extra data storage, such as avoid preserving DOM fidelity. It is also useful to store sub-trees or complex types as CLOBs by setting the **xdb: SQLTypes ="CLOB"** when no XPath-based queries on the content are required. Oracle XML DB will not shred this XML data, thus saving time and resources.

Finally, when working with small but unbounded XML elements you should store the content as VARRAYs by setting the **xdb:storeVarrayAsTable="false"**. For large unbounded XML elements, you can instead use nested tables by specifying the **xdb:storeVarrayAsTables="true**" in the **<schema>** element or even use nested tables by setting **xdb:maintainOrder="false"** on the element for better performance.

XML Data Loading

After you have defined the XMLType storage, you can load data into XMLType tables by using SQL, the protocol APIs, or the SQL*Loader utility.

Using SQL Command

The simplest way to load XML data into XMLType tables is through the INSERT SQL command, such as in the following example:

```
INSERT INTO customer VALUES(XMLType('<Customer>
  <NAME>Steve Joes</NAME>
  <EMAIL>Steve.Joes@example.com</EMAIL>
  <ADDRESS>Someroad, Somecity, Redwood Shores, CA 94065, U.S.A</ADDRESS>
  <PHONE>6505723456</PHONE>
  <DESCRIPTION>Very Important US Customer</DESCRIPTION>
</Customer>').CreateSchemaBasedXML(
      'http://localhost:8080/public/contact_simple_ann.xsd'));
```

Using this approach, you can construct the XMLType instance from XML in VARCHAR2, CLOB, or BFILE and optionally use the XMLType.**CreateSchemaBasedXML()** function to refer to a registered XML schema.

Without the XMLType.**CreateSchemaBasedXML()** function, you can insert XML into XML schema-based XMLTypes by including an XML Schema reference in the root element of the XML document using the XML schema location attributes, including the **xsi:schemaLocation** or **xsi:noNamespaceSchemaLocation** attribute:

```
INSERT INTO customer
 values(XMLType('<Customer xmlns:xsi="http://www.w3.org/2001/XMLSchema
   -instance"  xsi:noNamespaceSchemaLocation="http://localhost:8080/public/
   contact_simple_ann.xsd">
 <NAME>Steve Joes</NAME>
 <EMAIL>Steve.Joes@example.com</EMAIL>
  <ADDRESS>Someroad, Somecity, Redwood Shores, CA 94065, U.S.A</ADDRESS>
  <PHONE>6505723456</PHONE>
  <DESCRIPTION>Very Important US Customer</DESCRIPTION>
</Customer>'));
```

The **xmlns:xsi="http://www.w3.org/2001/XMLSchema-instance"** attribute declares the namespace for the XML Schema instance. The **xsi:noNamespaceSchemaLocation= "http://localhost:8080/public/contact_simple_ann.xsd"** attribute specifies the registered XML schema URL. In this example, since the XML document doesn't have a namespace, **xsi:noNamespaceSchemaLocation** is used. If the XML document contains a namespace, for example, the XML schema of the XML document defines a target namespace as **targetNamespace="http://www.example.com/customer"**, you need to use the **xsi:schemaLocation** attribute as follows:

```
xsi:schemaLocation= "http://www.example.com/customer http://localhost:8080/
public/contact_simple_ann.xsd"
```

The attribute contains the **targetNamespace**, **http://www.example.com/customer**, and the URL of the XML schema, **http://localhost:8080/public/contact_simple_ann.xsd**.

Using Oracle XML DB Repository Interfaces

The XML DB repository provides protocol interfaces, including FTP and WebDAV/HTTP interfaces, to insert XML and other types of documents. As discussed in Chapter 8, you can create a WebDAV folder and use it to copy or edit XML files in the XML DB repository as if it were another directory on your disk. When using the protocol interfaces, the XML document must have the XML schema location attributes to ensure that the data is inserted into the default tables created during the XML schema registration. The following example utilizes the FTP interface to insert a customer record to the default **customer** table after registering the **contact_simple_ann.xsd** to the XML DB:

```
D:\>ftp
ftp> open localhost 2100
Connected to [Machine_Name] 220 [Machine_Name].FTP Server (Oracle XML
DB/Oracle Database 10g Enterprise Edition Release X.X.X.X.X) ready.
User ([Machine_Name]:(none)): demo
331 pass required for DEMO
Password:
230 DEMO logged in
ftp> cd public
250 CWD Command successful
ftp> put customer1.xml
200 PORT Command successful
150 ASCII Data Connection
226 ASCII Transfer Complete
ftp: 444 bytes sent in 0.00Seconds 444000.00Kbytes/sec.
ftp> ls customer1.xml
200 PORT Command successful
150 ASCII Data Connection
customer1.xml
226 ASCII Transfer Complete
ftp: 15 bytes received in 0.00Seconds 15000.00Kbytes/sec.
ftp>bye
```

After the operations, the new customer record is inserted into both the XML DB repository in **/public** directory and the default **customer** table. In addition to the two records inserted using SQL, there are now three records in the **customer** table:

```
SQL> SELECT count(1) FROM customer;
  COUNT(1)
----------
         3
```

We will discuss the XML DB repository features in the "Oracle XML DB Repository" section. For now, you just need to know that no matter what directory in the XML DB repository is used to store the XML document, the new customer record will always be inserted into the default XMLType table as long as it refers to the corresponding URL of the registered XML schema.

Using SQL*Loader

SQL*Loader has been the predominant tool for loading data into the Oracle databases. In Oracle Database 10g, SQL*Loader supports loading XML data into XMLType columns or XMLType tables independent of the underlying storage. In other words, you can use this same method to load XML data to CLOBs or object-relational XMLTypes. Additionally, SQL*Loader allows XML data to be loaded using both conventional and direct path methods. The conventional path is the default mode that uses SQL to load data into Oracle databases. The direct path mode bypasses SQL and streams the data directly into the Oracle database files.

To load XML data using SQL*Loader, you need a control file describing the input data and the target table or table columns. For example, to insert two customer records as in **customer3.xml** and **customer4.xml** into the **customer** table, you can create a control file as shown in the following:

```
LOAD DATA
INFILE *
INTO TABLE customer
APPEND
XMLType(XMLDATA)(
 lobfn FILLER CHAR TERMINATED BY ',',
 XMLDATA LOBFILE(lobfn) TERMINATED BY EOF
 )
BEGINDATA
xml/customer3.xml,
xml/customer4.xml
```

The control file tells SQL*Loader to load data (LOAD DATA) by appending (APPEND) the new data contained within the control file (INFILE *) to the **customer** table (INTO TABLE **customer**). XMLType(XMLDATA) refers to new data as XMLType. Since this is an appending operation, it means that SQL*Loader will load the new data without overwriting the old customer records. If you use REPLACE instead, the old customer records will be deleted before new data is inserted.

The **lobfn** operator is a FILLER field. In SQL*Loader, FILLER fields are used to collect the data from the inputs. In other words, the FILLER fields are not mapped to any table columns; instead they are used to skip or select data from the input data. In this example, **lobfn** is used to get the names of the XML documents after BEGIN DATA and the names are delimitated by comas (TERMINATED BY ','). The actual XML data in the files are delimitated by the end-of-file (EOF).

After the control file is created, you can set the **$ORACLE_HOME\bin** directory in your PATH environment and run the following command to invoke the SQL*Loader command-line utility **sqlldr**:

```
D:\>sqlldr userid=demo/demo control=customerLoad.ctl
SQL*Loader: Release X on Thu Jun 26 22:26:53 2003
 (c) Copyright 2001 Oracle Corporation.  All rights reserved.
Commit point reached - logical record count 2
```

The **userid** specifies the username and password for the database user who owns the **customer** table. The **control** option specifies the filename for the control file. The result shows that two logical records are recognized by SQL*Loader. The further logging information for **sqlldr** can be find in the **<control_file_name>.log** file. You can specify **direct=y** if you want to use the direct path mode to load the XML data. Compared to the conventional path mode, the direct path mode is faster because it bypasses the SQL layer and streams XML data into the Oracle database files without invoking any triggers or constraint checking.

XML Schema Validation

During XML loading or after content updates on the XML Schema–based XMLTypes, Oracle XML DB simply checks to see if the XML document is well-formed augmented with object checks instead of performing a full XML Schema validation. In other words, Oracle XML DB performs only limited checks to make sure the XML document conforms to the object-relational storage. For example, the XML DB will check whether the **<PHONE>** element exists before inserting the customer records. It will not stop the data insertion when the phone numbers violate the string pattern defined in the XML schema.

To void invalid data that could be inserted into XMLTypes, you need to explicitly call for XML Schema validation. The simplest way to do this is to set up a TRIGGER before the INSERT actions as follows:

```
CREATE OR REPLACE TRIGGER customer_insert
  AFTER INSERT ON customer
  FOR EACH ROW
  DECLARE
  doc XMLType;
  BEGIN
    doc := :new.SYS_NC_ROWINFO$;
    XMLType.schemaValidate(doc);
  END;
```

After the trigger is created, full validation is performed when you insert sample data into the **customer** table:

```
INSERT INTO customer VALUES(
  XMLType('<CUSTOMER xmlns:xsi="http://www.w3.org/2001/XMLSchema-instance"
    xsi:noNamespaceSchemaLocation="http://localhost:8080/public/
    contact_simple_ann.xsd">
  <NAME>Steve Joes</NAME>
  <EMAIL>Steve.Joes@example.com</EMAIL>
  <ADDRESS>Someroad, Somecity, Redwood Shores, CA 94065, U.S.A</ADDRESS>
  <PHONE>6505723456</PHONE>
  <DESCRIPTION>Very Important US Customer</DESCRIPTION>
</CUSTOMER>'));
```

Thus this example returns the following errors:

```
INSERT INTO customer
*
ERROR at line 1:
ORA-31154: invalid XML document
ORA-19202: Error occurred in XML processing
LSX-00333: literal "6505723456" is not valid with respect to the pattern
ORA-06512: at "SYS.XMLTYPE", line 333
ORA-06512: at "DEMO.CUSTOMER_INSERT", line 5
ORA-04088: error during execution of trigger 'DEMO.CUSTOMER_INSERT'
```

As you see, the error message states that the phone number does not follow the string pattern defined in the XML schema. After you have updated the phone number, you can try again:

```
SQL> INSERT INTO customer VALUES(
  XMLType('<Customer xmlns:xsi="http://www.w3.org/2001/XMLSchema-instance"
      xsi:noNamespaceSchemaLocation="http://localhost:8080/public/
    contact_simple_ann.xsd">
 <NAME>Steve Joes</NAME>
 <EMAIL>Steve.Joes@example.com</EMAIL>
 <ADDRESS>Someroad, Somecity, Redwood Shores, CA 94065, U.S.A
 </ADDRESS>
 <PHONE>(650)572-3456</PHONE>
 <DESCRIPTION>Very Important US Customer</DESCRIPTION>
</CUSTOMER>'));
```

The new valid customer record is inserted. You can check the XML Schema validation status of an XMLType object using either the **XMLType.isSchemaValid()** function or the **XMLType .isSchemaValidated()** function:

```
SQL> SELECT x.isSchemaValid() FROM customer x;
X.ISSCHEMAVALID()
-----------------
                1
                0
             ...0
```

The preceding result shows that, so far, there is only one record in the table and it is valid against the XML schema. The records inserted previously do not have a valid status. This is because the **XMLType.schemaValidate()** function validates the XMLType object and updates the validation status of XMLType objects in the XML DB.

NOTE
Turning on full validation will have a significant negative effect on INSERT performance, thus should be used only if necessary. It is usually better to do validation checks at the time of document creation or in the middle tier.

Oracle XML DB Repository

Oracle XML DB Repository can function as a file system in the Oracle database. Any data in the Oracle XML DB Repository maps to a resouce which has a pathname (or a URL) and is stored either in a BLOB or an XMLType object. The XML DB repository provides extensive management facilities for these content resources.

You have learned how to load XML through the protocol interfaces of the XML DB repository. In this section, we will discuss other topics, such as applying version control to documents and creating links, and managing resources. We will also discuss the major PL/SQL packages that support this functionality:

- **DBMS_XDB** provides functions for resource and session management of the XML DB repository. It also provides functionality to rebuild the hierarchical indexes.
- **DBMS_XDB_VERSION** provides functions for the version control of the resources.

Resource Management

In Oracle Database 10*g*, you can use the DBMS_XDB package to create and delete resources, folders, and links for the resources. You can also use this package to lock/unlock resources when reading or updating XML data:

```
DECLARE
 res BOOLEAN;
 xr REF XMLType;
 x  XMLType;
BEGIN
  FOR po_rec IN (SELECT rownum id, ref(p) xref FROM customer p
      ORDER BY rowid)
  LOOP
    res:=DBMS_XDB.createResource('/public/customer'||po_rec.id||
    '.xml', po_rec.xref);
  END LOOP;
END;
```

In this example, all of the customer records are read out of the **customer** table, and XML resource documents are created in the **/public** directory of the XML DB repository using the **DBMS_XDB .createResource ()** function.You can additionally create a **/public/important_customer** folder in the XML DB repository as follows:

```
DECLARE
   retb BOOLEAN;
BEGIN
   retb := DBMS_XDB.createFolder('/public/important_customer');
   COMMIT;
END;
/
```

Then, you can create a resource such as **README.txt** to explain the content in this folder:

```
DECLARE
  res BOOLEAN;
BEGIN
  res :=
DBMS_XDB.createResource('/public/important_customer/README.txt',
   'This folder lists all of the US customer who are important to
   our business');
  COMMIT;
END;
/
```

Since you already have a set of customers listed in the **/public** directory, you can create a set of links instead of creating a second copy of the data:

```
EXEC DBMS_XDB.link('/public/customer1.xml',
                    '/public/important_customer/','SteveJones.xml');
```

If you want to delete a resource, you can use the **DBMS_XDB. DeleteResource()** function, as follows:

```
DBMS_XDB.DeleteResource('/public/important_customer/SteveJones.xml');
DBMS_XDB.DeleteResource ('/public/customer1.xml');
```

You can delete a resource with resources linking to it. However, after the original resource is removed, all the linked resoruces are no longer references. Each of them instead will hold a copy of the data.

Version Control

The DBMS_XDB_VERSION and DBMS_XDB PL/SQL packages implement Oracle XML DB versioning functions, which provide a way to create and manage different versions of a *Version-Controlled Resource (VCR)* in Oracle XML DB.

When an XML DB resource is turned into a VCR, a flag is set to mark it as a VCR and the current resource becomes the initail version. This version is not physically stored in the database. In other words, there is no extra copy of this resource stored when it is versioned. Subsequent versions are stored in the same tables. Since the version resource is a system-generated resource, it does not have a pathname. But you can still access the resource via the functions provided in the DBMS_XDB_VERSION package.

When the resource is checked out, no other user can make updates to it. When the resource is updated the first time, a copy of the resource is created. You can make several changes to the resource without checking it back in. You will always get the latest copy of the resource, even if you are a different user. When a resource is checked back in, the original version that was checked out is placed into historical version storage.

The versioning properties for the VCR are maintained within the XML DB repository. In this release, versioning *only* works for non-schema-based resources. Thus XMLTypes based upon shredded XML documents or XMLType CLOBs that have schemas attached are not officially supported to use VCRs. However, we have found that as long as you do not create unique meta-data associated with a particular version, such as an index, VCRs will work.

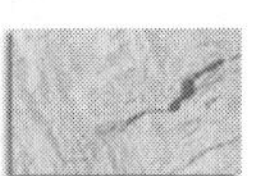

NOTE
You cannot switch a VCR back to a non-VCR.

Oracle XML DB provides functions to keep track of all changes on Oracle XML DB VCRs. The following code demonstrates these functions:

```
DECLARE
 resid DBMS_XDB_VERSION.RESID_TYPE;
BEGIN
 resid := DBMS_XDB_VERSION.MakeVersioned('/public/important_customer/
      SteveJones.xml');
END;
/
```

You can get the resource ID of the VCR as follows:

```
SET AUTOPRINT ON
VAR OUT CLOB
DECLARE
 resid DBMS_XDB_VERSION.RESID_TYPE;
 res XMLType;
BEGIN
 resid := DBMS_XDB_VERSION.MakeVersioned('/public/important_customer/SteveJones.xml');
 -- Obtain the resource
 res := DBMS_XDB_VERSION.GetResourceByResId(resid);
 SELECT res.getClobVal() INTO :OUT FROM dual;
END;
```

To update a VCR, you need to first check out the resource, make file updates, and then check them back in to the XML DB repository, as follows:

```
DECLARE
 resid DBMS_XDB_VERSION.RESID_TYPE;
BEGIN
 DBMS_XDB_VERSION.CheckOut('/public/important_customer/SteveJones.xml');
 resid :=
   DBMS_XDB_VERSION.CheckIn('/public/important_customer/SteveJones.xml');
END;
```

Note that the resource is not updated until the new file is checked in. If you want to cancel the updates after the checkout, you can "uncheck out" the resource as follows:

```
DECLARE
resid DBMS_XDB_VERSION.RESID_TYPE;
BEGIN
 resid :=
  DBMS_XDB_VERSION.UncheckOut('/public/important_customer/SteveJones.xml ');
END;
```

Storing XML Documents in Relational Tables

Relational tables are normally designed without considering XML storage. However, in many cases these tables can be used to store *shredded* XML documents and produce a useful XML representation by creating XMLType views using Oracle Database 10*g* XML features or generating XML using the Oracle XDK.

Storing XML data in relational tables is useful if your application needs to avoid the limitations of the XMLType storage, such as limited XML schema evolution and data replication. Relational storage is also widely used by applications that require fine-grained access to the data in XML documents while not needing to preserve the complete hierarchical structure of XML.

Oracle Database 10*g* provides extensive support for loading, exporting, and processing XML data into relational tables. To load XML data, you can use the *XML SQL Utility (XSU)*. XSU provides both Java and PL/SQL program interfaces and command-line utilities. Built on XSU, the *TransX*

Utility (XML Translation) further simplifies the character set conversion during data loading, and the *XSQL Servlet* provides the HTTP interfaces. If the functionality provided by these utilities is not sufficient for your application, you can always use their programmatic APIs in conjunction with other XDK libraries to build your own custom solution.

XML SQL Utility

XSU provides Java-based APIs, command-line utilities, and PL/SQL packages that support loading XML data into relational tables including tables with XMLType columns. We will discuss how you can use its functionality in the following sections.

Canonical Mapping

The first thing you need to understand before using XSU is the canonical mapping used by XSU to map XML to relational tables and render the results of SQL queries in XML. In this canonical mapping, the **<ROWSET>** element is the root element of the XML document, and its child **<ROW>** elements map to rows of data in tables. The names of the child elements for each **<ROW>** element map to the table column names or object names from which the results are returned. The **num** attributes of the **<ROW>** elements are numbers that provide the order information. The following is an XML Schema representation of this metadata structure:

```
<xs:schema xmlns:xs="http://www.w3.org/2001/XMLSchema"
    elementFormDefault="qualified" attributeFormDefault="unqualified">
 <xs:element name="ROWSET">
  <xs:complexType>
   <xs:sequence>
    <xs:element name="ROW">
     <xs:complexType>
      <xs:sequence>
       <xs:any/>
      </xs:sequence>
      <xs:attribute name="num" type="xs:string" use="optional"/>
     </xs:complexType>
    </xs:element>
   </xs:sequence>
  </xs:complexType>
  </xs:element>
</xs:schema>
```

XSU provides ways to change the names of the **<ROWSET>** and **<ROW>** elements. For example, a CUSTOMER_TBL table is defined as follows:

```
CREATE TABLE CUSTOMER_TBL (
  NAME VARCHAR2(100),
  ADDRESS VARCHAR2(200),
  EMAIL VARCHAR2(200),
  PHONE VARCHAR2(50),
  DESCRIPTION VARCHAR2(4000));
```

The XML document mapping to this table with the canonical mapping is shown as follows:

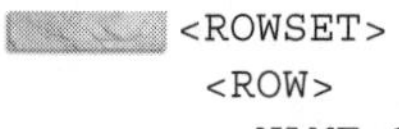

```
<ROWSET>
 <ROW>
  <NAME>Steve Jones</NAME>
  <EMAIL>Steve.Jones@example.com</EMAIL>
  <ADDRESS>Someroad, Somecity, Redwood Shores, CA 94065, U.S.A</ADDRESS>
  <PHONE>6505723456</PHONE>
  <DESCRIPTION>Very Important US Customer</DESCRIPTION>
 </ROW>
</ROWSET>
```

NOTE
By default, all table, column, and object names are uppercase; therefore, if you want to have mixed-case XML documents successfully inserted you need to specify the ***ignoreCase*** *options when using XSU.*

In order to run the XSU command-line utility, you need to set the following Java packages in your Java CLASSPATH:

- **xmlparserv2.jar** Oracle XML Parser for Java
- **classes12.jar** Oracle JDBC Drivers
- **xsu12.jar** Oracle XML SQL Utility

NOTE
You may need to add the ***orai18n.jar*** *package to your Java CLASSPATH when handling XML with different character sets. Or, you might get an oracle.xml.sql.OracleXMLSQLException: 'java.sql.SQLException: Non supported character set...'*

XSU depends on the XML parser to build a DOM and depends on the JDBC drivers to connect to the Oracle database and retrieve the table metadata. After the Java CLASSPATH is properly set, you can run the XSU command-line utility with `java OracleXML`, which has two options, **getXML** for querying the database and **putXML** for inserting data into the database.

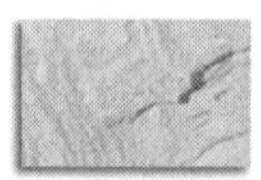

NOTE
Update and delete operations are not included in the XSU command-line utility but they are supported by XSU through the Java and PL/SQL APIs.

For example, to insert the XML data in **contact01.xml**, you can run the following command:

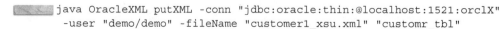

```
java OracleXML putXML -conn "jdbc:oracle:thin:@localhost:1521:orclX"
 -user "demo/demo" -fileName "customer1_xsu.xml" "customr_tbl"
```

The data is inserted into the CUSTOMER_TBL table in the **demo** schema. To query the content in the table and return the results in XML, you can run the following XSU command:

```
java OracleXML getXML -conn "jdbc:oracle:thin:@localhost:1521:orclX"
 -user "demo/demo" "SELECT * FROM customer_tbl"
```

The following XML document is returned:

```
<?xml version = '1.0'?>
<ROWSET>
 <ROW num="1">
  <NAME>Steve Jones</NAME>
  <ADDRESS>Someroad, Somecity, Redwood Shores, CA 94065, U.S.A</ADDRESS>
  <EMAIL>Steve.Jones@example.com</EMAIL>
  <PHONE>6505723456</PHONE>
  <DESCRIPTION>Very Important US Customer</DESCRIPTION>
 </ROW>
</ROWSET>
```

At this point, the XML document's data has been successfully loaded into the database. However, input XML documents are not always in the canonical format. How can you deal with these XML documents? The usual approach is to use an XSLT stylesheet to transform the XML document into the canonical format. On the other hand, you can create database object views mapping to the incoming XML format.

Object Views

If an XML document is not in the canonical format, you can create object views or XMLType views, to allow XSU to map XML documents to database tables. In the following **contact.xml** XML document, the contact information is stored as follows:

```
<Contact_List>
 <Contact>
  <User_id>userid</User_id>
  <First_Name>Steve</First_Name>
  <Last_Name>Jones</Last_Name>
  <Business>
   <Email>Steve.Jones@oracle.com</Email>
   <Phone>(650)5769801</Phone>
   <Address>
    <Street1>4op11</Street1>
    <Street2>500 Oracle Parkway</Street2>
    <City>Redwood Shores</City>
    <State>CA</State>
    <Zipcode>94065</Zipcode>
    <Country>USA</Country>
   </Address>
  </Business>
 </Contact>
</Contact_List>
```

The database schema is defined as follows:

```
CREATE TYPE address_typ AS OBJECT(
  street1 VARCHAR2(200),
  street2 VARCHAR2(200),
  city VARCHAR2(100),
  state VARCHAR2(20),
  zipcode VARCHAR2(20),
  country VARCHAR2(20));
/
CREATE TABLE contact_tbl(
  contactid VARCHAR2(15) PRIMARY KEY,
  firstname VARCHAR2(100),
  lastname VARCHAR2(200),
  midname VARCHAR2(50),
  business_phone VARCHAR2(20),
  home_phone VARCHAR2(10),
  cell_phone VARCHAR2(20),
  business_addr address_typ,
  business_email VARCHAR2(150));
```

Using the canonical mapping, the XML document cannot directly map to the table columns as the document contains multiple levels; thus, to insert this XML document, you need to create the following object view:

```
CREATE TYPE contactinfo_type AS OBJECT(
   phone VARCHAR2(20),
   email VARCHAR2(150),
   address address_typ);
/
 -- Create Object View
CREATE VIEW contact_view AS
   SELECT contactid AS user_id, firstname AS first_name, lastname AS
     last_name,midname AS mid_name,
     contactinfo_type(business_phone,business_email,
     business_addr) AS business
   FROM contact_tbl;
```

Then, you can run a similar command to load the XML file into CUSTOMER_VIEW:

```
java OracleXML putXML -conn "jdbc:oracle:thin:@localhost:1521:orclX"
 -user "demo/demo" -fileName "contacts.xml" "contact_view"
```

In this example, the **contact_view** is used by the Oracle database to map the XML data into underlying tables. However, in many cases these types of views are not updateable, when they include multiple table joins or object type inheritance. You then must create an INSTEAD-OF TRIGGER on the views to handle data population for these tables or objects.

Dividing XML Documents into Fragments

When storing XML documents, you sometimes do not want to map every XML element to relational table columns. Instead, you might want to store some of the XML fragments in XML into CLOBs or XMLTypes. The following example illustrates an approach using XSLT to create such XML fragments and insert those XML fragments into one XMLType table column using XSU. In the example, the input XML document is shown as follows:

```
<Contact_List>
 <Contact>
  <User_id>jwang</User_id>
  <First_Name>Jinyu</First_Name>
  <Last_Name>Wang</Last_Name>
  <Title>Senior Product Manager</Title>
  <Description>Jinyu manages the <PRODUCT>Oracle XML Developer's
    Kit</PRODUCT> product.</Description>
 </Contact>
</Contact_List>
```

The **<Description>** element contains mixed content, which we do not want to map to multiple table columns. A **contact_tbl** table is defined as follows:

```
CREATE TABLE contact_tbl(
  contactid VARCHAR2(15) PRIMARY KEY,
  firstname VARCHAR2(100),
  lastname VARCHAR2(200),
  midname VARCHAR2(50),
  description CLOB);
```

To map the **<Description>** element to the **description** column using XSU, you need to apply the following **setCDATA.xsl** XSL stylesheet:

```
<xsl:stylesheet version="1.0"
   xmlns:xsl="http://www.w3.org/1999/XSL/Transform">
 <xsl:output cdata-section-elements="CODE"/>
 <!-- Identity transformation -->
 <xsl:template match="*|@*|comment()|processing-instruction()|
     text()">
  <xsl:copy>
   <xsl:apply-templates select="*|@*|comment()|processing-
     instruction()|text()"/>
  </xsl:copy>
 </xsl:template>
 <xsl:template match="Description">
  <xsl:element name="Description">
   <xsl:copy-of select="@*|comment()|processing-instruction()"/>
   <xsl:text disable-output-escaping="yes">&lt;![CDATA[</xsl:text>
   <xsl:apply-templates select="*|./*/@*|./*/comment()|./*/
     processing-instruction()|text()"/>
   <xsl:text disable-output-escaping="yes">]]&gt;</xsl:text>
  </xsl:element>
 </xsl:template>
</xsl:stylesheet>
```

This XSLT transformation will transform the input XML document and include all the child elements of **<Description>** into one CDATA section so that each CDATA section can be stored to the **description** column by XSU.

You can modify the XSL stylesheet for your application by specifying different **match** attributes for the following template:

```
<xsl:template match="Description">… </ xsl:template>
```

The XPath in the **match** attribute specifies the root element of the XML fragment to be stored.

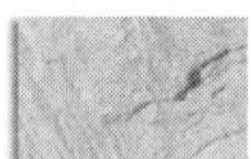

NOTE
Because XSLT requires a DOM to be built in memory, you may need to split the large documents before the transformation.

TransX Utility

When populating the Oracle database with multilingual data or data translations, or when encoding, validation is needed for each XML file. The traditional way is to switch the NLS_LANG setting as you switch loading files with different encoding information. The NLS_LANG setting has to reflect the character set of the file loaded into the database. This approach is error-prone because the encoding information is maintained separately from the data itself. Setting the NLS_LANG environment variable is also tedious work.

With the TransX Utility provided in the XDK, the encoding information is kept along with the data in an XML document of a predefined format so that multilingual data can be transferred without having to switch NLS_LANG settings. TransX Utility maintains the correct character set throughout the process of translating the data and successfully loading it into the database. We will not discuss the details of how to use the TransX Utility. However, we include some samples with the chapter source code for you to try its functionality.

DBMS_XMLSTORE

DBMS_XMLSTORE is a supplied PL/SQL package that supports inserting XML data into database tables. This C-based implementation provides better performance and system manageability than the Java-based DBMS_XMLSave package. This package eliminates the overhead of starting up Oracle JVM as well as translating Java class names for each method call. In addition, DBMS_XMLSTORE is built based on SAX parsing instead of DOM parsing. Therefore, it scales well for large XML documents. You can see this in the following comparison using the SH sample schema:

```
SQL> SELECT count(1) FROM sales;
  COUNT(1)
----------
   1136945
SQL> CREATE TABLE test AS SELECT * FROM sales;
Table created.
SQL> CREATE TABLE result AS SELECT * FROM sales WHERE 0=1;
Table created.
SQL> SELECT count(1) FROM test;
```

```
  COUNT(1)
----------
   1136945
SQL> SELECT count(1) FROM result;
  COUNT(1)
----------
         0
SQL> SET timing ON
SQL> DECLARE
      qryCtx DBMS_XMLQuery.ctxHandle;
      v_clob CLOB;
      savCtx DBMS_XMLSave.ctxType;
      v_rows NUMBER;
   BEGIN
      -- Query out the content
      qryCtx := DBMS_XMLQuery.newContext('SELECT * FROM test');
      v_clob := DBMS_XMLQuery.getXml(qryCtx);
      DBMS_OUTPUT.PUT_LINE('CLOB size = '||DBMS_LOB.GETLENGTH(v_clob));
      -- Save the content
      savCtx := DBMS_XMLSave.newContext('RESULT');
      v_rows := DBMS_XMLSave.insertxml(savCtx,v_clob);
      DBMS_XMLSave.closeContext(savCtx);
      DBMS_OUTPUT.PUT_LINE(v_rows || ' rows inserted...');
   END;
   /
DECLARE
*
ERROR at line 1:
ORA-29532: Java call terminated by uncaught Java exception:
java.lang.OutOfMemoryError
ORA-06512: at "SYS.DBMS_XMLSAVE", line 114
ORA-06512: at line 13
Elapsed: 00:11:57.05
```

In the preceding example, the **sales** table in the SH sample schema described in Chapter 8 is used to generate a large XML document that, when parsed, is too large for the configured Oracle JVM memory. You can increase the JAVA_POOL_SIZE to give more memory for processing; however, this may not be sufficient, especially when this memory takes away from the database memory pool. In Oracle Database 10g, you can use DBMS_XMLSTORE to resolve this issue as follows:

```
DECLARE
    v_clob CLOB;
    savCtx DBMS_XMLSTORE.ctxType;
    v_rows NUMBER;
  BEGIN
    -- Query out the content
    SELECT doc INTO v_clob FROM temp_clob;
    -- Save the content
    savCtx := DBMS_XMLSTORE.newContext('RESULT');
    -- Set the update columns to improve performance
```

```
    DBMS_XMLSTORE.SetUpdateColumn (savCtx, 'PROD_ID');
    DBMS_XMLSTORE.SetUpdateColumn (savCtx, 'CUST_ID');
    DBMS_XMLSTORE.SetUpdateColumn (savCtx, 'TIME_ID');
    DBMS_XMLSTORE.SetUpdateColumn (savCtx, 'CHANNEL_ID');
    DBMS_XMLSTORE.SetUpdateColumn (savCtx, 'PROMO_ID');
    DBMS_XMLSTORE.SetUpdateColumn (savCtx, 'QUANTITY_SOLD');
    DBMS_XMLSTORE.SetUpdateColumn (savCtx, 'AMOUNT_SOLD');
    -- Insert the document
    v_rows := DBMS_XMLSTORE.insertxml(savCtx,v_clob);
    DBMS_XMLSTORE.closeContext(savCtx);
    DBMS_OUTPUT.PUT_LINE(v_rows || ' rows inserted...');
  END;
```

It is recommended to use the DBMS_XMLSTORE **SetUpdateColumn()** function where applicable, as shown in the preceding example, because this allows the DBMS_XMLSTORE program to know the list of columns that need to be updated so as to use explicit SQL binding to the XML data. The previous example uses the following SQL statement when preparing the data insertion:

```
INSERT INTO sales(prod_id, cust_id, ..., amount_sold) values
  (:1, :2, ..., :6);
```

This speeds up the data-insertion process by eliminating the overhead of parsing of the SQL statements in the database.

Using External Tables

Introduced in Oracle9*i*, Oracle's external table feature offers a solution to define a table in the database while leaving the data stored outside of the database. Prior to Oracle Database 10*g*, external tables can be used only as read-only tables. In other words, if you create an external table for XML files, these files can be queries and the table can be joined with other tables. However, no DML operations, such as INSERT, UPDATE, and DELETE, are allowed on the external tables.

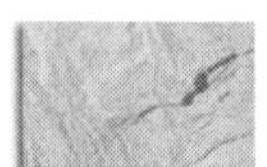

NOTE
*In Oracle Database 10*g*, by using the ORACLE_DATAPUMP driver instead of the default ORACLE_DRIVER, you can write to external tables.*

In Oracle Database 10*g*, you can define VARCHAR2 and CLOB columns in external tables to store XML documents. The following example shows how you can create an external table with a CLOB column to store the XML documents. First, you need to create a DIRECTORY to read the data files:

```
CREATE DIRECTORY data_file_dir AS 'D:\xmlbook\Examples\Chapter9\src\xml';
GRANT READ, WRITE ON DIRECTORY data_file_dir TO demo;
```

Then, you can use this DIRECTORY to define an external table:

```
CREATE TABLE customer_xt  (doc CLOB)
  ORGANIZATION EXTERNAL
  (
```

```
    TYPE ORACLE_LOADER
    DEFAULT DIRECTORY data_file_dir
    ACCESS PARAMETERS
    (
      FIELDS (lobfn CHAR TERMINATED BY ',')
      COLUMN TRANSFORMS (doc FROM lobfile (lobfn))
    )
    LOCATION ('xml.dat')
  )
REJECT LIMIT UNLIMITED;
```

The **xml.dat** file follows:

```
customer1.xml
customer2.xml
```

If you describe the table, you can see the following definition:

```
SQL> DESC customer_xt;
 Name                                      Null?    Type
 ----------------------------------------- -------- ------------------------
 DOC                                                CLOB
```

Then, you can query the XML document as follows:

```
SELECT XMLType(doc).extract('/Customer/EMAIL')
FROM customer_xt;
```

Though the query requires run-time XMLType creation and XPath evaluation, this approach is useful when applications just need a few queries on the XML data and don't want to upload the XML data into database. In Oracle Database 10*g*, you cannot create external tables that contain pre-defined XMLType column types.

Schema Evolution

XML schemas evolve when there are new requirements for the XML data. Your ability to reflect these changes in the database is highly dependent on the storage.

If you use relational tables, you can change the table structure and update the XML views to reflect the new mapping from XML to relational tables. If you use CLOB XMLTypes, your new XML data can be directly inserted because this storage allows you to store XML conforming to different XML schemas. However, for XML Schema–based XMLTypes, evolution of their XML schemas is an expensive process because it requires updating of the object-relational structure of the XMLTypes. In Oracle Database 10*g*, this type of evolution is limited to either performing export/import of the data or using the **CopyEvolution()** function in the DBMS_XMLSCHEMA package.

Best Practices

If you need to accept XML data and store it in the database, the first thing that you should consider is whether your application requires preserving the XML structure in the database. As we discussed in Chapter 8, you need to evaluate the pros and cons of the XML storage options and analyze how the storage affects the retrieving and updating of the XML data. Additionally, you sometimes need to choose a particular XML storage model in order to support receiving XML in the presence of evolving XML schemas.

After selecting the right XML storage model for your application, the following sections provide some guidelines of what you need to know when storing XML in Oracle Database 10*g*.

Handling Document Type Definitions

Although DTDs are not used to define the storage structure for XMLTypes, Oracle XML DB resolves all the DTD definitions and entities defined or referenced in the inserted XML document. This is performed during the inserting process of XMLType when all the incoming XML documents are parsed. In this process, all the entities, including external or internal entities defined in DTDs, are resolved. This means that all the entities are replaced with their actual values and hence the original entity references are lost.

If you would like to preserve these entity references, you have to store the XML in CLOBs, instead of CLOB XMLTypes. You then can create temporary XMLTypes from these CLOBs whenever you need to resolve all the entities and use the XML content.

Creating XML Schema–based XMLTypes

You can create XML Schema–based XMLTypes using the XMLType construction functions or the **XMLType.CreateXML()** function. However, when you are using these functions to create XML Schema–based XMLTypes, the XML documents have to contain the XML **SchemaLocation** attributes. Sometimes XML documents do not contain such attributes. How can you create an XML Schema–based XMLType without changing the original XML document?

As you have seen in Chapter 8, you can use the **XMLType.CreateSchemaBasedXML** function and specify the URL of the XML schema as follows:

```
INSERT INTO product(id, name, description)
  VALUES('xdk', 'XML Developer's Kit',
  XMLTYPE('<DESCRIPTION><KEYWORD>xdk</KEYWORD> is a set of
    standards-based utilities that helps to build
    <KEYWORD>XML</KEYWORD> applications. It contains XDK Java
    Components, XDK C Components and XDK C++ Components.
    </DESCRIPTION>').CreateSchemaBasedXML('http://xmlns.oracle.com/
    xml/content.xsd'));
```

The URL **http://xmlns.oracle.com/xml/content.xsd** is the registered URL of the XML schema, and it will be used to store the product DESCRIPTION.

Specifying Namespaces

If a stored XML document has namespaces, all of the XML queries on the document have to be namespace-qualified because the **<Namespace:Element>** is not the same as **<Element>** in XML. Both the **XMLType.existsNode()**and the **XMLType.extract()** functions allow the user to specify the namespace in the second parameter as follows:

```
MEMBER FUNCTION existsNode(xpath in varchar2, nsmap in varchar2)
   RETURN number deterministic
MEMBER FUNCTION extract(xpath IN varchar2, nsmap IN varchar2)
 RETURN XMLType deterministic
```

In this case, the XPath needs to use fully qualified XML names, which contain the element name and its namespace. For example, you can insert an XML document with two namespace declarations into XMLTypes as follows:

```
CREATE TABLE temp (doc XMLType);
DECLARE
  v_temp XMLType;
BEGIN
  v_temp:= XMLType.createXML('<foo xmlns="http://www.example.com"
     xmlns:xsd="http://www.w3c.org/2001/XMLSchema">
    <foo_type xsd:type="date">03-11-1998</foo_type>
  </foo>');
  INSERT INTO temp VALUES(v_temp);
END;
```

To query the document, you can define the namespace and its prefix in the second parameter of the **XMLType.extract()** function and qualify the XPath using the prefix, as shown in the following SQL query:

```
SELECT a.doc.extract('/a:foo/a:foo_type',
                     'xmlns:a="http://www.example.com"')
FROM temp a;
```

The result is

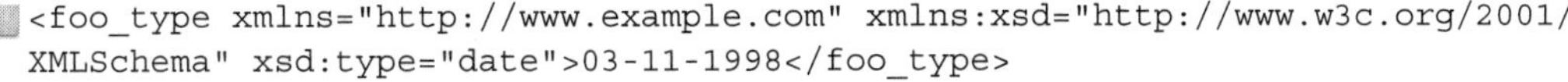

```
<foo_type xmlns="http://www.example.com" xmlns:xsd="http://www.w3c.org/2001/
XMLSchema" xsd:type="date">03-11-1998</foo_type>
```

NOTE
If you do not use the namespace-qualified name in the XPath after providing namespaces, you will get an ORA-31013: Invalid XPath expression *error.*

If you have multiple namespaces, you can list them in the second parameter of the **XMLType.existsNode()** and the **XMLType.extract()** function and separate them with white spaces, as shown in the following example:

```
SELECT a.doc.extract('/a:foo/a:lastupdate/@b:type',
           'xmlns:a="http://www.example.com"
            xmlns:b="http://www.w3c.org/2001/XMLSchema"') AS result
FROM temp a;
RESULT
----------------------------------------------------------------------
date
```

Summary

The chapter discusses various XML storage options and the associated data loading strategies in Oracle Database 10*g*. Table 9-1 shows the relationships between the XML storage and the functionality offered in the XML data-loading utilities. You can choose one of these utilities or use the SQL and PL/SQL interfaces to load XML documents into the Oracle database.

Utilities	Functionality	Relational Storage with XMLType Views	XMLType Tables	XMLType Columns
SQL*Loader	Command-line utility	Limited support	Yes	Yes
XML SQL Utility	Command-line utility and programmatic interfaces in Java and PL/SQL	Yes	Yes	Yes
TransX Utility	Command-line utility and programmatic interfaces in Java	Yes	Yes	Yes
XSQL Servlet	Command-line utility, program interfaces in Java and the HTTP interfaces provided in the built-in action handlers	Yes	Yes	Yes
HTTP/WebDAV	HTTP/WebDAV folders	No	Yes, but the table has to be the default table created during the XML schema registration.	No
FTP Interfaces	FTP interfaces	No	Yes, but the table has to be the default table created during the XML schema registration.	No

TABLE 9-1. *XML Data-Storage and Data-Loading Utilities*

CHAPTER 10

Generating and Retrieving XML

When data is incorporated along with its metadata in XML, it is more self-describing and portable and can be easily shared, transformed, and transported across applications and platforms. This has been the driving force in making XML a widely accepted format for encapsulating data and in a standard protocol for delivering services across software components in business systems. As a result, the ways of managing XML data greatly influence the architecture of modern databases.

Oracle Database 10*g* provides the built-in support for XML, which greatly simplifies the retrieval of XML content and the conversion between relational datasets and XML-formatted data. This chapter will cover the techniques to populate the data stored in object or relational tables into XML and to retrieve data from XML natively stored as XMLTypes. The detailed description includes how you can create, transform, extract, and concatenate XMLTypes into a preferred format.

The discussion starts by introducing the SQL/XML functions that allow you to create, access, and update XML with SQL statements. This set of standards-based methods bridges the gap between SQL and XML operations, enabling you to leverage the XML functionality when working on relational data and to utilize the relational SQL functions when dealing with XML operations. Through the examples, you will learn how this seamless integration of SQL and XML in the Oracle XML Database 10*g* (Oracle XML DB) provides great flexibility and functionality for solving business problems.

In addition to the SQL/XML functions, the DBMS_XMLGEN PL/SQL package provides complementary functionality to create XML. This chapter will show you typical examples and illustrate how and when to use this package.

After the discussion on how to create XML content from SQL data, XML processing techniques, such as how to access, update, and transform XML content stored in XMLTypes, are included. We will explore how to create XMLType Views and use the XML DB Repository to publish XML documents.

In the "Best Practices" section, we compare the database and mid-tier approaches, and describe solutions to some common problems when generating and retrieving XML data from the Oracle database.

Generating XML from SQL Data with SQL XML Functions

To generate XML from the SQL data stored in object or relational tables and process XML, Oracle XML DB provides support for the SQL/XML standard and a set of Oracle-provided SQL/XML functions.

The SQL/XML standard is part of the ISO/IEC (International Organization for Standardization/International Electrotechnical Commission) 9075 standard, which specifies the SQL standard for XML operations. Table 10-1 lists the SQL/XML functions and describes their functionality in the Oracle Database 10*g*. Because currently the SQL/XML standard is still a working draft, the syntax of the SQL/XML functions is subject to change in future releases.

Table 10-2 lists the Oracle-provided SQL/XML functions.

NOTE
The EXTRACTVALUE() is covered in a later section, when we discuss techniques on retrieving XML. The XMLTRANSFORM() function is not covered because **XMLType.*transform()*** *provides the same functionality.*

Function Name	Description
XMLELEMENT()	Returns an XML element in an XMLType when given the XML element name, an optional list of XML attributes (XMLATTRIBUTES()), and an optional list of values as the content of the new element. XMLELEMENT() can also contain other XML elements or XML fragments (XMLFOREST()) as its children.
XMLATTRIBUTES()	Used within XMLELEMENT() to specify attributes for the element.
XMLFOREST()	Returns an XML fragment in an XMLType when given a list of named expressions for the XML elements. Each expression specifies the name of an XML element and its content.
XMLCONCAT()	Returns an XML fragment in an XMLType by concatenating a list of XML elements/values.
XMLAGG()	Returns an XML fragment in an XMLType by aggregating XML fragments, with the option of XML element sorting.

TABLE 10-1. *ISO/IEC SQL/XML Functions*

Function	Description
SYS_XMLGEN()	Generates an XML document with the **<?XML?>** prolog from one scalar type, a user-defined object type, or an instance of XMLType.
XMLSEQUENCE()	Returns a collection of XMLTypes in an XMLSEQUENCEType, which is a VARRAY of XMLType instances in the database.
SYS_XMLAGG()	Aggregates XML elements from one scalar type, a user-defined object type, or an instance of XMLType.
XMLCOLATTVAL()	Generates a set of **<column/>** elements with the name attributes specifying the column names or the name aliases.
UPDATEXML()	Updates XML documents in XMLTypes using XPath expressions.
XMLTRANSFORM()	Applies XSL transformation on XML documents in XMLTypes.
EXTRACTVALUE()	Returns scalar content, such as numbers or strings, when passed an XPath expression pointing to an XML element with only a single text child.

TABLE 10-2. *Oracle-Provided SQL/XML Functions*

If you are familiar with SQL, it should not be difficult to use these SQL/XML functions in the SQL statements. The following is the basic syntax:

```
SELECT [XMLELEMENT |XMLATTRIBUTES |XMLFOREST|XMLCONCAT |XMLAGG|...]
FROM table_name, [table (XMLSEQUENCE)]
WHERE search_conditions
```

Using XMLELEMENT(), XMLATTRIBUTES(), and XMLFOREST() functions, you can create XML elements, the attributes for those elements, and XML document fragments. The XML elements and XML document fragments then can be concatenated and aggregated using XMLCONCAT() and XMLAGG(). The XMLSEQUENCE() function is different from the other functions. It creates a collection of XMLType instances, which can then be used to create temporary tables in the FROM clause of the SQL queries.

XMLELEMENT() and XMLATTRIBUTES()

XMLELEMENT() takes an element name and zero or more arguments that make up the element's content to create the XML element as an instance of XMLType. You can also specify the collection of attributes for the element using XMLATTRIBUTES(). For example, logging in to the HR sample schema, you can create an XML element by using the following SQL command:

```
SQL> SELECT
  2   XMLELEMENT("Employee",
  3    XMLATTRIBUTES(employee_id AS "empno",
  4                   job_id AS "job"),
  5    XMLELEMENT("Name",first_name||' '||last_name),
  6     'is hired on ',
  7     hire_date
  8    )AS result
  9  FROM employees
 10  WHERE rownum=1;
```

In line 2, an **Employee** element is defined with two attributes, **empno** and **job**. The content of the attributes comes from the **employee_id** and **job_id** column in the **employees** table. Then, a child element of **Employee** is created, called **Name**, with its content coming from the concatenation of the **first_name** and **last_name** columns. Additionally, you can add mixed content in the query; for example, **'is hired on '** is concatenated with the content of the **hire_date** column in lines 6 and 7, and the text is inserted after the **<Name>** element. The SQL query produces the following XML element with attributes, along with a child element with mixed content:

```
<Employee empno="100" job="AD_PRES">
 <Name>Steven King</Name>is hired on 17-JUN-87
</Employee>
```

Note that if the element name or attribute name is not specified, the table column name will be used by default.

SYS_XMLGEN()

Different from XMLELEMENT(), SYS_XMLGEN() function allows creating the **<?XML?>** XML prolog and adding the *XML Processing Instructions* (PIs), such as XSLT stylesheet PI, to the created XML documents. For example, you can create an XML document with a prolog with the following SQL command:

```
SELECT SYS_XMLGEN(XMLELEMENT("Employee",
         XMLATTRIBUTES(employee_id AS "empno", job_id AS "job"),
         XMLELEMENT("Name",first_name||' '||last_name),
                   'is hired on ',
                   hire_date))AS result
FROM EMPLOYEES
WHERE rownum=1;
```

Executing this query returns the following result:

```
<?xml version="1.0"?>
<ROW>
  <Employee empno="100" job="AD_PRES">
    <Name>Steven King</Name>is hired on 17-JUN-87
  </Employee>
</ROW>
```

The SYS_XMLGEN() requires taking one scalar value, a user-defined object type or an XMLType instance as the input. You can also use the XMLFORMAT object to specify the XML formatting options (PIs, root tag, etc.) for the XML document:

```
SELECT SYS_XMLGEN(XMLELEMENT("Employee",
  XMLATTRIBUTES(employee_id AS "empno", job_id AS "job"),
   XMLELEMENT("Name",first_name||' '||last_name),
  'is hired on ',
  hire_date),
  XMLFORMAT.createformat('EmployeeList','NO_SCHEMA',
             null,'http://www.oracle.com/','http://dburl',
    '<?xml-stylesheet href="htmlRend.xsl" type="text/xsl" ?>'))
FROM employees
WHERE rownum <3;
```

The XML created contains an XSL stylesheet PI and the default root element, the **<ROW>** element, is replaced by the **<EmployeeList>** element:

```
<?xml version="1.0"?>
<?xml-stylesheet href="htmlRend.xsl" type="text/xsl" ?>
<EmployeeList>
<Employee empno="100" job="AD_PRES">
  <Name>Steven King</Name>is hired on 17-JUN-87</Employee>
</EmployeeList>
```

XMLFOREST()

The XMLFOREST() function produces an XML fragment that contains a set of XML elements. The following example adds additional sub-elements to the **<Employee>** element:

```
SELECT
 XMLELEMENT("Employee",
   XMLATTRIBUTES(employee_id AS "empno", job_id AS "job"),
   XMLELEMENT("Name",first_name||' '||last_name),
   'is hired on ', hire_date,
   XMLFOREST(EMAIL, PHONE_NUMBER))AS result
FROM employees
WHERE rownum=1;
```

This produces the following result:

```
<Employee empno="100" job="AD_PRES">
 <Name>Steven King</Name>is hired on 17-JUN-87
 <EMAIL>SKING</EMAIL>
 <PHONE_NUMBER>515.123.4567</PHONE_NUMBER>
</Employee>
```

Note that some of the characters allowed in SQL identifiers are not valid for XML element names. When element or attribute names are not specified as quoted aliases such as using **XMLELEMENT("<element_name>")** or using the AS clauses as we did for the XMLATTRIBUTES() function, the *fully escaped* character mapping is used to map table column names to the XML element names, such as **<EMAIL>** and **<PHONE_NUMBER>** in the XMLFOREST() are fully escaped names from the corresponding table column names. The fully escaped character mapping will convert all of the invalid XML characters in the SQL names, such as the **:** character, to their Unicode representation in hexadecimal format starting with an **x** sign. For example, if the following object and table are created, where the object name contains a **:** character:

```
CREATE TYPE mydesc AS OBJECT ("my:desc" VARCHAR(200))
/
CREATE TABLE mydesc_tbl of mydesc
/
INSERT INTO mydesc_tbl VALUES('fully escaped character mapping');
```

After inserting the sample data, you can submit an SQL query as follows:

```
SELECT XMLELEMENT("Test", XMLFOREST("my:desc")) FROM mydesc_tbl;
```

It gives you the XML element **<my_x003A_desc>** with the SQL name fully escaped:

```
<Test><my_x003A_desc>fully escaped character mapping</my_x003A_desc>
</Test>
```

Because **:** is not a legal character for the name of XML elements, it is escaped to be **x003A**, which is its Unicode representation.

If you need to keep the **:** character in the XML element/attribute names, you need to specify the name aliases for the XML elements and attributes to enable *partially escaped* character mapping, as shown in the following SQL query:

```
SELECT XMLELEMENT("Test", XMLFOREST("my:desc" AS "my:desc"))
FROM mydesc_tb
```

This allows you to create XML elements and attributes with namespaces as follows:

```
SELECT XMLELEMENT("TEST",
          XMLATTRIBUTES('http://xmlns.oracle.com/xml/Employee.xsd'
             AS "xmlns:my"), XMLFOREST("my:desc" as "my:desc"))
FROM mydesc_tbl;
```

The result is

```
<TEST xmlns:my="http://xmlns.oracle.com/xml/Employee.xsd">
<my:desc>fully escaped character mapping</my:desc></TEST>
```

The XML document defines a namespace prefix **my** for the **<my:desc>** element.

XMLSEQUENCE()

The function XMLSEQUENCE() returns a sequence of XMLTypes in XMLSEQUENCEType, which is a VARRAY of XMLType instances. The following example shows the output of XMLSEQUENCE() when given a SQL cursor expression as the input:

```
SELECT XMLSEQUENCE(
         CURSOR(
               SELECT employee_id, first_name, last_name
               FROM employees where rownum <3)) AS result
FROM dual;
```

The result is

```
XMLSEQUENCETYPE(XMLTYPE( <ROW>
  <EMPLOYEE_ID>100</EMPLOYEE_ID>
  <FIRST_NAME>Steven</FIRST_NAME>
  <LAST_NAME>King</LAST_NAME>
 </ROW>
), XMLTYPE( <ROW>
  <EMPLOYEE_ID>101</EMPLOYEE_ID>
  <FIRST_NAME>Neena</FIRST_NAME>
  <LAST_NAME>Kochhar</LAST_NAME>
 </ROW>
))
```

The query returns a collection of XMLType instances containing the **<EMPLOYEE_ID>**, **<FIRST_NAME>**, and **<LAST_NAME>** elements in XML. Since the **<ROW>** element is used within each row of XMLTypes, you need to make sure it is included in the XPath expressions when accessing the XML data returned as follows:

```
SELECT value(e).extract('/ROW/EMPLOYEE_ID').getClobVal()
FROM TABLE(SELECT XMLSEQUENCE(
         CURSOR(
                SELECT employee_id, first_name, last_name
                FROM employees where rownum <3))
         FROM dual) e;
```

The result is

```
<EMPLOYEE_ID>100</EMPLOYEE_ID>
<EMPLOYEE_ID>101</EMPLOYEE_ID>
```

In the first line of the preceding SQL query, the XPath expression **/ROW/EMPLOYEE_ID** is used to extract the employees' IDs.

XMLCONCAT()

XMLCONCAT() takes an XMLSEQUENCEType or a number of XMLType instances and returns an XML fragment with all the passed-in XML content concatenated. For example, the following SQL concatenates all XML elements within an XML sequence:

```
SELECT (XMLCONCAT(
           XMLSEQUENCE(
             CURSOR(SELECT * FROM employees WHERE rownum<3))))
FROM dual;
```

You can also use XMLCONCAT() with a set of XMLTypes, as shown in the following SQL query:

```
SELECT XMLCONCAT(XMLELEMENT("Email",email),
                 XMLELEMENT("Name", first_name||' '||last_name))
FROM employees
WHERE ROWNUM<3;
```

This function is useful when creating a single XML fragment from multiple XMLTypes.

XMLAGG()

The XMLAGG() function aggregates all the XML elements returned by the SQL query into an XML document fragment and allows an optional ORDER BY clause to order the XML values during the aggregation. The following SQL query returns all the employees ordered by their **first_name**:

```
SELECT XMLAGG(value(e)
 ORDER BY EXTRACTVALUE(value(e),'/ROW/FIRST_NAME') DESC NULLS FIRST)
FROM TABLE(XMLSEQUENCE(CURSOR(SELECT first_name, last_name,salary
                              FROM employees))) e
WHERE EXTRACTVALUE(value(e), '/ROW/SALARY') BETWEEN 12000 AND 18000;
```

The difference between XMLCONCAT() and XMLAGG() is that XMLAGG() operates over the rows of data returned by the SQL query, while XMLCONCAT() doesn't work across rows.

SYS_XMLAGG()

SYS_XMLAGG() provides similar functionality to XMLAGG() except that SYS_XMLAGG() adds an additional **<ROWSET>** root element and the **<?XML?>** prolog to make sure the result is a well-formed XML document. Like SYS_XMLGEN(), SYS_XMLAGG() can use the XMLFORMAT object to specify the output formats. However, you need to make sure the input of SYS_XMLAGG() is a scalar type, an object type or an XMLType instance. Therefore, if multiple XMLType objects are needed for SYS_XMLAGG(), you need to use XMLCONCAT() to concatenate them into one XMLType object instead of passing them directly to the SYS_XMLAGG():

```
SELECT SYS_XMLAGG(XMLCONCAT(value(e)),
        XMLFORMAT.createFormat('EmployeeList'))
FROM TABLE(XMLSEQUENCE(CURSOR(SELECT first_name, last_name,salary
                              FROM employees))) e
WHERE EXTRACTVALUE(value(e), '/ROW/SALARY') BETWEEN 12000 AND 18000;
```

XMLCOLATTVAL()

The XMLCOLATTVAL() function creates an XML fragment containing a set of **<column>** elements where the **name** attributes are used to keep the column names or the name aliases provided by SQL queries. For example, the following SQL query returns three **<column>** elements with their **name** attributes coming from the **hire_date** and **job_id** column names and the **dept** name alias:

```
SELECT XMLELEMENT("Employee",
XMLATTRIBUTES(first_name||' '||last_name AS "name"),
XMLCOLATTVAL(hire_date, job_id, department_id AS "dept")) AS "result"
FROM employees e
WHERE rownum=1
```

The result is

```
<Employee name="Steven King">
 <column name = "HIRE_DATE">17-JUN-87</column>
 <column name = "JOB_ID">AD_PRES</column>
 <column name = "dept">90</column>
</Employee>
```

This function is useful when table column names contain illegal XML characters.

UPDATEXML()

The UPDATEXML() function is a useful XML extension function that accepts an XMLType instance and a set of XPath expression and string value pairs to update the XPath-referred elements or attributes with the provided values. It returns a new transient XMLType instance consisting of the original XMLType instance with appropriate XML nodes updated.

The UPDATEXML() function offers multiple updates on the XML document and allows multiple namespace declarations:

```
SELECT UPDATEXML(column_name, 'XPath1', 'text1', …'XPathN',
'textN','Namespace1 NamespaceN') FROM table_name;
```

The following example illustrates how to use namespaces in an update:

```
SQL> SELECT UPDATEXML(XMLType(
  2    '<Employee xmlns:app1="www.example.com/ns1"
                 xmlns:app2="www.example.com/ns2">
  3     <Name app1:type="Customer">Janet Jones</Name>
  4     <Job app2:type="IT">Manager</Job>
  5     <Salary app2:type="Hidden">12000</Salary>
  6     <Commission app2:type="Hidden">3400</Commission>
  7    </Employee>'),
  8    '/Employee/Name/text()', 'Janet Lee',
  9    '/Employee/Name/@app1:type', 'Important Customer',
 10    '/Employee/Job/@app2:type', 'Hidden',
 11    '/Employee//*[@app2:type="Hidden"]',null,
 12    'xmlns:app1="www.example.com/ns1"
 13     xmlns:app2="www.example.com/ns2"') AS result
 14 FROM dual;
```

The result is

```
<Employee xmlns:app1="www.example.com/ns1" xmlns:app2="www.example.com/ns2">
  <Name app1:type="Important Customer">Janet Lee</Name>
  <Job/>
  <Salary/>
  <Commission/>
</Employee>
```

The input XML document contains two namespaces, the **xmlns:app1="www.example.com/ns1"** and **xmlns:app2="www.example.com/ns2"**. However, you don't have to declare the namespaces for the UPDATEXML() unless the XML elements in the XPath expressions needed to be qualified by the namespaces. For example, you do not have to declare any namespace if you just need to update the **/Employee/Name/text()** node to be **Janet Lee**.

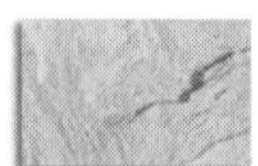

NOTE
When updating the text content in the XML elements, you should use the ***text()*** *function in XPath expressions. Otherwise, for example, if you want to update the* ***/Employee/Name*** *element, you need to specify the XPath as* ***/Employee/Name*** *and the update content as* ***<Name>Janet Lee</Name>.***

However, if XML elements in XPath need to be qualified by the namespaces, you have to declare the namespaces in UPDATEXML() as shown in line 12 and line 13, where namespaces are delimited by whitespaces.

The order of updates is determined by the order of the XPath expressions in the UPDATEXML() from left to right. Updates can be cascaded because each successive update is based on the result of the previous ones. Therefore, after updating the **/Employee/Job/@app2:type** to be **Hidden**, the next update, which sets the elements satisfied **/Employee//*[@app2:type="Hidden"]** to be NULL, updates the **<Job>** element in addition to the **<Salary>** and **<Commission>** elements.

To update the data stored in the tables, you can use UPDATEXML() in a SQL INSERT statement, as shown in this example:

```
UPDATE temp SET doc=UPDATEXML(doc,
     '/a:foo/a:lastupdate/text()',SYSDATE,
     'xmlns:a="http://www.example.com"');
```

The result is

```
<foo xmlns="http://www.example.com" xmlns:xsd="http://www.w3c.org/2001/XMLSchema">
  <lastupdate xsd:type="date">12-MAY-03</lastupdate>
</foo>
```

Now we have discussed the built-in SQL/XML functions in Oracle Database 10*g* to create XML elements, attributes, XML document fragments, and update XML documents. With these functions, you can create XML easily using SQL statements. In the next section, we will look at PL/SQL XML functions that can also be used to create XML supporting more complex logic.

Generating XML from SQL Data with DBM XMLGEN

DBMS_XMLGEN is a PL/SQL package supplied in Oracle Database 10*g* to generate XML in CLOBs or XMLTypes. It is a C-based implementation, which provides much better performance than the Java-based DBMS_XMLQUERY package in the Oracle8*i* and Oracle9*i* database. While DBMS_XMLGEN provides similar functionality to the SQL/XML functions, it is most useful when you need to

- Utilize the "fetching" interfaces in DBMS_XMLGEN for pagination
- Perform PL/SQL processing during the XML document generation

DBMS_XMLGEN is not limited to PL/SQL statements. You can also call its functions directly from any SQL statement using DBMS_XMLGEN.GETXML() or DBMS_XMGEN.GETXMLTYPE(). In many cases, you will find that this is easier than using the SQL/XML functions, as the input is simply a SQL statement. The following sections providing some typical examples and describe how you can use this package.

Canonical Mapping

Unlike the SQL/XML functions, DBMS_XMLGEN uses a canonical mapping to map the SQL data to XML. The format is exactly the same format used by the DBMS_XMLQUERY PL/SQL package or the XML SQL Utility (XSU) Java packages. The following example generates an XML document containing a set of employee records:

```
SQL> SET AUTOPRINT ON
SQL> SET LONG 100000
SQL> VAR result CLOB
SQL> DECLARE
```

```
  qryCtx DBMS_XMLGEN.CTXHANDLE;
BEGIN
  qryCtx :=
     DBMS_XMLGEN.NEWCONTEXT('SELECT employee_id AS "@id",
                                    first_name AS "FirstName",
                                    last_name AS "LastName",
                                    email AS "Email",
                                    phone_number AS "Phone"
                             FROM employees
                             WHERE salary > 20000');
  DBMS_XMLGEN.SETROWSETTAG(qryCtx,'EMPLOYEES');
  DBMS_XMLGEN.SETROWTAG(qryCtx,'EMPLOYEE');
  :result := DBMS_XMLGEN.GETXML(qryCtx);
   DBMS_XMLGEN.CLOSECONTEXT(qryCtx);
END;
```

The result is

```
<?xml version="1.0"?>
<EMPLOYEES>
 <EMPLOYEE id = "100">
  <FirstName>Steven</FirstName>
  <LastName>King</LastName>
  <Email>SKING</Email>
  <Phone>515.123.4567</Phone>
 </EMPLOYEE>
</EMPLOYEES>
```

NOTE
*In the example, the SQL*Plus command SET AUTOPRINT ON is used to automatically display the value of the bind variables (the* ***result*** *variable in the CLOB data type).*

The canonical mapping uses the **<ROW>** element to enclose each row of data returned by the SQL query. The **<ROW>** elements are then included by the **<ROWSET>** element to create the XML document. In the example, the **<ROWSET>** or **<ROW>** element names are changed to **EMPLOYEES** and **EMPLOYEE** respectively by calling the DBMS_XMLGEN.SETROWSETTAG() and DBMS_XMLGEN.SETROWTAG() procedures.

NOTE
By setting the parameters of DBMS_XMLGEN.SETROWSETTAG() and DBMS_XMLGEN.SETROWTAG() to NULL, you can suppress the ***<ROWSET>*** *and* ***<ROW>*** *elements. However, suppressing the* ***<ROWSET>*** *element may result in no root element for the XML document and the following error: ORA-19336: Missing XML root element.*

By default, the child elements of **<ROW>** use the table column names as their element names. There is no PL/SQL procedure provided in the DBMS_XMLGEN package to customize the names of these elements, but, you can modify them via the AS clause in the SQL query. In the example, the **LastName** is set as the alias for the **last_name** column, and the **employee_id** column uses the alias **@id**. The difference between aliases with or without @ in the aliases, is that the column with an alias with @ is mapped to an XML attribute instead of an XML element.

Print Formatting

Using DBMS_XMLGEN, you can set the output formats using the following procedures:

```
PROCEDURE SETINDENTATIONWIDTH(ctx IN CTXHANDLE, width IN NUMBER);
PROCEDURE SETPRETTYPRINTING(ctx IN CTXHANDLE, pp IN BOOLEAN);
```

By default, the output is in "pretty" print format with all the whitespaces, indentations and linefeeds between the XML elements, and you can set the number of whitespace characters used for indentation by calling DBMS_XMLGEN.SETINDENTATIONWIDTH(). By setting the second parameter of DBMS_XMLGEN.SETPRETTYPRINTING() to be FALSE, you can to get the XML documents generated in "compact" format with all the whitespaces between the XML element tags stripped out, as shown in the following example:

```
DECLARE
 qryCtx DBMS_XMLGEN.CTXHANDLE;
BEGIN
 qryCtx :=
  DBMS_XMLGEN.NEWCONTEXT('SELECT employee_id AS "@id",
                                   first_name as "FirstName",
                                    last_name as "LastName",
                                    email as "Email",
                                    phone_number as "Phone"
                             FROM employees
                             WHERE salary > 20000');
  DBMS_XMLGEN.SETPRETTYPRINTING(qryCtx, FALSE);
  :result := DBMS_XMLGEN.GETXML(qryCtx);
  DBMS_XMLGEN.CLOSECONTEXT(qryCtx);
END;
```

The result is

```
<?xml version="1.0"?>
<ROWSET><ROW><EMPLOYEE_ID>100</EMPLOYEE_ID>
<FIRST_NAME>Steven</FIRST_NAME><LAST_NAME>King</LAST_NAME>
<EMAIL>SKING</EMAIL><PHONE_NUMBER>515.123.4567</PHONE_NUMBER>
<HIRE_DATE>17-JUN-87</HIRE_DATE><JOB_ID>AD_PRES</JOB_ID>
<SALARY>24000</SALARY><DEPARTMENT_ID>90</DEPARTMENT_ID>
</ROW></ROWSET>
```

Though this output is not the pretty format that you can easily read, an XML parser considers the data to be equivalent.

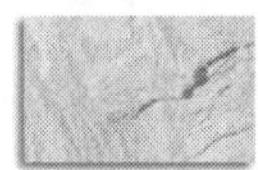

NOTE
The output format customization is the new feature for the DBMS_XMLGEN package in Oracle Database 10g.

Data Fetching

When a large amount of data is returned by the SQL query, it is not efficient to generate a single huge XML document containing all the data. This will result in memory issues when performing DOM-based processing or transmitting the document to another user. The data "fetching" feature in DBMS_XMLGEN allows you to generate a set of small XML documents using the following procedures:

```
FUNCTION GETNUMROWSPROCESSED(ctx IN CTXHANDLE) RETURN NUMBER;
PROCEDURE SETMAXROWS(ctx IN CTXHANDLE, maxRows IN NUMBER);
```

Here is an example using these functions in a PL/SQL FOR...LOOP:

```
SQL> SET SERVEROUTPUT ON SIZE 1000000
SQL> DECLARE
       qryCtx DBMS_XMLGEN.CTXHANDLE;
       res BOOLEAN;
       result XMLType;
       i NUMBER :=0;
     BEGIN
       -- Create the query context
       qryCtx := DBMS_XMLGEN.NEWCONTEXT(
                   'SELECT * FROM employees ORDER BY employee_id');
       DBMS_XMLGEN.SETMAXROWS(qryCtx,10);
       LOOP
         result:= DBMS_XMLGEN.GETXMLTYPE(qryCtx);
         EXIT WHEN DBMS_XMLGEN.GETNUMROWSPROCESSED(qryCtx) =0;
         i :=i+1;
         -- Create XML DB Resources
         res := DBMS_XDB.CREATERESOURCE('/public/emp'||i||'.xml',result);
         IF res = FALSE THEN
           DBMS_OUTPUT.PUT_LINE('Error creating XML DB resource');
         ELSE
           DBMS_OUTPUT.PUT_LINE('/public/emp'||i||'.xml'||' is created');
         END IF;
       END LOOP;
       COMMIT;
    END;
```

The SQL query gets all the employees in order of their **employee_id**. By setting **Max Rows** to be **10**, each XML document contains no greater than ten records. The DBMS_XMLGEN .GETNUMROWSPROCESSED() function keeps track of the number of rows that get decremented by **10** from the previous DBMS_XMLGEN.GETXML() calls. Once the loops have completed, the DBMS_XMLGEN.GETNUMROWSPROCESSED() returns zero, and the procedure exits.

During the creation of the outputs, DBMS_XMLGEN.GETXMLTYPE() is used to return the query result in XMLType. This XMLType is then used by DBMS_XDB.CREATERESOURCE() to create a resource file in the XML DB Repository. After the resource files are created, you can access the XML documents either through the WebDAV/HTTP or the FTP interfaces. For example, when you type the following HTTP address in Internet Explorer:

```
http://localhost:8080/public
```

A window pops up asking for login information. You can log in using any database username and its associated password. However, because the resource is created as a private resource by default, you need to log in as HR user to access the generated files from HR user, as shown in Figure 10-1. From these interfaces, you can easily download the files from the database server to other client systems.

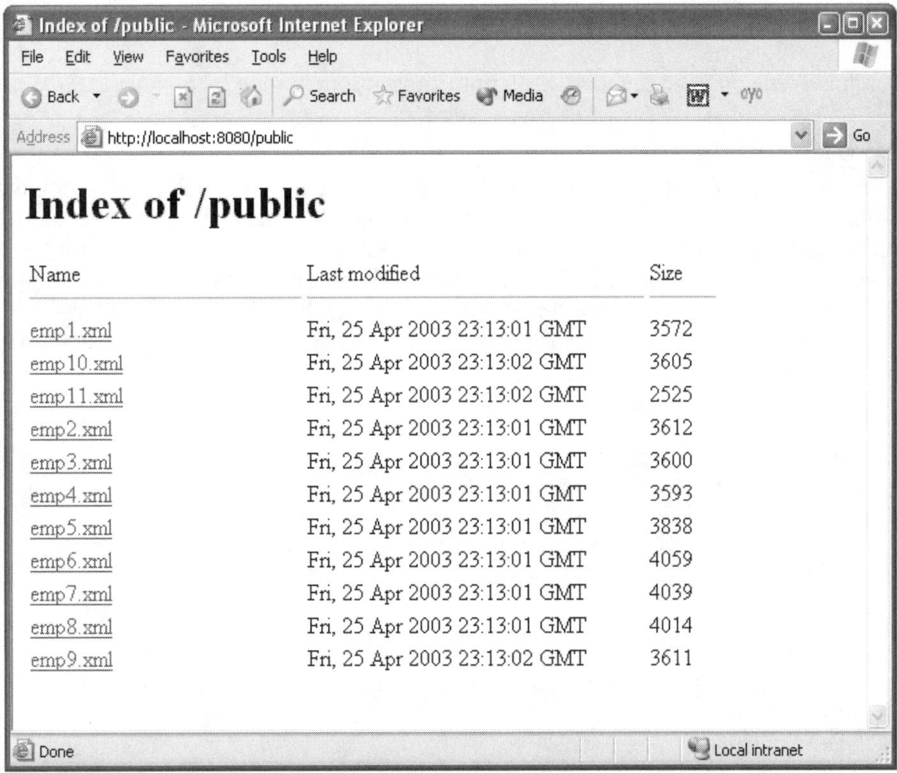

FIGURE 10-1. *HTTP access of XDB (XML DB) repository*

Using REF Cursor

In addition to creating the query context from SQL queries, DBMS_XMLGEN.NEWCONTEXT() allows you to create the query context based on REF cursors. This is done by specifying a SYS_REFCURSOR as the initialization parameter, as shown in the following example:

```
SQL> SET AUTOPRINT ON
SQL> VAR result CLOB;
SQL> DECLARE
     salary NUMBER :=20000;
     refcur SYS_REFCURSOR;
     qryCtx DBMS_XMLGEN.CTXHANDLE;
   BEGIN
   OPEN refcur FOR
       'SELECT * FROM employees WHERE salary> :1' USING salary;
     qryCtx := DBMS_XMLGEN.NEWCONTEXT(refcur);
     :result := DBMS_XMLGEN.GETXML(qryCtx,DBMS_XMLGEN.NONE);
     DBMS_XMLGEN.CLOSECONTEXT(qryCtx);
  END;
```

This is useful when you need to create XML from a result set returned by another PL/SQL process.

Using Bind Variables

Whenever you use a SQL query repeatedly by simply updating several variables, you should think about using bind variables, because they eliminate the need to reparse the SQL statement, thus saving processing time. In the following example, we open a SYS_REFCURSOR for the **department_id** in the **department** table and use it to find all the employees within each department. When creating the loop for each **department_id**, DBMS_XMLGEN.SETBINDVALUE() is used to set the bind variable for the SQL query, and DBMS_XMLGEN.CLEARBINDVALUE() is used to clear the bind variable data.

```
DECLARE
  qryCtx DBMS_XMLGEN.CTXTYPE;
  v_sql VARCHAR2(100);
  v_clob CLOB;
  TYPE deptType IS RECORD (department_id NUMBER(4));
  v_deprec deptType;
  v_refcur SYS_REFCURSOR;
BEGIN
  qryCtx := DBMS_XMLGEN.NEWCONTEXT(
          'SELECT * FROM employees WHERE department_id = :MID');
  -- Open Ref Cursor
  OPEN v_refcur FOR
    'SELECT department_id FROM departments WHERE location_id = 1700';
  -- Loop each department
  LOOP
    -- Fetch from cursor variable.
     FETCH v_refcur INTO v_deprec;
     EXIT WHEN v_refcur%NOTFOUND;
```

```
      DBMS_XMLGEN.SETBINDVALUE( qryCtx, 'MID', v_deprec.department_id);
      v_clob := DBMS_XMLGEN.GETXML( qryCtx );
      INSERT INTO temp VALUES(v_clob);
   END LOOP;
   DBMS_XMLGEN.CLOSECONTEXT(qryCtx);
EXCEPTION
   WHEN OTHERS THEN
      DBMS_XMLGEN.CLOSECONTEXT(qryCtx);
END;
```

Querying the V$SQL view in SYS user, we can see how many times the SQL query is parsed and executed:

```
SQL> SELECT parse_calls,executions
     FROM v$sql
     WHERE sql_text
        LIKE 'SELECT * FROM employees WHERE department_id =%';
PARSE_CALLS EXECUTIONS
---------- ----------
         1         21
```

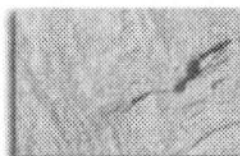

NOTE
The V$SQL view is one of the V$ views created on the dynamic performance tables, in which every parsed and stored SQL statement in the shared pool is presented as a row in the view. You need to run ***GRANT SELECT ON v_$sql TO HR*** *before running the query on V$sql.*

The result shows that the SQL query is executed 21 times but is only parsed once. This shows the value of using bind variables in SQL.

Dealing with Special Characters

Some characters—such as ‘, <, and >—are special characters in XML documents and must be in escaped format, also known as *character entities* format. For example, the escaped format for ‘ is **'**, the escaped format for > is **>**, and the escaped format for < is **<**. By default, all special characters are escaped. For example, the following SQL query contains a ‘ character:

```
SELECT DBMS_XMLGEN.GETXML(
        'SELECT ''Don''''t escape me!'' AS result FROM dual')
FROM dual;
```

The following XML document is generated with the ‘ escaped:

```
<?xml version="1.0"?>
<ROWSET>
 <ROW>
  <RESULT>Don&apos;t escape me!</RESULT>
 </ROW>
</ROWSET>
```

To avoid the character escaping, you can call the DBMS_XMLGEN.SETCONVERTSPECIALCHARS() procedure with FALSE, as in the following example:

```
DECLARE
  qryCtx DBMS_XMLGEN.CTXHANDLE;
BEGIN
  qryCtx :=
    DBMS_XMLGEN.NEWCONTEXT(
      'SELECT ''Don''''t escape me!'' as result FROM dual');
  DBMS_XMLGEN.SETCONVERTSPECIALCHARS(qryCtx, FALSE);
  :result := DBMS_XMLGEN.GETXML(qryCtx);
  DBMS_XMLGEN.CLOSECONTEXT(qryCtx);
END;
```

The generated XML document will have the following format:

```
<?xml version="1.0"?>
<ROWSET>
 <ROW>
  <RESULT>Don't escape me!</RESULT>
 </ROW>
</ROWSET>
```

Retrieving Using XMLType and SQL/XML Functions

So far, we have discussed various ways of generating XML from SQL data using the SQL/XML functions and the DBMS_XMLGEN package. In Oracle Database 10*g*, if you already have XML documents natively stored as XMLTypes, you can use the built-in XMLType member functions and the SQL/XML functions to retrieve and create XML. Table 10-3 summarizes the XMLType member functions and their respective XML processing functionalities.

We will not discuss all details of the functions listed in Table 10-3, because they are well covered by the online manual, *Oracle XML Database Developer's Guide*. Instead, in the following section, we will explore frequently used functionality to help you solve some real problems.

Name	Functionality
XMLType() createXML() createSchemaBasedXML() createNonSchemaBasedXML()	Create XMLTypes from XML data stored in VARCHAR2, CLOB, or other XMLTypes.
existsNode()	Checks if the XML nodes or node sets specified by XPath exist. It returns 1 if nodes or node sets are found; otherwise, it returns 0. If the XPath string is NULL or the document is empty, then a value of 0 is returned; otherwise, 1 is returned.

TABLE 10-3. *XMLType Member Functions*

Name	Functionality
extract()	Extracts nodes or node sets based on the XPath expression and returns an XMLType instance containing the resulting node(s).
isFragment()	Checks if the XMLType is an XML document fragment or a well-formed document. It returns 1 if the XMLType is an XML document fragment or a well-formed document. Otherwise, it returns 0. Determines if the XMLType instance corresponds to a well-formed document or a fragment. Returns `1` or `0` indicating if the XMLType instance contains a fragment or a well-formed document.
getClobVal() getNumberVal() getStringVal()	Gets the CLOB, NUMBER, or String value in VARCHAR2, respectively, from the XMLType. You can only use **getNumberVal()** when the content of XMLType is numeric.
transform()	Transforms the XML content in XMLType with the XSL stylesheet specified.
toObject()	Casts the XMLType to other object types.
isSchemaBased() getSchemaURL() getRootElement() getNamespace()	Checks the XML schema–related information of XMLType. If the XMLType is XML schema–based, **isSchemaBased()** returns TRUE. Then, **getSchemaURL(), getRootElement()**, and **getNamespace()** can be used to find out the registered XML schema URL, the defined root element and the namespace of the root element for the XMLType.
isSchemaValidate() isSchemaValid() schemaValidation() setSchemaValidate()	Checks and updates the XML Schema validation status of XMLType. If the XMLType is valid against the XML schema, then **isSchemaValidate()** returns 1. The **isSchemaValid()** function returns the validation status of the XMLType against the supplied XML schema.To update the status of the XMLType, **schemaValidation()** validates the XMLType against an XML schema and updates the status to validated after the validation. If you validated the XMLTypes, you can update the status through the **setSchemaValidate()** procedure.

TABLE 10-3. *XMLType Member Functions* (continued)

Both the SQL/XML extension functions and XMLType member functions can be used, along with SQL commands such as SELECT, UPDATE, and INSERT to perform XML operations. This section discusses how you can extract, transform, and update the content when XML is stored natively in XMLTypes.

extract() and existsNode()

The XMLType.**extract()** object member function extracts nodes or node sets based on the passed XPath expression and returns an XMLType instance containing the resulting node or nodes. You need to specify the table name alias to qualify the object. Otherwise, you will get an error message as follows:

```
SQL> SELECT description.extract('//KEYWORD').isFragment()
      FROM product;
SELECT description.extract('//KEYWORD').isFragment() FROM product
       *
ERROR at line 1:
ORA-00904: "DESCRIPTION"."EXTRACT": invalid identifier
```

In this example from Chapter 8, the **product** table contains a **description** XMLType column.

There are corresponding SQL/XML extension functions with the same name as the XMLType member functions, including EXTRACT()and EXISTSNODE(). They are functionally the same except that they take an XMLType as their first parameter and normally do not require the use of qualified names, as are needed by the XMLType member functions. The following example illustrates using the EXTRACT() SQL/XML function:

```
SQL> SELECT EXTRACT(description,'//KEYWORD') FROM product;
EXTRACT(DESCRIPTION,'//KEYWORD')
-----------------------------------------------------------------------------
<KEYWORD>xdk</KEYWORD>
<KEYWORD>XML</KEYWORD>
```

EXTRACTVALUE()

EXTRACTVALUE()does not belong to the XMLType object. It is an Oracle-provided SQL/XML function that returns scalar content, such as numbers or strings, when passed an XPath expression. This function is quite convenient to use because it automatically gets the value of the child text element of the specified XML node. However, make sure the XPath points to an XML element with only a single child text element, otherwise, you will get the following error:

```
<DESCRIPTION>This Oracle XML Parser supports <KEY>DOM</KEY> and
 <KEY>SAX</KEY> interfaces.</DESCRIPTION>
SQL> SELECT EXTRACTVALUE(description,'//DESCRIPTION/text()') FROM product;
SELECT EXTRACTVALUE(description,'//DESCRIPTION/text()') FROM product
                                                             *
ERROR at line 1:
ORA-19025: EXTRACTVALUE returns value of only one node
```

The EXTRACTVALUE() function always returns a VARCHAR2 by default for string values. Therefore, the node value cannot be greater than 4K. If larger sizes are needed, you can use XMLType.**extract()** to get the document and use the XMLType **getClobVal()** to get the content out in CLOB. When the XMLType storage is based on an XML schema, at query compile time, EXTRACTVALUE() can automatically return the appropriate data type based on the XML schema information, such as in a CLOB, DATE, or NUMBER.

Generating XML Schemas

XML schemas and DTDs define the metadata for XML and can ensure both data and structural integrity. In Oracle Database 10*g*, the DBMS_XMLQUERY PL/SQL package and the XML SQL Utility (XSU) Java package support XML schema generation from simple SQL statements. DBMS_XMLSCHEMA can generate XML schemas only from existing object types.

NOTE
DBMS_XMLGEN does not support XML schema or DTD generation.

Taking the **employees** table as an example and using DBMS_XMLQUERY, we can generate the corresponding XML schema:

```
SET AUTOPRINT ON
VAR result CLOB;
BEGIN
 :result:=DBMS_XMLQUERY.GETXML('SELECT employee_id AS "@id",
                                      email, department_id
                               FROM employees WHERE rownum=1',
                          DBMS_XMLQUERY.SCHEMA);
END;
```

The generated XML schema is

```
<?xml version = '1.0'?>
<DOCUMENT xmlns:xsd="http://www.w3.org/2001/XMLSchema">
 <xsd:schema xmlns:xsd="http://www.w3.org/2001/XMLSchema">
   <xsd:element name="ROWSET">
    <xsd:complexType>
     <xsd:sequence>
      <xsd:element name="ROW" minOccurs="0" maxOccurs="unbounded">
       <xsd:complexType>
         <xsd:sequence>
          <xsd:element name="EMAIL" nillable="true" minOccurs="0">
            <xsd:simpleType>
              <xsd:restriction base="xsd:string">
                 <xsd:maxLength value="25"/>
              </xsd:restriction>
            </xsd:simpleType>
           </xsd:element>
           <xsd:element name="DEPARTMENT_ID" type="xsd:integer" nillable="true" minOccurs="0"/>
           </xsd:sequence>
           <xsd:attribute name="num" type="xsd:integer"/>
           <xsd:attribute name="id" type="xsd:integer"/>
         </xsd:complexType>
       </xsd:element>
      </xsd:sequence>
     </xsd:complexType>
    </xsd:element>
 </xsd:schema>
   <ROWSET xmlns:xsi="http://www.w3.org/2001/XMLSchema-instance"
xsi:noNamespaceSchemaLocation="#/DOCUMENT/xsd:schema[not(@targetNamespace)]">
   <ROW num="1" id="100">
    <EMAIL>SKING</EMAIL>
```

```
    <DEPARTMENT_ID>90</DEPARTMENT_ID>
   </ROW>
   </ROWSET>
</DOCUMENT>
```

The generated XML schema maps database data types to the corresponding XML schema data types. In this case, VARCHAR2 maps to **xsd:string** and NUMBER maps to **xsd:integer**. The generated schema also includes the length constraints for the VARHAR2 columns using the **xsd:maxLength** for **xsd:string**. For table columns that can be NULL, the attribute **xsd:nillable="true"** is added. The generated XML documents specify the schema location using the special syntax in Oracle XML DB, which uses # to specify the current document followed by the XPath to the XML schema definition. Oracle XML schema processors are extended to validate the XML document using this "inline" XML schema location, though this is not defined in the W3C XML Schema Recommendation.

To generate the DTDs, you can use DBMS_XMLQUERY.DTD as the second parameter for the DBMS_XMLQUERY.GETXML() function, as shown in the following example:

```
SET AUTOPRINT ON
VAR result CLOB;
BEGIN
 :result:=DBMS_XMLQUERY.GETXML('SELECT * FROM employees
                                WHERE rownum=1',
                                DBMS_XMLQUERY.DTD);
END;
```

The XSU Java package provides similar interfaces to those provided by the DBMS_XMLQUERY package.

Using DBMS_XMLSCHEMA, you can create the following object types and use them as parameters as in the following example:

```
CREATE OR REPLACE TYPE EMP_T AS OBJECT
 ( "@id"  NUMBER(6),
  email  VARCHAR2(25),
  department_id  NUMBER(4));

SELECT DBMS_XMLSCHEMA.GENERATESCHEMA('HR', 'EMP_T') FROM dual;
```

If there is any related object, you must create the corresponding object. Otherwise, you will get the following error:

```
 PLS-00382: expression is of wrong type
```

Though using the DBMS_XMLSCHEMA package is complicated, it allows great flexibility in creating XML hierarchical structure. The advantage of using DBMS_XMLQUERY is that you need to pass only in SQL queries. However, it generates limited types of XML schemas.

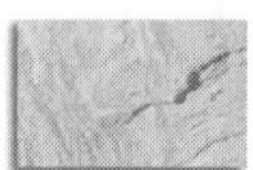

NOTE

If the objects belong to different user schemas, using DBMS_XMLQUERY.GETXML() or DBMS_XMLSCHEMA.GENERATESCHEMAS(), instead of DBMS_XMLSCHEMA.GENERATESCHEMA(), will create multiple XML schemas.

Creating XMLType Views

An XMLType view is an efficient way of encapsulating existing relational or object-relational data in XML. In Oracle Database 10*g*, you can use any SQL or PL/SQL functions that generate XMLTypes to create an XMLType view. There are two different ways of creating XMLType views—as columns or rows.

You can create a view where the XMLType is a single column, as shown in the following example using a SQL/XML statement:

```
CREATE OR REPLACE VIEW employee_vw AS
   SELECT XMLELEMENT("Employee",
             XMLATTRIBUTES(first_name||' '||last_name AS "name"),
             XMLFOREST(salary, phone_number))AS result,employee_id
FROM employees;
```

When you run **describe employee_vw**, you will see the following definition for the view:

```
SQL> describe employee_vw;
 Name                                      Null?    Type
 ----------------------------------------- -------- ------------------------
 RESULT                                             SYS.XMLTYPE
 EMPLOYEE_ID                               NOT NULL NUMBER(6)
```

The other way is to create an object XMLType view, where each row object is an XMLType instance and is associated with a unique *OBJECT ID* (OID). The resulting SYS_NC_ROWINFO$ is a virtual column referring to the XMLType instance in the XMLType object view or table:

```
CREATE OR REPLACE VIEW employee_vw OF XMLTYPE WITH OBJECT ID
   (EXTRACT(SYS_NC_ROWINFO$,'/Employee/@empno').getNumberVal())
   AS
   SELECT XMLELEMENT("Employee",
             XMLATTRIBUTES(e.employee_id AS "empno"),
             XMLFOREST(e.first_name, e.last_name, e.job_id))AS result
FROM employees e;
```

When creating XMLType object views, you need to specify the OBJECT ID via the **OF XMLType WITH OBJECT ID** syntax and assign the OBJECT ID by extracting a scalar value out of the XMLType. You can use the DEFAULT keyword to ask the database to create a default OBJECT ID. However, this is not recommended, because it will generate a 16-byte ID that is difficult to use when referring to the data in the view.

After you have created either view, you can query it as you would a relational table with XMLType columns or an XMLType object table:

```
SELECT * FROM employee_vw WHERE ROWNUM<2;
```

To optimize the queries on the XMLType object views to be able to use "query rewrite", you can associate an XML schema with it through the following SQL statement:

```
CREATE OR REPLACE VIEW employee_vw OF XMLTYPE
XMLSCHEMA "http://xmlns.oracle.com/xml/employee.xsd" ELEMENT "Employee"
WITH OBJECT ID
(EXTRACT(SYS_NC_ROWINFO$,'/Employee/@empno').getNumberVal())
AS
SELECT XMLELEMENT("Employee",
```

```
XMLATTRIBUTES(e.employee_id AS "empno"),
XMLFOREST(e.first_name, e.last_name, e.job_id))AS result
FROM employees e;
```

The advantage of using XMLType views is that you can have several views representing differing XML hierarchies with single data storage.

Processing XML

We have covered the basic techniques of generating XML from SQL data in object-relational tables and XMLTypes. In this section, we discuss how you can process the XML documents before passing them to applications. Specifically, we discuss how to convert XML fragments into XML documents and how to use DBMS_XMLDOM to create a DOM during XML document generation. PL/SQL transformations are discussed in Chapter 26.

Dealing with XML Fragments

XMLType operations may result in creating XMLTypes containing XML fragments instead of XML documents. Since you cannot insert an XML fragment into XMLType columns or tables, you need to use the following function to check whether or not the current XML type is an XML fragment:

```
SQL> INSERT INTO temp_emp
     SELECT XMLCONCAT(XMLELEMENT("Email",email),
                  XMLELEMENT("Name", first_name||' '||last_name))
     FROM employees
     WHERE ROWNUM<3;
insert into temp_emp
         *
ERROR at line 1:
ORA-19010: Cannot insert XML fragments
```

The following query checks if the result of the SQL/XML function is an XML document fragment:

```
SQL> SELECT XMLCONCAT(XMLELEMENT("Email",email),
  2       XMLELEMENT("Name", first_name||' '||last_name)).isFragment()
  3  FROM employees
  4  WHERE ROWNUM<2;

XMLCONCAT(XMLELEMENT("EMAIL",EMAIL),
XMLELEMENT("NAME",FIRST_NAME||''||LAST_NAME)
----------------------------------------------------------------------
                                                                     1
```

The result of the preceding query shows that the XMLType is an XML fragment. Normally, such XML fragments do not meet the single root element requirement for XML documents. Therefore, you need to create a well-formed XML document using XMLELEMENT() before instering it into XMLTypes as follows:

```
INSERT INTO temp_emp
SELECT XMLELEMENT"RESULT",
```

```
        XMLCONCAT(XMLELEMENT("Email",email),
                  XMLELEMENT("Name", first_name||' '||last_name)))
FROM employees
WHERE ROWNUM<2;
```

DOM Editing

As discussed in Chapter 2, the Document Object Model (DOM) is a set of standard APIs dealing with XML as a tree-type memory object. You can use the DOM APIs to delete, insert, and update XML elements, nodes, and attributes. In Oracle Database 10*g*, you can use the DBMS_XMLDOM package to perform these functions. From Chapter 2, you should be already familiar with the DOM operations, so the following examples show how these are performed from PL/SQL.

Operating on XMLType DOM

In Oracle Database 10*g*, you do not need to reparse an XML document if it is stored as an XMLType. There are two functions in the DBMS_XMLDOM package that directly support XMLType DOM operations:

```
FUNCTION NEWDOMDOCUMENT(xmldoc IN SYS.XMLType) RETURN DOMDOCUMENT;
FUNCTION GETXMLTYPE(doc IN DOMDOCUMENT) RETURN SYS.XMLType;
```

As a result, you can call DOM functions by creating an XMLType, using its construction function, and then passing it to DBMS_XMLDOM.NEWDOMDOCUMENT() as an input. After DOM processing, you can get the result in an XMLType by using the DBMS_XMLDOM.GETXMLTYPE() function. Here is an example of an update operation:

```
CREATE OR REPLACE PROCEDURE updateXMLElement(p_doc IN OUT XMLTYPE,
                                   p_ename IN VARCHAR2,
                                   p_content IN VARCHAR2) AS
   v_item NUMBER;
   v_doc DBMS_XMLDOM.DOMDOCUMENT;
   v_ndoc DBMS_XMLDOM.DOMNODE;
   v_nlist DBMS_XMLDOM.DOMNODELIST;
   v_node DBMS_XMLDOM.DOMNODE;
   v_elem DBMS_XMLDOM.DOMELEMENT;
   v_nelem DBMS_XMLDOM.DOMNODE;
   v_text DBMS_XMLDOM.DOMTEXT;
   v_ntext DBMS_XMLDOM.DOMNODE;
BEGIN
  -- Create DOM Object
  v_doc := DBMS_XMLDOM.NEWDOMDOCUMENT(p_doc);
  v_ndoc :=DBMS_XMLDOM.MAKENODE(DBMS_XMLDOM.GETDOCUMENTELEMENT(v_doc));
  -- Select the DOM Nodes
  v_nlist:= DBMS_XMLDOM.GETELEMENTSBYTAGNAME(v_doc,p_ename);
  IF DBMS_XMLDOM.GETLENGTH(v_nlist) > 0 THEN
    DBMS_OUTPUT.PUT_LINE('Update the: '||p_ename||' elements.');
    FOR v_item IN 0..DBMS_XMLDOM.GETLENGTH(v_nlist) LOOP
      v_node := DBMS_XMLDOM.ITEM(v_nlist, v_item);
      v_ntext := DBMS_XMLDOM.GETFIRSTCHILD(v_node);
      DBMS_OUTPUT.PUT_LINE(DBMS_XMLDOM.GETNODEVALUE(v_ntext));
      DBMS_XMLDOM.SETNODEVALUE(v_ntext, p_content);
    END LOOP;
```

```
  ELSE
    DBMS_OUTPUT.PUT_LINE('No '||p_ename||' element in the current
 document.');
  END IF;
  -- Free resources
  DBMS_XMLDOM.FREEDOCUMENT(v_doc);
EXCEPTION
  WHEN OTHERS THEN
  DBMS_OUTPUT.PUT_LINE('Exceptions during the process');
END;
```

In the example, the DBMS_XMLDOM.DOMDOCUMENT() creates the DOMDOCUMENT from the XMLType input **p_doc**. Then, a set of DOM operations is performed, which include using the DBMS_XMLDOM.GETELEMENTBYTAGNAME() function to get the XML elements with name **p_ename** for the updates and iterating each XML element item to update the content using the DBMS_XMLDOM.SETNODEVALUE().

Next, the created procedure can be used to update the telephone number for an employee with EMPLOYEE_ID of **199**. The original document contains the following:

```
<ROWSET>
  <ROW>
    <EMPLOYEE_ID>199</EMPLOYEE_ID>
    …
    <PHONE_NUMBER>650.507.9844</PHONE_NUMBER>
    …
  </ROW>
```

Then, run the **updateXMLElement()** function:

```
DECLARE
  v_doc XMLType;
BEGIN
  -- Create Sample XML Document
  SELECT XMLTYPE(DBMS_XMLGEN.GETXML('SELECT * FROM employees
                                    WHERE employee_id=199'))
     INTO v_doc FROM dual;
  -- Update the Element
  updateXMLElement(v_doc,'PHONE_NUMBER','650.506.9181');
  -- Print out the content
  SELECT v_doc.getClobVal() INTO :result FROM dual;
END;
```

The result is the XML document containing the updated phone number:

```
<ROWSET>
  <ROW>
    <EMPLOYEE_ID>199</EMPLOYEE_ID>
    …
    <PHONE_NUMBER>650.506.9181</PHONE_NUMBER>
    …
  </ROW>
</ROWSET>
```

If multiple employees were selected, all of them would be updated. You can try the sample yourself by updating the WHERE clause in the SQL statement.

Appending XML Document Fragments

If you have two XML documents and want to merge them together, you can use the following functions, which use DBMS_XMLDOM:

```
FUNCTION importNode(doc DOMDOCUMENT, importednode DOMNODE,
                    deep BOOLEAN) RETURN DOMNODE;
FUNCTION appendChild(n DOMNODE, newChild IN DOMNODE) RETURN DOMNODE;
```

For example, if you create one XML document containing the department information and want to merge this document with one containing the employees of this department, you could use the following code:

```
SQL> SET AUTOPRINT ON
SQL> VAR RESULT CLOB
SQL> DECLARE
  v_tdoc XMLType;
  v_tsubdoc XMLType;
  v_result CLOB;
  v_doc DBMS_XMLDOM.DOMDOCUMENT;
  v_subdoc DBMS_XMLDOM.DOMDOCUMENT;
  v_doc_elem DBMS_XMLDOM.DOMELEMENT;
  v_subdoc_elem DBMS_XMLDOM.DOMELEMENT;
   v_node DBMS_XMLDOM.DOMNODE;
  v_impnode DBMS_XMLDOM.DOMNODE;
BEGIN
  -- Create the Main XML document
  SELECT XMLType(DBMS_XMLGEN.GETXML('SELECT * FROM departments
                                     WHERE department_id =20'))
    INTO v_tdoc FROM dual;
  -- Create the Sub XML document
  SELECT XMLType(DBMS_XMLGEN.GETXML('SELECT * FROM employees
                                     WHERE department_id = 20'))
    INTO v_tsubdoc from dual;

  -- Merge the documents
  v_doc := DBMS_XMLDOM.NEWDOMDOCUMENT(v_tdoc);
  v_subdoc :=DBMS_XMLDOM.NEWDOMDOCUMENT(v_tsubdoc);
  v_doc_elem := DBMS_XMLDOM.GETDOCUMENTELEMENT(v_doc);
  v_subdoc_elem := DBMS_XMLDOM.GETDOCUMENTELEMENT(v_subdoc);
  v_impnode := DBMS_XMLDOM.IMPORTNODE(v_doc,
                 DBMS_XMLDOM.MAKENODE(v_subdoc_elem), true) ;
  v_node := DBMS_XMLDOM.APPENDCHILD(
             DBMS_XMLDOM.MAKENODE(v_doc_elem), v_impnode);
  --v_node := DBMS_XMLDOM.APPENDCHILD(
   --         DBMS_XMLDOM.MAKENODE(v_doc_elem),
  --          DBMS_XMLDOM.MAKENODE(v_subdoc_elem));
  DBMS_LOB.CREATETEMPORARY(v_result,true,DBMS_LOB.SESSION);
  DBMS_XMLDOM.WRITETOCLOB(v_doc,v_result);
  SELECT v_result INTO :result FROM dual;
  DBMS_LOB.FREETEMPORARY(v_result);
END;
```

This example uses the DBMS_XMLDOM.IMPORTNODE() and DBMS_XMLDOM.APPENDCHILD() functions to create the merged document. This is the suggested and standards-compliant way to add content from one document to another via the DOM. We explore the DBMS_XMLDOM package further in Chapter 26.

Best Practices

Before you start to explore the technical details of your XML application implementation, it is important to ask yourself the following questions:

- What information do I need to deliver?
- What is the format for the XML document?
- Are there any limits to the size of the XML document?
- Which tier can be used to create, process, and deliver the XML content?

The answers to these questions will help you to make your design decisions.

First, for point-to-point communications, where individual pairs of applications exchange data through their private tunnels, encapsulating the data in XML is not a good choice because it introduces processing overhead from the metadata. Without this need to share data in public, the proprietary data formats, such as the binary format, are much more efficient and provide better security for the data transmission over the network.

Second, when using XML, always make sure to pick the right data format. Also, avoid including presentation data in XML. It is a good practice to keep presentation data in the XSLT stylesheets.

Even though many people perceive the capability to create highly descriptive tag names as an advantage of XML, you should not forget that, in most cases, XML documents are used for application processing and the size of the XML can greatly impact on the scalability of XML applications. XML documents need to be designed for efficient application processing. For example, the human-readable element name **Employee_Salary** could be replaced by **EmpSal**, and certain empty XML elements that describe properties or context for the data can be replaced by XML attributes to simplify the data access and reduce document size.

As discussed earlier, whitespaces are used to format an XML document as human-readable. This creates additional overhead for most XML processing. Removing whitespaces in XML documents sometimes can reduce the DOM object size 50 to 70 percent!

Third, in addition to creating a compact data format, you should also avoid generating large XML documents from SQL queries. Just as databases utilize partitions to deal with large tables, you should also split large XML documents containing repeating subtrees or row sets into sets of smaller XML documents. Otherwise, your application may end up running out of memory or not being able to scale when deployed in production systems with high volumes of data and transactions.

Fourth, you should avoid overloading any application tier with XML processing. For example, sometimes XSL transformations are required before delivering the XML data. Depending on the nature of the XSL stylesheets and the size of the input documents, you can perform the XSL transformation in database tier, in mid-tier application servers or on the client side.

If the XSL process transforms large amounts of data from the database, it is a good practice to run them in database. This is because you can easily leverage the high-performance data management in database, such as the lazy DOM support in the Oracle XML DB. Additionally, transforming in database can facilitate sharing the transformed results between database applications.

If the XML documents are small but intensive processing is required, such as processing SOAP or other types of XML messages, the middle tier provides the advantage of scalability by offloading the database server and hence improving the overall system performance.

To further offload the servers, some XML processing can even be performed on the client side. Now, through their support for Java, PDAs and cell phones also provide XML support.

Caching XML is another way to save processing resources in servers. The Oracle database will cache the query results in its the shared pool. However, you can also simply store the result XML documents in CLOB tables for further use.

Fifth, if certain XML SQL queries are frequently used, XML views can be used to eliminate retyping and parsing the SQL statements, thus saving time.

Finally, though the built-in XML functions give you broad functionality in generating XML, you could implement customized solutions with Oracle XML Developer's Kit (Oracle XDK) APIs in C, C++, and Java when the built-in XML functionality cannot meet your business requirements. For example, since the SAX parsing is not available in the SQL/XML functions or any of the PL/SQL packages, you can create mid-tier applications using SAX APIs from the Oracle XDK to generate large XML documents as follows:

```
Connection conn;
String username = "sh";
String password = "sh";
String thinConn = "jdbc:oracle:thin:@localhost:1521:ORCLX";
try
{
  //Open a File and JDBC Connection
  OutputStream out = new FileOutputStream("out.xml");
  DriverManager.registerDriver(new oracle.jdbc.driver.OracleDriver());
  conn= DriverManager.getConnection(thinConn,username,password);
 // Create SAX Print Driver
  XMLSAXSerializer sample = new XMLSAXSerializer(out);
  // Using the OracleXMLQuery with SAX Output
  OracleXMLQuery qry = new OracleXMLQuery(conn,"select * from sales");
  qry.getXMLSAX(sample);
  sample.flush();
}
    catch(Exception ex)
    {
      ex.printStackTrace();
    }
```

The **XMLSAXSerializer** is a SAX Content Handler in Oracle XDK that provides SAX output serialization with many options to customize the output such as specifying "pretty" or "compact" formats, setting the encoding attribute in the **<?XML?>** prolog and so on. In this example, the XMLSAXSerializer is registered to the **OracleXMLQuery.getXMLSAX()** interface to receive SAX events for the XML created by the XML SQL Utility. It then serializes the output **out.xml**.

Summary

This chapter illustrated the techniques to produce XML from various data sources in Oracle Database 10*g*. We showed how to create XMLTypes from SQL data and how to extract, transform, aggregate, and concatenate XML data within SQL commands or PL/SQL programs.

This functionality, natively provided in Oracle Database 10*g*, permits a single source of data to be presented in multiple XML formats appropriate to individual clients or applications. This opens up information-sharing possibilities, resulting in better web publishing and data exchange across applications.

CHAPTER 11

Searching XML Data

ML is a widely accepted standard for enterprise applications to exchange business data and publish data over the Internet. By storing XML data in Oracle Database 10*g*, you can create SQL indexes and enable users to efficiently search XML data. Oracle Database 10*g* provides two types of search on XML: the XPath-based search provided along with the XMLType functions, and the full text search using the Oracle database component, Oracle Text.

The XPath-based searches are queries that are based on XPath expressions, which narrow down the scope of the search through the XML hierarchical structure. Using XPath expressions, you can specify XML namespaces and leverage a wide range of datatype comparisons, such as string, number, and date comparisons. Though Oracle Text currently does not support XML namespaces and provides limited XPath and datatype support, you may need to rely on it for its scalable full text search capabilities, optimized content indexes, rich linguistic rules, and analysis.

This chapter describes both approaches, and explains how to create indexes and ensure that your XML document searches are efficient. Then, in the "Best Practices" section, it explains how to choose between the two.

XPath-Based Searches

Using XPath-based queries is straightforward. You simply use the XPath expressions in XMLType functions to specify the content retrieval from XML documents. The following is an example product document in XML:

```
<Product>
 <Name>XSLT Processor</Name>
 <Description lastupdate="03-07-2003">
  <Whatis>XSLT Processor makes use of
      <Standard type="W3C">XSLT</Standard> language defined by the World
      Wide Web Consortium (<KEYWORD>W3C</KEYWORD>) to
      <Function>transform</Function> XML documents into other formats.
  </Whatis>
  <OracleSupport>Oracle supports XSLT in SQL, PL/SQL, JAVA and C/C++.
  </OracleSupport>
 </Description>
</Product>
```

To query the XML content, you can use the following XPath expressions:

1. What is the name of product?

   XPath: **/Product/Name**

2. What are the W3C standards supported by the product?

   XPath: **/Product//Standard[@type = "W3C"]**

3. What is the description of the product, which is updated after March 1, 2003?

   XPath: **/Product/Description[@lastupdate >"03-01-2003"]**

In Oracle Database 10*g*, these kinds of XPath expressions can be used within EXISTSNODE() to search the XML documents in XMLTypes.

Searching the XML Document Using XPath

To illustrate how to use XPath in EXISTSNODE(), a table called **product** is created, which includes the **product_id**, the product **name**, and the **description** column:

```
CREATE TABLE product(
  product_id NUMBER PRIMARY KEY,
  name VARCHAR2(200),
  description XMLType);
```

The **description** is defined as an XMLType column to store the product descriptions in XML. The **description** column uses CLOB as its storage, which by default holds up to 4GB of text. After the table is created, you can insert new product records as follows:

```
INSERT INTO product(product_id, name, description)
 VALUES(1, 'XSLT Processor', XMLType('<Description>
  <Whatis>Based on the <Standard type="W3C">XSLT</Standard> standard
  defined by the World Wide Web Consortium (<KEYWORD>W3C</KEYWORD>),
  XSLT Processors <Function>transform</Function> XML documents into
  other formats.</Whatis>
  <OracleSupport>Oracle supports XSLT in SQL, PL/SQL, JAVA and
     C/C++.</OracleSupport>
  <ProductDetails>
   <Product name="XSLT for C">
    <Description>XSLT for C in Oracle XDK 10g provides the high-performance
XSLT Virtual Machine, which compiles the XSL Stylesheets and performs the
XSLT transformation using the fixed memory stack.</Description>
        <Developer>
         <First_Name>John</First_Name>
         <Last_Name>Smith</Last_Name>
         <Email>John.Smith@oracle.com</Email>
        </Developer>
   </Product>
  </ProductDetails>
 </Description>'));

INSERT INTO product(product_id, name, description)
 VALUES(2, 'XSQL', XMLType('<Description>
  <Whatis>XSQL produces dynamic XML documents based on one or more SQL
 queries and can optionally apply <Standard type="W3C">XSL</Standard>
Stylesheets to <Function>transform</Function> XML documents. Its Java
Servlet interface provides rich HTTP management functionality, such as
Cookies, <Standard type="W3C">HTTP</Standard> session parameters
etc.</Whatis>
  <OracleSupport>Java command-line utility, run-time Servlet engine and
 extensible Java development framework are provided.</OracleSupport>
  <ProductDetails>
   <Product name="XSQL for Java">
    <Description>XSQL for Java support FOP serialization</Description>
     <Developer>
      <First_Name>Richard</First_Name>
```

```
      <Last_Name>Lee</Last_Name>
      <Email>Richard.Lee@oracle.com</Email>
     </Developer>
    </Product>
  </ProductDetails>
 </Description>'));
```

You can use the EXISTSNODE() function to search the product descriptions as follows:

```
SQL> SELECT product_id, name
  2  FROM product
  3  WHERE EXISTSNODE(description,
                  '//*[contains(.,"HTTP") and contains(.,"SQL")]')>0;
PRODUCT_ID NAME
---------- -----------------------------------
         2 XSQL
```

The EXISTSNODE() function takes an XMLType as the first parameter and an XPath expression as the second parameter. In the XPath expression, the XPath function **contains(string1,string2)** is used to handle the string matching. The **contains()** function returns TRUE if the first string argument (**string1**) contains the substring equal to the second argument (**string2**). According to the XPath standard, you can add **and** or **or** logic operators between two **contains()** functions. In the preceding example, the XPath-based query returns all products that contain both *HTTP* and *SQL* in the product description.

Note that all the text in XPath expressions is case sensitive and that all the logic predicates in XPath, such as **and** and **or**, have to be in lowercase. For example, the following query produces an *ORA-31013: Invalid XPath Expression* error because *AND* is used instead of *and* in the logic predicates:

```
SQL> SELECT product_id, name
  2  FROM product
  3  WHERE EXISTSNODE(description,
                    '//*[contains(.,"HTTP") AND contains(.,"SQL")]')>0;
   FROM product
        *
ERROR at line 2:
ORA-31013: Invalid XPath expression
```

Because the XPath expressions are case sensitive, *sql* and *SQL* are treated as different strings. As a result, the following query will not return the products containing the word *SQL* in their description:

```
SELECT product_id, name
FROM product
WHERE EXISTSNODE(description,'//*[contains(.,"HTTP")
                                    and contains(.,"sql")]')>0;
```

To make the search case insensitive, you can enumerate all the possible combinations of the characters in a word. For example, the following query will return all the products whose description contains either *SQL* or *sql*:

```
SELECT product_id, name
FROM product
WHERE EXISTSNODE (description,
'//*[contains(.,"HTTP") and ( contains(.,"SQL")
                              or contains(.,"sql"))]')>0;
```

However, covering all the possible combinations is annoying. In Oracle Database 10*g*, you can instead use the **ora:contains()** function, which provides case-insensitive text searches. Another reason to use **ora:contains()** is that the **contains()** XPath function does not have word semantics. It performs only consecutive character-by-character comparisons. This may result in unexpected query results, as shown in the following example. After the **<OracleSupport>** element in the product description of the XSQL Servlet has been updated, as follows:

```
SQL> UPDATE product SET description=UPDATEXML(description,
   '/Description/OracleSupport',
   '<OracleSupport>Oracle XSQL provides Java command-line utility,
    run-time Servlet engine and an extensible Java development framework.
    </OracleSupport>')
   WHERE product_id=2;
```

a query on the updated **product** table will return the following result:

```
SQL> SELECT product_id, name
  FROM product
  WHERE EXISTSNODE(description,
                   '//OracleSupport[contains(.,"SQL")]')>0;
PRODUCT_ID NAME
---------- -----------------------------------
         1 XSLT Processor
         2 XSQL
```

This query result is not anticipated! The reason that the **contains()** function returns TRUE is that in the **<OracleSupport>** element of the product description for XSQL Servlet, the string *XSQL* contains *SQL* as a substring. Using **ora:contains()** instead, with its support for word semantics, gives an accurate text search result, as shown in the following example:

```
SQL> SELECT product_id, name
   FROM product
   WHERE EXISTSNODE(description,
                   '//OracleSupport[ora:contains(.,"SQL")>0]',
                   'xmlns:ora="http://xmlns.oracle.com/xdb"')>0;

PRODUCT_ID NAME
---------- -----------------------------------
         1 XSLT Processor
```

In Oracle Database 10*g*, the **ora:contains()** function can be used at any place in the XPath expressions and can leverage the full text search functionality in Oracle Text, such as word stemming, fuzzy matching, proximity searching, specifying searching policies, and so on. For example, the following query uses word stemming to query the product descriptions:

```
SQL> SELECT product_id, name
       FROM product
       WHERE EXISTSNODE(description, '//*[ora:contains(.,"$base")>0]',
                     'xmlns:ora="http://xmlns.oracle.com/xdb"')>0;

PRODUCT_ID NAME
---------- -----------------------------------
         1 XSLT Processor
         2 XSQL
```

Though the word *base* is not shown in the XML document, the product is returned because the word *based* has the same word stem.

In Oracle Database 10*g*, the EXISTSNODE() function can be used in the WHERE clause of SQL queries along with any other SQL predicates or combinations of itself. Here is one example:

```
SELECT product_id, name
FROM product
WHERE EXISTSNODE(description, '//OracleSupport[ora:contains(.,"sql")>0]',
                 'xmlns:ora="http://xmlns.oracle.com/xdb"')>0
 AND EXISTSNODE(description,'//Standard[@type="W3C"]')>0;
```

This example specifies the query for *What are the Oracle products that support W3C standards and provide SQL interfaces?*

How XPath-Based Searching Works

When you specify an XPath expression in EXISTSNODE(), the Oracle XML DB evaluates the XPath expressions and executes queries based on the XMLType storage.

If XML is stored in CLOB XMLTypes, the Oracle XML DB functionally evaluates the XPath expressions by building the DOM tree of the XML document in memory and resolves the XPath programmatically using the methods provided by DOM. If a CTXXPATH index is created, the XML DB engine first uses the CTXXPATH index to get the superset of the result data set and then performs DOM-based functional evaluation. If the **ora:contains()** function is used in the XPath expressions, the selected XML data will be loaded into memory for additional full text-search analysis.

If XML is stored in XML Schema-based XMLTypes, the Oracle XML DB first rewrites the XPath expressions into equivalent SQL statements. Then, based on the object-relational (O-R) data structures, it utilizes whichever index is available to access the data in the object tables. This query-translation process is called the *query rewrite* of XPath-based queries. Because of the query rewrite process, the XML data retrieval can be as fast as accessing the SQL data.

In the Oracle XML DB, query rewrite is a different process than the query rewrite widely used in data warehouse applications, where users do not need the query rewrite privileges and do not need to create materialized views or summary tables. To make sure you understand the execution process, the following example creates another table that stores the product descriptions in XML Schema-based XMLTypes. First, you need to register an XML schema:

```
BEGIN
   DBMS_XMLSCHEMA.REGISTERSCHEMA('product.xsd',
          '<?xml version="1.0" encoding="UTF-8"?>
<xs:schema xmlns:xdb="http://xmlns.oracle.com/xdb"
xmlns:xs="http://www.w3.org/2001/XMLSchema"
       elementFormDefault="qualified">
 <xs:element name="Description">
  <xs:complexType xdb:SQLType="DESCRIPTION_TYPE">
   <xs:sequence>
    <xs:element name="Whatis" xdb:SQLName="WHATIS"
         xdb:SQLType="WHATIS_TYPE">
     <xs:complexType mixed="true">
      <xs:choice minOccurs="0" maxOccurs="unbounded">
       <xs:element name="Function" type="xs:string"/>
       <xs:element name="KEYWORD" type="xs:string"/>
       <xs:element name="Standard">
        <xs:complexType>
         <xs:simpleContent>
          <xs:extension base="xs:string">
           <xs:attribute name="type" type="xs:string" use="required"/>
          </xs:extension>
         </xs:simpleContent>
        </xs:complexType>
       </xs:element>
      </xs:choice>
     </xs:complexType>
    </xs:element>
    <xs:element name="OracleSupport" type="xs:string"/>
   </xs:sequence>
   <xs:attribute name="name" type="xs:string" use="required"/>
  </xs:complexType>
 </xs:element>
</xs:schema>', TRUE, TRUE, FALSE,FALSE);
END;
```

After you have registered the XML schema, you can create a **product** table by specifying the structured XMLType storage for the **description** column:

```
CREATE TABLE product(
  product_id NUMBER PRIMARY KEY,
  name VARCHAR2(200),
  description XMLType)
   XMLTYPE COLUMN description ELEMENT "product.xsd#Description";
```

You then can insert the same set of data into the table as shown in the previous examples, except that you need to use the XMLType.**CreateSchemaBasedXML()** function to specify the registered XML schema URLs during data insertions:

```
INSERT INTO product(product_id, name, description) VALUES(1, 'XSLT
Processor', XMLType('…').CreateSchemaBasedXML('product.xsd'));
```

Looking at the following XPath query:

```
SELECT product_id, name
FROM product
WHERE EXISTSNODE(description, '/Description[@name="XSQL"]')>0;
```

The Oracle XML DB parses and rewrites the XPath query to a SQL query that looks like the following:

```
SELECT VALUE(description)
FROM product p
WHERE description.XMLDATA.name='XSLT';
```

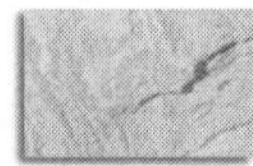

NOTE
In the object-relational storage of XMLTypes, XMLDATA refers to the root element of the XML document in the XMLType, and SYS_NC_ROWINFO$ represents the XMLType object.

However, not all XPath-based queries can be rewritten. In Oracle Database 10*g*, if the XPath expression contains the following items, the query cannot be rewritten:

- All XPath functions except **not()**, **floor()**, **ceiling()**, **substring()**, **string-length**(), and **translate()**
- XPath variable references
- Any axes except the child and attribute axes
- Recursive type definitions with descendent axis
- UNION operators

If the registered XML schema of an XMLType contains the following elements and the XPath expression includes nodes under these elements, the query also cannot be successfully rewritten:

- Elements containing open content, namely ANY content
- Elements mapped to SQL CLOBs

The advantage of query rewrite is that it enables the use of B*Tree or other indexes on the XML data to speed up the query response. Without query rewrite, the XPath queries require in-memory construction of the XML object tree and programmatic evaluation through the object tree traversal.

NOTE
Like the other Oracle-provided extension functions that are under the Oracle XML DB *namespace (http://xmlns.oracle.com/xdb), such as* ***ora:upper(), ora:lower(), ora:to_date(), ora:to_number()*** *and* ***ora:like()****, the* ***ora:contains()*** *function is rewritten to a SQL query. Additionally, it uses the CONTEXT index if available, and the XML element or attribute used by* ***ora:contains()*** *is an object in the O-R tables of the XMLType.*

Optimizing XPath-Based Queries Using Indexes

To speed up XPath-based queries, you can create indexes on XML documents. There are four main types of indexes available in Oracle Database 10*g* for XMLTypes: B*Tree indexes, bitmap indexes, function-based indexes, and CTXXPATH indexes. The following sections discuss how to use them.

B*Tree Indexes

If an XML document is stored in O-R XMLTypes, you can create B*Tree indexes on the XML content. Since XPath-based queries are rewritten to SQL queries, B*Tree indexes can speed up all rewritten SQL queries. In the following example, a B*Tree index is created on the **name** attribute of the **<Description>** element, and the EXPLAIN PLAN command is run to examine the query execution plan:

```
SQL> CREATE UNIQUE INDEX name_idx ON product(description.xmldata."name");
Index created.
SQL> EXPLAIN PLAN FOR
     SELECT count(*)
     FROM product x
     WHERE x.description.EXISTSNODE( '/Description[@name="XSLT"]')=1;
Explained.
SQL> @d:\oracle\rdbms\admin\utlxpls
PLAN_TABLE_OUTPUT
-------------------------------------------------------------------------------
|Id | Operation               | Name    |Rows | Bytes | Cost (%CPU)|  Time    |
-------------------------------------------------------------------------------
| 0 |SELECT STATEMENT         |         |  1 |   496 |    3  (34) |00:00:01|
| 1 | SORT AGGREGATE          |         |  1 |   496 |            |        |
| 2 |  TABLE ACCESS           |         |    |       |            |        |
|   |   BY INDEX ROWID        | PRODUCT| 1   |   496 |    3  (34) |00:00:01|
|*3 |    INDEX UNIQUE SCAN|NAME_IDX| 1   |       |      2  (50)|00:00:01|

Predicate Information (identified by operation id):
---------------------------------------------------
   3 - access("X"."SYS_NC00010$"='XSLT')

14 rows selected.
```

The INDEX UNIQUE SCAN that uses the NAME_IDX shows that the created B*Tree index is used when executing the XPath-based query.

Bitmap Indexes

Bitmap indexes store all the index keys in a bitmap instead of the list of ROWIDs, as in B*Tree indexes. Each bit in the bitmap corresponds to a possible ROWID. If the bit is set, it means that the row with the corresponding ROWIDs contains the key value. A mapping function converts the bit position to the actual ROWID, so the bitmap index provides the same functionality as a regular index even though it internally uses a different representation.

If the number of different key values is small, bitmap indexes are space efficient. For XML documents, you can create bitmap indexes on those XML elements containing a high duplication of data. In the following example, a bitmap index is created for the **types** attribute in the **<Standard>** element:

```
SQL> CREATE BITMAP INDEX bitmap_idx ON
 product(description.existsNode('/Description/Whatis/Standard@type'));
Index created.
```

Then, you can run the following EXPLAIN PLAN command to examine the query execution details:

```
SQL> EXPLAIN PLAN FOR
 SELECT /*+ index(x bitmap_idx) */ count(*) FROM product x
 WHERE x.description.EXISTSNODE('/Description/Whatis/Standard@type')=1;
Explained.

SQL>  @d:\oracle\rdbms\admin\utlxpls
PLAN_TABLE_OUTPUT
-----------------------------------------------------------------------
| Id |     Operation            |  Name      |Rows|Bytes|Cost (%CPU)| Time    |
-----------------------------------------------------------------------
| 0  |SELECT STATEMENT          |            | 1  | 496 |    69       |00:00:01|
| 1  | SORT AGGREGATE           |            | 1  | 496 |             |        |
|*2  |  TABLE ACCESS BY         |            |    |     |             |        |
|    |   INDEX ROWID            | PRODUCT    | 4  | 496 |    69       |00:00:01|
| 3  |   BITMAP CONVERSION      |            |    |     |             |        |
|    |    TO ROWIDS             |            |    |     |             |        |
| 4  |  BITMAP INDEX FULL SCAN|BITMAP_IDX|    |     |             |        |
-----------------------------------------------------------------------
Predicate Information (identified by operation id):
---------------------------------------------------
 2 - filter(EXISTSNODE(SYS_MAKEXML('0602BCF5CB2048E2BBA19796753F5D49',
     2812,X."SYS_NC00004$",X."SYS_NC00007$"),
     '/Description/Whatis/Standard@type')=1)
16 rows selected.
```

The BITMAP INDEX FULL SCAN that uses the BITMAP_IDX shows that the created bitmap index is used when executing the XPath-based query.

Function-Based Indexes

A function-based index is created based on the values returned by function expressions. After the values are computed and stored, SQL queries using the functions in their WHERE clauses will be sped up by use of the index. The function used for building the index can be either an arithmetic expression or an expression that contains a PL/SQL function, a C callout, or a SQL function.

In the Oracle XML DB, when query rewrite cannot be used on O-R XMLTypes because of the previously discussed limitations, you can create a function-based index using XMLType functions. The following example creates a function-based index and the EXPLAIN PLAN command is run to examine the query execution plan:

```
SQL> CREATE INDEX fidx_existnode ON PRODUCT(
EXTRACT(description,'/Description/Whatis/Function').getStringVal());
Index created.

SQL> EXPLAIN PLAN FOR
     SELECT count(*)
     FROM product x
     WHERE EXTRACT(description,
            '/Description/Whatis/Function').getStringVal()='transform';
Explained.
SQL> @d:\oracle\rdbms\admin\utlxpls
PLAN_TABLE_OUTPUT
```

```
---------------------------------------------------------------------------
| Id | Operation          |    Name         |Rows|Bytes|Cost (%CPU)|   Time   |
---------------------------------------------------------------------------
| 0 |SELECT STATEMENT   |                  |  1 | 496 |    2  (50) | 00:00:01|
| 1 |  SORT AGGREGATE   |                  |  1 | 496 |            |         |
|* 2|   INDEX RANGE SCAN| FIDX_EXISTNODE |  1 |496  |  2  (50)| 00:00:01 |
---------------------------------------------------------------------------
Predicate Information (identified by operation id):
---------------------------------------------------
   2 - access((EXTRACT(SYS_MAKEXML('1279EA6100D34050A95214274890C924',
3065,X."SYS_NC00004$",X."SYS_NC00007$"),'/Description/Whatis/Function'))
='transform')

15 rows selected.
```

The INDEX RANGE SCAN that uses the FIDX_EXISTNODE shows that the created function-based index is used when executing the XPath-based query.

CTXXPATH Indexes

To improve the performance of XPath-based searches, CTXXPATH index was introduced in Oracle9*i* R2 for XMLTypes, which serves primarily as a content filter for EXISTSNODE(). When CTXXPATH index is used by EXISTSNODE(), a superset of the results of the XPath expression is returned, as in the following query:

```
SELECT product_id, name
FROM product
WHERE EXISTSNODE(description,
'/Description[@name="XSLT"]/OracleSupport[ora:contains(.,"SQL")>0]',
                'xmlns:ora="http://xmlns.oracle.com/xdb"')>0;
```

The CTXXPATH index can't return the results for the complete XPath query since it can't process **ora:contains()**, but it can filter the content and return all the documents containing the path **/Description/[@name="XSLT"]**. Based on the superset returned by the CTXXPATH index, EXISTSNODE() then processes a significantly reduced number of XML documents.

Creating the CTXXPATH index is similar to creating the CONTEXT index provided by Oracle Text. For example, you can create a CTXXPATH index on the **description** column of the **product** table as follows:

```
CREATE INDEX ctxxpath_idx ON product(description)

INDEXTYPE IS CTXSYS.CTXXPATH;
```

As with the CONTEXT index, the CTXXPATH index requires index synchronizations after insert and update DML operations. Additionally, it supports only XPath without XML namespaces. If the XPath expression contains namespaces, the CTXXPATH index will not be used for XPath functions, numerical range operators, arithmetic operators, or XPath axes. The use of the CTXXPATH index also depends on the database optimizers. For example, if the *Cost Based Optimizer (CBO)* decides that the CTXXPATH index is too expensive to use, it also will not be used by the EXISTSNODE() function. In order to let the database optimizers properly estimate the cost, you can use the ANALYZE command or the DBMS_STATS package.

Full Text Search

Oracle Text, known as Oracle *interMedia Text* in Oracle8*i*, provides the full text search functionality that allows users to quickly find the documents that contain certain words or phrases.

To utilize the full text search functionality in Oracle Text, you can create a CONTEXT index provided by Oracle Text and specify searches in SQL using the CONTAINS() function. For example, you can create a CONTEXT index on the **description** column of the **product** table as follows:

```
CREATE INDEX desc_idx ON product(description)
INDEXTYPE IS CTXSYS.CONTEXT;
```

The CONTEXT index type is specified by the INDEXTYPE clause. After the CONTEXT index is created, you can submit a SQL query as follows:

```
SELECT name FROM product WHERE CONTAINS(description, 'XSLT')>0;
```

The first argument of the CONTAINS() function is the column being searched, and the second argument includes the search words or phrases. The CONTAINS() function returns a number for each row in the table, indicating how closely the document matches the query. If the returned number is greater than zero, the document matches the query. As a result, the example query returns the name of every product containing *XSLT* in its description.

By default, the CONTEXT index does not provide transactional support for the DML operations, including data insertions and updates. You need to synchronize the CONTEXT index to ensure that the index is up-to-date.

In Oracle Database 10*g*, a new index property called TRANSACTIONAL is introduced for the CONTEXT index to provide transactional support, as shown in the following example:

```
CREATE INDEX desc_idx ON product(description)
INDEXTYPE IS CTXSYS.CONTEXT
PARAMETERS('TRANSACTIONAL');
```

if the CONTEXT index is created with the TRANSACTIONAL property turned on. In addition to processing the synchronized ROWIDs in the CONTEXT index, the CONTAINS() function does in-memory indexing and processing for the updated or inserted ROWIDs that have not yet been synchronized. You still need to synchronize the index to bring the pending ROWIDs into the CONTEXT index for better performance.

In summary, the following is the basic procedure for using the full text search functionality provided by Oracle Text:

1. Create a CONTEXT index on VARCHAR2, CLOB, BLOB, BFILE, UriType, or XMLType columns.
2. Query table-indexed columns using the CONTAINS() function in SQL.
3. Synchronize the CONTEXT index after DML operations and optimize the index regularly to ensure better performance.

We will discuss the CONTEXT index optimization in the following sections.

NOTE
Oracle Text provides a transaction-based index called the CTXCAT index. However, normally it is not used for indexing XML documents because it supports only CHAR and VARCHAR2 columns and has limited support for structured document search.

Searching XML Using Oracle Text

In searching XML, you often want to use the structure of the XML document to restrict the search. In Oracle Text, *document sections* are used to define and add structure information from the XML document to the CONTEXT index. Each document section is defined based on the start tag/end tag of the XML elements or on certain XPath detections. During indexing, the CONTEXT index stores the document sections for every indexed token. This allows users to specify the scope of the text search either by using XPath expressions with INPATH/HASPATH operators or by using XML element names with the WITHIN operator.

Oracle Text provides three types of document section for XML documents: AUTO_SECTION_GROUP, PATH_SECTION_GROUP, and XML_SECTION_GROUP. Each section group is an object that consists of a collection of tags that should be indexed and a section type specification that indicates the format of the document and how to parse the format.

Both AUTO_SECTION_GROUP and XML_SECTION_GROUP index the document based on the element/attribute names. The difference between the two is that AUTO_SECTION_GROUP indexes every XML tag whereas XML_SECTION_GROUP indexes only the tags in its tag collection. PATH_SECTION_GROUP indexes all the element tags and attributes while maintaining the XPath information.

NOTE
Using AUTO_SECTION_GROUP in Oracle Database 10g is not recommended, because its searching functionality can be fully covered by the PATH_SECTION_GROUP index.

Using PATH_SECTION_GROUP

PATH_SECTION_GROUP is the default section group for XMLTypes. Since PATH_SECTION_GROUP indexes all the sections in the XML document, there is no need to declare the document sections to be indexed. Therefore, users normally use the default instance of PATH_SECTION_GROUP provided by Oracle Text to create the index. This default instance of PATH_SECTION_GROUP contains the predefined full text search preferences. For example, you can create a CONTEXT index called **product_idx** with PATH_SECTION_GROUP as follows:

```
CREATE INDEX product_idx ON product(description)
 INDEXTYPE IS CTXSYS.CONTEXT
 PARAMETERS('SECTION GROUP CTXSYS.PATH_SECTION_GROUP');
```

With PATH_SECTION_GROUP, you can use the WITHIN operator, but you can additionally choose from two more-powerful operators, the HASPATH or INPATH operators, to incorporate a subset of XPath expressions within the CONTAINS() function. HASPATH returns TRUE if the specified

XPath exists in the XML document, and INPATH returns TRUE if the text specified exists in the XML content selected out by the XPath expressions. Here are examples of both operators in action:

```
SQL> SELECT product_id, name
  FROM product
  WHERE CONTAINS(description,'SQL INPATH(/Description/
      OracleSupport)')>0;
PRODUCT_Id NAME
----------------------------------------------------------------------
        1  XSLT Processor
SQL> SELECT product_id, name
  FROM product
  WHERE CONTAINS(description,
              'HASPATH(/Description//Standard[@type="W3C"])')>0;

PRODUCT_ID  NAME
----------------------------------------------------------------------
         2  XSQL
         1  XSLT Processor
```

The first SQL query uses INPATH to limit the **<OracleSupport>** element to be a direct child of the root element, **<Description>**, which contains the word *SQL*. The HASPATH operator in the second query is used to evaluate the XPath expression and return TRUE if the XPath **/Description//Standard[@type="W3C"]** exists in the XML document.

NOTE
The text used in XPath is case sensitive; for example, INPATH(//Product) is different from INPATH(//product).

Using XML_SECTION_GROUP

The CONTEXT index in PATH_SECTION_GROUP is easy to use, but it can be expensive because it indexes all the document sections in the XML document, including those whose content will not be searched. To avoid the overhead, you can use XML_SECTION_GROUP to specify a limited number of document sections based on the XML elements. For example, you can create an instance of XML_SECTION_GROUP called **productGroup** and limit the index on one document section called **whatis_sec** containing content from the **<Whatis>** element:

```
EXEC CTX_DDL.CREATE_SECTION_GROUP('productGroup','XML_SECTION_GROUP');
EXEC CTX_DDL.ADD_ZONE_SECTION('productGroup','whatis_sec','Whatis');
```

Then, you can create a CONTEXT index using the **productGroup**:

```
CREATE INDEX desc_xml_idx ON product(description)
INDEXTYPE IS CTXSYS.CONTEXT
PARAMETERS('SECTION GROUP productGroup');
```

The SQL query can use the WITHIN operator to specify the document section:

```
SELECT name
FROM product
WHERE CONTAINS(description, 'java WITHIN whatis_sec')>0;
```

You can also add a new zone section named **orasupport_sec** using the tag name of the **<OracleSupport>** element by rebuilding the index:

```
ALTER INDEX desc_xml_idx REBUILD
PARAMETERS ('ADD ZONE SECTION orasupport_sec TAG OracleSupport');
```

However, the following SQL query will not return any rows:

```
SELECT name
FROM product
WHERE CONTAINS(description, 'java WITHIN orasupport_sec')>0;
```

This is because the rebuild process only modifies the index metadata, and does not rebuild the index in any way. This means that these section updates do not affect any indexed documents. To include the existing documents in the index with the new sections, you need to manually mark the documents for re-indexing or simply drop and re-create the index.

In contrast to PATH_SECTION_GROUP, XML_SECTION_GROUP is efficient. However, when the element names are not unique in the XML document, you cannot create zone sections to differentiate these elements in the full text searches.

Synchronizing the Index

Unlike the B*Tree index, where the database maintains the index on the basis of DML transactions, the CONTEXT index is not updated after the DML transactions, including the data insertions and updates. Instead, only the ROWIDs of the updated or inserted table records are kept for later index synchronization. Therefore, if there are any inserts or updates of documents in the base table, you need to synchronize the CONTEXT index for the records to be part of the searching content.

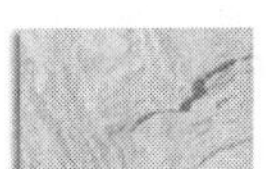

NOTE
The CONTEXT index transactionally supports data deletion operations.

You can decide whether synchronization is needed by reviewing the CTX_USER_PENDING view, where all ROWIDs related to DML operations are stored. For example, if the **product** table is updated, you can see new entries in the CTX_USER_PENDING view:

```
SQL> UPDATE product SET
  description=updateXML(description,'/Description/OracleSupport',
  '<OracleSupport>Oracle XSQL provides command-line utility, run-time
  Servlet engine and extensible Java development framework
  </OracleSupport>')
  WHERE product_id=2;
1 row updated.
```

```
SQL> SELECT pnd_index_name, pnd_rowid, TO_CHAR(pnd_timestamp,
  'dd-mon-yyyy') timestamp
  FROM CTX_USER_PENDING;

PND_INDEX_NAME                 PND_ROWID          TIMESTAMP
------------------------------ ------------------ -----------
PRODUCT_IDX                    AAAK6jAAEAAAAbsAAB 09-aug-2003
```

You can synchronize your index manually by calling the CTX_DDL.SYNC_INDEX() procedure. In order to have the execution privilege on the CTX_DDL PL/SQL package, you need to have the CTXAPP role granted by the CTXSYS user:

```
GRANT ctxapp TO &user_name;
```

The following example synchronizes the **product_idx** index using 2MB of memory:

```
SQL> BEGIN
  2    CTX_DDL.SYNC_INDEX('product_idx', '2M');
  3  END;
  4  /
PL/SQL procedure successfully completed.

SQL> SELECT pnd_index_name, pnd_rowid, TO_CHAR(pnd_timestamp,
  'dd-mon-yyyy') timestamp FROM CTX_USER_PENDING;
no rows selected
```

After index synchronization, the CTX_USER_PENDING view will not have any entries.

Alternatively, you can run CTX_DDL.SYNC_INDEX() automatically at regular intervals using the DBMS_JOB.SUBMIT() procedure. Oracle Text includes a SQL script you can use to do this:

```
$ORACLE_HOME/ctx/sample/script/drjobdml.sql

$ORACLE_HOME/ctx/sample/script/drbgdml.sql
```

To use this script, you must be the owner of the index and you must have execution privileges on the CTX_DDL package. You must also set the JOB_QUEUE_PROCESSES parameter in the Oracle initialization file. For example, to set the index synchronization to run every 360 minutes on **product_idx**, you can issue the following command in SQL*Plus:

```
SQL> @drjobdml product_idx 360;
```

You need to properly choose an interval for CONTEXT index synchronization. This is because synchronizing the CONTEXT indexes right after each data insertion or update may result in index fragmentation, which may dramatically reduce the performance of the full text search queries.

If the application requires frequent synchronization of the CONTEXT index or even requires the transactional update of the CONTEXT index, you then need to schedule additional regular CONTEXT index optimization to ensure high performance.

How Oracle Text Search Works

Knowing the details of how searching with Oracle Text works helps you build better searches. This is particularly useful when you want to know why the data is selected. This section discusses those features that help you understand the search process.

Whenever the CONTEXT index is created, all the XML documents are analyzed and a set of tables is created to store the indexed tokens. For example, along with the **product_idx** index, the following index tables are created:

```
SQL> SELECT table_name FROM user_tables
   WHERE table_name LIKE '%PRODUCT_IDX%';

TABLE_NAME
------------------------------
DR$PRODUCT_IDX$I
DR$PRODUCT_IDX$K
DR$PRODUCT_IDX$N
DR$PRODUCT_IDX$R
```

The Oracle Text engine creates four tables automatically. These tables start with the DR$ prefix and end with the suffix to be $I, $K, $N, or $R. Between the prefix and suffix is the index name.

The DR$<INDEX NAME>$K and DR$<INDEX NAME>$R tables store the mapping of the row information from the internal document identifiers (DOCIDs) to external ROWID values. The database optimizer (Cost Based Optimizer) determines the type of lookup. For functional lookups, the $K table is used. For indexed lookups, the $R table is used. Hence, you can easily find out whether a functional or indexed lookup is used by examining the SQL trace and looking for the $K or $R tables.

The $N table is used to maintain information for the deleted rows and the $I table is the one that stores all the tokens indexed by Oracle Text. The search queries will look up all the tokens stored in the $I table before returning the result. The following is the schema of the $I table:

```
SQL> DESC DR$product_idx$I;
 Name                                      Null?    Type
 --------------- ------------------- -------- ----------------
 TOKEN_TEXT                              NOT NULL VARCHAR2(64)
 TOKEN_TYPE                              NOT NULL NUMBER(3)
 TOKEN_FIRST                             NOT NULL NUMBER(10)
 TOKEN_LAST                              NOT NULL NUMBER(10)
 TOKEN_COUNT                             NOT NULL NUMBER(10)
 TOKEN_INFO                                       BLOB
```

The TOKEN_TEXT column stores the tokens and the TOKEN_INFO column stores the information about the row and word positions where the token occurs.

To ensure the preferred content is indexed by Oracle Text, you can use the following command to check the $I table:

```
SELECT TOKEN_TEXT FROM DR$product_idx$I
WHERE TOKEN_TEXT LIKE 'XSLT';
```

This SQL query checks whether the word *XSLT* is indexed by the CONTEXT index called **product_idx**.

Sometimes an indexing operation might fail or not complete successfully. When the system encounters an error indexing a row, it logs the error in an Oracle Text view. You can view these errors for specific users using the CTX_USER_INDEX_ERRORS view or query the CTXSYS errors for all users using the CTX_INDEX_ERRORS view. For example, to view the most recent index errors of the current logged in user, you can issue the following SQL command:

```
SELECT err_timestamp, err_text
FROM ctx_user_index_errors
ORDER BY err_timestamp DESC;
```

To clear the view of errors, you can issue the following command:

```
DELETE FROM CTX_USER_INDEX_ERRORS;
```

Optimizing Oracle Text Searches

We have discussed that you need to optimize the CONTEXT index after multiple index synchronizations. This is because index synchronization may result in index fragmentation that adversely affects query performance.

Additionally, in order to improve query response time, when many rows are deleted from the base table, you need to optimize the CONTEXT index in FULL mode. This is because the old data in the index table is marked only as deleted but is not cleaned up immediately. Because the old data takes up space and can cause extra overhead at query time, you must remove this data from the index by optimizing the index in FULL mode. This is called *garbage collection*. Optimizing in FULL mode for garbage collection is also necessary when you have had frequent updates or deletions to the base table. If you rarely delete or update data from a table, you can use the OPTIMIZE FAST option. Otherwise, you should use OPTIMIZE FULL.

You can also optimize the index in TOKEN mode, where you specify a specific token to be optimized. You can use this mode to optimize index tokens that are frequently searched, without spending time optimizing tokens that are rarely referenced. For example, you can specify that only the token "Functionality" in the product description be optimized in the index if you know that this token is updated and queried frequently. To optimize an index in TOKEN mode, you can use CTX_DDL.OPTIMIZE_INDEX() as follows:

```
BEGIN
CTX_DDL.OPTIMIZE_INDEX('product_idx','token',
    TOKEN=>'Functionality');
END;
```

An optimized token can improve its query response time. Again, the tokens can be found in the $I table.

To help you decide whether to optimize your index, you can create a statistical report on your index using the CTX_REPORT.INDEX_STATS() procedure. The report includes information on the optimal row fragmentation, a list of the most fragmented tokens, and the amount of garbage data in your index. Although this report might take a long time to run for large indexes, it really helps.

Advanced Text Searches

Oracle Text provides many full text search features. This section discusses techniques on how to return scores that reflect the relevance of the query and returned records, how to leverage the full text search on XML documents in the XML DB Repository, and how to set up categories for XML document searching.

Using Scores

When you issue a full text search query, Oracle Text returns a relevance score for each document returned. The score is between 1 and 10. The higher the score, the more relevant the document is to the query. The score can be selected using the SCORE() operator with a label of 1:

```
SQL> SELECT score(1) AS score, product_id, name
  FROM product
  WHERE CONTAINS(description,'W3C INPATH(//Standard/@type)',1)>0;

SCORE        PRODUCT_ID       NAME
-----------------------------------------------------------------
         6           2        XSQL
         3           1        XSLT Processor
```

You can use these scores to order the returned documents by showing the most relevant documents first.

Searching XML in the Oracle XML DB Repository

To add full text search for XML files stored in the Oracle XML DB repository, you can create a CONTEXT index using a subtype of the **UriType** called **XDBUriType**.

NOTE
Additionally, you can create CONTEXT indexes on files in HTTP server, FTP server, and OS file systems using the ***UriType*** *or its subtypes such as the* ***HTTPUriType****.*

For example, you can create a table with an **XDBUriType** column containing the Oracle XML DB repository URIs pointing to the files stored the XML DB repository. For example, the XML DB repository URI of the **xdbconfig.xml** file is **/xdbconfig.xml**:

```
CREATE TABLE myconfig(url SYS.XDBURITYPE);
INSERT INTO myconfig VALUES(SYS.XDBURITYPE.CREATEURI('/xdbconfig.xml'));
```

Then, you can create a CONTEXT index on this column:

```
CREATE INDEX config_idx ON myconfig(url) INDEXTYPE IS CTXSYS.CONTEXT;
```

After the index is created, you can use the following SQL CONTAINS query to search the content:

```
SELECT * FROM myconfig WHERE CONTAINS(url, 'http')>0;
```

Category-Based Searching

When searching a large number of XML documents, you can classify the documents and establish the document routing by creating a CTXRULE index. In Oracle Database 10*g*, you can build a CTXRULE index based on your XML document queries.

The first step is to create a table of queries that defines the classifications. For example, you can create a **QUERY_CAT** table to hold the category name and query text:

```
CREATE TABLE QUERY_CAT (
query_id NUMBER PRIMARY KEY,
category VARCHAR2(30),
query VARCHAR2(2000));
```

You then can populate the table with the classifications and the queries that define each category. For example, consider a classification for the subjects *XML* and *SQL*:

```
INSERT INTO QUERY_CAT VALUES(1, 'XML Product', 'xml');
INSERT INTO QUERY_CAT VALUES(2, 'SQL', 'ABOUT(sql)');
```

You can create the CTXRULE index as follows:

```
CREATE INDEX ctxrule_idx ON query_cat(query)
INDEXTYPE IS CTXSYS.CTXRULE;
```

After a CTXRULE index is created on the query set, you can use the MATCHES() function to classify the XML documents. In the following example, a **product_route** table is created to store results of the document classification:

```
create table product_route
(product_id number,
 category varchar2(30));
```

The following PL/SQL code populates the **product_route** table using MATCHES():

```
DECLARE
 CURSOR p_desc IS SELECT product_id, description FROM product;
BEGIN
 FOR item IN p_desc LOOP
  FOR c1 IN (SELECT category
             FROM query_cat
             WHERE MATCHES(query,item.description.getStringVal())>0)
  LOOP
    INSERT INTO product_route(product_id, category)
      VALUES (item.product_id, c1.category);
  END LOOP;
 END LOOP;
END;
```

Using this functionality, you can classify XML documents into a number of predefined categories.

Best Practices

Optimizing the performance of searches can be a trial-and-error process. You should regularly monitor the performance to establish a plan for maintaining the indexes. The following are some tips to maximize the query performance.

When to Use XPath-Based Searches

You should not overuse XPath-based queries on XML documents unless you can ensure that the query rewrite is performed properly. Without query rewrite, the in-memory building of DOM trees or text analysis for **ora:contains()** can be very expensive and prevent you from searching large numbers of XML documents.

In addition, you should know that without **ora:contains()**, XPath-based queries are limited to matching substrings and may result in unexpected results.

Finally, the CTXXPATH index and functional indexes are both very useful for XPath-based searches when the query rewrite cannot be used.

When to Use Oracle Text Searches

Compared to XPath-based queries, Oracle Text performs linguistic analysis and provides rich full text search features that go beyond substring matching. For example, it allows you to create a concise abstract, called gist, for the indexed XML documents:

```
CREATE TABLE ctx_gist (query_id  NUMBER,
                        pov       VARCHAR2(80),
                        gist      CLOB);

BEGIN
  FOR item IN (SELECT product_id FROM product) LOOP
   CTX_DOC.GIST('product_idx',item.product_id,'CTX_GIST',1,'P',
pov =>'GENERIC', numParagraphs => 1);
  END LOOP;
END;
```

This example uses the CTX_DOC.GIST() procedure to generate gists for the product descriptions, specifying the size of the gist to be no more than one paragraph and inserting the created abstracts into a gist table called **ctx_gist**.

Oracle Text provides better scalability for the searches on XML documents that cannot use query rewrite by substantially reducing the processing overhead introduced by XML DOM tree creation and traversal, and the in-memory text analysis for **ora:contains()**.

Additionally, Oracle Text can deal with a variety of documents from various sources in multiple languages. The document formats include Microsoft Word, PDF, Microsoft Excel, and HTML files. These documents can be stored inside the Oracle database as well as outside the database and accessed over HTTP, FTP, or from file servers. This, therefore, allows you to build Oracle Text indexes to optimally search XML documents stored both inside and outside the database.

When to Use Oracle Text Partitioned Indexes

Table partitioning is good to use when dealing with a large number of XML data sets. In Oracle9*i*, Oracle Text introduced the *Local Partitioned Index,* which is a partitioned index on a partitioned table with a one-to-one mapping of index partitions to table partitions. This virtually splits up a large table and the CONTEXT index into a set of smaller tables and indexes. It allows you to use local partitioned indexes instead of a global index.

For document systems, in which a large amount of new data is inserted every day, it is not practical to refresh the Oracle Text index for all the data, because that can take a long time. The local partitioned index makes the index more manageable, because after the DML operations you need to rebuild only the partition with the data changes, not the whole index.

On the other hand, with the local partitioning, index partitions can be synchronized in parallel, thus increasing uptime.

Finally, because the local partitioned CONTEXT index takes advantage of partition pruning and partition iteration to filter out the ROWIDs of the other partitions, it can provide faster mixed and sorted queries.

NOTE
The CTXXPATH index does not support local partitions.

Summary

This chapter discussed two types of searching strategies on XML documents: the XPath-based search using EXISTSNODE() with **ora:contains()** and the CTXXPATH index, and the full text search using Oracle Text.

Both approaches can be used with other SQL predicates. However, the EXISTSNODE() search provides better datatype comparisons and supports many XML native features such as namespaces, XPath functions, and entities. The EXISTSNODE() search also uses the XML schema to rewrite the XPath-based queries if the XMLType is stored in XML schema–based XMLType objects, which can greatly speed up the search process. CTXSYS.CTXXPATH index and **ora:contains()** function leverage the full text search functionality within XPath-based queries and enhance the searching capability of EXISTSNODE().

Oracle Text, although it supports only limited XML features and XPath syntax, has a powerful text-analysis and linguistic searching capability for an XML document management system. These features include the use of a thesaurus, the use of custom lexes, and the use of word stems and wildcards on indexes.

After reading this chapter, you should have a better understanding of Oracle Text and XPath-based queries, which you can use to search XML documents. The next step is to explore XPath functionality and the rich full text search feature in Oracle Text on your own to make your searches more accurate and intelligent.

CHAPTER 12

Managing the Oracle XML Database

This chapter covers Oracle XML Database 10*g* management topics, beginning with looking at the components that are installed. Then, it explores how to configure the Oracle XML Database (Oracle XML DB) to ensure functionality for XML applications. Finally, it shows configurations for user privileges and permissions to secure XML data and operations in the Oracle database.

Installed Oracle XML DB Components

After installing Oracle XML Database 10*g*, the XDB and ANONYMOUS users and an XDBADMIN role are created. The XDB user is created to maintain the PL/SQL packages, datatypes, and system object registries for Oracle XML DB. The ANONYMOUS user is created to allow for unauthenticated access of the Oracle XML DB Repository through the built-in HTTP server in the Oracle database. The XDBADMIN role is granted to all the DBA users by default so that DBA users can perform Oracle XML DB administration operations, such as registering global XML schemas.

NOTE
The ANONYMOUS user is created with the account LOCKED. Unless you need unauthenticated access to the Oracle XML DB Repository, do not *unlock the ANONYMOUS user; doing so will create a security hole.*

Table 12-1 lists the Oracle XML DB directory tables that are created to manage registered XML schemas, XMLType tables, and views. These tables can be viewed from SQL*Plus or Oracle Enterprise Manager.

Directory Name	Description
DBA_XML_SCHEMAS	All registered XML schemas in the Oracle XML DB
USER_XML_SCHEMAS	All registered XML schemas owned by the current user
ALL_XML_SCHEMAS	All registered XML schemas usable by the current user
DBA_XML_TABLES	All XMLType tables in the Oracle XML DB
USER_XML_TABLES	All XMLType tables owned by the current user
ALL_XML_TABLES	All XMLType tables usable by the current user
DBA_XML_TAB_COLS	All XMLType table columns in the Oracle XML DB
USER_XML_TAB_COLS	All XMLType table columns in tables owned by the current user
ALL_XML_TAB_COLS	All XMLType table columns in tables usable by the current user
DBA_XML_VIEWS	All XMLType views in the Oracle XML DB

TABLE 12-1. *Oracle XML DB Dictionary Tables*

Directory Name	Description
USER_XML_VIEWS	All XMLType views owned by the current user
ALL_XML_VIEWS	All XMLType views usable by the current user
DBA_XML_VIEW_COLS	All XMLType view columns in the Oracle XML DB
USER_XML_VIEW_COLS	All XMLType view columns in views owned by the current user
ALL_XML_VIEW_COLS	All XMLType view columns in views usable by the current user

TABLE 12-1. *Oracle XML DB Dictionary Tables* (continued)

All Oracle XML DB PL/SQL packages and the new XML data types, including XMLType and Oracle XML DB URI types, are installed with Oracle XML DB. Table 12-2 lists major PL/SQL packages, XML datatypes and their function descriptions. All the definition files are stored in the **ORACLE_HOME/rdbms/ADMIN** directory.

Package Name	Definition File	Functionality
XMLType XMLSequenceType XMLGenFormatType	dbmsxmlt.sql	New XML data types
UriType DBUriType FTPUriType XDBUriType HTTPUriType UriFactory	dbmsuri.sql	Oracle XML DB URI datatypes
DBMS_XMLGEN DBMS_XMLSTORE	dbmsxml.sql	PL/SQL packages generating XML from SQL queries and storing XML into relational tables via a canonical mapping
DBMS_XMLDOM	dbmsxmld.sql	PL/SQL DOM XML parsing API
DBMS_XMLPARSER	dbmsxmlp.sql	PL/SQL XML parser interface with support of XMLType
DBMS_XSLPROCESSOR	dbmsxsl.sql	PL/SQL XSL processor with support for XPath XML data extraction from DOM
DBMS_XMLSCHEMA	dbmsxsch.sql	PL/SQL XML Schema support
DBMS_XDB	dbmsxdb.sql	PL/SQL APIs to access and manage resource and data in Oracle XML DB Repository

TABLE 12-2. *PL/SQL Package Specifications and Functionality*

Package Name	Definition File	Functionality
DBMS_XDBZ	dbmsxdbz.sql	XML DB security support
DBMS_XDBT	dbmsxdbt.sql	PL/SQL package to set up an Oracle Text ConText index on the Oracle XML DB Repository hierarchy, create default preferences, and set up automatic synchronization of the CONTEXT index

TABLE 12-2. *PL/SQL Package Specifications and Functionality* (continued)

NOTE
*The corresponding PL/SQL package implementations are in the files with names starting with **prvt** followed by the letters after **dbms** in the name of the definition file. For example, the package body of DBMS_XDBT is in the **prvtxdbt.sql** file.*

If you need to reinstall Oracle XML DB, you can go to the **$ORACLE_HOME/rdbms/admin** directory on UNIX and the **%ORACLE_HOME%/rdbms/admin** directory on Windows, connect to the Oracle database as SYS user, and follow these steps:

1. Log in to a SQL*Plus session and connect as the SYS user with SYSDBA privileges:

```
> sqlplus "SYS/<sys_password> as SYSDBA"
```

2. Run **catnoqm.sql**:

```
SQL> @catnoqm
```

This step drops the XDB user, and all information in the Oracle XML DB Repository will be lost as will all information in the schema-based XMLType tables and columns.

3. Shut down and restart the database:

```
SQL> shutdown immediate;
SQL> startup
```

4. Run **catqm.sql** script and specify the password (such as **XDBPW**), the default tablespace (such as **XDB**), and the temporary tablespace (TEMP) for the XDB user:

```
SQL> @catqm XDBPW XDB TEMP
```

5. Run **catxdbj.sql** to install the XML DB Java packages:

```
SQL> @catxdbj
```

Configuring the Oracle XML DB

To configure the Oracle XML DB, you can update the **xdbconfig.xml** file using the DOM PL/SQL APIs and DBMS_XDB package or the graphical interface provided in Oracle Enterprise Manager

(OEM). The OEM allows you to insert, remove, or update the content of the XML elements in **xdbconfig.xml**. In this section, we discuss the PL/SQL operations.

Understanding xdbconfig.xml

The **xdbconfig.xml** file is an XML file that is stored as a resource in the Oracle XML DB Repository. It conforms to the XML schema defined in **/sys/schemas/PUBLIC/xmlns.oracle.com/xdb/xdbconfig.xsd** in the Oracle XML DB Repository File. It has the following data structure:

```
<xdbconfig>
 <sysconfig> ... </sysconfig>
 <userconfig> ... </userconfig>
</xdbconfig>
```

The top-level **<xdbconfig>** tag contains two sections:

- **<sysconfig>** Lists all the system-specific setups and the built-in parameters.
- **<userconfig>** Lists all parameters that allow users to customize the setups.

The **<sysconfig>** section contains the following content:

```
<sysconfig>
 General parameters
 <protocolconfig> ... </protocolconfig>
</sysconfig>
```

It stores the general parameters that apply to the Oracle XML DB; for example, the maximum age for an access control list (ACL), whether Oracle XML DB should be case sensitive, and so on. In **<sysconfig>**, the protocol parameters are grouped inside the **<protocolconfig>** tag, which has the following data structure:

```
<protocolconfig>
 <common> ... </common>
 <httpconfig> ... </httpconfig>
 <ftpconfig> ... </ftpconfig>
</protocolconfig>
```

The **<common>** element stores the parameters that apply to all protocols, such as MIME type information. The HTTP- and FTP-specific parameters are stored under the sections **<httpconfig>** and **<ftpconfig>**, respectively. The **<httpconfig>** section contains the **<webappconfig>** element for web-based application configurations, including the icon name and display name for the applications, and a list of servlets in Oracle XML DB.

Configuring xdbconfig.xml

In SQL*Plus, you can use DBMS_XMLDB.CFG_GET() to retrieve the current content of **xdbconfig.xml** as follows:

```
VAR out CLOB
SET AUTOPRINT ON
```

```
BEGIN
  :out := DBMS_XDB.CFG_GET().GETCLOBVAL();
END;
```

NOTE
*To be able to see the content, you need to run SET LONG 100000 to increase the size of the display buffer for SQL*Plus.*

The DBMS_XDB.CFG_GET() function returns a copy of the **xdbconfig.xml** configuration as an XMLType and it automatically commits after each execution:

```
DBMS_XDB.CFG_GET() RETURN SYS.XMLTYPE
```

If you have many parameters to update in the **xdbconfig.xml** file, you can use the DBMS_XDB.CFG_UPDATE() function. It replaces the content of the **xdbconfig.xml** file with the content in the input XMLType:

```
DBMS_XDB.CFG_UPDATE(newconfig SYS.XMLTYPE)
```

After the configuration parameters are updated, you need to call the DBMS_XDB.CFG_REFRESH() function to make sure the Oracle XML DB picks up the new updated configuration:

```
DBMS_XDB.CFG_REFRESH();
```

For example, if you need to configure the port numbers for Oracle XML DB HTTP and FTP servers to use other than the default values (HTTP: 8080, FTP: 2100), you can follow these steps:

1. Log in to a SQL*Plus session and connect as the XDB user (assuming the password for XDB user is **xdbpw**):

   ```
   > sqlplus xdb/xdbpw
   ```

2. Call DBMS_XDB.CFG_UPDATE() to update the HTTP port:

   ```
   DECLARE
      config XMLType;
   BEGIN
     config := DBMS_XDB.CFG_GET();
     SELECT UPDATEXML(config,
      '/xdbconfig/sysconfig/protocolconfig/httpconfig/http-port/text()',
       8081,
       '/xdbconfig/sysconfig/protocolconfig/ftpconfig/ftp-port/text()',
        2121) into config
       FROM DUAL;
     DBMS_XDB.CFG_UPDATE(config);
   END;
   ```

3. Call DBMS_XDB.CFG_REFRESH() to ensure the Oracle XML DB picks up the new settings:

   ```
   SQL> EXEC DBMS_XDB.CFG_REFRESH();
   ```

4. To check the HTTP and FTP port numbers, you can use the following SQL query:

```
SELECT
  EXTRACTVALUE(DBMS_XDB.CFG_GET(),
   '/xdbconfig/sysconfig/protocolconfig/httpconfig/http-port/text()')
   AS httpport,
  EXTRACTVALUE(DBMS_XDB.CFG_GET(),
   '/xdbconfig/sysconfig/protocolconfig/ftpconfig/ftp-port/text()')
    AS ftpport
FROM dual;
```

Normally, you just need to update the content in the configuration file. However, sometimes you need to insert a new element into this file. For example, if you want the Oracle XML DB Repository to properly handle Scalar Vector Graphics (SVG) files, you need to add a new MIME entry in **xdbconfig.xml**, as follows:

```
<mime-mapping
xmlns="http://xmlns.oracle.com/xdb/xdbconfig.xsd">
 <extension>svg</extension>
 <mime-type>image/svg+xml</mime-type>
</mime-mapping>
```

Since the current UPDATEXML() function does not append new XML child elements, you need to update the content of **<mime-mappings>**, which includes all the MIME mapping definitions. In such cases, using the DOM API in PL/SQL provides efficient XML updates:

```
CREATE OR REPLACE PROCEDURE AddNewElement(p_xpath IN VARCHAR2,
                                          p_content IN VARCHAR2,
                                          p_namespace IN VARCHAR2) AS
  v_config XMLType;
  v_mimemap XMLType;
  v_doc DBMS_XMLDOM.DOMDocument;
  v_doc_elem  dbms_xmldom.DOMElement;
  v_xsl  DBMS_XSLPROCESSOR.Processor;
  v_subdoc dbms_xmldom.DOMDocument;
  v_subdoc_elem dbms_xmldom.DOMElement;
  v_node dbms_xmldom.DOMNode;
  v_impnode dbms_xmldom.DOMNode;
BEGIN
  v_mimemap := XMLType.createXML(p_content);
  v_config := DBMS_XDB.CFG_GET();
  v_doc := DBMS_XMLDOM.newDOMDocument(v_config);
  v_doc_elem := DBMS_XMLDOM.getDocumentElement(v_doc);
  v_node := DBMS_XSLPROCESSOR.selectSingleNode(DBMS_XMLDOM.makeNode(v_doc),
           p_xpath, p_namespace);
  v_subdoc :=DBMS_XMLDOM.newDOMDocument(v_mimemap);
  v_subdoc_elem := DBMS_XMLDOM.getDocumentElement(v_subdoc);
  v_impnode := DBMS_XMLDOM.importNode(v_doc,
    DBMS_XMLDOM.makeNode(v_subdoc_elem), true);
  v_node := DBMS_XMLDOM.appendChild(v_node, v_impnode);
  DBMS_XDB.CFG_UPDATE(v_config);
END;
/
```

Using this procedure, we can add a new MIME mapping for SVG files:

```
BEGIN
AddNewElement(
'/xdbconfig/sysconfig/protocolconfig/common/extension-mappings/
mime-mappings', '<mime-mapping xmlns="http://xmlns.oracle.com/xdb/xdbconfig.xsd">
<extension>svgjinyu</extension>
<mime-type>image/svg+xml</mime-type></mime-mapping>',
'xmlns="http://xmlns.oracle.com/xdb/xdbconfig.xsd"');
END;
/
```

Security Management

In Oracle XML Database 10*g*, security should be set up to protect against unauthorized access of data and any XML processes that could affect database system operations.

Protecting Data in the Oracle XML DB Repository

The security for the Oracle XML DB resources is based on an ACL, which is a standard security mechanism used in Java, Windows NT, and other systems. The ACL maintains a list of object-level restrictions on database users or roles to access the resources in the Oracle XML DB Repository hierarchy.

Before a user performs an operation or method on a resource, a check of privileges for the user on the resource takes place. The set of privileges checked depends on the operation or method performed. For example, to update the Oracle XML DB configurations, READ and WRITE privileges are needed for the **xdbconfig.xml** resource.

Data access is controlled by the ACL document that specifies the database users, roles, and groups who are able to access certain resources. The default ACL includes the following:

- **all_all_acl.xml** Grants all privileges to all users
- **all_owner_acl.xml** Grants all privileges to owner/creator user
- **ro_all_acl.xml** Grants read privileges to all users

The DBMS_XDBZ PL/SQL package provides the APIs to check and update the ACL in the Oracle XML DB Repository. The following example shows how you can create a user group and set up the ACL for the group to access the Oracle XML DB Repository. The access privilege for each principal, who can be a user or a role, is stored in *access control entries (ACEs)* in the ACL:

```
CREATE USER USER1 IDENTIFIED BY USER1;
GRANT CONNECT, RESOURCE TO USER1;

CREATE USER USER2 IDENTIFIED BY USER2;
GRANT CONNECT, RESOURCE TO USER2;

CREATE ROLE DEMOGROUP NOT IDENTIFIED;
GRANT CONNECT, RESOURCE to DEMOGROUP;

GRANT DEMOGROUP to USER1;
GRANT DEMOGROUP to USER2;
```

By default, all file and directory resources created by a user are accessible to all database users. To limit these users to the group, DEMOGROUP, you first need to create a new ACL resource file and store it in the Oracle XML DB Repository as the file **/sys/acls/all_demogroup_acl.xml**. The file looks like the following:

```
<acl description="Private:All privileges to OWNER only"
xmlns="http://xmlns.oracle.com/xdb/acl.xsd"
xmlns:dav="DAV:"
xmlns:xsi="http://www.w3.org/2001/XMLSchema-instance"
xsi:schemaLocation="http://xmlns.oracle.com/xdb/acl.xsd http://xmlns.oracle.com/xdb/acl.xsd">
 <ace>
  <principal>DEMOGROUP</principal>
  <grant>true</grant>
  <privilege>
   <all/>
  </privilege>
 </ace>
</acl>
```

The preceding ACL specifies grants of all privileges to the owner of the document using the ACE elements. Each ACE element specifies access privileges for a given principal using values set for the elements described in Table 12-3.

To have some resources to work with, you can connect as USER1 and create a folder in the Oracle XML DB Repository for User1:

```
DECLARE
retval BOOLEAN;
BEGIN
retval := DBMS_XDB.createfolder('/public/folder1');
retval := DBMS_XDB.createResource('/public/folder1/doc1.xml',
XMLType('<xml1/>'));
END;
/
```

To confirm that User1 and User2 can currently view this resource, either use your FTP client to see the **/public/folder1** directory or execute the following query while connected as each user:

```
SELECT count(*) from RESOURCE_VIEW;
```

Now you can restrict access to these resources by changing the ACL file to **all_all_acl.xml** by executing the following command:

```
BEGIN
  DBMS_XDB.SetACL('/public/folder1',
                  '/sys/acls/all_all_acl.xml');
COMMIT;
END;
/
```

Element	Description
<principal>	Specifies the principal (user or group).
<grant>	A Boolean value that specifies whether the principal has been granted access to the resource. A value of **true** specifies that the access is granted. A value of **false** specifies that access is denied.
<privilege>	Specifies the privileges granted to the principal.

TABLE 12-3. *Access Control Entry Definitions*

Once again check for resource access and count and you will see that User2 has fewer resources and no access to **/public/folder1**. If role/group ownership is in effect, both users could have the same number of accessible resources. You can do this by switching the ACL file again to **all_demogroup_acl.xml** by executing the following connected as SYS:

```
BEGIN
  DBMS_XDB.SetACL('/public/folder1',
                  '/sys/acls/all_demogroup_acl.xml');
COMMIT;
END;
/
```

Using the same query, USER1 and USER2 now have the same number of accessible resources:

```
SELECT count(*) from RESOURCE_VIEW;
```

Each DBMS_XDB security management method takes a path (resource_path, abspath, or acl_path) as a parameter. You can then use any or all of the following DBMS_XDB methods to perform security management tasks:

- getAclDocument()
- ACLCheckPrivileges()
- checkPrivileges()
- getPrivileges()
- changePrivileges()
- setACL()

Oracle XML DB ACLs are cached for very fast evaluation. When a transaction that modifies an ACL is committed, the modified ACL is picked up after the time-out specified in the Oracle XML DB configuration file. The XPath for this configuration parameter is **/xdbconfig/sysconfig/acl-max-age**.

Securing DBUri Operations

DBUri servlet security is handled by Oracle Database 10g by using roles. When users log in to the servlet, they use their database username and password. The servlet will check to make sure the user logging in belongs to one of the roles specified in the configuration file. The roles that are allowed to access the servlet are specified in the **security-role-ref** tag. By default, the servlet is available to the special role **authenticatedUser**. Any user with a valid database username and password belongs to this role and thus can use the servlet.

The parameter updated in the following example restricting the list of authenticated users can be changed to restrict access to any role(s) in the database. To change from the default authenticated-user role to a role that you have created, for example, **servlet-users**, run the following connected as a user with XDBADMIN role:

```
DECLARE
  doc XMLType;
  doc2 XMLType;
  doc3 XMLType;
BEGIN
  doc := dbms_xdb.cfg_get();
  select updateXML(doc, '/xdbconfig/sysconfig/protocolconfig/httpconfig/webappconfig
/servletconfig/servlet-list/servlet[servlet-name="DBUriServlet"]
/security-role-ref/role-name/text()', 'servlet-users') into doc2
from dual;
  select updateXML(doc2, '/xdbconfig/sysconfig/protocolconfig/httpconfig/webappconfig
/servletconfig/servlet-list/servlet[servlet-name="DBUriServlet"]
/security-role-ref/role-link/text()', 'servlet-users') into doc3
from dual;
  DBMS_XDB.CFG_UPDATE(doc3);
  COMMIT;
END;
/
```

Summary

In this chapter, we discussed how you can manage the Oracle XML DB to ensure the proper functionality and security protection for stored resources. In the samples, we also provided the utility package that simplifies update operations to the **xdbconfig.xml** file to manage these resources.

PART III

Oracle XML for Java Developers

CHAPTER 13

Getting Started with Oracle XML and Java

he previous chapters introduced the overall XML functionality provided by the Oracle XDK and Oracle Database 10*g*. Over the next several chapters, you will learn how to actually develop applications in Java with these products by exploring sample applications derived from actual Oracle customer use cases. To get the greatest benefit from the following chapters, you need to be familiar with the Oracle XDK Java libraries, the JDK environment (both within and without the database), and how to use the XDK with Oracle JDeveloper 10*g*. This chapter provides a general overview of these topics. This chapter supplements the **Getting_Started_Java.html** documentation provided with the Oracle XDK within the **$XDK_HOME\xdk\doc\java** directory either in the OTN distribution or in the Oracle XML Application Developer's Guide included with the Oracle Database 10*g* release.

The Oracle XDK Java Libraries

Although you learned about the Oracle XDK functionality in the previous chapters, you may not know where all the XDK components are stored, because the XDK is packaged within a set of JAR files that combine functions. The XDK components are delivered in the **\lib** directory of the OTN distribution and the **ORACLE_HOME\lib** directory. There is an additional JAR called **orai18n.jar** in the corresponding **ORACLE_HOME\jlib** directories. The following is a functional description of each.

xmlparserv2.jar

The **xmlparserv2.jar** is much more than its name implies, though it started life in Oracle8*i* as simply the DOM and SAX interfaces. In Oracle XDK 10*g*, this library contains those classes as well as the XML Schema processor classes, XSLT Processor classes, XML compression classes, JAXP classes, W3C interfaces for DOM and SAX, and utility functionality such as the XMLSAXSerializer and asynchronous DOM Builder.

xml.jar

The **xml.jar** is a new library for Oracle XDK 10*g* and is an attempt to consolidate a number of JARs. It includes all the classes from **oraclexsql.jar**, **xsqlserializers.jar**, **xmlcomp.jar**, **xmlcomp2.jar**, and **transx.zip**, as well as the new JAXB and Pipeline Processor classes. This greatly simplifies your **CLASSPATH**. You might wonder why **xmlparserv2.jar** is not included as well. The answer is that this JAR has been around since the start and has so many products depending on it that it would be too great a risk to existing code to collapse it.

xschema.jar

Although the XML Schema classes are already contained in the **xmlparserv2.jar**, the **xschema.jar** is still included for backward compatibility reasons. In previous versions, these classes have resided in this JAR; however, it will eventually disappear. Therefore, you should ignore this JAR for all new development.

oraclexsql.jar and xsqlserializers.jar

The **oraclexsql.jar** contains most of the XSQL Servlet classes needed to deploy XSQL pages. If, however, you want to create serialized output, such as PDFs, you need the **xsqlserializers.jar** because it contains these serializer classes. Both of these JARs have been superceded by the **xml.jar** and are only included for backward compatibility. You should not continue to use them in new development.

xmlcomp.jar, xmlcomp2.jar, xmldemo.jar, and jdev-rt.zip

The **xmlcomp.jar** contains the XML JavaBeans that do not depend on the database, while the **xmlcomp2.jar** contains the JavaBeans that do, and thus depends on **xdb.jar**, which is the library that includes the Java classes that support the XML DB functionality. These JARs are included only for backward compatibility, because their classes are now included in **xml.jar**.

The **xmlcomp.jar** contains the DOMBuilder, XSLTransformer, DBAccess, XSDValidator, and XMLDiffer Beans, while the **xmlcomp2.jar** contains only the XMLDBAccess and XMLCompress Beans. You will not find future XML JavaBeans in these JARs, so you should not use them for new development. You also won't find the visual Beans that were in previous releases. The XMLTreeView, XMLTransformPanel, XMLSourceView, and DBViewer Beans are now considered demos and are included in the **xmldemo.jar**. The **jdev-rt.zip** is used when working with the demos within the JDeveloper IDE.

xsu12.jar

The **xsu12.jar** contains the classes that implement the XML SQL Utility's Java functionality. These classes also have a dependency on the **xdb.jar** for XMLType access.

classgen.jar

The **classgen.jar** contains the Class Generator for Java classes. In Oracle XDK 10*g*, only the run-time classes are included, as the JAXB Class Generator included in **xml.jar** has superceded their functionality. Only Oracle9*i* applications that cannot be rewritten should continue to use this JAR.

xdb.jar

The **xdb.jar** contains the classes that are needed by **xml.jar** and **xmlcom2.jar** to access XMLTypes. It also includes the SPI and XDBServlet classes to access the XML DB Repository, and the XMLType DOM classes for direct manipulation of the XMLType DOM tree. Note that this is not as complete a DOM implementation as in **xmlparserv2.jar** and thus will not be covered in this book.

xmlmesg.jar

The **xmlmesg.jar** is only necessary for development that requires non-U.S. English error messages that are available by default in all the other JARs. This JAR contains 27 additional translations and can simply be added to your CLASSPATH. The selected language will be based on your Java Locale setting.

transx.zip

The **transx.zip** archive contains the TransX Utility classes. This archive has been supplanted by **xml.jar** and is retained only for backward compatibility. New development should use the classes from **xml.jar**.

orai18n.jar

The **orai18n.jar** contains the Oracle National Language Supported (NLS) character set encodings. Distinct from the previous JARs, it resides in the **XDK_HOME/xdk/jlib** directory for OTN distributions and **ORACLE_HOME/jlib** for Oracle Database 10*g*. You will need it to support the normalization functions in XPath and on XSLT output for the proper collations.

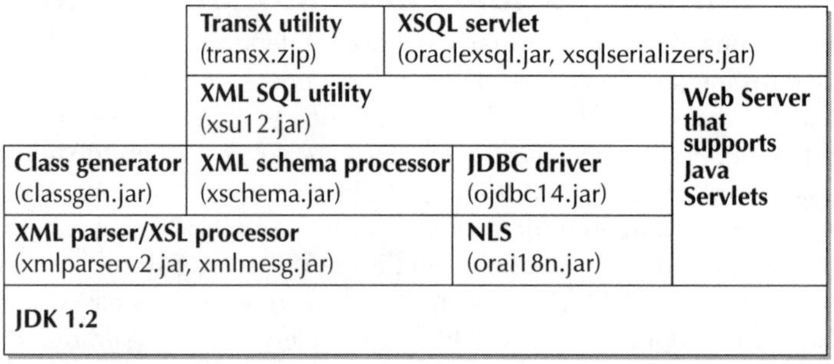

<table>
<tr><td></td><td>TransX utility
(transx.zip)</td><td colspan="3">XSQL servlet
(oraclexsql.jar, xsqlserializers.jar)</td></tr>
<tr><td></td><td colspan="3">XML SQL utility
(xsu12.jar)</td><td rowspan="3">Web Server that supports Java Servlets</td></tr>
<tr><td>Class generator
(classgen.jar)</td><td colspan="2">XML schema processor
(xschema.jar)</td><td>JDBC driver
(ojdbc14.jar)</td></tr>
<tr><td colspan="3">XML parser/XSL processor
(xmlparserv2.jar, xmlmesg.jar)</td><td>NLS
(orai18n.jar)</td></tr>
<tr><td colspan="5">JDK 1.2</td></tr>
</table>

FIGURE 13-1. *XDK library dependencies*

classes12.jar and ojdbc14.jar

The **classes12.jar** and **ojdbc14.jar** are the Oracle JDBC drivers for Java 1.2/1.3 and 1.4, respectively. These JARs also depend upon **orai18n.jar** for their character set support when additional character sets beyond UTF-8, ISO8859-1, and JA16SJIS are required. These JARs are not part of the XDK distribution on OTN but are in the **ORACLE_HOME\jdbc\lib** directory of the database.

Figure 13-1 illustrates the dependencies between these XDK classes so that you can understand which ones are required when in your CLASSPATH.

The JDK Environment

The Oracle XDK supports all currently supported JDK and JRE versions at the time of this writing—JDK 1.2, 1.3, and 1.4 and their associated JREs. Oracle 10*g* products, including the database, application server, and XDK, no longer support JDK 1.1 because of Sun's de-support of that version. This can also be said for the JDBC drivers, as the 1.1 version is no longer supplied. The Oracle JServer JVM is its own special implementation and has unique requirements that were discussed in Chapter 8.

Setting Up the JDK Environment

There is nothing special about setting up your Java environment for developing with the Oracle XDK and Oracle Database 10*g*. You should note that when installing an Oracle Home, no changes are made to your CLASSPATH settings even though significant Java functionality is being used. This is because Oracle Java applications are invoked with their required **CLASSPATHs** on the command line or in a script.

While the Oracle database requires you to manually set the CLASSPATH, the OTN XDK distribution supplies an **env.bat** file on Windows and an **env.csh** file on UNIX to automate the setup of your environment and serve as a template for customizations. These files need certain variables set in order to create a working environment. Tables 13-1 and 13-2 provide the definitions on Windows and UNIX, respectively, for the various JDK versions.

Using **env.bat** as an example, if you have %JAVA_HOME% and %ORACLE_HOME% set up in your environment and you use JDK 1.4, which is suggested for use with Oracle XDK 10*g*, you

Variable Name	Values	Customize
%INSTALL_ROOT%	Installation root of XDK, which is the directory we refer to as %XDK_HOME%.	NO
%JAVA_HOME%	Directory where the Java SDK, Standard Edition is installed. Path linked to the Java SDK needs to be modified.	YES
%CLASSPATHJ%	For 1.2 and 1.3: CLASSPATHJ=%ORACLE_HOME%\jdbc\lib\classes12.jar; %ORACLE_HOME%\jdbc\lib\orai18n.jar For 1.2 and 1.3: CLASSPATHJ=%ORACLE_HOME%\jdbc\lib\ojdbc14.jar; %ORACLE_HOME%\jdbc\lib\orai18n.jar	YES
%PATH%	PATH=%JAVA_HOME%\bin;%ORACLE_HOME%\bin; %PATH%;%INSTALL_ROOT%\bin	NO
%CLASSPATH%	.;%CLASSPATHJ%;%INSTALL_ROOT%\lib\xmlparserv2.jar; %INSTALL_ROOT%\lib\xsu12.jar; %INSTALL_ROOT%\lib\xml.jar;	NO

TABLE 13-1. *Windows XDK Environment Variables for env.bat*

Variable Name	Values	Customize
$INSTALL_ROOT	Installation root of XDK, which is the directory we refer to as $XDK_HOME.	NO
$JAVA_HOME	Directory where the Java SDK, Standard Edition is installed. Path linked to the Java SDK needs to be modified.	YES
$CLASSPATHJ	For 1.2 and 1.3: CLASSPATHJ=${ORACLE_HOME}\jdbc\lib\classes12.jar; ${ORACLE_HOME}\jdbc\lib\orai18n.jar For 1.2 and 1.3: CLASSPATHJ=${ORACLE_HOME}\jdbc\lib\ojdbc14.jar; ${ORACLE_HOME}\jdbc\lib\orai18n.jar	YES
$PATH	PATH=$JAVA_HOME\bin; $PATH;${INSTALL_ROOT}\bin	NO
$CLASSPATH	.;$CLASSPATHJ;${INSTALL_ROOT}\lib\xmlparserv2.jar; ${INSTALL_ROOT}\lib\xsu12.jar; ${INSTALL_ROOT}\lib\xml.jar;	NO
$LD_LIBRARY_PATH	For OCI JDBC connections: ${ORACLE_HOME}/lib:${LD_ LIBRARY_PATH}	NO

TABLE 13-2. *UNIX XDK Environment Variables for env.csh*

can simply go to the **%XDK_HOME%/bin** directory and run **env.bat**. The batch file will set the PATH environment variable so that you can run the command-line executables provided along with the XDK. Additionally, the batch file sets the Java CLASSPATH variable, which includes **ojdbc14.jar**, **orai18n.jar**, **xmlparserv2.jar**, **xml.jar**, **xmlmesg.jar**, **xsu12.jar**, and **oraclexsql.jar**.

Using the XDK with Oracle JDeveloper

Oracle JDeveloper has added more XML functionality with each release. At the time of this writing, Oracle JDeveloper 10*g* has just been released, so this section is current to that version. Every version has included the Oracle XDK's Java libraries, and each version has seen them better integrated. Regardless of the version you are using, the content in this section will be applicable unless specifically stated otherwise.

Setting Up an XDK Environment

Each Java project in JDeveloper has a set of properties that can be accessed by right-clicking the project filename in the Navigator window and selecting Project Properties. Project files are identified by a **.jpr** extension. Select Libraries to display the dialog box shown in Figure 13-2.

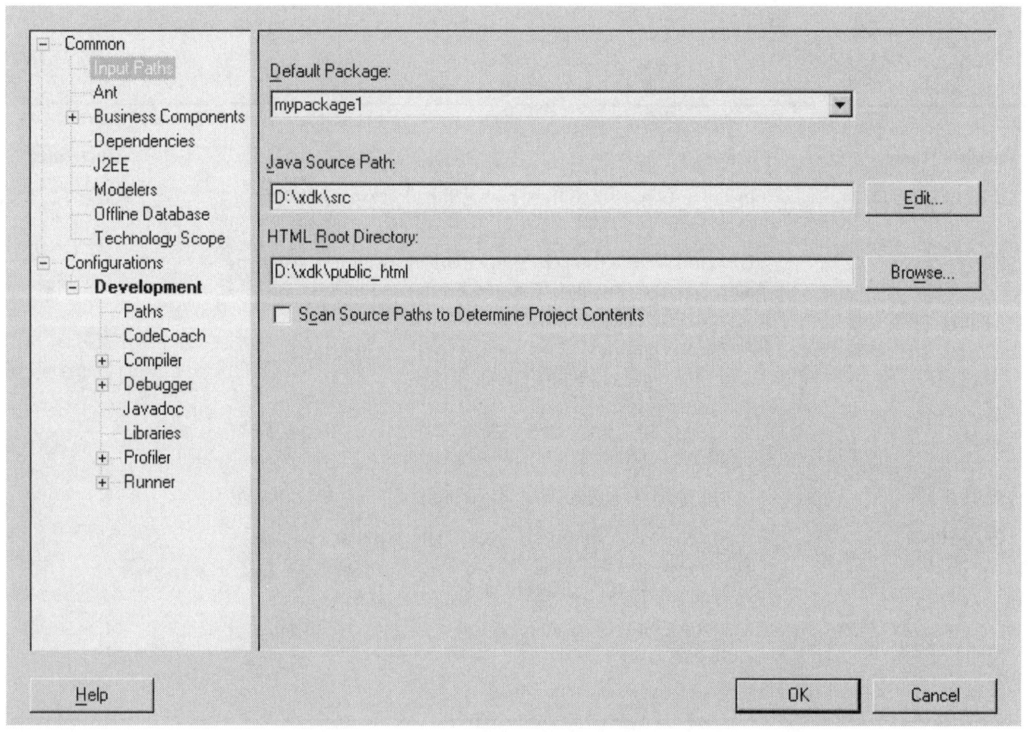

FIGURE 13-2. *Selecting your project properties' libraries*

Since Oracle JDeveloper includes the Oracle XDK's Java libraries, you already have entries for them. Should you wish to add newer versions, you can easily add them by clicking New or Edit and defining a different library name from existing ones. While you will not have the path to the source code, you can download the Javadocs for the newer libraries from OTN and provide their path for easy use within the IDE.

The other use of the Libraries dialog box is to indicate what libraries are missing when compiling or deploying a project. This is especially true for imported projects. Missing libraries will be indicated in red and you can resolve them simply by either adding a new one or editing it so that it refers to the local library.

Setting Up a Database Connection

JDeveloper has the functionality to connect to a database for run-time access; however, this connection must be configured globally before you can use it. Access to this configuration is not intuitive, so the following are the instructions. However, before you start you should have a database instance running and the user ID, password, and optionally the role you want to use to connect.

Types of JDBC Drivers

One additional important preparation step is to ensure that JDeveloper knows about the Oracle Database 10*g* JDBC drivers. This is important because, starting in this release, the naming convention has changed. JDeveloper comes configured for version 9 JDBC drivers, which, while they will work against Oracle Database 10*g*, will have poorer performance and will not have support for all the features. The following sections describe the JDBC drivers included in your **ORACLE_HOME/jdbc/lib** directory along with their dependencies and purpose.

JDBC Thin Driver 10.1.0.2.0 This is a 100 percent Java driver designed for client applications, midtier servers, and applets. It is contained within **classes12.jar** for use with JDK 1.2 and 1.3 and contained within **ojdbc14.jar** for use with 1.4. If you require complete NLS support for objects and collection types, you also need **orai18n.jar**. This driver will not support XMLType on the client. The connection string is

```
Connection conn = DriverManager.getConnection(
                         "jdbc:oracle:thin:@<database>",
                         "my_user", "my_password");
```

where **<database>** is either a string of the form *host*:*port*:*sid*, a SQL*NET name-value pair, or a service name.

JDBC OCI Driver 10.1.0.2.0 This is the "thick" Java driver that utilizes OCI to provide client-side full datatype support, including XMLType. It is contained within **classes12.jar** for use with JDK 1.2 and 1.3 and contained within **ojdbc14.jar** for use with 1.4. If you require complete NLS support for objects and collection types, you also need **orai18n.jar**. On Windows, you also need to have ***ORACLE_HOME*\bin** in your PATH to locate the needed C libraries. The connection string is

```
Connection conn = DriverManager.getConnection(
                         "jdbc:oracle:oci:@<database>",
                         "my_user", "my_password");
```

where **<database>** is either an entry in **tnsnames.ora** or a SQL*NET name-value pair.

JDBC Server-Side Internal Driver 10.1.0.2.0 This is the internal JDBC driver that runs in the OJVM in the database. It is also known as the **kprb** JDBC driver. All classes and libraries are already loaded for it to work supporting all data types. The connection string is

```
Connection conn = DriverManager.getConnection(
                          "jdbc:oracle:kprb:");
```

Note that the trailing ";" is necessary.

Creating a Database Connection

To create a database connection, first select File | New to open the New Gallery dialog box. Expand the General category and select Connections, as shown in Figure 13-3. In the list of items on the right side, double-click Database Connection. This starts the Database Connection Wizard. The

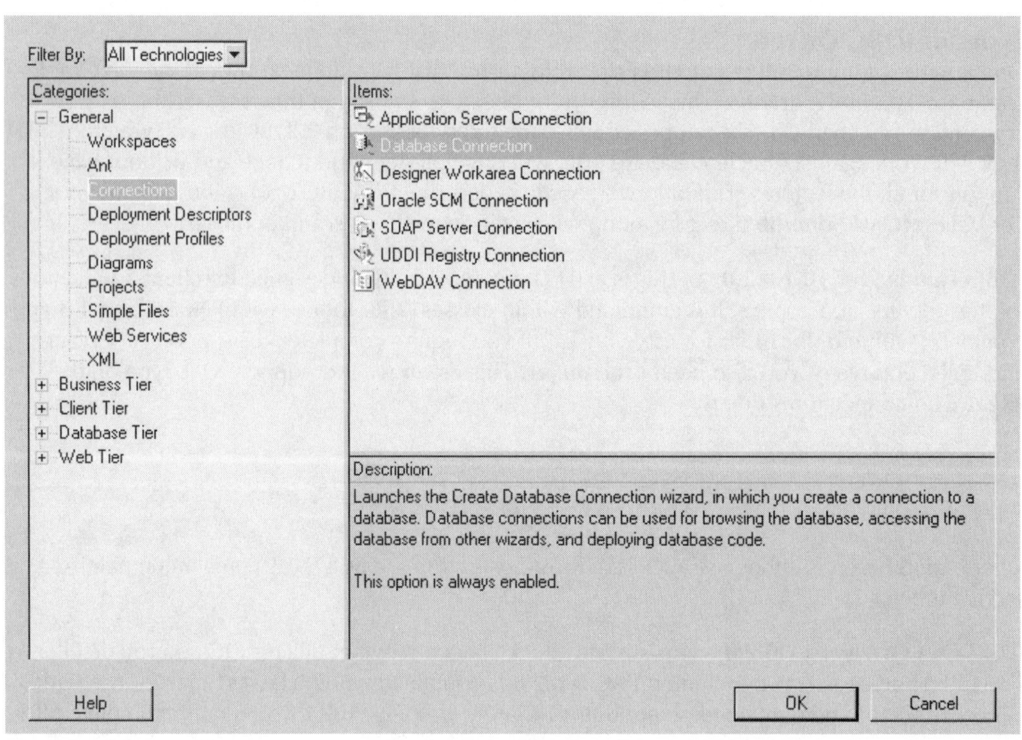

FIGURE 13-3. *JDeveloper database connection selection*

same wizard can also be triggered from the Connection Navigator, by right-clicking the Database Connection node and selecting the New Database Connection shortcut menu.

Select OK on the first wizard page to go to Step 1, which allows you to name the connection (for example, DBConnection10*g*). At this point, the Connection Type drop-down list box enables you to select the type of JDBC driver you want to use. To use either the thin or thick JDBC driver, select Oracle (JDBC), which takes you to the Authentication step to enter your login information (e.g., SYS, ORACLE, SYSDBA). Check Deploy Password to avoid the password prompt each time you connect. Click Next to go to the Connection step, where you select either the thin or oci8 (thick) driver along with the Hostname, JDBC Port, and SID (e.g., localhost, 1521, ORCL).

Select Next to go to the final Test step, which lets you test the JDBC connection. If your setup is correct, you will see "Success!" displayed; otherwise, you will see the error you need to correct. Even if you plan to use the thick driver to get full XMLType support, if you get an error, we suggest that you try the thin connection because that will confirm that your database parameters and strings are correct.

When you create connections using Oracle's JDBC/OCI drivers, be aware of the following platform-specific requirements:

- You must have the required native libraries (DLL files on Windows, and SO/SL files on UNIX). With the Oracle thick driver (JDBC/OCI), the version of the JDBC driver must match the version of the Oracle Home. For example, the Oracle JDBC Driver version 10.1.0 requires that the Oracle Home contain version 10.1.0 of the **ocijdbc10.dll**, as well as the Oracle Network software and supporting libraries, message files, encodings, etc., within an Oracle Home. If you are connecting to a local database that is a different version from the JDBC driver you are using, then you must install the Oracle client software into a separate Oracle Home, and connect via the Oracle Net Listener.
- You must place the **ORACLE_HOME** directory in which the client-side files for the required native libraries reside in your PATH environment variable. On Windows, you need the **%ORACLE_HOME%\bin** directory in which the client-side DLL files reside in your PATH environment variable. If you have multiple Oracle Homes installed on your machine, use the Oracle Home Switch utility to choose the correct Oracle Home. On UNIX, you need the **$ORACLE_HOME/lib** directory in which the client-side SO/SL files reside in your PATH environment variable.
- If your Oracle Home for the OCI driver is not the same as the Oracle Home in which JDeveloper is installed, you must either set the ORACLE_HOME environment variable or edit **/jdev/bin/jdev.conf** with a line similar to the following, replacing the path shown with the full path to your Oracle Home:
  - On Windows: "AddNativeCodePath C:\ORACLE\ORA10\BIN"
  - On UNIX: "AddNativeCodePath /u01/app/oracle/product/10.1.0/lib"

This command allows JDeveloper to properly update the **java.library.path** in which the Java VM searches for shared libraries. Connections set up this way are available globally and are automatically available to your projects.

Creating an XDK Component Palette

Oracle XDK 10*g* includes a collection of XML JavaBeans that can be easily integrated into JDeveloper as an XDK palette. You can add pages to the Component Palette to group your XDK JavaBeans components, or you can add components to existing pages. Once you add JavaBeans to the palette, you can insert them into any file you have open in the UI Editor by selecting them from the Component Palette.

The XDK JavaBeans are contained in **xml.jar** and **xmlparserv2.jar**; therefore, you need to first make sure JDeveloper knows about these JARs. Select Tools | Manage Libraries to display a listing of User Libraries, Addin Libraries, and System Libraries. Selecting any one will allow you to add a new library to the list by clicking New. Enter **XDK Components** for Library Name and edit the Class Path to point to the location at, for example, C:\oracle\ora10\lib\xml.jar. Leave the Source Path and Doc Path blank unless you downloaded the Javadocs from OTN. Click OK and you are done.

To create an XDK JavaBeans Component Palette, follow these steps:

1. From the main menu, select Tools | Configure Palette to open the Configure Component Palette dialog box.
2. Click Add to open the New Palette Page dialog box.
3. Enter a page name, such as XDK JavaBeans, and click OK. You now see your new entry highlighted in the Configure Component Palette dialog box.
4. Click Add on the Components side, and an Add JavaBeans dialog box will appear with a picklist of register libraries.
5. Select XDK Components, and for the filter, select JavaBeans with BeanInfo Only from the Filter drop-down list. Expanding the **oracle.xml** class tree displays the list shown in Figure 13-4.
6. You can now select the DBAccess, XSDValidator, XMLDiffer, XMLDBAccess, and XMLCompress JavaBeans by clicking each and then clicking OK.

NOTE
Although you can select multiple Beans by holding down the CTRL *key, the associated Bean images will not be correctly assigned.*

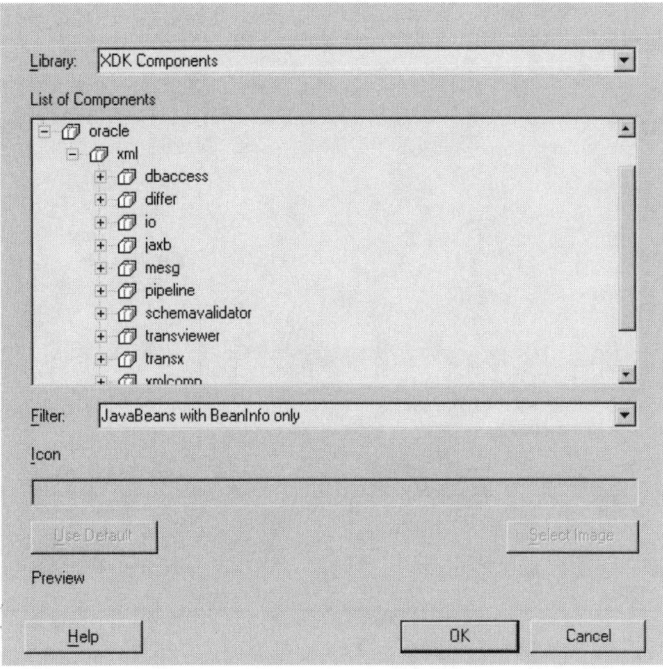

FIGURE 13-4. *Adding a JavaBeans XDK Components list*

7. Once you have completed these, you can add the DOMBuilder and XSLTransformer JavaBeans from **xmlparserv2.jar**, giving you seven JavaBeans, as shown in Figure 13-5.

This palette now is available whenever you activate the Component Palette from View | Component Palette for all Java programs. You can drag and drop its components onto Swing or AWT panels when using the UI Designer of JDeveloper.

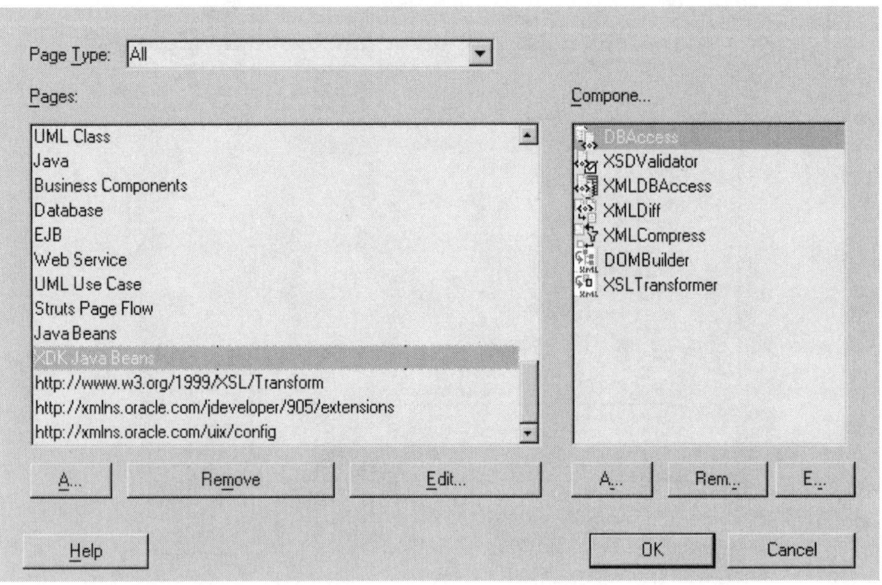

FIGURE 13-5. *XDK Component Palette*

Summary

This chapter walked you through the basics of getting your Java development environment configured and set up for either command-line development or using the Oracle JDeveloper IDE. It also introduced you to the JDK and JDBC driver configurations and requirements that you will use in the following chapters. In those chapters, you will learn how to build real Java XML-enabled applications covering a range of solution scenarios.

CHAPTER 14

Building an XML-Powered Web Site

hroughout this book, we have presented the wide range of Oracle products that have become XML-enabled, and we have introduced many of the XML standards. In this chapter, we will explore the development and deployment of a real-world application that uses these standards with the Oracle XDK and the new XML features of Oracle Database 10*g*. In this application, we explore the important capabilities of XSLT, the XSQL Servlet, the XML SQL Utility, Oracle Text, and the XML data types and operators in Oracle Database 10*g*.

An XML-Enabled FAQ Web Site

A frequent requirement for companies that maintain a web presence is to have a support area for their products. This area may range from simple electronic versions of their owner's manuals to a moderated discussion forum. A popular support area feature is to have an FAQ (frequently asked questions) section for each product.

Visitors to the site will be able to see all the FAQ subject areas on the home page and can also search and select from the most frequently viewed FAQs. Whenever the list of FAQs appears, users can see the answers as well as find related FAQs by following the presented links. Inside each FAQ answer are links to an online glossary for technical or special terms. This functionality will be described in detail later in the chapter.

As you no doubt have realized, the Oracle XML-enabled products and components are quite extensive and include components in the quite disparate programming languages of C, C++, PL/SQL, and Java. However, underneath they all provide XML functionality that is programming-language independent. This gives rise to an awkward model for providing technical support, because many questions that are XML-based are equally applicable across all the XDKs, yet there are many language-specific questions that only make sense in only one XDK. Therefore, providing an Oracle XML FAQ site that can store all questions within a database and designing the schema in a way that FAQs can be tagged as relevant for one or more of the languages as well as the XML-enabled database features is a basic requirement for this site.

Besides simply displaying a listing of FAQs per XML component and feature, users would expect a full text search facility. Since we plan to store the FAQs in the Oracle XML database, we can take advantage of Oracle Text (formerly interMedia Text) search engine with its XML support. We also need a mechanism for submitting FAQs, which can be provided by FTP access to the Oracle XML DB repository.

In most cases, the content for web sites is delivered from HTML pages stored in file systems on servers. For this application, we will deliver as much of the content as possible from the database. This will give us maximum manageability of the content while at the same time demonstrating most of the Oracle XML database functionality.

Designing the Framework

This application will use the Oracle XML database as its repository for the FAQs. We will create this storage by registering an FAQ XML schema with the database that will then create the underlying objects and indexes that will store the XML. Additionally, we will create SQL tables to manage the categorization and glossary functionality of the site.

Once the database schema is designed, we will set up the application using the XSQL Servlet as the back end and an Internet browser as the front end. We will create a set of XSQL XML pages that will use the XML SQL Utility to submit queries via JDBC and then create a set of XSL stylesheets using the XDK's XSLT Processor to transform the result into HTML that is returned to the browser. To support paging of the FAQs, we will create an XSQL custom action handler in Java.

To implement the search functionality, we will use Oracle Text in the database. Since it has been enhanced with XML support, we will be able to submit queries as either text expressions or XPaths. To extend the functionality of term searching, we will implement a glossary that will be accessible through links in the content of FAQ answers.

Creating the FAQ Database

Since this is a database-backed application, you will need to design a database schema to store the FAQs and their metadata. Obviously, since the individual FAQs will be XML documents, there can also be an XML schema that describes their format. As you learned in Chapter 8, you can register this XML schema, and the XML database will create the database schema for you. On the other hand, you can start with the database schema and generate an XML schema using the XML SQL Utility introduced in Chapter 10. In this application, you will create the FAQ storage with an FAQ schema and create metadata tables using SQL to improve search performance and extend the functionality of the site.

Designing the FAQ Schema

Many developers feel it is easier to design an XML schema from a sample instance XML document, whereas other developers design the XML schema from a data-modeling perspective. In either case, you need to start by enumerating the data types that you will need. From the FAQ site requirements, you can determine the types and their content as set forth in Table 14-1.

XML TYPE	Description	Database Type
FAQ	Complex type of entire FAQ document	OBJECT
TITLE	Simple type string with restricted length to specify an FAQ question for one-line display	VARCHAR2
QUESTION	Mixed content to support keyword and code markup	OBJECT
ANSWER	Mixed content to support keyword and code markup	OBJECT
CATEGORY	String describing component type	VARCHAR2
LANGUAGE	String describing language type	VARCHAR2
PARAGRAPH	Mixed content of text, code, keywords, and links	OBJECT
CODE	String for embedded source code	VARCHAR2
KEYWORD	String for identifying glossary terms	VARCHAR2
LINK	Complex type of two strings for hrefs and type	OBJECT
SAMPLE	Complex type of two strings for hrefs and type	VARCHAR2

TABLE 14-1. *XML Datatypes Needed to Describe FAQ*

Note that even though LANGUAGE and CATEGORY each will be a specific list, they have not been identified as such in the schema. While the choice to do this has the consequence of limiting the storage model, the selection can be handled on the insert side by presenting a list of languages or categories when the FAQ is generated. It is important not to unnecessarily constrain your storage, because doing so limits extensibility. In this case, regardless of whether there is a finite list, the selections are stored as strings in a column and any index created would accommodate additional strings with negligible impact.

Besides the actual FAQ content, the site maintenance would benefit from additional metadata about the FAQ, such as the following:

TYPE	Description	Database Type
id	Positive integer identifying the FAQ	NUMBER
lastupdate	Date of the FAQ insertion or update	DATE
status	String indicating the publication status of the FAQ	VARCHAR2

With these types enumerated, you can design an XML schema that takes into account what types are needed within other types. For example, you would like **<ANSWER>** to be able to contain **<PARAGRAPH>**, **<KEYWORD>**, and **<CODE>** elements, and you would like the metadata information, such as the **status**, **id**, and **lastupdate**, to be attributes instead of child elements of **<FAQ>**. Taking these dependencies into account, you could produce the following FAQ XML schema:

```
<?xml version="1.0" encoding="UTF-8"?>
<xs:schema xmlns:xdb="http://xmlns.oracle.com/xdb"
    xmlns:xs="http://www.w3.org/2001/XMLSchema"
    elementFormDefault="qualified">
 <!-- Defile the CONTENT_TYPE-->
 <xs:complexType name="CONTENT_TYPE" mixed="true" xdb:SQLType="CLOB"
  <xs:choice minOccurs="0" maxOccurs="unbounded">
   <xs:element name="CODE" type="xs:string"/>
   <xs:element name="PARAGRAPH" nillable="true">
    <xs:complexType mixed="true">
     <xs:choice minOccurs="0" maxOccurs="unbounded">
      <xs:element name="LINK" nillable="true">
       <xs:complexType mixed="true">
        <xs:attribute name="href" type="xs:string"/>
        <xs:attribute name="type" type="xs:string"/>
       </xs:complexType>
      </xs:element>
      <xs:element name="KEYWORD" type="xs:string"/>
      <xs:element name="CODE" type="xs:string"/>
     </xs:choice>
    </xs:complexType>
   </xs:element>
```

```
  <xs:any processContents="skip"/>
 </xs:choice>
</xs:complexType>
 <!-- Define FAQ Element -->
 <xs:element name="FAQ" xdb:maintainDOM="false" xdb:defaultTable="FAQ">
  <xs:complexType>
   <xs:sequence>
    <xs:element name="TITLE" xdb:SQLName="TITLE">
     <xs:simpleType>
      <xs:restriction base="xs:string">
       <xs:maxLength value="100"/>
      </xs:restriction>
     </xs:simpleType>
    </xs:element>
    <xs:element name="QUESTION" type="CONTENT_TYPE" nillable="true"
         xdb:SQLName="QUESTION"/>
    <xs:element name="ANSWER" type="CONTENT_TYPE" xdb:SQLName="ANSWER"/>
    <xs:element name="CATEGORY" type="xs:string" xdb:SQLType="VARCHAR2"
         xdb:SQLName="CATEGORY"/>
    <xs:element name="LANGUAGE" type="xs:string" minOccurs="0"
         xdb:SQLType="VARCHAR2" xdb:SQLName="LANGUAGE"/>
  </xs:element>
  </xs:sequence>
   <xs:attribute name="id" type="xs:positiveInteger" default="0001"
      xdb:SQLType="NUMBER" xdb:SQLName="ID"/>
   <xs:attribute name="lastupdate" type="xs:date" default="2003-03-11"
      xdb:SQLType="DATE" xdb:SQLName="LASTUPDATE"/>
   <xs:attribute name="status" type="xs:string" default="pending"
      xdb:SQLType="VARCHAR2" xdb:SQLName="STATUS"/>
  </xs:complexType>
 </xs:element>
</xs:schema>
```

There are several points to note about this schema. First, there are attributes with the name **xdb:SQLType** that are used to tell the registration process to which database type XML types should be mapped and **xdb:SQLName** to specify the column or object name.

Next, note that a type called CONTENT_TYPE is defined and is used in both the definition of QUESTION and ANSWER elements. This is a useful technique when you are using the same XML datatype for more than one element definition. Also to add content flexibility within these types, **<xs:anyprocessContents="skip">** is added. This tells the XML schema processor in the Oracle XML DB to ignore any elements within **<QUESTION>** or **<ANSWER>** other than the **<CODE>** and **<PARAGRAPH>** elements.

Finally, note the attribute within the FAQ element, **xdb:maintainDOM="false"**. This is a special notation to the XML database that specifies that it is not important for this application to have these documents stored with all white space, comments, processing instructions, etc. preserved. This lets the XML database create only the necessary objects and indexes to retrieve the content, thereby improving performance.

Creating a Database User

Before proceeding with the database operations, you need to create a user with the appropriate privileges to store, query, and search FAQs using Oracle XML DB. To create, in this case, an *xdkus* user, you need to use the sys/password logon as SYSDBA and execute the following commands from SQLPlus:

```
CREATE USER xdkus IDENTIFIED BY xdkus
 DEFAULT TABLESPACE users
 TEMPORARY TABLESPACE temp;
```

Then, to make sure this user has the necessary privileges to access the resources needed, such as the Oracle Text index and Oracle XML DB repository, execute the following:

```
GRANT CONNECT, RESOURCE TO xdkus;
GRANT ctxapp TO xdkus;
```

Registering the FAQ Schema

Now that you have the FAQ schema, you need to register it with the XML database to create the database schema. While you can use the FTP or WebDAV interface to load the XML schema file to the Oracle XML DB repository, as discussed in Chapter 8, we simply copy the file into the **/public** directory. You can do this from SQL, connected as XDKUS/XDKUS, using the **DBMS_XMLSCHEMA.registerURI()** function that takes an XML DB repository URI path from which to retrieve the schema file as follows:

```
begin

  DBMS_XMLSCHEMA.registerURI('http://localhost:8080/public/faq.xsd',
      '/public/faq.xsd',TRUE,TRUE,FALSE,TRUE);

end;
/
```

Note that this file is being retrieved from the **/public** directory; however, this is a directory inside the Oracle XML DB repository and not your local file system. There are two important reasons to store the schema in the database. First, XML documents are sensitive to the character encoding they were created in. This cannot be overridden by specifying the encoding in the XML declaration, as that attribute is only a hint to the parser if it can't determine it from the first few bytes. By storing the schema in the database, the encoding is converted, if necessary, to the database encoding, thus ensuring the document will be successfully parsed.

NOTE
An error stating that an unexpected character was found when < was expected at the start of the file usually means the document has an incompatible encoding.

The other reason to use the repository is that you can be assured the schema will always be available as a link without the need to configure proxies or firewalls and instantly retrievable for validation.

You can easily store the FAQ schema by using FTP or creating a WebDAV folder under Windows. With the XML database running, launch Internet Explorer and select File | Open. Enter **http://localhost:8080/public/**, check the Open As Web Folder check box, and then click OK. You will now see the **/public** directory in the XML database repository and can copy **faq.xsd** to it. Now you can register the schema.

Loading the FAQs

Now that you have created the database schema, you can store the FAQs. But first, to prevent duplicate FAQs, you can create a SQL unique constraint on the value of **<TITLE>**. This can be done from SQL with the following:

```
ALTER TABLE faq
ADD CONSTRAINT TITLE_IS_UNIQUE
UNIQUE(xmldata."TITLE");
```

As discussed in the previous chapter, the XMLDATA refers to the XML Type Object storing the FAQs and XMLDATA. "TITLE" can be used to refer to its child TITLE element.

To load **Glossary.xml**, the database directory XMLDIR is created using BFILE, by using the sys/password logon as SYSDBA and executing the following commands from SQLPlus:

```
CREATE DIRECTORY XMLDIR AS '&os_directory';
GRANT READ ON DIRECTORY XMLDIR TO xdkus;
```

At this point you have an option of uploading the FAQs via FTP or using web folders that use WebDAV as xdkus user. When attempting to use FTP, you should use a client that permits copying files by generating successive PUT commands. Since the XML database's FTP server only supports the basic set of FTP commands, multiple file operations and wildcard expansions are not available.

You can also create new directories or just use an existing directory in the repository to load the FAQs. However, to ensure the FAQs are stored in the default table created by the XML schema registration, which is called FAQ, the **schemaLocation** attribute in each FAQ has to be the registered XML schema URL in the Oracle XML DB. In this example, it is **xsi:noNamespaceSchemaLocation= "http://localhost:8080/public/faq.xsd"**. Therefore, each FAQ must look like the following:

```
<FAQ xmlns:xsi="http://www.w3.org/2001/XMLSchema-instance"
     xsi:noNamespaceSchemaLocation="http://localhost:8080/public/faq.xsd"
     id="0001" lastupdate="2002-02-26">…</FAQ>
```

Once you have the files loaded, you can confirm their successful storage by issuing this command from SQL*Plus:

```
SQL> SELECT COUNT(1) FROM FAQ;
  COUNT(1)
----------
       108
```

Now that the XML and database schema is designed and the data loaded, you can turn to interfacing the database to the web site using the XSQL Servlet from the XDK.

Connecting the FAQ Web Site to the XML Database

The XSQL servlet, introduced in Oracle8*i* and refined in Oracle9*i* and Oracle Database 10*g*, provides a robust and flexible platform for this type of application. We will use it in the following ways:

- To generate the content from data stored in the database
- To provide a keyword search interface
- To display the results from the various queries in the browser using an interactive interface
- To manage the database connections

Figure 14-1 illustrates the FAQ web site's home page, which is dynamically generated from the XSQL Servlet using a combination of XML and XSL files.

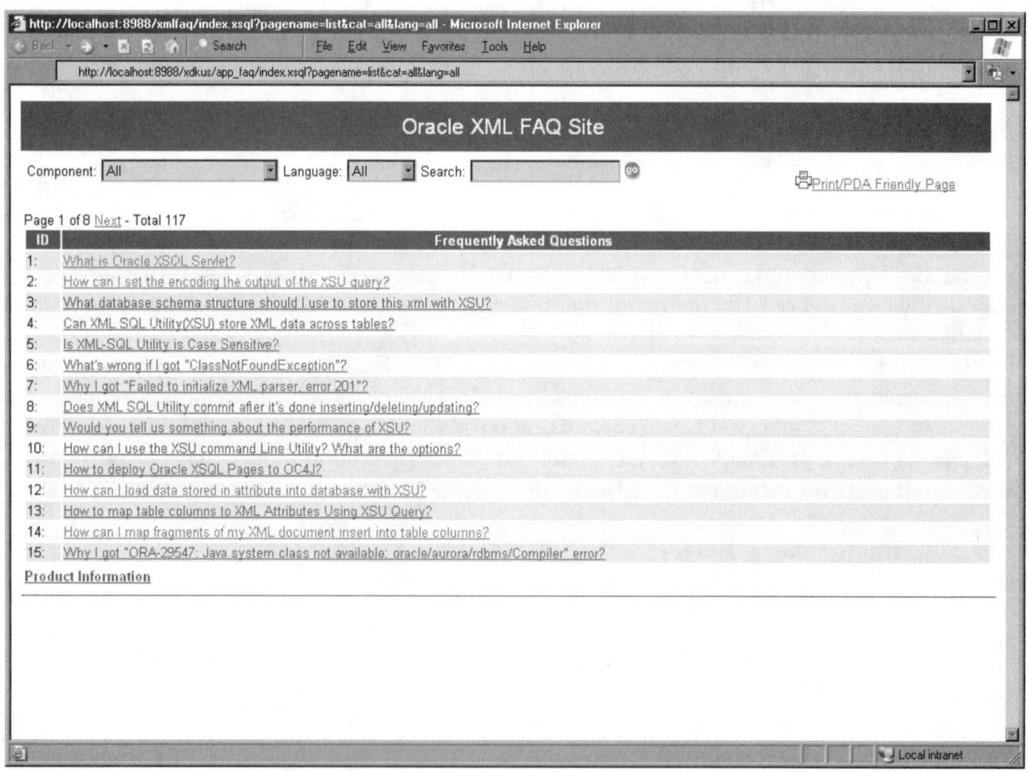

FIGURE 14-1. *FAQ web site*

Building the XSQL Home Page

From previous chapters, you know that the elements of an XSQL page consist of the following sections:

```
<?xml version="1.0" encoding='UTF-8'?>
<!-- Stylesheet PIs -->
<!-- Database Connection -->
<!-- XSQL code and database queries -->
```

However, to allow the web site to be modular and extensible, we will be parameterizing the XSQL pages where their content will be added using XML files passed as an HTTP parameter. The following is the **index.xsql** page that will serve as the base module:

```
<?xml version="1.0"?>
<?xml-stylesheet type="text/xsl" media="msie" href="xsl/xdkus.xsl"?>
<?xml-stylesheet type="text/xsl" media="mozilla"
      href="xsl/xdkus_ns.xsl"?>
<page xmlns:xsql="urn:oracle-xsql">
 <content>
  <xsql:if-param name="pagename" exists="yes">
   <xsql:include-xsql reparse="yes" href="{@pagename}.xsql"/>
  </xsql:if-param>
  <xsql:if-param name="pagename" exists="no">
   <xsql:include-xsql reparse="yes" href="list.xsql?cat=all&amp;
      lang=all"/>
  </xsql:if-param>
 </content>
</page>
```

Note that it uses the **<xsql:if-param>** element introduced in Oracle Database 10*g* XDK to conditionally include XML files. The first **<xsql:if-param>** element is called if a **pagename** parameter supplying the filename of an XSQL page is passed in, while the second is called when no parameter is supplied. Therefore, when this page is first invoked, as shown in Figure 14-1, the **list.xsql** page is included with parameters that specify the query should return *all* FAQs across *all* programming languages.

Also included are two **<?xml-stylesheet?>** processing instructions. These differ by the **media** and **href** attributes that the XSQL Servlet uses to perform the appropriate stylesheet transformation for the requesting browser.

Creating the FAQ List

The **list.xsql** page is the one that queries the database, returning XML from which the HTML page is created after the stylesheet processing. To create this page, you need to specify the database queries that will be submitted as well as the connection information for JDBC access.

You can begin by setting up the database connection. The following element declares the title of the page, the XSQL namespace, and the alias for the database connection located in the **XSQLConfig.xml** file:

```
<page title="Oracle XML FAQ Demo" connection="xdkus" id="1" xmlns:xsql=
      "urn:oracle-xsql">
```

The **xdkus** entry in the **XSQLConfig.xml** file that will be used to connect to the database is as follows:

```
<connection name="xdkus">
      <username>xdkus</username>
      <password>xdkus</password>
      <dburl>jdbc:oracle:thin:@localhost:1521:orcl</dburl>
      <driver>oracle.jdbc.driver.OracleDriver</driver>
    </connection>
```

Since the FAQs are stored as complete XML documents, if you want to produce an initial summary listing, as shown in Figure 14-1, you need to extract the information instead of displaying the entire document. Although applying a stylesheet on each returned FAQ could do this, it would be very inefficient and doesn't leverage the power of the XML database. Instead, you can use XPaths as illustrated in the following SQL query to retrieve only the data required:

```
SELECT extractValue(value(x),'/FAQ/TITLE') as title,
                 extractValue(value(x),'/FAQ/@status') as status,
                 extractValue(value(x),'/FAQ/@id') as id
           FROM faq x
           order by id
```

Retrieving the IDs for each FAQ allows you to use them to construct a link to the full question and answer. This can be done in the following XSL template included within **list.xsl**:

```
<xsl:for-each select="page/ROWSET/ROW">
   <tr>
   <xsl:attribute name="class">
   <xsl:choose>
    <xsl:when test="position() mod 2 = 1">rowodd</xsl:when>
    <xsl:when test="position() mod 2 = 0">roweven</xsl:when>
  </xsl:choose>
 </xsl:attribute>
 <td>
   <xsl:value-of select="ID"/>:</td>
 <td>
 <a href="showAnswer.xsql?id={ID}"
   Onclick="NewWindow('showAnswer.xsql?id={ID}','{ID}','600','400',
     'yes');
     return false;">
  <xsl:value-of select="TITLE"/>
 </a>
   <xsl:if test="STATUS ='hot'">
    <img src="/xdkus/images/{STATUS}.gif"/>
   </xsl:if>
  </td>
 </tr>
</xsl:for-each>
```

This template does several things. First, it produces the alternating row colors in the table by using **<xsl:choose>** to add a CSS attribute **ROWODD** or **ROWEVEN**. It then makes a link of **<TITLE>** using JavaScript to pass the FAQ ID to **showanswer.xsql** to display a new window with the answer. Finally, to indicate popular FAQs, the template adds the **hot.gif** image.

Filtering the FAQ List

Since the FAQs are categorized by programming language and component, you will want to retrieve only relevant FAQs. You can do this by passing parameters into a query. The XSQL Servlet facilitates your capability to do this, as illustrated in the following section from **list.xsql**:

```
<xsql:if-param name="lang" not-equals="all">
 <xsql:action handler="oracle.xml.sample.xsql.portal.Paging"
     rows-per-page="15" url-pagename="index.xsql?pagename=list&amp;
     cat={@cat}&amp;lang={@lang}&amp;">
   <![CDATA[
          SELECT count(1)
          FROM faq x
          where extractValue(value(x),'/FAQ/LANGUAGE/text()') ='{@lang}'
          and  extractValue(value(x),'/FAQ/CATEGORY/text()') ='{@cat}'
       ]]>
    </xsql:action>
    <xsql:query skip-rows="{@paging-skip}" max-rows="{@paging-max}">
      <![CDATA[
          SELECT extractValue(value(x),'/FAQ/TITLE') as title,
                    extractValue(value(x),'/FAQ/@status') as status,
                    extractValue(value(x),'/FAQ/@id') as id
         FROM faq x
         where extractValue(value(x),'/FAQ/LANGUAGE/text()') ='{@lang}'
            and extractValue(value(x),'/FAQ/CATEGORY/text()') ='{@cat}'
           order by id
        ]]>
 </xsql:query>
</xsql:if-param>
```

Once again, **<xsql:if-param>** is used to be able to switch in another application section. Once the category parameter, **@cat**, and the language parameter, **@lang**, are initialized by selecting from the pick lists, the queries are populated and submitted. The first query returns the FAQ count that is used for pagination and the second query returns the list of FAQs. Note that you can use XPaths in both sections of the query and that, when used in the predicate, **text()** is appended in order to perform the string match.

Adding Pagination to the FAQ Listing

Since there are over a hundred FAQs, you obviously will not want to return all of them at once. You can set up pagination in an XSQL custom action handler that calls a Java class. In this case, we have created **paging.java**, which accepts parameters from the XSQL page to set up the number of rows per page, **rows-per-page**, the URL for the page to invoke, **url-pagename**, the next page parameter name, **p**, and the parameters to pass in the URL, **url-params**. The following is a Java code fragment that performs the pagination:

```
public class Paging extends XSQLActionHandlerImpl {
  private static final String PAGE_PARAM_NAME = "p";
  private static final String ROWSPERPAGE     = "rows-per-page";
  private static final String TARGETPAGEARGS  = "url-params";
  private static final String PAGENAME        = "url-pagename";

  public void handleAction(Node root) throws SQLException {
    XSQLPageRequest req = getPageRequest();
    Element actElt  = getActionElement();
    // Get the count query from the action element content
    String query    = getActionElementContent();
    // Get the number of rows per page, defaulting to 10
    long pageSize   = longVal(getAttributeAllowingParam(ROWSPERPAGE,actElt)
      ,10);
    long totalRows  = longVal(firstColumnOfFirstRow(root,query),0);
    long curPage = longVal(variableValue(PAGE_PARAM_NAME,actElt),1);
    // Get the name of the current page to use as the target
    //String pageName = curPageName(req);
    // Get any URL param names that need to be echoed into paging URL's
    String pageArgs = getAttributeAllowingParam(TARGETPAGEARGS,actElt);
    String pageName = getAttributeAllowingParam(PAGENAME,actElt);
    // Calculate the total number of pages
    long totalPages = totalRows / pageSize;
    long fract = totalRows % pageSize;
    if (fract > 0) totalPages++;
    // Make sure current page is between 1 < cur < totalPages
    if (curPage < 1) curPage = 1;if (curPage > totalPages)
        curPage = totalPages;
    // Create the <paging> fragment to add to the "data page"
    Document d = actElt.getOwnerDocument();
    Element e = d.createElement("paging");
    root.appendChild(e);
      addResultElement(e,"total-rows",Long.toString(totalRows));
      addResultElement(e,"total-pages",Long.toString(totalPages));
      addResultElement(e,"current-page",Long.toString(curPage));
      if (curPage < totalPages)
        addResultElement(e,"next-page",Long.toString(curPage+1));
      if (curPage > 1)
        addResultElement(e,"prev-page",Long.toString(curPage-1));
      addResultElement(e,"target-page",pageName);
      if (pageArgs != null && !pageArgs.equals(""))
        addResultElement(e,"target-args",expandedUrlParams(pageArgs,
          actElt));
    // Set to page-level parameters that the <xsql:query> can use
    req.setPageParam("paging-skip",
          Long.toString((curPage-1)*pageSize));
```

```
    req.setPageParam("paging-max",Long.toString(pageSize));
  }
  // Get the name of the current page from the current page's URI
  private String curPageName(XSQLPageRequest req) {
    String thisPage = req.getSourceDocumentURI();;
    int pos = thisPage.lastIndexOf('/');
    if (pos >=0) thisPage = thisPage.substring(pos+1);
    pos = thisPage.indexOf('?');
    if (pos >=0) thisPage = thisPage.substring(0,pos-1);
    return thisPage;
  }
}
```

This class is invoked by the **<xsql:action handler>** element, as in the following example from **list.xsql**:

```
<xsql:action handler="oracle.xml.sample.xsql.portal.Paging"
       rows-per-page="15" url-pagename="index.xsql?
       pagename=list&amp;cat={@cat}&amp;lang={@lang}&amp;">
      <![CDATA[
            SELECT count(1) FROM faq
       ]]>
    </xsql:action>
```

Invoking this element will pass the three parameters to the **paging** class that will compute the total number of 15-row pages from the total number of FAQs. This class will also set the **paging-skip** and **paging-max** parameters that will be used in the following query to retrieve the correct set of questions:

```
<xsql:query skip-rows="{@paging-skip}" max-rows="{@paging-max}">
  <![CDATA[
       SELECT extractValue(value(x),'/FAQ/TITLE') as title,
              extractValue(value(x),'/FAQ/@status') as status,
              extractValue(value(x),'/FAQ/@id') as id
       FROM faq x
       order by id
    ]]>
</xsql:query>
```

Now all that you need to do is create a Next link that increments the **p** parameter to display successive FAQ pages. This is done by creating the following link to pass a new set of parameters to **index.xsql** and subsequently **list.xsql**:

```
http://localhost:8988/xdkus/app_faq/index.xsql?
     pagename=list&cat=all&lang=all&p=2
```

Each time **p** is incremented, a new set of 15 FAQs is displayed until the maximum is reached.

Displaying the FAQ and Answers

In a previous section, you saw how the link is created to invoke the **showanswer.xsql** page that displays the FAQ. Now we will discuss how this actually works. This page is invoked by passing the selected FAQ **id** as a parameter in the following URL:

```
http://localhost:8988/xdkus/app_faq/showAnswer.xsql?id=16
```

Figure 14-2 shows the XML transformed into the HTML display of the output.

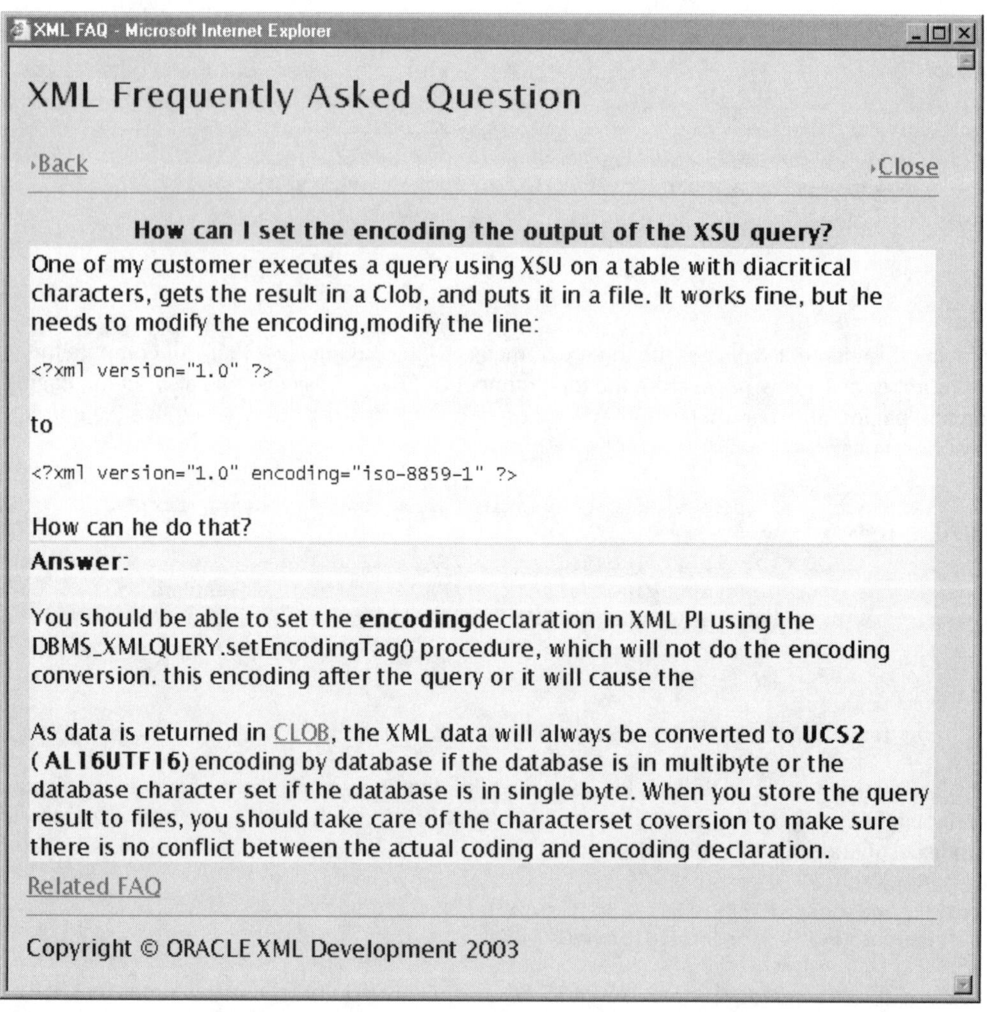

FIGURE 14-2. *FAQ answer in HTML*

The **id** is then passed into the following query to retrieve the FAQ data:

```
<xsql:include-xml>
    <![CDATA[
      select  xmlelement("FAQ",
                xmlforest(extract(value(x),'/FAQ/ANSWER') as answer,
                     extract(value(x),'/FAQ/TITLE/text()') as title,
                     extract(value(x),'/FAQ/QUESTION') as question,
                     extract(value(x),'/FAQ/@id') as id)).getClobVal()
        from faq x
     where extractValue(value(x),'/FAQ/@id')='{@id}'
   ]]>
  </xsql:include-xml>
```

If you examine this query, you'll see that it uses the SQL/XML extensions in the database to construct a new XML document. To simply include the XML output from SQL/XML queries, you can use **<xsql:include-xml>** instead of **<xsql:query>** as it doesn't add the **<ROWSET>** and **<ROW>** elements. The following is an example of this document before it is transformed into HTML by the **showAnswer.xsl** stylesheet:

```
<page id="1">
 <FAQ>
  <ANSWER>
   <ANSWER>
    <PARAGRAPH> You should be able to set the
       <KEYWORD>encoding</KEYWORD> declaration in XML PI using the
       DBMS_XMLQUERY.setEncodingTag() procedure,
       which will not do the encoding conversion.</PARAGRAPH>
    <PARAGRAPH> As data is returned in <KEYWORD>CLOB</KEYWORD>,
    the XML data will  always be converted to <KEYWORD>UCS2</KEYWORD>
    ( <KEYWORD>AL16UTF16</KEYWORD> ) encoding by database if the
    database is in multibyte or the database character set if the
    database is in single byte. When you store the query result
    to files, you should take care of the characterset conversion
    to make sure there is no conflict between the actual coding and
    encoding declaration. </PARAGRAPH>
  </ANSWER>
 </ANSWER>
 <TITLE>How can I set the encoding the output of the XSU query?</TITLE>
 <QUESTION>
  <QUESTION>
   <PARAGRAPH>One of my customers executes a query using XSU on a
   table with diacritical characters, gets the result in a CLOB,
   and puts it in a file. It works fine, but he needs to modify the
   encoding, modify the line:</PARAGRAPH>
   <CODE><?xml version="1.0" ?></CODE> to <CODE><?xml version="1.0"
   encoding="iso-8859-1" ?></CODE>
  <PARAGRAPH>How can he do that?</PARAGRAPH>
  </QUESTION>
```

```
  </QUESTION>
    <ID>2</ID>
</FAQ>
```

Note that the four top-level elements, **<ANSWER>**, **<TITLE>**, **<QUESTION>**, and **<ID>**, were retrieved using the **extract()** function passing in the respective XPaths.

To display this FAQ in HTML, you need to apply a stylesheet. This is done for you by including a stylesheet processing instruction in **showanswer.xsql** and having the XSQL Servlet apply it for you. The following is in our example:

```
<?xml-stylesheet type="text/xsl" href="xsl/showAnswer.xsl" ?>
```

This stylesheet is quite long because it sets up tables, but it is useful to examine the templates that actually operate over the input FAQ XML document. First, the **<PARAGRAPH>** sections need to be formatted. This is done with the identity transform template, introduced in Chapter 3, as follows:

```
<xsl:template match="PARAGRAPH">
  <p>
    <xsl:apply-templates select="*|@*|comment()|processing-instruction()
      |text()"/>
  </p>
</xsl:template>
```

Next, the **<CODE>** elements need to be presented in a fixed font. This is accomplished with the following template:

```
<xsl:template match="CODE">
      <pre>
        <xsl:value-of select="."/>
      </pre>
</xsl:template>
```

Next, turning to the main sections of the answer, these will be formatted in the main template of the stylesheet. First, we see that the FAQ title has special formatting. This is done with the following section, which uses a CSS class to provide the special formatting:

```
<tr valign="top">
  <th class="portletTitle">
    <xsl:value-of disable-output-escaping="yes" select="page/FAQ/TITLE"/>
  </th>
</tr>
```

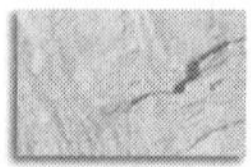

NOTE
Throughout these examples, you will see that CSS classes are used to provide formatting. You should adopt this technique, because it makes your stylesheets easier to build, and the formatting is reusable.

Next, we see that the answer is identified with **Answer:** and a different background color. The following section shows how this is done:

```
<tr bgcolor="#F0F0F0">
  <td width="100%">
   <b>Answer: </b>
   <br/>
   <xsl:apply-templates select="page/FAQ/ANSWER/ANSWER"/>
  </td>
</tr>
```

Finally, you need to add navigational controls to this page, such as Back and Close. You can do this by adding JavaScript commands to the template as follows:

```
<tr>
 <td>
  <img src="images/r_arrow.gif" width="8" height="9"/>
   <a href="#" onClick="history.back()">Back</a>
 </td>
 <td align="right">
  <img src="images/r_arrow.gif" width="8" height="9"/>
  <a href="#" onClick="self.close()">Close</a>
 </td>
</tr>
```

Note that both the text of the commands and an arrow graphic are inserted when the template is applied.

Creating a Glossary

A useful function in any FAQ site is to have an online glossary that displays definitions of important technical terms when users click on the corresponding words. You can implement this feature in your FAQ site by marking up terms as **<KEYWORD>** elements and then creating links dynamically through XSLT to retrieve their definitions from a glossary table in the database. In this example, we have already created a glossary file in XML format that can be used.

Creating the Glossary Schema

First you need to create a glossary table in the database in which to store the definitions. It is not important that the glossary data is stored as XML; therefore, you can create a simple table as follows:

```
CREATE TABLE GLOSSARY(
 ID NUMBER,
 NAME VARCHAR2(30),
 CONTENT VARCHAR2(4000)
 );

CREATE SEQUENCE glossary_seq START WITH 100;

CREATE or replace TRIGGER glossary_insert
BEFORE INSERT ON glossary
FOR EACH ROW
```

```
BEGIN
  select glossary_seq.nextval into :new.id from dual;
END;
/
show errors;
```

This SQL script creates a simple three-column table to store the ID, NAME, and CONTENT for each term. It also creates a sequence and a trigger to update the sequence so that the IDs are generated automatically every time a new entry is inserted.

Loading the Glossary

The supplied glossary file is called **glossary.xml** and will be loaded directly into the table using the DBMS_XMLSave package available in the database. The XML format for the glossary data is provided in the required canonical form:

```
<ROW num="1">
 <NAME>API</NAME>
 <CONTENT>(Application Program Interface) A set of public programmatic
  interfaces that consist of a language and message format to communicate
  with an operating system or other programmatic environment such as
  databases, Web servers, JVMs, etc.  These messages typically call
  functions and methods available for application development.
 </CONTENT>
</ROW>
```

All of these entries are contained within a **<ROWSET>** root element that will permit the entire document to be inserted at one time. The following PL/SQL script performs the insert:

```
DECLARE
  insCtx DBMS_XMLSave.ctxType;
  rows NUMBER;
BEGIN
  insCtx := DBMS_XMLSave.newContext('GLOSSARY');
  rows := DBMS_XMLSave.insertXML(insCtx, FileToClob('glossary.xml'));
  DBMS_XMLSave.closeContext(insCtx);
  DBMS_OUTPUT.put_line(rows||' of data in glossary have been updated.');
END;
/
show errors;
```

Note that even though a **num=""** attribute is included in the file, this is not used to index the entry. This is because attributes are not mapped by **DBMS_XMLSAVE** nor by **DBMS_XMLSTORE** or **oracle.xml.sql.query.OracleXMLQuery()** for data insertions. The CREATE SEQUENCE command ends up creating the ID to retrieve the item. In order to do the insertion, you need to first set the context to your table, in this case GLOSSARY. Then you can populate the rows in the table by using **insertXML()**, which accepts a CLOB that was populated using **FiletoCLOB()** to load **glossary.xml**. All that is left to do is to close the context, thus committing the changes.

Linking to the Glossary

Now that the glossary is loaded, you just need to be able to associate keywords within **<KEYWORD>** elements in your FAQs with the glossary and insert links. To do this, you need to query the retrieved FAQ answer for keywords. This is done in **showAnswer.xsql** with the following code:

```
<page>
<GLOSSARY>
 <xsql:query>
  <![CDATA[
   SELECT name, id FROM glossary
   WHERE name in (
     SELECT extractValue(value(e), 'KEYWORD') FROM faq p,
        table(xmlsequence(p.extract('/FAQ//KEYWORD'))) e
     WHERE p.xmldata.id={@id})  ]]>
 </xsql:query>
</GLOSSARY>
</page>
```

The query first uses the **EXTRACT('/FAQ//KEYWORD')** function to get the **<KEYWORD>** elements in the FAQ. Then using **XMLSEQUENCE()** and **TABLE()**, a table is created containing the set of **<KEYWORD>** elements in XMLType. This table is then used to create a collection of values of keywords using **EXTRACTVALUE()** and only the NAME and ID for each glossary item are returned by the query.

Note that you are only trying to retrieve the set of IDs associated with the keywords found anywhere in the FAQ, as specified by the double-slash (//) in front of **KEYWORD** in **p.extract()**. Don't confuse the two IDs specified in the query: the one in the SELECT is the glossary ID and the one in the predicate is the FAQ ID. An example of the actual query output is as follows:

```
<GLOSSARY>
 <ROWSET>
  <ROW num="1">
   <NAME>CLASSPATH</NAME>
   <ID>113</ID>
  </ROW>
 </ROWSET>
</GLOSSARY>
```

In this case, one keyword was found and it has 113 as its ID. Only those keywords that have glossary entries are returned.

With the keyword IDs retrieved, the remaining task is to create a link in the HTML page. This is done in a template in **showAnswer.xsl** as follows:

```
<xsl:template match="KEYWORD">
 <xsl:variable name="content">
  <xsl:value-of select="./text()"/>
 </xsl:variable>
 <xsl:variable name="glossary">
```

```
    <xsl:value-of select="/page/GLOSSARY/ROWSET/ROW[NAME/text()=
      $content]/ID"/>
  </xsl:variable>
  <xsl:choose>
    <xsl:when test="$glossary">
     <a href="showGlossary.xsql?id={$glossary}">
      <xsl:value-of select="."/>
     </a>
    </xsl:when>
  <xsl:otherwise>
    <b>
     <xsl:value-of select="."/>
    </b>
  </xsl:otherwise>
 </xsl:choose>
</xsl:template>
```

Because this template is complex, we will examine it closely. First, variables are used, because you need to pass in the ID dynamically to the link. These variables are used together. The **content** variable is simply the keyword. This is then reused in the **glossary** variable to create the XPath that selects the ID.

The functional portion of the template is a choice between two formatting actions. If there is an instance of the **glossary** variable, then the test in **<xsl:when>** returns true and a link is created that passes the ID to a new page, **showGlossary.xsql**, to display the glossary item. If the test fails, then the **<xsl:otherwise>** section is executed, formatting the keyword in bold. This formatting flags these keywords for inclusion in the glossary.

Displaying the Glossary Definitions

Now that the links to keywords in the FAQ answers are added, we can turn to examine how the page displaying the definition is created. As specified by the following example link, this is once again performed by an XSQL page:

```
http://localhost:8988/xdkus/app_faq/showGlossary.xsql?id=100
```

The **showglossary.xsql** page is very simple, as shown here:

```
<?xml version="1.0" encoding='UTF-8'?>
<?xml-stylesheet type="text/xsl" href="xsl/showGlossary.xsl" ?>
<page id="1" connection="xdkus" xmlns:xsql="urn:oracle-xsql">
 <xsql:query>
  <![CDATA[
       SELECT NAME, CONTENT
       FROM GLOSSARY
       WHERE id={@id}
    ]]>
 </xsql:query>
</page>
```

This page simply executes one query to retrieve the NAME and CONTENT from the GLOSSARY table and apply the **showGlossary.xsl** stylesheet to convert to HTML. The following is the XML output for CLASSPATH:

```
<?xml version="1.0" encoding="UTF-8" ?>
<?xml-stylesheet type="text/xsl" href="xsl/showGlossary.xsl" ?>
<page id="1">
 <ROWSET>
  <ROW num="1">
  <NAME>CLASSPATH</NAME>
  <CONTENT>The operating system environmental variable that the JVM uses
   to find the classes it needs to run applications.</CONTENT>
  </ROW>
 </ROWSET>
</page>
```

This stylesheet incorporates the same types of transformations discussed previously for **showAnswer.xsl** in the section "Displaying the FAQ and Answers."

Searching the FAQs

No FAQ site would be fully functional without the ability to perform text searches. This site uses the Oracle Text search engine to search XML either as content or structurally using XPaths. The **index.xsql** page combines these text searches with category searches to create a single result, as evidenced by the following sample query for all Java components that reference DOM:

```
http://localhost:8988/xdkus/app_faq/index.xsql?
       pagename=search&search=DOM&cat=all&lang=JAVA
```

This URL links to a new XSQL page, **search.xsql**, that performs a direct search instead of the browse action discussed previously. This page has all the same elements as **list.xsql** except that it takes an additional parameter, **search**, and it has an additional predicate, as shown in the following query:

```
<xsql:query skip-rows="{@paging-skip}" max-rows="{@paging-max}">
  <![CDATA[
   SELECT extractValue(value(x),'/FAQ/TITLE') as title,
          extractValue(value(x),'/FAQ/@id') as id
   FROM faq x
    where extractValue(value(x),'/FAQ/LANGUAGE/text()') ='{@lang}'
    and contains(value(x),'{@search}')>0
    order by id
        ]]>
</xsql:query>
```

Note that the Oracle Text **CONTAINS()** function is now added to the WHERE clause to narrow the selection process further. The output from this page will again be a list of FAQs that is displayed using the identical paging and listing code discussed earlier.

Summary

In this chapter you have seen how to create a content management and web publishing application utilizing Oracle XML DB 10*g* features and Oracle XDK components, including the powerful functionality of the XSQL Servlet. We have combined XML documents, XML Schema, and XSLT with Java, JavaScript, and SQL to create a compelling application. Using this application as a base, we will add more sophisticated features in Chapter 15, transforming it into a portal site.

CHAPTER 15

Creating a Portal Site with XML and Web Services

eb sites are moving from static sets of pages to dynamic personalized portals of information. Oracle has obviously recognized this movement, as demonstrated by its sophisticated Oracle Portal product, but what isn't often realized is that this functionality can be set up on a smaller scale with the XML technology offered in the Oracle XDK and XML database. In this chapter, you will take the FAQ web site put together in the previous chapter and add Portal functionality to it. This will include building a login area, dynamic page areas, web service areas, and a customization area.

Designing the Framework

The idea behind this portal site is to build it to serve the purposes of a development team who can use it as a home page for all documentation, tips, latest developments, status, and FAQs. This site needs to leverage the previously introduced concept of modularity so that the site can continually be customized and expanded as needed. This framework consists of a set of XSQL pages that were called from each other with appropriate parameters to alter behavior or display dynamic content. What we are going to introduce now is how to combine this modularity into single container pages whose content is supplied by several XSQL pages firing at once.

Figure 15-1 shows what the finished site will look like. As you can see, it contains new areas that were not on the FAQ site. Reviewing clockwise, you'll note a new What's New area (where the FAQ list was) that has links to the latest interesting XML articles, displaying ten links at a time. Next is a new login area for XDK users, with the requisite Name and Password fields. This area serves as the major user action area of the page and is handled by a separate XSQL page. It also will be used as a role-specific link area after a successful login.

Below the login area is the Hot Topics area, which appears as a list of links but actually is dynamically generated from a web service that is supplied by the Oracle Technology Network (OTN) site. The web service provider, employing a push model, keeps this area current; you will include it on your site by using another XSQL page. Below the Hot Topics area is a Hot Links area, which is actually populated by XML content from a file. Finally, the left-hand bar serves as a static area that repopulates the center area when its links are clicked with content from queries executed by the series of XSQL pages linked here.

You will also be creating an administrative page to facilitate adding users, content, links, etc. This will be a separate role based upon the permission level of the user login, using the page illustrated in Figure 15-2. Note that the login area has specific links for this role and that the left-hand bar now displays administrative tasks, such as inserting or updating a news item, adding links, and approving new users.

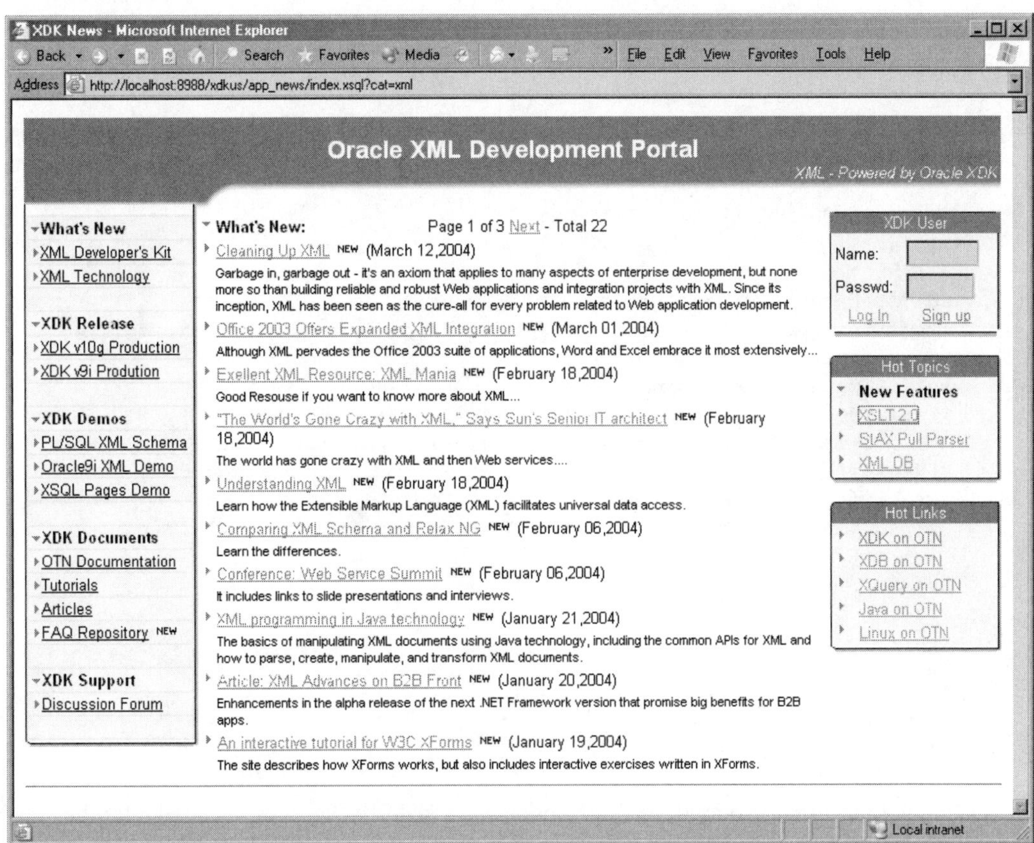

FIGURE 15-1. *Finished Oracle XML Development Group portal site*

Turning to how this web site is designed, an XSQL container page is used to call additional XSQL pages to populate the areas, as shown in the following listing for **index.xsql**:

```
<?xml version="1.0"?>
<?xml-stylesheet type="text/xsl" media="msie" href="xsl/xdkus.xsl"?>
<?xml-stylesheet type="text/xsl" media="mozilla"
   href="xsl/xdkus_ns.xsl"?>
```

```
<page xmlns:xsql="urn:oracle-xsql">
  <login>
    <xsql:include-xsql reparse="yes" href="login.xsql"/>
  </login>
  <nav>
    <xsql:include-xml href="xml/nav.xml"/>
  </nav>
  <link>
    <xsql:include-xml href="xml/link.xml"/>
  </link>
  <content>
    <xsql:if-param name="appname" exists="yes">
      <xsql:include-xsql reparse="yes" href="app_{@appname}/index.xsql"/>
    </xsql:if-param>
    <xsql:if-param name="appname" exists="no">
      <xsql:if-param name="pagename" exists="yes">
        <xsql:include-xsql reparse="yes" href="{@pagename}.xsql"/>
      </xsql:if-param>
      <xsql:if-param name="pagename" exists="no">
        <xsql:include-xsql reparse="yes" href="app_news/news.xsql?
           cat=xdk"/>
       </xsql:if-param>
    </xsql:if-param>
 </content>
 <topic>
  <xsql:include-xsql href="app_news/otnnews.xsql"/>
 </topic>
</page>
```

Examining this listing, you will see the familiar XSLT stylesheet entries to account for the different behavior between Netscape and Internet Explorer, this distinction being made by using the **media** attribute of the **<?xml-stylesheet?>** processing instruction. You then see element groups defining the different areas of the page, as follows:

- **<login>** Calls **login.xsql** to populate the login area.
- **<nav>** Loads **nav.xml** to populate the left-hand navigation bar.
- **<link>** Loads **link.xml** to populate the Hot Links area.
- **<content>** Calls specify XSQL pages depending on the appname and pagemane input. By default, it calls **news.xsql** to populate the What's New section as well as iteratively calling the paging engine as described in the previous chapter to create pages of entries.
- **<topic>** Calls **otnnews.xsql** to populate the Hot Topics area.

This page demonstrates retrieving content not only from the database but also from a file system and a web service, thus demonstrating a broad range of functionality that you can implement with this architecture. We will discuss each of these forms of retrieval in the following sections.

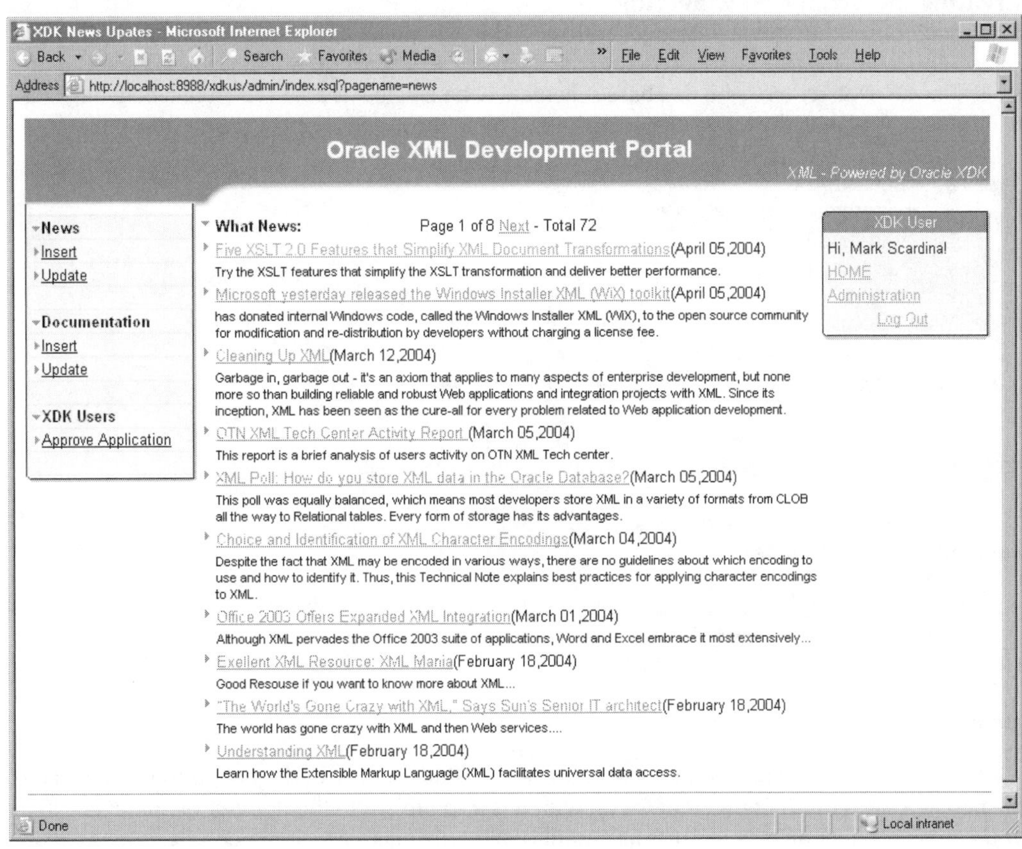

FIGURE 15-2. *Development Group portal administrative page*

Designing the Static and Dynamic Areas

In this section, you will see how to populate the various content areas with their data and links. In this discussion, a *static* area is one that gets its content from the local file system, and a *dynamic* area is one that is populated from a remote source where the content is unknown to the web server at request time. In this example, this dynamic content will be from database queries and web services. For ease of development and the ability to support multiple browsers, all content will be delivered in XML, and the XSQL servlet will apply the appropriate XSLT stylesheet to produce HTML or another device-appropriate markup language such as WML.

Creating the Dynamic Areas

For this sample page, there are two dynamic areas: What's New and Hot Topics. The What's New area is created by retrieving listings from the database, while the Hot Topics area is generated from a web service offered on OTN.

Creating the What's New Section

This section uses the same techniques introduced in Chapter 14 for retrieving and displaying FAQs. Therefore, the first task is to define the database schema for these news items. Instead of registering an XML schema, the database schema will be created as a NEWS table where the data will be stored relationally but retrieved as XML. The following SQL script creates this table:

```
CREATE TABLE NEWS(
  news_id NUMBER PRIMARY KEY,
  title  VARCHAR2(100),
  notes VARCHAR2(200),
  link VARCHAR2(200),
  createtime DATE,
  category VARCHAR2(10),
  status varchar2(10)
);

CREATE SEQUENCE news_seq START WITH 1;

CREATE or replace TRIGGER news_insert
BEFORE INSERT ON news
FOR EACH ROW
BEGIN
  select news_seq.nextval into :new.news_id from dual;
END;
/
show errors;
```

Since you would want to store information such as title, notes, and a link, these columns are created as VARCHAR2. The size of each column is also limited to the number of characters that you can reasonably display in a listing. Additionally, metadata about the entry can be added, such as the date, category, and publication status. Finally, you will need to generate IDs for the items, which will be useful in creating a link for retrieval of the entry for updating. These IDs are generated by the NEWS_SEQ trigger created in the second part of the script.

Now that the schema is created, we can examine the XSQL page that retrieves its contents. The following fragment does this retrieval from the main **index.xsql** page:

```
<content>
  <xsql:if-param name="pagename" exists="yes">
   <xsql:include-xsql reparse="yes" href="{@pagename}.xsql"/>
  </xsql:if-param>
  <xsql:if-param name="pagename" exists="no">
   <xsql:include-xsql reparse="yes" href="app_news/news.xsql?cat=xdk"/>
  </xsql:if-param>
</content>
```

As in the FAQ listing, the first iteration of this section is without a **pagename**, so the first **xsql:if-param>** will be skipped and the second one executed by calling the **app_news/index.xsql** page with a category parameter of **xdk**. Taking a look at this page in the following listing, you'll see that it has its own stylesheet, **news.xsl**, to handle the specific formatting of the XML. It also uses the **xdkus** database connection in the **XSQLConfig.xml** file and calls the same **Paging.java** class used for the FAQs, located in the package **oracle.xml.sample.xsql.portal**.

```
<?xml version="1.0"?>
<?xml-stylesheet type="text/xsl" href="xsl/news.xsl"?>
<page id="1" title="News of XDK" connection="xdkus" xmlns:xsql="urn:oracle-xsql">
  <xsql:action handler="oracle.xml.sample.xsql.portal.Paging" rows-per-page="10"
     url-pagename="index.xsql?cat={@cat}&amp;">
      <![CDATA[
            SELECT count(1)
            FROM news
            where category='{@cat}'
         ]]>
    </xsql:action>
    <xsql:query rowset-element="NEWS" row-element="NEWS_ITEM"
                skip-rows="{@paging-skip}" max-rows="{@paging-max}">
      <![CDATA[
            SELECT news_id as id,title,link,status,
                   TO_CHAR(createtime,'Month DD,YYYY') as time, notes as note
            FROM news
            where category='{@cat}'
            ORDER BY createtime DESC
         ]]>
    </xsql:query>
</page>
```

Taking a look at the queries, the first one simply generates the overall count of items. The second one uses the capability of the XML SQL Utility to encapsulate the result in XML. The following is an example result returned in XML:

```
<page>
...

<NEWS>
 <NEWS_ITEM num="4">
  <ID>124</ID>
  <TITLE>XDK eSeminar</TITLE>
  <LINK>http://ilearning.oracle.com/ilearn/en/learner/jsp/
     offering_details_home.jsp?classid=58377231</LINK>
   <STATUS>new</STATUS>
   <TIME>July 05,2003</TIME>
   <NOTE>Overview of the XML standards support by the Oracle XDK and an
      in-depth discussion on the XML features.</NOTE>
 </NEWS_ITEM>
</NEWS>
...
</page>
```

This result is then processed by the **news.xsl** stylesheet to create the entry, as shown in this fragment:

```
<xsl:for-each select="page/NEWS/NEWS_ITEM">
 <tr>
  <td width="10" align="right" valign="top">
   <img src="images/r_arrow.gif" width="10" height="10"/>
  </td>
  <td colspan="2" width="600" align="left" class="fbox">
   <a href="{LINK}" target="_new" class="fbox">
      <xsl:value-of select="TITLE"/></a>
   <xsl:if test="STATUS[text()!='']">
    <img src="/xdkus/images/{STATUS}.gif"/>
   </xsl:if>
   <xsl:text>(</xsl:text><xsl:value-of select="TIME"/><xsl:text>)</xsl:text>
  </td>
 </tr>
 <tr>
  <td width="10"><xsl:text> </xsl:text></td>
  <td colspan="2" width="600" class="footnt">
   <xsl:value-of select="NOTE"/>
  </td>
 </tr>
</xsl:for-each>
```

Of note is the **<xsl:if>** element, which tests for a value in the **<STATUS>** element. If found, an icon corresponding to its value is displayed. This is accomplished by using {STATUS} in the XPath to construct the name of the image. Looking at our example result, **new.gif** would be chosen. This technique is also used to construct the HREF attribute for the link to the news item.

Notice that the XSL statement

```
<img src="/xdkus/images/{STATUS}.gif"/>
```

is equivalent to

```
<img>
  <xsl:attribute name="src">
    <xsl:text>/xdkus/images/</xsl:text><xsl:value-of select="STATUS"/>
          <xsl:text>.gif</xsl:text>
  </xsl:attribute>
</img>
```

but is easier to write, read, and maintain.

Finally, different CSS classes are used to vary the formatting and text size of the **<TITLE>** and **<NOTE>** values, as shown in the stylesheet, where the **class** attribute of some **<td>** elements takes the values **fbox** and **footn**.

Creating the Hot Topics Area

Up to this point, the content on the site has been supplied locally. Web services provide the advantage of supplying changing content without requiring maintenance on your part. For this area, you'll use a web service provided by OTN as an XML document sent as the payload of a SOAP message. This XML service, while of a *Really Simple Syndication (RSS)* type, has a Web Services Description Language (WSDL) service description available at **http://otn.oracle.com/ws/oracle.otn.ws.news.OTNNews?WSDL**. These services are available from a variety of web sites, from retailers such as amazon.com to personal blogs.

To connect this service to the site, you need to create a Java class—usually called a stub, or a proxy—to generate the request and receive the XML response that can then be transformed into HTML by a stylesheet. This class, acting as a SOAP client, needs to call the **getRSS** method available at **oracle.otn.ws.news.OTNNews**. You can set up an XSQL custom action handler to invoke the class from within an XSQL page. In this case, the following section from the main **index.xsql** page calls the **otnnews.xsql** page, invoking the service:

```
<topic>
 <xsql:include-xsql href="app_news/otnnews.xsql"/>
</topic>
```

The **otnnews.xsql** page is very simple, as shown in the following section, but needs to be its own page in order for the **otnnews.xsl** stylesheet to be applied:

```
<?xml version="1.0"?>
<?xml-stylesheet type="text/xsl" href="xsl/otnnews.xsl"?>
<xsql:action xmlns:xsql="urn:oracle-xsql"
 handler="oracle.xml.sample.xsql.portal.OTNNewsStub"/>
```

To implement the **OTNNewsStub.java** class, you need to use the Oracle SOAP implementation that is part of the XDK. The following are the code fragments. First, you need to initialize an HTTP connection:

```
public OTNNewsStub()
   {
     m_httpConnection = new OracleSOAPHTTPConnection();}
```

Next, you need to set up the connection session and properties:

```
public void setMaintainSession(boolean maintainSession)
{
     m_httpConnection.setMaintainSession(maintainSession); }
public boolean getMaintainSession()
{
  return m_httpConnection.getMaintainSession(); }
public void setTransportProperties(Properties props)
{
  m_httpConnection.setProperties(props); }
public Properties getTransportProperties()
{
  return m_httpConnection.getProperties(); }
```

Then, you need to create the method to invoke the web service:

```
public void getRss(Node root)
  {
    String resultVal = null;
try
    {
    //Initialize the URL location of the service
    URL endpointURL = new
               URL("http://otn.oracle.com/ws/oracle.otn.ws.news.OTNNews");
    //Build the call.
    Call call = new Call();
    //Associate connection with call
    call.setSOAPTransport(m_httpConnection);
    // configure the call (i.e. targetObjectURI, methodName, etc.)
    call.setTargetObjectURI("oracle.otn.ws.news.OTNNews");
    call.setMethodName("getRss");
    call.setEncodingStyleURI(Constants.NS_URI_SOAP_ENC);
    //Make the call
    Response response = call.invoke(endpointURL, "");
if   (!response.generatedFault())
    {
      Parameter result = response.getReturnValue();
      resultVal = (String)result.getValue();
      DOMParser p=new DOMParser();
      p.parse(new ByteArrayInputStream(returnVal.getBytes()));
      XMLDocument doc = p.getDocument();
      appendCopyOfSecondaryDocument(root, doc);
     // return doc.getDocumentElement();
    }
else { … }
catch { … )
```

Finally, you need to connect up the XSQL plumbing to call the service and return the data:

```
public void handleAction(Node root)
  {
    //Initialize the returned data
    String m_title=null;
    String m_question=null;
    String m_answer=null;
    String m_category=null;
    String m_language=null;
    String m_path = null;
    if(getPageRequest().getRequestType().equals("Servlet"))
    {
      // Get the XSQL Page Request
      XSQLServletPageRequest xspr = (XSQLServletPageRequest)getPageRequest();
      HttpServletRequest req = xspr.getHttpServletRequest();
```

```
    // Call the Web Service
    getRss(root); }
}
```

Upon invoking **getRSS()**, an XML document is returned, as shown in the following listing:

```
<rss version="0.91">
 <channel>
  <title>Oracle Technology News</title>
  <link>http://otn.oracle.com</link>
  <description>Oracle Technology News</description>
  <language>en-us</language>
  <copyright>Copyright 2002, Oracle Corporation. All rights reserved</copyright>
  <managingEditor>otn_us@oracle.com</managingEditor>
  <webmaster>otn_us@oracle.com</webmaster>
  <textinput>
  <title>Search OTN</title>
   <description>Enter your search terms</description>
   <name>keyword</name>
   <link>http://otn.oracle.com/ws/searchwrapper</link>
  </textinput>
  <image>
   <title>Oracle Technology Network</title>
   <url>http://otn.oracle.com/otn116x65_center.gif</url>
   <link>otn.oracle.com</link>
   <width>116</width>
   <height>65</height>
   <description>Developer news from Oracle Technology Network.</description>
  </image>
  <item num="1">
   <title>New Oracle Portal Development Kit (PDK)</title>
   <link>http://otn.oracle.com/products/iportal/files/pdk105ea/index.html</link>
   <description><a  href=\"/products/iportal/index2.htm?
    Info&/products/iportal/files/pdk105ea/index.html\">The Oracle Portal
    Development Kit (PDK)</a> is the pre-eminent resource for developing
    portlets. It contains utilities and articles that assist in every step
    of portlet development. This release of the PDK illustrates how to extend
    the <a href=\"/products/iportal/\"> Oracle Portal</a> and includes the
    JPDK utilities for building portlets in Java.</description>
  </item>
  ...
 </channel>
</rss>
```

For the purpose of this site, you are only interested in displaying the title and link for a subset of items. Therefore, a very simple stylesheet, **otnnews.xsl**, is all that is required:

```
<xsl:stylesheet version="1.0" xmlns:xsl="http://www.w3.org/1999/XSL/Transform">
<xsl:template match="/">
 <top_topics>
  <topic name="OTN News">
```

```
    <link uri="{rss/channel/item[1]/link}"><xsl:value-of
          select="rss/channel/item[1]/title"/></link>
    <link uri="{rss/channel/item[2]/link}"><xsl:value-of
          select="rss/channel/item[2]/title"/></link>
  </topic>
</top_topics>
</xsl:template>
</xsl:stylesheet>
```

As you can see, this stylesheet retrieves the values of **<title>** and **<link>** of the first two items and creates a small XML document that is returned to the calling **index.xsql** page to be converted into HTML by the included **topic.xsl** that creates the Hot Topics area. These links are created in the same way as the News items previously discussed.

Creating the Static Areas

For the portal page, there are two areas that will be populated from XML files: the left-hand navigation bar, which is a constant across pages, and the Hot Links area, a set of links that is easy to update and maintain.

To retrieve XML from a file on the local system running the XSQL servlet, you simply use the **<xsql:include-xml>** element, as in the following example from **index.xsql**:

```
<nav>
 <xsql:include-xml href="xml/nav.xml"/>
</nav>
<link>
 <xsql:include-xml href="xml/link.xml"/>
</link>
```

Each of these files contains **<link>** elements made up of the URI, descriptive text, and optional status, as follows:

```
<link status="new" uri="/xdkus/app_release/index.xsql?pagename=beta&amp;rel=beta">
XDK v10 Beta</link>
```

These links are transformed into HTML by associated stylesheets that extract each part. Here is a simple template section that performs this transformation:

```
<xsl:for-each select="link">
 <tr bgcolor="#f7f7e7">
 <td>
  <img src="/xdkus/images/r_arrow.gif" width="10" height="10"/>
  <xsl:choose>
   <xsl:when test="./@uri">
    <a href="{./@uri}" class="navs">
     <xsl:value-of select="./text()"/>
    </a>
   <xsl:if test="@status">
    <img src="/xdkus/images/{@status}.gif"/>
   </xsl:if>
```

```
  </xsl:when>
  <xsl:otherwise>
   <xsl:value-of select="./@name"/>
  </xsl:otherwise>
  </xsl:choose>
  </td>
  </tr>
</xsl:for-each>
```

Note that this template is conditional based upon finding a **uri** attribute in the link element and turning it into an HTML **href** using the link's text value as the new HTML **href** text. As before, an image is optionally added based upon finding a **status** attribute. The **<xsl:otherwise>** element selects the value of the **name** attribute that could be used as subdivision text.

Adding the Portal Functionality

The characteristic that separates a portal site from a normal web site is its ability to be personalized for the specific user. This can be done by creating a login area that, once successfully accessed, retrieves a profile that results in a version of the site that is customized to the user. In this section, we will define that customization based on roles.

To set up this personalization feature, you need to first define a database schema for the user information, create a form to sign up new users, create an administrative page to approve users and assign roles, and create a login area for users to sign in.

Creating the User Schema

To define the database schema, you first must determine what information is required to identify the user uniquely and what information that you want to maintain for each user. For this application, you will store the following information for each user:

- **user_id** Generated primary key
- **uname** User login name
- **first_name** User's first name
- **last_name** User's last name
- **email** User's e-mail address
- **password** User's password
- **role** User's role (user, admin, manager, developer)
- **status** User's approval status
- **register_date** User's registration date
- **last_visit** Date of user's last visit
- **comments** Notes regarding the user

All of these values can be stored in a single USERS table because there is no data that requires nesting. You can create this table by using the following SQL script:

```
CREATE TABLE USERS(
 user_id VARCHAR2(20) PRIMARY KEY,
 uname varchar2(20),
 first_name VARCHAR2(100),
 last_name VARCHAR2(100),
 email VARCHAR2(200),
 password varchar2(20),
 role VARCHAR2(10),
 status varchar2(20),
 register_date DATE,
 last_visit date,
 comments varchar2(4000)
);
ALTER TABLE USERS
ADD CONSTRAINT CK_ROLE
CHECK (role IN ('user', 'admin', 'manager', 'developer'));

CREATE SEQUENCE users_seq START WITH 100;

CREATE or replace TRIGGER users_insert
BEFORE INSERT ON users
FOR EACH ROW
BEGIN
  select users_seq.nextval into :new.user_id from dual;
  select sysdate into :new.register_date from dual;
  select 'pending' into :new.status from dual;
END;
/
show errors;
```

Note that you need to define a trigger to handle the following:

- Inserting the **user_id** from a sequence
- The registration date and time from the database current date and time
- Adding *pending* into the status column as an initial value

Creating the Login Area

Before discussing how to create the user application form, we will discuss how to add the login area to the main page. Referring to this page, you see the following section that adds the area:

```
<login>
    <xsql:include-xsql reparse="yes" href="login.xsql"/>
</login>
```

This element calls **login.xsql** to create the box and provide the functionality. This is the most sophisticated XSQL file presented, so we will examine it in detail:

```
<?xml version="1.0"?>
<?xml-stylesheet type="text/xsl" media="msie" href="xsl/login.xsl"?>
<?xml-stylesheet type="text/xsl" media="mozilla" href="xsl/login_ns.xsl"?>
<page connection="xdkus" xmlns:xsql="urn:oracle-xsql">
  <xsql:if-param name="action" equals="login">
    <xsql:set-session-param name="usr" ignore-empty-value="no">select uname
    from users
    where uname='{@logusr}' and password='{@passwd}'</xsql:set-session-param>
  </xsql:if-param>
  <xsql:if-param name="action" equals="logout">
    <xsql:set-session-param name="usr" value=" "/>
  </xsql:if-param>
  <xsql:if-param name="usr" not-equals=" ">
      <xsql:query>
    select first_name ||', '|| last_name as name, role
    from users
    where uname='{@usr}'</xsql:query>
    <xsql:dml commit="yes">
     update users set last_visit=sysdate where uname='{@usr}'
    </xsql:dml>
    <xsql:set-session-param name="role" ignore-empty-value="no">
     select role
     from users
     where uname='{@usr}'</xsql:set-session-param>
  </xsql:if-param>
  <xsql:if-param name="usr" exists="no">
    <backtohome/>
  </xsql:if-param>
  <xsql:include-param name="usr"/>
  <xsql:include-param name="action"/>
  <xsql:include-xml href="xml/nav_login.xml"/>
</page>
```

This page has a number of conditional sections based upon both the way it is called and the parameters passed. The first set of conditions defines a Login and Logout action. Intrinsic in handling a Login action is the ability to set up a session. This is accomplished using the **<xsql:set-session-param>** element and insuring that a **uname** is return by setting the attribute, **ignore-empty-value**, equal to **no**. This initializes **usr**, which then satisfies the condition **not-equals=" "** permitting the query inside **<xsql:query>** to be executed as well as inserting the current date using the **<xsql:dml>** element content. Finally, the **nav_login.xml** page is included as follows:

```
<nav_bar>
   <category name="admin">
      <link uri="/xdkus/admin/index.xsql?pagename=news">Administration</link>
      <link uri="/xdkus/app_document/doc.xsql?pagename=xdk_perf">Performance
        test</link>
```

```
      <link uri="/xdkus/app_customer/index.xsql">Customer Reference</link>
      <link status="new" uri="/xdkus/app_document/doc.xsql?
         pagename=schemamapping">SchemaMapping</link>
    </category>
   <category name="manager">
    <link uri="/xdkus/app_document/doc.xsql?pagename=xdk_perf">Performance
      Test</link>
    <link uri="/xdkus/app_customer/index.xsql">Customer Reference</link>
    <link status="new"  uri="/xdkus/app_document/doc.xsql?
         pagename=schemamapping">SchemaMapping</link>
    </category>
   <category name="user">
    <link uri="/xdkus/app_customer/index.xsql">Customer Reference</link>
    <link uri="/xdkus/app_document/doc.xsql?pagename=xdk_perf">Performance
     Test</link>
   </category>
   <category name="developer">
     <link uri="/xdkus/app_document/doc.xsql?pagename=xdk_perf">Performance
          Test</link>
      <link uri="/xdkus/app_customer/index.xsql">Customer Reference</link>
   </category>
</nav_bar>
```

The stylesheet declared at the top of the Login page then selects the proper category based upon the role specified in the **name** attribute of the **<category>** element. This illustrates how you can mix file-based dynamic content with database content. Obviously, these roles and links could also be retrieved from the database.

Finally, the Login XSQL page handles the conditions of Logout by nulling **usr**, which returns the user to the home page, as well as conditions where parts of the login are missing.

Creating the User Application Form

The XSQL Servlet makes it easy to create web forms that are designed for submitting data into a database. The full range of input types is available. Figure 15-3 shows the finished form displayed within the center window.

This form is created by passing the name of the XSQL page to **index.xsql** and refreshing the page. In this case, the URL is **http://localhost:8988/xdkus/index.xsql?pagename=register**.

Referring to the code in the **index.xsql** page, the existence of the **pagename** parameter causes its value to be used to identify the XSQL page that is to be loaded. In this case, it is **register.xsql**, which is as follows:

```
<?xml version="1.0"?>
<page id="1" title="XDK User Registration" connection="xdkus"
     xmlns:xsql="urn:oracle-xsql">
  <xsql:include-xml href="xml/register.xml"/>
</page>
```

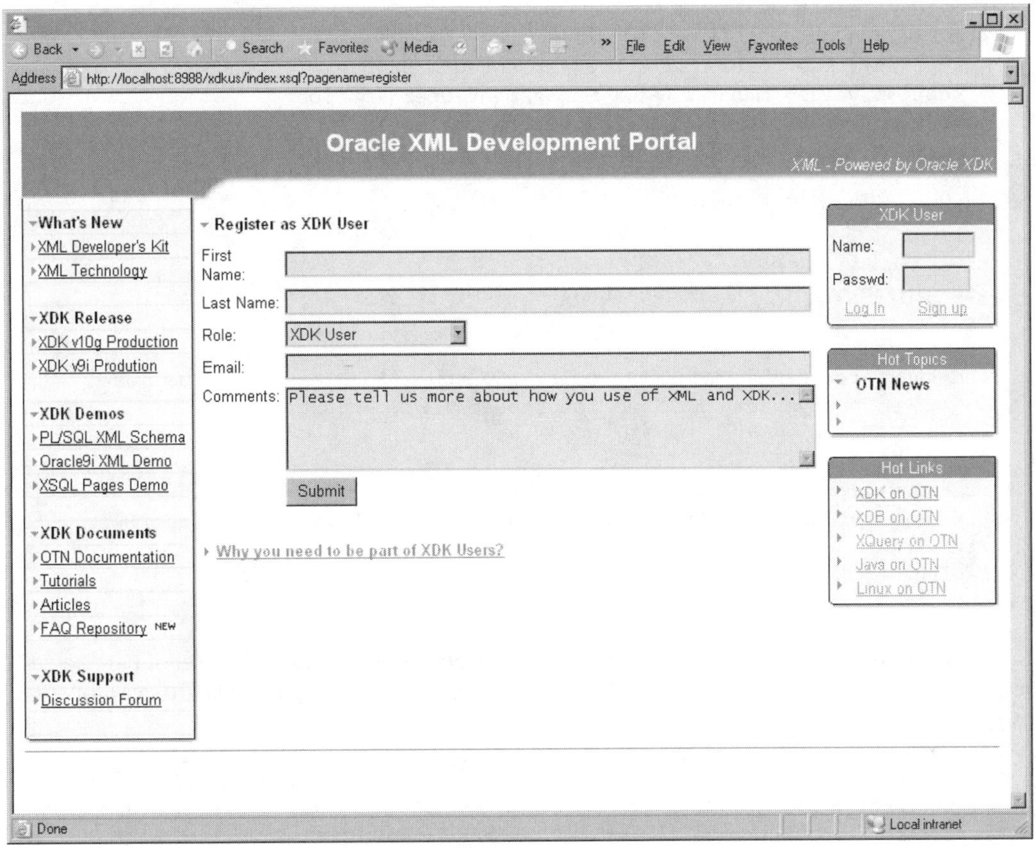

FIGURE 15-3. *User application form*

This page includes an XHTML fragment—located in the document named **register.xml**—that adds the form and its associated fields. This form uses the POST method and another XSQL page to submit the data as follows:

```
<form method="post" action="registerAction.xsql" name="adduser">
 <table width="60%" border="0">
  <tr> <td>First Name:</td>
    <td><input type="text" name="FIRST_NAME" size="70"/></td>
  </tr>
  <tr><td>Last Name:</td>
   <td><input type="text" name="LAST_NAME" size="70"/></td>
```

```
  </tr>
  <tr><td>Role:</td>
   <td><select name="ROLE">
     <option value="user" selected="selected">XDK User</option>
     <option value="manager">XDK Management User</option>
     <option value="admin">XDK Administrator</option>
     <option value="developer">XDK Development User</option>
    </select>
   </td>
  </tr>
  <tr><td>Email:</td>
   <td><input type="text" name="EMAIL" size="70"/></td>
  </tr>
  <tr><td valign="top">Comments:</td>
   <td><textarea name="COMMENTS" cols="55" rows="5">Please tell us more
       about how you use XML and the Oracle XDK...</textarea>
   </td>
  </tr>
  <tr><td valign="top" height="8"> </td>
   <td height="8"><input type="submit" name="Submit" value="Submit"/></td>
  </tr>
 </table>
</form>
```

This form uses a combination of **<input>** and **<select>** elements to build a set of parameters to pass to the **registerAction.xsql** page. This page handles the insert into the database as follows:

```
<?xml version="1.0"?>
<?xml-stylesheet type="text/xsl" media="mozilla" href="xsl/registerAction.xsl"?>
<page title="Add new XDK User" connection="xdkus" xmlns:xsql="urn:oracle-xsql">
  <xsql:insert-request date-format="MM/dd/yyyy" table="USERS"
       transform="xsl/generateXML.xsl"/>
</page>
```

This XSQL page has two stylesheet references. The **registerAction.xsl** stylesheet simply transforms the output as has been done previously. However, the following **generateXML.xsl** stylesheet performs a different function. When used as part of the **<xsql:insert-request>** element, it creates the XML document from the form's data passed as parameters and passes it into a SQL query as follows:

```
<?xml version="1.0"?>
<xsl:stylesheet version="1.0" xmlns:xsl="http://www.w3.org/1999/XSL/Transform">
<xsl:output method="xml"/>
 <xsl:template match="/">
  <ROWSET>
   <ROW>
    <xsl:copy-of select="request/parameters//*[name() !='Submit' and name()
       !='table' and name() !='keycolmn']"/>
```

```
    </ROW>
   </ROWSET>
 </xsl:template>
 <xsl:template match="node()|@*">
    <!- Copy the current node ->
    <xsl:copy>
      <!- Including any attributes it has and any child nodes ->
      <xsl:apply-templates select="@*|node()"/>
    </xsl:copy>
  </xsl:template>
</xsl:stylesheet>
```

After an application is successfully submitted, it is useful to send an e-mail acknowledgement. Since this depends upon a successful database insertion, you can use an INSERT TRIGGER command to generate not only a notification to the user but also a copy to the administrator to act upon. The Oracle database provides the UTL_SMTP package, which can be used to write PL/SQL procedures to send e-mails inside a PL/SQL trigger. The procedure is included in the provided sample code for this chapter. The following is the SQL that can be added to the previously defined **users_insert** trigger:

```
sendEmail_pkg.send_email('smtp.foo.com',
       'xdkadmin@foo.com', 'XDK Product Management<xdkadmin@foo.com>',
       :new.email,
       'John.Smith@foo.com', null, 'XDK.US Registration',
       'Thanks for your registration. We will review the request and
       get back to you soon.');
```

Once the administrator receives the mail, there must be a way to approve the user's application. This is done by creating a new form that is populated by the inserted data. This will be described in the next section.

Creating an Administration Page

The user administration page needs to be able to list the users and their status as well as provide a method to retrieve a specific user record and update it. Figure 15-4 shows a listing of users and their status retrieved by passing **users** as a pagename parameter to **index.xsql** linked from Approve Application.

This **users.xsql** page uses the same paging techniques as discussed earlier but executes the following query:

```
<xsql:query skip-rows="{@paging-skip}" max-rows="{@paging-max}">
   <![CDATA[
      SELECT user_id, first_name,last_name, role,status,last_visit,
        TO_CHAR(register_date,'Month DD,YYYY') as register_date,email
      FROM users
      ORDER BY status desc, first_name
   ]]>
</xsql:query>
```

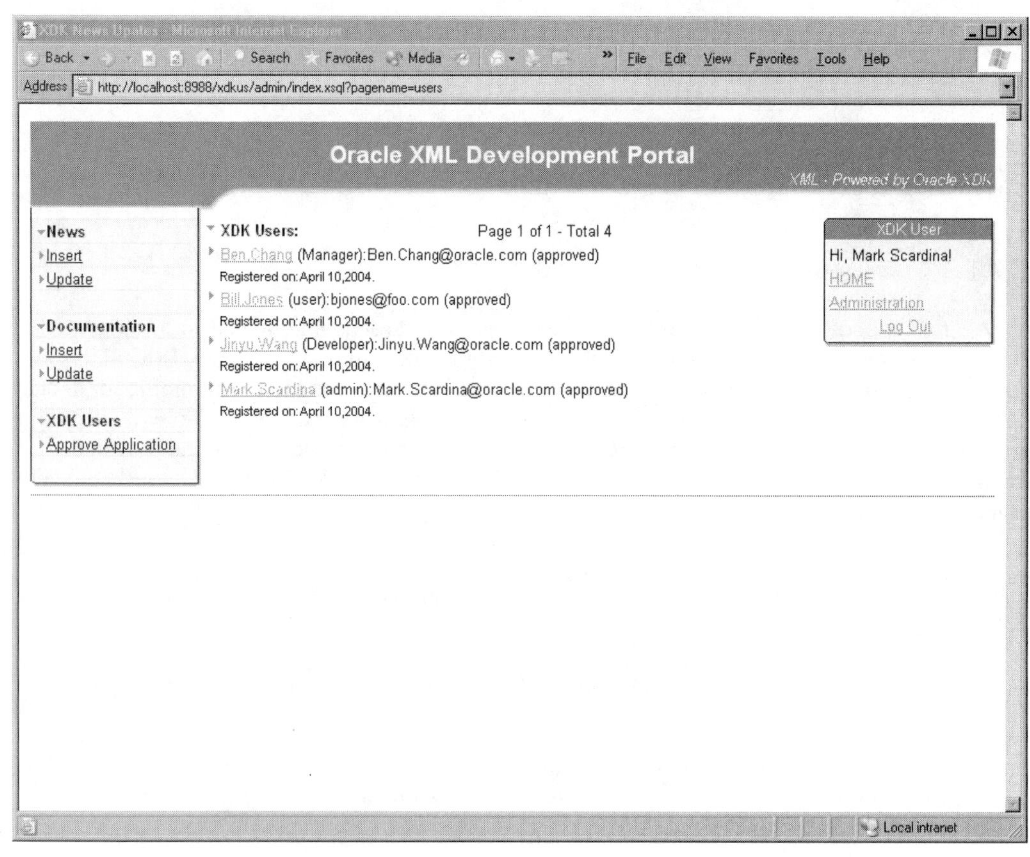

FIGURE 15-4. *Listing of XDK users and their status*

The results are returned in XML to be transformed into a list with user record links as follows:

```
<xsl:template name ="news_content" match="/">
<page title="XDK News Updates">
   <table width="100%" border="0">
     <tr>
       <td width="10" align="right" valign="top">
            <img src="images/d_arrow.gif" width="10" height="10"/>
       </td>
       <td>
           <b>XDK Users:</b>
        </td>
       <td> <xsl:apply-templates select="page/paging"/>
       </td>
```

```
 </tr>

<xsl:for-each select="page/ROWSET/ROW">
   <tr>
     <td width="10" align="right" valign="top">
       <img src="images/r_arrow.gif" width="10" height="10"/>
     </td>
     <td colspan="2" width="600" align="left" class="fbox">
       <a href="index.xsql?pagename=generateForm&amp;
                 amp;updateid={USER_ID}&amp;u
                              ="fbox">
                              FIRST_NAME"/>,
                              LAST_NAME"/></a>
                              ROLE"/>):<xsl:value-of select="EMAIL"/>
                              ><xsl:value-of
                              ><xsl:text>)</xsl:text>



                              /xsl:text></td>
                               class="footnt">
                              of select="REGISTER_DATE"/>.
                              MENTS"/>
```

or can then select a pending application and be
ser information ready for update, as shown in

ink calling the **generateForm.xsql** page:

```
index.xsql?pagename=generateForm
ecolmn=user_id
```

parameters at the same time you are passing in a
page is as follows:

```
                           media="mozilla" href="xsl/generateForm.xsl"?>
<page title="Insert New XDK ...   se" connection="xdkadmin"
     xmlns:xsql="urn:oracle-xs     ">
  <xsql:include-param name="table" value="{@table}"/>
  <xsql:include-param name="updateid" value="{@updateid}"/>
  <xsql:include-param name="updatecolmn" value="{@updatecolmn}"/>
```

```
  <xsql:query>select column_name as name, data_type as type, data_length as
length,
            NULLABLE
     from user_tab_columns
     where table_name=upper('{@table}')
  </xsql:query>
  <xsql:if-param name="updateid" exists="yes">
    <data>
      <xsql:query date-format="MM/dd/yyyy">
      select * from {@table}
      where {@updatecolmn}='{@updateid}'
      </xsql:query>
    </data>
  </xsql:if-param>
</page>
```

NOTE
Since the page allows users to update the content of the SQL WHERE clause, it should not be accessable without proper security verification. It is also suggested that these types of administration pages should be hosted separately from the public XSQL pages and preferably on a machine behind a firewall.

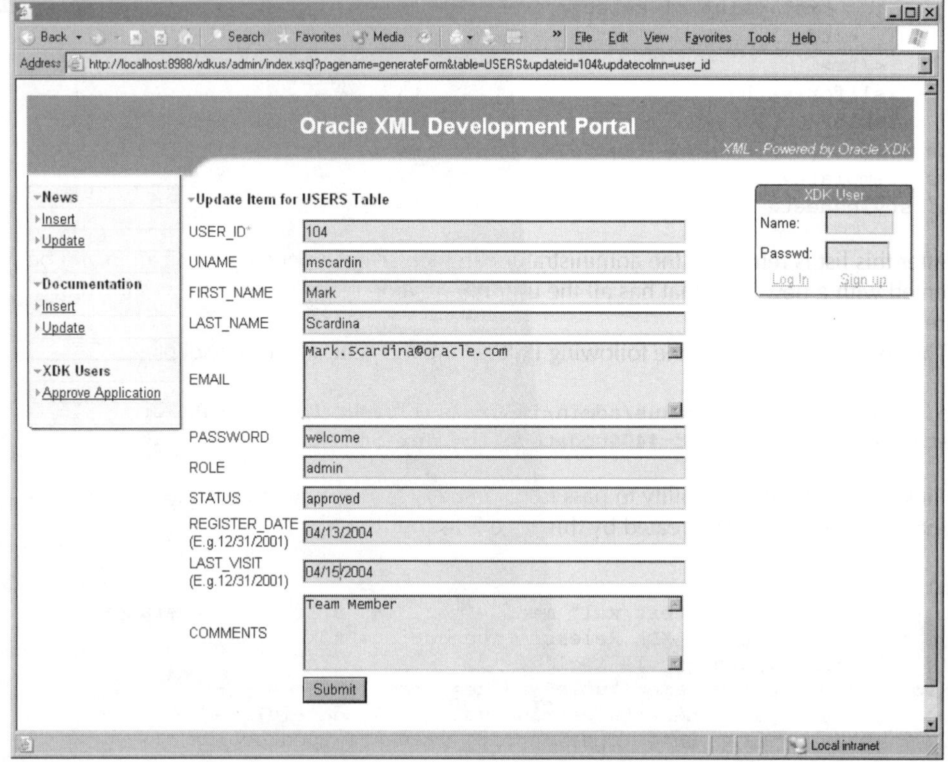

FIGURE 15-5. *Update form for users*

Note that this page uses a different database connection alias, **xdkadmin**, because you need to have administrative database privileges to perform updates and maintenance. The query also returns an XML document that is transformed to HTML by **generateForm.xsl** in the same way as the user application form, with the distinction that the fields are populated with the results of the query. This allows the administrator to assign a username and a password.

Once again, the form submission can not only insert the data but also deliver an e-mail to the user that his application was accepted and include the login information using an INSERT trigger.

Summary

In this chapter, you learned how you can extend the XSQL Servlet along with the XML database to create sophisticated portal sites with powerful functionality. You have combined XML documents, XSLT stylesheets, AQ, and SQL triggers to create a useful site that you can easily extend. Finally, you have seen how this site's modular structure, consisting of associated XML, XSL, and XSQL files, fits within this framework.

CHAPTER 16

Developing an XML Gateway Application with SOAP and AQ

hile XML generally has become the language of choice for e-business, many companies have not adopted it, typically because they perceive that adding this functionality to currently working applications is difficult. Many applications still depend on manually keying in data, such as a purchase order (PO), and businesses neither want nor can afford to have two entirely different applications to perform the same function differing only in their input methods. Additionally, many companies have brick-and-mortar stores and simply want to extend their presence by plugging in the Internet application into exiting applications. In this chapter, you will build an application that provides this functionality by leveraging the Oracle XDK, Oracle Streams Advanced Queuing (AQ), and Oracle XML Database 10*g*.

Designing the Framework

For the example scenario in this chapter, assume that you work for a widget business that has a perfectly satisfactory order-entry application. This application works as follows: When a clerk receives a PO via mail or the phone, the clerk types the information into a form provided by the order-entry application, which in turn creates a database entry for each PO. This application has been working fine for years and the company has no interest in rewriting it or deploying a new one; however, it does want to begin using the Internet to accept orders.

This company has several requirements that this new functionality must satisfy. First, the company does business with a wide range of companies and organizations, including the government, but is not big enough to require customers to use a particular format for the PO. The information the company needs to capture is quite simple: the customer's Bill To Address, Ship To Address, and Items ordered. Optionally, a customer can specify which carrier to use to deliver the order. In the past, the widget company's clerks extracted this information from a variety of POs, but now this must be handled electronically. Therefore, the application has to be able to extract information from POs in various schemas. Second, the requisite confirmations, notifications, etc., need to be generated and sent electronically.

To implement this application, you will be using a little-known but very useful and robust feature of the Oracle database called Oracle Streams Advanced Queuing(AQ). This feature, which was developed to implement replication, provides a rich and secure messaging infrastructure to connect the database to the outside world. AQ is capable of natively understanding SOAP messages, as discussed in Chapter 6, and you will be using that capability in this chapter. You will also be using new interfaces within the Oracle XDK XML Schema processor.

A Conventional Solution

A conventional way to design this application would be to have companies supply an XML schema for their POs when they open an account. Each company's XML schema would then be used to validate the POs received from that company via SOAP messages. Once validated, the PO would then need to be transformed into an XML document that is compliant with your database schema, before the data could be inserted into database tables. This would involve designing an XSL stylesheet that is specific to each PO type, which would then be applied to a DOM of the PO.

The conventional approach presents a number of issues. First, it involves creating a stylesheet for every PO type and updating those stylesheets whenever there are changes. Secondly, XSLT requires building DOM for the entire PO, which can be expensive because it generally requires up to ten times the memory of the original PO text file. Finally, for every PO, your application must load and parse its schema to validate it, and then load and parse its stylesheet to transform it. These operations take both time and memory, thus degrading performance and scalability.

You may be wondering why you cannot use the native capability of the XML database to register these PO schemas and directly insert them into the database. There are several reasons why you can't:

- You need to use the existing database schema, because that application still needs to work. Registering a PO schema would create a new database schema that would be difficult to integrate into the old one.
- There is also the problem of dealing with any changes in companies' XML schemas over time. Your company is not big enough to dictate which schema customers must use.
- You are going to need to process POs from a variety of customers and companies; this would mean registering PO schemas for each, which would quickly become a nightmare for the DBA.

A Stream-Based One-Step Solution

The previous, conventional solution focused first on the input XML and then on defining an approach to transform it into a compatible database format. An alternative is to start with the XML requirements for your database schema and build the system from there. First, you know which information you need from each PO for your application to work. Any other information in the PO is not useful, as it cannot be consumed by your application. Therefore, validating the entire PO is unnecessary and may actually cause you to reject a PO that has an error in a portion that you don't even use. Instead, your design needs to validate only the data that your application requires. It also needs to extract only the needed data. This can be done in one processing step by using Oracle XDK 10*g*.

Figure 16-1 shows the process flow of the application. First, note that it uses SAX-based processing, thus eliminating expensive DOM construction. Second, only the XML Schema processor is employed. This processor is unique in its ability to perform XML Schema validation using SAX and expose the status of its validator through APIs. When an XML document is validated, the processor starts validating once it finds a type that is included in the XML schema, and can ignore parts it knows nothing about. What makes this design effective is that the XML schema is not simply the one associated with the submitted PO. Instead, it is a master schema that includes only those types you are interested in, but from every customer and company you do business with. Therefore, you need to load and parse only one schema at initialization time, with every type being a very quick hash table lookup.

Now that your application can do very efficient streaming validation, you need to handle the transformation into your database schema–compatible format. This can be done by communicating with the processor during validation and adding annotations to the schema types to indicate the necessary transformation. As the gateway processor gets events from its SAX handler, it queries the schema processor to find out whether validation has started. If it hasn't started, the parsed content is just skipped. If it has, it buffers the content from the type until it receives a successful validation response after the last element of the type. It then queries the schema processor for the type annotation that tells it the type of transformation it needs to perform to make the type acceptable to the database. Finally, it marks off that type from its list of required types for a complete PO. Once all types are satisfied, the document is inserted into your database for further processing.

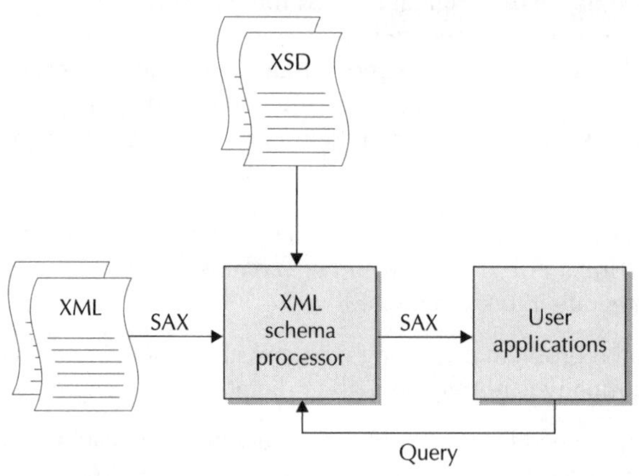

FIGURE 16-1. *Stream-based XML processing solution*

Interfacing to the Internet

Now that you know how the processing is done, you need to be able to receive and send messages using the Internet. To do this, you will use AQ's capability to receive and unpack SOAP messages, send confirmations, perform workflow within its message queue, and send e-mail responses. Figure 16-2 shows the entire system.

SOAP messages that contain POs are sent across the Internet to your company, where they pass through the firewall and are received by the AQ servlet that unwraps the PO and places it in

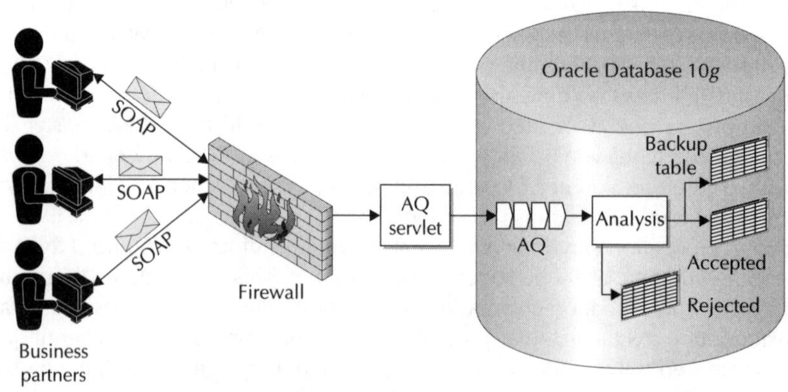

FIGURE 16-2. *PO messaging gateway architecture*

its queue. Once a PO is received, it triggers the validation and gateway process that either rejects or transforms and inserts the data. For this deployment, you will be using Oracle JVM, which is a Java VM that runs within the Oracle database. This application easily could be built to run in the middle tier by using the XDK's SOAP implementation and inserting data using JDBC.

It is important to note that this design satisfies the requirement to maintain the existing database schema and application while providing a high-performance and scalable Internet gateway. Thus, your company can painlessly expand its business to a whole new range of customers.

Creating the Framework

Because your widget company already has an existing application that must be maintained, you first need to set up the database schema, after which you can begin configuring AQ and the SOAP service for your application. This will provide the framework for the application.

Creating the Database Schema

Instead of using XMLType functionality that didn't exist when your original application was written, you will continue to use relational storage. This type of storage is not complicated, because your company has very straightforward requirements. But before you create the database schema, you need to create the administrator after logging in as SYSDBA, as follows:

```
CREATE USER poadmin IDENTIFIED BY poadmin
   DEFAULT tablespace USERS;
GRANT CONNECT, RESOURCE TO poadmin;
-- Grant AQ Privileges
GRANT aq_administrator_role TO poadmin;
GRANT execute ON dbms_aqadm TO poadmin;
/
```

Don't worry about the AQ privileges, as these will be discussed later. Recalling the schema description, the following SQL script will create your database schema:

```
CREATE TABLE PO(
  po_id raw(16) PRIMARY KEY,
  sendby_csname VARCHAR2(50),
  sendby_street VARCHAR2(100),
  sendby_city VARCHAR2(200),
  sendby_state VARCHAR2(20),
  sendby_zip VARCHAR2(20),
  sendby_country VARCHAR2(30),
  shipping_csname VARCHAR2(50),
  shipping_street VARCHAR2(100),
  shipping_city VARCHAR2(200),
  shipping_state VARCHAR2(20),
  shipping_zip VARCHAR2(20),
  shipping_country VARCHAR2(30),
  billing_csname VARCHAR2(50),
  billing_street VARCHAR2(100),
  billing_city VARCHAR2(200),
```

```
  billing_state VARCHAR2(20),
  billing_zip VARCHAR2(20),
  billing_country VARCHAR2(30)
);
CREATE TABLE LineItems(
  po_id raw(16),
  product_id VARCHAR2(10)
);
CREATE TABLE LineItem(
  product_id VARCHAR2(10) primary key,
  product_name VARCHAR2(10),
  product_quantity NUMBER(30),
  product_price VARCHAR2(20)
);
 CREATE SEQUENCE poobj_seq START WITH 1;
/
```

This script defines three different addresses: SENDBY for the shipper, SHIPPING for the destination, and BILLING for the invoice. A LINEITEMS table is created to associate the individual PO with its lineitems stored in the LINEITEM table.

Since there are multiple tables, you have to manage a single PO insertion as a multitable insert. This requires additional code and the creation of several objects and an object view. These objects link the columns together into types, and the object view defines the relationship between the tables in a way that they can be queried as one table. The following SQL script creates the first objects you need:

```
CREATE TYPE address_typ AS OBJECT(
  customer_name VARCHAR2(50),
  street  VARCHAR2(100),
  city VARCHAR2(200),
  state VARCHAR2(20),
  zip VARCHAR2(20),
  country VARCHAR2(30)
);
/
CREATE TYPE lineitem_typ AS OBJECT(
  product_id VARCHAR2(10),
  product_name VARCHAR2(10),
  product_quantity NUMBER(30),
  product_price VARCHAR2(20)
);
/
CREATE TYPE lineitem_list AS TABLE OF lineitem_typ;
/
CREATE TYPE po_typ AS OBJECT(
 po_id raw(16),
 sendby_addr address_typ,
 shipping_addr address_typ,
 billing_addr address_typ,
 lineitems lineitem_list
);
/
```

Note that the final **po_typ** object is made up of the four object types. This provides the linkage you need to treat the entire PO as a single document insert. Now you can create a PO view to represent the XML structure of the PO, as follows:

```
CREATE OR REPLACE VIEW purchaseorder OF po_typ
WITH OBJECT OID (po_id) AS
  select po_id, address_typ(sendby_csname,
                            sendby_street,
                            sendby_city,
                            sendby_state,
                            sendby_zip,
                            sendby_country),
                address_typ(shipping_csname,
                            shipping_street,
                            shipping_city,
                            shipping_state,
                            shipping_zip,
                            shipping_country),
                 address_typ(billing_csname,
                            billing_street,
                            billing_city,
                            billing_state,
                            billing_zip,
                            billing_country),
                cast(multiset(
                             select lineitem.product_id, product_name,
                             product_quantity, product_price
                             from lineitem, lineitems
                             where lineitems.po_id=po.po_id and
                                   lineitem.product_id=lineitems.product_id
                             ) as lineitem_list
                     ) lineitems
     from po;
/
```

With the database schema created, you need to add one more piece of code to perform inserts. This function is called an INSTEAD OF trigger and is executed by the database in place of the normal DML operation. In this case, because you need to perform inserts, you need to create an INSTEAD OF INSERT trigger, as follows:

```
CREATE TRIGGER purchaseorder_insert_trigger
INSTEAD OF INSERT ON purchaseorder
FOR EACH ROW
DECLARE
  v_lineitems lineitem_list;
  v_lineitem  lineitem_typ;
  v_id RAW(16);
  v_num number;
BEGIN
```

```
    -----------------------------------------------------------------------------
    -- Insert into PO table
    -----------------------------------------------------------------------------
    SELECT current_id into v_id from poid  where rownum=1;
    INSERT INTO po
      values (v_id,
                  :new.sendby_addr.customer_name,
                  :new.sendby_addr.street,
                  :new.sendby_addr.city,
                  :new.sendby_addr.state,
                  :new.sendby_addr.zip,
                  :new.sendby_addr.country,
                  :new.shipping_addr.customer_name,
                  :new.shipping_addr.street,
                  :new.shipping_addr.city,
                  :new.shipping_addr.state,
                  :new.shipping_addr.zip,
                  :new.shipping_addr.country,
                  :new.billing_addr.customer_name,
                  :new.billing_addr.street,
                  :new.billing_addr.city,
                  :new.billing_addr.state,
                  :new.billing_addr.zip,
                  :new.billing_addr.country);
    -----------------------------------------------------------------------------
    -- Insert into LineItem and LineItems table
    -----------------------------------------------------------------------------
    v_lineitems := :new.lineitems;
    FOR i in 1..v_lineitems.count loop
      v_lineitem := v_lineitems(i);
      SELECT count(1) INTO v_num FROM lineitem
      WHERE product_id = v_lineitem.product_id;
      IF v_num = 0 THEN
      INSERT INTO lineitem
        VALUES(v_lineitem.product_id,
               v_lineitem.product_name,
               v_lineitem.product_quantity,
               v_lineitem.product_price);
       END IF;
      INSERT INTO lineitems VALUES(v_id, v_lineitem.product_id);
    END LOOP;
END;
/
SHOW ERRORS;
```

The first thing to note is that you attach the trigger to the view, not to the object. The reason you do this is that you are inserting the data in an XML document using XSU, and you must insert into a compliant structure. Next, since there is an ID relationship that is not conveyed within the document, you need to declare variables to store the calculated result. The same holds true for the master-detail relationship in the LINEITEMS and LINEITEM relationship. The actual SQL code is identical to what you would use to insert into these objects manually.

Creating the XML Purchase Orders

Now that you have the database schema set up to accept XML POs in addition to keyed-in ones, you need to create a valid XML PO. You can generate an XML schema for the PO by using XSU's capability to generate a schema from the object view. The following query will generate an XML schema for the **po_typ** object:

```
SET LONG 10000;
SELECT DBMS_XMLSCHEMA.generateschema('POUSER', 'PO_TYP').getClobVal()
FROM DUAL;
```

This query generates the following schema:

```
<?xml version="1.0"?>
<xsd:schema xmlns:xsd="http://www.w3.org/2001/XMLSchema"
xmlns:xsi="http://www.w3.org/2001/XMLSchema-instance"
xmlns:xdb="http://xmlns.oracle.com/xdb"
xsi:schemaLocation="http://xmlns.oracle.com/xdb
http://xmlns.oracle.com/xdb/XDBSchema.xsd">
 <xsd:element name="PO_TYP" type="PO_TYPType" xdb:SQLType="PO_TYP"
xdb:SQLSchema="POUSER"/>
 <xsd:complexType name="PO_TYPType" xdb:SQLType="PO_TYP"
xdb:SQLSchema="POUSER" xdb:maintainDOM="false">
  <xsd:sequence>
   <xsd:element name="PO_ID" type="xsd:hexBinary" xdb:SQLName="PO_ID"
xdb:SQLType="RAW"/>
   <xsd:element name="SENDBY_ADDR" type="ADDRESS_TYPType"
xdb:SQLName="SENDBY_ADDR" xdb:SQLSchema="POUSER"
xdb:SQLType="ADDRESS_TYP"/>
   <xsd:element name="SHIPPING_ADDR" type="ADDRESS_TYPType"
 xdb:SQLName="SHIPPING_ADDR" xdb:SQLSchema="POUSER"
 xdb:SQLType="ADDRESS_TYP"/>
   <xsd:element name="BILLING_ADDR" type="ADDRESS_TYPType"
 xdb:SQLName="BILLING_ADDR" xdb:SQLSchema="POUSER"
 xdb:SQLType="ADDRESS_TYP"/>
   <xsd:element name="LINEITEMS" type="LINEITEM_TYPType"
maxOccurs="unbounded" minOccurs="0" xdb:SQLName="LINEITEMS"
xdb:SQLCollType="LINEITEM_LIST" xdb:SQLType="LINEITEM_TYP"
xdb:SQLSchema="POUSER" xdb:SQLCollSchema="POUSER"/>
  </xsd:sequence>
</xsd:complexType>
<xsd:complexType name="ADDRESS_TYPType" xdb:SQLType="ADDRESS_TYP"
xdb:SQLSchema="POUSER" xdb:maintainDOM="false">
```

```
    <xsd:sequence>
     <xsd:element name="CUSTOMER_NAME" xdb:SQLName="CUSTOMER_NAME"
xdb:SQLType="VARCHAR2">
      <xsd:simpleType>
       <xsd:restriction base="xsd:string">
        <xsd:maxLength value="50"/>
       </xsd:restriction>
      </xsd:simpleType>
     </xsd:element>
     <xsd:element name="STREET" xdb:SQLName="STREET" xdb:SQLType="VARCHAR2">
      <xsd:simpleType>
       <xsd:restriction base="xsd:string">
        <xsd:maxLength value="100"/>
       </xsd:restriction>
      </xsd:simpleType>
     </xsd:element>
     <xsd:element name="CITY" xdb:SQLName="CITY" xdb:SQLType="VARCHAR2">
      <xsd:simpleType>
       <xsd:restriction base="xsd:string">
        <xsd:maxLength value="200"/>
       </xsd:restriction>
      </xsd:simpleType>
     </xsd:element>
     <xsd:element name="STATE" xdb:SQLName="STATE" xdb:SQLType="VARCHAR2">
      <xsd:simpleType>
       <xsd:restriction base="xsd:string">
        <xsd:maxLength value="20"/>
       </xsd:restriction>
      </xsd:simpleType>
     </xsd:element>
     <xsd:element name="ZIP" xdb:SQLName="ZIP" xdb:SQLType="VARCHAR2">
      <xsd:simpleType>
       <xsd:restriction base="xsd:string">
        <xsd:maxLength value="20"/>
       </xsd:restriction>
      </xsd:simpleType>
     </xsd:element>
     <xsd:element name="COUNTRY" xdb:SQLName="COUNTRY"
xdb:SQLType="VARCHAR2">
      <xsd:simpleType>
       <xsd:restriction base="xsd:string">
        <xsd:maxLength value="30"/>
       </xsd:restriction>
      </xsd:simpleType>
     </xsd:element>
    </xsd:sequence>
   </xsd:complexType>
   <xsd:complexType name="LINEITEM_TYPType" xdb:SQLType="LINEITEM_TYP"
xdb:SQLSchema="POUSER" xdb:maintainDOM="false">
    <xsd:sequence>
```

```
    <xsd:element name="PRODUCT_ID" xdb:SQLName="PRODUCT_ID"
xdb:SQLType="VARCHAR2">
     <xsd:simpleType>
      <xsd:restriction base="xsd:string">
       <xsd:maxLength value="10"/>
      </xsd:restriction>
     </xsd:simpleType>
    </xsd:element>
    <xsd:element name="PRODUCT_NAME" xdb:SQLName="PRODUCT_NAME"
xdb:SQLType="VARCHAR2">
     <xsd:simpleType>
      <xsd:restriction base="xsd:string">
       <xsd:maxLength value="10"/>
      </xsd:restriction>
     </xsd:simpleType>
    </xsd:element>
    <xsd:element name="PRODUCT_QUANTITY" type="xsd:double"
xdb:SQLName="PRODUCT_QUANTITY" xdb:SQLType="NUMBER"/>
    <xsd:element name="PRODUCT_PRICE" xdb:SQLName="PRODUCT_PRICE"
xdb:SQLType="VARCHAR2">
     <xsd:simpleType>
      <xsd:restriction base="xsd:string">
       <xsd:maxLength value="20"/>
      </xsd:restriction>
     </xsd:simpleType>
    </xsd:element>
   </xsd:sequence>
  </xsd:complexType>
</xsd:schema>
```

In the first part of your application, you will use this schema to validate incoming POs that are submitted as SOAP messages. Once a PO is validated, a confirmation e-mail can be sent to the customer via AQ's e-mail functionality and the data will be added to your application's schema. In the second part, you will extend the design to accept POs that do not conform to your application's schema but do map to it.

Creating the XML Messaging Gateway

Since the whole point of this application is to extend the widget company's business to the Internet, you must set up Internet access to its database schema. This can be done in a number of ways. The traditional approach is to use the middle tier to container-manage the database through object-relational applications such as Oracle Toplink, EJBs, etc. However, these applications can be difficult to set up and maintain. Therefore, instead, you will use Oracle Database 10*g*'s built-in messaging infrastructure, Oracle Streams Advance Queuing (AQ), and its AQ servlet to send and receive SOAP messages. This robust system can be extended to perform application processing upon the messages in the manner of workflow. To use AQ Streams, you need to set up the servlet as well as create the messaging schema for storing accepted and rejected POs.

Creating the Messaging Schema

Since this portion of your database will have exposure to the Internet, you need to create a separate user and restrict access. This can be done by logging in as SYSDBA and creating POUSER, as follows:

```
CREATE USER pouser IDENTIFIED BY pouser
   DEFAULT tablespace USERS;
GRANT CONNECT, RESOURCE TO pouser;
-- Grant AQ privileges
GRANT execute ON dbms_aq TO pouser;
GRANT execute ON dbms_aqin TO pouser;
ALTER USER pouser GRANT CONNECT through pouser;
/
```

As you did for POADMIN earlier in the chapter, the preceding code grants to POUSER a number of AQ privileges as well as the ability to connect to the database.

You also need to set up the tables that will be needed by the AQ messaging queue to receive the POs and store copies of accepted and rejected POs. You can set up these tables with the following script:

```
CREATE TABLE po_tbl(
 msgid RAW(16),
 consumer VARCHAR2(100),
 sender VARCHAR2(200),
 podoc XMLTYPE
);
CREATE TABLE po_rejected_tbl(
 msgid RAW(16),
 consumer VARCHAR2(100),
 sender VARCHAR2(200),
 reason VARCHAR2(500),
 podoc XMLTYPE
);
CREATE TABLE po_backup_tbl(
 msgid RAW(16),
 consumer VARCHAR2(100),
 sender VARCHAR2(200),
 podoc XMLTYPE
);
grant SELECT,DELETE on po_tbl to poadmin;
grant SELECT,DELETE  on po_rejected_tbl to poadmin;
grant SELECT,DELETE  on po_backup_tbl to poadmin;
/
```

Note that you need to grant specific privileges on these tables to the administrator in order to review and maintain them.

Finally, you need to set up specific user accounts in order to accept a PO. This permits you to set up a user ID and password for each company you wish to do business with. The following SQL script creates a PO Users table and seeds it with sample data:

```
CREATE TABLE POUSER(
  user_id VARCHAR(10) PRIMARY KEY,
  name VARCHAR2(50),
  street VARCHAR2(100),
  city VARCHAR2(200),
  state VARCHAR2(20),
  zip VARCHAR2(20),
  country VARCHAR2(30)
);
INSERT INTO POUSER values('bob', 'Bob Smith','400 Oracle parkway',
         'Redwood shores', 'CA', '94065','US');
INSERT INTO POUSER values('scott', 'Scott Tiger','400 Oracle parkway',
         'Redwood shores', 'CA', '94065','US');
/
```

As you can see, there is no entry in the table for a password. This is because you will be using the JAZN support provided by the OC4J J2EE container in which you are going to deploy this application. JAZN is the *Java Authentication and Authorization Service (JAAS)* provider, which can be configured either with the *Oracle Internet Directory (OID)* LDAP repository or with an XML repository file. For simplicity, you will use the latter configuration, because it only requires adding a **jazn-data.xml** file to the deployment. To set this up, you need to create an AQ agent for each user and give the user the necessary execution privileges for database access, as in the following SQL script:

```
BEGIN
   DBMS_AQADM.create_aq_agent(agent_name=>'"jazn.com/bob"',
                              enable_http =>true);
END;
/
EXECUTE dbms_aqadm.enable_db_access('JAZN.COM/BOB', 'pouser');
```

Note that the agent name refers to "jazn.com/bob". This is the JAZN realm set for your J2EE application as defined in the **myjazn-data.xml** file that gets deployed with your application. This XML file defines not only the set of users and their passwords but also the policies and permissions for the realm.

Creating the AQ Agent and Queue

While AQ is built into the Oracle database, it still must be set up to supply messages to a predefined queue and then to your previously created tables. This is done with special functions that are part of the included DBMS_ADMIN package. The queue is nothing more than special tables for the messages, and since these POs are XML documents, you can use an XMLType table, as follows:

```
BEGIN
 dbms_aqadm.create_queue_table(queue_table=>'poxml_qt',
                 queue_payload_type=>'SYS.XMLTYPE',
                 COMMENT=>'Purchase Order Queue Table',
                 multiple_consumers=>TRUE,
                 primary_instance=>1,
                 secondary_instance=>2);
```

```
END;
/
BEGIN
  dbms_aqadm.create_queue(queue_name => 'poxml_q',
                          queue_table =>'poxml_qt');
END;
/
BEGIN
   dbms_aqadm.start_queue (queue_name => 'poxml_q');
END;
/
```

POs as SOAP messages come into the database from the AQ servlet. Therefore, you need to extend the AQ servlet to handle these messages. This can be done by creating the following **MyAQServlet** class:

```
package oracle.xml.sample.XMLIntegration;
import java.io.PrintStream;
import java.io.FileOutputStream;
import javax.servlet.ServletConfig;
import javax.servlet.ServletException;
import oracle.AQ.xml.AQxmlException;
import oracle.AQ.xml.AQxmlDebug;
import oracle.AQ.xml.AQxmlDataSource;
import oracle.AQ.xml.AQxmlCallback;

public class MyAQServlet extends oracle.AQ.xml.AQxmlServlet {
  public void init(ServletConfig p_config) throws ServletException {
    // Database Variables
    String username="pouser";
    String password="pouser";
    String sid="ORCL";
    String host="localhost";
    String port="1521";

    AQxmlDataSource  db_drv = null;
    try {
      // Set the log file
      PrintStream debugFile = new PrintStream (new
             FileOutputStream("aqdebug.log"));
      debugFile.println("Function Called");
      debugFile.flush();
      super.init(p_config);

      AQxmlDebug.setTraceLevel(5);
      AQxmlDebug.setDebug(true);
      AQxmlDebug.setLogStream(new FileOutputStream("aqlogfile"));

      // Get and Set DataSource
```

```
      db_drv = new AQxmlDataSource(username, password, sid, host, port);
      this.setAQDataSource(db_drv);
    }
    catch (AQxmlException aq_ex) {
      aq_ex.printStackTrace();
      aq_ex.getNextException().printStackTrace();
    }
    catch (Exception ex) {
      ex.printStackTrace();
    }
  }
}
```

There are several things you should note about the preceding code:

- You need to use the **javax.servlet** classes that are part of the **servlet.jar** file included with OC4J to configure this class as an extension.
- To aid in debugging, the **AQxmlDebug** functionality is set up and initialized to create a log file. The database communication is configured by using **AqxmlDataSource** to pass in the necessary login and database parameters.
- An option to include a stylesheet is provided. The reason is that once a submission is made, the AQ Servlet provides a response in XML, as in the following example, and you may want to format it for better presentation if the response will be viewed by a person. The classes of the package ORACLE.AQ.XML are delivered with the database distribution, in a file called **aqxml.jar**.

```
<?xml version="1.0" ?>
<Envelope xmlns="http://ns.oracle.com/AQ/schemas/envelope">
 <Body>
  <AQXmlPublishResponse xmlns="http://ns.oracle.com/AQ/schemas/access">
   <status_response>
    <status_code>0</status_code>
   </status_response>
   <publish_result>
    <destination>POADMIN.poxml_q</destination>
    <message_id>21238FFE4B5D41E89E670D8CC147CD75</message_id>
   </publish_result>
  </AQXmlPublishResponse>
 </Body>
</Envelope>
```

Every AQ submission has an associated ID that is generated by the database and that uniquely identifies the message. Therefore, this number can be used by customers to trace the disposition of their POs, regardless of the PO numbers they might have assigned.

Creating the AQ PO Process Procedures

Now that your messaging queue is configured to be able to accept POs, you can finally create the procedures to actually process them. You are going to do this by using a combination of PL/SQL and Java. The reason that you are going to use PL/SQL is that this processing is being done within the database itself. Had you chosen to implement this design with a midtier SOAP service and a messaging protocol such as JMS, everything could have been done in Java, with the data inserted using JDBC. In this case, the data is already in the database and you will use Java within a stored procedure only to validate and analyze the PO using the new XDK validator class.

Once a message is submitted, it is considered to be *in the queue* and needs to be dequeued to be processed. Then, the PO must be extracted from the SOAP envelope and validated against its schema. Finally, the PO must be inserted into the PO database schema to be fulfilled. This is done in a single PL/SQL procedure called **dequeueXMLAnalysis()**, which is listed in this section and then explained in its component parts because it is quite long.

First, you must load some subprocedures. As mentioned earlier, you are going to use Java to perform the validation and analysis; the following Java stored procedure will set this up:

```
CREATE OR REPLACE FUNCTION XMLSemanticProcessing(xml IN CLOB,
                xsd IN CLOB,
                result IN OUT CLOB)
RETURN VARCHAR2
IS LANGUAGE JAVA NAME
'oracle.xml.sample.semantics.XMLAnalysis.analyze(oracle.sql.CLOB,
      oracle.sql.CLOB,oracle.sql.CLOB[]) returns java.lang.String';
/
```

The PO and the XSD schema are passed in as CLOBs. Even though these are XML documents, there is no need to use an XMLType here because the Java class will parse them; thus, they are simply character strings at input.

The other subprocedure performs the actual XML data insert and uses the PL/SQL versions of the XML SQL Utility that have the DBMS_ prefix. These are recommended over the older, unprefixed packages because they are written over C (versus calling Java in JServer), thus improving performance significantly.

```
CREATE OR REPLACE PROCEDURE insProc(xmlDoc IN CLOB,
                                    tableName IN VARCHAR2) IS
   insCtx DBMS_XMLSave.ctxType;
   rows NUMBER;
 BEGIN
    insCtx := DBMS_XMLSave.newContext(tableName);
    DBMS_XMLSave.setRowtag(insCtx,'purchaseorder');
    rows := DBMS_XMLSave.insertXML(insCtx,xmlDoc);
    DBMS_OUTPUT.put_line(rows||' rows inserted');
    DBMS_XMLSave.closeContext(insCtx);
END;
/
```

Note that you are inserting into **<purchaseorder>** instead of the **<PO>** table of your original schema, because the POUSER schema spans multiple tables and you need to use the object view that you defined earlier. Upon insert, the INSTEAD OF INSERT trigger will fire, properly inserting the data and creating the appropriate keys to link the rows.

Now you get to the main procedure. Because this has many parts and calls other procedures, you need to have a set of variables declared as follows:

```
CREATE OR REPLACE PROCEDURE dequeueXMLAnalysis(p_consumer IN VARCHAR2,
                    p_queue IN VARCHAR2)
   AS
    v_msgid             RAW(16);
    v_dopt              dbms_aq.dequeue_options_t;
    v_mprop             dbms_aq.message_properties_t;
    v_payload           XMLTYPE;
    no_messages         EXCEPTION;
    PRAGMA EXCEPTION_INIT(no_messages, -25228);
    v_xml   CLOB;
    v_xsd   CLOB;
    v_result CLOB;
    v_insert CLOB;
    v_out VARCHAR2(32767);
    v_temp XMLType;
    v_sendby VARCHAR2(32767);
    v_id VARCHAR2(10);
    v_i NUMBER;
    v_name VARCHAR2(100);
    v_doc XMLTYPE;
```

Note that **v_dopt** and **v_mprop** are simply aliases for longer function names. Now you begin the body by retrieving the XML document:

```
BEGIN
   -- Setup Dequeue Options
   v_dopt.consumer_name := p_consumer;
   v_dopt.dequeue_mode := DBMS_AQ.REMOVE;
   v_dopt.wait := DBMS_AQ.NO_WAIT;
   v_dopt.navigation := DBMS_AQ.FIRST_MESSAGE;
   LOOP
     DBMS_AQ.dequeue(queue_name => p_queue,
                   dequeue_options => v_dopt,
                   message_properties => v_mprop,
                   payload => v_payload,
                   msgid => v_msgid);
     v_xml := v_payload.getClobVal();
```

In the preceding code you start a loop to process each PO message. Once you have a PO, you need to get the schema to validate:

```
SELECT xsd INTO v_xsd FROM xsd_tbl WHERE id=1;
```

Then, perform the validation and analysis:

```
DBMS_LOB.createtemporary(v_result,TRUE,DBMS_LOB.SESSION);
DBMS_LOB.createtemporary(v_insert,TRUE,DBMS_LOB.SESSION);
     v_out := XMLSemanticProcessing(v_xml,v_xsd,v_result);
     IF v_out = 'OK' THEN
       INSERT INTO po_tbl(msgid, consumer, podoc)
        VALUES(v_msgid,p_consumer, XMLTYPE(v_result));
       INSERT INTO po_backup_tbl(msgid, consumer, podoc)
        VALUES(v_msgid,p_consumer, XMLTYPE(v_xml));
```

Note that based upon a successful validation and analysis returning OK, you store the results in two tables—one for further processing and one for archiving. Finally, you insert the data into the tables with XSU and end the loop:

```
       DBMS_LOB.OPEN(v_insert, DBMS_LOB.LOB_READWRITE);
       DBMS_LOB.writeappend(v_insert,length('<ROWSET>'),'<ROWSET>');
       DBMS_LOB.append(v_insert,v_result);
       DBMS_LOB.writeappend(v_insert,length('</ROWSET>'),'</ROWSET>');
       DBMS_LOB.CLOSE(v_insert);
       dbms_output.put_line(v_msgid);
       INSERT INTO poid values(v_msgid);
       insProc(v_insert,'purchaseorder');
       DBMS_LOB.freetemporary(v_insert);
       DBMS_LOB.freetemporary(v_result);
       -- Commit the transaction
       DELETE FROM poid;
     ELSE
       DBMS_OUTPUT.put_line(v_out);
       INSERT INTO po_rejected_tbl(msgid, consumer, podoc,reason)
          VALUES(v_msgid,p_consumer, XMLTYPE(v_xml),v_out);
     END IF;
     COMMIT;
     v_dopt.navigation := DBMS_AQ.NEXT_MESSAGE;
   END LOOP
```

Note that the XML was encapsulated in **<ROWSET>** elements. This is done to make the XML data acceptable by XSU because the document listed at the end would not have a single root. Also, rejected POs are stored in a separate **po_rejected_tbl**. The procedure then ends by handling possible errors:

```
EXCEPTION
    WHEN no_messages THEN
      DBMS_OUTPUT.put_line( 'Error:'||'No more messages in queue.');
END;
/
```

Now that you have walked through the process, you can see the transformation that took place between the original PO and the XML that was inserted by XSU. The following is the original PO:

```
<purchaseOrder orderDate="2003-10-20"
          xmlns="http://ns.oracle.com/AQ/schemas/access">
  <ShipTo country="US">
    <name>California Whirligig</name>
    <street>123 Maple Street</street>
    <city>Mill Valley</city>
    <state>CA</state>
    <zip>90952</zip>
  </ShipTo>
  <BillTo country="US">
    <name>U.S. Whirligig</name>
    <street>8 Oak Avenue</street>
    <city>Old Town</city>
    <state>PA</state>
    <zip>95819</zip>
  </BillTo>
  <LineItems>
    <LineItem partNum="872-AA">
      <ProductName>Micro Widget</ProductName>
      <Quantity>1</Quantity>
      <UnitofPrice>148.95</UnitofPrice>
    </LineItem>
    <LineItem partNum="926-AA">
      <ProductName>Multi-Widget</ProductName>
      <Quantity>1</Quantity>
      <UnitofPrice>39.98</UnitofPrice>
    </LineItem>
  </LineItems>
  <comment>Hurry, I can't stop this thing!</comment>
</purchaseOrder>
```

The original PO was transformed into the following:

```
<ROWSET>
 <ROW num="1">
  <PO_ID>7F2F2FED620F4400A2F598B23965492F</PO_ID>
  <SHIPPING_ADDR>
   <CUSTOMER_NAME>California Whirligig</CUSTOMER_NAME>
   <STREET>123 Maple Street</STREET>
   <CITY>Mill Valley</CITY>
   <STATE>CA</STATE>
   <ZIP>90952</ZIP>
   <COUNTRY>US</COUNTRY>
  </SHIPPING_ADDR>
  <BILLING_ADDR>
   <CUSTOMER_NAME>U.S. Whirligig</CUSTOMER_NAME>
```

```
      <STREET>8 Oak Avenue</STREET>
      <CITY>Old Town</CITY>
      <STATE>PA</STATE>
      <ZIP>95819</ZIP>
      <COUNTRY>US</COUNTRY>
    </BILLING_ADDR>
    <LINEITEMS>
      <LINEITEMS_ITEM>
        <PRODUCT_ID>872-AA</PRODUCT_ID>
        <PRODUCT_NAME>Micro Widget</PRODUCT_NAME>
        <PRODUCT_QUANTITY>1</PRODUCT_QUANTITY>
        <PRODUCT_PRICE>148.95</PRODUCT_PRICE>
      </LINEITEMS_ITEM>
      <LINEITEMS_ITEM>
        <PRODUCT_ID>926-AA</PRODUCT_ID>
        <PRODUCT_NAME>Multi-Widget</PRODUCT_NAME>
        <PRODUCT_QUANTITY>1</PRODUCT_QUANTITY>
        <PRODUCT_PRICE>39.98</PRODUCT_PRICE>
      </LINEITEMS_ITEM>
    </LINEITEMS>
  </ROW>
</ROWSET>
```

Note that the **<comment>** element was ignored and the element names were transformed. This process occurred during the analysis phase in Java. The next section discusses this phase in detail.

Extending the Framework

Although your company is a successful one, it is not in position to dictate that all of your customers use your PO XML schema. Therefore, when companies want to do business with your company, they will provide their own PO schemas. You could store each of them and load them individually each time you get a PO, to validate it. This is expensive, because you not only need to retrieve it but also need to parse it and build a compiled schema object that will be thrown away each time. Instead of using these separately for each respective PO instance, you can extract the types you are interested in and add them to your base schema. The following is an example of a schema that semantically meets your requirements but uses different syntax:

```
<xsd:schema targetNamespace="http://ns.oracle.com/AQ/schemas/access"
            xmlns:xsd="http://www.w3.org/2001/XMLSchema"
            xmlns:xdk="http://xmlns.oracle.com/xdk"
            xmlns="http://ns.oracle.com/AQ/schemas/access"
            elementFormDefault="qualified" xdk:TableName="ORDERS">
  <!-- Address Type -->
  <xsd:complexType name="AddressType">
    <xsd:sequence>
      <xsd:element name="name" type="xsd:string"
                             xdk:SQLName="CUSTOMER_NAME"/>
      <xsd:element name="street" type="xsd:string"
                               xdk:SQLName="STREET"/>
      <xsd:element name="city" type="xsd:string"
```

```
                                    xdk:SQLName="CITY"/>
      <xsd:element name="state" type="xsd:string"
                                     xdk:SQLName="STATE"/>
      <xsd:element name="zip" type="xsd:string"
                                     xdk:SQLName="ZIP"/>
    </xsd:sequence>
    <xsd:attribute name="country" type="xsd:string"
                                     xdk:SQLName="COUNTRY"/>
    <xsd:anyAttribute processContents="skip"/>
  </xsd:complexType>
  <!--Sendby Address Element-->
  <xsd:element name="sendby" type="AddressType"
                                 xdk:SQLName="SENDBY_ADDR"/>
  <!--Shipping Address Element-->
  <xsd:element name="DeliverTo" type="AddressType"
                                 xdk:SQLName="SHIPPING_ADDR"/>
  <xsd:element name="ShipTo" type="AddressType"
                                 xdk:SQLName="SHIPPING_ADDR"/>
  <!--Billing Address Element-->
  <xsd:element name="BillTo" type="AddressType"
                                 xdk:SQLName="BILLING_ADDR"/>
  <xsd:element name="InvoiceTo" type="AddressType"
                                 xdk:SQLName="BILLING_ADDR"/>
  <!--Line Item Type-->
  <xsd:complexType name="LineItemType">
    <xsd:all>
      <xsd:element name="ProductName" type="xsd:string"
                   xdk:SQLName="PRODUCT_NAME"/>
      <xsd:element name="Quantity" type="xsd:string"
                   xdk:SQLName="PRODUCT_QUANTITY"/>
      <xsd:element name="UnitofPrice" type="xsd:string"
                   xdk:SQLName="PRODUCT_PRICE"/>
    </xsd:all>
    <xsd:attribute name="partNum" type="xsd:string"
                                 xdk:SQLName="PRODUCT_ID"/>
  </xsd:complexType>
 <xsd:complexType name="POItemType">
    <xsd:all>
      <xsd:element name="ProductID" type="xsd:string"
                   xdk:SQLName="PRODUCT_ID"/>
      <xsd:element name="Quantity" type="xsd:string"
                   xdk:SQLName="PRODUCT_QUANTITY"/>
      <xsd:element name="UnitofPrice" type="xsd:string"
                   xdk:SQLName="PRODUCT_PRICE"/>
    </xsd:all>
    <xsd:attribute name="name" type="xsd:string"
                                 xdk:SQLName="PRODUCT_NAME"/>
  </xsd:complexType>

  <!-- Line Items Element -->
```

```
  <xsd:element name="LineItems" xdk:SQLName="LINEITEMS">
    <xsd:complexType>
      <xsd:sequence>
        <xsd:element name="LineItem" type="LineItemType"
                          maxOccurs="unbounded"
                          xdk:SQLName="LINEITEM"/>
      </xsd:sequence>
    </xsd:complexType>
  </xsd:element>
  <xsd:element name="POLines" xdk:SQLName="LINEITEMS">
    <xsd:complexType>
      <xsd:choice>
        <xsd:element name="POItem" type="POItemType"
                          maxOccurs="unbounded"
                          xdk:SQLName="LINEITEM"/>
      </xsd:choice>
    </xsd:complexType>
  </xsd:element>
</xsd:schema>
```

There are a few unexpected aspects to this schema that allow you to use it for more than simple validation. First, each named element and attribute has an additional **xdk:SQLName=""** annotation that corresponds to the column name in your database schema. These annotations can be retrieved by your application by using the new **XSDValidator** class in the **xmlparserv2.jar** file. These annotations conform to the extension mechanisms provided for in the XML Schema 1.0 specification and provide a similar function to the **xdb:SQLType** annotations used to direct the XML DB upon schema registration.

Additionally, note that there are multiple elements that map to the same **xdk:SQLName**, such as "ShipTo" and "DeliverTo". These reflect the addition of company schemas into your master schema, thus allowing you to only load one schema regardless of the PO being received. In fact, your application can keep its compiled schema object in memory for all validations. Because you extracted these types from the original company PO schemas, any changes to them that do not change the specific types you need will not cause you to reject the PO. This is an important feature that promotes the reliability of your application.

Now you are ready to analyze the Java code that will use this XML schema to deliver a validated and transformed PO that can be successfully inserted into your PO database schema. This code is organized into two source files, **XMLAnalysis.java** and **XMLAnalysisHandler.java**, the latter of which is called by the former to perform most of the work. The following are code fragments from **XMLAnalysis.java**:

```
public class XMLAnalysis {
  public XMLAnalysis() {
  }
  public static String analyze(CLOB xml_doc, CLOB xsd_doc,
                               CLOB[] res_doc) {
    Reader rd;
    Writer wt = null;

    // Check the Result CLOB
```

```
    if(res_doc[0] == null) {
      return "CLOB to write can not be null.";
    }
    try {
      wt =res_doc[0].getCharacterOutputStream();
      //Build up XML Schema Object
      rd = xsd_doc.getCharacterStream();
      XSDBuilder builder = new XSDBuilder();
    XMLSchema schemadoc = (XMLSchema)builder.build(rd,null);
    // Create Content Handlers
    XMLAnalysisHandler POHandler =
                          new XMLAnalysisHandler(new PrintWriter(wt));
    // Setup for SAX XML Schema Validation
    SAXParser parser = new SAXParser();
    parser.setContentHandler(POHandler);
    POHandler.setXMLProperty(XSDConstantValues.FIXED_SCHEMA,schemadoc);
    POHandler.setXMLProperty(XSDConstantValues.VALIDATION_MODE,
                              XSDConstantValues.LAX_VALIDATION);
      // Parse the XML document
      rd = xml_doc.getCharacterStream();
      parser.parse(rd);
    } catch(Exception e) {
      e.printStackTrace();
      return e.getMessage();
    }
    return "OK";
  }
```

This is the method that gets the XML document and performs a SAX-based validation by using LAX mode and registering the **XMLAnalysisHandler** to receive the SAX events. The reason for using LAX mode is that the instance document may contain content that you are not interested in or that your application is not set up to consume, such as the **<comment>** element included earlier. In LAX mode the schema processor skips unknown content but performs STRICT mode validation on known content.

All of the actual work is done in the **XMLAnalysisHandler**. The following listing includes the declarations and constructor of this handler:

```
public class XMLAnalysisHandler extends XSDValidator {
   private PrintWriter out;
  private boolean isSelect;
  private StringBuffer buf;
  private int level;
  private Hashtable po_tbl;
  private Hashtable name_tbl;
  private DMElement cur_elem;
  private XMLError err;
  private XSDElement elementNode;

public XMLAnalysisHandler(PrintWriter out)
                              throws XSDException,SAXException
```

```
{
  po_tbl = new Hashtable();
  name_tbl = new Hashtable();
  buf = new StringBuffer();
  err = new XMLError();
  setError(err);
  isSelect= false;
  level = 0;
  this.out= out;
  write("<PURCHASEORDER>\n");
}
```

Note that the **java.util.Hashtable** class is used to store the elements of the PO and that an initial **<purchaseOrder>** element is the root tag of the transformed output.

Since this is a SAX parse, you need to register event handlers for each type of SAX event you use. In this case, you need **startElement()**, **endElement()**, and **endDocument()**. The following lists their respective code fragments:

```
public void startElement(String namespaceURI, String localName,
             String qName, Attributes atts) throws SAXException
{
  String schemaName = null;

  super.startElement(namespaceURI,localName,qName,atts);
  // Create the DMElement at the start of Strict validation
  if(getCurrentMode()==_strict && level==0)
  {
    isSelect=true;
    cur_elem= new DMElement();
    //level=curState;
    level=0;
  }
  if (isSelect == true) {
    level++;
     //Get mapped name based upon localName
    String elementName = getElementName(localName);
    if(elementName != null)
    {
   //store in hashtable with localName as key
     name_tbl.put(localName, elementName);
  //write into buffer new mapped tag name and its attributes
     writeElement("<"+elementName+">");
     printAttributes(atts);
    }
  }
}
```

This handler is using the **getCurrentMode** method in the **XSDValidator** class to query the state of its schema validation. If the mode returned is **_strict**, the content will be buffered for transformation in **DMElement**, as this is a known element, and subsequently written to the

name_tbl hash table. On the other hand, any **_lax** results indicate an unrecognized element that will be ignored. Note also the use of the **level** variable as a way to handle the nesting of XML elements. Once a strict validation starts, it is used as a stack to indicate the process is continuing. Finally, this handler calls **getElementName()**, which is an internal method to retrieve the mapped name based upon the local name. The following is the code:

```
String getElementName(String localName) {
    String elementName="";
    //Call new interface to get schema node associated with localname
      elementNode = getElementDeclaration();

    // Find the XDK Annotation from the attributes
    if (elementNode != null) {
      XSDAnnotation ann = elementNode.getAnnotation();
      if ( ann != null) {
        Vector attrs = ann.getAttributes();
        int attrs_size = attrs.size();
        for (int i =0; i< attrs_size; i++) {
          XMLAttr xsd_attr = (XMLAttr)attrs.get(i);
          String name = xsd_attr.getName();
          if (name.equals("xdk:SQLName")) {
            elementName= xsd_attr.getValue();
            break;
          }
        }
      }
       //if no annotation let elementName=localName;
      if (elementName.equals("")) return null;
    }
    return elementName;
  }
}
```

This method uses **getElementDeclaration**, which is another of the **XSDValidator** methods, and returns the node from the master XML schema in order to retrieve the **xdk:SQLName** annotation. This is done by populating a vector with all the annotations by calling the **getAnnontation()** method from the **XSDAnnotation** class. Once populated, the **attrs** vector can be traversed to find the matching name. If no SQLName annotation is found, then the element name is returned unchanged.

While XML documents have the concept of attributes that may contain data, relational databases do not. Therefore, any data-conveying attributes must be transformed, or *canonicalized,* into XML elements in order for them to be stored relationally. This is the purpose of the **printAttributes()** method in the **startElement()** handler. The following is the associated code:

```
void printAttributes(Attributes atts) {
    String attr_name;

    int len = atts.getLength();
    if (len <1) return;
```

```
    for (int i=0; i< len; i++) {
      attr_name = getAttributeName(atts.getLocalName(i));
      if(attr_name != null)
      {
        writeElement("<"+attr_name+">");
        writeElement(atts.getValue(i));
        writeElement("</"+attr_name+">");
      }
    }
  }
```

Note that it needs to walk through the list of attributes for the XML element, and when a mapping is found by a string returned from **getAttributeName()**, write out its value as a mapped XML element. The code to check for this match is a derivation of the **getElementName()** method, as follows:

```
String getAttributeName(String localName) {
    String attrName="";
    if(elementNode == null) return localName;

    elementNode = getElementDeclaration();
    XSDAttribute[] attrNode = elementNode.getAttributeDeclarations();

    for (int j=0;j<attrNode.length; j++) {
      if (attrNode[j].getName().equals(localName)) {
        XSDAnnotation ann = attrNode[j].getAnnotation();
        if ( ann != null) {
          Vector attrs = ann.getAttributes();
          int attrs_size = attrs.size();
          for (int i =0; i< attrs_size; i++) {
            XMLAttr xsd_attr = (XMLAttr)attrs.get(i);
            String name = xsd_attr.getName();
            if (name.equals("xdk:SQLName")) {
              attrName= xsd_attr.getValue();
              break;
            }
          }
        }
      }
    }
    if (attrName.equals("")) return null;  //attrName = localName;

    return attrName;
  }
```

Similar to **getElementDeclaration()**, there is a corresponding attribute version called **getAttributeDeclarations()** that returns all the attribute nodes associated with an element. However, since there can be many nodes, it returns them in an array, and thus your code must walk through the **attrNode** array of **attrs** vectors.

Turning now to the **endElement()** code, you can see how the complete element is processed in the following code:

```
public void endElement(String namespaceURI, String localName,String qName)
  throws SAXException
  {
    XSDAnnotation ann;
    String elementName;

    super.endElement(namespaceURI, localName,qName);

    if (isSelect == true) {
      level--;
      flushChar();
      // Output the endTag of the Element
      elementName = (String)name_tbl.get(localName);
      writeElement("</"+elementName+">");
      // If validation errors exists, exit the process
      int i = err.getFirstError();
      if (i!=-1)
        throw new
        SAXException("(Line,Column)("+err.getLineNumber(i)+","+
                     err.getColumnNumber(i)+"):"+err.getMessage(i));
      // Save the Validated Element
      cur_elem.level = level;
      cur_elem.isValid=true;
      po_tbl.put(elementName, cur_elem);
         if(level==0){
        isSelect=false;
      }
    } else {
      flushChar();
    }
  }
```

First, note that although the validation is namespace aware, your database schema is not; therefore, you are only interested in the local name of the element for processing. Since this is the end tag and you have already done the mapping for the start tag, it can be written by using a simple hash table lookup based upon the **localName**. If the element correctly validates, it is sent to the **po_tbl** hash table, from which it will be evaluated.

Once all the elements are processed, the **endDocument()** event is received. This event triggers several actions, as illustrated in the following handler code:

```
  public void endDocument() throws SAXException
  {
    String[] ship_elems = new String[]{"SHIPPING_ADDR"};
    String[] bill_elems = new String[]{"BILLING_ADDR"};
    String[] line_elems = new String[]{"LINEITEMS"};
    DMElement ck_elem = null;
```

```
  //Check Required Shipping Address
    ck_elem = (DMElement) po_tbl.get(ship_elems[i]);
    if (ck_elem != null)
        write(ck_elem.content);

  if (ck_elem == null)
    throw new SAXException("Missing required Shipping Address!");
  else if (ck_elem.content == null)
    throw new SAXException("Shipping Address doesn't have content!");

  //Check Required Billing Address
  ck_elem = null;
   ck_elem = (DMElement) po_tbl.get(bill_elems[i]);
    if (ck_elem != null)
        write(ck_elem.content);

    if (ck_elem == null)
    throw new SAXException("Missing required Billing Address!");
  else if (ck_elem.content == null)
    throw new SAXException("Billing Address doesn't have content!");

  //Check Required LineItems
  ck_elem = null;
    ck_elem = (DMElement) po_tbl.get(line_elems[i]);
    if (ck_elem != null)
       write(ck_elem.content);
    if (ck_elem == null)
    throw new SAXException("Missing required LineItems!");
  else if (ck_elem.content == null)
    throw new SAXException("LineItems don't have content!");

    //Write new PO closing tag
  write("</PURCHASEORDER>");
  out.flush();
}
```

First, the essential types that you need to have a complete PO are initialized as strings.

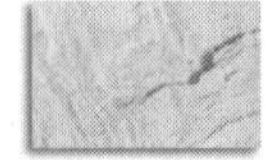

NOTE
Instead of being hard-coded, these strings could be read from an external configuration file or the DB itself, thus making the code more generic and extensible.

Then, you use these strings to look up the elements from the **po_tbl** hash table and check to see not only whether the element is there but also whether it contains content as is done in each **ck_elem()** function. If either of these conditions fails, then the appropriate error message is returned. If both conditions pass, then the closing element tag is printed and the validated and transformed document is returned for submission by XSU into the database.

Extending the Application's Functionality

As you should have seen, this use of a master schema with Oracle Streams AQ and SOAP is quite powerful functionality yet simple in its configuration. Adding new customers is simply a matter of adding new types to your master schema. Performance is not affected because additional elements and attributes are looked up efficiently by using hash tables. Note however, that the client schema may be complex in situations where the types you need are not at the top level. This is not a problem, because the application won't get the mode change signal from LAX to STRICT until the validator encounters the known type, no matter how buried it is. There are several features or conditions you may need to accommodate. We will close the chapter with a brief discussion of these.

Submitting SOAP Messages

Thus far, we have covered only the processing of SOAP-based POs, not the generation of them. Generation can be done in several ways, but a very easy method is to do it as part of the PO generation process. For example, you could use the XDK JAXB Class Generator to create a set of classes corresponding to your PO schema and use this code in a JSP- or XSQL-based web form to generate both the SOAP message and its PO content. An example of such an XSQL page is included in the book's downloadable source code.

Handling of xsi:types in POs

XML Schema allows users to override built-in types by adding **xsi:type** annotations to attributes within the instance document. These attributes must be retrieved differently in your **getAttributeName()** method because of their reserved status. The following code will retrieve them:

```
if (currNode.getNodeType() == TYPE)
  XSDAttribute[] attrNode = currNode.getAttributeDeclarations();
```

Conveying type overrides in an instance document is not a good design practice and thus should be avoided.

Generating an E-Mail Confirmation

Even though a user has received a transaction confirmation from AQ, it would be useful to provide to the user a notification of successful or failed PO processing. This functionality is built into AQ's **AQXmlRegister()** and **AQXmlCommit()** methods, so you can set up a mail URL such as the following to notify users upon commit:

```
<?xml version="1.0"?>
<Envelope xmlns= "http://ns.oracle.com/AQ/schemas/envelope">
 <Body>
   <AQXmlRegister xmlns = "http://ns.oracle.com/AQ/schemas/access">
     <register_options>
      <destination>AQUSER.EMP_TOPIC</destination>
      <consumer_name>WHIRLIGIG</consumer_name>
```

```
      <notify_url>mailto:bob.smith@hotmail.com</notify_url>
     </register_options>
    <AQXmlCommit/>
  </AQXmlRegister>
 </Body>
</Envelope>
```

Summary

In this chapter, you learned how the Oracle XDK and little-known yet powerful features such as AQ can create applications that solve real business problems. Even though XML started off as a document technology, its use for data exchange has rapidly become prevalent. The gateway application presented here is a very real one, as most business data is stored relationally and will continue to be stored in this manner in the future. It is not realistic in these economic times to have businesses totally rewrite their applications or database schemas in order to do business on the Internet. This approach satisfies both the preservation and expansion requirements and should be seriously considered when designing Internet applications.

CHAPTER 17

Developing XML-Based Reusable Components

In this chapter we begin to look at higher-order XML functionality. In previous chapters you have been introduced to the components that make up an XML infrastructure—XML parser, XSLT processor, XML Schema validator, etc. Now you will use this functionality in an XML-powered framework that supports building whole application processing blocks that can be easily configured by XML files instead of compiled code. This configuration not only covers the logic flow of your application but its schema as well. This functionality allows for the creation of reusable software components that reduce development time and improve application reliability. In the past such a framework would have had performance disadvantages; however, the design we will be discussing uses SAX streaming to mitigate these disadvantages and allow form-managed scalability.

Designing the Framework

Consider a fictitious book reseller, Big Barrel Books (BBB), who does business over the Internet with a wide variety of suppliers. However, BBB is not the size of Amazon.com and thus cannot dictate to its suppliers the particular book listing XML format that they use. Under these conditions, BBB needs to validate each entry against each partner's XML schema before accepting the entry. To improve the system performance, these schemas are stored locally. However, this opens up a potential problem area because BBB may not be informed of a change or update to these schemas and thus could reject valid listings. Therefore, the system must include the capability to check for this condition without the overhead of always fetching the XSD file from the partner.

The block diagram in Figure 17-1 illustrates such a system organized as a streaming pipeline. The strategy is to parse and validate incoming XML book listings using the SAX validation capabilities in Oracle XDK 10*g* against the local copies of partners' schemas. If the listing validates, then it is passed through the pipeline to the output. However, if it fails validation, then the listing may be invalid, its associated schema may need updating, or both. You need to evaluate this condition and validate the listing against the new schema; then, you need to decide whether schema changes have occurred and whether the listing is truly invalid.

To perform this processing, you could custom design an application from scratch; however, you need a number of generic XML processing components, which means that you could design this in a modular form using a pipeline strategy. This is exactly how we will proceed, using the new XML Pipeline Processor in Oracle XDK 10*g*. (See Chapter 7 for an introduction to the XML Pipeline Processor.) The following components constitute the required functionality, as shown in Figure 17-1:

- **SAXParserProcess** Parses incoming XML and outputs SAX events
- **XSDValProcess** Validates against the local schema, analyzes the results, and reports any errors if necessary
- **XSDSchemaBuilder** Parses an XML schema and outputs a schema object for validation
- **XSDConditionalValProcess** Receives the SAX stream as well as the **isCheck** from which it either passes on the stream or compares and revalidates against the remote schema
- **XMLDiffProcess** Compares two XML schemas, checking for differences, and returns an XSL stylesheet to convert one to the other if one or more differences are found
- **SAXPrintProcess** Writes the SAX event output stream to a file

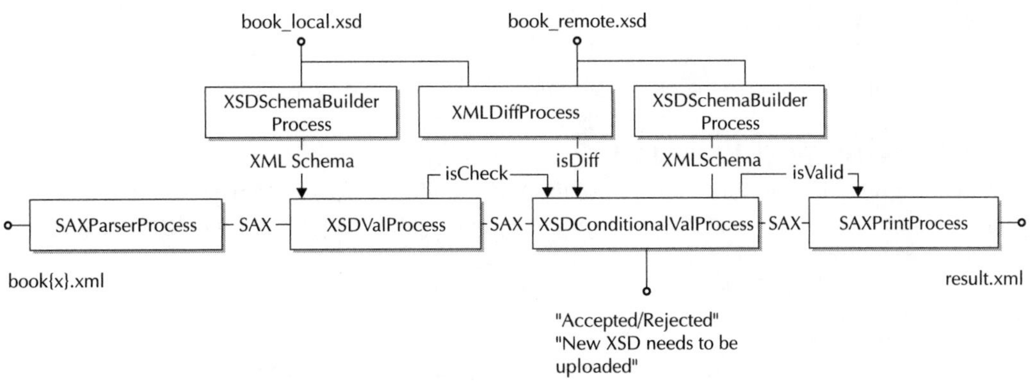

FIGURE 17-1. *Book listing streaming pipeline*

These components and processes can be connected together through a combination of the Pipeline Processor and an XML pipeline control file. Before we build this application, let's start with a couple simple pipeline processes.

Simple Pipeline Examples

The Oracle XDK 10*g* XML Pipeline Processor provides a command-line utility that makes it easy to prototype and test pipeline applications. **Oracle.xml.pipeline.controller.orapipe** is a utility that can be launched from Java and has the following parameters:

- **–help** Prints the help message
- **–version** Prints the release version
- **–sequential** Executes the pipeline in a sequential mode; the default is parallel
- **–validate** Validates the XML pipeline control file with the pipeline schema; by default, does not validate
- **–log <*logfile*>** Writes the errors/logs to the output file; by default, writes to **pipe.log**
- **–noinfo** Doesn't log any info items; default is on
- **–nowarning** Doesn't log any warnings; default is on
- **–force** Executes pipeline even if target is up-to-date; by default, no force is specified

It also turns out that there is a very useful parameter that was not documented in the initial release that lets you pass in parameters into the XML pipeline control file:

- **–attr <*name*> <*value*>** Sets the value of $name

We will use this utility and its parameters in the following simple examples.

SAX Parsing and Printing

This first example demonstrates how to use the XML Pipeline Processor to parse and print an input XML document. An example of an instance document that should validate against this schema is as follows:

```
<?xml version="1.0"?>
<book inStock="Yes">
  <title>Compilers: Principles, Techniques, and Tools</title>
  <author>Alfred V.Aho, Ravi Sethi, Jeffrey D. Ullman</author>
  <ISBN>0-201-10088-6</ISBN>
  <edition>Second</edition>
  <publisher>Addison Wesley</publisher>
</book>
```

You could obviously write Java code to parse, validate, and write this document to a file. Instead, you could create an XML pipeline control file that calls generic classes to perform the same functions. The following file, **pipeprocessing_1.xml**, is an example:

```
<pipeline xmlns="http://www.w3.org/2002/02/xml-pipeline">
  <param name="target" select="result1.xml"/>

  <processdef name="saxparser.p"
            definition="oracle.xml.pipeline.processes.SAXParserProcess"/>
  <processdef name="saxprint.p"
            definition="oracle.xml.sample.pipeline.SAXPrintProcess"/>

  <process id="p1" type="saxparser.p" ignore-errors="true">
    <input name="xmlsource" label="$source"/>
    <output name="sax" label="saxevents"/>
  </process>

  <process id="p2" type="saxprint.p" ignore-errors="true">
    <input name="pxmlsource" label="saxevents"/>
    <param name="isPrint" select="true"/>
    <output name="printxml" label="$result"/>
 </process>
</pipeline>
```

Note that two named processes are called, **saxparser.p** and **saxprint.p**, and that these are associated with actual Java classes. This allows them to be used in the process sections identified by **id** attributes **p1** and **p2**. These processes supply the parameters required by the XML Pipeline Processor and the called classes. In this case you see **$source** as the parameter for specifying the input filename and **$result** for the output filename. The following is the command line for executing this process after you have added the **xml.jar** in **ORACLE_HOME/lib** and the compiled **oracle.xml.sample.pipeline.SAXPrintProcess class** to your Java CLASSPATH:

```
java oracle.xml.pipeline.controller.orapipe -sequential -force
  -attr source xml/book1.xml -attr result result1.xml
  pipeline/pipeProcessing_1.xml
```

As noted, there are two classes that need to be created that implement the pipeline interfaces. The **oracle.xml.pipeline.processes.SAXParserProcess** method is a built-in class, and the following is a listing for the other, **oracle.xml.sample.pipeline.SAXPrintProcess**:

```
package oracle.xml.sample.pipeline;

import java.io.IOException;
import java.io.OutputStream;
import java.io.PrintWriter;
import java.io.StringWriter;
import oracle.xml.parser.v2.XMLSAXSerializer;
import oracle.xml.pipeline.controller.Process;
import oracle.xml.pipeline.controller.Input;
import oracle.xml.pipeline.controller.Output;
import oracle.xml.pipeline.controller.PipelineException;
import org.xml.sax.ContentHandler;

public class SAXPrintProcess extends Process {
  StringWriter sw=new StringWriter();
  PrintWriter out= new PrintWriter(sw);

  public SAXPrintProcess() {
  }
  public void initialize() {
    /* Set the supported xml infoset types for the inputs and outputs */
    Input i = getInput("pxmlsource");
    i.supportType(SAXSOURCE);
    i.supportType(DOCUMENT);
    Output o = getOutput("printxml");
    o.supportType(STREAMRESULT);
    o.supportType(DOCUMENT);
  }
  public ContentHandler SAXContentHandler() throws PipelineException
  {
    printHandler = new XMLSAXSerializer(out);
    return printHandler;
  }
  public void execute() throws PipelineException {
    Object isPrint= getInParamValue("isPrint");
    if(isPrint == null) isPrint="false";
    if(isPrint.equals("true")) {
```

```
        try {
          OutputStream outstream = getOutputStream("printxml");
          outstream.write(sw.toString().getBytes());
          out.flush();
        } catch(IOException ex) {
          ex.printStackTrace();
        }
      }
    }
    XMLSAXSerializer printHandler;
  }
```

The steps needed to implement a customized XML pipeline processor are to extend the **oracle.xml.pipeline.controller.Process** class and implement the **initialize()** and **execute()** function. In order to create SAX-based pipeline processors, you also need to implement the **SAXContentHandler()** to process SAX events.

Parsing and Checking for Differences

Another simple example and a task we will incorporate into the application is the comparison of two XML files by using the **XMLDiff** class from the Oracle XDK 10g. In this case, you will compare two XML schemas. The following **book_local.xsd** schema specifies the format for the book listing files:

```
<xsd:schema xmlns:xsd="http://www.w3.org/2001/XMLSchema">
  <xsd:element name="book" type="bookType"/>
  <xsd:complexType name="bookType">
    <xsd:sequence>
      <xsd:element ref="title"/>
      <xsd:choice>
        <xsd:element ref="author"/>
        <xsd:element ref="editor"/>
      </xsd:choice>
      <xsd:element ref="ISBN"/>
      <xsd:element ref="edition" minOccurs="1"/>
      <xsd:element ref="publisher"/>
    </xsd:sequence>
    <xsd:attribute name="inStock" use="required">
      <xsd:simpleType>
        <xsd:restriction base="xsd:string">
          <xsd:enumeration value="Yes"/>
          <xsd:enumeration value="No"/>
        </xsd:restriction>
      </xsd:simpleType>
    </xsd:attribute>
  </xsd:complexType>
  <xsd:element name="title" type="xsd:string"/>
  <xsd:element name="author" type="nameType"/>
  <xsd:element name="ISBN" type="xsd:string"/>
  <xsd:element name="edition" default="First">
```

```
    <xsd:simpleType>
      <xsd:restriction base="xsd:string">
        <xsd:enumeration value="First"/>
        <xsd:enumeration value="Second"/>
        <xsd:enumeration value="Third"/>
        <xsd:enumeration value="Fourth"/>
        <xsd:enumeration value="Fifth"/>
      </xsd:restriction>
    </xsd:simpleType>
  </xsd:element>
  <xsd:element name="publisher" type="xsd:string"/>
  <xsd:element name="editor" type="nameType"/>
  <xsd:simpleType name="nameType">
    <xsd:restriction base="xsd:string">
      <xsd:minLength value="4"/>
    </xsd:restriction>
  </xsd:simpleType>
</xsd:schema>
```

A second schema, **book_remote.xsd**, differs only in the **<edition/>** element, changing from a mandatory occurrence to an optional one, as follows:

```
<xsd:element ref="edition" minOccurs="0"/>
```

The two schemas can be compared using a very simple pipeline control file, **pipeProcessing_2.xml**:

```
<pipeline xmlns="http://www.w3.org/2002/02/xml-pipeline">

  <param name="target" select="result2.xsl"/>

  <processdef name="xmldiff.p"
        definition="oracle.xml.sample.pipeline.XMLDiffProcess"/>

 <process id="p1" type="xmldiff.p" ignore-errors="true">
  <input name="xmlsource1" label="$source1"/>
  <input name="xmlsource2" label="$source2"/>
  <outparam name="isDiff" label="isDiffStatus"/>
  <output name="xsl" label="result2.xsl"/>
 </process>
</pipeline>
```

This file specifies a single **xmldiff.p** process to be called and process two input files, **source1** and **source2**, and print the output to **result2.xsl** if there is a difference. This file is executed with the following command line:

```
java oracle.xml.pipeline.controller.orapipe -sequential -force
-attr source1 xsd/book_local.xsd -attr source2 xsd/book_remote.xsd
 pipeline/pipeProcessing_2.xml
```

In this case a difference is found, so you get a **result2.xsl** stylesheet detailing the expected change in the **<edition>** element:

```
<xsl:stylesheet version="1.0" xmlns:xsl="http://www.w3.org/1999/XSL/Transform">
   <xsl:output xmlns:ora="http://www.oracle.com/XSL/Transform/java"
      ora:omit-xml-encoding="yes"/>
   <!--Select all nodes-->
   <xsl:template match="node()|@*">
      <xsl:copy>
         <xsl:apply-templates select="node()|@*"/>
      </xsl:copy>
   </xsl:template>
   <xsl:template match="/xsd:schema[1]/xsd:complexType[1]/xsd:sequence[1]
/xsd:element[3]/@minOccurs">
      <xsl:attribute name="minOccurs">0</xsl:attribute>
   </xsl:template>
</xsl:stylesheet>
```

As with the previous example, you need to implement **oracle.xml.sample.pipeline .XMLDiffProcess** with the proper pipeline interfaces. The following is an example of such an implementation:

```
package oracle.xml.sample.pipeline;

import java.io.FileInputStream;
import java.io.InputStream;
import java.io.OutputStream;
import java.io.Reader;
import java.net.URL;
import javax.xml.transform.Source;
import javax.xml.transform.dom.DOMResult;
import javax.xml.transform.stream.StreamSource;
import oracle.xml.differ.XMLDiff;
import oracle.xml.parser.v2.DOMParser;
import oracle.xml.parser.v2.XMLDocument;
import oracle.xml.parser.v2.XMLParser;
import oracle.xml.pipeline.controller.Input;
import oracle.xml.pipeline.controller.Output;
import oracle.xml.pipeline.controller.PipelineException;
import oracle.xml.pipeline.controller.Process;
import org.xml.sax.InputSource;

public class XMLDiffProcess extends Process {
  public XMLDiffProcess() {
  }

  public void initialize() {
    // Initialized inputs
    Input input1 = getInput("xmlsource1");
    input1.supportType(DOMSOURCE);
```

```
    input1.supportType(DOCUMENT);
    Input input2 = getInput("xmlsource2");
    input2.supportType(DOMSOURCE);
    input2.supportType(DOCUMENT);
    // Initialized Output
    Output output = getOutput("xsl");
    output.supportType(STREAMRESULT);
    output.supportType(DOCUMENT);
  }

  public void execute() throws PipelineException {
    XMLDocument doc1=null, doc2=null;
    boolean res=false;
    DOMParser parser = new DOMParser();

    /* get input stream source */
    Source xmlSource1 = getInputSource("xmlsource1");
    Source xmlSource2 = getInputSource("xmlsource2");
    XMLDiff xmlDiff = new XMLDiff();
    if(xmlSource1 instanceof StreamSource) {
      StreamSource xmlstream = (StreamSource)xmlSource1;
      Object instream;
      try {
        if((instream = xmlstream.getInputStream()) != null) {
          parser.parse((InputStream)instream);
        } else {
          error(30005, FATAL_ERROR, new String[]{"xmlsource"});
        }
        doc1= parser.getDocument();
         } catch(Exception e) {
        e.printStackTrace();
      }
    } else {
      error(30002, FATAL_ERROR, new String[]{"StreamSource"});
    }
    if(xmlSource2 instanceof StreamSource) {
      StreamSource xmlstream = (StreamSource)xmlSource2;
      Object instream;
      try {
        if((instream = xmlstream.getInputStream()) != null) {
          parser.parse((InputStream)instream);
        } else {
          error(30005, FATAL_ERROR, new String[]{"xmlsource"});
        }
        doc2= parser.getDocument();
      } catch(Exception e) {
        e.printStackTrace();
      }
    } else {
      error(30002, FATAL_ERROR, new String[]{"StreamSource"});
```

```
    }
    if(doc1!=null && doc2 !=null) {
      xmlDiff.setInput1(doc1);
      xmlDiff.setInput2(doc2);
      res = xmlDiff.diff();
      if(res == true) setOutParam("isDiff","true");
      else setOutParam("isDiff","false");
    } else setOutParam("isDiff","N/A");
    if(res==true){
      try {
        XMLDocument doc = xmlDiff.generateXSLDoc();
        OutputStream outstream = getOutputStream("xsl");
        doc.print(outstream);
      } catch(Exception e) {
        e.printStackTrace();
      }
    }
    return;
  }
  public void endExecute() throws PipelineException
  {
    System.out.println("End of XMLDiffProcess!!");
  }
}
```

Building the Pipeline Application

Obviously, if you simply wanted to invoke one or two processes, you would not need to use a pipeline framework. That, however, is not the case for our application. Building upon the previous examples, our application needs to invoke additional processes, and thus your pipeline control file becomes more sophisticated, as shown here in **pipeProcessing_3.xml**:

```
<pipeline xmlns="http://www.w3.org/2002/02/xml-pipeline">
  <param name="target" select="result3.xml"/>
  <processdef name="saxparser.p"
        definition="oracle.xml.pipeline.processes.SAXParserProcess"/>
  <processdef name="XSDVal.p"
        definition="oracle.xml.sample.pipeline.XSDValProcess"/>
  <processdef name="xsdschemabuilder.p"
        definition="oracle.xml.pipeline.processes.XSDSchemaBuilder"/>
  <processdef name="conditionvalidation.p"
        definition="oracle.xml.sample.pipeline.XSDConditionalValProcess"/>
 <processdef name="xmldiff.p"
        definition="oracle.xml.sample.pipeline.XMLDiffProcess"/>
 <processdef name="saxprint.p"
        definition="oracle.xml.sample.pipeline.SAXPrintProcess"/>

<!-- Parse and build the local schema -->
 <process id="p1" type="xsdschemabuilder.p" ignore-errors="true">
  <input name="schema" label="$Lschema"/>
```

```
  <param name="baseURL" select="url"></param>
  <outparam name="xmlschema" label="xmlschemaobj"/>
 </process>

<!--Parse the source XML -->
  <process id="p2" type="saxparser.p" ignore-errors="true">
     <input name="xmlsource" label="$source"/>
     <output name="sax" label="saxevents"/>
     <param name="preserveWhitespace" select="false"></param>
    </process>

<!--Check for validation errors and switch the output accordingly -->
  <process id="p3" type="XSDVal.p" ignore-errors="true">
    <input name="xml" label="saxevents"/>
    <param name="sschemaObj" label="xmlschemaobj"></param>
    <outparam name="isCheckXSDDiff" label="isCheckStatus"></outparam>
    <output name="validatedxml" label="xsdsaxevents"/>
  </process>

<!--Parse and build the remote schema -->
 <process id="p4" type="xsdschemabuilder.p" ignore-errors="true">
  <input name="schema" label="$Rschema"/>
  <param name="baseURL" select="url"></param>
  <outparam name="xmlschema" label="txmlschemaobj"/>
 </process>

<!--Compare local and remote schemas and report result -->
<process id="p5" type="xmldiff.p" ignore-errors="true">
  <input name="xmlsource1" label="$Lschema"/>
  <input name="xmlsource2" label="Rschema"/>
  <outparam name="isDiff" label="isDiffStatus"/>
  <output name="xsl" label="result.xsl"/>
 </process>

<!--Optionally validates input if remote schema is different -->
<process id="p6" type="conditionvalidation.p" ignore-errors="true">
   <input name="csax" label="xsdsaxevents"/>
   <param name="txmlschema" label="txmlschemaobj"/>
   <param name="isCheck" label="isCheckStatus"/>
   <param name="isXSDDiff" label="isDiffStatus"/>
   <outparam name="isValid" label="isConditionalValid"/>
   <output name="xmlout" label="valsaxevents"/>
 </process>

<!-- Print validated document if successful -->
<process id="p7" type="saxprint.p" ignore-errors="true">
    <input name="pxmlsource" label="valsaxevents"/>
    <param name="isPrint" label="isConditionalValid"/>
    <output name="printxml" label="result3.xml"/>
 </process>
</pipeline>
```

In this application, no fewer than seven processes are pipelined, each process passing its results to the next. We have already reviewed four of these processes. Let's review the remaining three.

The XSDSchemaBuilder Process

The XSDSchemaBuilder process is built into the XML Pipeline Processor and builds schema objects that are used for validating XML documents. In this case, it is used for both the local and remote schemas and returns the XML schema objects **xmlschemaobj** and **txmlschemaobj** respectively, which can then be passed into other processes for validation.

The XSDValProcess Process

The **XSDValProcess** class performs a validation of the source file input via SAX events and reports the result of a validation error analysis. The following is its code listing:

```
package oracle.xml.sample.pipeline;

import java.io.IOException;
import java.io.ObjectOutputStream;
import java.io.OutputStream;
import java.io.PrintWriter;
import java.io.StringWriter;
import javax.xml.transform.Source;
import javax.xml.transform.dom.DOMSource;
import oracle.xml.comp.CXMLContext;
import oracle.xml.comp.CXMLStream;
import oracle.xml.parser.schema.XSDConstantValues;
import oracle.xml.parser.v2.XMLDocument;
import oracle.xml.pipeline.controller.Input;
import oracle.xml.pipeline.controller.Output;
import oracle.xml.pipeline.controller.Process;
import oracle.xml.pipeline.controller.PipelineException;
import org.xml.sax.ContentHandler;
import org.xml.sax.ErrorHandler;

public class XSDValProcess extends Process {
  StringWriter sw=new StringWriter();
  PrintWriter out= new PrintWriter(sw);
  boolean isCheckXSDDiff=false;
  boolean isValid=true;

  public XSDValProcess() {
  }

  public void initialize() {
    /* Set the supported xml infoset types for the inputs and outputs */
    Input i = getInput("xml");
    i.supportType(SAXSOURCE);
    i.supportType(DOCUMENT);
    Output o = getOutput("validatedxml");
```

```
    //o.supportType(DOMRESULT);
    o.supportType(SAXRESULT);
    o.supportType(STREAMRESULT);
    o.supportType(DOCUMENT);
  }

  public ContentHandler SAXContentHandler() throws PipelineException {
    try {
      Output output = getOutput("validatedxml");
      // if dependents are not available then return null
      ContentHandler hdlr = getSAXContentHandler(output);
      if (hdlr == null)
         return null;
      Object schemaObj = getInParamValue("sschemaObj");
      if (schemaObj == null)
         return null;
      exXsdHandler = new ExXSDHandler(new PrintWriter(out), this);
      exXsdHandler.addContentHandler(hdlr);
      exXsdHandler.setXMLProperty(XSDConstantValues.VALIDATION_MODE,
                                  XSDConstantValues.STRICT_VALIDATION);
      Object obj = ExXSDHandler.setXMLProperty(XSDConstantValues.FIXED_SCHEMA,
                                         schemaObj);
      if(obj== null)
        throw new PipelineException("The XML Schema Object is not correct.");

    } catch(Exception ex) {
      ex.printStackTrace();
    }

    return exXSDHandler;
  }

  public void execute() throws PipelineException {
    super.execute();
    if(isValid==true) {
      setOutParam("isCheckXSDDiff","ignore");
    } else {
      //Set the output parameter
      if(isCheckXSDDiff == true) setOutParam("isCheckXSDDiff","true");
      else {
        setOutParam("isCheckXSDDiff","false");
           }
      }
  }

  ExXSDHandler exXsdHandler;
}
```

After initializing the objects, the XSDValProcess takes the input schema object, **schemaObj**, and sets the type of validation and confirms its validity in **SAXContentHandler()**, returning

exXsdHandler. This handler, along with the SAX stream, is passed to **execute()** to perform the validation. The SAX stream by way of **exXsdHandler** is output along with the validation result in the **isCheckASDiff** output parameter. The **exXsdHandler** performs an error analysis to determine whether the error is one that should trigger a check of the remote schema. Here is its code listing:

```
package oracle.xml.sample.pipeline;

import java.io.PrintWriter;
import java.util.Hashtable;
import oracle.xml.parser.schema.XSDException;
import oracle.xml.parser.schema.XSDValidator;
import oracle.xml.parser.v2.DefaultXMLDocumentHandler;
import oracle.xml.parser.v2.XMLError;
import org.xml.sax.Attributes;
import org.xml.sax.ContentHandler;
import org.xml.sax.SAXException;

public class ExXSDHandler extends XSDValidator {
  private MyXMLError err;
  Hashtable ht;
  PrintWriter out;
  XSDValProcess parentProcess;
  int errorIndex=0;

  public ExXSDHandler(PrintWriter out, XSDValProcess parentProcess) throws
 XSDException,SAXException {
    this.out= out;
    this.parentProcess=parentProcess;
    parentProcess.isValid=true;
    err = new MyXMLError();
    setError(err);
 //Initialize hashtable for error numbers to track
    ht =new Hashtable();
// XML-24536 Missing ''{0}'' Attribute
    ht.put(new Integer(24536),"24536");
// XML-24534 "Element ''{0}'' not expected.
    ht.put(new Integer(24534),"24534");
  }
  public void startDocument() throws SAXException  {
    super.startDocument();
  }
  public void startElement(String namespaceURI, String localName,
          String qName, Attributes atts) throws SAXException {
    super.startElement(namespaceURI,localName,qName,atts);
  }
  public void endElement(String namespaceURI, String localName,String qName)
  throws SAXException  {
    super.endElement(namespaceURI, localName,qName);
    // If validation errors exist, exit the process
    int i = err.getNumMessages();
```

```
    if(i>errorIndex) {
      errorIndex=i;
      parentProcess.isValid=false;
      int j= err.getErrorCode(i-1);
            if(ht.get(new Integer(j)) != null) {
        parentProcess.isCheckXSDDiff=true;
      }
    }
  }
  public void endDocument() throws SAXException  {
    super.endDocument();
  }
}
```

Note that this class creates a hash table of error numbers to be compared to the validation errors. The reason for this analysis is to minimize the round trips to compare the remote schema with the local one. The schema validator returns error messages and associated numbers from 24000 to 24999. These numbers are available in **errid**, which can be retrieved by extending the **XMLError** class as follows:

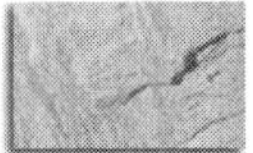

```
package oracle.xml.sample.pipeline;

import oracle.xml.parser.v2.XMLError;
import oracle.xml.parser.v2.XMLParseException;

public class MyXMLError extends XMLError {
  public MyXMLError() {
  }

  public int getErrorCode(int index) {
    return errid[index];
  }
}
```

NOTE
The error codes and their messages were not included in the Oracle Database 10g release. However, their documentation is available on OTN in the Oracle XDK Development section of the XML Technology Center.

The XSDConditionalValProcess Process

The XML Pipeline Processor does not include the capability for conditional logic branching. The specification intentionally omits this capability so that it remains simple. However, sometimes you may need branching, as in this chapter's application. The final process, **XSDConditionalValProcess**, adds conditional logic to the pipeline. The process takes an input XML document parsed into SAX events, the schemaObject, **txmlschema**, the conditional, **isCheck**, and an **isXSDDiff** input parameter. If **isCheck** is true, it validates the XML document against an XSD file. Otherwise, no action is taken. The following is its code listing:

```
package oracle.xml.sample.pipeline;

import java.io.IOException;
import java.io.ObjectOutputStream;
import java.io.OutputStream;
import java.io.PrintWriter;
import java.io.StringWriter;
import javax.xml.transform.Source;
import javax.xml.transform.dom.DOMSource;
import oracle.xml.comp.CXMLContext;
import oracle.xml.comp.CXMLStream;
import oracle.xml.parser.schema.XSDConstantValues;
import oracle.xml.parser.v2.XMLDocument;
import oracle.xml.pipeline.controller.Input;
import oracle.xml.pipeline.controller.Output;
import oracle.xml.pipeline.controller.Process;
import oracle.xml.pipeline.controller.PipelineException;
import org.xml.sax.ContentHandler;

public class XSDConditionalValProcess extends Process {
  StringWriter sw=new StringWriter();
  PrintWriter out= new PrintWriter(sw);
  boolean isValid=true;

  public XSDConditionalValProcess() {
  }

  public void initialize() {
    /* Set the supported xml infoset types for the inputs and outputs */
    Input i = getInput("csax");
    i.supportType(SAXSOURCE);
    i.supportType(DOCUMENT);
    Output o = getOutput("xmlout");
    o.supportType(SAXRESULT);
    o.supportType(STREAMRESULT);
    o.supportType(DOCUMENT);
  }

  public ContentHandler SAXContentHandler() throws PipelineException
  {
    try {
      Object schemaObj = getInParamValue("txmlschema");
      if (schemaObj == null)
         return null;
      Output output = getOutput("xmlout");
      xsdHandler = new XSDValidationHandler(new PrintWriter(out), this);
      xsdHandler.setXMLProperty(XSDConstantValues.VALIDATION_MODE,
                                XSDConstantValues.STRICT_VALIDATION);
```

```
      Object obj = xsdHandler.setXMLProperty(XSDConstantValues.FIXED_SCHEMA,
                                             schemaObj);
      if(obj== null)
        throw new PipelineException("The XML Schema Object is not correct.");
      ContentHandler hdlr = getSAXContentHandler(output);
      xsdHandler.addContentHandler(hdlr);
    } catch(Exception ex) {
      ex.printStackTrace();
    }
    return xsdHandler;
  }

  public void execute() throws PipelineException
  {
    super.execute();
    Object isCheck = getInParamValue("isCheck");
    if(isCheck.equals("true")) {
      Object isDiff = getInParamValue("isXSDDiff");
      if(isDiff.equals("true")) {
        System.out.println("XSD documents are not consistent.");
        System.out.println("Please upload the new XSD file.");
        if(isValid==true) {
          System.out.println("XML document accepted.");
          setOutParam("isValid","true");
        } else {
          System.out.println("XML document rejected.");
          setOutParam("isValid","false");
        }
      } else {
        System.out.println("XSD documents are consistent.");
        System.out.println("XML document rejected.");
        setOutParam("isValid","false");
      }
    } else if(isCheck.equals("ignore")) {
      setOutParam("isValid","true");
      System.out.println("XML document accepted.");
    } else if(isCheck.equals("false")) {
      setOutParam("isValid","false");
      System.out.println("XML document rejected.");
    }
  }
  XSDValidationHandler xsdHandler;
}
```

If the validation process is performed and the XML document is valid, **isXSDDiff** is checked. If it is true, then the message indicates that the XML document is valid according to the local XSD but that the local XSD and the remote XSD are not consistent. If **isXSDDiff** is false, the message indicates that the XML document is valid according to the local XSD and that the local and remote XSDs are consistent (this is not shown in the example because **isCheck** is false in this case).

When the validation process is performed and the XML document is invalid, **isXSDDiff** is checked. If it is true, then the message indicates that the XML document is invalid according to the local XSD but that the XSDs are not consistent. If **isXSDDiff** is false, the message shows that the XML document is invalid according to the local XSD and that the XSDs are consistent.

Running the Pipeline Application

As you have done with the two simple examples, you can use the **orapipe** utility to run the pipeline application. Referring to its pipeline control file, you see the following three parameters that need to be passed:

- **source** The input XML book listing file
- **Lschema** The local schema
- **Rschema** The remote schema

Even though you pass the remote schema filename or URL, it is not actually retrieved unless the condition calls for it. The following is the command line for the **book1.xml** file:

```
java oracle.xml.pipeline.controller.orapipe -sequential -force
-attr source xml/book1.xml -attr Lschema xsd/book_local.xsd
-attr Rschema xsd/book_remote.xsd pipeline/pipeProcessing_3.xml
```

Because this is a valid book listing, you will see the message "XML document accepted" and an identical **result3.xml** file written.

Processing an Invalid Document

In the previous sections, we discussed the details of each process in the XML pipeline application. Now, we will show you how the XML pipeline application behaves under different scenarios. First consider an invalid book listing, called **book2.xml**:

```
<?xml version="1.0"?>
<book inStock="true">
  <title>Compilers: Principles, Techniques, and Tools</title>
  <author>Alfred V.Aho, Ravi Sethi, Jeffrey D. Ullman</author>
  <ISBN>0-201-10088-6</ISBN>
  <edition>Second</edition>
  <publisher>Addison Wesley</publisher>
</book>
```

Instead of the **instock** attribute having a value of "Yes" or "No" as per the schema, it is "true." Recall that this error is not one that we track and therefore the document should be rejected with additional processing. The following is the command line and the result:

```
java oracle.xml.pipeline.controller.orapipe -sequential -force
 -attr source xml/book2.xml -attr Lschema xsd/book_local.xsd
-attr Rschema xsd/book_remote.xsd pipeline/pipeProcessing_3.xml

XML document rejected.
```

Processing a Document That Is Valid Against the Remote Schema

This section considers the situation in which a partner has altered its schema but without your knowledge. In this case, the partner has decided that the **<edition>** element could be optional and has changed **minOccurs="1"** to **minOccurs="0"**. Now you have received **book3.xml** with the following listing:

```
<?xml version="1.0"?>
<book inStock="Yes">
  <title>Compilers: Principles, Techniques, and Tools</title>
  <author>Alfred V.Aho, Ravi Sethi, Jeffrey D. Ullman</author>
  <ISBN>0-201-10088-6</ISBN>
  <publisher>Addison Wesley</publisher>
</book>
```

The initial validation against the local XML schema should fail with an **errid** of 24534, indicating that there is an XSD error. This causes the remote XML schema to be retrieved and compared with the local XML schema. If the XML document is valid against the remote XSD, changes found in the remote XML schema will be noted and the XML document will be finally accepted, as shown in the following command line and its result:

```
java oracle.xml.pipeline.controller.orapipe -sequential -force
 -attr source xml/book3.xml -attr Lschema xsd/book_local.xsd
 -attr Rschema xsd/book_remote.xsd pipeline/pipeProcessing_3.xml

XSD documents are not consistent.
Please upload the new XSD file.
XML document accepted.
```

Processing an Invalid XML Document with Consistent Local and Remote XSDs

If the invalidating error happens to return one of the watched numbers, there is a chance that the remote schema has not changed and thus it was simply an error in the input XML document. This case triggers a comparison between the two schemas as well as a second validation, but ultimately the XML document or, in this case, **book4.xml** will be rejected, as shown in the following command line and result:

```
java oracle.xml.pipeline.controller.orapipe -sequential -force -attr source
xml/book4.xml -attr Lschema xsd/book_local.xsd -attr Rschema xsd/book_remote_
same.xsd pipeline/pipeProcessing_3.xml

XSD documents are consistent.
XML document rejected.
```

Processing an Invalid Document Against Both Schemas with Change

In this final case, the invalidating error again returns one of the watched numbers, and a check of the schemas detected a difference. However, in this case, the second validation failed, as shown in the following:

```
java oracle.xml.pipeline.controller.orapipe -sequential -force -attr source
xml/book4.xml -attr Lschema xsd/book_local.xsd -attr Rschema xsd/book_remote_
same.xsd pipeline/pipeProcessing_3.xml

XSD documents are not consistent.
Please upload the new XSD file.
XML document rejected.
```

Summary

In this chapter you had the chance to build an application that was truly *XML-powered,* using the new Oracle XML Pipeline Processor. The example application was multimodal in that its logic was implemented with a combination of compiled and declarative code. While this can initially appear foreign to developers, it is not much different than JSPs, XSQL pages, ASP pages, etc. With development and support costs going up, the ability to create stable, bug-free components that can be assembled in a declarative way can yield significant efficiencies, thereby reducing time to deployment and increasing the bottom line. A particularly apt comparison is to the electronics industry at the time when the switch was made from discrete components to integrated circuits, which not only lowered costs but improved reliability.

PART IV

Oracle XML for C Developers

CHAPTER 18

Getting Started with Oracle XML and C

racle Database 10*g* includes in its default installation the Oracle XDK 10*g* C libraries and utilities. They provide portable XML functionalities that allow you to easily develop stand-alone or Oracle Call Interface (OCI) XML-enabled applications. In this chapter, we describe the various libraries and utilities, set up both the compile-time and run-time environments, and cover the basics of the configuration that is necessary to get connected to the Oracle database.

The Oracle XDK C Libraries

The Oracle XDK C components contain functionalities for reading, manipulating, transforming, and validating XML documents. All the Oracle XDK C components reside in the **ORACLE_HOME/lib** directory, and are split into the libraries described in the following sections.

libxml10.a, libxml10.so, and oraxml10.dll

In previous releases the C XML components have been in multiple libraries. In Oracle XDK 10*g*, these components have been consolidated into a single **libxml10.a** library on UNIX and an **oraxml10.dll** library on Windows.

Within **libxml10.a** are the following XML components:

- **XML parser** Checks whether an XML document is well-formed and, optionally, validates it against a DTD or XML schema. The parser can construct an object tree that can be accessed via a DOM interface or operate serially via a SAX interface.
- **XSLT processor** Provides the capability to transform an XML document according to an XSLT stylesheet and is bundled with the parser.
- **XSLT Compiler** Compiles XSL stylesheets into byte code, to be used later by the XSLT Virtual Machine (VM).
- **XSLT VM** High-performance XSLT transformation engine that accepts compiled XSL stylesheets for faster processing, using less memory than the regular XSLT engine.
- **XML Schema processor** Supports parsing and validating XML files against an XML Schema Definition (XSD) file.

While all of the XML functionality resides in these XML libraries, they do depend on two additional libraries and an optional third one as described in the following section.

libcore10.a, libcoresh10.so, and libcore10.dll

The C common run-time functions that permit Oracle code to be portable across platforms are contained in **libcore10.a** on UNIX and **libcore10.dll** on Windows. An additional library that is new in Oracle Database 10*g*, **libcoresh10.so**, supports dynamic linking on the UNIX platforms. It is also used to build **libxmlsh10.so**, which is why it is considerably smaller than **libxml10.a**.

libnls10.a and oranls10.dll

One of the advantages of the Oracle C XML implementation over others resides in its extensive internationalization support. Support for the UTF-8, UTF-16, and ISO-8859-1 character sets is provided in **libnls10.a** on UNIX and **oranls10.dll** on Windows. These libraries also depend on the environment to find their encoding and message files. The setup of the environment will be covered in a later section.

libunls10.a and oraunls10.dll

When you need support for other character sets, you also need to use **libunls10.a** on UNIX and **oraunls10.dll** on Windows. Generally, these character sets can be classified as Asian, European, or Middle Eastern language character sets. Because over 300 character sets are supported, we are not listing them here, but you can find them in Appendix A of the *Oracle Data Globalization Support Guide 10g*. As with the previous libraries, these also depend on the environment to find their encoding and message files.

Setting Up Your C XML Development Environment

While much of your environment is already set up by an Oracle Database 10*g* installation, there are several steps that are platform-specific that you need to perform to both compile and run your Oracle C XML-enabled applications.

Note that in later sections the XDK directory is referred to as **$XDK_HOME** or **%XDK_HOME%** and the Oracle Home is referred to as **$ORACLE_HOME** or **%ORACLE_HOME%**.

UNIX Setup of XDK C Components

In order to successfully run your UNIX C application, several environment variables need to be set for the various components so they can find their support files.

ORA_NLS10

The environment variable ORA_NLS10 is set to point to the location of the NLS character-encoding definition files. If you have installed Oracle Database 10*g*, then you can set it as follows:

```
setenv ORA_NLS10 ${ORACLE_HOME}/nls/data
```

If you don't have an Oracle database installed, you can use the NLS character-encoding definition files that come with the OTN Oracle XDK release, as follows:

```
setenv ORA_NLS10 ${XDK_HOME}/nls/data
```

NOTE
The XDK-included encoding files contain a subset of the character sets that are in the Oracle database release. While it contains only 34 character-encoding files, they are the most common ones.

ORA_XML_MESG

The environment variable ORA_XML_MESG is set to point to the location of the XML error message files. These files are provided in the **xdk/mesg/** directory. Files ending in **.msb** are machine-readable and needed at runtime; files ending in **.msg** are human-readable and include cause and action descriptions for each error. For Oracle database installations, these message files exist in the **$ORACLE_HOME/xdk/mesg** directory and no environment variable is necessary. If no Oracle database is installed, you should set the environment variable ORA_XML_MESG to point to the absolute path of the **xdk/mesg/** directory:

```
setenv ORA_XML_MESG ${XDK_HOME}/xdk/mesg
```

Checking Your C Run-Time Environment

Several ready-to-run XML utilities are included in Oracle XDK 10*g*. These make it easy for you to confirm that your run-time environment is properly configured. They all reside in **$ORACLE_HOME/bin** for Oracle database installations and **$XDK_HOME/bin** for OTN XDK installations. The following sections describe these XML utilities along with their command-line options.

xml

The C XML parser may be called as an executable by invoking **xml** from your **$ORACLE_HOME/bin** or **$XDK_HOME/bin** as follows:

```
xml options URI
```

The following is the list of options:

- **-c** Perform conformance check only, no validation
- **-e** *encoding* Specify default input file encoding ("incoding")
- **-E** *encoding* Specify DOM/SAX encoding ("outcoding")
- **-f** *file* Interpret as filespec, not as URI
- **-l** *language* Specify language for error reporting
- **-n** *number* Perform DOM traversal and report number of elements
- **-p** Print document after parsing it
- **-v** Display parser version then exit
- **-w** Preserve all white spaces
- **-W** Stop parsing after a warning
- **-x** Exercise SAX interface and print document

xsl

The C XSLT processor may be called as an executable by invoking **bin/xsl** as follows:

```
xsl options URI
```

The following is the list of options:

- **-f** *file* Interpret as filespec, not as URI
- **-h** Show usage help and full list of flags
- **-i** *n* Specify number of times to iterate the XSLT processing
- **-l** *language* Specify language for error reporting
- **-o** *XSL outfile* Specify output file of XSLT processor
- **-r** Do not ignore <xsl:output> instruction in XSLT processing
- **-s** *stylesheet* Specify the XSL stylesheet
- **-v** Display XSLT processor version then exit
- **-V** *var value* Test top-level variables in C XSLT

schema

The Schema Validator may be called as an executable by invoking **bin/schema**, which takes two arguments: the XML instance document and, optionally, a default schema to apply:

```
schema options document schema
```

The following is the list of options:

- **-0** Always exit with code 0 (success)
- **-e** *encoding* Specify default input file encoding ("incoding")
- **-E** *encoding* Specify output/data/presentation encoding ("outcoding")
- **-i** Ignore provided schema file
- **-o** *num* Specify validation options
- **-p** Print instance document to standard output on success
- **-u** Force the Unicode code path
- **-v** Display version and then exit

Setting Up Your C Compile-Time Environment

To compile your code, you need to have the run-time environment set up and you need to have the header files for the components that you are using. These header files reside in the **xdk/include** directory in either installation. The following is a listing of each and its corresponding description:

- **oratypes.h** Includes all the private Oracle C data types independent of XML.
- **oraxml.h** Includes all the Oracle9*i* XML ORA data types and all the public ORA APIs in **libxml**. This is for backward compatibility only.
- **oraxmlcg.h** Includes the C APIs for the C++ Class Generator.
- **oraxsd.h** Includes the Oracle9*i* XSD validator data types and APIs. This is for backward compatibility only.
- **xml.h** Is the header to handle the Unified DOM APIs transparently, whether using OCI or standalone.
- **xmlerr.h** Includes the XML errors and their numbers.
- **xmlotn.h** Includes all the other headers based upon whether you are compiling standalone or using OCI and the Unified DOM.
- **xmlproc.h** Includes all the Oracle 10*g* XML data types and XML public parser APIs in **libxml10**.
- **xmlsch.h** Includes all the Oracle 10*g* XSD validator public APIs.
- **xmlptr.h** Includes all the XPointer data types and APIs. These are not currently documented or supported.
- **xmlxsl.h** Includes all the XSLT processor data types and public APIs.
- **xmlxvm.h** Includes all the XSLT compiler and VM data types and public APIs.

Confirming Your C Compile-Time Environment

You can confirm your setup by compiling the demo programs, by using **makefile** in the **$XDK_HOME/xdk/demo** directory of the OTN release. The demos are not shipped with the Oracle Database 10*g* CD but are on the Companion CD and will be in the **$ORACLE_HOME/xdk/demo** directory once installed.

Windows Setup of XDK C Components

In order to successfully run your Windows C application, several environment variables need to be set for the various components so they can find their support files.

ORA_NLS10

The environment variable ORA_NLS10 is set to point to the location of the NLS character-encoding definition files. If you have installed Oracle Database 10*g* (and assuming that the variable **ORACLE_HOME** has been set), then you can set it as follows:

```
set ORA_NLS10 %ORACLE_HOME%\nls\data
```

If you don't have an Oracle database installed, after setting a variable called **XDK_HOME**, you can use the NLS character-encoding definition files that come with the OTN Oracle XDK release as follows:

```
set ORA_NLS10 %XDK_HOME%\nls\data
```

NOTE
The XDK-included encoding files contain a subset of the character sets that are in the Oracle database release. While it contains only 34 character-encoding files, they are the most common ones.

ORA_XML_MESG

The environment variable ORA_XML_MESG is set to point to the location of the XML error message files. These files are provided in the **xdk\mesg** directory. Files ending in **.msb** are machine-readable and needed at runtime; files ending in **.msg** are human-readable and include cause and action descriptions for each error. For Oracle database installations, these message files exist in the **$ORACLE_HOME\xdk\mesg** directory and no environment variable is necessary. If no Oracle database is installed, you should set the environment variable, ORA_XML_MESG, to point to the absolute path of the **xdk\mesg** directory:

```
set ORA_XML_MESG %XDK_HOME%\xdk\mesg
```

Checking Your C Run-Time Environment

Several ready-to-run XML utilities are included in Oracle XDK 10*g*. They help you to make sure that your run-time environment is properly configured. They all reside in **%ORACLE_HOME%\bin** for Oracle database installations and **%XDK_HOME%\bin** for OTN XDK installations. The following sections describe these XML utilities. Their command-line options are the same as in the previous UNIX section.

xml.exe

The C XML parser may be called as an executable by invoking **xml.exe** in the **bin** directory as follows:

```
xml.exe options URI
```

xsl.exe

The C XSLT processor may be called as an executable by invoking **xsl.exe** in the **bin** directory as follows:

```
xsl.exe options URI
```

schema.exe

The Schema Validator may be called as an executable by invoking **schema.exe in the bin** directory, which takes two arguments: the XML instance document and, optionally, a default schema to apply:

```
schema options document schema
```

Setting Up Your C Compile-Time Environment

To compile your code, you need to have the run-time environment set up and you need to have the header files for the components that you are using. These header files reside in the **xdk\include** directory in either installation. These are the same files as described in the previous UNIX section.

Confirming Your C Compile-Time Environment

You can confirm your setup by compiling the demo programs, by using **make.bat** in the **%XDK_HOME%\xdk\demo** directory of the OTN release only. The demos are not shipped with the Oracle Database 10*g* release. The make file assumes you are using **cl.exe** and that you have it in your PATH. You also have to edit **make.bat** to provide the paths to the header files as well as the corresponding **.lib** files located in **%ORACLE_HOME%\lib** or **%XDK_HOME%\lib**.

Setting Up Microsoft Visual C/C++

Because much of the Windows C development is done using Microsoft Visual C/C++, we will show you how to set up a project and its settings for the applications covered in the later chapters. These instructions can also be used for the demos that are included in Oracle XDK 10*g*. These instructions assume Microsoft Visual C/C++ version 6.0a is compatible.

Creating a New Project

Projects need to be attached to workspaces; therefore, if you don't already have one that you would like to use, you will need to create a blank one. You do so by clicking File I New I Workspaces and entering a name, after which you can click the now activated OK button to give you a new workspace.

To add a project to this new workspace or to an existing one, you need to click File I NewI Projects at which point you will see the screen shown in Figure 18-1. For the applications in this book as well as the Oracle XDK 10*g* demos, you need to select Win32 Console Application and enter the name of your project. In Figure 18-1, this is **CXMLApp**.

NOTE
This name will be used as the one for your executable unless you specify an alternate debug executable under the Project Settings / Link / General category.

Once you click OK, you will be asked the kind of console application you wish to create. You can select an empty project and click Finish. This will add your new project to your workspace in the FileView pane.

Configuring Your Project

Once you have created a project, you can then configure its settings. This is done by right-clicking the project name, selecting Settings, and then clicking C/C++ in the Project Settings window that appears. You'll find numerous settings here, but, as you can see in Figure 18-2, you can keep them in their default configuration with or without Debug optimizations.

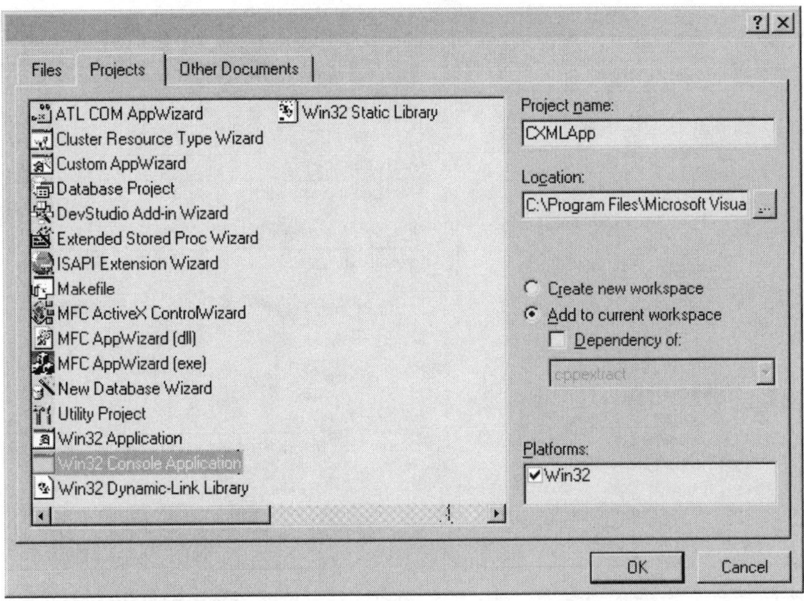

FIGURE 18-1. *New Projects window*

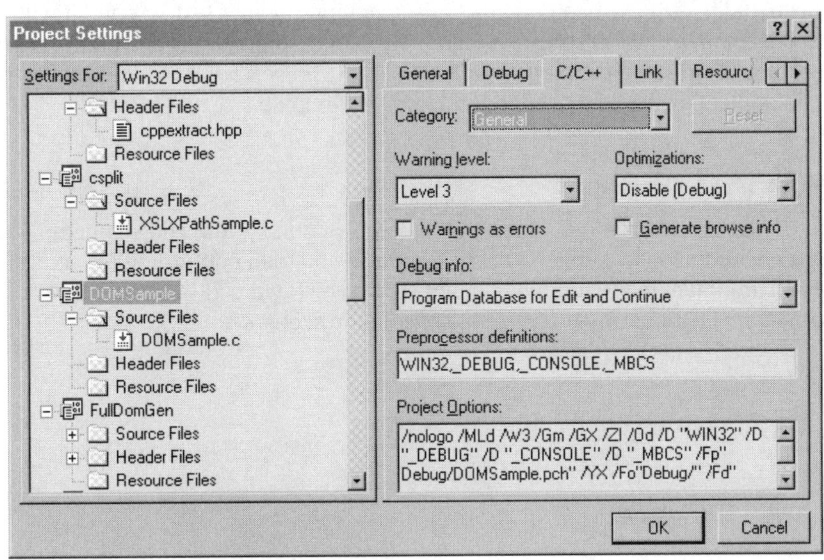

FIGURE 18-2. *Project Settings: C/C++ window*

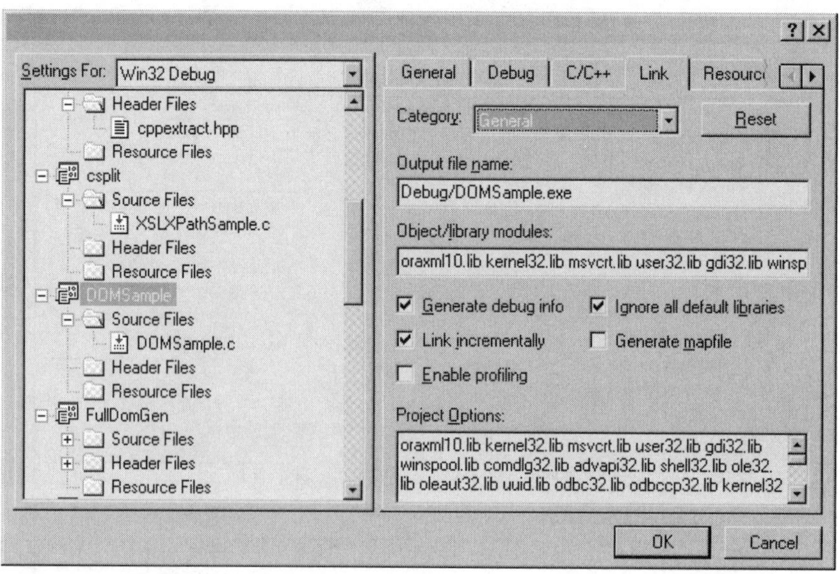

FIGURE 18-3. *Project Settings: Link window*

At this point you can set up your link configuration by selecting the Link tab in the Project Settings window. You will then see the window shown in Figure 18-3.

Add **oraxml10.lib** as the first entry in the Object/Library Modules text box and it will be added to your link line automatically as shown in Figure 18-3. At runtime you will need the **oraxml10.dll**, **oracore10.dll**, and **oranls10.dll** to be in your PATH for the objects to be found. You can now click OK and begin populating the Source Files and Header Files folders.

Summary

In this chapter, we have walked you through the basics of configuring and setting up your XDK C development environment for either UNIX or Windows and then confirming proper setup. You will use this environment in the following chapters, in which we will show you how to build real C XML-enabled applications covering a range of solution scenarios.

CHAPTER 19

Building an XML-Managed Application

any software applications, from servers to simple client applications, use configuration files to set up their environment, run-time options, look and feel, and other persisted conditions and options. In the past these files have usually been simply a collection of name-value pairs with specified delimiters. It turns out that this format suffers significant limitations. For example, it is a very fragile format, because misplacement of a single character may invalidate every subsequent entry. Also, there is no random access to this type of format, so if you want a single bit of information, it has to be processed linearly until the data appears. Finally, a flat list of pairs may not be sufficient to support the required semantics. For these reasons and more, these flat files are being replaced by XML files, which eliminate or mitigate these issues.

In this chapter, you will build a C XML application that is configured by an XML file. The scenario is a simple one that is easily extensible and involves publishing XML content to a variety of devices by using XSLT and the XML configuration file to specify the stylesheets and profiles that control the transformations.

Designing the Framework

For this example, you are going to build a media catalog application, called **publishcat**, for a fictitious company that brokers the sale of books, CDs, and DVDs. It receives its catalogs in XML and must publish them in a way that optimizes their presentation on a variety of devices, such as PCs, PDAs, and cell phones. You could implement this by using a custom-built stylesheet for each device; however, you can use a single stylesheet and have the device profile passed in as parameters read from an XML configuration file. This is the approach we will examine and implement.

To build this application, you will need the XML-formatted catalog entries for books, CDs, and DVDs. Since each of these media types has differing semantics for its description, and thus different DTDs, you will have a different stylesheet for each. The configuration file will also have a schema that contains not only the XSL stylesheets to be applied to each type but also the three profiles and their elements. To optimize the display characteristics, you will need to specify the following parameters when applying the stylesheet:

- **Character Set** The proper character encoding for the device
- **OutputFileType** The markup language to use for the display
- **LinesPerPage** The number of lines to display per screen page
- **Graphics** An option to display graphics
- **Color Depth** The number of colors supported to display the best graphics

Because these parameters are numerous and a mixture of data types, instead of passing each one in on the command line, you will group them as named profiles that the application can read from the configuration file.

The **publishcat** application will be a command-line application that functionally performs the following steps to produce the appropriate output from a set of XML input files:

1. Parses the command line.
2. Validates and creates a DOM from the input XML media documents.
3. Retrieves the schema URL for each DOM.
4. Parses **XSLConfig.xml** using SAX.
5. Retrieves XSLT Stylesheet and profile parameters.
6. Performs XSLT transformation on the DOMs passing the profile parameters to the stylesheet.
7. Serializes the result to the specified output file. If no output file is specified, it prints to the screen.
8. Cleans up and terminates.

Each of these steps will be discussed and implemented in the following sections.

The XML Media Files

To illustrate this use case, it is sufficient to use simple XML data files for the catalogs of the different media types. These files could be based upon either DTDs or XML schemas. In this case we chose to use DTDs as most of this type of content is based on DTDs and there are no datatypes used beyond strings that would benefit from an XML Schema data model.

Even though each book, CD, and DVD listing has common components, since you will be using the DOCTYPE value to differentiate the type of processing, we have chosen to create three DTDs:

bookcatalog.dtd

```
<?xml version="1.0" encoding="UTF-8"?>
<!ELEMENT color64K (#PCDATA)>
<!ATTLIST color64K URL ENTITY #REQUIRED>
<!ELEMENT color256 (#PCDATA)>
<!ATTLIST color256 URL ENTITY #REQUIRED>
<!ELEMENT color16 (#PCDATA)>
<!ATTLIST color16 URL ENTITY #REQUIRED>
<!ELEMENT graphics (color256 | color16 | color64K)>
<!ELEMENT price (#PCDATA)>
<!ELEMENT publisher (#PCDATA)>
<!ELEMENT year (#PCDATA)>
<!ELEMENT ISBN (#PCDATA)>
<!ELEMENT title (#PCDATA)>
<!ELEMENT author_lastname (#PCDATA)>
<!ELEMENT publisher (#PCDATA)>
<!ELEMENT book (ISBN,  title, author_lastname, publisher,
       year, graphics, price )>
<!ELEMENT Bookcatalog (book+)>
```

cdcatalog.dtd

```
<?xml version="1.0" encoding="UTF-8"?>
<!ELEMENT color64K (#PCDATA)>
<!ATTLIST color64K URL ENTITY #REQUIRED>
<!ELEMENT color256 (#PCDATA)>
<!ATTLIST color256 URL ENTITY #REQUIRED>
<!ELEMENT color16 (#PCDATA)>
<!ATTLIST color16 URL ENTITY #REQUIRED>
<!ELEMENT graphics (color256 | color16 | color64K)>
<!ELEMENT ISBN (#PCDATA)>
<!ELEMENT title (#PCDATA)>
<!ELEMENT artist_lastname (#PCDATA)>
<!ELEMENT producer (#PCDATA)>
<!ELEMENT price (#PCDATA)>
<!ELEMENT cd (ISBN, title, artist_lastname, producer,
       year, graphics, price )>
<!ELEMENT CDcatalog (cd+)>
```

dvdcatalog.dtd

```
<?xml version="1.0" encoding="UTF-8"?>
<!ELEMENT color64K (#PCDATA)>
<!ATTLIST color64K URL ENTITY #REQUIRED>
<!ELEMENT color256 (#PCDATA)>
<!ATTLIST color256 URL ENTITY #REQUIRED>
<!ELEMENT color16 (#PCDATA)>
<!ATTLIST color16 URL ENTITY #REQUIRED>
<!ELEMENT graphics (color256 | color16 | color64K)>
<!ELEMENT ISBN (#PCDATA)>
<!ELEMENT title (#PCDATA)>
<!ELEMENT director_lastname (#PCDATA)>
<!ELEMENT studio (#PCDATA)>
<!ELEMENT price (#PCDATA)>
<!ELEMENT dvd (ISBN,  title, director_lastname, studio, year,
       graphics, price )>
<!ELEMENT DVDcatalog (dvd+)>
```

Note that each book, CD, and DVD catalog element has a plus appended to indicate that there needs to be one or more records for the input files to be valid. Also, we are using the element content for each graphic for its name and an attribute of type ENTITY to point to its location.

Creating an XML Configuration File

You need to create a configuration file format that can contain all the parameterized information that will be needed at runtime to produce the proper result. Since this file is an integral part of the application and is designed to be updated, it needs to be validated and thus should have a DTD or XML schema. For this application, we will use an XML schema. The following is the XML schema derived from the requirements, which is divided into two parts for ease of discussion.

Defining the XSLT Stylesheets

The configuration XML schema file is called **XSLConfig.xsd** and initially defines the stylesheets used in your application:

```
<?xml version="1.0"?>
<xsd:schema xmlns:xsd="http://www.w3.org/2001/XMLSchema"
   xmlns:xsi="http://www.w3.org/2001/XMLSchema-instance">
<xsd:element name="Styles">
 <xsd:complexType>
   <xsd:sequence>
    <xsd:element name="Stylesheets" type="Stylesheets"/>
    <xsd:element name="Profiles" type="Profiles" maxOccurs="unbounded"/>
   </xsd:sequence>
  </xsd:complexType>
 </xsd:element>
<!-- Define Stylesheets Type made up of Books, CDs, and DVDs -->
 <xsd:complexType name="Stylesheets">
  <xsd:sequence maxOccurs="unbounded">
   <xsd:element name="Books">
    <xsd:complexType>
     <xsd:sequence>
      <xsd:element name="bookxsl" maxOccurs="unbounded">
       <xsd:complexType>
        <xsd:simpleContent>
         <xsd:extension base="xsd:string">
          <xsd:attribute name="dtd" type="xsd:string"/>
         </xsd:extension>
        </xsd:simpleContent>
       </xsd:complexType>
      </xsd:element>
     </xsd:sequence>
    </xsd:complexType>
   </xsd:element>
   <xsd:element name="CDs">
    <xsd:complexType>
     <xsd:sequence>
      <xsd:element name="cdxsl" maxOccurs="unbounded">
       <xsd:complexType>
        <xsd:simpleContent>
         <xsd:extension base="xsd:string">
          <xsd:attribute name="dtd" type="xsd:string"/>
         </xsd:extension>
        </xsd:simpleContent>
       </xsd:complexType>
      </xsd:element>
     </xsd:sequence>
    </xsd:complexType>
   </xsd:element>
   <xsd:element name="DVDs">
    <xsd:complexType>
```

```
      <xsd:sequence>
       <xsd:element name="dvdxsl" maxOccurs="unbounded">
        <xsd:complexType>
         <xsd:simpleContent>
          <xsd:extension base="xsd:string">
           <xsd:attribute name="dtd" type="xsd:string"/>
          </xsd:extension>
         </xsd:simpleContent>
        </xsd:complexType>
       </xsd:element>
      </xsd:sequence>
     </xsd:complexType>
    </xsd:element>
   </xsd:sequence>
  </xsd:complexType>
```

This first section defines the root element to be **<Styles>** and its child elements to be **<Stylesheets>** and **<Profiles>** elements of the corresponding types. It then defines the **Stylesheets** type to contain **<Books>**, **<CDs>**, and **<DVDs>** elements, which contain their respective **<bookxsl>**, **<cdxsl>**, and **<dvdxsl>** elements. These *xsl elements specify the stylesheets to apply when the corresponding DTDs are retrieved from the DOCTYPE of the input XML document. Note that more than one *xsl element can be specified for each media type and that more media types can be added because of the presence of the **maxOccurs= "unbounded"** attribute on the **<xsd:sequence>** elements. The following is a conformant and valid **Stylesheets** instance XML fragment:

```
<Stylesheets>
 <Books>
  <bookxsl dtd="bookcatalog.dtd">booklist.xsl</bookxsl>
 </Books>
 <CDs>
  <cdxsl dtd="cdcatalog.dtd">cdlist.xsl</cdxsl>
 </CDs>
 <DVDs>
  <dvdxsl dtd="dvdcatalog.dtd">dvdlist.xsl</dvdxsl>
 </DVDs>
</Stylesheets>
```

The application will retrieve the DOCTYPE DTD declaration and execute the matching XSL stylesheet.

Defining the Profiles

The second section of **XSLConfig.xsd** defines the profiles for each device's parameter set as of type **Profileset**. In this case, we are defining one for **PC**, **PDA**, and **PHONE**.

```
<xsd:element name="Profileset" type="Profileset"/>
 <xsd:complexType name="Profiles">
  <xsd:choice maxOccurs="unbounded">
   <xsd:element name="PC" type="Profileset"/>
```

```
   <xsd:element name="PDA" type="Profileset"/>
   <xsd:element name="PHONE" type="Profileset"/>
  </xsd:choice>
 </xsd:complexType>
 <xsd:complexType name="Profileset">
  <xsd:sequence>
   <xsd:element name="CharacterSet" type="CharacterSetType"/>
   <xsd:element name="OutputFileType" type="OutputFileTypeType"/>
   <xsd:element name="Graphics" type="OnOffType"/>
   <xsd:element name="ColorDepth" type="ColorDepthType"/>
  </xsd:sequence>
 </xsd:complexType>
 <xsd:simpleType name="ColorDepthType">
  <xsd:restriction base="xsd:string">
   <xsd:enumeration value="16"/>
   <xsd:enumeration value="256"/>
   <xsd:enumeration value="64K"/>
  </xsd:restriction>
 </xsd:simpleType>
 <xsd:simpleType name="OnOffType">
  <xsd:restriction base="xsd:string">
   <xsd:enumeration value="ON"/>
   <xsd:enumeration value="OFF"/>
  </xsd:restriction>
 </xsd:simpleType>
 <xsd:simpleType name="CharacterSetType">
  <xsd:restriction base="xsd:string">
   <xsd:enumeration value="UTF-8"/>
   <xsd:enumeration value="8859-1"/>
   <xsd:enumeration value="US-ASCII"/>
  </xsd:restriction>
 </xsd:simpleType>
 <xsd:simpleType name="OutputFileTypeType">
  <xsd:restriction base="xsd:string">
   <xsd:enumeration value="WML"/>
   <xsd:enumeration value="HTML"/>
  </xsd:restriction>
 </xsd:simpleType>
</xsd:schema>
```

Note that instead of using **<xsd:sequence>** to specify the named profiles, as we did with the different media types, we used **<xsd:choice>**. The distinction is that a valid configuration file must be able to transform all of the specified types; however, it needs to optimize the output only for one or more devices. Obviously, this is an option that you can eliminate by using **<xsd:sequence>** instead.

Also note that the **Profileset** type is made up of element types that use enumerations to further restrict their content. This means that only those values specified are legal.

Finally, there are two other options of note in the second section of **XSLConfig.xsd**. The first is the definition of **OnOffType** as a restriction of **xsd:string**. As we are using "ON" and "OFF" as the values for better semantic understanding, we chose to restrict to a string enumeration.

You could also select a Boolean, should you wish to instead have TRUE/FALSE or 1/0 as the values. A similar option holds true for **LinesPerPage** type; however, in this case we are enumerating over actual numerical values. In the case of XSLT 1.0, these will be implicitly cast anyway.

The following is a conformant and valid **Profiles** XML instance section from an **XSLConfig.xml** file:

```
<Profiles>
  <PC>
   <CharacterSet>UTF-8</CharacterSet>
   <OutputFileType>HTML</OutputFileType>
   <Graphics>ON</Graphics>
   <ColorDepth>64K</ColorDepth>
  </PC>
  <PDA>
   <CharacterSet>US-ASCII</CharacterSet>
   <OutputFileType>HTML</OutputFileType>
   <Graphics>ON</Graphics>
   <ColorDepth>256</ColorDepth>
  </PDA>
  <PHONE>
   <CharacterSet>8859-1</CharacterSet>
   <OutputFileType>WML</OutputFileType>
   <Graphics>OFF</Graphics>
   <ColorDepth>16</ColorDepth>
  </PHONE>
 </Profiles>
```

The application will retrieve these parameters along with the stylesheets using the SAX parser because there is no need to build a DOM of the configuration document, as you are not altering it.

The following is an example **dvdlist.xml** instance document:

```
<?xml version="1.0" encoding="UTF-8" standalone="no"?>
<!DOCTYPE DVDcatalog SYSTEM "dvdcatalog.dtd">
<DVDcatalog>
 <dvd>
  <ISBN>2222</ISBN>
  <title>Titanic</title>
  <director_lastname>Cameron</director_lastname>
  <studio>MGM</studio>
  <year>2003</year>
  <graphics>
   <color64K URL="http:/pictures.foo.com/64K/2222.jpg">
      Don Quixote Cover</color64K>
   <color256 URL="http:/pictures.foo.com/256/2222.jpg">
      Don Quixote Cover</color256>
   <color16 URL="http:/pictures.foo.com/16/2222.jpg">
      Don Quixote Cover</color16>
  </graphics>
  <price>9.99</price>
 </dvd>
</DVDcatalog>
```

Creating the XSL Stylesheets

It is now time to turn to the stylesheet that will be used to produce HTML or WML pages based upon the specific device. We will examine the stylesheet for DVDs; however, the book and CD stylesheets are the same except for the names of a few elements. Because this is a complex stylesheet, we will discuss each template.

The following section is where the parameter values are passed into the stylesheet. In this case, we use the optional **select="value"** attribute to set a default value if a parameter is missing. This is also an effective way to debug a stylesheet that uses a variety of parameter values.

```
<?xml version="1.0" encoding="UTF-8"?>
<xsl:stylesheet version="1.0" xmlns:xsl=
       "http://www.w3.org/1999/XSL/Transform">

<xsl:param name="Graphics" select="'ON'"/>
<xsl:param name="ColorDepth" select="'16'"/>
<xsl:param name="Profile" select="'PC'"/>
```

The following **xsl:choose** section handles the setting of the character set and the output file type since this cannot be done within a template in XSLT 1.0. It chooses between inserting the HTML and WML DOCTYPE declarations as well as the specific output encoding, which in this case is UTF-8, based upon the active **Profile**.

```
<xsl:choose>
 <xsl:when select="$Profile='PC'">
    <xsl:output encoding="UTF-8" method="HTML"/>
 </xsl:when>
 <xsl:otherwise>
   <xsl:choose>
    <xsl:when test="$Profile='PHONE'">
     <xsl:output encoding="UTF-8" method="XML"
          doctype-public="-//WAPFORUM//DTD WML 1.1//EN"
          doctype-system="http://www.wapforum.org/DTD/wml_1.1.xml"/>
    </xsl:when>
    <xsl:otherwise>
     <xsl:output encoding="UTF-8" method="HTML"/>
    </xsl:otherwise>
  </xsl:choose>
 </xsl:otherwise>
</xsl:choose>
```

The following mode template allows you to control execution based upon the **Profile** passed in and sets the basis for executing the following mode-specific templates:

```
<xsl:template match="/">
 <xsl:if test="$Profile='PC'">
   <xsl:apply-templates mode="PC" select="/" />
 </xsl:if>
 <xsl:if test="$Profile='PDA'">
```

```
    <xsl:apply-templates mode="PC" select="/" />
  </xsl:if>
  <xsl:if test="$Profile='PHONE'">
    <xsl:apply-templates mode="PHONE" select="/" />
  </xsl:if>
</xsl:template>
```

The following is the template that is executed if the mode is **PC** or **PDA** and uses the corresponding mode parameters to configure the display for **Graphics** and **ColorDepth**. Note that the images are differentiated by different paths in the HREF attribute, which is created from the **URL** attribute in the input XML document.

```
<xsl:template match="DVDcatalog" mode="PC | PDA">
 <html>
  <body>
    <table>
     <tr>
     <th>ISBN</th>
     <td>Title</td>
     <td>Director</td>
     <td>Studio</td>
     <td>Year</td>
     <xsl:if test="$Graphics='ON'">
       <td>Picture</td>
     </xsl:if>
     <td>Price</td>
    </tr>
    <xsl:for-each select="dvd">
     <tr>
      <td><xsl:value-of select="ISBN"/></td>
      <td><xsl:value-of select="title"/></td>
      <td><xsl:value-of select="director_lastname"/></td>
      <td><xsl:value-of select="studio"/></td>
      <td><xsl:value-of select="year"/></td>
      <xsl:if test="$Graphics='ON'">
      <td>
        <xsl:if test="$ColorDepth = 16">
          <img href="{graphics/color16/@URL}"/>
        </xsl:if>
        <xsl:if test="$ColorDepth = 64">
          <img href="{graphics/color64K/@URL}"/>
        </xsl:if>
       </td>
      </xsl:if>
      <td><xsl:value-of select="price"/></td>
     </tr>
    </xsl:for-each>
    </table>
  </body>
 </html>
</xsl:template>
```

This final template produces the WML output for the **PHONE** mode. Since for our example this mode does not support graphics, you don't have to handle them within the template. Figure 19-1 shows an example of the output on a phone.

```
<xsl:template match="DVDcatalog" mode="PHONE">
 <wml>
   <card>
  <xsl:for-each select="dvd">
   <p>
  ISBN: <xsl:value-of select="ISBN"/><br/>
  Title: <xsl:value-of select="title"/><br/>
  Director: <xsl:value-of select="director_lastname"/><br/>
  Studio: <xsl:value-of select="studio"/><br/>
  Year: <xsl:value-of select="year"/><br/>
  Price: <xsl:value-of select="price"/><br/>
   </p>
   </xsl:for-each>
   </card>
   </wml>
 </xsl:template>
</xsl:stylesheet>
```

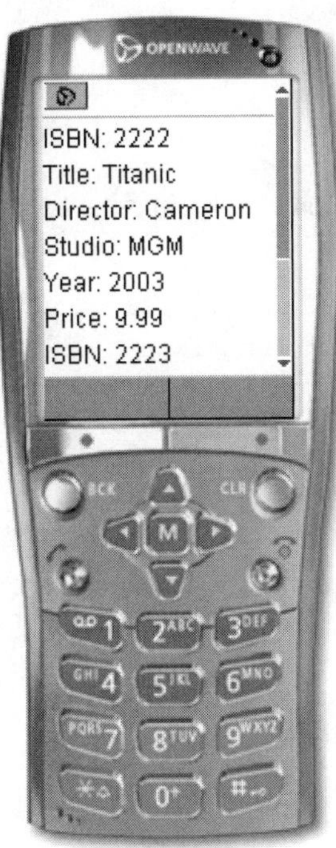

FIGURE 19-1. *DVD listing on WML phone*

Creating the publishcat Application

Now that we have explained all of the supporting files, we can discuss the **publishcat** application itself. It uses the C SAX parser to read the **XSLConfig.xml** file and the DOM parser to prepare the input document for stylesheet transformation that is done with the XSLT processor.

This section declares the header files and sets up a global structure to hold the profile parameters that will be retrieved from the configuration file:

```
#include <stdio.h>
#include <string.h>
#include <stdlib.h>

#ifndef XML_ORACLE
# include <xml.h>
#endif

typedef struct {
    xmlctx   *xctx;
    oratext *sskeyword;
    size_t   sskeylen;
    oratext *elem;
    oratext  characterset[80];
    oratext  outputfile[80];
    oratext  graphics[80];
    oratext  colordepth[80];
    oratext  stylesheets[80];
    oratext  profiles[80];
} saxctx;
```

The **findsub()** support function is used to handle the SAX character events that we are not interested in:

```
/*-----------------------------------------------------
                        support functions
-----------------------------------------------------*/
static oratext *findsub(oratext *buf, size_t bufsiz,
                        oratext *sub, size_t subsiz)
{
    uword i;

    if (!buf || !bufsiz || (subsiz > bufsiz))
        return NULL;
    if (!sub || !subsiz)
        return buf;
    for (i = 0; i < bufsiz - subsiz; i++, buf++)
    {
        if (!memcmp(buf, sub, subsiz))
            return buf;
    }
    return NULL;
}
```

The following is the SAX callback section in which you declare the content handlers for the SAX event stream. Note that you need to handle expected content types, which in this case are **startDocument**, **endDocument**, **startElement**, **endElement**, and **characters**.

```
/* ------------------------------------------
                              SAX callbacks
------------------------------------------*/

static XMLSAX_START_DOC_F(startDocument, ctx)
{
    return 0;
}

static XMLSAX_END_DOC_F(endDocument, ctx)
{
    return 0;
}

static XMLSAX_START_ELEM_F(startElement, ctx, name, attrs)
{
    ((saxctx *) ctx)->elem = name;
    return 0;
}

static XMLSAX_END_ELEM_F(endElement, ctx, name)
{
    ((saxctx *) ctx)->elem = (oratext *) "";
    return 0;
}

static XMLSAX_CHARACTERS_F(characters, ctx, ch, len)
{
    saxctx *sc = (saxctx *) ctx;

    if (!strcmp((char *) sc->elem, "Stylesheets"))
    {
        memcpy(sc->stylesheets, ch, len);   /* set current ss */
        sc->stylesheets[len] = 0;
    }
    else if (!strcmp((char *)sc->elem, "Profiles"))
    {
        memcpy(sc->profiles, ch, len);   /* set current profiles */
        sc->profiles[len] = 0;
    }
    else if (!strcmp((char *)sc->elem, "CharacterSet"))
    {
        memcpy(sc->characterset, ch, len);
        sc->characterset[len] = 0;
    }
    else if (!strcmp((char *)sc->elem, "OutputFileType"))
```

```
    {
        memcpy(sc->outputfile, ch, len);
        sc->outputfile[len] = 0;
    }
    else if (!strcmp((char *)sc->elem, "Graphics"))
    {
        memcpy(sc->graphics, ch, len);
        sc->graphics[len] = 0;
    }
    else if (!strcmp((char *)sc->elem, "ColorDepth"))
    {
        memcpy(sc->colordepth, ch, len);
        sc->colordepth[len] = 0;
    }
    else if (!strcmp((char *)sc->elem, "LinesPerPage"))
    {
        memcpy(sc->linesperpage, ch, len);
        sc->linesperpage[len] = 0;
    }
    else if (findsub((oratext *) ch, len, sc->sskeyword, sc->sskeylen))
    return 0;
}

static xmlsaxcb saxcb = {
    startDocument,
    endDocument,
    startElement,
    endElement,
    characters
};
```

The following is the main function of **publishcat** that initially processes the command-line parameters by assigning them to variables. The code is commented to describe its flow.

```
/*--------------Main function ---------------*/
int main(int argc, char *argv[])
{
    xmlctx      *xctx = NULL;
    xslctx      *xslx = NULL;
    saxctx      sc;
    xmlerr      err;
    oratext     *xmlfile, *outfile, *xslconfigFile, *xslfile, *schemaURL;
    xmldocnode  *doc = NULL, *ss_doc = NULL;

    if (argc < 4) {
     printf("\nUsage error: publishcat -h -i<inputXML> -o<outputFile>
        -p<XSLConfig.xml>\n\
     \n - h show commandline and parameters \n\
     \n - i input XML \n\
```

```
 \n - o output file (extension optional as it will use default
       for format)\n\
 \n - p profile (defined in XSLConfig.xml)\n\n");
  return 0;
}

xmlfile = (oratext *)argv[2];
xmlfile = xmlfile+2;
outfile = (oratext *)argv[3];
outfile = outfile+2;

xslconfigFile = (oratext *)argv[4];
xslconfigFile = xslconfigFile + 2;

/* Creates the context */
if (!(xctx = XmlCreate(&err, (oratext *)"xslsample_xctx", NULL)))
{
    printf("Failed to create XML context, error %u\n", (unsigned)err);
    goto terminate;
}

/* Creates the DOM and parses */
if (!(doc=XmlLoadDom(xctx, &err, "file", xmlfile,
      "validate", TRUE, "discard_whitespace", TRUE, NULL)))
{
    printf("Parse failed, code %d\n", (int)err);
    goto terminate;
}

/* Retrieves Schema URL from DOM */
schemaURL = XmlDomGetSchema(xctx, doc);

/* Init SAX context */
memset(&sc, sizeof(sc), 0);
sc.sskeyword = (oratext *)"xsl";
sc.sskeylen = strlen(sc.sskeyword);
sc.elem = (oratext *) "";

/* Parse XSLConfig.xml using SAX */
if (!(err=XmlLoadSax(xctx, &saxcb, &sc, "file", xslconfigFile,
      "validate", TRUE, "discard_whitespace", TRUE,  NULL)))
{
    printf("Parse failed, code %d\n", (int)err);
    goto terminate;
}

/* Retrieves XSL stylesheet using SAX and profile parameters */
xslfile = sc.stylesheets;
```

```
/* Parsing stylesheet */
if (!(ss_doc = XmlLoadDom(xctx, &err, "file", xslfile,
      "validate", TRUE, "discard_whitespace", TRUE, NULL)))
{
    printf("Parse failed, error %u\n", (unsigned)err);
    goto terminate;
}

/* Initialize the result context */
xslx = XmlXslCreate(xctx, ss_doc, xslfile, &err);

/* Set Profile Parameters */
if (err=XmlXslSetTextParam(xslx, (oratext *)"CharacterSet",
    sc.characterset))
{
   printf("Setting failed, error %u\n", (unsigned)err);
}

if (err=XmlXslSetTextParam(xslx, (oratext *)"OutputFileType",
     sc.outputfile))
{
   printf("Setting failed, error %u\n", (unsigned)err);
}
if (err=XmlXslSetTextParam(xslx, (oratext *)"Graphics", sc.graphics))
{
   printf("Setting failed, error %u\n", (unsigned)err);
}
if (err=XmlXslSetTextParam(xslx, (oratext *)"ColorDepth",
     sc.colordepth))
{
   printf("Setting failed, error %u\n", (unsigned)err);
}
if (err=XmlXslSetTextParam(xslx, (oratext *)"LinesPerPage",
    sc.linesperpage))
{
   printf("Setting failed, error %u\n", (unsigned)err);
}

/* XSL processing */
if (err = XmlXslProcess(xslx, doc, FALSE))
{
    printf("Processing failed, error %u\n", (unsigned)err);
    goto terminate;
}

/* Serialize result to specified output file */
XmlSaveDom(xctx, &err, doc, "outFile", NULL);
```

```
/* Clean up and terminate contexts */
terminate:
        if (doc)
           XmlFreeDocument(xctx, doc);
        if (ss_doc)
           XmlFreeDocument(xctx, ss_doc);
        if (xctx)
           XmlDestroy(xctx);
        if (xslx)
           XmlXslDestroy(xslx);
        return 1;
}
```

The following is an example command line for execution:

```
publishcat -i dvdlist.xml -o dvdlist.html -p XSLConfig.xml
```

Summary

In this chapter we have discussed an application that uses XML to convey not only data and content but configuration information as well. In fact, this is exactly how many of the Oracle products interface with Oracle Enterprise Manager to handle configuration and maintenance. In creating **publishcat**, you have used many of the C components in Oracle XDK 10*g*, including the DOM and SAX parsers and the XSLT processor.

CHAPTER 20

Build an XML Database OCI Application

any applications require access to database data, because they typically are designed to return large result sets or to update and retrieve data frequently. While Oracle offers PL/SQL as an *in the database* programming language, many applications need the flexibility and functionality of C or need to offload program logic from the database. This is where building your application using the Oracle Class Interface (OCI) libraries can be a real value. Previous Oracle Database releases included no OCI support for the XMLType. Applications had to serialize the output from a query and reparse using DOM or SAX APIs on the client to process XML. This processing model has distinct disadvantages when the datasets become large, especially when using the DOM APIs, because you need to materialize the entire dataset on the client in order to access and modify or update it.

Oracle Database 10*g*, by way of the Oracle XDK 10*g*, now provides XMLType support to OCI applications through a set of new APIs that have the prefix *XML*. The reason that these do not have the prefix *OCI* is that they are the same APIs that can be used for stand-alone XDK applications.

In this chapter we show you how to create an OCI program by using these new APIs and connecting to the database. There is a fair amount of boilerplate OCI code that is necessary for all OCI applications. We are not going to spend time explaining this code since it can simply be copied and pasted into your application without alteration.

Designing the Framework

The premise for all OCI applications is that they need to connect to Oracle databases and retrieve, insert, or update data. In the case of XML, this data may be stored in XML format or generated from relational tables. For this example application, you will use OCI to generate an XMLType from a SQL/XML query over relational tables from the SH sample schema. However, instead of simply returning a serialized stream of the data that would need to be reparsed, you will return an XMLType DOM called an XOB (XML object) that can be accessed directly through the new XML* APIs. You will then update the XOB and serialize it for consumption or display. You can also save it back to the database.

The steps to create such an application are as follows:

1. Initialize the OCI application context, handles, environment, etc., with the boilerplate code.
2. Initialize the OCIXMLDB and XDK contexts to operate on an XOB.
3. Log on to the database and submit the SQL/XML query.
4. Cast the result to an XDK **xmldocnode** to prepare it for DOM operations.
5. Perform DOM operations with the XML* APIs.
6. Save the XOB.
7. Serialize the XOB or save it back to the database with OCI.

These steps are used in the following command-line **xmlupdate** application that can accept as parameters the SQL/XML query, the XPath expression to the location to be updated, and the update data.

Setting Up the OCI Application Environment

To build OCI XML applications, you need to set up the necessary headers and libraries and make files. Fortunately, you already have these items if you have installed the companion CD-ROM and specified as the destination directory $ORACLE_HOME on Unix or %ORACLE_HOME% on Windows.

The OCI XML Application Headers

The headers in Oracle Database 10*g* are installed into your Oracle Home by performing a companion CD installation. Once you have done this, you will have two directories that include the necessary header files: **$ORACLE_HOME/rdbms/public** and **$ORACLE_HOME/xdk/include** on Unix, and **%ORACLE_HOME%/oci/include** and **%ORACLE_HOME%/xdk/include** on Windows. The following is **xmlupdate.h,** the application header file that lists the required Oracle headers along with the application functions:

```
#ifndef STDIO
#include <stdio.h>
#endif

#ifndef STDLIB
#include <stdlib.h>
#endif

#ifndef STRING
#include <string.h>
#endif

#ifndef OCIAP_ORACLE
#include <ociap.h>
#endif

#ifndef XML_ORACLE
#include <xml.h>
#endif

/*----------------- End of including files -----------------*/
/*----------------- Public Constants and Variables ---------*/
/* constants */
#define MAXBUFLEN     2000
#define SCHEMA        "SYS"
```

```
#define TYPE          "XMLTYPE"
/*----------------- End of Constants and Variables -----------------*/
/*--------------------- Functions Declaration --------------------*/
int  main(/*_ int argc, char *argv[] _*/);
static void checkerr(/*_ OCIError *errhp, sword status _*/);
static void cleanup(/*_ OCIEnv *envhp _*/);
static sb4 connect_server(/*_ OCIServer *srvhp, OCIError *errhp,
     OCISvcCtx *svchp, OCISession *authp, text *user, text *password _*/);
static void disconnect_server(/*_ OCIEnv *envhp, OCISvcCtx *svchp,
     OCIError errhp, OCISession *authp, OCIServer *srvhp, OCIStmt *stmthp,
     boolean tab_exists _*/);
static sb4 init_env_handle(/*_ OCIEnv **envhp, OCISvcCtx **svchp,
     OCIError *errhp, OCIServer **svrhp, OCISession **authp,
     OCIStmt **stmthp _*/);
 static sb4 select_xml(/*_ OCIEnv *envhp, OCISvcCtx *svchp,
     OCIError *errhp, OCIStmt *stmthp, ub4 row, text *sel, text*xpath,
     text *value_*/);
static sb4 do_xml(/*_ OCIEnv *envhp, OCISvcCtx *svchp,
     OCIError *errhp, OCIXMLType *xml, text *xsl_file,
     text *xpathexpr, text *value _*/);
int update_xml(/* struct xmlctx *xctx, xmldocnode *doc,
      text *xpathexpr, text *value;_*/);
/*----------------- End of Functions Declaration ----------------*/
```

Note that while there are only two explicit Oracle header files, **ociap.h** and **xml.h**, they include others from their respective directories. We discuss the functions when we get to the code throughout the chapter.

The OCI XML Application Libraries

OCI applications are dynamically linked on both Unix and Windows using **libclntsh.so**, located in **$ORACLE_HOME/lib32** on Unix, and **oci.lib/ociw32.lib**, located in **%ORACLE_HOME%\oci\lib\Msvc** on Windows. In the past the Solaris library has been in the **lib** directory, but since Oracle Database 10*g* is now only a 64-bit release, the 32-bit libraries are located in their own directory. On Windows you also need to link with the **user32.lib**, **kernel32.lib**, **msvcrt.lib**, **advapi32.lib**, **oldnames.lib**, and **winmm.lib** Windows libraries.

The OCI libraries do not contain the XML APIs; therefore, you also need to link with **libxml10.a** on Unix and **oraxml10.lib** on Windows. The Unix library is not a shared one like the OCI library and thus the objects you need will be pulled into your executable.

The OCI XML Application Make Files

As previously mentioned, the make files necessary to compile and link your application are provided with the database. On Unix this make file is **demo_rdbms.mk**, and it resides in your **$ORACLE_HOME/rdbms/demo** directory. This is a complicated make file because it works for various builds and thus you need a specific command line for our example:

```
make -f demo_rdbms32.mk build EXE=xmlupdate OBJS="xmlupdate.o"
```

Now, this make file includes **$ORACLE_HOME/rdbms/lib/env_rdbms.mk**, which includes the actual compile and link lines. Therefore, to ensure that your XML library is linked, you need to add **libxml10.a** to the end of the OCISHAREDLIBS variable as follows:

```
OCISHAREDLIBS=$(LLIBCLNTSH) $(LDLIBS) $(LLIBTHREAD) -lxml10
```

On Windows the make file is **make.bat** and is located in the **%ORACLE_HOME%\oci\samples** directory. Only one section is used for stand-alone applications, as follows, with **oraxml10.lib** added to the link portion:

```
cl -I%ORACLE_HOME%\oci\include -I. -D_DLL -D_MT %1.c /link /LIBPATH:%ORACLE_
HOME%\oci\lib\msvc oci.lib kernel32.lib msvcrt.lib
%ORACLE_HOME\Lib\Oraxml10.lib /nod:libc
```

This section is called with the following command line for our example:

```
make xmlupdate
```

The Update Application

Now that you understand the mechanics of creating an OCI XML application, we can examine the Update application's Main function:

```
#include "xmlupdate.h"

/*--------------------------Main function ----------------------------*/
int main(argc, argv)
int argc;
char *argv[];
{
  /* OCI Handles and Variables */
 OCIEnv          *envhp = (OCIEnv *) 0;
 OCIServer       *srvhp = (OCIServer *) 0;
 OCISvcCtx       *svchp = (OCISvcCtx *) 0;
 OCIError        *errhp = (OCIError *) 0;
 OCISession      *authp = (OCISession *) 0;
 OCIStmt         *stmthp = (OCIStmt *) 0;

  /* database login information */
 text            *user=(text *)"SH";
 text            *password=(text *)"SH";
 /*Service Name for DB instance if remote DB */
 text            *conn=(text *)"";

  /* Miscellaneous */
 boolean          tab_exists = TRUE;
 ub4              row = 1;
```

```
  if (argc < 3) {
    printf("\nUsage error: xmlupdate \"<SQL/XML Query>\" \"<XPath>\"
      \"<value>\"\n\n");
    return OCI_ERROR;
  }
  /* Initialize the environment and allocate handles */
  if (init_env_handle(&envhp, &svchp, &errhp, &srvhp, &authp, &stmthp))
  {
    printf("FAILED: init_env_handle()!\n");
    return OCI_ERROR;
  }
  /* Log on to the server and begin a session */
  if (connect_server(srvhp, errhp, svchp, authp, user, password))
  {
    printf("FAILED: connect_server()!\n");
    cleanup(envhp);
    return OCI_ERROR;
  }
  /* Select an xmltype column by defining it to an xmltype instance,
        apply some OCIXMLType and unified DOM APIs */
  row = 1;
  if (select_test_xml(envhp, svchp, errhp, stmthp, row, (text *)argv[1],
       (text *)argv[2], (text *)argv[3]))
  {
    printf("FAILED: select_test_xml()!\n");
    disconnect_server(envhp, svchp, errhp, authp, srvhp, stmthp, tab_exists);
    return OCI_ERROR;
  }
  /* Detach from a server and clean up the environment */
  disconnect_server(envhp, svchp, errhp, authp, srvhp, stmthp, tab_exists);

  return OCI_SUCCESS;
}
```

Note that the application has the software steps of initialization; connecting to the database; submitting the query; performing the application logic on the results; and cleaning up before exiting. In the following sections, you will see the details of each of these steps as the application is built out.

Initializing the OCI Application

The first step when creating an OCI application is to perform all of the necessary OCI initializations and allocations. These steps are required for all OCI applications, as the following code illustrates:

```
/*---------------------------------------------------------*/
/* Initialize the environment and allocate handles */
/*---------------------------------------------------------*/
sb4 init_env_handle(envhp, svchp, errhp, srvhp, authp, stmthp)
OCIEnv **envhp;
OCISvcCtx **svchp;
OCIError **errhp;
```

```
OCIServer **srvhp;
OCISession **authp;
OCIStmt **stmthp;
{
 sword status = 0;

 /* Environment initialization and creation */
 if (OCIEnvCreate((OCIEnv **) envhp, (ub4) OCI_OBJECT, (dvoid *) 0,
             (dvoid * (*)(dvoid *,size_t)) 0,
             (dvoid * (*)(dvoid *, dvoid *, size_t)) 0,
             (void (*)(dvoid *, dvoid *)) 0, (size_t) 0, (dvoid **) 0))
 {
   printf("FAILED: OCIEnvCreate()\n");
   return OCI_ERROR;
 }
  /* allocate error handle */
 if (OCIHandleAlloc((dvoid *) *envhp, (dvoid **) errhp,
            (ub4) OCI_HTYPE_ERROR, (size_t) 0, (dvoid **) 0))
 {
   printf("FAILED: OCIHandleAlloc() on errhp\n");
   return OCI_ERROR;
 }

 /* allocate server handle */
 if (status = OCIHandleAlloc((dvoid *) *envhp, (dvoid **) srvhp,
            (ub4) OCI_HTYPE_SERVER, (size_t) 0, (dvoid **) 0))
 {
    printf("FAILED: OCIHandleAlloc() on srvhp\n");
   checkerr(*errhp, status);
   return OCI_ERROR;
 }
 /* allocate service context handle */
 if (status = OCIHandleAlloc((dvoid *) *envhp, (dvoid **) svchp,
             (ub4) OCI_HTYPE_SVCCTX, (size_t) 0, (dvoid **) 0))
 {
   printf("FAILED: OCIHandleAlloc() on svchp\n");
   checkerr(*errhp, status);
   return OCI_ERROR;
 }
 /* allocate session handle */
 if (status = OCIHandleAlloc((dvoid *) *envhp, (dvoid **) authp,
             (ub4) OCI_HTYPE_SESSION, (size_t) 0, (dvoid **) 0))
 {
   printf("FAILED: OCIHandleAlloc() on authp\n");
   checkerr(*errhp, status);
   return OCI_ERROR;
 }
 /* Allocate statement handle */
 if (status = OCIHandleAlloc((dvoid *) *envhp, (dvoid **) stmthp,
                        (ub4) OCI_HTYPE_STMT, (size_t) 0, (dvoid **) 0))
 {
```

```
    printf("FAILED: OCIHandleAlloc() on stmthp\n");
    checkerr(*errhp, status);
    return OCI_ERROR;
  }

 return OCI_SUCCESS;
}
/*---------------------Subfunctions --------------------*/
/* Return corresponding messages in different cases-------*/
/*-------------------------------------------------------*/
void checkerr(errhp, status)
OCIError *errhp;
sword     status;
{
  text  msgbuf[512];
  sb4   errcode = 0;

  memset((void *) msgbuf, (int)'\0', (size_t)512);

  switch (status)
  {
  case OCI_SUCCESS: break;
  case OCI_SUCCESS_WITH_INFO:
    printf("status = OCI_SUCCESS_WITH_INFO\n");
    OCIErrorGet((dvoid *) errhp, (ub4) 1, (text *) NULL, &errcode,
            msgbuf, (ub4) sizeof(msgbuf), (ub4) OCI_HTYPE_ERROR);
    printf("ERROR CODE = %d\n", errcode);
    printf("%.*s\n", 512, msgbuf);
    if (errcode == 436 || errcode == 437 || errcode == 438 ||
      errcode == 439) exit(1);
    break;
  case OCI_NEED_DATA:
    printf("status = OCI_NEED_DATA\n");
    break;
  case OCI_NO_DATA:
     printf("status = OCI_NO_DATA\n");
    break;
  case OCI_ERROR:
     printf("status = OCI_ERROR\n");
     OCIErrorGet((dvoid *) errhp, (ub4) 1, (text *) NULL, &errcode,
             msgbuf, (ub4) sizeof(msgbuf), (ub4) OCI_HTYPE_ERROR);
     printf("ERROR CODE = %d\n", errcode);
     printf("%.*s\n", 512, msgbuf);
    if (errcode == 436 || errcode == 437 || errcode == 438
       || errcode == 439)
      exit(1);
    break;
  case OCI_INVALID_HANDLE:
     printf("status = OCI_INVALID_HANDLE\n");
    break;
```

```
  case OCI_STILL_EXECUTING:
     printf("status = OCI_STILL_EXECUTE\n");
    break;
  case OCI_CONTINUE:
     printf("status = OCI_CONTINUE\n");
    break;
  default:
    break;
  }

  return;
}
/*---------------------------------------------------------*/
/* Free the envhp whenever there is an error--------------*/
/*---------------------------------------------------------*/
void cleanup(envhp)
OCIEnv *envhp;
{
 if (envhp) {
    OCIHandleFree((dvoid *)envhp, OCI_HTYPE_ENV);
 }

 return;
}
```

No part of this code is specific to an application, thus it can be pasted into your OCI applications without modification.

Retrieving a DOM of the Record List via OCI

Since the application queries a set of relational tables and then encapsulates the data returned in XML as dictated by the SQL/XML query, we don't want to return the XML directly but rather return it as an XOB-based DOM so that it can be directly accessed. However, first you need to connect to the database as follows:

```
/*---------------------------------------------------------*/
/* Attach to server, set attributes, and begin session----*/
/*---------------------------------------------------------*/
sb4 connect_server(srvhp, errhp, svchp, authp, user, password)
OCIServer *srvhp;
OCIError *errhp;
OCISvcCtx *svchp;
OCISession *authp;
text *user;
text *password;
{
 sword status = 0;
 /* attach to server */
 if (status = OCIServerAttach((OCIServer *) srvhp, (OCIError *) errhp,
             (text *) conn, (sb4) strlen(conn), (ub4) OCI_DEFAULT))
 {
```

```
    printf("FAILED: OCIServerAttach() on srvhp\n");
    checkerr(errhp, status);
    return OCI_ERROR;
  }
  /* set server attribute to service context */
  if (status = OCIAttrSet((dvoid *) svchp, (ub4) OCI_HTYPE_SVCCTX,
             (dvoid *) srvhp, (ub4) 0, (ub4) OCI_ATTR_SERVER,
             (OCIError *) errhp))
  {
    printf("FAILED: OCIAttrSet() on svchp\n");
    checkerr(errhp, status);
    return OCI_ERROR;
  }
  /* set user attribute to session */
  if (status = OCIAttrSet((dvoid *) authp, (ub4) OCI_HTYPE_SESSION,
               (dvoid *) user, (ub4) strlen((char *)user),
               (ub4) OCI_ATTR_USERNAME, (OCIError *) errhp))
  {
    printf("FAILED: OCIAttrSet() on authp for user\n");
    checkerr(errhp, status);
    return OCI_ERROR;
  }
  /* set password attribute to session */
  if (status = OCIAttrSet((dvoid *) authp, (ub4) OCI_HTYPE_SESSION,
               (dvoid *) password, (ub4) strlen((char *)password),
               (ub4) OCI_ATTR_PASSWORD, (OCIError *) errhp))
  {
    printf("FAILED: OCIAttrSet() on authp for password\n");
    checkerr(errhp, status);
    return OCI_ERROR;
  }
  /* Begin a session  */
  if (status = OCISessionBegin((OCISvcCtx *) svchp, (OCIError *) errhp,
               (OCISession *) authp, (ub4) OCI_CRED_RDBMS,
               (ub4) OCI_DEFAULT))
  {
    printf("FAILED: OCISessionBegin()\n");
    checkerr(errhp, status);
    return OCI_ERROR;
  }
  /* set session attribute to service context */
  if (status = OCIAttrSet((dvoid *) svchp, (ub4) OCI_HTYPE_SVCCTX,
               (dvoid *) authp, (ub4) 0, (ub4) OCI_ATTR_SESSION,
               (OCIError *) errhp))
  {
    printf("FAILED: OCIAttrSet() on svchp\n");
    checkerr(errhp, status);
    return OCI_ERROR;
  }
  return OCI_SUCCESS;
}
```

After successfully connecting to the database and opening a session, you can submit the query that was passed in on the command line as follows:

```
/*--------------------------------------------------------------*/
/* select an xml column from the table into an xmltype instance */
/*--------------------------------------------------------------*/
sb4 select_xml(envhp, svchp, errhp, stmthp, row, selstmt,
     xpathexpr, value)
OCIEnv *envhp;
OCISvcCtx *svchp;
OCIError *errhp;
OCIStmt *stmthp;
ub4 row;
text *selstmt;
text *xpathexpr;
text *value;
{
 ub4 colc = row;
 ub4 xmlsize = 0;
 sword status = 0;
 OCIDefine *defnp = (OCIDefine *) 0;
 OCIBind *bndhp = (OCIBind *) 0;
 OCIXMLType *xml = (OCIXMLType *) 0;
 OCIType *xmltdo = (OCIType *) 0;
 OCIInd ind = OCI_IND_NULL;
 OCIInd *xml_ind = &ind;

 printf("\n=> Selecting row %d by defining to an XMLType
          instance...\n", row);

  /* get the tdo for the xmltype */
 if(status = OCITypeByName(envhp, errhp, svchp, (const text *) SCHEMA,
          (ub4) strlen((char *)SCHEMA), (const text *) TYPE,
          (ub4) strlen((char *)TYPE), (CONST text *) 0,
          (ub4) 0, OCI_DURATION_SESSION, OCI_TYPEGET_HEADER,
          (OCIType **) &xmltdo)) {
   printf("FAILED: OCITypeByName()\n");
   checkerr(errhp, status);
   return OCI_ERROR;
 }
 if(!xmltdo)
 {
   printf("NULL tdo returned\n");
   return OCI_ERROR;
 }
  /* create a new xmltype instance */
 if(status = OCIObjectNew((OCIEnv *)envhp, (OCIError *)errhp,
     (CONST OCISvcCtx *)svchp, (OCITypeCode) OCI_TYPECODE_OPAQUE,
     (OCIType *) xmltdo, (dvoid *) 0, (OCIDuration)
             OCI_DURATION_SESSION, FALSE,
```

```
        (dvoid **) &xml)) {
   printf("FAILED: OCIObjectNew()\n");
   checkerr(errhp, status);
   return OCI_ERROR;
  }
  if(status = OCIStmtPrepare(stmthp, errhp, (OraText *)selstmt,
          (ub4)strlen((char *)selstmt),
          (ub4) OCI_NTV_SYNTAX, (ub4) OCI_DEFAULT)) {
   printf("FAILED: OCIStmtPrepare()\n");
   checkerr(errhp, status);
   return OCI_ERROR;
  }
   /* define it to an xmltype instance */
  if(status = OCIDefineByPos(stmthp, &defnp, errhp, (ub4) 1, (dvoid *) 0,
          (sb4) 0, SQLT_NTY, (dvoid *) 0, (ub2 *)0,
          (ub2 *)0, (ub4) OCI_DEFAULT)) {
    printf("FAILED: OCIDefineByPos()\n");
    checkerr(errhp, status);
    return OCI_ERROR;
  }
  if(status = OCIDefineObject(defnp, errhp, (OCIType *) xmltdo,
          (dvoid **) &xml, &xmlsize, (dvoid **) &xml_ind, (ub4 *) 0)) {
    printf("FAILED: OCIDefineObject()\n");
    checkerr(errhp, status);
    return OCI_ERROR;
  }
  if(status = OCIStmtExecute(svchp, stmthp, errhp, (ub4) 1, (ub4) 0,
         (CONST OCISnapshot*) 0, (OCISnapshot*) 0, (ub4) OCI_DEFAULT)) {
    printf("FAILED: OCIStmtExecute()\n");
    checkerr(errhp, status);
    return OCI_ERROR;
  }
```

At this point you have an OCI context, the OCIXMLType member called **xml**, populated with an XMLType XOB corresponding to the result set in XML format. However, it is not quite ready to be accessed, because you need to initialize one more context and perform a cast as follows:

```
/*-----------------------------------------------------*/
/* Initialize XML context and call DOM APIs---------------*/
/*-----------------------------------------------------*/
sb4 do_xml(envhp, svchp, errhp, xml, xpathexpr, value)
OCIEnv *envhp;
OCISvcCtx *svchp;
OCIError *errhp;
OCIXMLType *xml;
text *xpathexpr;
text *value;
{
 boolean result = 0;
 OCIXMLType *newxml = (OCIXMLType *) 0;
```

```
OCIXMLType *xmltran = (OCIXMLType *) 0;
sword  status = 0;
/* For XML DOM APIs */
OCIStmt *stmthp = (OCIStmt *)0;
OCIDuration dur = OCI_DURATION_SESSION;
struct xmlctx *xctx = (xmlctx *)0;
xmldocnode *doc = (xmldocnode *)0;
ocixmldbparam params[1];

/* Get an XML context */
 params[0].name_ocixmldbparam = XCTXINIT_OCIDUR;
 params[0].value_ocixmldbparam = &dur;
 xctx = OCIXmlDbInitXmlCtx(envhp, svchp, errhp, params, 1);

   /* cast the xmltype value to an xmldomctx */
 doc = (xmldocnode *) xml;

   /* test xml unified C APIs */
 if(update_xml((xmlctx *)xctx, doc, xpathexpr, value)) {
   printf("FAILED: update_xml()\n");
   return OCI_ERROR;
 }

  /* free the statement handle */
 if (stmthp) {
   OCIHandleFree((dvoid *)stmthp, OCI_HTYPE_STMT);
 }

  /* free the xmlctx */
  OCIXmlDbFreeXmlCtx(xctx);

   /* free xml instances using OCIObjectFree */
 if(newxml &&
    (status = OCIObjectFree(envhp, errhp, (dvoid *) newxml, (ub2)
    OCI_OBJECTFREE_FORCE))) {
   printf("FAILED: OCIObjectFree()\n");
   checkerr(errhp, status);
   return OCI_ERROR;
 }

 return OCI_SUCCESS;
}
```

Note the pair of functions called **OCIXmlDbInitXmlCtx()** and **OCIXmlDbFreeXmlCtx()**. These set up and free the XML context that will be used by the DOM APIs. These are also only used when you are working with an XOB, as distinct from an XDK DOM. Additionally, there is an important cast of **xml** context to an xmldocnode, **doc**. This is equivalent to providing the **XMLDocument** from the parse operation for DOM access.

Performing Unified DOM Operations

At this point the XML DOM functions can operate on the document node in exactly the same way as if it were parsed from a file. The Xml* APIs are identical and thus your code can be portable for the actual application logic you need to perform. In the following update example, you use both XmlDom* and XmlXPath* functions to find the node and update it with the data passed in on the command line:

```
/*--------------------------------------------------------*/
/* Test XML unified C XML APIs----------------------------*/
/*--------------------------------------------------------*/
sword update_xml(xctx, doc, xpathexpr, value)
xmlctx *xctx;
xmldocnode *doc;
OraText *xpathexpr;
OraText *value;
{
 xpctx *xpathctx = (xpctx *) 0;
 OraText *baseuri = (OraText *) 0;
 ub2 ctxpos = 1;
 ub2 ctxsize = 1;
 xpexpr *exprtree = (xpexpr *) 0;
 xpobj *xpathobj = (xpobj *) 0;
 xmlerr xerr = (xmlerr)0;
 boolean nodes_exists = 0;
 xmlnode *foo, *foobar;

  /* print out the xml doc before updating it */
 printf("\nThe xml instance before updating with the unified APIs:\n");
 XmlSaveDom(xctx, &xerr, (xmlnode *)doc, "stdio", stdout, NULL);

  /* create an XPath context */
 xpathctx = XmlXPathCreateCtx(xctx, baseuri, (xmlnode *)doc,
     ctxpos, ctxsize);

  /* parse XPath expression */
 exprtree = XmlXPathParse((xpctx *)xpathctx, (OraText *)xpathexpr,
    (xmlerr)&xerr);

  /* evaluate XPath expression */
 xpathobj = XmlXPathEval((xpctx *)xpathctx, (xpexpr *)exprtree,
    (xmlerr *)&xerr);

 foobar = XmlXPathGetObjectNSetNode(xpathobj, 0);
 foo = XmlDomGetFirstChild(xctx, foobar);
 XmlDomSetNodeValue(xctx, foo, (oratext *)value);

 printf("\nThe xml instance after updating with the unified APIs:\n");
 XmlSaveDom(xctx, &xerr, (xmlnode *)doc, "stdio", stdout, NULL);
```

```
 return OCI_SUCCESS;
}
XML_ERRMSG_F(tkpgerr, ectx, msg, err)
{
  if (err)
  {
    printf("Error: %d\n", (int)err);
    printf("%s\n", msg);
  }
}
```

To demonstrate that the XML is actually updated, the function initially prints the XML document as it was received from the database query. It then must find the node that needs updating. This could be found by walking the DOM tree, but that can be tedious because it requires many lines of code. Instead, you can make use of XmlXpath functions to have the search done for you. **XmlXpathParse()** converts the XPath string into an expression form, which can then be passed to **XmlPathEval()** to actually find the node. Now you can call **XmlXPathGetObjectNSetNode()** to return the node, traverse to the first child, which is the text node, and perform the update with **XmlDomGetFirstChild()** and **XmlDomSetNodeValue()**.

At this point you have an updated XOB and need to send it on its way. In **update_xml()**, the **XmlSaveDom()** function is called to send it to standard I/O. It just as easily could have been saved as a file or saved back to the database with another OCI SQL statement.

Running the xmlupdate Application

You can run **xmlupdate** from the command line, passing in the specified parameters. You need to have Oracle Database 10*g* up and running locally. If connecting to a remote database, then you will need to set the service name of your DB instance to the **conn** variable. The following command line queries the SH schema in the database for all of the products whose list prices are greater than 1000 and returns the result as an XML document. It also queries that XML document for the item whose ProductID is 17 and updates its price to 999.99.

```
xmlupdate "select XMLELEMENT("ProductList", XMLAGG(XMLELEMENT(
      "Product", XMLATTRIBUTES(PROD_ID AS "ProductID"),
       XMLELEMENT("Name", PROD_NAME), XMLELEMENT("Price",
       PROD_LIST_PRICE)))) AS result from products
       where PROD_LIST_PRICE>1000"
       "//Product[@ProductID=17]/Price/text()"
       "999.99"
```

The preceding SQL/XML query constructs a single XML document containing multiple products by first specifying the root XML element **<ProductList>** and then using the **XMLAGG()** function to aggregate the set of products meeting the query constraint. The following is the resulting XML document retrieved as a XOB before it is updated. Note the price of 1099.99 for the first item.

```
<ProductList>
  <Product ProductID="17">
    <Name>Mini DV Camcorder with 3.5&quot; Swivel LCD</Name>
```

```
    <Price>1099.99</Price>
  </Product>
  <Product ProductID=18>
    <Name>Envoy Ambassador</Name>
    <Price>1299.99</Price>
  </Product>
</ProductList>
```

This next XML document is the same as the preceding one except the first item's price has been updated to be 999.99.

```
<ProductList>
  <Product ProductID="17">
    <Name>Mini DV Camcorder with 3.5&quot; Swivel LCD</Name>
    <Price>999.99</Price>
  </Product>
  <Product ProductID=18>
    <Name>Envoy Ambassador</Name>
    <Price>1299.99</Price>
  </Product>
</ProductList>
```

This application simply prints the results to the screen. The **XMLSaveDOM()** function performing this can also be used to write the results to a file or stream. Alternatively, the XOB can be saved back to the database using standard OCI statement binding.

Summary

In this chapter you have built an OCI XML application by using the new unified XML APIs that are available in Oracle Database 10*g* by way of the Oracle XDK. This functionality has not been available in the past and answers a real need when operating close to large datasets where serializing this data only to reparse it before working on it produces an application that doesn't scale or perform. These interfaces also enable an OCI application developer to work natively with XMLTypes, thereby utilizing the full flexibility and power of the Oracle XML DB and XMLTypes.

CHAPTER 21

Create an XML-Configured High-Performance Transformation Engine

Transforming XML documents from one markup language to another or from one schema to another is the responsibility of an XSLT processor. This process can be expensive in terms of time and memory even with the high-performance C and Java processors that are included in Oracle XDK 10*g*. This expense is largely due to the complexity and reiterative nature of the XSLT process. Therefore, to improve performance further, Oracle took an alternative approach and created the Oracle XDK 10*g* XSLT Compiler and XSLT virtual machine (XSLTVM). In this chapter we show you how you can put these to use for an application that requires dynamic selection of an XSLT stylesheet and the fastest, most efficient transformation. This will be done by creating a high-performance transformation engine that is XML-configured to apply precompiled stylesheets.

Designing the Framework

To create high-performance XSLT transformation, we must first examine the individual steps that go into the XSLT process and then see which steps can be optimized, combined, or even eliminated. For example, if you have a **records.xml** input XML file to be transformed by a **publish.xsl** XSLT stylesheet into a **report.html** output file, you need to perform the following functional steps:

1. Parse **records.xml** into a DOM.
2. Parse **publish.xsl** into an XSLT stylesheet object.
3. Apply the XSLT templates from the stylesheet object to the input DOM to create an XSLT result object.
4. Serialize the result object to **report.html**.

One way to optimize run-time performance is to introduce precompilation wherever possible. Although the input XML documents are not known ahead of time, the XSLT stylesheets usually are; however, standard XSLT processors do not serialize out nor read in their object formats. There is an XSLT compiler in Oracle XDK 10*g* that effectively does exactly this. Only instead of creating a serializable object, it creates XSLT byte code that can be understood by a purpose-built XSLT virtual machine. The advantage of this approach is that it can optimize Step 3 because it translates XSLT templates and functions into ready-to-execute byte-code instructions. Finally, Step 4 is usually not a bottleneck and, in fact, is very fast in the case of the VM, which is written in C.

A question remains as to how these compiled stylesheets become associated with the input XML files if there is more than one to choose from. XML files that require XSLT transformation usually include a stylesheet processing instruction (PI) in their prolog:

```
<?xml version="1.0"?>
<?xml-stylesheet type="text/xsl" href="publish.xsl"?>
```

Since this is a reference to the stylesheet file and not the compiled version, you must create a mapping of one to the other. For this engine, you do this with an XSLT mapping file of the following form:

```
<?xml version = "1.0"?>
 <xslmap>
  <xsl xsb="booklist.xsb">booklist.xsl</xsl>
  <xsl xsb="cdlist.xsb">cdlist.xsl</xsl>
  <xsl xsb="dvdlist.xsb">dvdlist.xsl</xsl>
</xslmap>
```

By parsing this **xslmap.xml** file on startup, the engine can create a mapping table so that when it gets the stylesheet PI from the input document, it knows what compiled stylesheet to load into the VM.

To implement this engine, you will create two command-line applications. The first, **xslcompile**, creates the compiled XSLT stylesheets and adds a corresponding entry in the map file. The second, **xsbtransform**, applies the stylesheets to the input XML file to create the output file.

Compiling Stylesheets with xslcompile

Because the Oracle XSLT Compiler resides in **oraxml10.lib** on Windows NT and **libxml10.a**, it can be used either as a stand-alone application or from within another application. Using the compiler from within an application requires these steps:

1. Create an instance of the XDK context using **XmlCreate()**.
2. Create an instance of the XSLT compiler using **XmlXvmCreateComp()**.
3. Compile the XSLT file using **XmlXvmCompileFile()**.

At this point, you can either pass the compiled stylesheet to the VM or, as you will do in this application, write it to a file. The following is the code for **xslcompile**:

```
#include <stdio.h>
#include <stdarg.h>
#include <string.h>

#ifndef XML_ORACLE
# include <xml.h>
#endif

/* Deposit xsb and insert into the map file function */
void depositxsb(char *fileargv, ub2 *code, ub4 len, char *filemap)
{
    char filename[200], *name;
    char *input, *inputxsl;
    FILE *xsb;
    xmlctx *ctx;
    xmlerr *ecode;
    xmltextnode *textnode;
    xmlattrnode *attr1;
    xmldocnode  *doc;
```

```
    xmlelemnode *node, *elem;

    name = (char *)strtok(fileargv, ".");
    strcpy(filename, name);
    strcat(filename, ".xsb");
    xsb = fopen(filename, "w");
    fwrite((void *)code, len, 1, xsb);
    fclose(xsb);

  /* Assuming the XML declaration and root node already exist
   * in the map file.  Init and deal with xml map file
   */
    if (!(ctx = XmlCreate(ecode, (oratext *)"xml_context", NULL)))
    {
        printf("Failed to initialize XML parser, error \n");
    }

    if (!(doc=XmlLoadDom(ctx, ecode, filemap, NULL)))
    {
        printf("Parse failed, code %d\n", (int) ecode);
    }

  /* Get root element */
  node = XmlDomGetDocElem(ctx, doc);

  /* Create the element, add data, create the attribute */
  if (!(elem = XmlDomCreateElem(ctx, doc, (oratext *)"xsl")))
  {
     printf("Element creation failed\n");
  }
  if (!(textnode = XmlDomCreateText(ctx, doc, (oratext *)inputxsl)) ||
        !XmlDomAppendChild(ctx, elem, textnode))
  {
     printf("Text node creation failed\n");
  }
  if (!(attr1 = XmlDomCreateAttr(ctx, doc, (oratext*)"xsb",
    (oratext*)input)))
  {
     printf("Attribute creation failed\n");
  }
  if (!XmlDomSetAttrNode(ctx, elem, attr1))
  {
     printf("Attribute setting failed\n");
  }

  /* insert the element */
  if (!XmlDomAppendChild(ctx, (xmlnode *)node, (xmlnode *)elem))
  {
     printf("Appending to root element failed \n");
```

```
  }

  XmlFreeDocument(ctx, doc);

}
```

The **depositxsb()** function performs three supporting tasks. First, it creates the file to which the compiled stylesheet will be saved. Second, it updates the **xslmap.xml** file with an entry for the compiled stylesheet and associates it with the actual stylesheet that will be in the input XML document PI. Finally, it cleans up after itself before returning to the main function, which follows:

```
/* ====================================================================
                                main
  ------------------------------------------------------------------*/
int main (sword argc, char *argv[])
{
    xmlctx       *xctx = NULL;
    xmlxvmcomp   *comp = NULL;
    xmlerr        err;
    ub2          *code;
    ub4           len;
    oratext      *xslFile;

    if (argc < 2) {
        printf("Usage is: xslcompile <input xsl>\n");
        return -1;
    }
    xslFile = (oratext*)argv[1];
    xctx = XmlCreate(&err, (oratext *) "sample",
           "data_encoding", "US-ASCII", NULL);
    if (!xctx) {
        printf("Failed to create xctx: %d\n",err);
        goto terminate;
    }
    comp = XmlXvmCreateComp (xctx);
    if (!comp) {
          printf("Failed to create Compiler.");
          goto terminate;
    }

    code = XmlXvmCompileFile (comp, xslFile, NULL, 0, &err);
    if (err != XMLERR_OK) {
        printf("Failed to Compile:%u\n", err);
        goto terminate;
    }
    len = XmlXvmGetBytecodeLength(code, &err);

    /* Deposit in xsb */
```

```
        depositxsb(argv[1], code, len, argv[2]);

    terminate:
        /* clean the memory */
        if (comp)
            XmlXvmDestroyComp(comp);
        if (xctx)
            XmlDestroy(xctx);
        return 0;
}
```

The preceding is the main routine in the program. It first initializes the XML context, **xctx**, which is the necessary first step for all C XDK applications. To compile stylesheets, you must first initialize the XSLT compiler, which is done using **XmlXvmCreateComp()** and passing in your XML context. Now you can compile by calling **XmlXvmCompileFile()** and passing in the stylesheet file. Note that this function supports passing in a file path and/or base URI in order to locate the stylesheet. For this example, since the file is local, the base URI in not used.

Once you have the compiled stylesheet, all that is left is to get its length, since it is a binary file, and pass it to **depositxsb()** along with the map filename to have it saved and to have the map file updated.

Once **xslcompile** is compiled and linked, you can execute it with the following command line and any supported XSLT file:

```
xslcompile bookcatalog.xsl xslmap.xml
```

Note that the Oracle XSLT Compiler supports only XSLT 1.0 and XPath 1.0 in the Oracle XDK 10*g* release and thus the stylesheets must be limited to this version.

Running the XSLT Virtual Machine with xsbtransform

Now that you have one or more stylesheets and their associated compiled XSB files, you can use them in your applications, as shown in this section as we discuss how **xsbtransform** works.

To use this resource from an application, you must perform the following steps:

1. Create an instance of the XDK context using **XmlCreate()**.
2. Create a parser to read the map file using **XMLLoadSax()**.
3. Parse the map file for its entries using SAX callbacks.
4. Create a parser to read the input XML file using **XmlLoadDom()**.
5. Retrieve the stylesheet PI to get the filename using **XmlDomGet*()**.
6. Match the **XSL** filename to its **XSB** filename.
7. Create the XSLT virtual machine using **XmlXvmCreate()**.

8. Perform the transformation by passing in the input XML and XSB file using **XmlXvmSetBytecodeFile()** and **XmlXvmTransformFile()**.

9. Get the DOM and output the result of the transformation using **XmlXvmGetOutputDom()** and **XmlSaveDom()**.

The following code for **xsbtransform** implements these steps:

```
#include <stdio.h>
#include <stdlib.h>
#include <stdlib.h>
#include <string.h>

#ifndef XML_ORACLE
#include <xml.h>
#endif

/* Obtains XSL compiled code filename */
oratext *getXSBFileName (xmlctx *xctx, xmldocnode *doc,
     oratext *xslmapfile)
{
   oratext        *p, *filename;
   static oratext input[100];

   xmlpinode      *stpinode, *pinode;
   xmlnode        *stnode;

   filename = (oratext *)malloc(200);

   /* Get first PI */
   pinode = (xmlpinode *)XmlDomGetFirstChild(xctx, (xmlnode *)doc);
   /* Get stylesheet PI */
   stpinode = (xmlpinode *)XmlDomGetNextSibling(xctx,
     (xmlnode *)pinode);
   /* Get href node as last child */
   stnode = XmlDomGetLastChild(xctx, (xmlnode *)stpinode);
   /* Get attribute value, which is the filename */
   filename = XmlDomGetAttrValue(xctx, (xmlattrnode *)stnode);

   p = (oratext*)strtok((char*)filename, ".");
   strcpy((char*)input, (char*)p);
   strcat((char*)input, ".xsb");

   return input;
}
```

The support function **getXSBFileName()** receives the input XML file DOM and walks the DOM tree using **XMLDomGetFirstChild()**, **XMLDomGetNextSibling()**, and **XmlDomGetLastChild()** to retrieve the stylesheet PI and then calls **XmlDomGetAttrValue()** to retrieve the stylesheet attribute. Finally, it tokenizes the string to retrieve the filename, less its extension, and returns the compiled stylesheet by appending its extension as follows:

```
/* ================================================================
                              main
  ---------------------------------------------------------------*/
int main (sword argc, char *argv[])
{
    xmlctx       *xctx = NULL;
    xmlxvm       *vm   = NULL;
    xmlerr        err;
    oratext      *xmlFile, *outFile, *xslmapFile, *codeFile;
    xmldocnode   *doc, *odoc;
    xmlfragnode  *root;

    if (argc < 3) {
        printf("Usage is: xsbtransform <xmlfile> <outputfile>
          <xslmap file>\n");
        return 0;
    }

    xmlFile = (oratext *)argv[1];
    outFile = (oratext *)argv[2];
    xslmapFile = (oratext *)argv[3];

    /* Get the xsl compiled code */

    /* Creates the context */
    xctx = XmlCreate(&err, (oratext *) "sample",
             "data_encoding", "US-ASCII", NULL);
    if (!xctx) {
        printf("Failed to create xctx: %d\n", err);
        goto terminate;
    }
    if (!(doc=XmlLoadDom(xctx, &err, xmlFile, NULL)))
   {
      printf("Parse failed, code %d\n", (int) err);
   }
    codeFile = getXSBFileName(xctx, doc, xslmapFile);

    /* Creates the VM */
    vm = XmlXvmCreate (xctx, NULL);
    if (!vm) {
        printf("Failed to create VM");
        goto terminate;
    }

    /* Create the output document node */
```

```
    odoc = XmlCreateDocument(xctx, NULL, NULL, NULL, &err);
    err = XmlXvmSetOutputDom(vm, odoc);

    err = XmlXvmSetBytecodeFile(vm, codeFile);
    if (err != XMLERR_OK) {
        printf("Failed to set the bytecode: %u\n", err);
        goto terminate;
    }

    err = XmlXvmTransformDom (vm, doc);
    if (err != XMLERR_OK) {
        printf("Failed to transform: %u\n", err);
        goto terminate;
    }

    /* Get DOM of transformed XML file and write into output file */
    root = XmlXvmGetOutputDom(vm);
    XmlSaveDom(xctx, &err, root, "outFile", NULL);

    terminate:
    /* clean the memory */
    if (vm)
        XmlXvmDestroy(vm);
    if (xctx)
        XmlDestroy(xctx);

    return 0;
}
```

Once again, the main function is where most of the application work is performed. After the XML context is initialized by **XmlCreate()**, the input XML file is parsed into a DOM with **XmlLoadDom()**. At this point you need to retrieve the stylesheet PI, therefore you call the custom **getXSBFileName()** function, which returns the compiled stylesheet name to use.

The next step initializes the XSLT virtual machine with **XmlXvmCreate()** and sets it up by setting the output root with **XmlCreateDocument()** and the output DOM with **XmlXvmSetOutputDom()**. Finally, the initialization is completed by setting the compiled stylesheet with **XmlXvmSetBytecodeFile()**.

At this point the XSL transformation can take place by calling **XmlXvmTransformDom()** and passing in the DOM of the input file, **doc**. You now can get the output document's DOM by calling **XmlXvmGetOutputDom()** and print it to a file with **XmlSaveDom()**. This output method is quite flexible because it can also print to a URI, buffer, stream, or STDIO. You can also specify "pretty printing," by setting the number of spaces to indent, specifying the output encoding to use, and choosing whether to print the XML declaration.

It is now time to run the program. Make sure that the XML, XSB, and map files are local if specified without paths and then run this example command line:

```
xsbtransform booklist.xml bookcatalog.html xslmap.xml
```

Summary

In this chapter we have discussed in detail the Oracle XDK 10*g* XSLT Compiler and XSLTVM. We have also showed you how to use them to create one of the fastest software XSLT engines available when the stylesheets can be compiled in advance. You also realized one of the smallest memory footprints during XSLT transformation. In this particular implementation, these compiled stylesheets reside on your file system, but you could just as readily create an implementation in which they are retrieved from a database or URL.

PART V

Oracle XML for C++ Developers

CHAPTER 22

Getting Started with Oracle XML and C++

racle Database 10*g* includes in its default installation the Oracle XDK 10*g* C++ libraries and utilities. These provide portable XML functionality that permits you to easily develop stand-alone or database XML-enabled applications. In this chapter we describe the various libraries and utilities, set up both the compile-time and run-time environments, and cover the basics of the configuration that is necessary to connect to the Oracle database.

The Oracle XDK C++ Libraries

The Oracle XDK C++ components are built upon the C components and contain the same functionality for reading, manipulating, transforming, and validating XML documents. In addition, a class generator is available for constructing XML documents. The Oracle XDK C++ components reside in the same libraries as the C components. These libraries all reside in **ORACLE_HOME\lib** and in **XDK_HOME/lib** if installed from the OTN distribution.

libxml10.a, libxml10.so, and libxml10.dl

In previous releases the C and C++ XML components have been in multiple libraries. In Oracle XDK 10*g*, these components have been consolidated into a single **libxml10.a** library on UNIX and an **oraxml10.dll** library on Windows.

Within **libxml10.a** are the following XML components:

- **XML parser** Checks whether an XML document is well-formed and, optionally, validates it against a DTD or XML schema. The parser constructs an object tree that can be accessed via a DOM interface or operate serially via a SAX interface.
- **XSLT processor** Provides the functionality to transform an XML document according to an XSLT stylesheet and is bundled with the parser.
- **XSLT Compiler** Compiles XSLT stylesheets into byte code for use by the XSLT Virtual Machine.
- **XSLTVM** High-performance XSLT transformation engine that accepts compiled XSLT stylesheets for faster processing using less memory.
- **XML Schema processor** Supports parsing and validating XML files against an XML Schema Definition (XSD) file.
- **XML Class Generator** Creates a set of C++ source files based on an input DTD or XML Schema. These classes can then be used to construct XML documents conforming to the DTD or XML schema.

While all of the XML functionality resides in this library, it does depend on an additional library to provide run-time support and an optional third library to provide globalization support as described in the following section.

libcore10.a, libcoresh10.so, and libcore10.dll

The C common run-time functions that permit Oracle code to be portable across platforms are contained in **libcore10.a** on UNIX and **libcore10.dll** on Windows. An additional library that is new in Oracle Database 10*g*, **libcoresh10.so**, supports dynamic linking on the UNIX platforms. Even though these are C libraries, they are used for C++ applications and need to be linked in.

libnls10.a and oranls10.dll

One of the advantages of the Oracle C++ XML implementation over others resides in its extensive internationalization support. Support for the UTF-8, UTF-16, and ISO-8859-1 character sets is provided in **libnls10.a** on UNIX and **oranls10.dll** on Windows. These libraries also depend on the environment to find their encoding and message files. The environment setup will be covered in a later section.

libunls10.a and oraunls10.dll

When you need support for other character sets, you also need to use **libunls10.a** on UNIX and **oraunls10.dll** on Windows. Generally, these character sets can be classified as Asian, European, or Middle Eastern language character sets. Because over 300 character sets are supported, we are not listing them here, but you can find them in Appendix A of the *Oracle Data Globalization Support Guide 10*g. As with the previous libraries, these also depend on the environment to find their encoding and message files.

Setting Up Your C++ XML Development Environment

While much of your environment is already set up by an Oracle Database 10*g* installation, there are several steps that are platform-specific that you need to performed to both compile and run your Oracle C++ XML-enabled applications.

Note that in later sections the XDK directory is referred to as **$XDK_HOME** on UNIX or **%XDK_HOME%** on Windows and that the Oracle Home is referred to as **$ORACLE_HOME** on UNIX or **%ORACLE_HOME%** on Windows.

UNIX Setup of XDK C++ Components

In order to successfully run your UNIX C++ XML application, you need to set several environment variables for the various components so that the components can find their support files, and you need to establish the run-time configuration.

ORA_NLS10

The environment variable ORA_NLS10 is set to point to the location of the NLS character-encoding definition files. If you have installed Oracle Database 10*g*, then you can set it as follows:

```
setenv ORA_NLS10 $ORACLE_HOME/nls/data
```

If you don't have an Oracle database installed, you can use the NLS character encoding definition files which come with the OTN Oracle XDK release as follows:

```
setenv ORA_NLS10 $XDK_HOME/nls/data
```

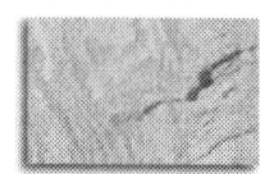

NOTE
The XDK-included encoding files contain a subset of the character sets that are in the Oracle database release. While it contains only 34 character-encoding files, they are the most common ones.

ORA_XML_MESG

The environment variable ORA_XML_MESG is set to point to the location of the XML error message files. These files are provided in the **xdk/mesg/** directory. Files ending in **.msb** are machine-readable and needed at runtime; files ending in **.msg** are human-readable and include cause and action descriptions for each error. For Oracle database installations, these message files exist in the **$ORACLE_HOME/xdk/mesg** directory and no environment variable is necessary. If an Oracle database is not installed, you should set the environment variable, ORA_XML_MESG, to point to the absolute path of the **xdk/mesg/** directory:

```
setenv ORA_XML_MESG $XDK_HOME/xdk/mesg
```

Checking Your C++ Run-Time Environment

Several ready-to-run XML utilities are included in Oracle XDK 10g. These make it easy for you to confirm that your run-time environment is properly configured. They all reside in **$ORACLE_HOME/bin** for Oracle database installations and **$XDK_HOME/bin** for OTN XDK installations. The following sections describe these XML utilities along with their command-line options.

xml

There is no command-line C++ XML parser utility; however, the C XML parser may be called as an executable by invoking **xml** from your **$ORACLE_HOME/bin** or **$XDK_HOME/bin** as follows:

```
xml options URI
```

The following is the list of options:

- **–c** Perform conformance check only, no validation
- **–e *encoding*** Specify default input file encoding ("incoding")
- **–E *encoding*** Specify DOM/SAX encoding ("outcoding")
- **–f** Interpret as filespec, not as URI
- **–l *language*** Specify language for error reporting
- **–n** Perform DOM traversal and report number of elements
- **–p** Print document after parsing it
- **–v** Display parser version then exit
- **–w** Preserve all whitespace
- **–W** Stop parsing after a warning
- **–x** Exercise SAX interface and print document

xsl

There is no command-line C++ XSLT processor; however, the C XSLT processor may be called as an executable by invoking **xsl** from your **$ORACLE_HOME/bin** or **$XDK_HOME/bin** as follows:

```
xsl options URI
```

The following is the list of options:

- **-f** Interpret as filespec, not URI
- **-h** Show usage help and full list of flags
- **-i *n*** Specify number of times to iterate the XSLT processing
- **-l *language*** Specify language for error reporting
- **-o *XSLoutfile*** Specify output file of XSLT processor
- **-r** Do not ignore <xsl:output> instruction in XSLT processing
- **-s *stylesheet*** Specify the XSL stylesheet
- **-v** Display XSLT processor version then exit
- **-V *var value*** Test top-level variables in C XSLT

schema There is no command-line C++ schema validator; however, the C XML Schema Validator may be called as an executable by invoking **bin/schema**, which takes two arguments: the XML instance document and a default schema to apply:

```
schema options document schema
```

The following is the list of options:

- **-0** Always exit with code 0 (success)
- **-e *encoding*** Specify default input file encoding ("incoding")
- **-E *encoding*** Specify output/data/presentation encoding ("outcoding")
- **-i** Ignore provided schema file
- **-o *num*** Specify validation options
- **-p** Print instance document to stdout on success
- **-u** Force the Unicode code path
- **-v** Display version then exit

xmlcg The stand-alone C++ XML Class Generator may be called as an executable by invoking **xmlcg** from your **$ORACLE_HOME/bin** or **$XDK_HOME/bin**. The following is the command line with its syntax and options:

```
xmlcg [flags] <input file>
```

The following are the option flags and their descriptions:

- **-d** ***name*** Generate **name.cpp** and **name.h** when there is an external DTD
- **-o** ***directory*** Display output directory for generated files (default is current directory)
- **-e** ***encoding*** Specify default input file encoding
- **-h** Show this usage help
- **-s** ***name*** Generate **name.cpp** and **name.h** when input is an XML schema;
- **-v** Show the Class Generator version

Setting Up Your C++ Compile-Time Environment

To compile your code, you need to have the run-time environment set up and you need to have the header files for the components that you are using. These header files reside in the **xdk/include** directory in either installation. Refer to Chapter 18 for a description of the C header files. The following is a listing of the C++ files and their corresponding description:

- **oraxml.hpp** Includes all the Oracle9*i* XML ORA data types and all the public ORA APIs in **libxml**. This is for backward compatibility only.
- **oraxmlcg.h** Includes the C APIs for the C++ class generator.
- **oraxsd.hpp** Includes the Oracle9*i* XSD validator data types and APIs. This is for backward compatibility only.
- **xml.hpp** Is the header to handle the Unified DOM APIs transparently, whether using OCI or standalone.
- **xmlotn.hpp** Includes all the common APIs, whether you are compiling standalone or using OCI and the Unified DOM.
- **xmlctx.hpp** Includes all the initialization and exception-handling public APIs.

Confirming Your C++ Compile-Time Environment

You can confirm your setup by compiling the demo programs, by using **makefile** in the **$XDK_HOME/xdk/demo/cpp** directory of the OTN release or in the **$ORACLE_HOME/xdk/demo/cpp** directory if you have installed the Oracle Database 10*g* Companion CD in **$ORACLE_HOME**.

Windows Setup of XDK C++ Components

In order to successfully run your Windows C++ XML application, you need to set several environment variables for the various components so that the components can find their support files, and you need to establish the run-time configuration.

ORA_NLS10

The environment variable ORA_NLS10 is set to point to the location of the NLS character-encoding definition files. If you have installed Oracle Database 10*g*, then you can set it as follows:

```
set ORA_NLS10 %ORACLE_HOME%\nls\data
```

If you don't have an Oracle database installed, you can use the NLS character-encoding definition files that come with the OTN Oracle XDK release as follows:

```
set ORA_NLS10 %XDK_HOME%\nls\data
```

NOTE
The XDK-included encoding files contain a subset of the character sets that are in the Oracle database release. While it contains only 34 character-encoding files, they are the most common ones.

ORA_XML_MESG

The environment variable ORA_XML_MESG is set to point to the location of the XML error message files. These files are provided in the **xdk\mesg** directory. Files ending in **.msb** are machine-readable and needed at runtime; files ending in **.msg** are human-readable and include cause and action descriptions for each error. For Oracle database installations, these message files exist in the **$ORACLE_HOME\xdk\mesg** directory and no environment variable is necessary. If an Oracle database is not installed, you should set the environment variable, ORA_XML_MESG, to point to the absolute path of the **xdk\mesg** directory:

```
set ORA_XML_MESG %XDK_HOME%\xdk\mesg
```

Checking Your C++ Run-Time Environment

Several ready-to-run XML utilities are included in Oracle XDK 10*g*. They make it easy for you to confirm that your run-time environment is properly configured. They all reside in **%ORACLE_HOME%\bin** for Oracle database installations and **%XDK_HOME%\bin** for OTN XDK installations. The following sections describe these XML utilities. Their command-line options are the same as in the previous UNIX section.

xml.exe

There is no command-line C++ XML parser utility; however, the C XML parser may be called as an executable by invoking **xml.exe** from your **%ORACLE_HOME%/bin** or **%XDK_HOME%/bin** as follows:

```
xml.exe options URI
```

xsl.exe

There is no command-line C++ XSLT processor; however, the C XSLT processor may be called as an executable by invoking **xsl.exe** from your **%ORACLE_HOME%/bin** or **%XDK_HOME%/bin** as follows:

```
xsl.exe options URI
```

schema.exe

There is no command-line C++ XML; however, the Schema Validator may be called as an executable by invoking **schema.exe** from your **%ORACLE_HOME%/bin** or **%XDK_HOME%/**

bin, which takes two arguments: the XML instance document and, optionally, a default schema to apply:

```
schema.exe options document schema
```

xmlcg.exe

The stand-alone C++ XML class generator may be called as an executable by invoking **xmlcg.exe** from your **%ORACLE_HOME%/bin** or **%XDK_HOME%/bin.** The following is the command line with its syntax and options:

```
        xmlcg.exe [flags] <input file>
```

Setting Up Your C++ Compile-Time Environment

To compile your code, you need to have the run-time environment set up and you need to have the header files for the components that you are using. These header files reside in the **xdk\include** directory in either installation. These are the same files as described in the previous UNIX section.

Confirming Your C++ Compile-Time Environment

You can confirm your setup by compiling the demo programs, by using **makefile.bat** in the **%XDK_HOME%\xdk\demo\new** directory of the OTN release only or in the **%ORACLE_HOME%\xdk\demo\cpp\new** directory if you have installed the Oracle Database 10*g* Companion CD in **$ORACLE_HOME**.

The make file assumes you are using **cl.exe** for compiling and **link.exe** for linking and that you have both in your PATH. You also have to edit the **make.bat** file to provide the paths to the header files as well as the corresponding **.lib** files located in **%ORACLE_HOME%\lib** or **%XDK_HOME%\lib**.

Setting Up Microsoft Visual C/C++

Since much of the Windows C++ development is done using Microsoft Visual C/C++, we will show you how to set up a project and its settings for the applications covered in later chapters. These instructions can also be used for the demos that are included in Oracle XDK 10*g*. These instructions assume Microsoft Visual C/C++ version 6.0a or compatible.

Creating a New Project

Projects need to be attached to workspaces; therefore, if you don't already have one that you would like to use, you will need to create a blank workspace. You do so by choosing File | New | Workspaces and entering a name, after which the OK button is activated, and clicking it gives you a new workspace.

To add a project to this new workspace or to an existing one, you need to select File | New | Projects, at which point you will see the screen in Figure 22-1. For the applications in this book as well as the Oracle XDK 10*g* demos, you need to click Win32 Console Application and enter the name of your project. In Figure 22-1 the name of the project is "CPPXMLApp".

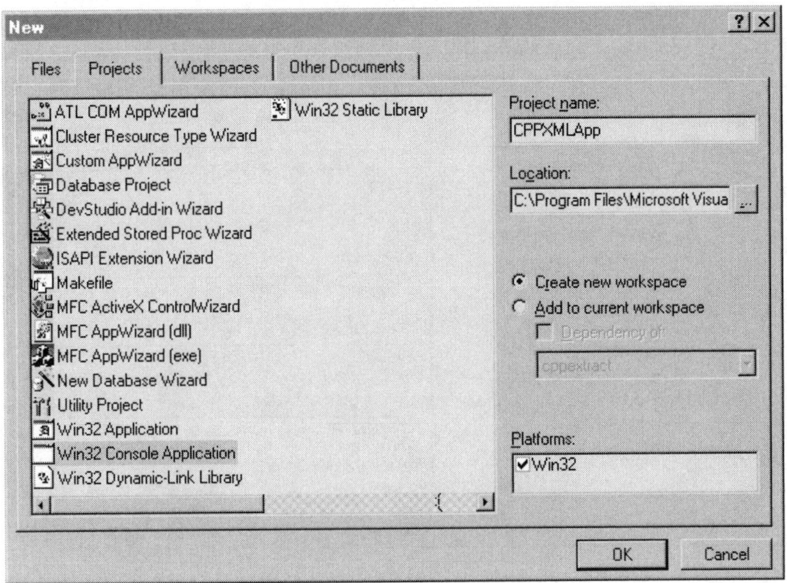

FIGURE 22-1. *New projects window*

NOTE
This name will be used for your executable unless you specify an alternate debug executable under the Project Settings | Link | General category.

Once you click OK, you will be asked what kind of console application you wish to create. You can simply select an empty project and click Finish. This will add your new project to your workspace in the FileView pane.

Configuring Your Project

Once you have a project you can then configure its settings. This is done by right-clicking the project name, selecting Settings and then clicking C/C++ in the Project Settings window that appears. There are numerous settings here but, as you can see in Figure 22-2, you can keep them in their default configuration with or without Debug optimizations.

At this point you can set up your link configuration using another tab in the Project Settings window. Click the Link tab and you will see the window shown in Figure 22-3. Enter "oraxml10.lib" in the Object/Libraries Modules text box to add it to your link line automatically, as shown here. Note, at runtime you will need the **oraxml10.dll**, **oracore10.dll**, and **oranls10.dll** to be in your PATH for the objects to be found. You can now click OK and begin populating the source files and header files folders.

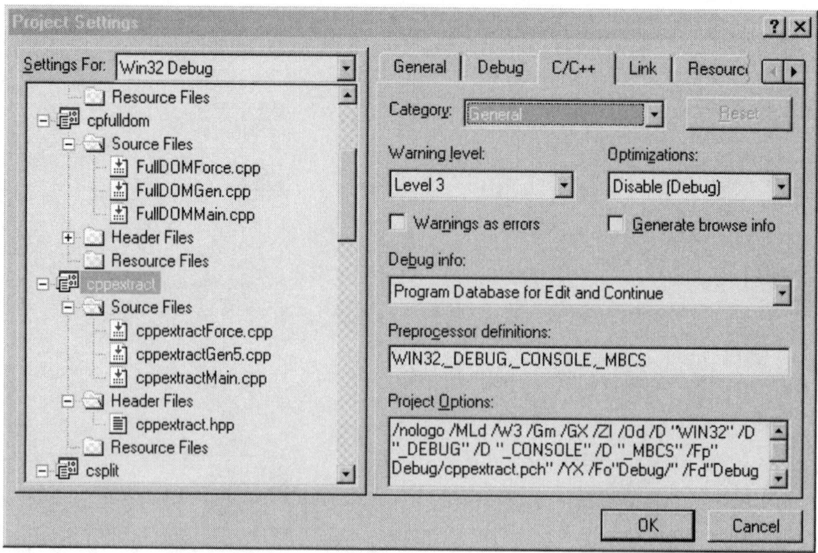

FIGURE 22-2. *Project Settings: C/C++ window*

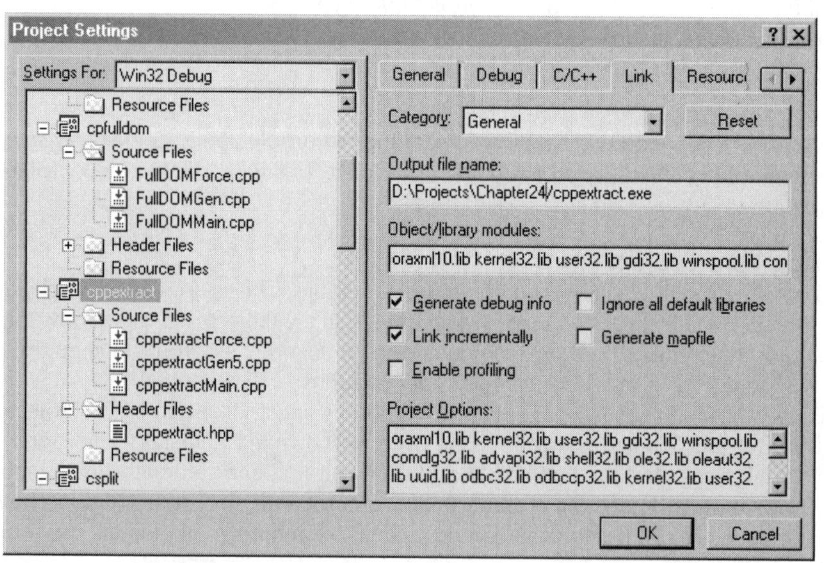

FIGURE 22-3. *Project Settings: Link window*

Summary

In this chapter, we have walked you through the basics of configuring and setting up your XDK C++ development environment for either UNIX or Windows and then confirming proper setup. You will use this environment in the following chapters, in which we will show you how to build real C++ XML-enabled applications covering a range of solution scenarios.

CHAPTER 23

Build an XML Database OCI C++ Application

any C++ applications require direct access to database data, typically because they are designed to work with large data sets or to retrieve and update data frequently. While Oracle offers PL/SQL as an *in the database* programming language, many applications need the flexibility and functionality of C++ or need to offload program logic from the database. This is where building your C++ application using the Oracle C++ Call Interface (OCCI) libraries can be a real value. However, unlike the Oracle Call Interface (OCI) for C, OCCI has not had XMLType support added. Generally, this means that C++ programs must use C code and thus OCI. However, as you will discover in this chapter, you can use the Oracle XDK C++ components with some C++ wrappers of OCI code to enable C++ XMLType support.

C++ applications that would have had to serialize the output from a query and reparse using DOM or SAX APIs on the client in order to process XML no longer need to do so because they can take advantage of a DOM within the database as an XMLType. Thus, when the data sets become large, especially when using the DOM APIs, you'll be able to preserve memory resources because you no longer need to materialize the entire data set on the client in order to access and modify or update it.

Oracle Database 10*g* with the inclusion of Oracle XDK 10*g* now offers XMLType support to C++ applications through a set of new APIs located in the **xml*.hpp** header files. The reason these APIs are not included in the OCCI header files is that they are the same APIs that can be used for stand-alone XDK applications.

Designing the Framework

The premise for all C++ database applications is that they need to connect to Oracle databases and retrieve, insert, or update data. In the case of XML, this data may be stored in XML format or generated from relational tables. While Oracle Database 10*g* provides an OCCI library to support these types of applications, OCCI cannot be used for an XML application because currently the unified DOM support (discussed in Chapter 20) is not available. For this example application, you will use special C++ classes that call OCI functions to generate an XMLType from a SQL/XML query over relational tables from the SALES sample schema. However, instead of simply returning a serialized stream of the data that would need to be reparsed, you will return an XMLType DOM called an XOB (XML object) that can be accessed directly through the new C++ XML APIs. You will then query the XOB with an XPath and serialize it for consumption or display. You can also save it back to the database.

The steps to create such an application are as follows:

1. Initialize the OCI environment from C++ and create a connection.
2. Initialize the OCIXMLDB and XDK contexts to operate on an XOB.
3. Log on to the database and submit the SQL/XML query.
4. Cast the result to an xmldocnode to prepare it for DOM operations.
5. Perform DOM operations with the XML* APIs.
6. Serialize the DOM or save back to the database with a C++ class calling OCI.

These steps are used in the following specific example, which creates a command-line **selectxpq** application that can accept as parameters the SQL/XML query and the XPath to evaluate and print the result. The following is an example **selectxpq** command line:

```
selectxpq 'select xmlelement("Exec", xmlattributes(s.ENAME "Name"),
     xmlforest(s.JOB as "Job", s.SAL as "Salary")) from EMP s where
     s.SAL>3000;" /Exec/Job"
```

The SQL/XML query returns this XML document using the sample schema:

```
<Exec Name="KING">
  <Job>PRESIDENT</Job>
  <Salary>5000</Salary>
</Exec>
```

The following is the XPath evaluation result:

```
<Job>PRESIDENT</Job>
```

Setting Up the C++ OCI XML Application Environment

To build C++ XML database applications, you need to set up the necessary headers and libraries and make files. Fortunately, you already have these items if you have installed the companion CD and specified as your destination directory $ORACLE_HOME on Unix or %ORACLE_HOME% on Windows. You will be using both the OCI and XDK header files for this application. You will not be using the OCCI header files.

The OCI XML Application Headers

The headers in Oracle Database 10*g* are installed into your Oracle Home when you perform the initial companion CD installation. Once you have done this, you will have two directories that include the necessary header files: **$ORACLE_HOME/rdbms/demo** and **$ORACLE_HOME/xdk/include** on Unix, and **%ORACLE_HOME%/rdbms/demo** and **%ORACLE_HOME%/xdk/include** on Windows. The following is the application header file that lists the required Oracle headers along with the application functions:

```
#ifndef STDIO
#include <stdio.h>
#endif

#ifndef STDLIB
#include <stdlib.h>
#endif

#ifndef STRING
#include <string.h>
#endif

extern "C" {
```

```
#ifndef OCIAP_ORACLE
#include <ociap.h>
#endif
}

extern "C" {
#ifndef XML_ORACLE
#include <xml.h>
#endif
}

#ifndef XMLCTX_CPP_ORACLE
#include <xmlctx.hpp>
#endif

/* constants */
#define MAXBUFLEN     2000
#define SCHEMA        "SYS"
#define TYPE          "XMLTYPE"

/* classes */

class ociapi {
public:

  /* constructors and destructors */
  ociapi();
  ~ociapi();

  /* member functions */
  sb4 init_env_handle();
  sb4 connect_server( text* user, text* password);
  void disconnect_server( boolean tab_exists);
  void cleanup();

  sb4 select_and_query(text* select_stmt, text* xpathexp);
  sb4 select_from_doc( OCIXMLType* xml, text *xpathexpr);

  /* get member functions for private variables */
  OCIEnv* getEnv() const;

private:
  /* OCI Handles and Variables */
  OCIEnv       *envhp;
  OCIServer    *srvhp;
  OCISvcCtx    *svchp;
  OCIError     *errhp;
  OCISession   *authp;
  OCIStmt      *stmthp;
};
```

```
/* functions */

void checkerr( OCIError* errhp, sword status);

/* generic functions */

template< typename TCtx, typename Tnode>
sb4 doXPath( TCtx* ctxp, DocumentRef< Tnode>& doc_ref,
    char* xpath_exp);
/*----------------- End of Functions Declaration -----------------*/
```

In examining this file, first note that there are two Oracle C header files, **xml.h** and **ociap.h**. These contain the C XML APIs and OCI APIs, respectively. The **xmlctx.hpp** file is the header file for the constructor class for OCI XML initialization. We discuss the functions when we get to the code throughout the chapter.

The OCI and C++ XML Application Libraries

OCI applications are dynamically linked on both Unix and Windows using **libclntsh.so**, located in **$ORACLE_HOME/lib32** on Unix, and **oci.lib** plus **ociw32.lib**, located in **%ORACLE_HOME%\oci\lib\Msvc** on Windows. In the past the Solaris library has been in the **lib** directory, but since Oracle Database 10*g* is now only a 64-bit release, the 32-bit libraries are located in their own directory. On Windows you also need to link with the **user32.lib**, **kernel32.lib**, **msvcrt.lib**, **advapi32.lib**, **oldnames.lib**, and **winmm.lib** Windows libraries.

The OCI libraries do not contain the XML APIs; therefore, you also need to link with **libxml10.a** on Unix and **oraxml10.lib** on Windows, which include both the C and C++ XML APIs. The Unix library is not a shared one like the OCI library and thus the objects you need will be pulled into your executable.

Creating the C++ OCI Helper Class

To use the XML APIs from C++, you must create a compatible context. In the case of a midtier or client application, you do this with the built-in **xmlinit()** method in the **XMLParser** class. However, in the case of working with the database, you need to call a method to initialize the OCI context along with the XML context. At the same time, you need to establish a database connection and submit your query in order to return the DOM of the XMLType you are interested in. You do all of this with the **ociapi** class specified in the previous header file, which has the following member functions:

- **init_env_handle()** Creates and initializes and the OCI environment
- **connect_server()** Creates a database connection and passes in the user ID and password
- **disconnect_server()** Disconnects from the server, ending the session
- **cleanup()** Cleans up the OCI environment
- **select_and_query()** Submits the SQL/XML statement and returns the DOM of the XMLType result while calling out to the DOM APIs to do the XPath query
- **query_xmlApi()** Performs C++ XPath operations on XMLType and prints the result

The following sections examine the actual source code for the **ociapi** class implementation, broken down by its member functions.

Initializing the C++ Database XML Application

The first step when creating a C++ database application is to perform all of the necessary OCI initializations and allocations. These steps are required for all OCI applications, as the following code illustrates. This **init_env_handle()** function creates and initializes the OCI environment that requires an allocation of several handles that will be populated by the subsequent member functions. This function is not application-specific and thus can be used as-is in your applications.

```
/*---------------------------------------------------------*/
/* Initialize the environment and allocate handles         */
/*---------------------------------------------------------*/
sb4 ociapi::init_env_handle()
{ sword status = 0;
  /* Environment initialization and creation */
  if (OCIEnvCreate((OCIEnv **) &envhp, (ub4) OCI_OBJECT, (dvoid *) 0,
   (dvoid * (*)(dvoid *,size_t)) 0,
   (dvoid * (*)(dvoid *, dvoid *, size_t)) 0,
   (void (*)(dvoid *, dvoid *)) 0, (size_t) 0, (dvoid **) 0))
  { printf("FAILED: OCIEnvCreate()\n");
    return OCI_ERROR;
  }
  /* allocate error handle */
  if (OCIHandleAlloc( (dvoid *)envhp, (dvoid **) errhp,
      (ub4) OCI_HTYPE_ERROR, (size_t) 0, (dvoid **) 0))
  { printf("FAILED: OCIHandleAlloc() on errhp\n");
    return OCI_ERROR;
  }
  /* allocate server handle */
  if (status = OCIHandleAlloc( (dvoid*)envhp, (dvoid **) &srvhp,
      (ub4) OCI_HTYPE_SERVER, (size_t) 0, (dvoid **) 0))
  { printf("FAILED: OCIHandleAlloc() on srvhp\n");
    checkerr( errhp, status);
    return OCI_ERROR;
  }
  /* allocate service context handle */
  if (status = OCIHandleAlloc(( dvoid*)envhp, (dvoid **) &svchp,
             (ub4) OCI_HTYPE_SVCCTX, (size_t) 0, (dvoid **) 0))
  { printf("FAILED: OCIHandleAlloc() on svchp\n");
    checkerr( errhp, status);
    return OCI_ERROR;
  }
  /* allocate session handle */
  if (status = OCIHandleAlloc( (dvoid*)envhp, (dvoid **) &authp,
      (ub4) OCI_HTYPE_SESSION, (size_t) 0, (dvoid **) 0))
  { printf("FAILED: OCIHandleAlloc() on authp\n");
    checkerr( errhp, status);
    return OCI_ERROR;
  }
```

```
  /* Allocate statement handle */
  if (status = OCIHandleAlloc( (dvoid*)envhp, (dvoid **) stmthp,
      (ub4) OCI_HTYPE_STMT, (size_t) 0, (dvoid **) 0))
  { printf("FAILED: OCIHandleAlloc() on stmthp\n");
    checkerr( errhp, status);
    return OCI_ERROR;
  }
  return OCI_SUCCESS;
}
```

Handling OCI Errors

It is necessary to include error checking within this application. This can be done with the following **checker()** function. This generic code can be copied and pasted into your applications without customization.

```
void checkerr( OCIError* errhp, sword status) {
  text  msgbuf[512];
  sb4   errcode = 0;

  memset((void *) msgbuf, (int)'\0', (size_t)512);

  switch (status)
  {
  case OCI_SUCCESS: break;
  case OCI_SUCCESS_WITH_INFO:
    printf("status = OCI_SUCCESS_WITH_INFO\n");
    OCIErrorGet((dvoid *) errhp, (ub4) 1, (text *) NULL, &errcode,
             msgbuf, (ub4) sizeof(msgbuf), (ub4) OCI_HTYPE_ERROR);
    printf("ERROR CODE = %d\n", errcode);
    printf("%.*s\n", 512, msgbuf);
    if (errcode == 436 || errcode == 437 || errcode == 438
    || errcode == 439)
      exit(1);
    break;
  case OCI_NEED_DATA:
    printf("status = OCI_NEED_DATA\n");
    break;
  case OCI_NO_DATA:
     printf("status = OCI_NO_DATA\n");
    break;
  case OCI_ERROR:
     printf("status = OCI_ERROR\n");
     OCIErrorGet((dvoid *) errhp, (ub4) 1, (text *) NULL, &errcode,
              msgbuf, (ub4) sizeof(msgbuf), (ub4) OCI_HTYPE_ERROR);
     printf("ERROR CODE = %d\n", errcode);
     printf("%.*s\n", 512, msgbuf);
    if (errcode == 436 || errcode == 437 || errcode == 438
    || errcode == 439)
      exit(1);
    break;
```

```
    case OCI_INVALID_HANDLE:
       printf("status = OCI_INVALID_HANDLE\n");
      break;
    case OCI_STILL_EXECUTING:
       printf("status = OCI_STILL_EXECUTE\n");
      break;
    case OCI_CONTINUE:
       printf("status = OCI_CONTINUE\n");
      break;
    default:
      break;
    }

    return;
}
```

This is a standard case-statement-error-routine checking for the OCI error condition constants defined in **oci.h.** Now that the generic code is complete, we can begin discussing the application-specific code.

Connecting to the Database

Since this is a database application, you need to connect to it using the Oracle Net services provided by OCI. The **connect_server()** function passes in the user ID and password to initialize a database session. It does this by populating data fields within the session handle and then sets the session handle into the service context. While your user ID and password is passed in, the code itself is generic and independent of your application.

Since the example is querying a set of relational tables to return the result in XML as dictated by the SQL/XML query, we don't want to return the XML directly but rather return it as an XOB-based DOM so that it can be directly accessed. However, first you need to connect to the database as follows:

```
*-----------------------------------------------------------------------*/
/* connect_server member function to connect to the DB                 */
*-----------------------------------------------------------------------*/
sb4 ociapi::connect_server( text* user, text* password)
{ sword status = 0;
  /* attach to server */
  if (status = OCIServerAttach((OCIServer *) srvhp, (OCIError *) errhp,
       (text *) "", (sb4) strlen(""), (ub4) OCI_DEFAULT))
  { printf("FAILED: OCIServerAttach() on srvhp\n");
    checkerr(errhp, status);
    return OCI_ERROR;
  }
  /* set server attribute to service context */
  if (status = OCIAttrSet((dvoid *) svchp, (ub4) OCI_HTYPE_SVCCTX,
        (dvoid *) srvhp, (ub4) 0, (ub4) OCI_ATTR_SERVER,
        (OCIError *) errhp))
  { printf("FAILED: OCIAttrSet() on svchp\n");
    checkerr(errhp, status);
```

```
    return OCI_ERROR;
  }
  /* set user attribute to session */
  if (status = OCIAttrSet((dvoid *) authp, (ub4) OCI_HTYPE_SESSION,
        (dvoid *) user, (ub4) strlen((char *)user),
        (ub4) OCI_ATTR_USERNAME, (OCIError *) errhp))
  { printf("FAILED: OCIAttrSet() on authp for user\n");
    checkerr(errhp, status);
    return OCI_ERROR;
  }
  /* set password attribute to session */
  if (status = OCIAttrSet((dvoid *) authp, (ub4) OCI_HTYPE_SESSION,
              (dvoid *) password, (ub4) strlen((char *)password),
              (ub4) OCI_ATTR_PASSWORD, (OCIError *) errhp))
  { printf("FAILED: OCIAttrSet() on authp for password\n");
    checkerr( errhp, status);
    return OCI_ERROR;
  }
  /* Begin a session  */
  if (status = OCISessionBegin((OCISvcCtx *) svchp, (OCIError *) errhp,
              (OCISession *) authp, (ub4) OCI_CRED_RDBMS,
              (ub4) OCI_DEFAULT))
  { printf("FAILED: OCISessionBegin()\n");
    checkerr( errhp, status);
    return OCI_ERROR;
  }

  /* set session attribute to service context */
  if (status = OCIAttrSet((dvoid *) svchp, (ub4) OCI_HTYPE_SVCCTX,
        (dvoid *) authp, (ub4) 0, (ub4) OCI_ATTR_SESSION,
        (OCIError *) errhp))
  { printf("FAILED: OCIAttrSet() on svchp\n");
    checkerr( errhp, status);
    return OCI_ERROR;
  }
  return OCI_SUCCESS;
}
```

Disconnecting from the Database and Cleaning Up

Once your database session is completed, you need to detach from the database and clean up the context by freeing all of the allocated handles. You do this by calling **detach_server()** in the following generic code, which is not application-dependent.

```
/*----------------------------------------------------------*/
/* End the session, detach server, and free handles.        */
/*----------------------------------------------------------*/
void ociapi::disconnect_server( boolean tab_exists)
```

```
{ sword status = 0;

  printf("\n\nLogged off and detached from server.\n");

 /* End a session */
  if (status = OCISessionEnd((OCISvcCtx *)svchp, (OCIError *)errhp,
                  (OCISession *)authp, (ub4) OCI_DEFAULT)) {
    checkerr( errhp, status);
    cleanup();
    return;
  }
  /* Detach from the server */
  if (status = OCIServerDetach((OCIServer *)srvhp, (OCIError *)errhp,
                  (ub4)OCI_DEFAULT)) {
    checkerr( errhp, status);
    cleanup();
    return;
  }
  /* Free the handles */
  if (stmthp) {
    OCIHandleFree((dvoid *)stmthp, (ub4) OCI_HTYPE_STMT);
  }
  if (authp) {
    OCIHandleFree((dvoid *)authp, (ub4) OCI_HTYPE_SESSION);
  }
  if (svchp) {
    OCIHandleFree((dvoid *)svchp, (ub4) OCI_HTYPE_SVCCTX);
  }
  if (srvhp) {
    OCIHandleFree((dvoid *)srvhp, (ub4) OCI_HTYPE_SERVER);
  }
  if (errhp) {
    OCIHandleFree((dvoid *)errhp, (ub4) OCI_HTYPE_ERROR);
  }
  if (envhp) {
    OCIHandleFree((dvoid *)envhp, (ub4) OCI_HTYPE_ENV);
  }
}
```

To perform the final bit of housekeeping, you call the **cleanup()** function to free the OCI environment as a whole:

```
/*-------------------------------------------------------*/
/* Clean up OCI handles.                                 */
/*-------------------------------------------------------*/
void ociapi::cleanup()
{ if (envhp) {
    OCIHandleFree((dvoid *)envhp, OCI_HTYPE_ENV);
  }
}
```

Creating the C++ Query Application

Now that you understand the mechanics of creating an OCI XML application, we can examine the Query application's Main function:

```
#include "sample.hpp"
/*------------------------Main function -------------------------*/

int main( int argc, char* argv[])
{
  /* database login information */
  text           *user=(text *)"HR";
  text           *password=(text *)"HR";

  /* OCI environment variables */
  ociapi* ociobjp;

  /* Miscellaneous */
  boolean         tab_exists = TRUE;
  ub4             row = 1;

  if (argc < 2) {
    printf( "\nUsage error: \"<SQL-XML Query>\" \"<XPath>\" \n\n");
    return OCI_ERROR;
  }

  ociobjp = new ociapi();

  /* Initialize the environment and allocate handles */
  if (ociobjp->init_env_handle())
  {
    printf("FAILED: init_env_handle()!\n");
    delete ociobjp;
    return OCI_ERROR;
  }

  /* Log on to the server and begin a session */
  if (ociobjp->connect_server( user, password))
  {
    printf("FAILED: connect_server()!\n");
    delete ociobjp;
    return OCI_ERROR;
  }

  /* Select an xmltype column by defining it to an xmltype instance,
     and query the XOB using the Xpath expression with
     the unified DOM APIs */

  if (ociobjp->select_and_query((text *)argv[1], (text *)argv[2])
```

```
  {
    printf("FAILED: select_and_query!\n");
    ociobjp->disconnect_server( tab_exists);
    delete ociobjp;
    return OCI_ERROR;
  }

  /* Detach from a server and clean up the environment */
  ociobjp->disconnect_server( tab_exists);
  delete ociobjp;

  return OCI_SUCCESS;
}
```

The application has the software steps of initialization; connecting to the database; submitting the query; performing the application logic on the results; and cleaning up before exiting. In the following sections, you will see the details of each of these steps as the application is built out. Note that there is a series of *if* statements to call the code we have discussed that set up the environment, connect to and disconnect from the database, and clean up. What is left is the **select_and_query()** function that does all the work.

Selecting into an XMLType

After successfully connecting to the database and opening a session, you can submit the query that was passed in on the command line. This is the *select* section of the **select_and_query()** function:

```
sb4 ociapi::select_and_query( text* select_stmt, text *xpathexpr)
{
  ub4 xmlsize = 0;
  sword status = 0;
  OCIDefine *defnp = (OCIDefine *) 0;
  OCIBind *bndhp = (OCIBind *) 0;
  OCIXMLType *xml = (OCIXMLType *) 0;
  OCIType *xmltdo = (OCIType *) 0;
  OCIInd ind = OCI_IND_NULL;
  OCIInd *xml_ind = &ind;

  printf("\n=> \"%select_stmt\" as an XMLType instance......\n", row);

  /* get the tdo for the xmltype */
  if (status = OCITypeByName(envhp, errhp, svchp, (const text *) SCHEMA,
           (ub4) strlen((char *)SCHEMA), (const text *) TYPE,
           (ub4) strlen((char *)TYPE), (CONST text *) 0,
           (ub4) 0, OCI_DURATION_SESSION, OCI_TYPEGET_HEADER,
           (OCIType **) &xmltdo))
  {
    printf("FAILED: OCITypeByName()\n");
    checkerr( errhp, status);
    return OCI_ERROR;
  }
```

```
if (!xmltdo)
{
  printf("NULL tdo returned\n");
  return OCI_ERROR;
}

/* create a new xmltype instance */
if (status = OCIObjectNew( (OCIEnv*)envhp, (OCIError*)errhp,
          (CONST OCISvcCtx *)svchp,
          (OCITypeCode) OCI_TYPECODE_OPAQUE,
          (OCIType *) xmltdo, (dvoid *) 0,
          (OCIDuration) OCI_DURATION_SESSION, FALSE,
          (dvoid **) &xml))
{
  printf("FAILED: OCIObjectNew()\n");
  checkerr( errhp, status);
  return OCI_ERROR;
}

if(status = OCIStmtPrepare( stmthp, errhp, (OraText *)select_stmt,
          (ub4)strlen((char*)select_stmt),
          (ub4) OCI_NTV_SYNTAX, (ub4) OCI_DEFAULT))
{
  printf("FAILED: OCIStmtPrepare()\n");
  checkerr( errhp, status);
  return OCI_ERROR;
}

/* define it to an xmltype instance */
if(status = OCIDefineByPos( stmthp, &defnp, errhp, (ub4) 1, (dvoid *) 0,
          (sb4) 0, SQLT_NTY, (dvoid *) 0, (ub2 *)0,
          (ub2 *)0, (ub4) OCI_DEFAULT))
{
  printf("FAILED: OCIDefineByPos()\n");
  checkerr( errhp, status);
  return OCI_ERROR;
}

if(status = OCIDefineObject( defnp, errhp, (OCIType *) xmltdo,
           (dvoid **) &xml, &xmlsize,
           (dvoid **) &xml_ind, (ub4 *) 0))
{
  printf("FAILED: OCIDefineObject()\n");
  checkerr(errhp, status);
  return OCI_ERROR;
}

if(status = OCIStmtExecute( svchp, stmthp, errhp, (ub4) 1, (ub4) 0,
          (CONST OCISnapshot*) 0, (OCISnapshot*) 0,
          (ub4) OCI_DEFAULT))
```

```
{
  printf("FAILED: OCIStmtExecute()\n");
  checkerr(errhp, status);
  return OCI_ERROR;
}
```

At this point, assuming the statement execution was successful, you have an OCI context, **xml**, populated with an XMLType XOB corresponding to the result set in XML format. You now need to initialize the XDK context and bind it to the XOB so you can use the C++ unified XDK APIs on the XOB.

Initializing the XDK for XMLType XOB Access

The XDK C++ XML APIs need an XML context from which to operate. When using the C APIs this is done by calling **OCIXmlDbInitXmlCtx()** and then casting its return context to **xmlnode**. This can't be done directly in C++; therefore, the following function wraps the C one to produce a C++ context you can use with the C++ XDK APIs.

```
sb4 ociapi::select_from_doc(OCIXMLType* xml, text *xpathexpr){
  boolean result = 0;
  OCIXMLType *newxml = (OCIXMLType *) 0;
  OCIXMLType *xmltran = (OCIXMLType *) 0;
  sword  status = 0;

  /* For XML C++ APIs */
  OCIDuration dur = OCI_DURATION_SESSION;
  struct xmlctx *xctx = (xmlctx *)0;
  xmldocnode *doc = (xmldocnode *)0;
  ocixmldbparam params[1];


  /* Get an XML C and C++ context */
  params[0].name_ocixmldbparam = XCTXINIT_OCIDUR;
  params[0].value_ocixmldbparam = &dur;
  xctx = OCIXmlDbInitXmlCtx( envhp, svchp, errhp, params, 1);
  CXmlCtx* cxctxp = new CXmlCtx( xctx);

   /* convert the xmltype value to C++ DocumentRef */
  doc = (xmldocnode *) xml;
  DOMImplRef< CXmlCtx, xmlnode>
    impl_ref( cxctxp, new DOMImplementation< xmlnode>( FALSE));
  DocumentRef< xmlnode>* doc_refp = impl_ref.formDocument( (xmlnode*)doc);

  /* test xml unified C APIs */
  if (doXPath< CXmlCtx, xmlnode>( cxctxp, *doc_refp, (char*)xpathexpr)) {
    printf("FAILED: doXPath()\n");
    return OCI_ERROR;
  }
```

```
  /* free the statement handle */
  if (stmthp) {
    OCIHandleFree((dvoid *)stmthp, OCI_HTYPE_STMT);
  }

  /* free the xmlctx */
  OCIXmlDbFreeXmlCtx(xctx);

  /* free xml instances using OCIObjectFree */
  if (newxml &&
      (status = OCIObjectFree(envhp, errhp, (dvoid *) newxml,
                             (ub2)OCI_OBJECTFREE_FORCE))) {
   printf("FAILED: OCIObjectFree()\n");
   checkerr(errhp, status);
   return OCI_ERROR;
 }

 return OCI_SUCCESS;
}
```

The **OCIXmlDbInit()** function returns the C context, **xctx**, which is then passed to the **CXmlCtx()** constructor to return the C++ context, **cxctxp**. This context can then be used to create the C++ DocumentRef, **doc_refp**, that points to the XOB DOM and can be used with the C++ XDK APIs.

Querying an XMLType with the C++ XDK APIs

At this point, the C++ XML functions can operate on the document node in exactly the same way as if it were parsed from a file. These APIs are identical and thus your code can be portable for the actual application logic you need to perform. The following generic template, **doXPath()**, evaluates the XPath expression, **doXPath**, and prints out the result to the screen:

```
/* generic template to handle XPath processing */
template< typename TCtx, typename Tnode>
sb4 doXPath( TCtx* ctxp, DocumentRef< Tnode>& doc_ref, char* xpath_exp) {
  printf("Initializing Tools Factory\n");
  Factory< TCtx, Tnode>* fp = NULL;
  try {
  fp = new Factory< TCtx, Tnode>( ctxp); }
  catch (FactoryException& fe) {
    unsigned ecode = fe.getCode();
    printf( "Failed to create factory, error %u\n", ecode);
    return ecode;}
  printf("Creating XPath processor\n");
  XPath::Processor< TCtx, Tnode>* prp = NULL;
  try {
    prp = fp->createXPathProcessor( XPathPrCXml, NULL);}
  catch (FactoryException& fe1) {
    unsigned ecode = fe1.getCode();
    printf( "Failed to create XPath processor, error %u\n", ecode);
```

```
    return ecode; }
  printf( "Create DOM source for the DOM tree\n");
  InputSource* isrcp = new DOMSource< Tnode>( doc_ref);
  printf("Processing DOM tree with  '%s' ...\n", xpath_exp);
  XPathObject< Tnode>* objp = NULL;
  try {
    objp = prp->process (isrcp, (oratext*)xpath_exp); }
  catch (XPathException& xpe) {
    unsigned ecode = xpe.getCode();
    printf( "Failed to process the document, error %u\n", ecode);
    return ecode; }
  NodeSet< Tnode>* np = NULL;
  boolean varb = FALSE;
  double num = 0.0;
  oratext* str = NULL;
  unsigned i = 0;
  switch (objp->getObjType()) {
  case XPOBJ_TYPE_NDSET:
    np = objp->getNodeSet();
    printf("NodeSet:\n");
    for (i = 0; i < np->getSize(); i++ ) {
      NodeRef< Tnode>* nrefp = np->getNode( i);
      switch( nrefp->getNodeType()) {
      case ELEMENT_NODE:
      case ATTRIBUTE_NODE:
      printf("Node Name : %s\n",
             nrefp->getNodeName());
      break;
      default:
      printf("Other Node: %s\n" nrefp->getNodeValue() );
      break; }
    }
    break;
  case XPOBJ_TYPE_BOOL:
    varb = objp->getObjBoolean();
    printf("Boolean Value : %d\n", varb);
    break;
  case XPOBJ_TYPE_NUM:
    num = objp->getObjNumber();
    printf("Numeric Value : %10.2f\n", num);
    break;
  case XPOBJ_TYPE_STR:
    str = objp->getObjString();
    printf("String Value : %s\n", str);
    break;
  default:
    printf( "Failed to create valid object\n");
  }
  return 0;
}
```

This code has several sections. First, you must create an XPath processor, which can accept as parameters your XPath expression and database DOM tree and then return the result. Since the result may be a collection of nodes, a string, a number, or a Boolean, you need to set up a case statement because the code to print these items is not the same.

For a node set, you need to iterate over each item and properly detect whether they are a set of attributes or elements. You must convert Boolean and number values to strings before you can print them. Even though they started out as lexical representations, the XPath processor implicitly cast them per the 1.0 specification.

Running the Application

Once you have the source code compiled and linked, it can be run connecting to the database specified by your ORACLE_SID environment setting and using the HR/HR userID/Password. The following is an example command line with its result.

```
selectxpq "select XMLELEMENT("EmployeeList", XMLAGG(XMLELEMENT("Employee",
 XMLATTRIBUTES( employee_id AS "EmpID"), XMLELEMENT("Name", first_name
|| ' '|| last_name), XMLELEMENT("Salary", salary))))AS result FROM
hr.employees where Salary > 13000" "//Employee/Name[../Salary="17000"]"
```

This query returns the following XML document from the **employees** table:

```
<EmployeeList>
 <Employee EmpID="100">
  <Name>Steven King</Name>
  <Salary>24000</Salary>
 </Employee>
 <Employee EmpID="101">
  <Name>Neena Kochhar</Name>
  <Salary>17000</Salary>
 </Employee>
 <Employee EmpID="102">
  <Name>Lex De Haan</Name>
  <Salary>17000</Salary>
 </Employee>
  <Employee EmpID="145">
  <Name>John Russell</Name>
  <Salary>14000</Salary>
 </Employee>
 <Employee EmpID="146">
   <Name>Karen Partners</Name>
   <Salary>13500</Salary>
 </Employee>
</EmployeeList>
```

The XPath expression **//Employee/Name[../Salary="17000"]** asks for all the names of employees whose salary is equal to 17000 and returns the following XML fragment:

```
<Name>Neena Kochhar</Name>
<Name>Lex De Haan</Name>
```

Summary

In this chapter you have built an OCI XML application by using the new unified XML APIs that are available in Oracle Database 10*g* by way of the Oracle XDK. This functionality has not been available in the past and answers a real need to allow operating close to large datasets. The alternative of serializing this data only to reparse it before working on it produces an application that doesn't scale or perform. These interfaces also enable an OCI application developer to work natively with XMLTypes and thereby utilize the full flexibility and power of the XML database and XMLTypes.

CHAPTER 24

Building an XML Data-Retrieval Application

s XML becomes the industry standard for exchanging business data, the capability to retrieve selective data from large XML documents becomes increasingly more important. Because XPath is the XML navigational language, it lies at the foundation of standards-based data-retrieval solutions. XPath-supported solutions such as XSLT require creation and traversal of the input XML's Document Object Model (DOM). In practice, DOMs require up to ten times the memory of the original document because DOMs include traversal APIs that are difficult to optimize. Other XML processing methods, such as SAX and StAX, are event-based and require less memory; however, they lack the desired XPath support for retrieving XML data.

XPath allows you to retrieve XML data based not only on its content but also on the XML document structure. In Oracle XDK 10*g*, you have access to an XPath processor in C and C++ that can evaluate an XPath and return a set of nodes or values as appropriate.

In this chapter, we first examine typical requirements for data retrieval from XML documents, and then discuss the design of an application that provides XPath-based XML data retrieval. Then you will build a lightweight data-extraction engine that can efficiently match XPaths and retrieve the results. Finally, we describe how this engine can be easily integrated into a content-management application in an actual use case.

Designing the Framework

In much the same way that SQL is used to query a relational database, XPath expressions can be used to query an XML document. While the W3C XPath standard is not meant to stand alone, any implementation of XSLT or XQuery requires an internal XPath processor. Since Oracle has exposed its XPath processor, you can use it for a variety of applications. The example framework presented in this chapter supports two specific applications that are quite common.

To work with XML documents that are stored in your database, you need to be able to query them for information. One approach is to simply index them within your database; however, that is expensive. Another approach is to extract from the document, prior to or upon its insertion, key data that can be stored relationally and linked to the document itself through an ID. This results in far faster and more efficient queries.

The second application enables you to process large XML documents that consist of repeating subtrees, which are quite common in database data. Instead of processing the document as a whole, this application enables you to split it based on an XPath and return a set of smaller documents that are easier to process.

Both of these applications have in common the use of an XPath processor. The first application returns a set of values, the second a set of nodes. Therefore, your design must be able to handle both conditions. To do this, you will build a framework around the C++ XPath processor. For ease of testing, this framework will be packaged as a command-line utility, but it can easily be plugged into a larger application.

Building the cppextract Application

Since the Oracle XDK 10*g* C++ libraries have been converted to use C++ templates, you will use this design approach for the application called **cppextract**. It will be made up of the following three object files and their associated source files:

- **cppextractGen.cpp** The generic functions used within the application
- **cppextractForce.cpp** The specific instantiation of the generic functions in the application
- **cppextract.cpp** The user interface to the application

The following sections discuss these files and their usage within the application.

Creating the Generic Functions

The **cppextractGen.cpp** file contains the code of the templates that are used in the application. Its only dependencies are on the standard C I/O library, **stdio.h**, and the XDK C/C++ library, **oraxml10**, which is referenced by including **xml.hpp**:

```
#ifndef XML_CPP_ORACLE
#include <xml.hpp>
#endif
```

The processXPath() Template

The **processXPath()** template performs the actual XPath evaluation by wrapping the **process()** function with the necessary code to parse the input XML document and to handle the resulting output. Let's examine the template in detail.

This first section handles the initialization of the XDK context and is a call that all C++ XDK applications need to make. It needs to be made only one time because it can be reused throughout the application.

```
template< typename TCtx, typename Tnode> unsigned processXPath(
               char* dname, char* xpath_exp);

extern "C" {

#include <stdio.h>
}
#include "cppextract.hpp"

template< typename Tnode> void printSubtree( NodeRef< Tnode>& nrefp);

template< typename TCtx, typename Tnode> unsigned processXPath(
                                 char* dname, char* xpath_exp) {

  TCtx* ctxp = NULL;

  cout << "XML C++ XPath Extract\n";

  try
  {
    ctxp = new TCtx();
  }
```

```
catch (XmlException& e)
{
  unsigned ecode = e.getCode();

  cout << "Failed to initialize XML context, error " <<ecode<< "\n";
  return ecode;
}
```

The next section creates an instance of the XPath processor by first creating a new Tools Factory instance, **fp**, and then using it to create the processor, **prp**, with **createXPathProcessor()**:

```
Factory< TCtx, Tnode>* fp = NULL;

try
{
  fp = new Factory< TCtx, Tnode>( ctxp);
}
catch (FactoryException& fe)
{
  unsigned ecode = fe.getCode();

  cout << "Failed to create factory, error " <<ecode <<"\n";
  return ecode;
}

printf("Creating XPath processor\n");

XPath::Processor< TCtx, Tnode>* prp = NULL;

try
{
  prp = fp->createXPathProcessor( XPathPrCXml, NULL);
}
catch (FactoryException& fe1)
{
  unsigned ecode = fe1.getCode();

  cout << "Failed to create XPath processor, error " <<ecode <<"\n";
  return ecode;
}
```

Next, the input XML document is passed in by calling **Filesource()**:

```
InputSource* isrcp = new FileSource( (oratext*)dname);
```

The following section invokes the XPath processor through its **process()** function by passing in the document object, **isrcp**, and the XPath expression, **xpath_exp**. The result is returned as **objp** (which is analyzed in the next section).

```
cout<< "Processing "<<dname;
cout<<"using"<<"\""<<xpath_exp<<"\""<<"\n";

XPathObject< Tnode>* objp = NULL;

try
{
  objp = prp->process (isrcp, (oratext*)xpath_exp);

}
catch (XPathException& xpe)
{
  unsigned ecode = xpe.getCode();

  cout << "Failed to process the document, error " <<ecode <<"\n";
  return ecode;
}
```

The next section queries the result object, **objp**, and the case statement branches the resulting processing:

```
NodeSet< Tnode>* np = NULL;
boolean varb = FALSE;
double num = 0.0;
oratext* str = NULL;
unsigned i = 0;

switch (objp->getObjType())
{
case XPOBJ_TYPE_NDSET:
  np = objp->getNodeSet();
  cout << "NodeSet:\n";
  for (i = 0; i < np->getSize(); i++ )
  {
    NodeRef< Tnode>* nrefp = np->getNode( i);
    switch( nrefp->getNodeType())
    {
    case ELEMENT_NODE:
    NodeRef< Tnode> elref( (*np), nrefp);
    cout << "<?xml version=\"1.0\" encoding=\"UTF-8\"?>\n";
    printSubTree< Tnode>( *nrefp);
     break;

    case ATTRIBUTE_NODE:
      cout << "Attribute Name :" <<nrefp->getNodeName()<<"\n";
    break;
default:
```

```
          cout<<("Node Value : "<<nrefp->getNodeValue()<<"\n";
        break;
          }
      }
      break;

    case XPOBJ_TYPE_BOOL:
      varb = objp->getObjBoolean();
      cout<<("Boolean Value : "<<varb<<"\n";
      break;
    case XPOBJ_TYPE_NUM:
      num = objp->getObjNumber();
      cout<<("Numeric Value : "<<num<<"\n";
      break;

    case XPOBJ_TYPE_STR:
      str = objp->getObjString();
      cout << "String Value : " << str << "\n";
      objp = prp->process (isrcp, (oratext*)xpath_exp);

    default:
      cout<<( "Failed to create valid object\n");
    }
    return 0;
}
```

Since **objp** may represent a set of nodes, values, strings, etc., you need to loop through them as is done in the FOR loop. If the result is XPOBJ_TYPE_NDSET, then the return type is a node set. An additional case statement further processes it to determine the type of nodes. If the nodes are elements, it treats this as a request for splitting the document into subtrees and thus first prints out the XML processing instruction and then calls the **printSubTree()** function. If the result is one or more attribute nodes, it prints their names. If the node type is neither an element nor attribute node, it prints its value. For example, consider the following document:

```
<?xml version="1.0" encoding="UTF-8"?>
<Bookcatalog>
 <book ISBN = "7564">
  <title>The Adventures of Don Quixote</title>
  <author_lastname>Cervantes</author_lastname>
  <publisher>Oracle Press</publisher>
  <year>2000</year>
  <price>50.00</price>
 </book>
 <book ISBN= "5354">
  <title>The Iliad</title>
  <author_lastname>Homer</author_lastname>
  <publisher>Oracle Press</publisher>
  <year>1000</year>
  <price>5.00</price>
</book>
</Bookcatalog>
```

The XPath **/bookcatalog/book** will print each book record. The XPath **//book/@*** will print the name of each attribute, which in this case is **ISBN**. The XPath **string(//book/@*)** will return the ISBN values of 7564 and 5354 since the case statement will break out under XPOBJ_TYPE_STR. If the node is neither an element nor an attribute, such as a text node, the **NodeSet** case statement executes its default section and returns the associated string values as in **//book/title/text()** which returns "The Adventures of Don Quixote" and "The Iliad".

This file also includes the **cppextract.hpp** header file that declares the main template, **processXPath()**, as follows:

```
#ifndef XML_CPP_ORACLE
#include <xml.hpp>
#endif

template< typename TCtx, typename Tnode> unsigned processXPath(
                                char* dname, char* xpath_exp);
```

The printSubTree() Template

The **printSubTree()** template is used to print the subtrees rooted at the specified element to separate documents:

```
template< typename Tnode> void printSubTree( NodeRef< Tnode>& nref)
{
  oratext* tag = nref.getNodeName();
  if (tag == NULL)
  {
    cout << " Element has no name - error\n";
    return;
  }
  // print opening tag
   cout << "<" << tag;

  //Get attributes on element
  NamedNodeMap< Tnode>* attrs = nref.getAttributes();
  NamedNodeMapRef< Tnode> attref( nref, attrs);
  ub4 n_attrs = attref.getLength();
  NodeRef< Tnode>* attrefp = NULL;
  for (unsigned a = 0; a < n_attrs; a++)
  {
    Tnode* ap = attref.item( a);
    if (a == 0)
      attrefp = new NodeRef< Tnode>( nref, ap);
    else
      attrefp->resetNode( ap);
// print attribute
    cout << " " << attrefp->getNodeName() << " = " << attrefp->getNodeValue();
  }
  cout << ">";
  NodeRef< Tnode>* nrefp = NULL;
  if (nref.hasChildNodes())
  {
```

```
    NodeList< Tnode>* lp = nref.getChildNodes();
    NodeListRef< Tnode> lref( nref, lp);

    ub4 len = lref.getLength();
    for (unsigned i = 0; i < len; i++)
    {
      Tnode* np = lref.item( i);
      if (i == 0)
                    nrefp = new NodeRef< Tnode>( nref, np);
      else
                    nrefp->resetNode( np);

      if  (nrefp->getNodeType() == ELEMENT_NODE)
      {
//Continue iterration
                printSubTree< Tnode>( *nrefp);
      }
      else if (nrefp->getNodeType() == TEXT_NODE)
//Print Text value
                cout << nrefp->getNodeValue();
    }
  }
//Print closing tag
  cout << "</" << tag << ">";
}
```

This is a useful template for serializing an XML document or fragment as there currently is not a version of **XmlSaveDOM()** for C++. First it sends out the opening angle bracket and tag name. Then it must check for attributes. This is done with a FOR loop to iterate over them by first getting a pointer, **attrefp**, to each one and serializing its name and value. Then the closing angle bracket is serialized. Since an element can have element content, text content, or both, an IF statement is created to check for this. By calling **getChildNodes()** and then checking the number returned, you can iterate over them with a FOR loop and either call **printSubTree()** again for element nodes or serialize the value for text nodes. Finally, once the node list, **lp**, is completed, you can serialize the end tag.

Instantiating the Generic Functions with cppextractForce

Once the generic functions are completed, you need to instantiate them in the schema of your application. This is done in **cppextractForce.cpp**:

```
#ifndef XMLCTX_CPP_ORACLE
#include <xmlctx.hpp>
#endif

#include "cppextractGen.cpp"

unsigned force( char* dname, char* xpath_exp)
{
  return processXPath< CXmlCtx, xmlnode>( dname, xpath_exp);
}
```

Note that this file includes the generic functions created in **cppextractGen.cpp**.

Creating the Main Program with cppextractMain

It is now time to create the user interface for the application. This is done in **cppextractMain.cpp**. Since this is a command-line application, you need to pass in the appropriate parameters, which in this case are the XML file to query and the XPath expression to use:

```
#include <iostream.h>
#include <string.h>

#ifndef XMLCTX_CPP_ORACLE
#include <xmlctx.hpp>
#endif

#include "cppextract.hpp"

int main( int argc, char* argv[])
{
    if (argc < 3)
    {
      cout << "Usage is cppextract <xmlfile> <xpath>\n";
      return 1;
    }
    if (processXPath< CXmlCtx, xmlnode>( argv[1], argv[2]))
        return 1;
}
```

Besides parsing the command line, the only thing the application needs to do is call your main **processXPath()** function as it encapsulates the application's functionality. Obviously, if you were using this function from within a more sophisticated application, as we will discuss shortly, the **processXPath()** function could return the actual nodes or subtree DOMs for further processing, such as performing an XSLT transformation or inserting into a database.

Running the cppextract Application

Cppextract implements both application types described in the beginning of the chapter through different sets of command-line parameters: Since **cppextract** only depends upon the C run-time library and the **oraxml10** library, it can be run with no explicit setup from the command line.

Running cppextract in Extraction Mode

Using the **booklist.xml** document you can extract a variety of data by passing in the appropriate XPath expression as the XPath parameter. The following are example command lines and their resulting extractions:

```
cppextract booklist.xml //book/title/text()

Node Value : The Adventures of Don Quixote
Node Value : The Iliad
```

```
booklist.xml number(//book[2]/price/text())

Numeric Value : 5

cppextract booklist.xml string(//book[2]/@*)

String Value : 5354
```

Running cppextract in Splitter Mode

In order to split an XML document with repeating subtrees, you can pass in the XPath expression that points to the element at the root of the subtree as the XPath parameter. Using these specific parameters will return the following XML documents:

```
cppextract booklist.xml "/bookcatalog/book"

<?xml version="1.0" encoding="UTF-8"?>
<book ISBN = "7564">
  <title>The Adventures of Don Quixote</title>
  <author_lastname>Cervantes</author_lastname>
  <publisher>Oracle Press</publisher>
  <year>2000</year>
  <price>50.00</price>
 </book>

<?xml version="1.0" encoding="UTF-8"?>
<book ISBN= "5354">
  <title>The Iliad</title>
  <author_lastname>Homer</author_lastname>
  <publisher>Oracle Press</publisher>
  <year>1000</year>
  <price>5.00</price>
</book>
```

Extending the Framework

As mentioned at the beginning of this chapter, there are many uses for an application that can extract data from an XML document using XPath expressions. While the framework presented here is simple, it is also powerful, as it can easily be extended as described in the next sections.

An XML Document Pruning Use Case for cppextract

Because they are hierarchical with no limits on the size of element content or the number of attributes, XML documents can be large. In many cases, the actual data is buried several levels into the hierarchical structure. While the extracting and splitting techniques presented can simplify some types of processing, *document pruning* can selectively remove nodes while maintaining a single DOM tree.

This can be accomplished using a variation of the code in **cppextract** within the **printSubTree()** template. Since the nodes returned as a result of processing the XPath expression are not copies of the document nodes but references to them, you can perform DOM operations before printing the results. For example, you could produce separate book documents without the price by passing in "//book" and calling **removeChild()** to remove the **<Price>** element. You can also use similar techniques to replace content. The key point to remember is that you have full access to the DOM tree.

A Content-Management Use Case for cppextract

Since XPath is a rich language that is expanding even further in 2.0, you can encapsulate operations on the nodes or values extracted within the expression itself. For example, if you want to find out the number of books listed in **booklist.xml**, the following command line would give you the result in one process step:

```
cppextract booklist.xml "count(/bookcatalog/book)"
...
Numeric Value : 2.0
```

A complete content-management extraction system could be put together in a manner similar to the system shown in the diagram in Figure 24-1. This content-management system extracts the XML data and metadata by using the Extractor that encapsulates the **cppextract** functionality and inserts it into the relational database tables in an Oracle database. The XML data extraction is based on the XPaths stored in an XPath table associated with a DTD and uses the DTD's sysID and docID or an XML schema's location URL to retrieve the appropriate set. When initializing the Extractor, the content-management application retrieves the DTD's sysID and docID or the XML schema location URL from the XML document and uses them to query the XPath table. After it gets a list of

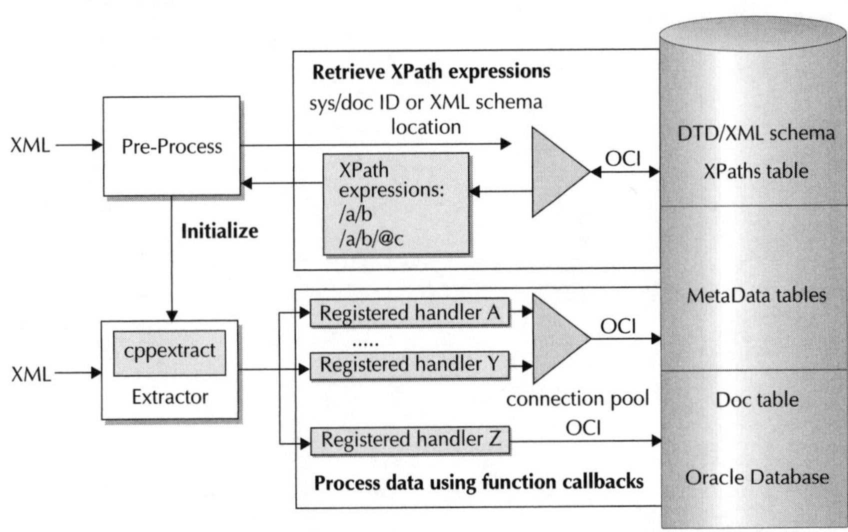

FIGURE 24-1. *cppextract content-management use case*

XPaths, the application then registers the XPaths to the Extractor and specifies instances of callback functions to receive the retrieved data. The Extractor retrieves the XML data for each XPath and disseminates the data to the corresponding content handlers. The content handlers then insert the extracted data into either metadata or data tables in the database.

Summary

In this chapter you were introduced to the XPath processor that is included in the Oracle XDK 10*g* C/C++ library. You used it to build a simple yet powerful XPath data-extraction application that can be used as a basis for broader content-management tasks, as described. You also used the new C++ template architecture for the XML interfaces that replaces the older ones in **oraxml.h** from Oracle9*i*.

PART VI

Oracle XML for PL/SQL Developers

CHAPTER 25

Getting Started with Oracle XML and PL/SQL

PL/SQL is Oracle's procedural language extension to SQL. The PL/SQL XML support allows Oracle DBAs and database application developers to process XML data within the Oracle database. In Oracle Database 10*g*, in addition to the PL/SQL packages that generate XML, store XML, and manage the XML DB Repository, three built-in XML PL/SQL packages are available that provide application programatic interfaces:

- **DBMS_XMLPARSER** Provides the PL/SQL XML parser APIs for parsing XML documents
- **DBMS_XMLDOM** Provides the PL/SQL DOM 1.0 and 2.0 APIs for accessing and updating XML documents
- **DBMS_XSLPROCESSOR** Provides the PL/SQL XSLT Processing APIs for transforming XML documents into other text formats using XSLT

In this chapter, we work through examples that show you how to parse XML, retrieve XML data, and transform XML documents using PL/SQL in Oracle Database 10*g*. At the end of the chapter, we discuss how to set up Oracle JVM to further enable Java XML programming within the Oracle database.

Setting Up the Environment

Since the three XML PL/SQL packages are created during the database installation, you do not need to perform additional setup. During the creation of the three PL/SQL packages, public synonyms—XMLPARSER, XMLDOM, and XSLPROCESSOR—are created for DBMS_XMLPARSER, DBMS_XMLDOM, and DBMS_XSLPROCESSOR, respectively, to substitute for the XMLPARSER, XMLDOM, and XSLPROCESSOR packages in Oracle9*i* Database. The execution privileges of the XML PL/SQL packages are also granted to PUBLIC, which means all users by default are able to run these packages. If you have any security concerns, you need to withdraw these privileges from PUBLIC and grant them to specific users.

To check whether you can run the PL/SQL packages, you can use the following SQL command:

```
SQL> desc <PL/SQL package name>
```

For example, you can check whether you can run the DBMS_XMLPARSER package by using the following command:

```
SQL> desc DBMS_XMLPARSER
```

If you have the execution privilege, you will see the definitions of the procedures and functions defined in the DBMS_XMLPARSER package.

PL/SQL XML Processing Techniques

After you get the privileges to run the XML PL/SQL packages, you can use them to process XML data. However, unlike in Oracle9*i* Database, you do not have to use these packages in certain cases because Oracle Database 10*g* has many SQL/XML features available that often are easier to use than the XML PL/SQL packages to process XML data. For example, you will not normally use DBMS_XSLTPROCESSOR to transform XML documents because the **XMLType.transform()** function provides the same functionality and is easier to use. Therefore, in this section, we discuss the PL/SQL XML processing techniques only if they are distinct from the SQL/XML functions.

Parsing XML

Parsing XML is an operation that reads XML documents, processes the XML documents, and provides programmatic access to the XML data.

In Oracle Database 10*g*, you can use either the DBMS_XMLPARSER package or the **XMLType()** constructor function to parse XML. The difference is that DBMS_XMLPARSER returns the parsed XML document as a **DBMS_XMLDOM.DOMDocument** object, while the **XMLType()** function returns parsed XML as an **XMLType** object. In order to process the parsed **XMLType** objects using DBMS_XMLDOM, you can use the **DBMS_XMLDOM.newDOMDocument()** function to create **DBMS_XMLDOM.DOMDocument** objects from XMLTypes objects.

The DBMS_XMLPARSER package in Oracle Database 10*g* provides three interfaces that allow you to parse XML documents from a string buffer, from a CLOB, or from a file that is stored in the local file system, in the XML DB Repository, or in a web server:

- **parse (p Parser, url VARCHAR2)** Parses XML stored in the given URL or file and returns the built DOM document
- **parseBuffer(p Parser, doc VARCHAR2)** Parses XML stored in the given string buffer
- **parseClob(p Parser, doc CLOB)** Parses XML stored in the given CLOB

Since parsing from a string buffer or a CLOB inside the Oracle database is very straightforward, in the following sections, we only explain the techniques of how to parse XML from files using UTL_FILE_DIR, BFILE, and database URL types.

Parsing XML from Local File Systems

You can either set up UTL_FILE_DIR or use BFILE to parse XML documents from the local file system.

Setting Up UTL_FILE_DIR to Parse XML Documents When you set up UTL_FILE_DIR to parse XML documents, you first need to use the following command to set up the database system parameter, UTL_FILE_DIR, to include the directory in which the XML documents are stored:

```
SQL> ALTER SYSTEM
 SET UTL_FILE_DIR='D:\xmlbook\Examples\Chapter26\src\xml' SCOPE=SPFILE;
```

In this example, **D:\xmlbook\Examples\Chapter26\src\xml** is set to UTL_FILE_DIR. After you run this command as a SYS user, you have to restart the Oracle database to make this change take effect.

After you restart the Oracle database, you can parse XML documents by using DBMS_XMLPARSER. Within your PL/SQL procedure, you first have to initialize an XML parser by using the **DBMS_XMLPARSER.newParser()** function:

```
v_parser DBMS_XMLPARSER.parser;
...
v_parser := DBMS_XMLPARSER.newParser;
```

You can choose whether to validate XML against a DTD and whether to preserve whitespace in the parsed XML documents by specifying the parsing parameters, as follows:

```
DBMS_XMLPARSER.setValidationMode(v_parser, FALSE);
DBMS_XMLPARSER.setPreserveWhiteSpace(v_parser, TRUE);
```

To parse an XML file from UTL_FILE_DIR, you need to set the XML file directory specified in UTL_FILE_DIR to be the base URL of the XML parser by using **DBMS_XMLPASER.setBaseURL**() as follows:

```
v_dir VARCHAR2(200) :=
     'D:\xmlbook\Examples\Chapter26\src\xml';
...
DBMS_XMLPARSER.setBaseDir(v_parser, v_dir);
```

Then, you can use the **DBMS_XMLPARSER.parse(p Parser, url VARCHAR2)** procedure to parse XML files. For example, you can parse a **contact.xml** file stored in this directory as follows:

```
DBMS_XMLPARSER.parse(v_parser, 'contact.xml');
```

You then can get the **DBMS_XMLDOM.DOMDocument** from the XML parser:

```
v_xmldoc := DBMS_XMLPARSER.getDocument(v_parser);
```

You can perform DOM operations on the returned DOM document and we will discuss how you can perform such operations later in this chapter.

After you perform DOM operations, you can write the XML DOM document to a CLOB, a string buffer, or a file by using the following procedures:

- **DBMS_XMLDOM.writetoBuffer**() writes XML into a string buffer.
- **DBMS_XMLDOM.writetoClob**() writes XML into a CLOB.
- **DBMS_XMLDOM.writetoFile**() writes XML into a file in the local file system.

In the following example, the document is written to a CLOB whose content is displayed on the SQL*Plus screen and to an XML file named **out.xml** that is created in the directory specified in UTL_FILE_DIR:

```
DBMS_LOB.createtemporary(v_out,FALSE,DBMS_LOB.SESSION);
DBMS_XMLDOM.writetoClob(v_xmldoc, v_out);
DBMS_XMLDOM.writetoFile(v_xmldoc,v_dir||'/out.xml');
:out := v_out;
DBMS_LOB.freetemporary(v_out);
```

In summary, the following is the example PL/SQL program that parses an XML document stored in a local file system by using UTL_FILE_DIR:

```
SET LONG 100000
SET AUTOPRINT ON
```

```
VAR out CLOB
DECLARE
 v_xmldoc DBMS_XMLDOM.DOMDocument;
 v_parser DBMS_XMLPARSER.parser;
 v_out CLOB;
 v_dir VARCHAR2(200) :=
        'D:\xmlbook\Examples\Chapter26\src\xml';
BEGIN
  -- New parser
  v_parser := DBMS_XMLPARSER.newParser;
  -- Setting up the parsing parameters
  DBMS_XMLPARSER.setValidationMode(v_parser, FALSE);
  DBMS_XMLPARSER.setPreserveWhiteSpace(v_parser, TRUE);
  -- The v_dir has to be a valid directory in the UTL_FILE_DIR
  DBMS_XMLPARSER.setBaseDir(v_parser, v_dir);
  -- Parsing the XML file
  DBMS_XMLPARSER.parse(v_parser, 'contact.xml');
  -- Getting the XML DOMDocument
  v_xmldoc := DBMS_XMLPARSER.getDocument(v_parser);
  -- Print out the result
  DBMS_LOB.createtemporary(v_out,FALSE,DBMS_LOB.SESSION);
  DBMS_XMLDOM.writetoClob(v_xmldoc, v_out);
DBMS_XMLDOM.writetoFile(v_xmldoc,v_dir||'/out.xml');
  :out := v_out;
  DBMS_LOB.freetemporary(v_out);
END;
/
```

Compared to DBMS_XMLPARSER, the **XMLType()** function doesn't allow files to be read from UTL_FILE_DIR. Moreover, by using DBMS_XMLPARSER, you can parse DTDs and use them to validate the XML documents, which is not possible with **XMLType()**.

Using BFILE In the Oracle database, you can create a database directory and use BFILE to read XML files from the local file system. After loading the data into BFILEs, you then get the data into CLOBs where you can parse them by using either DBMS_XMLPARSER or the **XMLType()** function.

To create a database directory, you need to log in as a SYS user and run the following commands:

```
CREATE DIRECTORY xmldir AS 'D:\xmlbook\Examples\Chapter26\src\xml';
GRANT READ ON DIRECTORY xmldir TO demo;
```

These two commands create a database directory called **xmldir** and grant the **read** privilege to the user **demo**.

To load XML documents using BFILE, you can use the following PL/SQL procedure after you have connected as **demo/demo**:

```
CREATE OR REPLACE FUNCTION BfileToClob(fname VARCHAR2) RETURN CLOB IS
fclob CLOB;
theBFile BFILE;
```

```
num NUMBER := 0;
src_offset NUMBER   := 1;
dest_offset NUMBER  := 1;
lang_context NUMBER := 1;
BEGIN
  DBMS_LOB.createtemporary(fclob,FALSE,DBMS_LOB.SESSION);

  theBFile := BFileName('XMLDIR',fname);
  DBMS_LOB.fileOpen(theBFile);
  DBMS_LOB.loadClobFromFile(dest_lob=>fclob,
                            src_bfile=>theBFile,
                            amount=>dbms_lob.getLength(theBFile),
                            dest_offset=>dest_offset,
                            src_offset=>src_offset,
                            bfile_csid=>0,
                            lang_context=>lang_context,
                            warning=>num);
  DBMS_LOB.fileClose(theBFile);
  RETURN fclob;
END;
/
```

In this procedure, a BFILE is opened in the **XMLDIR** database directory by using the **BFileName()** function. To ensure the character set conversion is properly performed, the current language context—the **lang_context** parameter—is set to 1 for the **DBMS_LOB.loadClobFromFile()** function.

After the XML document is loaded from a BFILE into a CLOB, you can use the **DBMS_XMLPARSER.ParseCLOB()** or **XMLType()** function to parse the document in Oracle Database 10*g* as follows:

```
SET AUTOPRINT ON
VAR out CLOB
DECLARE
 v_xmldoc DBMS_XMLDOM.DOMDocument;
 v_xmltype XMLType;
 v_out CLOB;
BEGIN
  v_xmltype := XMLType(BFiletoClob('contact.xml'));
  v_xmldoc :=DBMS_XMLDOM.newDOMDocument(v_xmltype);
  DBMS_LOB.createtemporary(v_out,FALSE,DBMS_LOB.SESSION);
  DBMS_XMLDOM.writetoClob(v_xmldoc, v_out);
  :out := v_out;
  DBMS_LOB.freetemporary(v_out);
END;
/
show errors;
```

In this example, **XMLType()** parses the XML in the CLOB returned by the **BFiletoClob()** procedure.

If an XML document contains DTD references, both UTL_FILE_DIR and BFILE approaches might not work properly. For example, assume that you have an XML document, **test01.xml**, that refers to a DTD document called **test01.dtd**, as follows:

```
<?xml version="1.0" encoding="UTF-8"?>
<?xml-stylesheet type="text/xsl" href="display.xsl"?>
<!DOCTYPE SIGNATURE SYSTEM "test01.dtd">
<SIGNATURE>
  <NAME>&AUTHOR_NAME;</NAME>
  <COPYRIGHT>&COPYRIGHT;</COPYRIGHT>
  <EMAIL>&AUTHOR_EMAIL;</EMAIL>
  <LAST_MODIFIED>&LAST_MODIFIED;</LAST_MODIFIED>
  <PHOTO SOURCE="FUN_IMG">Lovely Kevin</PHOTO>
</SIGNATURE>
```

Parsing this document using BFILE or UTL_FILE_DIR will return the ORA-31001: Invalid Resource Handle or Path Name "/test01.dtd" error.

To avoid this error, you can load the DTD files to the XML DB Repository and update the DTD URLs in the XML files to be the **XMLDBURIs** for the DTD files. Otherwise, you have to rewrite the **EntityResolvers** for the XML parsers. In Chapter 27, we will discuss how to create Java stored procedures to rewrite the **EntityResolvers** so that XML parsers can resolve reference URLs in XML by reading data from files in the local file system, from URLs, or even from database tables.

NOTE
Turning off DTD validation does not prevent the DTD lookup as DTDs are also used for entity expansion and whitespace handling. To turn off the lookup for the DTD references in XML when parsing XML documents, you can use the command

```
Alter session set events '31156 trace name context
forever, level 2';
```

Parsing XML from URLs

To parse an XML document from a URL, you can leverage the **UriType** datatypes that are provided in the Oracle XML DB, such as **HTTPUriType**, **DBUriType**, and **XDBUriType**.

Using HTTPUriType The following example parses an XML document from a web server by using **HTTPUriType**:

```
SET LONG 100000
SET AUTOPRINT ON
VAR out CLOB
DECLARE
  v_xmldoc DBMS_XMLDOM.DOMDocument;
  v_xmltype XMLType;
  v_out CLOB;
BEGIN
v_xmltype := sys.HTTPUriType.createURI(
'http://otn.oracle.com/syndication/rss_otn_news.xml').getXML();
v_xmldoc :=DBMS_XMLDOM.newDOMDocument(v_xmltype);
  DBMS_LOB.createTemporary(v_out,FALSE,DBMS_LOB.SESSION);
  DBMS_XMLDOM.writetoClob(v_xmldoc, v_out);
  :out:=v_out;
  DBMS_LOB.freeTemporary(v_out);
END;
/
```

In this example, an **HTTUriType** object is created for the XML document with the URL **http://otn.oracle.com/syndication/rss_otn_news.xml**, as follows:

```
sys.HTTPUriType.createURI(
'http://otn.oracle.com/syndication/rss_otn_news.xml')
```

To get the XML document, the **HTTPUriType.getXML()** function is then used. The content of the XML document is returned in an XMLType, which is then used to create a **DBMS_XMLDOM.DOMDocument** object for further processing.

Using XDBUriType A similar approach to parse an XML document stored in the XML DB Repository is to use **XDBUriType**. The following procedure assumes that you have loaded **contact.xml** into the XML DB repository's **/public** directory.

```
SET LONG 100000
SET AUTOPRINT ON
VAR out CLOB
DECLARE
 v_xmldoc DBMS_XMLDOM.DOMDocument;
 v_xmltype XMLType;
 v_out CLOB;
BEGIN
v_xmltype :=
SYS.XDBUriType.createUri('/public/contact.xml').getXML();
v_xmldoc :=DBMS_XMLDOM.newDOMDocument(v_xmltype);
  DBMS_LOB.createtemporary(v_out,FALSE,DBMS_LOB.SESSION);
  DBMS_XMLDOM.writetoClob(v_xmldoc, v_out);
  :out := v_out;
  DBMS_LOB.freetemporary(v_out);
END;
/
```

The **XDBUriType** object is created using the **SYS.XDBUriType.createUri()** function and the XML data is returned as an XMLType by using the **XDBUriType.getXML()** function.

Setting Up HTTP Proxy and User Authentication If an XML document has URL references to external files outside the intranet, you need to set up the proxy server to retrieve them. Otherwise, you will get the ORA-29273: HTTP Request Failed error. To set up a proxy server, you can use the **UTL_HTTP.SET_PROXY()** procedure as follows:

```
BEGIN
  UTL_HTTP.SET_PROXY('proxy.mycompany.com:80', 'mycompany.com');
END;
/
```

The first parameter is the proxy URL in *host:port* format. The second parameter includes the domains that can be accessed without the proxy server. The proxy will stay in effect for the current database connection session.

If the URL requires user authentication, you need to create the URL with the username and password in a format as follows:

```
[http://][user[:password]@]host[:port][/]
```

For example, **contact.xml** is created by user **demo** as a private resource in the **/public** directory in the XML DB Repository. To access its content, you need to log in as user **demo**. If the demo user's password is **demo** and the HTTP port number for the XML DB Repository is **8080**, you need to specify the URL to be **http://demo:demo@localhost:8080/public/contact.xml**. Otherwise, you will get an ORA-29273: HTTP Request Failed error. The following example shows how to parse an XML document from an HTTP server that requires user authentication:

```
SET LONG 100000
SET AUTOPRINT ON
VAR out CLOB
DECLARE
 v_xmldoc DBMS_XMLDOM.DOMDocument;
 v_xmltype XMLType;
 v_out CLOB;
BEGIN
  v_xmltype := sys.httpuritype.createuri(
   'http://demo:demo@localhost:8080/public/contact.xml').getXML();
  v_xmldoc :=DBMS_XMLDOM.newDOMDocument(v_xmltype);
  DBMS_LOB.createtemporary(v_out,FALSE,DBMS_LOB.SESSION);
  DBMS_XMLDOM.writetoClob(v_xmldoc, v_out);
  :out:=v_out;
  DBMS_LOB.freetemporary(v_out);
END;
/
```

NOTE
*Including the username and password in the URL should only be used with caution due to security concerns but it is supported in Oracle Database 10*g.

An alternative approach that does not have the security issue is to use UTL_HTTP to get the XML file as follows:

```
set long 100000
set autoprint on
var out clob
declare
 v_xmldoc DBMS_XMLDOM.DOMDocument;
 v_xmltype XMLType;
 v_out clob;
 v_req  UTL_HTTP.req;
 v_resp UTL_HTTP.resp;
 v_text VARCHAR2(32767);
 BEGIN
   v_req :=
     UTL_HTTP.begin_request(‘localhost:8080/public/contact.xml’);
```

```
    UTL_HTTP.set_authentication(r=>v_req,
                                username=>'demo',
                                password=>'demo');
    v_resp := UTL_HTTP.get_response(v_req);
    UTL_HTTP.read_text(r=>v_resp,data=>v_text);
    UTL_HTTP.end_response(v_resp);v_xmltype :=XMLType(v_text);
    v_xmldoc :=DBMS_XMLDOM.newDOMDocument(v_xmltype);
    DBMS_LOB.createtemporary(v_out,FALSE,DBMS_LOB.SESSION);
    DBMS_XMLDOM.writetoClob(v_xmldoc, v_out);
    :out:=v_out;
   DBMS_LOB.freetemporary(v_out);
END;
/
```

Both the **DBMS_XMLPARSER.PARSE()** and **XMLType()** functions use UTL_HTTP to request the data from remote web servers. Therefore, the proxy setup and the user authentication setup are the same.

Parsing with DTDs

Similar to XML schemas, DTDs can be used to define the structure and metadata of XML documents, which then can be used to validate XML documents. While they are not supported to the same extent as XML schemas, you can control the use of DTDs in Oracle Database 10*g* using the following command:

```
Alter session set events '31156 trace name context forever, level 2';
```

This turns off the DTD parsing and validation when parsing XML in either the **XMLType()** functions or the DBMS_XMLPARSER XML parsing functions.

In addition, and distinct from XML schemas, DTDs can also define entities for an XML document, which have to be resolved before XML parsers can check the well-formedness of XML documents. In this case, you cannot turn off DTD parsing; therefore, DTD files must have a URL that can be resolved by the Oracle XML DB. In Oracle Database 10*g*, it should be an XML DB URI like **/public/author.dtd** pointing to a resource file stored in the Oracle XML DB Repository.

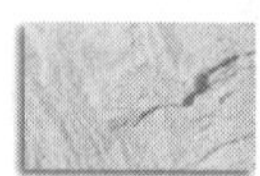

NOTE
*In Oracle Database 10gR1, **DBMS_XMLPARSER.parseDTD()**, **DBMS_XMLPARSER.parseDTDBuffer()**, and **DBMS_XMLPARSER.parseDTDClob()** are not supported. Therefore, you can't parse external DTDs and set them to XML parsers.*

Processing XML Using DOM

After XML documents are parsed by DBMS_XMLPARSER or **XMLType()** constructor functions, the XML parser builds XML documents as in-memory object trees. Therefore, you can navigate the object tree by using the DOM APIs in the DBMS_XMLDOM package to retrieve XML data or to update the object tree by inserting or deleting XML elements or their content. In this section, we do not explain every DOM API but rather focus on discussing the solutions for some common problems that are encountered when dealing with XML using DOM in PL/SQL.

NOTE
Oracle Database 10g does not provide built-in SAX XML parsing in PL/SQL. However, in Chapter 27, we will discuss techniques that use Java stored procedures to process XML data using SAX in PL/SQL.

Dealing with XML Namespaces

XML namespaces are collections of names identified by URI references, which are then used on XML elements and attributes to qualify XML elements or attributes for different applications. The following example, which uses the DBMS_XMLDOM package, shows how you can create an XML element with a namespace in Oracle Database 10*g*:

```
CREATE OR REPLACE FUNCTION appendChild(p_doc xmltype)
RETURN XMLType AS
  v_doc DBMS_XMLDOM.DOMDocument;
  v_docn DBMS_XMLDOM.DOMNode;
  v_lcn DBMS_XMLDOm.DOMNode;
  v_nelem DBMS_XMLDOM.DOMNode;
  v_elem DBMS_XMLDOM.DOMElement;
  v_attr DBMS_XMLDOM.DOMAttr;
  v_nattr DBMS_XMLDOM.DOMNode;
  v_tx DBMS_XMLDOM.DOMText;
  v_ntx DBMS_XMLDOM.DOMNode;
BEGIN
  -- Create DOM document
  v_doc := DBMS_XMLDOM.newDOMDocument(p_doc);
  v_docn := DBMS_XMLDOM.makeNode(
                DBMS_XMLDOM.getDocumentElement(v_doc));
  -- Locate the element where the new element will be inserted
  v_lcn := DBMS_XMLDOM.getLastChild(v_docn);

  -- Create a new XML element with namespace
  v_elem :=DBMS_XMLDOM.CreateElement(v_doc,
                                  'my:notes',
                                  'http://www.example.com');

  -- Create the attribute to include namespace declaration
  v_attr :=DBMS_XMLDOM.CreateAttribute(v_doc,'xmlns:my');
  v_nattr := DBMS_XMLDOM.makeNode(v_attr);
  DBMS_XMLDOM.setNodeValue(v_nattr, 'http://www.example.com');
  -- Set the attribute to the XML element
  v_attr := DBMS_XMLDOM.setAttributeNode(v_elem,
                      v_attr,'http://www.example.com' );

  -- Insert Text Node to XML Element
  v_nelem := DBMS_XMLDOM.makeNode(v_elem);
  v_tx :=DBMS_XMLDOM.createtextnode(v_doc, 'Address is not complete.');
  v_ntx:=DBMS_XMLDOM.makenode(v_tx);
  v_ntx:= DBMS_XMLDOM.appendchild(v_nelem, v_ntx);
```

```
  -- Insert the new element
  v_nelem := DBMS_XMLDOM.insertBefore(v_docn, v_nelem, v_lcn);

  RETURN p_doc;
END;
/
show errors;
```

This example shows that you can create XML elements or attributes qualified by namespaces in Oracle Database 10*g* by specifying the third parameter of the **DBMS_XMLDOM.CreateElement()** or **DBMS_XMLDOM.CreateAttribute()** function. In this sample, the new XML element is created with its namespace to be **http://www.example.com**:

```
  v_elem :=DBMS_XMLDOM.CreateElement(v_doc,
                                    'my:notes',
                                    'http://www.example.com');
```

However, according to the DOM specification, the namespace declarations are not added by default. Therefore, you need to add the namespace declaration attributes explicitly as shown in the following example, which adds an **xmlns:my** attribute to the **my:note** element:

```
  v_attr :=DBMS_XMLDOM.CreateAttribute(v_doc,'xmlns:my');
  v_nattr := DBMS_XMLDOM.makeNode(v_attr);
  DBMS_XMLDOM.setNodeValue(v_nattr, 'http://www.example.com');
  -- Set the attribute to the XML element
  v_attr := DBMS_XMLDOM.setAttributeNode(v_elem,
                      v_attr,'http://www.example.com' );
```

After the PL/SQL function is created, you then test it as follows:

```
set autoprint on
var out clob
BEGIN
  SELECT appendChild(XMLType('<person>
                          <name> John Smith </name>
                          <address> XYZ street, CA 12345</address>
</person>')).getClobVal() INTO :out
FROM DUAL;
END;
/
```

The output of the procedure is the XML with the new element inserted, as follows:

```
<person>
  <name> John Smith </name>
  <my:notes xmlns:my="http://www.example.com"/>
  <address> XYZ street, CA 12345</address>
</person>
```

Retrieving XML Data Using XPath

The **UPDATEXML()** function in Oracle Database 10*g* can update XML elements selected by XPaths in XMLTypes. However, instead of updating the original XML document, **UPDATEXML()**

creates a new XML document with the updates. To edit and update the original XML document, you need to use DOM APIs provided by DBMS_XMLDOM.

In Chapter 10, we showed an example that selects XML elements using **DBMS_XMLDOM .GetElementsByTagName()** and updates their content. In this section, we extend this example on discussing how to select XML elements using three XPath functions in the DBMS_XSLPROCESSOR package and update the selected content using DBMS_XMLDOM. The following are the three XPath interfaces provided in DBMS_XSLPROCESSOR:

- **SelectNodes (n DOMNode, pattern VARCHAR2, namespace VARCHAR2)** Selects nodes from a DOM tree that match the given XPath pattern. It returns the result as the **DBMS_XMLDOM.NodeList** object.
- **SelectSingleNodes (n DOMNode, pattern VARCHAR2, namespace VARCHAR2)** Selects the first node as a **DBMS_XMLDOM.DOMNode** object from the DOM tree that matches the given XPath pattern.
- **ValueOf (n DOMNode, pattern VARCHAR2, value VARCHAR2, namespace VARCHAR2)** Retrieves the value of the *first node* in a string from the DOM tree that matches the given XPath pattern.

To update XML elements using XPath, you need to first select the XML elements by using **DBMS_XSLPROCESSOR.SelectNodes()**. Before you use this interface, you need to get the **DBMS_XMLDOM.DOMDocument** object either parsed by DBMS_XMLPARSER or created using the **DBMS_XMLDOM.newDocument()**. Next, you need to get the document element and create a DOM node using **DBMS_XMLDOM.MakeNode()** that you can process:

```
v_doc     DBMS_XMLDOM.DOMDocument;
v_ndoc    DBMS_XMLDOM.DOMNode;
...
v_ndoc := DBMS_XMLDOM.makeNode(dbms_xmldom.getDocumentElement(v_doc));
```

Then, you get the first child of the document node, which will be the root of the DOM document:

```
v_fnode := DBMS_XMLDOM.getFirstChild(v_node);
```

Next, you can call **DBMS_XSLPROCESSOR.SelectNodes()** function with the document root node as the first parameter and the XPath as the second parameter, as follows:

```
v_nodeList := DBMS_XSLPROCESSOR.selectNodes(v_fnode, '/Txn/Data/@value');
```

A DOM node list will be returned from the **DBMS_XSLPROCESSOR.SelectNodes()** function. Then, you can iterate over each node to update the DOM object using the **DBMS_XMLDOM.setNodeValue()** function:

```
v_nl := DBMS_XMLDOM.getLength(v_nodeList);
v_sum := 0;
 IF v_nl > 0 THEN
  FOR j in 0..v_nl-1 LOOP
```

```
    v_node := DBMS_XMLDOM.item(v_nodeList,j);
  DBMS_XMLDOM.setNodeValue(v_node,'<new value>');
 END LOOP;
```

Processing XML Using XSLT

In Oracle Database 10*g*, you can use **XMLType.transform()** to apply XSL stylesheets on XML documents, which is normally a process to transform XML documents. However, in this section, we discuss how you can leverage XSLT to process XML data. We compare the XSLT approach with the DOM approach. You will see that using XSLT to process XML data sometimes is much easier than using DOM.

The example is a process, which gets an input XML document containing a collection of data from an application transaction and needs to calculate the sum of all the data **values**. The input document is as follows:

```
<Txn>
  <Data value="18.75"/>
  <Data value="17.32"/>
  <Data value="16.45"/>
  <Data value="15.82"/>
</Txn>
```

Using DOM, you need to iterate over all the **<Data>** nodes, read out the numbers in the **value** attributes, and add them together. The sample code is as follows:

```
DECLARE
  v_xmlbuf      VARCHAR2(512);
  v_parser      DBMS_XMLPARSER.Parser;
  v_xmldoc      DBMS_XMLDOM.DOMDocument;
  v_outbuf      VARCHAR2(600);
  v_node        DBMS_XMLDOM.DOMNode;
  v_fnode       DBMS_XMLDOM.DOMNode;
  v_nodeList    DBMS_XMLDOM.DOMNodeList;
  v_nl          NUMBER;
  v_value       NUMBER;
  v_sum         NUMBER :=0;
 BEGIN
   v_xmlbuf := '<Txn><Data value="18.75"/><Data value="17.32"/>' ||
               '<Data value="16.45"/><Data value="15.82"/></Txn>';
   -- Initialize the XML parser
   v_parser := DBMS_XMLPARSER.newParser;
   -- Parse XML document
   DBMS_XMLPARSER.parseBuffer(v_parser, v_xmlbuf);
   v_xmldoc := DBMS_XMLPARSER.getDocument(v_parser);
   v_node := DBMS_XMLDOM.makenode(v_xmldoc);
   v_fnode := DBMS_XMLDOM.getfirstchild(v_node);

   -- Select <Data> elements
```

```
    v_nodeList:=DBMS_XSLPROCESSOR.selectNodes(v_fnode,
                                                   '/Txn/Data/@value');
    v_nl := DBMS_XMLDOM.getLength(v_nodeList);
    DBMS_OUTPUT.put_line('The length of the node list:'||v_nl);
    -- Iterate the <Data> elements and sum the value attributes
    v_sum:=0;
    IF v_nl > 0 THEN
     for j in 0..v_nl-1 loop
       v_node := DBMS_XMLDOM.item(v_nodeList,j);
       v_value := DBMS_XMLDOM.getNodeValue(v_node);
       v_sum := v_sum+v_value;
     END LOOP;
     DBMS_OUTPUT.put_line('Sum='||v_sum);
   ELSE
   DBMS_OUTPUT.put_line('No node selected');
   END IF;
END;
/
show errors;
```

The DOM operation requires parsing the XML document, selecting the **<Data>** elements, and iterating all the **<Data>** elements to calculate the sum of all the values. Instead of doing that, you can use the following XSL stylesheet, which can do the same job:

```
<xsl:stylesheet version="2.0"
                xmlns:xsl="http://www.w3.org/1999/XSL/Transform">
<xsl:template match="/">
 <xsl:value-of select="sum(Txn//Data/@v)"/>
</xsl:template>
</xsl:stylesheet>
```

Thus, the operation can be done in a single SQL command as follows:

```
SELECT XMLType('<Txn>
                 <Data value="18.75"/>
                 <Data value="17.32"/>
                 <Data value="16.45"/>
                 <Data value="15.82"/>
</Txn>').transform(XMLType('<xsl:stylesheet version="2.0"
                xmlns:xsl="http://www.w3.org/1999/XSL/Transform">
<xsl:template match="/">
  <xsl:value-of select="sum(Txn//Data/@value)"/>
 </xsl:template>
</xsl:stylesheet>')) AS result
FROM DUAL;
```

Using XSLT, you don't have to write programs to traverse DOM objects, and it is much more efficient. Therefore, XSLT is not limited to transforming XML documents. You sometimes can leverage its functionality, especially using XPath functions, to process XML data.

Setting Up Oracle JVM

With Oracle JVM, you can leverage Java programming within the Oracle database. When you are creating databases with Oracle Database Configuration Assistant (DBCA), Oracle JVM is an option. If you select the Oracle JVM option, the number of loaded Java schema objects in the database should be more than 8000 for Oracle Database 10*g* when you are querying as **SYS** using the following SQL command:

```
SELECT count (*)
FROM user_objects
WHERE object_type='JAVA CLASS';
```

Otherwise, you need to connect to the Oracle database as **SYS** user and run the **$ORACLE_HOME/javavm/install/initjvm.sql** and **$ORACLE_HOME/rdbms/admin/catjava.sql** scripts, as follows:

```
SQL>@javavm/install/initjvm.sql
SQL>@rdbms/admin/catjava.sql
```

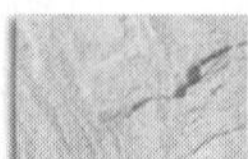

NOTE

While Oracle XDK Java libraries can be loaded into the ***SYS*** *user schema by running the* ***$ORACLE_HOME/xdk/admin/initxml.sql*** *in* ***SYS****, it is not recommended to do so because you may wish to reload the libraries to leverage new XDK features or bug fixes in a release on OTN. To simplify the maintenance of XDK Java libraries in Oracle JVM, you can create a new database user, for example* ***XDK****, and load the Java libraries into this user schema instead of* ***SYS****.*

To run **initjvm.sql** successfully, you also need reasonable sizes for SHARE_POOL_SIZE and JAVA_POOL_SIZE. The recommended sizes are as follows:

```
shared_pool_size = 50000000
java_pool_size = 20000000
```

After you install Oracle JVM, you can load, compile, and run Java programs in the Oracle database by creating Java stored procedures. In Chapter 27, we will discuss how you can leverage Java Stored Procedures to process XML using SAX from PL/SQL.

Summary

In this chapter, we introduced you to the SQL XMLType and PL/SQL XML functionality within Oracle Database 10*g* and showed you through several examples how to use the functions to process XML data in the Oracle database. The easy-to-use SQL functions should be your first choice when processing XML in Oracle Database 10*g*. You should use the PL/SQL XML processing APIs only when you require fine-grained XML processing of XML documents that is not available in the SQL/XML or XMLType functions.

CHAPTER 26

Building PL/SQL Web Services

he open and standards-based web services are gaining more and more attention in the software industry because they provide a way for heterogeneous systems to interoperate by sharing data over the Internet. In Oracle Database 10*g*, web service features are provided to facilitate publishing database data, metadata, and PL/SQL computing resources as web services. Additionally, the web service features allow database users to consume external web services within the database server.

In this chapter, we work through examples that illustrate how you can publish database resources as web services and consume web services in Oracle Database 10*g*. We assume in this discussion that you understand the basic concepts of web services, such as the format of SOAP messages and WSDL files. If you are not familiar with these web service protocols, read Chapter 6 before you move on to the content in this chapter.

In the "Extending the Application" section, we discuss in which situations you need to implement a web service inside the Oracle database, how to protect your database from destructive users, and the different kinds of web services that you can create.

Building and Publishing the First Database Web Service

In this section, we discuss building a web service for a fictitious bookstore, Big Barrel Books (BBB), that needs to enable its partners to promote and sell its books. Through web services, BBB's partners will be able to query and update its catalog of books in the Oracle database.

Setting Up the Database Schema

In real applications, the database schema that is set up to manage a bookstore may be very complicated. It may require more than one table, with many columns in each table, such as a separate table to store data for the authors of the book. However, in this example, to help you focus on the techniques of building web services, we have greatly simplified the definition of these tables. Therefore, the following table, called **book**, is created to store the records of books:

```
CREATE TABLE book(
  ISBN VARCHAR2(200) PRIMARY KEY,
  author varchar2(200),
  title VARCHAR2(200),
  price FLOAT,
  instock_num NUMBER(20)
  );
```

In addition to the **book** table, a **partner** table is created to store information about the bookstore's partners and a **book_sale** table is created to store the partners' transactions that are executed within the database:

```
CREATE TABLE partner(
  partner_id NUMBER PRIMARY KEY,
  partner_name VARCHAR2(200),
  discount_rate NUMBER);
```

```
CREATE TABLE book_sale(
  ISBN VARCHAR2(12),
  op_time DATE,
  partner_id NUMBER,
  checkout_num NUMBER);
```

In this example, a discount rate is assigned for each partner that is stored in the **partner** table. The **book_sale** table keeps the details of each transaction on the **book** table, including the ISBN of the book, the time of the transaction, the ID of the partner that performs the transaction, and the number of items checked out of the inventory. You can insert the sample data into the **book** table as follows:

```
INSERT INTO book VALUES('0072225211','Kevin Loney,
 George Koch, Tusc','Oracle9i: The Complete Reference',74.99,1000);
INSERT INTO book VALUES('0072229527',
'Mark Scardina, Ben Chang, Jinyu Wang',
'Oracle Database 10g XML and SQL',49.99,1000);
```

You can insert partners into the database as follows:

```
INSERT INTO partner VALUES(1,'book wholesale',0.6);
```

This example inserts a sample partner called Book Wholesale and assigns it a 60 percent price discount from this bookstore.

In the example, two web services will be provided. The first one allows the partners to query the database and list all the information about the books they can sell, including the title, author, and price of each book. The query shows both the original price and the price the partner can get after applying the discount rate. The second web service is a transactional operation that allows the partners to check out books from the bookstore's inventory. After each transaction, the transaction information is stored in the **book_sale** table for later reference. A PL/SQL package called **booksale_pkg** is created to allow transaction operations as follows:

```
CREATE OR REPLACE PACKAGE booksale_pkg AS
  FUNCTION query(p_partner_id IN NUMBER) RETURN XMLType;
  FUNCTION checkout(p_partner_id IN NUMBER, p_isbn in VARCHAR2,
                    p_book_num IN NUMBER) RETURN VARCHAR2;
END booksale_pkg;
/
```

The two functions in the PL/SQL package can be used to provide the services, and the PL/SQL package body for **booksale_pkg** is created as follows:

```
CREATE OR REPLACE PACKAGE BODY booksale_pkg AS
  FUNCTION query(p_partner_id IN NUMBER) RETURN XMLType AS
    out XMLType;
    qryCtx DBMS_XMLGEN.ctxHandle;
  BEGIN
    qryCtx := DBMS_XMLGEN.NEWCONTEXT(
       'SELECT b.partner_id AS "@partner_id", a.isbn, a.author,
```

```
    a.title, a.price, a.price*discount_rate AS sale_price
          FROM book a, partner b
          WHERE b.partner_id=:PARTNER_ID');
     DBMS_XMLGEN.setBindValue(qryCtx, 'PARTNER_ID', p_partner_id);
     out := DBMS_XMLGEN.GETXMLTYPE(qryCtx);
     DBMS_XMLGEN.closeContext(qryCtx);

     RETURN out;
   END query;

   FUNCTION checkout(p_partner_id IN NUMBER,p_isbn IN VARCHAR2,
                     p_book_num IN NUMBER) RETURN VARCHAR2 AS
     out XMLType;
     current_num NUMBER;
   BEGIN
     INSERT INTO book_sale VALUES(p_isbn,sysdate,p_partner_id,
                                  p_book_num);
     UPDATE book
     SET instock_num=instock_num-p_book_num
     WHERE isbn=p_isbn;
     COMMIT;
     RETURN 'OK';
   EXCEPTION
    WHEN OTHERS THEN
       RETURN 'FAILED';
       RAISE;
   END checkout;
END booksale_pkg;
/
show errors;
```

In the **query()** function, DBMS_XMLGEN is used to generate the result in XML and return it as an XMLType. To get the XMLType, you need to use the DBMS_XMLGEN.GETXMLTYPE() function. In the **checkout()** procedure, the **book** table is updated by subtracting the requested number of books from the inventory and returning a string in VARCHAR2, which returns OK if enough books exist in inventory to fill the order, and otherwise returns FAILED.

Before you deploy the PL/SQL package to web services, you need to test it within the Oracle database, because debugging a web service is difficult. For example, the query to test Book Wholesale can be as follows:

```
LONG 10000
SET AUTOPRINT ON
VAR out CLOB
BEGIN
  :out := booksale_pkg.query(1).getCLOBVal();
END;
/
```

The output is the listing of the books stored in the **book** table, including the actual price and the discount price for the Book Wholesale partner:

```
<ROWSET>
 <ROW partner_id = "1">
  <ISBN>0072225211</ISBN>
  <AUTHOR>Kevin Loney, George Koch, Tusc</AUTHOR>
  <TITLE>Oracle9i: The Complete Reference</TITLE>
  <PRICE>74.99</PRICE>
  <SALE_PRICE>44.994</SALE_PRICE>
 </ROW>
 <ROW partner_id = "1">
  <ISBN>0072229527</ISBN>
  <AUTHOR>Mark Scardina, Ben Chang, Jinyu Wang</AUTHOR>
  <TITLE>Oracle Database 10g XML and SQL</TITLE>
  <PRICE>49.99</PRICE>
  <SALE_PRICE>29.994</SALE_PRICE>
 </ROW>
</ROWSET>
```

A similar test applies for the **checkout()** function, which is provided along with the samples for this chapter.

So far, we have built the database schema for a simplified book management system. In the following section, we publish the PL/SQL package as a web service and show you how to call the web service from its clients.

Publishing the PL/SQL Web Service Using Oracle JDeveloper 10*g*

The bookstore has provided the PL/SQL functions to operate on the **book** table and track the transactions. In this section, we discuss how to publish PL/SQL functions as web services. There are different ways to provide web services, as we will discuss in depth later. However, to create a web service, you need provide at least the following:

- A proxy program, residing within the server, that processes the incoming SOAP messages, calls the PL/SQL procedure, and then returns the result to the client via SOAP messages
- A dedicated server running the proxy program to receive SOAP messages
- A WSDL file that describes the web service, so that clients can easily develop client applications to call the service

If you build everything from scratch, a lot of work is required. To help you simplify the process, Oracle JDeveloper 10*g* provides a wizard that can automatically generate the proxy program, the WSDL file, and the stub program for the web service client, as well as the deployment profile, and the required features to debug them. All you need to do is provide the name of the PL/SQL package. Therefore, before we present the alternate approach that requires more work, we will discuss the procedures for creating PL/SQL web services via the wizard.

First, open the Oracle JDeveloper 10*g* project provided along with the book and set up a database connection, as discussed in Chapter 13. For example, create a database connection called **demo**, which connects to the database using the user for whom you just set up the book management schemas.

After the connection is set up, right-click the project name and select New. In the **New Gallery** dialog box, select **Business Tier | Web Services | PL/SQL Web Service**. This launches the Oracle JDeveloper 10*g* wizard that enables you to create PL/SQL web services through which you can access the PL/SQL procedures.

After you click **Next** on the Welcome screen, you should see the dialog box shown in Figure 26-1, which requires you to specify the database connection, the PL/SQL package, the name of the web service, and the name of the Java package that is used for the generated proxy program.

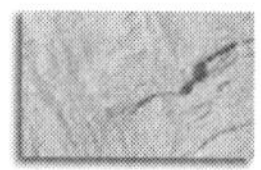

NOTE
You can access the same wizard by right-clicking the package itself when it is displayed in the Connection Navigator.

After you select the database connection, select the BOOKSALE_PKG from the available PL/SQL packages in the drop-down list. In this step, you can specify any name for the web service and the Java package. In the example, **BookSaleService** is the name of the web service and **demo** is the name of the Java package of the proxy program. Click **Next** after you have completed the page.

Step 2 of the wizard requires you to select the PL/SQL procedures from the PL/SQL package to publish as part of the web service, as shown in Figure 26-2. In this example, both the **checkout()** and **query()** procedures are selected. After selecting the PL/SQL procedures, you can continue by clicking the **Next** button.

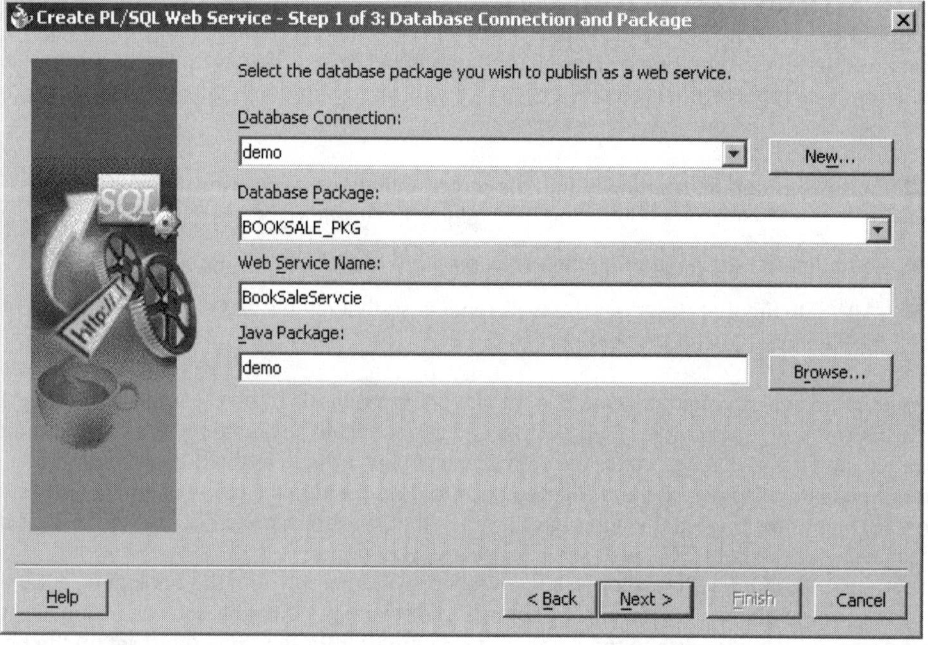

FIGURE 26-1. *Step 1 of the Create PL/SQL Web Service wizard*

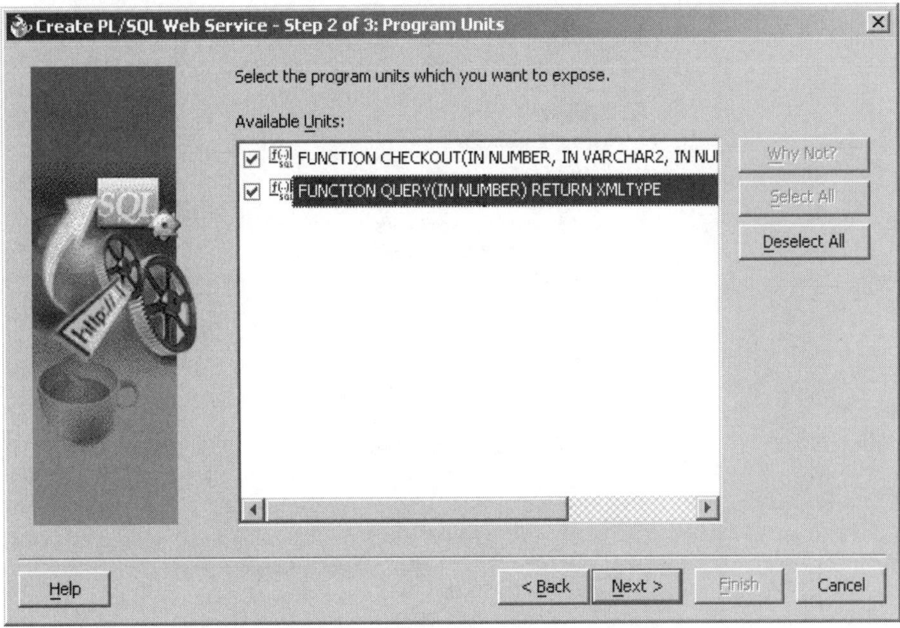

FIGURE 26-2. *Select the PL/SQL procedures.*

Before you complete the PL/SQL web service creation step, you are requested to specify the endpoint URL for the web service and its target namespace. The endpoint URL needs to reflect the J2EE server you want to deploy the web service to. For example, in the provided sample project, the J2EE application name is set to be **Chapter26**, and you will deploy the web service to the embedded Oracle J2EE Container (OC4J) of Oracle JDeveloper 10*g*, which runs on port 8988 by default. Therefore, the endpoint URL for **BookSaleService** is **http://127.0.0.1:8988/Chapter26/BookSaleService**. You can specify any target namespace here. In this example, we use **http://demo/BookSaleService.wsdl**.

After you complete the wizard, a set of files are created, as shown in Figure 26-3.

You now have all the prerequisites to build a web service:

- **The proxy program** You can download and review the source code via the web service user interface, as discussed later in this section.
- **The server running the deployed proxy program** This is the embedded OC4J in Oracle JDeveloper 10*g*. However, a deployment file, called **WebServices.deploy**, has been created to allow you to deploy the proxy program to other OC4J containers. In the example, this server is the OC4J web server.
- **The WSDL file** This file summarizes the signatures of the methods exposed by the web service. To review this file, right-click the **BookSaleService** description file in the **Applications Navigator** and choose **Go to WSDL**.

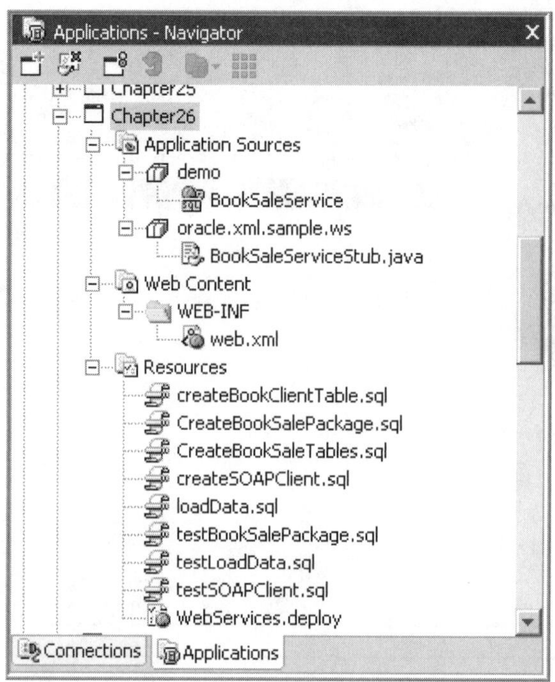

FIGURE 26-3. *Generated web service for the PL/SQL package*

You are ready to run the web service. Right-click the **BookSaleService** description file and select Run. In the message window of Oracle JDeveloper 10*g*, you will see the following messages:

```
04/02/10 11:52:26 Oracle Application Server Containers for J2EE 10g
 (9.0.4.0.0) initialized
04/02/10 11:52:26 Web service BookSaleService has been started on
the embedded server
The application can be accessed at location:
http://169.254.74.222:8988/Chapter26/BookSaleService
```

Pay no attention to the IP address that is displayed, because it is the IP address automatically detected by Oracle JDeveloper 10*g* when you run the samples. The IP address will be different when you run it. Now you can launch your browser and enter the URL, **http://127.0.0.1:8988/Chapter26/BookSaleService**, to access your up-and-running web service, as shown in Figure 26-4.

Through this web interface, you can download the Java package and source code for the proxy program, test each operation, and review the WSDL file.

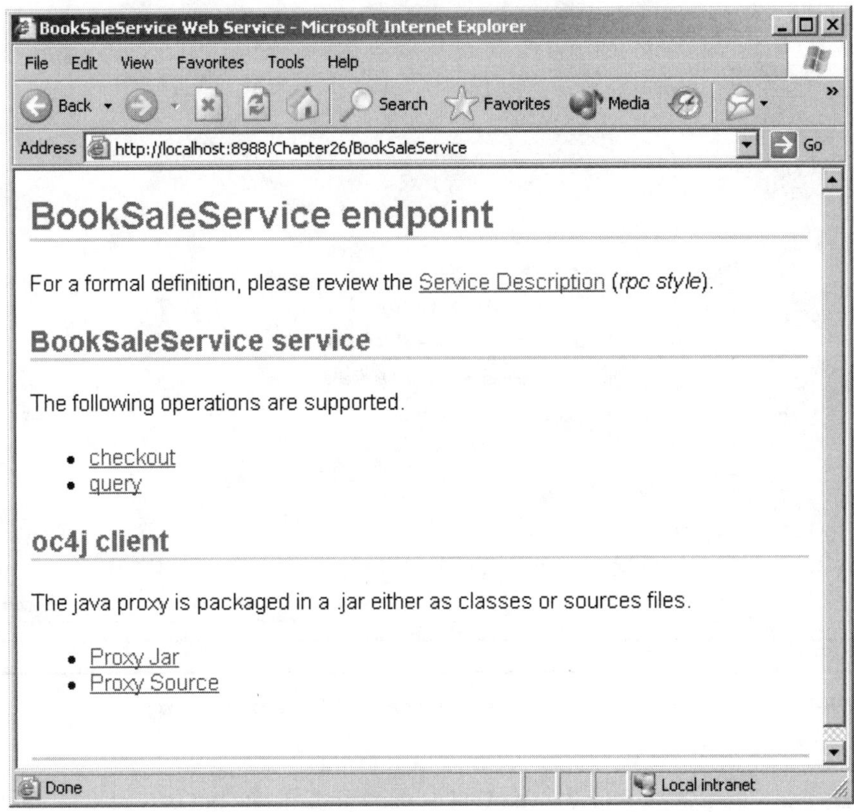

FIGURE 26-4. *Published web service user interface*

Calling the Web Service from Clients

Because web services are open and standards-based, they have little restriction on the clients that can invoke them. As long as the client follows the standards and sends the SOAP message in the correct format, the web service will respond whether it is written in Java, JavaScript, ASP, JSP, or Perl. However, in Oracle JDeveloper 10*g*, you can easily generate Java client programs that call web services. You just need to right-click the **BookSaleService** description file and choose Generate Web Service Stub. You can also choose Generate Simple Java Client to get a simplified version of the client program.

Figure 26-5 shows the dialog box in which you set up the wizard to generate the client stub program by right-clicking the **BookSaleService** and choosing Generate Web Service Stub.

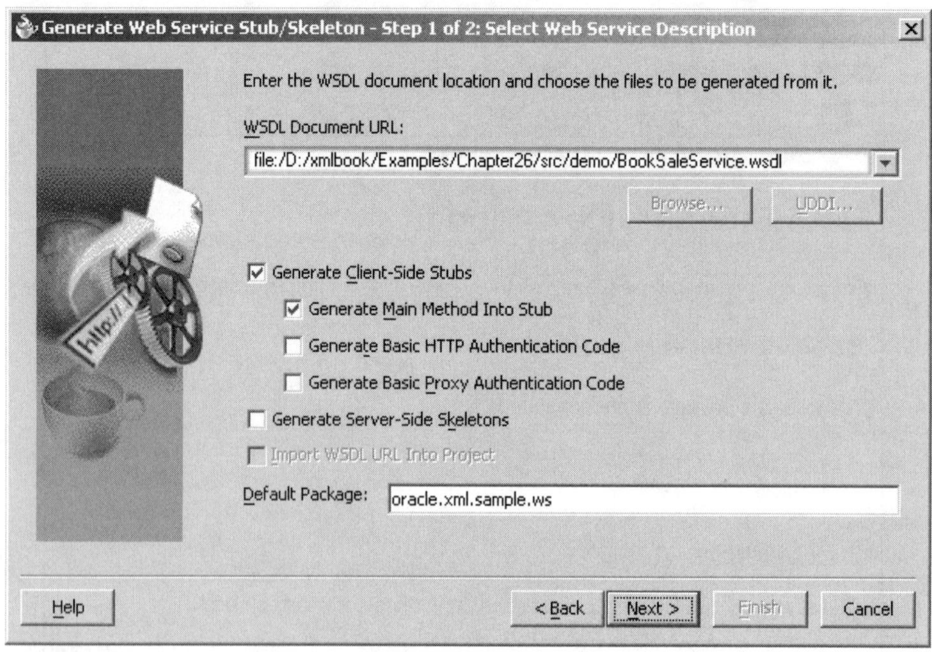

FIGURE 26-5. *Step 1 of the Generate Web Service Stub/Skeleton wizard*

As shown in Figure 26-5, from a given WSDL, you can generate not only client-side stubs but also a server-side skeleton. However, in this example, we need only a simple client stub. After you choose the options shown in Figure 26-5 and click Next, you then need to choose the necessary functions for the client and the package name for the Java package that will be generated. In the example, a **BookSaleServiceStub.java** file will be created in the **oracle.xml .sample.ws** package.

After the wizard generates the code, you need to update the code so that it can be used within your application.

In this example, you first need to modify the generated code so that it can properly handle the XMLType, which will be returned by the book query service (all the updated content is bold):

```
import oracle.xdb.XMLType;

public XMLType query(BigDecimal pPartnerId) throws Exception
{
  XMLType returnVal = null;
  URL endpointURL = new URL(_endpoint);
  Call call = new Call();
  call.setSOAPTransport(m_httpConnection);
  call.setTargetObjectURI("BookSaleService");
  call.setMethodName("query");
```

```
  call.setEncodingStyleURI(Constants.NS_URI_SOAP_ENC);

  Vector params = new Vector();
  params.addElement(new Parameter("pPartnerId",
                    java.math.BigDecimal.class, pPartnerId, null));
  call.setParams(params);
  call.setSOAPMappingRegistry(m_smr);

  Response response = call.invoke(endpointURL, "");
  if (!response.generatedFault()) {
    Parameter result = response.getReturnValue();
    returnVal = (XMLType)result.getValue();
  } else {
    Fault fault = response.getFault();
    throw new SOAPException(fault.getFaultCode(),
         fault.getFaultString());
  }

  return returnVal;
}
```

This proper datatype casting allows better use of XMLType functionality within Oracle XML DB.

Then, for the **main()** function, you need to add your code to specify how you call the web service. In the example, we simply dump the result to the screen:

```
public static void main(String[] args)
{
  try {
    BookSaleServiceStub stub = new BookSaleServiceStub();
    // Add your own code here.
    System.out.println(
       stub.checkout(new BigDecimal(1),"0072225211",new BigDecimal(10)));
    System.out.println(stub.query(new BigDecimal(1)).getStringVal());
  }catch(Exception ex){
    ex.printStackTrace();
  }
}
```

When calling the **stub.checkout()**, you need to provide the partner_id, ISBN, and number of the book to be checked out. However, the call to **stub.query()** needs some explanation. The **stub.query()** function returns the XMLType that contains the book list in XML for the specified partner. Because the returned content is in the XMLType, which provides the **XMLType.getStringVal()** procedure, the call finally returns the content in **String** so that it can be printed.

Debugging the Web Service

If you follow the instructions, everything should work fine when you generate and call the example web service. However, in the real world, something usually happens that requires you to debug the problem. A useful debug technique is to peek at the SOAP messages that are actually sent and received. In Oracle JDeveloper 10*g*, you can do this by using TCP Packet Monitor (select

View | TCP Packet Monitor). After you open TCP Package Monitor, click the green Play button to start the monitor. Each SOAP message is then recorded in the History window, and the Data window shows both the incoming and outgoing SOAP message content.

For the **checkout** service call, the outgoing SOAP message is shown as follows:

```
<?xml version = '1.0' encoding = 'UTF-8'?>
<SOAP-ENV:Envelope
   xmlns:SOAP-ENV="http://schemas.xmlsoap.org/soap/envelope/"
   xmlns:xsi="http://www.w3.org/2001/XMLSchema-instance"
   xmlns:xsd="http://www.w3.org/2001/XMLSchema">
 <SOAP-ENV:Body>
  <ns1:checkout xmlns:ns1="BookSaleService"
     SOAP-ENV:encodingStyle="http://schemas.xmlsoap.org/soap/encoding/">
    <pPartnerId xsi:type="xsd:decimal">1</pPartnerId>
     <pIsbn xsi:type="xsd:string">0072225211</pIsbn>
     <pBookNum xsi:type="xsd:decimal">10</pBookNum>
    </ns1:checkout>
   </SOAP-ENV:Body>
</SOAP-ENV:Envelope>
```

It returns a SOAP message as follows:

```
<?xml version = '1.0' encoding = 'UTF-8'?>
<SOAP-ENV:Envelope
    xmlns:SOAP-ENV="http://schemas.xmlsoap.org/soap/envelope/"
    xmlns:xsi="http://www.w3.org/2001/XMLSchema-instance"
    xmlns:xsd="http://www.w3.org/2001/XMLSchema">
  <SOAP-ENV:Body>
   <ns1:checkoutResponse xmlns:ns1="BookSaleService"
    SOAP-ENV:encodingStyle="http://schemas.xmlsoap.org/soap/encoding/">
     <return xsi:type="xsd:string">OK</return>
</ns1:checkoutResponse>
   </SOAP-ENV:Body>
</SOAP-ENV:Envelope>
```

The SOAP messages contain a lot of information, including namespaces. However, you do not have to create SOAP messages yourself. The SOAP messages can be simply generated using the supplied tools in Oracle JDeveloper 10*g*.

So far, the web service communication protocol and the interoperation between the bookstore owner and its partners have been set up. From the example, you can see that publishing a PL/SQL web service for Oracle Database 10*g* can be a very simple process.

Consuming a Web Service Within the Oracle Database

Now that you have learned how to build and publish PL/SQL procedures as web services, we will discuss how to consume an external web service within the Oracle database. There are two ways to do this in Oracle Database 10*g*:

- Generate Java web service clients using Oracle JDeveloper 10*g* and create Java stored procedures. In this approach, you need to load the Java web service clients and the Oracle SOAP support libraries into the Oracle JVM.
- Send out SOAP messages to the web service providers using the UTL_HTTP or UTL_SMTP PL/SQL packages.

Because there are many examples on Oracle Technology Network that illustrate the first approach, we discuss only the second approach, which does not require Oracle JVM. In this example, we will use UTL_HTTP to consume the bookstore web service that you just built.

Constructing SOAP Messages

By applying the XML processing techniques discussed in Chapter 10 and Chapter 25, you have several SOAP message construction options in Oracle Database 10*g*. To simplify the example, you can use the PL/SQL string operation to construct a SOAP message as follows (all the customized fields are bold):

```
<?xml version = '1.0' encoding = 'UTF-8'?>
<SOAP-ENV:Envelope
    xmslns:SOAP-ENV="http://schemas.xmlsoap.org/soap/envelope/"
     xmlns:xsi="http://www.w3.org/2001/XMLSchema-instance"
     xmlns:xsd="http://www.w3.org/2001/XMLSchema">
 <SOAP-ENV:Body>
  <ns1:query xmlns:ns1="BookSaleService"
    SOAP-ENV:encodingStyle="http://schemas.xmlsoap.org/soap/encoding/">
    <pPartnerId xsi:type="xsd:decimal">1</pPartnerId>
   </ns1:query>
 </SOAP-ENV:Body>
</SOAP-ENV:Envelope>
```

The message is assigned to a PL/SQL variable to be used in your PL/SQL procedure as follows:

```
soap_request := '<?xml version = "1.0" encoding = "UTF-8"?>
<SOAP-ENV:Envelope
    xmlns:SOAP-ENV="http://schemas.xmlsoap.org/soap/envelope/"
    xmlns:xsi="http://www.w3.org/2001/XMLSchema-instance"
    xmlns:xsd="http://www.w3.org/2001/XMLSchema">
   <SOAP-ENV:Body>
      <ns1:query xmlns:ns1="BookSaleService"
         SOAP-ENV:encodingStyle=
                       "http://schemas.xmlsoap.org/soap/encoding/">
         <pPartnerId xsi:type="xsd:decimal">'|| p_partner_id||'
         </pPartnerId>
      </ns1:query>
   </SOAP-ENV:Body>
</SOAP-ENV:Envelope>';
```

In this example, you can update the partner ID in the SOAP messages by using the **p_partner_id** parameter.

Sending Out SOAP Messages Using UTL_HTTP

After you create the SOAP message, you need to send it to the web service provider by using the UTL_HTTP package as follows:

```
CREATE OR REPLACE FUNCTION query_request(p_partner_id IN number)
RETURN XMLType
as
  soap_request VARCHAR2(32767);
  soap_respond VARCHAR2(32767);
  http_req  UTL_HTTP.req;
  http_resp UTL_HTTP.resp;
  resp XMLType;
  i NUMBER;
  len NUMBER;
BEGIN
  soap_request := '<?xml version = "1.0" encoding = "UTF-8"?>
<SOAP-ENV:Envelope
    xmlns:SOAP-ENV="http://schemas.xmlsoap.org/soap/envelope/"
    xmlns:xsi="http://www.w3.org/2001/XMLSchema-instance"
    xmlns:xsd="http://www.w3.org/2001/XMLSchema">
   <SOAP-ENV:Body>
      <ns1:query xmlns:ns1="BookSaleService"
         SOAP-ENV:encodingStyle=
                       "http://schemas.xmlsoap.org/soap/encoding/">
         <pPartnerId xsi:type="xsd:decimal">'|| p_partner_id||'
         </pPartnerId>
      </ns1:query>
   </SOAP-ENV:Body>
</SOAP-ENV:Envelope>';


  -- Invoke the SOAP message using UTL_HTTP package
  http_req := utl_http.begin_request(
   'http://127.0.0.1:8988/Chapter27/BookSaleService',
         'POST','HTTP/1.0');
    UTL_HTTP.set_header(http_req, 'Content-Type', 'text/xml');
    UTL_HTTP.set_header(http_req, 'Content-Length',
                        length(soap_request));
    UTL_HTTP.set_header(http_req, 'SOAPAction', 'query');
    UTL_HTTP.write_text(http_req, soap_request);
    http_resp := UTL_HTTP.get_response(http_req);
    UTL_HTTP.read_text(http_resp, soap_respond);
    UTL_HTTP.end_response(http_resp);
  resp := XMLType.createxml(soap_respond);
  resp := resp.extract('/soap:Envelope/soap:Body/child::node()',
      'xmlns:soap="http://schemas.xmlsoap.org/soap/envelope/"');
  -- Print out the result
  i := 1;
  len := LENGTH(soap_respond);
```

```
  WHILE (i <= len) LOOP
   DBMS_OUTPUT.PUT_LINE(substr(soap_respond, i, 60));
   i := i + 60;
  END LOOP;
  RETURN resp;
END;
/
show errors;
```

The UTL_HTTP package is provided within the Oracle database, allowing you to send out the constructed SOAP messages via HTTP. You need to set the HTTP URL for the web service provider, the data transmission method, and the HTTP version. In this example, the target URL for the web service is **http://127.0.0.1:8988/Chapter26/BookSaleService**, the data transmission method is **POST**, and the HTTP version is **HTTP 1.0**:

```
http_req := UTL_HTTP.begin_request(
   'http://127.0.0.1:8988/Chapter26/BookSaleService', 'POST','HTTP/1.0');
```

Because SOAP messages are XML messages, the HTTP **Content-Type** is set to be **text/xml**:

```
UTL_HTTP.set_header(http_req, 'Content-Type', 'text/xml');
```

Using the **PL/SQL LENGTH()** function, you can get the length of the SOAP message:

```
UTL_HTTP.set_header(http_req, 'Content-Length', length(soap_request));
```

The **SOAPAction** HTTP request parameter is needed in the HTTP header. In this example, it is the **query()** function we want to call. Therefore, the **SOAPAction** HTTP request parameter is set to be **query**:

```
UTL_HTTP.set_header(http_req, 'SOAPAction', 'query');
```

After the HTTP header is set up, the SOAP message is sent out by calling the UTL_HTTP .WRITE_TEXT() function and the response is received from the web service by using **UTL_HTTP.GET_RESPONSE()** and **UTL_HTTP.READ_TEXT()**:

```
UTL_HTTP.write_text(http_req, soap_request);
http_resp := utl_http.get_response(http_req);
UTL_HTTP.read_text(http_resp, soap_respond);
UTL_HTTP.end_response(http_resp);
```

After you run the PL/SQL procedure, you can create an XMLType from the SOAP message received in the text:

```
resp := xmltype.createxml(soap_respond);
resp := resp.extract('/soap:Envelope/soap:Body/child::node()',
      'xmlns:soap="http://schemas.xmlsoap.org/soap/envelope/"');
```

This allows for further XML processing on the data. In this example, the **XMLType.extract()** function is used to extract the response content. To test the procedure, you can run the following command:

```
SQL> DECLARE
      res XMLType;
     BEGIN
      res := query_request(1);
      :out := res.getClobVal();
     END;
     /
```

The following is the result:

```
<ns1:queryResponse xmlns:ns1="BookSaleService"
   xmlns:SOAP-ENV="http://schemas.xmlsoap.org/soap/envelope/"
   SOAP-ENV:encodingStyle="http://schemas.xmlsoap.org/soap/encoding/">
  <return xmlns:ns2="http://xmlns.oracle.com/xml-soap"
     xmlns:xsi="http://www.w3.org/2001/XMLSchema-instance"
      xsi:type="ns2:DocumentFragment">
  <ROWSET>
      <ROW partner_id="1">
        <ISBN>0072225211</ISBN>
        <AUTHOR>Kevin Loney, George Koch, Tusc</AUTHOR>
        <TITLE>Oracle9i: The Complete Reference</TITLE>
        <PRICE>74.99</PRICE>
        <SALE_PRICE>44.994</SALE_PRICE>
      </ROW>
      <ROW partner_id="1">
        <ISBN>0072229527</ISBN>
        <AUTHOR>Mark Scardina, Ben Chang, Jinyu Wang</AUTHOR>
        <TITLE>Oracle Database 10g XML and SQL</TITLE>
        <PRICE>49.99</PRICE>
        <SALE_PRICE>29.994</SALE_PRICE>
      </ROW>
    </ROWSET>
  </return>
</ns1:queryResponse>
```

Because of the native XML support in Oracle Database 10*g*, we can integrate the data from web services into the client database environment. For example, in the client database, you can create a MY_BOOK view as follows:

```
CREATE OR REPLACE VIEW MY_BOOK AS
 SELECT EXTRACT(value(a),'/ROW/ISBN/text()').getNumberVal() AS ISBN,
  EXTRACT(value(a),'/ROW/AUTHOR/text()').getStringVal() AS AUTHOR,
  EXTRACT(value(a),'/ROW/PRICE/text()').getNumberVal() AS PRICE,
  EXTRACT(value(a),'/ROW/TITLE/text()').getStringVal() AS TITLE,
  EXTRACT(value(a),'/ROW/SALE_PRICE/text()').getNumberVal()
        AS SALE_PRICE
 FROM TABLE(XMLSEQUENCE(
```

```
    query_request(1).extract('ns1:queryResponse/return/ROWSET/ROW',
                             'xmlns:ns1="BookSaleService"'))) a;
```

In this example, the SOAP request is made by calling the **query_request()** procedure. The returned XMLType is then extracted to create an XMLSEQUENCE, which is used to build a temporary table. Looking at the definition of the view, you can see that it can be used just as any other views in the database:

```
SQL> desc my_book;
 Name                                      Null?    Type
 ----------------------------------------- -------- ----------------
 ISBN                                               NUMBER
 AUTHOR                                             VARCHAR2(4000)
 PRICE                                              NUMBER
 TITLE                                              VARCHAR2(4000)
 SALE_PRICE                                         NUMBER
```

The data from the web service is seamlessly integrated with other data that is locally stored in the Oracle database.

Extending the Application

Because the PL/SQL web services run within the Oracle database and share the run-time database resources, there are special considerations when building PL/SQL web services. In this section, we discuss the best practices to implement when using PL/SQL web services.

When to Build Web Services in the Database Server

You have learned the techniques for building web services within the Oracle database. However, since many midtier web service products are available, you should consider whether you really need to build a web service inside the database server, instead of simply leveraging a widely used midtier web service framework. We believe that several issues need to be evaluated to make an informed decision.

The first issue is application complexity and code reuse. If you have many PL/SQL programs in the database and you do not want to spend too much development time building a new web service application, you can use the approach discussed in this chapter to publish the PL/SQL packages or procedures as web services.

The second issue is data access efficiency. If you want to build new web services that are highly dependent on the data stored in the database and require intensive data computation or large dataset evaluations, running them close to the data within the database server can greatly reduce the overhead needed for cross-tier data communication and synchronization. This sets a clean separation of data-centric logic that runs in the database from business logic that runs in the middle tier. It also lets you leverage the high-performance and highly scalable PL/SQL computing functionality provided by the Oracle database.

The third issue is operation efficiency. In this chapter, to illustrate the basic techniques, we built web services that perform simple DML operations. However, in real-world applications, you should not build web services to perform such fine-grained operations, because the benefits of these services do not outweigh the SOAP overhead. Instead, web services should be those services, such as data-mining analysis, that require expensive computational processing in the database.

The fourth issue is the efficiency for processing SOAP message requests. If the web service processes clients that send thousands of SOAP messages every minute, you could overload the database by simply collecting the incoming messages. The Oracle database might have much more important jobs to perform, such as managing and processing the data. In such cases, a better choice would be to build in the middle tier a web service that provides advanced caching and load balancing of the incoming messages.

Finally, your decision should not be limited to these considerations. You may also need to evaluate the application design on other issues, such as the security and scalability of your web service application.

Setting Up the Security Protection

Using web services, you can build an open infrastructure that allows easy cooperation and sharing of data and resources within your organization and among your business partners. However, you may also be open to a destructive user attacking your system. In Oracle Database 10g, the database web service is protected both by the servlet security setup within the OC4J server and by the username and password for JDBC connections within the deployed proxy program.

In addition to these safeguards, other techniques are available to protect your database web services. For example, you can have security validation of the SOAP messages through either XML Schema validation or other techniques used when processing the XML messages. Alternatively, before the execution of the PL/SQL web service, your application can perform logic-based validations. For example, in the **BookSaleService** service, you can confirm the partner's validity by requiring them to provide a password.

Because data is critical to business systems, you need to carefully design your application to protect the data when you expose it from database web services.

Building Different Types of Web Services

The approach we have discussed is not the only way for you to publish database computing and data resources as web services, though it might currently be the simplest way to do it. In this section, we discuss other types of web services you can build.

Synchronous vs. Asynchronous Web Services

A web service is just another type of messaging protocol. The service that we created in this chapter is a synchronous service. It works like a remote procedure call (RPC) where, after the SOAP request, the client-side program keeps waiting for the response from the server. However, this is not the only way to design it. In Oracle Database 10g, you can build asynchronous web services by using Oracle Streams Advanced Queuing. This is a useful way for web service providers to use the message queues in the Oracle database to handle a large number of simultaneous requests.

Push vs. Pull Web Services

In the examples of this chapter, the web service is in pull mode, where the service consumers request the service explicitly by sending SOAP messages to the service providers. However, web service communication can be bidirectional, which means that web services can also be implemented in push mode. For example, let's say the **book** table on the server side is updated by adding a new column called **reviews**, which includes the reviews for the books. Then, the bookstore can notify its partners about the changes by sending out SOAP messages using the UTL_HTTP package. Additionally, using XSLT 2.0, you can use **<xsl:result-document>** to send out SOAP messages by writing into URLs the SOAP messages created by the XSLT transformations.

Summary

In this chapter, we have shown you one very effective and simple way to expose PL/SQL procedures as Web Services. Database web service support in Oracle Database 10*g* simplifies the way you can expose database data and computing resources. However, you need to carefully evaluate the requirements of your application so that you can protect the data and ensure that the database runs properly and efficiently.

CHAPTER 27

Extending PL/SQL XML Functionality with Java

Starting with Oracle8*i* 8.1.5, Oracle Java Virtual Machine (Oracle JVM) has been provided as an execution environment for Java code running inside the Oracle databases. This functionality enables you to leverage Java functionality in PL/SQL by writing *Java stored procedures.*

In this chapter, we will help you understand how to build Java stored procedures to process XML data inside the database, including how to resolve URL references when parsing the XML data, and how to implement PL/SQL procedures to process XML in SAX. We will further provide suggestions to help you decide when to use Java stored procedures, and present some debugging and performance tips in the "Best Practices" section.

Creating the Java Stored Procedure to Process XML

To create a Java stored procedure, you need to follow these general steps, which are described in detail in the following sections:

1. Implement the Java code, and include it within a static method (or methods) that can be deployed as a Java stored procedure.
2. Deploy the Java code to Oracle JVM inside the database.
3. Create the PL/SQL specification for the Java stored procedure.

After the Java stored procedure is created, you can call it in PL/SQL procedures, SQL commands, or database triggers, just like any other PL/SQL objects. In fact, the caller of such a stored procedure can ignore that it has been written and implemented using Java. In this section, we follow these steps to create a Java stored procedure that parses and validates XML Schema documents.

Implementing the Java Code

Before you implement the Java code that can be deployed as Java stored procedures, you need to understand the datatype conversions between Java and PL/SQL arguments. A complete list of the available data types and their mapping is provided in the Oracle Database 10g online manuals. With regard to XML processing, XMLType, VARCHAR2, and CLOB are the three most frequently used data types for storing XML data and they have the following mappings:

- XMLType maps to **oracle.xdb.XMLType**
- VARCHAR2 maps to **oracle.sql.CHAR**
- CLOB maps to **oracle.sql.CLOB**

For example, if you want to read XML Schema documents from VARCHAR2, you can create a Java stored procedure as follows:

```
import java.io.ByteArrayInputStream;
import java.io.StringWriter;
```

```
import java.lang.Exception;
import oracle.sql.CHAR;
import oracle.xml.parser.schema.XMLSchema;
import oracle.xml.parser.schema.XSDBuilder;
import oracle.xml.parser.schema.XSDException;

public class XSDDBBuilder {
  public static String build(CHAR xsd) {
    StringWriter sw = new StringWriter();
    try {
      XSDBuilder builder = new XSDBuilder();
      byte [] docbytes = xsd.getBytes();
      ByteArrayInputStream in = new ByteArrayInputStream(docbytes);
      XMLSchema schemadoc = (XMLSchema)builder.build(in,null);
      sw.write("The input XSD parsed without errors.\n");
    } catch(Exception ex) {
      sw.write("Exception:"+ex.getMessage());
    }
    return sw.toString();
  }
}
```

In this example, the input parameter is **oracle.sql.CHAR**, which maps to the VARCHAR2 data type in PL/SQL. You can then get a **ByteArrayInputStream** and parse it using **oracle.xml.parser.schema.XSDBuilder** provided by Oracle XDK. The **XSDBuilder** will not only parse the XML Schema document but also validate the syntax and resolve all the URL references in the XML schema.

In order to be exposed as a PL/SQL procedure, the **build()** method in the **XSDDBBuilder** class should be a *static* method in Java.

Deploying the Java Code to the Oracle JVM

Oracle JVM is both a JRE and a JDK; therefore, it not only can run your programs but also compile your Java code. You can deploy and compile the Java code to Oracle JVM by using the following syntax:

```
CREATE OR REPLACE AND COMPILE
JAVA SOURCE NAMED "XSDDBBuilder" AS
{...Java Code...}
```

After running in SQL*Plus successfully, you will get a Java Created message, which means the Java code is compiled to byte code and stored in Oracle JVM ready for use. If there are any errors, you can use the SHOW ERROR command to show details of the errors.

NOTE
You need to set up Oracle JVM before you deploy the Java code. Refer to Chapter 25 for the setup instructions.

Creating the PL/SQL Specification

After the Java code is deployed to Oracle JVM, you need to create a PL/SQL call specification. For example, you can create an **xsd_build()** specification for **XSDDBBuilder.build()** as follows:

```
CREATE OR REPLACE FUNCTION xsd_build(xsd IN VARCHAR2) RETURN VARCHAR2
AUTHID CURRENT_USER
 AS LANGUAGE JAVA
 NAME 'XSDDBBuilder.build(oracle.sql.CHAR) return java.lang.String';
```

The AS LANGUAGE JAVA syntax indicates that the PL/SQL procedure is created based on a loaded Java class. The AUTHID CURRENT_USER syntax limits the running privileges of the procedure to the current user who is creating the specification. In this step, you need to properly specify the mapping between the PL/SQL and Java arguments. Otherwise, when executing the procedure, the Oracle database will give you a No Method Found error.

To simplify the deployment procedure and avoid typographical errors, you can use Oracle JDeveloper 10*g* to deploy and create Java stored procedures, which we will discuss in later sections.

Running the Java Stored Procedure

After you have successfully created the Java stored procedure, you can test it by creating a table that stores the XML Schema documents and loading the sample data in SQL*Plus as follows:

```
CREATE TABLE xsd_tbl(
  name VARCHAR2(30) PRIMARY KEY,
  doc VARCHAR2(4000));

INSERT INTO xsd_tbl VALUES('Product.xsd','<?xml version="1.0"?>
<xsd:schema xmlns:xsd="http://www.w3.org/2001/XMLSchema"
            elementFormDefault="qualified">
  <xsd:complexType name="ProductType">
    <xsd:sequence>
      <xsd:element name="Type" type="xsd:string"/>
    </xsd:sequence>
  </xsd:complexType>
</xsd:schema>');
commit;
```

You then can call the **xsd_build()** Java stored procedure to parse the XML schema document stored in the **xsd_tbl** table by using the following PL/SQL code:

```
SET AUTOPRINT ON
VAR out VARCHAR2(2000)
DECLARE
  xsd VARCHAR2(4000);
BEGIN
  SELECT doc INTO xsd FROM xsd_tbl WHERE name='Product.xsd';
  :out := xsd_build(xsd);
END;
```

If there are no errors in the XML Schema document, you will receive a message stating The Input XSD Parsed Without Errors. Otherwise, any error messages will be printed on the screen because all messages printed to a **StringWriter** in a Java program are returned and printed using the DBMS_OUTPUT package.

Simplifying Deployment of Java Stored Procedures Using Oracle JDeveloper 10*g*

The previous section demonstrated how the CREATE OR REPLACE AND COMPILE command is used to deploy the Java code. The CREATE OR REPLACE AND COMPILE command is useful when you would like to create a Java stored procedure from a small piece of Java code. However, if your Java code includes several Java classes, using the **loadjava** and **dropjava** command-line utilities included in Oracle Database 10*g* is a better choice. You can run these utilities by using the following commands:

```
loadjava -resolve -user <UserName>/<Password> <Java Classes or
Libraries in jar files>
dropjava -resolve -user <UserName>/<Password> <Java Classes or
Libraries in jar files>
```

However, you need to properly set up the Java CLASSPATH before you run these utilities, which can be complicated in some environments. To simplify this, you can use Oracle JDeveloper 10*g* to perform this deployment.

Using the previous example, you can create a Java class in a file called **XSDDBBuilder.java** and create a Loadjava and Java Stored Procedures deployment profile by right-clicking on the project name in Oracle JDeveloper and selecting New. In the pop-up dialog box, you then need to select **General | Deployment Profiles | Loadjava and Java Stored Procedures**. After inputting the deployment filename, click **OK**, and the dialog box will ask you to specify the classes and libraries that need to be loaded to the Oracle JVM. You can select Java classes and libraries under the **Files Groups | Project Output | Filters** option. However, before you can select the libraries in **Filters**, you need to add the directories storing the libraries by clicking the **Add** button in the dialog box under the **Files Groups | Project Output | Contributor** option. For example, if you want to load a new version of **xmlparserv2.jar** into Oracle JVM, you can add the **$ORACLE_HOME/lib** directory to the **Contributor** option. You then need to select the Java classes and libraries in the **Filter** option.

After the deployment file has been created, you can compile and load the Java classes into the database by right-clicking on the filename and selecting Deploy. You can deploy the Java classes to any Oracle database connections that you have set up in Oracle JDeveloper, as discussed in Chapter 13.

NOTE

*Make sure you use **xmlparserv2.jar** in the **$ORACLE_HOME/lib** directory when compiling the Java classes in Oracle JDeveloper because it is the library that is loaded into Oracle JVM by default. Otherwise, you need to make sure the libraries used both inside and outside the Oracle database are consistent. Any inconsistency will result in ORA-29532: Java Call Terminated by Uncaught Java Exception: java.lang.NoSuchMethodError.*

Using Oracle JDeveloper 10*g*, you now do not have to set up Java CLASSPATH when loading the Java classes into the Oracle database. Additionally, you can use Oracle JDeveloper to create PL/SQL specifications. You just need to right-click on the name of the created deployment profile of the Java stored procedure and choose Add Stored Procedures. You can select any available static Java methods to create respective Java stored procedures. Selecting the **build()** method in the **oracle.xml.sample.schema.XSDDBBuilder** class as an example, you can set the properties for the PL/SQL procedure as shown in Figure 27-1.

In this example, the PL/SQL **xsd_build(xsd IN VARCHAR2)** specification is created. After you click OK, you will see the name, **xsd_build**, listed under the deployment file. To review the generated PL/SQL code, shown next, right-click on the procedure name and choose Preview SQL Statement:

```
CREATE OR REPLACE FUNCTION xsd_build(xsd IN VARCHAR2) RETURN VARCHAR2
AUTHID CURRENT_USER
AS LANGUAGE JAVA NAME
'oracle.xml.sample.schema.XSDDBBuilder.build(oracle.sql.CHAR)
return java.lang.String';
```

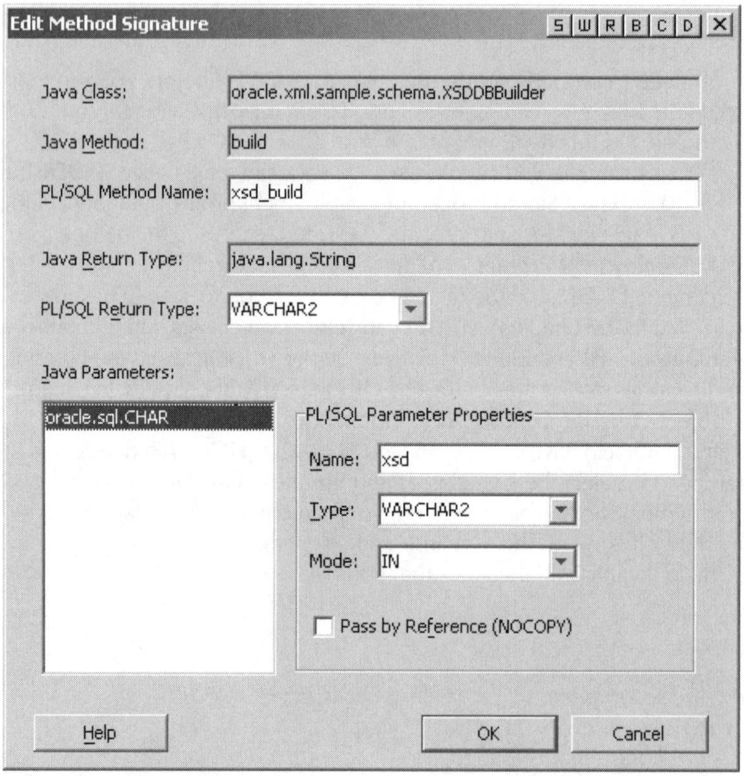

FIGURE 27-1. *SQL call specification for a Java stored procedure*

By using Oracle JDeveloper 10*g*, you can avoid the typographical errors, which may be problematic when debugging Java stored procedures.

Processing XML in the Oracle JVM

Having introduced the basic steps for creating Java stored procedures, we will present two useful examples for processing XML data. The first example shows how to resolve URL references when parsing XML, XSL stylesheets, and XML Schema documents. The second example illustrates how to perform SAX XML processing in Oracle JVM.

Resolving URL References

URL references are widely used in XML, XSL, and XML Schema documents to include external data, such as external entities in XML, external XSL documents included in XSL stylesheets by **<xsl:include>** and **document()**, and external XML Schema documents included in XML schemas by **<xsd:include>** and **<xsd:import>**.

When processing XML data, the URL references are resolved by a Java class called **EntityResolver**. You can set a base URL by using the **setBaseURL()** method, and this base URL is used by the **EntityResolver** to update all the relative URLs in XML documents to absolute URLs. Then, the **EntityResolver** will use these absolute URLs, and use the Java URL support, to retrieve the data.

In Oracle JVM, if external data is stored in a file directory, you need to grant the current database user read permission on that directory:

```
DBMS_JAVA.GRANT_PERMISSION(
   grantee=>'DEMO',
   permission_type=>'SYS:java.io.FilePermission',
   permission_name=>' <DirectoryName>',
   permission_action=>'read');
```

If external data is stored on a web server, you need to grant socket reading permission to the user:

```
DBMS_JAVA.GRANT_PERMISSION (
   grantee=> 'DEMO',
   permission_type=>'SYS:java.net.SocketPermission',
   permission_name=>'<WebServerorDomainName>',
   permission_action=>'connect,resolve');
```

However, when the referenced data is stored in database tables, which is common when processing XML data inside Oracle databases, the URL references cannot be resolved without additional help. In other words, in this case, instead of using the default **EntityResolver**, you need to implement a customized **EntityResolver** and register it to an XML parser, XSL processor, or XML schema processor. The customized **EntityResolver** is responsible for resolving the URL references and retrieving the data for the XML processors.

For example, in the following **company.xsd** XML schema file, there are **<xsd:include>** elements that include two additional XML schema files, **Person.xsd** and **Product.xsd**:

```
<?xml version="1.0"?>
<xsd:schema xmlns:xsd="http://www.w3.org/2001/XMLSchema"
            targetNamespace="http://www.company.org"
            xmlns="http://www.company.org"
            elementFormDefault="qualified">
<xsd:include schemaLocation="Person.xsd"/>
<xsd:include schemaLocation="Product.xsd"/>
<xsd:element name="Company">
 <xsd:complexType>
  <xsd:sequence>
   <xsd:element name="Person" type="PersonType" maxOccurs="unbounded"/>
   <xsd:element name="Product" type="ProductType" maxOccurs="unbounded"/>
   </xsd:sequence>
 </xsd:complexType>
</xsd:element>
</xsd:schema>
```

The **Person.xsd** schema defines the **PersonType**:

```
<?xml version="1.0"?>
<xsd:schema xmlns:xsd="http://www.w3.org/2001/XMLSchema"
            elementFormDefault="qualified">
  <xsd:complexType name="PersonType">
    <xsd:sequence>
      <xsd:element name="Name" type="xsd:string"/>
      <xsd:element name="SSN" type="xsd:string"/>
    </xsd:sequence>
  </xsd:complexType>
</xsd:schema>
```

The **Product.xsd** schema defines the **ProductType**:

```
<?xml version="1.0"?>
<xsd:schema xmlns:xsd="http://www.w3.org/2001/XMLSchema"
            elementFormDefault="qualified">
  <xsd:complexType name="ProductType">
   <xsd:sequence>
    <xsd:element name="Type" type="xsd:string"/>
   </xsd:sequence>
  </xsd:complexType>
</xsd:schema>
```

All the XML schema files are stored in the created **xsd_tbl** table, which uses the filename as the primary key and stores the content in a VARCHAR2 column.

If you use the previously created **xsd_build()** procedure to parse the XML schema document, you will get a No Protocol error. To solve this problem, you need to set a customized **EntityResolver** to the XML schema builder:

```
XSDBuilder builder = new XSDBuilder();
DBEntityResolver resolver = new DBEntityResolver();
builder.setEntityResolver(resolver);
byte [] docbytes = xsd.getBytes();
ByteArrayInputStream in = new ByteArrayInputStream(docbytes);
XMLSchema schemadoc = (XMLSchema)builder.build(in,null);
```

DBEntityResolver is a class that implements the **org.xml.sax.EntityResolver** interface as follows:

```
import java.io.IOException;
import java.io.InputStream;
import java.sql.Connection;
import java.sql.DriverManager;
import java.sql.PreparedStatement;
import java.sql.ResultSet;
import org.xml.sax.EntityResolver;
import org.xml.sax.InputSource;
import org.xml.sax.SAXException;
import java.sql.Driver;

//Define new custom EntityResolver class using the
// internal Oracle JVM KPRB JDBC driver to connect to
public class DBEntityResolver implements EntityResolver {
  Connection conn;
  DBEntityResolver() {
    try {
      Driver d = new oracle.jdbc.driver.OracleDriver();
      conn = DriverManager.getConnection("jdbc:oracle:kprb:");
    } catch(Exception ex) {
      ex.printStackTrace();
    }
  }
 //Define a method to resolve entities by retrieving schema files
 //from the xsd_tbl table.
  public InputSource resolveEntity (String publicId,  String systemId)
  throws SAXException, IOException{
    InputSource mySource = null;
    String location = systemId;
    InputStream xsd= null;

    try {
      PreparedStatement st =
      conn.prepareStatement("select doc from xsd_tbl where name=?");
```

```
        st.setString(1,location);
        ResultSet rset= st.executeQuery();
        while(rset.next()) {
          xsd    = rset.getBinaryStream(1);
        }
        rset.close();
        st.close();
      } catch(Exception ex) {
        ex.printStackTrace();
      }
      // Create the inputSource with an InputStream as input
      mySource = new InputSource(xsd);
      return mySource;
    }
}
```

Once this code has been written, you need to redeploy your Java stored procedure, after modifying your deployment profile so that it includes this new class. The signature of the method to expose as well as the signature of the matching PL/SQL procedure remain unchanged.

This class is used by the XML schema processor to resolve the URL references and retrieve referenced data from **Person.xsd** and **Product.xsd**. Since this is an important issue, let's discuss the code in greater detail.

First, in order to retrieve data from tables, you need to set up a JDBC connection to connect the Oracle database. Therefore, in the constructor function of the **DBEntityResolver** class, a server-side internal JDBC driver is initialized. In Oracle Database 10*g*, there are three JDBC drivers provided:

- JDBC *Oracle Call Interface (OCI)* driver (also known as *thick*) with the JDBC link: **jdbc:oracle:oci8:<UserName>/<Password>**
- JDBC thin driver with the JDBC link: **jdbc:oracle:thin:<UserName>/<Password>@<HostName>:<ListenerPort>:<DBSID>**
- JDBC server-side internal driver with the JDBC link: **jdbc.oracle.kprb**

Unlike the OCI and thin drivers, which are used primarily by the client applications to connect to the Oracle database, the internal JDBC driver is used for Java code running inside Oracle JVM. Because it will connect the currently connected database user running the Java program, it does not require specifying the username or password:

```
Driver d = new oracle.jdbc.driver.OracleDriver();
conn = DriverManager.getConnection("jdbc:oracle:kprb:");
```

This is an optimally tuned JDBC driver that runs directly inside the Oracle database, thereby providing the fastest access to Oracle data from Java stored procedures.

Next, you need to retrieve data from tables when the XML schema processor needs help to resolve the URL references. In this case, the **resolveEntity()** method will be called with the URLs passed in as the **systemId**. You need to overwrite the method by querying the **xsd_tbl** table using the URLs, which are filenames for the XML schemas, and return the data as a Java **InputSource**.

Finally, you need to follow the steps discussed in the previous sections to deploy the Java code and create a new Java stored procedure specification. This time, the XML schema can be parsed without errors. You can apply the same approach to resolve URLs for XML document parsing and XSLT transformation.

SAX XML Processing

Due to the nature of PL/SQL, it does not support event-based processing such as is required for SAX XML processing. However, in many cases, the large size of your XML documents requires you to use SAX to streamline the XML processing and reduce the strain on memory resources. Additionally, batch-mode SAX XML processing is more efficient than DOM XML processing when your only requirement is to read XML data. In this section, we discuss how to leverage this SAX functionality in the Oracle database.

First, whereas the previous section described how to create a Java stored procedure to parse XML Schema documents, this section discusses how to use the Java stored procedure to validate XML documents in SAX. The Java stored procedure is created after the Java method, defined as follows:

```
public static String validation(CLOB xml, CHAR xsd) throws Exception
{
   //Build Schema Object
   XSDBuilder builder = new XSDBuilder();
   EntityResolver resolver = new DBEntityResolver();
   builder.setEntityResolver(resolver);
   byte [] docbytes = xsd.getBytes();
   ByteArrayInputStream in = new ByteArrayInputStream(docbytes);
   XMLSchema schemadoc = (XMLSchema)builder.build(in,null);
   //Parse the input XML document with Schema Validation
   SAXParser parser = new SAXParser();
   parser.setXMLSchema(schemadoc);
   parser.setValidationMode(XMLParser.SCHEMA_VALIDATION);
   StringWriter sw = new StringWriter();
   try {
     parser.parse(xml.getCharacterStream());
     sw.write("The input XML parsed without errors.\n");
   } catch (XMLParseException pe) {
     sw.write("Parser Exception: " + pe.getMessage());
   } catch (Exception e) {
     sw.write("NonParserException: " + e.getMessage());
   }
   return sw.toString();
}
```

To validate the XML document, the SCHEMA_VALIDATION option for the SAX XML parser is turned on, and an XML Schema object is created and set to the SAX XML parser as follows:

```
parser.setXMLSchema(schemadoc);
parser.setValidationMode(XMLParser.SCHEMA_VALIDATION);
```

Then, the XML document is retrieved using **oracle.sql.CLOB.getCharacterStream()** and parsed by the SAX parser:

```
parser.parse(xml.getCharacterStream());
```

NOTE
*The **oracle.sql.CLOB** provides two methods to retrieve data: **getAsciiStream()** and **getCharacterStream()**. The **getAsciiStream()** method only supports ASCII characters and returns an **InputStream**. The **getCharacterStream()** method supports all characters and returns a **Reader**. Using **getCharacterStream()** is always recommended, unless you know there are only ASCII characters stored in the CLOB.*

After the Java code is deployed, a Java stored procedure called **xsd_validation()** can be created by the following statement:

```
CREATE OR REPLACE FUNCTION xsd_validation(xml IN CLOB, xsd IN VARCHAR2)
RETURN VARCHAR2 AUTHID CURRENT_USER AS LANGUAGE JAVA NAME
'XSDDBBuilder.validation(oracle.sql.CLOB, oracle.sql.CHAR) return
java.lang.String';
```

You can use it to validate XML documents in PL/SQL as follows:

```
SET SERVEROUTPUT ON
DECLARE
   out VARCHAR2(2000);
  xsd VARCHAR2(4000);
  xml CLOB;
BEGIN
  SELECT doc INTO xsd FROM xsd_tbl WHERE name='company.xsd';
  SELECT doc INTO xml FROM xml_tbl WHERE name='company.xml';
  out := xsd_validation(xml, xsd);
  DBMS_OUTPUT.PUT_LINE(out);
END;
```

For this example, the XML documents are stored in the **xml_tbl** table, created as follows:

```
CREATE TABLE xml_tbl(
    name VARCHAR2(30) PRIMARY KEY,
    docCLOB);
```

The **company.xml** can then be inserted into the Oracle database with the following command:

```
INSERT INTO xml_tbl VALUES('company.xml','<?xml version="1.0"?>
<Company xmlns="http://www.company.org">
  <Person>
    <Name>Foo</Name>
    <SSN>123-45-6789</SSN>
```

```
  </Person>
  <Product>
    <Type>Good Type</Type>
  </Product>
</Company>');
}
```

The XML Schema validation processing is performed in SAX streams. If any error occurs, the error messages will be printed on the screen. Otherwise, the processes will be successfully completed with an Input XML Parsed Without Errors message.

Second, if you need to manipulate the XML data, you can also create content handlers and register them to SAX parsers. For example, the following content handler is created to remove the white spaces in XML documents:

```
public class MyDocumentHandler extends XMLSAXSerializer {
  public MyDocumentHandler(OutputStream out) {
    super(out);
  }
  public void characters(char ch[], int start, int length)
  throws SAXException
  {
    String str = new String(ch, start, length);
    //Replace
    str = str.replace('\t',' ');
    str = str.replace('\n',' ');
    str = str.replace('\r',' ');
    // Collapse
    str = str.trim();
    char[] ca = str.toCharArray();
    int i, j;
    boolean seenWS = false;
    for(i=0,j=0; j< str.length(); j++) {
      if(ca[j] != ' ' || !seenWS) {
        ca[i++] = ca[j];
        if(ca[j] == ' ')
          seenWS = true;
        else
          seenWS = false;
      }
    }
    super.characters(ca,0,i);
  }
}
```

XMLSAXSerializer is a new class in Oracle XDK 10*g*, which is defined as follows:

```
public class XMLSAXSerializer extends
org.xml.sax.helpers.DefaultHandler implements
oracle.xml.parser.v2.XMLConstants, org.xml.sax.ext.LexicalHandler
{…}
```

This Java class in Oracle XDK 10*g* provides serialization for SAX processing. It prints out XML data to an **OutputStream** or a **PrintWriter** with printing formats that can be customized by the users. After implementing the document handler that is handling the SAX events, you can register it to the SAX parser with the following code:

```
public class XMLNormalize {
  public static String normalized(XMLType xml, CLOB[] result)
  {
    StringWriter sw = new StringWriter();
    SAXParser saxParser = new SAXParser();
    try {
    Writer out =result[0].getCharacterOutputStream();
    MyDocumentHandler docHandler =
           new MyDocumentHandler(new PrintWriter(out));
    saxParser.setContentHandler(docHandler);
    saxParser.parse(xml.getInputStream());
    out.close();
    } catch(XMLParseException ex) {
      sw.write("XSD Error:"+ex.getMessage());
    }catch(Exception ex) {
      sw.write("Error:"+ex.getMessage());
    }
    return sw.toString();
  }
}
```

In this example, we create a Java method that reads the XML document from an XMLType column and uses SAX to parse and normalize the document. If the original XML document is as follows:

```
<rootElement> This is the test
        <childElement test="true">
Value
        </childElement>
</rootElement>
```

After the normalization, the resulting XML document will be as follows:

```
<rootElement>This is the test<childElement test="true">Value</childElement></
rootElement>
```

Because Oracle JDeveloper 10*g* doesn't support XMLType when defining Java stored procedures, you need to write your own as follows:

```
CREATE OR REPLACE FUNCTION normalize(p1 IN XMLType,
                                     p2 IN OUT NOCOPY CLOB)
RETURN VARCHAR2
AUTHID CURRENT_USER
AS LANGUAGE JAVA NAME
'oracle.xml.sample.parser.XMLNormalize.normalized(oracle.xdb.XMLType,
 oracle.sql.CLOB[]) return java.lang.String';
```

This time, you also need to add the **$ORACLE_HOME/rdbms/jlib** directory in the **Files Groups | Project Output | Contributor** option to load the **xdb.jar** needed for XMLType processing.

By working through the examples, you should have a better understanding of how to process XML data in SAX using Java stored procedures. Because the processing is in SAX streams, you have the advantage of using less memory, which is especially important when processing large XML documents.

Developing Your Own Java Stored Procedures

In this section, we discuss when to use and how to debug Java stored procedures. Since Java stored procedures run within the Oracle database's memory space and consume database resources, there are special considerations when using Oracle JVM.

When to Use Java Stored Procedures

In practice, because the Oracle XML DB provides high-performance native XML features, its use should be your first choice for XML processing in your applications. If these features do not meet your requirements, you can implement Java stored procedures or leverage midtier or client-side XML support.

However, for data-intensive Java code that constantly connects to a database, you need to deploy it inside Oracle JVM and run it as a Java stored procedure. Because Java stored procedures run inside the RDBMS, they have less round-trip overheads for data transport.

On the other hand, though the round-trip expenses for Java stored procedures are less than the midtier or client-side programs, they still have high costs for data round trips between Oracle JVM and the database server. This can be especially true if there are many datatype conversions between SQL and Java.

Another performance bottleneck can result if there is a high number of Java method calls within a Java stored procedure or overall database application. Every Java call needs to be translated into an internal Oracle JVM method call. This translation is performed by using a very large lookup table to find the name mapping between PL/SQL and Java. Even though this table is indexed, the lookup process time can easily exceed the Java code execution time. The trick is to put as much Java code into the Java source file and make very few Java calls from the Java stored procedure.

Therefore, when designing your Java code, you need to make sure to minimize the interactions between the Oracle database and the Java program. For example, if you would like to use SAX to extract data from an XML document using XPath, instead of designing a Java stored procedure that allows the user to pass one XPath expression at a time, you can design it to allow the user to pass in all the XPath expressions in an array, and let the Java code process all of them in one batch process.

To tune the performance of the Java stored procedures, you also need to properly set the SHARED_POOL_SIZE, JAVA_POOL_SIZE, and JAVA_MAX_SESSIONSPACE_SIZE. All of these affect the memory usage of Java stored procedures. To avoid getting Out Of Memory errors from Oracle JVM, you need to give a reasonably large size for SHARED_POOL_SIZE and JAVA_POOL_SIZE and limit the size for JAVA_MAX_SESSIONSPACE_SIZE. These are set in your **init.ora** file and can be changed from Enterprise Manager or in SQL*Plus.

How to Debug Java Stored Procedures

You can debug Java stored procedures by printing out success and error messages. In these examples, we printed all the messages to a **StringWriter** and passed the content back as a return value. Alternatively, you can output the debug messages using **System.out** or **System.err**. By default, the messages will be printed to the current database trace files. In Chapter 9, we discussed how to check the current session ID to locate the correct trace file in USER_DUMP_DIR. However, if you want to redirect the output to the SQL*Plus text buffer, you can use the following command:

```
SQL> SET SERVEROUTPUT ON
SQL> CALL DBMS_JAVA.SET_OUTPUT(2000);
```

If this is not sufficient to discover the problem, you can also use the *Remote PL/SQL Debugging* feature of Oracle JDeveloper 10g to debug Java stored procedures.

To set up remote PL/SQL debugging you first need to open the **Tools | Project Properties** dialog box and check the **Remote Debugging** check box under the **Profiles | Development | Debugger | Remote** option. You then choose **Listen for JPDA** from the radio buttons and locate an appropriate database connection that you will run the PL/SQL code from.

Next, you can set breakpoints in the Java code and click the **Debug** button to start your debugging session. A dialog box will pop up asking you which port you want to listen on. You can enter any available port, "4000" as an example, and click OK. You will see a **Debug Listen** icon under the Processes folder in the **View | Application Navigator** window, which shows that the debugger is listening.

After this, you can open SQL*Plus and issue the following command:

```
ALTER SESSION SET PLSQL_DEBUG=TRUE
CALL DBMS_DEBUG_JDWP.CONNECT_TCP( '127.0.0.1', '4000' );
```

The address 127.0.0.1 is the IP address for the machine running Oracle JDeveloper, and 4000 is the port that the debugger is listening on. At this point, the Oracle JDeveloper debugger should have accepted the debugging connection, and you will see a new debugging process under the Processes folder. In addition, the log window should have the message Debugger Accepted Connection From Remote Process On Port 4000.

You then can return to SQL*Plus and issue a command that invokes your PL/SQL procedure calling the Java stored procedures. When the breakpoints are hit, the Oracle JDeveloper debugger will stop at the breakpoints and show all the related debugging information.

NOTE
To run the procedure to debug, you need to grant the DEBUG CONNECT SESSION and DEBUG ANY PROCEDURE privileges to the database user.

In addition to code debugging, you can check the validity of the Java classes using the database connection in Oracle JDeveloper 10*g*. Alternatively, you can use the following SQL command to query the USER_OBJECT view, which shows the Java classes owned by the current DB user and the status of the classes:

```
SELECT DBMS_JAVA.LONGNAME (object_name), status
FROM USER_OBJECTS
WHERE OBJECT_TYPE = 'JAVA CLASS';
```

You can use the ALL_OBJECTS view to check all the Java classes available to the current user. If the status of any Java class is shown as INVALID, you need to reload the class.

Summary

Using Java stored procedures is one of the options that you can leverage to process XML inside Oracle Database 10*g*. It should serve as complimentary functionality to the native XML DB functionality and provide additional development and deployment options when you are optimizing the performance of your XML-enabled applications.

CHAPTER 28

Putting It All Together

Looking back over the previous chapters, it is obvious that Oracle has an extensive XML platform across all major Oracle development languages. In this chapter, we discuss design and application decisions that you must make when you approach the implementation of your solution on Oracle. First we take a look at the platform from a tier-to-tier functionality point of view and the issues associated with performing XML processing on each. Then we discuss XML support in the database and the various strategies, including their advantages and disadvantages. Next we focus on the individual language decision from a functionality and run-time point of view. Finally, we finish up by exploring how the Oracle XML platform can be extended.

The Oracle XML Platform

What has been learned at Oracle over the last five years and echoed by enterprise customers is that XML processing cannot be done in one place. Thus it is vitally important that XML processing functionality is available on all tiers, from the database through to the client. Figure 28-1 shows the available standards-based support provided by the Oracle 10*g* XML platform on each tier.

As you can see in Figure 28-1, there is rich XML functionality on every tier that is compliant with open XML standards. In many cases this lets you move the XML processing between tiers to optimize performance, as we discuss in the next section. Since this support is standards-based, you can move between Oracle's XML platform and others such as IBM and Sun without having to migrate your code.

One thing to note is that Oracle XDK 10*g* serves as the foundation for XML functionality in all tiers. Therefore, there is a consistent level of functionality to develop against. In the case of the database tier, the XDK's C libraries are linked into the RDBMS server and are used by Oracle

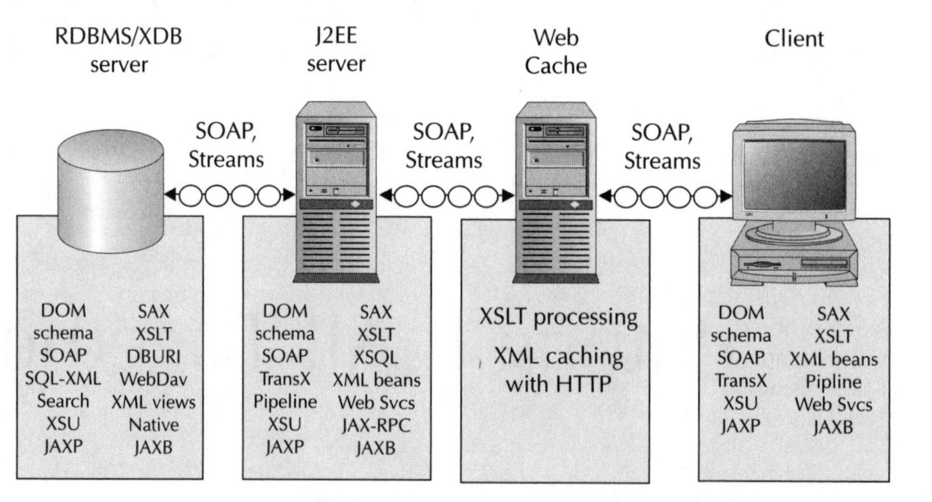

FIGURE 28-1. *Oracle 10g XML platform*

XML DB as well as AQ Streams. The Oracle JVM provides Java functionality that enables the XDK's Java libraries to be loaded and called from Java stored procedures. In the middle tier, the Oracle J2EE container includes the XDK's Java libraries and the XSQL Servlet, along with Web Services. Even Oracle Web Cache has smart XML functionality, as it caches XML message responses and performs XSLT transformations using the XDK's C libraries. Finally, rounding out the platform, all of the XDK's C, C++, and Java libraries can be used for client application development.

XML Processing Tier Decisions

A distributed or Internet application will be successful only if it can scale to meet its peak demands. In the case of XML-enabled applications and services, this cannot be guaranteed by simply throwing more and more hardware into the deployment. Instead, you need to intelligently design the system to perform XML processing on appropriate tiers and you need to choose the right type of processing.

First you need to realize that XML moving between tiers can require up to ten times the bandwidth of binary data. Interoperability comes at a cost because metadata is included along with the data. In many data-interchange applications, the metadata, element, and attribute names may be an order of magnitude greater than the data being conveyed. This is a current issue, as evidenced by the fact that two major analyst groups, Forester Research and Burton Group, both have warned enterprises to consider how XML traffic will likely affect their networks. Even Cisco reports that interest is growing in higher-throughput network products due to increasing XML traffic. What does this mean for your distributed applications?

This network bandwidth issue means that you need to consider doing XML processing close to the data if remote processing would mean shipping large quantities between tiers. For example, many applications that generate reports from large datasets produce better throughput by performing XSLT processing in the database where the application needs to ship only the finished product across the wire. This is also true if you want to extract only a small subset of data from large XML documents stored in the database.

On the other hand, in situations where XML messages are small and the number of transactions per second is high, you don't want your database to do anything but inserts. This is where midtier processing has the advantage over database tier processing, especially if validation of the XML is required. For example, the XDK's Java XML schema processor performs validation using SAX streaming and performs it significantly faster than the database. If you are storing in XMLTypes, XML that you know is already well-formed or valid, you should turn off the well-formedness checking on insert because that can significantly reduce throughput.

One area of consideration that is often missed is to make sure the correct parsing techniques are being used. Due to its higher standards' visibility, DOM parsing is the first choice for most XML document access. In fact, unless the document is being modified and written back, DOM is a bad choice compared to SAX when it comes to throughput and scalability. The same holds true for XSLT processing. Since it requires a DOM to be built, large-document processing may be very memory-intensive or may even fail. The Oracle XML DB's lazy DOM is used by its internal XSLT processor, eliminating the high memory costs.

Because XML has become more prevalent, its support is being built into many unexpected areas. One such area is web cache. As more and more demands are placed on having web sites and portal sites that have up-to-the-minute or -second data, there is no opportunity to create static pages. XML in combination with XSLT provides this dynamic publishing functionality but can be expensive if every request needs to start the process from scratch. Oracle Web Cache incorporates the capability to perform XSLT transformations on cached XML data, thereby significantly improving performance. Because it is written in C and runs entirely in memory, Oracle Web Cache's performance improvement can be much greater than that of Java-based approaches in the middle tier.

One often-overlooked processing tier is the client. Enhancements to Internet browsers to support XML and XSLT can move the processing off of servers while not dramatically affecting performance. Applets using Oracle XDK's XML JavaBeans can provide rich XML functionality using a JRE plug-in to your Internet browser. Validating XML input on the client usually degrades the user experience much less than having a server or the database processing hundreds of documents a minute.

The Oracle 10*g* XML platform is designed to be thread-safe down to the component level. Since there are some XML processes such as DOM parsing, XML Schema validation, and XSLT transformation that can take hundreds of milliseconds or even seconds, designing your application to use multithreading may be critical. Both the DOM and SAX parsers can work asynchronously, freeing your application to perform other tasks.

Finally, data security has to be a consideration for any XML tier-to-tier serialization. XML is, after all, a text-based protocol and therefore vulnerable. New standards such as Digital Signatures and XML Encryption are just being rolled out but have a processing/performance cost. The best security strategy is to not transmit data unless it really needs to be transmitted, and thus perform the processing close to or on the tier on which the data resides. Fortunately, Oracle provides several strategies, including the Oracle JVM, Oracle XDK XMLType support, and external tables, to minimize data exposure as clear, serialized XML.

If you create, whenever possible, functional software blocks or even applications that can run on any tier, you improve the likelihood of a successful deployment as you are able to partition the processing to meet load demands.

Database Design Decisions for XML

The challenges of storing and manipulating XML in a database are many, and can be daunting for those of you out there who know it "has" to be done but don't exactly know how. Databases are relational and XML is hierarchical, so until recently there has been no simple, elegant way to integrate the two. Traditionally, developers have had two choices: either use a parser to deconstruct the document data into relational data and store it as such in the database, or store the entire document as a text file, preserving its text-based structure.

The important thing to remember is that moving XML into the back end with the database is not a one-size-fits-all process. Each storage option has its advantages and disadvantages. Knowing which XML storage model is best for the purposes of your application, rather than modeling your application after an XML storage model, is critical. Let's look at each XML storage model's advantages and disadvantage to help you determine which type to use.

XMLType CLOB

In some sense, using an XMLType CLOB is the simplest way to store an XML file. It treats the XML document as exactly that: a document. The file is preserved as a complete text document in storage (with whitespace, comments, and so on intact), by storing it simply as a single, character-based entry in the database. Consequently, files of any size and depth can be stored as long as they are well-formed XML. However, although you may have defined data types in the document for validation against a schema, the data is not typed in the sense that it can be manipulated or retrieved using SQL queries.

Because of this clear limitation, the document must be searched using a text search engine—in contrast to SQL queries, which can leverage the functionality of query rewrites, functional indexes, and so on. Efficiently updating the document is limited because it involves parsing the entire file into memory using DOM, making the change, and replacing it. If, however, the primary purpose of your XML documents is to encapsulate content in a structure for transformation (as might be the focus in web publishing, content management, document archiving, and so on), and most changes to content are made at a document level, then the XMLType CLOB is your best choice for XML data storage. In these cases, you aren't likely to need a SQL context for your data, and you get a guarantee of byte-for-byte fidelity.

XMLType Views

An alternative to using the XMLType CLOB is to create a virtual XML document on top of a set of relational tables as an XMLType view. This approach permits a user to insert, update, and delete data in the XML file just as though it were SQL data. Because you are defining a virtual XML document on top of the data store, you aren't limited to just one representation of the data as with CLOB; rather, you can have multiple XML "documents."

Storing data in relational tables also means that you can update individual elements without pulling the entire document. In general, with XMLType views, you get all the advantages and efficiency that come with SQL operations, because the relational database engine is optimized for these kinds of retrievals. Finally, you can use the SQL datatype operations on the XML data types, instead of treating them simply as text. (For example, a date can be treated as a true date from a SQL standpoint, rather than simply a string of characters.)

This approach has some disadvantages, however. Defining XMLType views where the structure is deep (that is, deeper than eight to ten tiers) can degrade performance significantly due to table joins. Inserting and updating views requires INSTEAD-OF triggers and these are more difficult to maintain, because you need to include application code in the trigger. The great virtue of the CLOB approach is the complete preservation of structure and byte-for-byte fidelity. But with the XMLType view, you lose the guarantee of strict document order; also, many items (such as whitespace comments and processing instructions) will have disappeared while shredding the document data into tables.

None of this matters, of course, if you are shredding your data for use by data-centric applications that don't "care" about document structure. If your goal is to move data in and out of the database, and keep metadata intact only as context, and have all the advantages of DML operations, XMLType views are ideal. You can start from the database schema and generate the corresponding XML schema. Here there is no concept of document order; any required section ordering can be explicitly defined via ROWIDs or other application-specific methods. Functions are provided in the database and XDK to create XML schemas automatically from XMLType views.

This method is also especially useful if you are working with several XML schemas of differing tag names and structure and do not want them to define your underlying database schema (as when extending an existing legacy database application to support XML while preserving its legacy functionality). In a typical example, you can repurpose the same data store for a variety of customers who are dictating formats and templates to you. You simply define an XML Type view for each customer, and when you retrieve or insert the data to that view, it will have the format appropriate to the corresponding customer.

XML Stored in the Oracle XML DB Repository

With regards to storing XML, it is possible to have your cake and eat it too, at least to an extent: You can store your document as a native XMLType in the Oracle XML DB repository, which will preserve byte-for-byte document fidelity and also shred it into SQL tables. This approach gives you complete validation while allowing you to do all the DML operations on the document that you get with XML views. You still get fine-grained data management, and you can create multiple views and documents based on the SQL data. When your XML schema is registered, you store your XML data in your database, by simply inserting an XML document file using SQL, PL/SQL, Java, FTP, HTTP, or WebDAV. Getting XML data out of your database can be as simple as executing a SQL query or reading a file using one of those Internet-standard protocols. This functionality is made possible through the built-in query rewrite support, eliminating the need for the INSTEAD-OF triggers.

Besides the ease of working with XML in either its document or data form, you get an enhancement to the W3C-standard Document Object Model (DOM) APIs when programmatically using them. When parsing XML from a file, you can build an in-memory tree representation of the entire file in order to manipulate it. (This approach is shared by other XML processors such as XSLT.) With the "virtual DOM" feature of the native XMLType, you build the tree on demand—this preserves resources when using DOM APIs and XSLT, and, in cases of large documents or row sets, your application simply works instead of crashing.

There are many advantages to using the Oracle XML DB repository, but its use isn't right for every application. Overhead is involved in maintaining the relationship between the full document and its shredded data. However, the biggest problem comes with schema evolution. Because the document dictates the storing process (mapping which data to which tables), when you want to change the document schema, it is no longer a simple abstraction but is intimately bound to the database schema whose structure it dictated. That means you can't do most nontrivial changes of either the database or the document schema without having to export all the data and reimport it into the database. Oracle Database 10*g* is better than 9.2 in this regard; however, it is still an expensive operation and you have to decide how to handle the existing data. If there is no need for document fidelity, these changes can be abstracted from your database schema using the XMLType view storage model described previously.

By comparing and contrasting the three different DB storage options for XML data, the preceding discussion should give you a better idea of which is most appropriate for your purposes. Choosing carefully according to your applications' needs is very important. This choice can literally mean the difference between merely creating a successful prototype and bringing it successfully to production.

Java, C, C++, and PL/SQL Decisions

Oracle's XML platform allows development in Java, C, C++, and PL/SQL, thus providing rich XML functionality; however, all languages are not created equal in terms of performance and support on each tier. A survey of the Oracle development community has revealed that language usage for XML development follows this order: Java, then PL/SQL, then C++, with C a distant fourth. However, this is not the order of performance, which in most cases has C in first place. Let's compare and contrast these languages from a performance and functionality viewpoint.

Oracle XDK 10*g* is the first release that brings C XML functionality to all the tiers. Previously, you could not develop OCI programs directly against XMLTypes in the database. Now, with C support on each tier, you can develop with Oracle's highest-performance libraries. These libraries are the same ones that are linked into the database kernel and used by Oracle XML DB. They do not have the full range of XML technology support when compared to the Java versions. For example, they do not include support for XSLT 2.0, XPath 2.0, or DOM 3.0, nor are the interfaces object-oriented; however, they do include full internationalization support as well as the XSLT compiler and virtual machine, which you can leverage. While the C libraries are platform-specific, they are ported to all platforms that Oracle supports for the database and the interfaces are the same, thus producing cross-platform code usually requires only compiling and linking from a single source with the appropriate headers. Finally, if you are not concerned with interfacing to an Oracle database, you can use the XDK C libraries with only the CORE and NLS libraries, instead of an entire Oracle Home.

The Oracle XDK 10*g* C++ interfaces are implemented as code wrappers over the C ones. Therefore, there is a one-to-one mapping of functionality. For version 10*g*, this extends to support for XMLType, as we have previously discussed. One component is not present in the C libraries: the Class Generator, discussed in Chapter 23. Otherwise, the only additional overhead compared to the performance of C is a function call.

Portability of C++ code is an issue for cross-platform development. Oracle XDK 10*g* introduces for the first time namespaces for the C++ packages, to prevent collisions with other libraries or your application's functions. This is implemented using C++ templates. Since the C++ compiler *mangles* the class and method names into a unique string, issues may arise with certain compilers on various platforms. Oracle makes only one compilation available on each platform. This compilation has to be supported by your development compilation. For example, the Solaris 32-bit libraries are compiled with version 2.6 of Sun's compiler, Windows with Visual C++ 6.0, etc.

A tremendous amount of XML development is being done using PL/SQL. As you saw in Chapters 25 to 27, there are numerous built-in PL/SQL XML packages to facilitate XML development. However, they all are not created equal from both a functionality and performance perspective. Oracle Database 10*g* has ceased shipping XMLDOM, XMLPARSER, XSLPROCESSOR, and all other XML packages that are not prefixed with DBMS_, because of the migration from Java stored procedures to native C code, which is now exposed in DBMS_XMLDOM, DBMS_XMLPARSER, DBMS_XMLSCHEMA, and DBMS_XSLPROCESSOR. Thus, performance of the PL/SQL XML packages is greatly improved. There are a couple of XSU packages that still call Java. These are the DBMS_XMLSave and DBMS_XMLQuery packages, but these should be used only if you need functionality that is not available in the DBMS_XMLStore and DBMS_XMLGEN packages, respectively.

The biggest issue with PL/SQL development is the lack of available XML functionality, as compared to the other languages. For example, no event-driven interfaces, such as those in SAX or the Pipeline Processor, are available due to the limitations of PL/SQL. Also, there is no support for XSLT 2.0, XPath 2.0, or DOM 3.0. However, there is rich functionality for developing against XMLType and the XML DB using DBMS_XDB, DBMS_XDB_VERSION, DBMS_XDBT, and DBMS_XDBZ.

Finally, we turn to Java, the most popular XML development language. Within Oracle XDK 10*g*, the Java libraries support the most advanced standards levels, including all three versions of DOM, XSLT 1.0 and 2.0, XPath 1.0 and 2.0, XML Pipeline, and the Java extensions, JAXP and

JAXB. Much work has been done on the performance side of these libraries to both reduce memory resources and increase throughput.

One issue that has been raised since the introduction of JDK 1.4 is why should you not simply use Sun's XML components that are now included. There are several reasons. First, the XML functionality offered is quite limited compared to Oracle's, as shown in Table 28-1, and there are object compatibility issues if you attempt to mix and match.

As important as functionality in this comparison is technical support. As an Oracle Support customer, you get the same level of support as you would for the Oracle servers, which includes backports, patches, and one-offs. Sun offers only quarterly update releases, except in rare cases, and no backports whatsoever.

As an architect or developer faced with this many languages, you may be tempted to simply pick the most comfortable language and use it regardless of the tier you are running on. This will not produce optimum performance. Just as critical is the decision to apportion your XML processing across tiers so is your decision on the best language for that tier. As the XML is serialized between tiers, it is possible to process in the database using PL/SQL, deliver to the midtier for Java processing, and ultimately process it in C or C++ on the client.

Sun JDK 1.4	**Oracle XDK 10*g***
DOM 1.0/2.0	DOM 1.0/2.0/3.0 plus extensions
SAX 1.0/2.0	SAX 1.0/2.0 plus SAXSerializer
XML Schema 1.0	XML Schema 1.0 plus Streaming
XSLT 1.0	XSLT 1.0/2.0 plus extensions
XPath 1.0	XPath 1.0/2.0
JAXP 1.2	JAXP 1.2
	JAXB 1.0
	XML Beans
	XML Compression
	XML Pipeline Processor
	XML SQL Utility
	TransX Utility
	SOAP 1.1
	XSQL Servlet

TABLE 28-1. *Sun JDK 1.4 Versus Oracle XDK 10g Java XML Support*

Extending the Oracle XML Platform

We conclude this chapter with a discussion of the ways in which you can extend the Oracle XML platform. Extensibility and interoperability are such important XML characteristics that they are required to be carried through to the application level. This section addresses two types of extension: functional extension and code extension.

Oracle Database 10*g* and Oracle XDK 10*g* provide many ways in which you can extend the built-in XML functionality. With Oracle Database 10*g*, when you are using PL/SQL, you can create Java stored procedures to invoke Oracle's or your own Java code from the Oracle JVM. A great example of this is using the XDK's Java SAX parser to provide SAX parsing support to PL/SQL, as documented in an excellent code sample that is available on OTN. As long as you are not making continuous, fine-grained calls to Java—as you would when accessing the DOM—this method works extremely well. Moving to the midtier, you can extend XSLT stylesheets by means of extension elements that can invoke Java, which allows you to execute Java methods from an XSLT process. You can create custom XML Pipeline modules (as shown in Chapter 17) to extend the functionality of the Oracle XML Pipeline Processor. Finally, you can create custom action handlers to use with the XSQL Servlet to perform special server-side XML processing.

Code extension or reusability is a key design goal for cost-efficient, maintainable, and reliable applications. By including data and its metadata in a single document, XML offers the capability to build generic functionality that derives its processing from the metadata. Examples include applications that key off of a doctype or schema declaration to determine the type of processing required, such as XPaths to search or a stylesheet to apply, applications whose GUI or controls are configured by XML files, and applications that automatically configure themselves for the client devices they are communicating with. The first five years in the life of XML technology has broadened and matured the infrastructure that is necessary for serious enterprise-level XML-enabled application development. We predict that the next five years will see XML power applications as support is built into hardware, bringing XML processing anywhere...and fast everywhere.

APPENDIX

XML Standards Bodies and Open Specifications

pen software standards are defined as open to use by anybody and standard in the way they specify particular functionality; however, these three simple words convey meaning far beyond what's stated. For example, in an ideal situation, with open software standards, software developers could write programs with components from different vendors and not fear interoperability problems. The problem of being locked into a particular vendor would go away.

The role of the World Web Consortium (W3C) and other standards bodies is to come up with enough quality functionality to satisfy a majority of the software development community. And because requirements change at different times for different parts of the community, these standards bodies must be constantly attuned to the needs of their users and respond with additional functionality specifications or risk the possibility of their standards becoming obsolete. These software standards are especially important when certain industries need to standardize on new technologies such as XML. Not having such standards or having deficient standards would make it very difficult for businesses to interoperate on the Internet. The standards produced by W3C and other standards bodies are the key to pointing the way toward future work and applications.

Introducing the W3C Specifications

Currently, the most important standards body for the XML industry is W3C. According to its web site:

> The World Wide Web Consortium was created in October 1994 to lead the World Wide Web to its full potential by developing common protocols that promote its evolution and ensure its interoperability.... By promoting interoperability and encouraging an open forum for discussion, W3C commits to leading the technical evolution of the Web.

Basically, W3C is a consortium composed of W3C employees and companies, such as Oracle, IBM, Microsoft, and Sun Microsystems, that pay membership dues to place their representatives on a number of committees that produce open software standards specifications according to which developers in the industries code. In short, it is a very powerful consortium.

Although some member companies do not wait for the committees to formalize such specifications before they develop company-proprietary APIs, and although some APIs—such as the SAX APIs developed by Dave Megginson—don't fall under the auspices of W3C, developers know when it comes to the Internet that open standards are the way to go. When W3C comes out with a new API specification, developers flock to it unless the specification is horribly flawed. After the industry developers flock to it, company-proprietary APIs often fall by the wayside. The implications are that many companies can then participate in an industry mechanism, such as an electronic exchange, rather than being subjected to one company dictating what all others should do. W3C's home page is located at **http://www.w3.org**, and a free companion tutorial site on the XML family of standards is at **http://www.w3schools.com**.

W3C XML Specification

The seminal XML specification produced by W3C is the XML 1.0 specification, currently in its third edition, which describes a class of data objects called XML documents and explains how software modules, such as an XML parser, are used by applications to read such documents and provide them with access to the documents' content and structure. The URL for the XML 1.0 (third edition) specification is **http://www.w3.org/TR/2004/REC-xml-20040204/**.

The XML 1.1 specification, located at **http://www.w3.org/TR/2004/REC-xml11-20040204/**, updates the XML 1.0 specification so that it uses the latest Unicode version and adds checking of normalization. If you do not need these features, then you can develop your XML documents per the XML 1.0 specification. XML parsers should be able to understand both versions of the specification.

W3C DOM Specification

DOM is based on an object structure that closely resembles the structure of the documents it models. In DOM, the documents have a logical structure that is similar to a tree, with a root node, leaf nodes, and operations that traverse and extract information from the tree. The DOM 1.0 specification, located at **http://www.w3.org/TR/1998/REC-DOM-Level-1-19981001/**, covers this object structure.

A subsequent version of the DOM specification, the 2.0 specification, splits the specification into the following different modules to address the expanded requirements of the user community:

- **DOM Level 2 Core** http://www.w3.org/TR/2000/REC-DOM-Level-2-Core-20001113/
- **DOM Level 2 Views** http://www.w3.org/TR/2000/REC-DOM-Level-2-Views-20001113/
- **DOM Level 2 Events** http://www.w3.org/TR/2000/REC-DOM-Level-2-Events-20001113/
- **DOM Level 2 Style** http://www.w3.org/TR/2000/REC-DOM-Level-2-Style-20001113/
- **DOM Level 2 Traversal and Range** http://www.w3.org/TR/2000/REC-DOM-Level-2-Traversal-Range-20001113/
- **DOM Level 2 HTML** http://www.w3.org/2003/06/Process-20030618/tr.html#rec-publication

The final version of the DOM specification, the 3.0 specification, addresses further needs of the user community with these modules:

- **DOM Level 3 Core** http://www.w3.org/TR/2004/REC-DOM-Level-3-Core-20040407/
- **DOM Level 3 Load and Save** http://www.w3.org/TR/2004/REC-DOM-Level-3-LS-20040407/
- **DOM Level 3 Validation** http://www.w3.org/TR/2004/REC-DOM-Level-3-Val-20040127/

SAX Specification

The SAX specification is not a W3C specification, but because many XML application developers think that it is, it is included in this section. Many XML application developers believe that SAX is a W3C specification because it is a W3C Note and its APIs and the DOM APIs are the main APIs that they use to access and manipulate XML documents. SAX parsing is event-based XML parsing, meaning that when certain events occur or are encountered when processing the XML document—for example, when the root node of the document is encountered—the event handlers or functions are then invoked through function callbacks.

Compared to DOM parsing, SAX is much faster and less memory-intensive because it does not construct an in-memory tree representation. The documentation for both SAX 1.0 and SAX 2.0 with support for XML Namespaces and filters is located at **http://www.saxproject.org/**.

W3C Namespace Specifications

An XML namespace is a collection of names, identified by a URI reference, that is used in XML documents to differentiate element and attribute names. A namespace is useful when a single XML document contains elements and attributes that are defined for and used by multiple software modules. A namespace is introduced in an XML document by defining a special namespace prefix and prepending that prefix (followed by a colon) to the names of elements and attributes. Namespace prefixes are attributes that are themselves defined using a special prefix called xmlns. The specification is located at **http://www.w3.org/TR/1999/REC-xml-names-19990114/**.

W3C XML Schema Specification

The W3C XML Schema specification describes the XML Schema language, which provides a more structured and informative constraint on the XML document than a DTD, namely one that also, among other things:

- Supports both primitive and complex data types
- Supports restrictions or extensions on data types
- Is written in XML

Divided into two documents, the Structures portion is located at **http://www.w3.org/TR/xmlschema-1/** and the Datatypes portion is located at **http://www.w3.org/TR/xmlschema-2/**. If you need help understanding XML Schema, there is a non-normative Primer at **http://www.w3.org/TR/xmlschema-0/**.

W3C XML Query Specification

The W3C XML Query standards effort is made up of several specifications (at the time of this writing, all are in Last Call Working Draft form) and provides flexible query facilities to extract data from XML documents, treating collections of XML documents as databases on the Web. It is a query language that is based on expressions, and it is a typed language.

- **XQuery 1.0: An XML Query Language** is the language specification. Located at **http://www.w3.org/TR/xquery/**.
- **XML Syntax for XQuery 1.0 (XQueryX)** is the XML syntax specification. Located at **http://www.w3.org/TR/xqueryx/**.
- **XQuery 1.0 and XPath 2.0 Formal Semantics** is the formal semantics or algebra specification used by XQuery and XPath. Located at **http://www.w3.org/TR/xquery-semantics/**.

- **XQuery 1.0 and XPath 2.0 Data Model** is the data model specification used by XQuery and XPath. Located at **http://www.w3.org/TR/xpath-datamodel/**.
- **XQuery 1.0 and XPath 2.0 Functions and Operators** is the functions and operators specification for both XQuery and XPath. Located at **http://www.w3.org/TR/xpath-functions/**.
- **XSLT 2.0 and XQuery 1.0 Serialization** is the optional serialization specification for XSLT and XQuery. Located at **http://www.w3.org/TR/xslt-xquery-serialization/**.

To get a feel for the language and its capabilities, take a look at the use case specification located at **http://www.w3.org/ TR/xmlquery/query-usecases** and the requirements document located at **http://www.w3.org/TR/xmlquery/query-requirements**.

W3C XSLT and XPath Specification

The W3C XSL working group produces several specifications, which are divided into three areas: Formatting Objects, Transformations, and XPath.

The XSL Formatting Objects specification is located at **http://www.w3.org/TR/xsl/** and describes in XML the semantics for formatting an XML document.

The XSL Transformations (XSLT) specification has two versions. XSLT 1.0 (**http://www.w3.org/TR/xslt**) describes the language for transforming XML documents. XSLT 2.0 (**http://www.w3.org/TR/xslt20/**), in Last Call Working Draft form at the time of this writing, introduces not only additional functional support but also the use of XML Schema data types.

Similarly, the XML Path Language (XPath) specification has two versions. XPath 1.0 (**http://www.w3.org/TR/xpath**) describes the expression language used by XSLT to access or describe different parts of the XML document. Version 2.0 (**http://www.w3.org/TR/xpath20/**) is shared with the XML Query (XQuery) specification but is partitioned for XSLT 2.0 use. Its companion functions and operators specification is located at **http://www.w3.org/TR/xpath-functions/**, and its optional serialization specification is located at **http://www.w3.org/TR/xslt-xquery-serialization/**.

W3C XML Pipeline Definition Language Specification

The W3C XML Pipeline Definition Language specification (**http://www.w3.org/TR/2002/NOTE-xml-pipeline-20020228/**), which is still a W3C Note and not a Recommendation, provides a language in XML to describe the processing relationships between XML resources. A pipeline document would be coded in such a language to allow the inputs and outputs to be specified so that a pipeline processor can process this document to get a certain result.

W3C XML Protocol

The W3C XML Protocol working group, now part of the Web Services working group, has produced the SOAP 1.2 specification. This specification is divided into two parts. Part 1, called Messaging Framework (**http://www.w3.org/TR/2003/REC-soap12-part1-20030624/**), provides a messaging framework that contains a message construct that can be exchanged over a number of protocols. Part 2, called Adjuncts (**http://www.w3.org/TR/2003/REC-soap12-part2-20030624/**), covers topics such as the data model, encoding, and SOAP RPC representation.

Java Community Process Specifications

The Java development community under Sun Microsystems sponsorship has also come up with a number of specifications that are specific to the Java programming language. Sun embodies some of these specifications in Java Specification Requests (JSRs), to incorporate ideas from the developer community through the Java Community Process. Though the obvious intent is to package reference implementations within Sun's JDKs and spread their usage, the stated purpose of these additional specifications is to provide Java "friendliness" and additional functionality to the W3C specifications.

Sun JAXB Specification

The Sun XML Data Binding (JAXB) specification, located at **http://www.jcp.org/en/jsr/detail?id=31**, describes functionality that can bind an XML schema to Java classes so that XML documents that conform to the XML schema can be constructed, accessed, and manipulated programmatically.

Sun JAXP Specification

The Sun XML Parsing (JAXP) specification, located at **http://www.jcp.org/en/jsr/detail?id=5**, provides Java APIs to applications to process and transform XML documents independently of the particular XML processor.

Sun StAX Specification

The Sun Streaming API for XML (StAX) specification, located at **http://www.jcp.org/en/jsr/detail?id=173**, provides Java-based APIs to pull-parse XML.

ISO SQL/XML Specification

The SQL/XML specification, developed as Part 14 of the SQL standard, addresses such issues as the following:

- Representing SQL in XML form, and vice versa
- Mapping SQL schemata to and from XML schemata
- Representing SQL schemas in XML
- Representing SQL actions (insert, update, delete)
- Messaging for XML when used with SQL
- Using the SQL language with XML

Copies of this specification can be purchased from ISO's web site at **http://www.iso.ch**.

Oracle Technical Resources

Oracle has a huge repository of resources located at **http://otn.oracle.com**. Your first stop should be the XML Technology Center, located at **http://otn.oracle.com/tech/xml**. This is the location of the following resources:

- Oracle XML Developer's Kits documentation and releases
- XDK and XML DB forums
- XDK and XML DB samples, tutorials, and technical papers
- XML Technology Preview releases (current XQuery and StAX parser)

You can also find development versions of the latest Oracle product releases at OTN, such as the following:

- Oracle Database 10*g*, at **http://otn.oracle.com/products/database/**
- Oracle Application Server 10*g*, at **http://otn.oracle.com/products/ias/**
- Oracle JDeveloper 10*g*, at **http://otn.oracle.com/products/jdev/**

Other Helpful Resources

For open source software, check out The Apache XML Project at **http://xml.apache.org**. A good source of industry-specific DTDs or XML schemas is RosettaNet, at **http://www.rosettanet.org**. For other XML-related standards, go to the OASIS site at **http://www.oasis-open.org**. XML.org is a good source of XML industry updates and software, at **http://www.xml.org**.

Companies with XML sites and resources include Sun, **http://www.sun.com/xml**; Microsoft, **http://www.microsoft.com/xml**; and IBM, **http://www.ibm.com/xml**.

Finally, there is a wide array of general Oracle and XML educational sites. Some of our favorites are **http://www.zvon.org**, **http://asktom.oracle.com**, and **http://www.xmlfiles.com**.

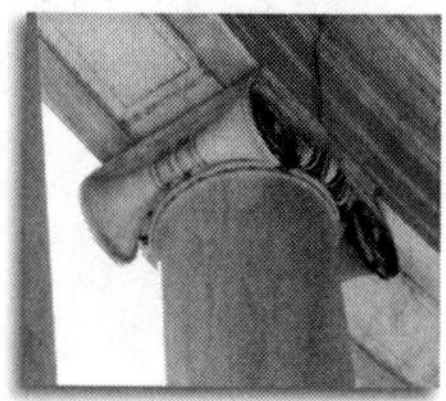

Glossary

API *See* application program interface.

application program interface (API) A set of public programmatic interfaces that consists of a language or message format to communicate with an operating system or other programmatic environment, such as a database, web server, JVM, and so forth. When formatted as messages, they will typically call functions and methods that are available for application development.

application server A server that is designed to host applications and their environments, permitting server applications to run. A typical example is Oracle Application Server 10*g*, which is able to host Java, C, C++, and PL/SQL applications in cases in which a remote client controls the interface. *See also* Oracle Application Server.

attribute A property of an element that consists of a name and a value separated by an equal sign and contained within the start tag after the element name. In the example **<Price units= "USD">5</Price>**, *price* is the attribute and *USD* is its value, which must be in single or double quotes. Elements may have many attributes, but their retrieval order is not defined.

BFILE A Large Object (LOB) data type that is an external binary file that exists outside the database files and tablespaces residing in the operating system. BFILEs are referenced from the database semantics and are also known as *External LOBs.*

Binary Large Object (BLOB) A LOB data type whose content consists of binary data. This data is considered *raw* because its structure is not recognized by the database.

BLOB *See* Binary Large Object.

business-to-business (B2B) The electronic exchange of goods and services between businesses. The software infrastructure to enable this is referred to as an *exchange.*

business-to-consumer (B2C) The electronic exchange of goods and services between businesses and consumers in the selling of goods and services.

callback A programmatic technique in which one process starts another and then continues. The second process then calls the first as a result of an action, value, or other event. This technique is used in most programs that have a user interface to allow continuous interaction.

cartridge A stored program in Java or PL/SQL that adds the necessary functionality for the database to understand and manipulate a new data type. Cartridges interface through the Extensibility Framework within Oracle 8*i* or later. Oracle Text is such a cartridge, adding support for reading, writing, and searching text documents stored within the database.

CDATA *See* character data.

CGI *See* Common Gateway Interface.

character data (CDATA) Text in a document that should not be parsed is put within a CDATA section. This allows for the inclusion of characters that would otherwise have special functions, such as &, <, >, and so on. CDATA sections can be used in the content of an element or in attributes. The syntax for element content is **<![CDATA[*put the text here*]]>**.

Character Large Object (CLOB) A LOB data type whose value is composed of character data that corresponds to the database character set. A CLOB may be indexed and searched by the Oracle Text search engine.

child element An element that is wholly contained within another element, which is referred to as its *parent element*. For example, ***<Parent><Child></Child></Parent>*** illustrates a child element nested within its parent element.

CLASSPATH The operating system environmental variable that the JDK or JRE uses to find the Java source, classes, and resources it needs to run applications.

client/server The application architecture in which the actual application runs on the client but accesses data or other external processes on a server across a network.

CLOB *See* Character Large Object.

command line The interface method in which the user enters commands at the command interpreter's prompt.

Common Gateway Interface (CGI) Industry-standard programming interfaces that enable web servers to execute other programs and pass their output to HTML pages, graphics, audio, and video sent to browsers.

Common Object Request Broker API (CORBA) An Object Management Group standard for communicating between distributed objects across a network. These CORBA objects are self-contained software modules that can be used by applications that run on different platforms or operating systems. CORBA objects and their data formats and functions are defined in the *Interface Definition Language (IDL),* which can be compiled in a variety of languages, including Java, C, C++, Smalltalk, and COBOL.

Common Oracle Runtime Environment (CORE) The library of functions written in C that enables developers to create code that can be easily ported to virtually any platform and operating system.

CORBA *See* Common Object Request Broker API.

Database Access Descriptor (DAD) A virtual path for Oracle's PL/SQL cartridge and a named set of configuration values used for database access. A DAD specifies information such as the database name or the SQL*Net V2 service name; the ORACLE_HOME directory; and the Globalization Support language configuration information, such as language, sort type, and date language.

datagram A text fragment, which may be in XML format, that is returned to the requester embedded in an HTML page from a SQL query processed by the XSQL Servlet.

DBUriType The Oracle XML DB data type used for storing instances of the data type that permits XPath-based navigation of database schemas.

DOCTYPE The tag name that designates the DTD or its reference within an XML document. For example, **<!DOCTYPE person SYSTEM "person.dtd">** declares the root element name as *person* and an external DTD as *person.dtd* in the file system. Internal DTDs are declared within the DOCTYPE declaration.

Document Object Model (DOM) An in-memory tree-based object representation of an XML document that enables programmatic access to its elements and attributes. The DOM object and its interface is a W3C recommendation.

Document Type Definition (DTD) A set of rules that defines the allowable structure of an XML document. DTDs are text files that derive their format from SGML and can be included in an XML document either by using the DOCTYPE element or by using an external file through a DOCTYPE reference.

DOM *See* Document Object Model.

DTD *See* Document Type Definition.

element The basic logical unit of an XML document that may serve as a container for other elements, such as children, data, and attributes and their values. Elements are identified by start tags, ***<tagname>***, and end tags, ***</tagname>*** or, in the case of empty elements, ***<tagname/>***.

empty element An element without text content or child elements. It may contain only attributes and their values. Empty elements are of the form ***<tagname/>*** or ***<tagname>*** ***</tagname>*** (with no space between the tags).

Enterprise Java Beans (EJB) An independent program module that runs within a JVM on the server. Oracle Application Server 10*g* provides the infrastructure for EJBs, and a container layer provides security, transaction support, and other common functions on any supported server.

entity A string of characters that may represent either another string of characters or special characters that are not part of the document's character set. Entities, and the text that is substituted for them by the parser, are declared in the DTD.

ExistNode The SQL operator provided in Oracle9*i* and Oracle Database 10*g* that returns TRUE or FALSE based upon the existence of an XPath expression within an XMLType.

Extensible Markup Language (XML) An open standard developed by W3C for describing data using a subset of the SGML syntax. XML is designed for Internet use. Version 1.0 is the current standard, published as a W3C recommendation in February 1998.

Extensible Stylesheet Language (XSL) The language used within stylesheets to transform or render XML documents. There are two W3C recommendations covering XSL stylesheets—XSL Transformations (XSLT) and XSL Formatting Objects (XSLFO).

Extensible Stylesheet Language Formatting Objects (XSLFO) The W3C standard specification that defines an XML vocabulary for specifying formatting semantics.

Extensible Stylesheet Language Transformations (XSLT) The XSL W3C standard specification that defines a transformation language to convert one XML document into another.

Extract The SQL operator provided in Oracle9*i* and Oracle Database 10*g* that retrieves fragments of XML documents stored as XMLTypes.

function-based index A database index built on an expression, which can be an arithmetic expression or an expression that contains a PL/SQL function, package function, C callout, or SQL function. Function-based indexes also support linguistic sorts based on collation keys, efficient linguistic collation of SQL statements, and case-insensitive sorts. They extend your indexing capabilities beyond indexing on a column and increase the variety of ways in which you can access data.

HASPATH The SQL operator provided in Oracle9*i* and Oracle Database 10*g* that is part of Oracle Text and used for querying XMLType data types for the existence of a specific XPath.

HTML *See* Hypertext Markup Language.

HTTP *See* Hypertext Transport Protocol.

HTTPUriType The SQL operator provided in Oracle9*i* and Oracle Database 10*g* that is used for storing instances of the data type that permits XPath-based navigation of database schemas in remote HTTP servers.

Hypertext Markup Language (HTML) The markup language that is used to create the files sent to web browsers and that serves as the basis of the World Wide Web. HTML's next version is *XHTML* and is an XML application.

Hypertext Transport Protocol (HTTP) The protocol used for transporting HTML files across the Internet between web servers and browsers.

IDE *See* Integrated Development Environment.

iFS *See* Internet File System.

INPATH The SQL operator provided in Oracle9*i* and Oracle Database 10*g* that is part of Oracle Text and used to query XMLType data types for specific text within a specific XPath.

instantiate In object-based languages such as Java and C++, refers to the creation of an object of a specific class.

Integrated Development Environment (IDE) A set of programs designed to aid in the development of software that is run from a single user interface. Oracle JDeveloper is an IDE for Java development because it includes an editor, compiler, debugger, syntax checker, help system, and so on, to permit Java software development through a single user interface.

Internet File System (iFS) The Oracle file system that has a Web GUI and a Java-based development environment (called Oracle Content Management SDK) and that runs on a middle tier and provides a means of creating, storing, and managing multiple types of documents in a single database repository. The Oracle Content Management SDK is available only in Oracle Application Server. The Oracle Files is only shipped with the Oracle Collaboration Suite.

Internet Inter-ORB Protocol (IIOP) The protocol used by CORBA to exchange messages on a TCP/IP network such as the Internet.

Java A high-level programming language developed and maintained by Sun Microsystems in which applications run in a Java Virtual Machine (JVM). The JVM is responsible for all interfaces to the operating system. This architecture permits developers to create Java applications and applets that can run on any operating system or platform that has a JVM.

JavaBeans Java objects whose implementations conform to a set of conventions designed to promote modularity and reusability. They are one example of a component-programming model and can be deployed in a servlet, an applet, or a JSP page.

Java Database Connectivity (JDBC) The programming API that enables Java applications to access a database through the SQL language. JDBC drivers are written in Java for platform independence but are specific to each database.

Java Developer's Kit (JDK) The collection of Java classes, run-time environment, compiler, debugger, and usually source code that comprises a Java development environment for a particular Java version. JDKs are designated by versions, and Java 2 is used to designate versions from 1.2 onward.

Java Runtime Environment (JRE) The collection of compiled classes that makes up the JVM on a platform. JREs are designated by versions, and Java 2 is used to designate versions from 1.2 onward.

JavaServer pages (JSP) An extension to the servlet functionality that enables a simple programmatic interface to web pages. JSPs are HTML pages with special tags and embedded Java code that is executed on the web or application server to provide dynamic functionality to HTML pages. JSPs are actually compiled into servlets when first requested and are run in the server's JVM.

Java Virtual Machine (JVM) The Java interpreter that converts the compiled Java byte code into the machine language of the platform and runs it. JVMs can run on a client, in a browser, on a web server, on an application server such as Oracle Application Server 10*g*, or on a database server such as Oracle Database 10*g*.

JAXB Class Generator A utility that accepts an input file and creates a set of output classes that has corresponding functionality. In the case of the XML JAXB Class Generator, which is compliant with JSR-031 XML Binding Specification (JAXB), the input file is an XML schema and the output is a series of Java classes that can be used to create XML documents that conform to the XML schema.

JDBC *See* Java Database Connectivity.

JDeveloper Oracle's Java IDE that enables application, applet, and servlet development and includes an editor, compiler, debugger, syntax checker, help system, and so on. In version 10g, JDeveloper has been enhanced to support XML-based development by including the Oracle XDK's Java libraries integrated for easy use along with XML support in its editor.

JDK *See* Java Developer's Kit.

JServer The JVM that runs within the memory space of the Oracle8*i* or later database. In Oracle 8*i* Release 1, the JVM was Java 1.1 compatible, while Release 2 is Java 1.2 compatible. In Oracle Database 10*g*, the JVM is compatible with JDK 1.4. It is also known as the OJVM.

JVM *See* Java Virtual Machine.

LAN *See* local area network.

Large Object (LOB) The class of SQL data type that is further divided into *Internal LOBs* and *External LOBs*. Internal LOBs include BLOBs, CLOBS, and NCLOBs, while External LOBs include BFILES. *See also* BFILES, Binary Large Object, Character Large Object, and Non-Character Large Object.

listener The server process that listens for and accepts incoming connection requests from client applications. Oracle listener processes start up Oracle database processes to handle subsequent communications with the client.

LOB *See* Large Object.

local area network (LAN) A computer communications network that serves users within a restricted geographical area. LANs consist of servers, workstations, communications hardware (routers, bridges, network cards, and so on), and a network operating system.

namespace A set of related element names or attributes within an XML document. The namespace syntax and its usage are defined by a W3C recommendation. For example, the **<xsl:apply-templates/>** element is identified as part of the XSL namespace. Namespaces are declared in the XML schema or in the XML document before they are used by using the attribute syntax **xmlns:xsl="http://www.w3.org/TR/WD-xsl"**.

NCLOB *See* Non-Character Large Object.

node In XML, each addressable entity in the DOM tree.

Non-Character Large Object (NCLOB) A CLOB that contains Unicode characters, with a maximum size of 4GB.

NOTATION In XML, the definition of a content type that is not part of the types understood by the XML parser. These types include audio, video, and other multimedia. For example, to include a GIF image in your XML document you would use **<!NOTATION GIF system "image/gif">**.

n-tier The designation for a computer communications network architecture that consists of one or more tiers made up of clients and servers. Typically, *two-tier systems* are made up of one client level and one server level. A *three-tier system* utilizes two server tiers, typically a database server as one tier and a web or application server as the other tier, along with a client tier.

OASIS *See* Organization for the Advancement of Structured Information.

object-relational A relational database system that can also store and manipulate higher-order data types, such as text documents, audio, video files, and user-defined objects.

Object Request Broker (ORB) Software that manages message communications between requesting programs on clients and between objects on servers. ORBs pass the action request and its parameters to the object and return the results. Common implementations are CORBA and EJB. *See also* Common Object Request Broker and Enterprise JavaBeans.

Object view A tailored presentation of the data contained in one or more object tables or other views. The output of an Object view query is treated as a table. Object views can be used in most places where a table is used.

Oracle Application Server (Oracle AS) The Oracle server that integrates all the core services and features required for building, deploying, and managing high-performance, n-tier, transaction-oriented web applications within an open standards framework.

Oracle Enterprise Manager A separate Oracle product that combines a graphical console, agents, common services, and tools to provide an integrated and comprehensive systems management platform for managing Oracle products.

ORACLE_HOME The operating system environmental variable that identifies the location of the Oracle database installation for use by applications.

Oracle Text An Oracle tool that provides full-text indexing of documents and the capability to do SQL queries over documents, along with XPath-like searching.

Oracle XML DB A high-performance XML storage and retrieval technology provided with Oracle database server beginning with Oracle9*i* Release 2. It is based on the W3C XML data model.

ORB *See* Object Request Broker.

Organization for the Advancement of Structured Information (OASIS) An organization of members chartered with promoting public information standards through conferences, seminars, exhibits, and other educational events. Oasis is actively promoting XML as well as SGML.

parent element An element that surrounds another element, which is referred to as its child element. For example, ***<Parent><Child></Child></Parent>*** illustrates a parent element wrapping its child element.

Parsed Character Data (PCDATA) The element or attribute content consisting of text that should be parsed but is not part of a tag or unparsed data (CDATA).

parser In XML, a software program that accepts as input an XML document, determines whether it is well formed and, optionally, valid, and provides programmatic access to XML data. The Oracle XML parser supports both SAX and DOM, and JAXP interfaces.

PCDATA *See* Parsed Character Data.

PL/SQL The Oracle procedural database language that extends SQL to create programs that can be run within the database.

prolog The opening part of an XML document that contains the XML declaration, a possible language encoding, and any DTD or other declarations needed to process the document.

PUBLIC Specifies the Internet location of the reference that follows it.

renderer A software processor that outputs a document in a specified format.

result set The output of a SQL query consisting of one or more rows of data.

root element The element that encloses all the other elements in an XML document and is located between the optional prolog and epilog. An XML document is permitted to have only one root element.

SAX *See* Simple API for XML.

schema The definition of the structure and data types within a database. It can also be used to refer to an XML document that supports the XML Schema W3C recommendation.

Secure Sockets Layer (SSL) The primary security protocol on the Internet; utilizes a public key/private key form of encryption between browsers and servers.

Server-Side Include (SSI) The HTML command used to place data or other content into a web page before sending it to the requesting browser.

servlet A Java application that runs in a server, typically a web or application server, and performs processing on that server. Servlets are the Java equivalent to CGI scripts.

session The active connection between two tiers.

SGML *See* Structured Generalized Markup Language.

Simple API for XML (SAX) An XML standard interface provided by XML parsers and used by event-based applications.

Simple Object Access Protocol (SOAP) Lightweight, XML-based protocol for exchanging information in a decentralized, distributed environment.

SQL *See* Structured Query Language.

SQL/XML Part of the ANSI/ISO SQL standard, SQL/XML provides a number of standards-based functions that enable you to query relational data and return XML documents.

SSI *See* Server-Side Include.

SSL *See* Secure Sockets Layer.

SOAP *See* Simple Object Access Protocol

Structured Generalized Markup Language (SGML) An ISO standard for defining the format of a text document, implemented using markup and DTDs.

Structured Query Language (SQL) The standard language used to access and process data in a relational database.

stylesheet In XML, an XML document that consists of XSL processing instructions used by an XSL processor to transform or format an input XML document into an output markup text document (XML, HTML, WML, SVG, etc.).

SYSTEM Specifies the location on the host operating system of the reference that follows it.

tag A single piece of XML markup that delimits the start or end of an element. A tag starts with < and ends with >. In XML, there are start tags (**<*tagname*>**), end tags (**</*tagname*>**), and empty tags (**<*tagname*/>**). Unlike HTML, XML tags are case sensitive.

TCP/IP *See* Transmission Control Protocol/Internet Protocol.

thread In programming, a single message or process execution path within an operating system that supports multiple operating systems, such as Windows, UNIX, and Java.

Transmission Control Protocol/Internet Protocol (TCP/IP) The communications network protocol that consists of TCP, which controls the transport functions, and IP, which provides the routing mechanism. It is the standard for Internet communications.

Uniform Resource Identifier (URI) The address syntax that is used to create URLs and XPaths.

Uniform Resource Locator (URL) The address that defines the location and route to a file or resource on the Internet. URLs are used by browsers to navigate the Web and consist of a protocol prefix, port number, domain name, directory and subdirectory names, and the filename. For example, **http://technet.oracle.com:80/tech/xml/index.htm** specifies the location and path a browser travels to find Oracle Technology Network's XML site on the Web.

URI *See* Uniform Resource Identifier.

URL *See* Uniform Resource Locator.

user interface (UI) The combination of menus, screens, keyboard commands, mouse clicks, and command language that defines how a user interacts with a software application.

valid The status of an XML document when its structure and element content is consistent with that declared in its referenced or included DTD or its XML schema.

W3C *See* World Wide Web Consortium.

WAN *See* wide area network.

well formed Describes an XML document that conforms to the syntax of the XML version declared in its XML declaration. This includes having a single root element, properly nested tags, and so forth.

wide area network (WAN) A computer communications network that serves users within a wide geographic area, such as a state or country. WANs consist of servers, workstations, communications hardware (routers, bridges, network cards, and so on), and a network operating system.

Working Group (WG) A committee within W3C that is made up of industry members that implement the recommendation process in specific Internet technology areas.

World Wide Web Consortium (W3C) An international industry consortium started in 1994 to develop standards for the Web. It is located at **http://www.w3c.org**.

wrapper A data structure or software that *wraps around* other data or software, typically to provide a generic or object interface.

XML *See* Extensible Markup Language.

XML Developer's Kit (XDK) The set of libraries, components, and utilities that provides software developers with the standards-based functionality to XML-enable their applications. In the case of the Oracle XDK for Java, the kit contains an XML parser, an XSLT processor, the XML JAXB Class Generator, the XML SQL Utility, and the XSQL Servlet.

XML Query (XQuery) W3C's effort to create a standard for the language and syntax to query XML documents.

XML Schema W3C's effort to create a standard to express simple data types and complex structures within an XML document.

XMLType An Oracle data type that stores XML data using an underlying CLOB column or object-relational columns within a table or view.

XMLType views Oracle XML DB provides XMPType views as a way to wrap existing relational and object-relational data in XML format. This is especially useful if, for example, your legacy data is not in XML but you have to migrate it to an XML format.

XPath The open standard syntax for addressing elements within a document used by XSL and XPointer. XPath is currently a W3C recommendation.

XPointer A reference to an XML document fragment. An XPointer can be used at the end of an XPath-formatted URI. XPointer is also the name of the W3C recommendation that describes the use of XPointers.

XQuery *See* XML Query.

XSL *See* Extensible Stylesheet Language.

XSLFO *See* Extensible Stylesheet Language Formatting Objects.

XSLT *See* Extensible Stylesheet Language Transformations.

XSQL The name of the Oracle Servlet providing the ability to produce dynamic XML documents from one or more SQL queries, optionally transform the document in the server using an XSL stylesheet, and provide HTTP session management.

Index

A

B

C

E

F

L

M

N

O

P

T

U

V

W

X

INTERNATIONAL CONTACT INFORMATION

AUSTRALIA
McGraw-Hill Book Company
Australia Pty. Ltd.
TEL +61-2-9900-1800
FAX +61-2-9878-8881
http://www.mcgraw-hill.com.au
books-it_sydney@mcgraw-hill.com

CANADA
McGraw-Hill Ryerson Ltd.
TEL +905-430-5000
FAX +905-430-5020
http://www.mcgraw-hill.ca

GREECE, MIDDLE EAST, & AFRICA (Excluding South Africa)
McGraw-Hill Hellas
TEL +30-210-6560-990
TEL +30-210-6560-993
TEL +30-210-6560-994
FAX +30-210-6545-525

MEXICO (Also serving Latin America)
McGraw-Hill Interamericana Editores
S.A. de C.V.
TEL +525-1500-5108
FAX +525-117-1589
http://www.mcgraw-hill.com.mx
carlos_ruiz@mcgraw-hill.com

SINGAPORE (Serving Asia)
McGraw-Hill Book Company
TEL +65-6863-1580
FAX +65-6862-3354
http://www.mcgraw-hill.com.sg
mghasia@mcgraw-hill.com

SOUTH AFRICA
McGraw-Hill South Africa
TEL +27-11-622-7512
FAX +27-11-622-9045
robyn_swanepoel@mcgraw-hill.com

SPAIN
McGraw-Hill/
Interamericana de España, S.A.U.
TEL +34-91-180-3000
FAX +34-91-372-8513
http://www.mcgraw-hill.es
professional@mcgraw-hill.es

UNITED KINGDOM, NORTHERN, EASTERN, & CENTRAL EUROPE
McGraw-Hill Education Europe
TEL +44-1-628-502500
FAX +44-1-628-770224
http://www.mcgraw-hill.co.uk
emea_queries@mcgraw-hill.com

ALL OTHER INQUIRIES Contact:
McGraw-Hill/Osborne
TEL +1-510-420-7700
FAX +1-510-420-7703
http://www.osborne.com
omg_international@mcgraw-hill.com

Mc
Graw
Hill
OSBORNE
www.osborne.com

GET YOUR FREE SUBSCRIPTION TO ORACLE MAGAZINE

***Oracle Magazine* is essential gear for today's information technology professionals. Stay informed and increase your productivity with every issue of *Oracle Magazine*. Inside each free bimonthly issue you'll get:**

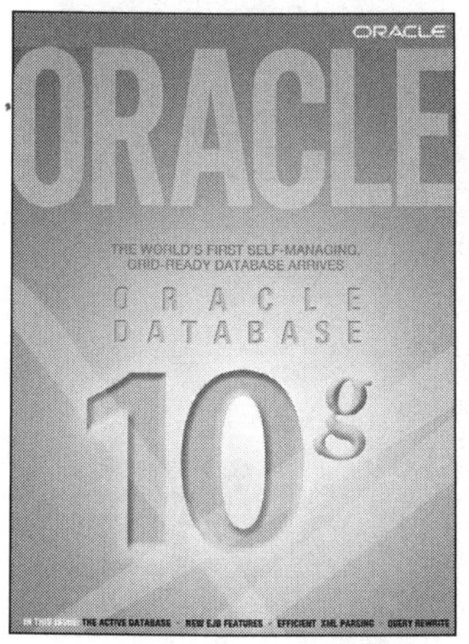

- Up-to-date information on Oracle Database, Oracle Application Server, Web development, enterprise grid computing, database technology, and business trends
- Third-party vendor news and announcements
- Technical articles on Oracle and partner products, technologies, and operating environments
- Development and administration tips
- Real-world customer stories

IF THERE ARE OTHER ORACLE USERS AT YOUR LOCATION WHO WOULD LIKE TO RECEIVE THEIR OWN SUBSCRIPTION TO ORACLE MAGAZINE, PLEASE PHOTOCOPY THIS FORM AND PASS IT ALONG.

Three easy ways to subscribe:

① Web
Visit our Web site at otn.oracle.com/oraclemagazine. You'll find a subscription form there, plus much more!

② Fax
Complete the questionnaire on the back of this card and fax the questionnaire side only to +1.847.763.9638.

③ Mail
Complete the questionnaire on the back of this card and mail it to P.O. Box 1263, Skokie, IL 60076-8263

ORACLE®

FREE SUBSCRIPTION

○ **Yes, please send me a FREE subscription to *Oracle Magazine*.** ○ **NO**

To receive a free subscription to *Oracle Magazine*, you must fill out the entire card, sign it, and date it (incomplete cards cannot be processed or acknowledged). You can also fax your application to +1.847.763.9638. **Or subscribe at our Web site at otn.oracle.com/oraclemagazine**

○ From time to time, Oracle Publishing allows our partners exclusive access to our e-mail addresses for special promotions and announcements. To be included in this program, please check this circle.

○ Oracle Publishing allows sharing of our mailing list with selected third parties. If you prefer your mailing address not to be included in this program, please check here. If at any time you would like to be removed from this mailing list, please contact Customer Service at +1.847.647.9630 or send an e-mail to oracle@halldata.com.

signature (required) X   date

name   title

company   e-mail address

street/p.o. box

city/state/zip or postal code   telephone

country   fax

YOU MUST ANSWER ALL TEN QUESTIONS BELOW.

① **WHAT IS THE PRIMARY BUSINESS ACTIVITY OF YOUR FIRM AT THIS LOCATION?** (check one only)
- □ 01 Aerospace and Defense Manufacturing
- □ 02 Application Service Provider
- □ 03 Automotive Manufacturing
- □ 04 Chemicals, Oil and Gas
- □ 05 Communications and Media
- □ 06 Construction/Engineering
- □ 07 Consumer Sector/Consumer Packaged Goods
- □ 08 Education
- □ 09 Financial Services/Insurance
- □ 10 Government (civil)
- □ 11 Government (military)
- □ 12 Healthcare
- □ 13 High Technology Manufacturing, OEM
- □ 14 Integrated Software Vendor
- □ 15 Life Sciences (Biotech, Pharmaceuticals)
- □ 16 Mining
- □ 17 Retail/Wholesale/Distribution
- □ 18 Systems Integrator, VAR/VAD
- □ 19 Telecommunications
- □ 20 Travel and Transportation
- □ 21 Utilities (electric, gas, sanitation, water)
- □ 98 Other Business and Services

② **WHICH OF THE FOLLOWING BEST DESCRIBES YOUR PRIMARY JOB FUNCTION?** (check one only)

Corporate Management/Staff
- □ 01 Executive Management (President, Chair, CEO, CFO, Owner, Partner, Principal)
- □ 02 Finance/Administrative Management (VP/Director/ Manager/Controller, Purchasing, Administration)
- □ 03 Sales/Marketing Management (VP/Director/Manager)
- □ 04 Computer Systems/Operations Management (CIO/VP/Director/ Manager MIS, Operations)

IS/IT Staff
- □ 05 Systems Development/ Programming Management
- □ 06 Systems Development/ Programming Staff
- □ 07 Consulting
- □ 08 DBA/Systems Administrator
- □ 09 Education/Training
- □ 10 Technical Support Director/Manager
- □ 11 Other Technical Management/Staff
- □ 98 Other

③ **WHAT IS YOUR CURRENT PRIMARY OPERATING PLATFORM?** (select all that apply)
- □ 01 Digital Equipment UNIX
- □ 02 Digital Equipment VAX VMS
- □ 03 HP UNIX
- □ 04 IBM AIX
- □ 05 IBM UNIX
- □ 06 Java
- □ 07 Linux
- □ 08 Macintosh
- □ 09 MS-DOS
- □ 10 MVS
- □ 11 NetWare
- □ 12 Network Computing
- □ 13 OpenVMS
- □ 14 SCO UNIX
- □ 15 Sequent DYNIX/ptx
- □ 16 Sun Solaris/SunOS
- □ 17 SVR4
- □ 18 UnixWare
- □ 19 Windows
- □ 20 Windows NT
- □ 21 Other UNIX
- □ 98 Other
- 99 □ None of the above

④ **DO YOU EVALUATE, SPECIFY, RECOMMEND, OR AUTHORIZE THE PURCHASE OF ANY OF THE FOLLOWING?** (check all that apply)
- □ 01 Hardware
- □ 02 Software
- □ 03 Application Development Tools
- □ 04 Database Products
- □ 05 Internet or Intranet Products
- 99 □ None of the above

⑤ **IN YOUR JOB, DO YOU USE OR PLAN TO PURCHASE ANY OF THE FOLLOWING PRODUCTS?** (check all that apply)

Software
- □ 01 Business Graphics
- □ 02 CAD/CAE/CAM
- □ 03 CASE
- □ 04 Communications
- □ 05 Database Management
- □ 06 File Management
- □ 07 Finance
- □ 08 Java
- □ 09 Materials Resource Planning
- □ 10 Multimedia Authoring
- □ 11 Networking
- □ 12 Office Automation
- □ 13 Order Entry/Inventory Control
- □ 14 Programming
- □ 15 Project Management
- □ 16 Scientific and Engineering
- □ 17 Spreadsheets
- □ 18 Systems Management
- □ 19 Workflow

Hardware
- □ 20 Macintosh
- □ 21 Mainframe
- □ 22 Massively Parallel Processing
- □ 23 Minicomputer
- □ 24 PC
- □ 25 Network Computer
- □ 26 Symmetric Multiprocessing
- □ 27 Workstation

Peripherals
- □ 28 Bridges/Routers/Hubs/Gateways
- □ 29 CD-ROM Drives
- □ 30 Disk Drives/Subsystems
- □ 31 Modems
- □ 32 Tape Drives/Subsystems
- □ 33 Video Boards/Multimedia

Services
- □ 34 Application Service Provider
- □ 35 Consulting
- □ 36 Education/Training
- □ 37 Maintenance
- □ 38 Online Database Services
- □ 39 Support
- □ 40 Technology-Based Training
- □ 98 Other
- 99 □ None of the above

⑥ **WHAT ORACLE PRODUCTS ARE IN USE AT YOUR SITE?** (check all that apply)

Oracle E-Business Suite
- □ 01 Oracle Marketing
- □ 02 Oracle Sales
- □ 03 Oracle Order Fulfillment
- □ 04 Oracle Supply Chain Management
- □ 05 Oracle Procurement
- □ 06 Oracle Manufacturing
- □ 07 Oracle Maintenance Management
- □ 08 Oracle Service
- □ 09 Oracle Contracts
- □ 10 Oracle Projects
- □ 11 Oracle Financials
- □ 12 Oracle Human Resources
- □ 13 Oracle Interaction Center
- □ 14 Oracle Communications/Utilities (modules)
- □ 15 Oracle Public Sector/University (modules)
- □ 16 Oracle Financial Services (modules)

Server/Software
- □ 17 Oracle9*i*
- □ 18 Oracle9*i* Lite
- □ 19 Oracle8*i*
- □ 20 Other Oracle database
- □ 21 Oracle9*i* Application Server
- □ 22 Oracle9*i* Application Server Wireless
- □ 23 Oracle Small Business Suite

Tools
- □ 24 Oracle Developer Suite
- □ 25 Oracle Discoverer
- □ 26 Oracle JDeveloper
- □ 27 Oracle Migration Workbench
- □ 28 Oracle9*i* AS Portal
- □ 29 Oracle Warehouse Builder

Oracle Services
- □ 30 Oracle Outsourcing
- □ 31 Oracle Consulting
- □ 32 Oracle Education
- □ 33 Oracle Support
- □ 98 Other
- 99 □ None of the above

⑦ **WHAT OTHER DATABASE PRODUCTS ARE IN USE AT YOUR SITE?** (check all that apply)
- □ 01 Access
- □ 02 Baan
- □ 03 dbase
- □ 04 Gupta
- □ 05 IBM DB2
- □ 06 Informix
- □ 07 Ingres
- □ 08 Microsoft Access
- □ 09 Microsoft SQL Server
- □ 10 PeopleSoft
- □ 11 Progress
- □ 12 SAP
- □ 13 Sybase
- □ 14 VSAM
- □ 98 Other
- 99 □ None of the above

⑧ **WHAT OTHER APPLICATION SERVER PRODUCTS ARE IN USE AT YOUR SITE?** (check all that apply)
- □ 01 BEA
- □ 02 IBM
- □ 03 Sybase
- □ 04 Sun
- □ 05 Other

⑨ **DURING THE NEXT 12 MONTHS, HOW MUCH DO YOU ANTICIPATE YOUR ORGANIZATION WILL SPEND ON COMPUTER HARDWARE, SOFTWARE, PERIPHERALS, AND SERVICES FOR YOUR LOCATION?** (check only one)
- □ 01 Less than $10,000
- □ 02 $10,000 to $49,999
- □ 03 $50,000 to $99,999
- □ 04 $100,000 to $499,999
- □ 05 $500,000 to $999,999
- □ 06 $1,000,000 and over

⑩ **WHAT IS YOUR COMPANY'S YEARLY SALES REVENUE?** (please choose one)
- □ 01 $500, 000, 000 and above
- □ 02 $100, 000, 000 to $500, 000, 000
- □ 03 $50, 000, 000 to $100, 000, 000
- □ 04 $5, 000, 000 to $50, 000, 000
- □ 05 $1, 000, 000 to $5, 000, 000

100103